NetBeans™
The Definitive Guide

NetBeans™
The Definitive Guide

Tim Boudreau, Jesse Glick, Simeon Greene,
Vaughn Spurlin, and Jack Woehr

O'REILLY®

Beijing · Cambridge · Farnham · Köln · Paris · Sebastopol · Taipei · Tokyo

NetBeans™: The Definitive Guide
by Tim Boudreau, Jesse Glick, Simeon Greene, Vaughn Spurlin and Jack Woehr

Published by O'Reilly & Associates, Inc., 1005 Gravenstein Highway North, Sebastopol, CA
95472.

O'Reilly & Associates books may be purchased for educational, business, or sales promotional
use. Online editions are also available for most titles (*safari.oreilly.com*). For more information,
contact our corporate/institutional sales department: (800) 998-9938 or *corporate@oreilly.com*.

Editor:	Brett McLaughlin
Production Editor:	Philip Dangler
Cover Designer:	Hanna Dyer
Interior Designer:	David Futato
Production Services:	Argosy

Printing History:

October 2002:	First Edition.

ISBN: 0-596-00280-7
[M]

Table of Contents

Preface

Is NetBeans for You?

Is NetBeans for you? The algorithm for answering this question is:

1. Determine what NetBeans does.
2. Decide if that functionality is for you.

NetBeans is first and foremost a well-crafted open source programmer's integrated development environment (IDE). It's powerful, it's useful, it's extensible, it's open, and it's free.

Sometimes it is incorrectly thought that integrated development environments are intended to make Java™ programming easier. You know already, though, that advanced tools don't save work so much as they make the same amount of work yield more effective results. That's what NetBeans does; it allows you to trade one set of practices for another. The practices that NetBeans imposes are fully as intricate as your current development practices. More intricate, perhaps, because if you are a real programmer, you will want to supplement your work style with NetBeans rather than attempting to use NetBeans to completely replace your current work style. The practice of NetBeans development is not easier. It's just more effective than what you were doing before NetBeans. You get more done with NetBeans.

Is This Book for You?

Well, for a start, *NetBeans: The Definitive Guide* is a book written by a select team of NetBeans enthusiasts and experts, all of whom are talented and experienced programmers. Some have used NetBeans almost since the beginning. Each has had his theories about programming using NetBeans tested in real world software engineering.

Also, members of the NetBeans development team watched over the evolution of this book, making suggestions, correcting misapprehensions, sometimes disagreeing with the authors' conclusions in the course of a long-distance group authorship project conducted over the Internet, a project that took almost two years to complete.

What's more, during the period in which the authors were preparing this book, Net-Beans was changing. Features came and went. Visual layout changed, thus rendering carefully arranged screenshots out of date. Whole components appeared in and disappeared from the NetBeans core. If you've ever studied the computer science heuristic of "simulated annealing," you'll recognize the process that this book underwent: like a seven-folded samurai sword, our work has been melted and hammered out flat over and over again.

NetBeans: The Definitive Guide presumes that you are a NetBeans beginner, not a beginner programmer. We are not going to teach you programming; we're going to teach you how to use NetBeans to enhance your programming productivity.

NetBeans and Java

Sun Microsystems' Java programming environment has transformed the software development model of many programming teams. Designed not only for portability and rapid prototyping, Java is as much a prefabricated software development methodology as a programming language. Life isn't always as simple as the Java approach tries to make it, but it is that simple often enough that Java is a good bet for many projects.

If you have no extraordinary requirements, the basic Java model of development is handy to use. If you happen to have special requirements, the power and flexibility of Java combined with access to other code bodies via language resources such as the Java Native Interface (JNI) and runtime protocols such as Transport Control Protocol/ Internet Protocol (TCP/IP) and Java's Remote Method Invocation (RMI) layer tend to assure that some Java-based solution is within practical reach.

Java is huge, yet still hugely consistent. The core Java development tools sprang from the same collective brow as did the language itself. For documentation, there's Javadoc. For client-server communication, there's RMI. Even the IDE, or rather, any number of IDEs from any number of vendors, were anticipated.

What Is JavaBeans™?

Java was intended from its earliest days to cater to the integrated development model of drag-and-drop program composition. Apropos this requirement, among the core methodologies designed into Java development you will find the *http://java.sun.com/ beans/docs/spec.html*, JavaBeans specification.

JavaBeans is an instance of the general design pattern of mapping a single fundamental entity onto a multiple-class implementation. As handy as the metaphor of object orientation has proven, real programming goes well beyond "just objects" in complexity of structure. Performing design decomposition on modern programs reveals that they tend to consist of fundamental entities that cannot conveniently be mapped just to single classes in any practical programming language. JavaBeans is one possible multiple-class mapping of a design concept.

If you think objects should communicate and cooperate reflexively, JavaBeans agrees with you. JavaBeans represents the object's ability to communicate with other entities, usually beyond runtime to design, compile, and configuration times.

Sun engineers identified early on in the life of Java one particularly interesting category of entity requiring a multiple-class implementation, that of the *reusable visual component*. Such a component has both a runtime and a design-time persona. Components of this sort are used in an integrated development environment such as NetBeans. Each drag-and-drop component used in an IDE to design programs needs both a runtime class that embodies the component functionality and a design-time class that the IDE employs for the visual representation and manipulation of the class.

The JavaBeans framework, although widely applicable beyond the creation of visual design components, has received its broadest exposure in that domain. Visual JavaBeans allows a component author to map the design persona of the component onto a separate Java class the BeanInfo class—from the component's runtime class in a fashion portable between different IDEs. This design-time persona is critical to establishing a visual representation of the component to the user and to establishing a properties metaphor for configuring the component in the design tool. On the other hand, the design-time persona is excess baggage at runtime. The packaging of the design-time persona of a reusable visual entity into a secondary class allows superfluous information to be discarded at runtime.

Java as an object-oriented programming environment possesses a more complete object model than does, say, C++. Java objects are capable of *reflection*. This means that objects and methods exist within Java to allow examination (often called *reflection*, sometimes called *introspection*) of an object's methods and data.

The JavaBeans framework takes advantage of Java reflection by creating classes whose main purpose is to be a repository of information about another class. These Bean classes each typically bear the name of the first-order class they shadow with "BeanInfo" appended to the name. A BeanInfo class can itself be composed algorithmically in software, either by automated examination of the source code for the first-order class or by using reflection to examine the compiled form of the first-order class. Additional information about the first-order class may be contained within the BeanInfo class; for example, in the case of a visual widget, the BeanInfo class contains information about the default size, title, colors, and orientation of the first-order class and often an embedded icon to be used to represent the first-order class on the toolbar. Additionally, the Bean may possess methods that communicate application-specific information to tools aware of the significance of that information.

The Core Concept of NetBeans

The basic JavaBeans design pattern was conceived primarily to ensure that factoring and component reuse would become the norm in Java programming. The core concept of NetBeans visual development is the design pattern of composing program components packaged as JavaBeans out of subcomponents also packaged as JavaBeans.

This might be called the "matryoshka doll pattern" of software design, after the Russian folk art of nested dolls, each of which is structurally complete in itself yet whose "semantic" resides in its recursively containing other structurally complete dolls.

NetBeans makes use of JavaBeans and the generation of new JavaBeans so automatic that it's almost always easier to generate a simple component, "bean" it, and drag it into the next-higher-level component you wish to compose than to do things any other way.

The architects of Java were largely successful in achieving this goal of providing a usable and compelling model for component packaging. And in the vanguard of this success we find *NetBeans*, the subject of our book.

 In case you were wondering, many programmers use NetBeans productively without often (or ever) straying into Bean construction.

NetBeans as the "Visual JDK"

NetBeans is an IDE. As such, it resembles other IDEs used in modern software engineering for authoring programs in languages such as C/C++, Forth, Ada, FORTRAN, COBOL, and RPG. NetBeans, however, is integrated with the code that is developed under NetBeans in a way that is impossible in many other languages (though Forth, Smalltalk, and LISP foreshadowed this sort of introspective language structure). It is as if NetBeans were itself the visual manifestation of the Java Development Kit (JDK) and of the Java Foundation Classes (Swing).

Per the core concept of NetBeans, the essential model of visual programming is as follows:

1. Use JavaBeans from the NetBeans component palette to create a visual component.
2. Wrap that component as a JavaBean.
3. Add that component to the NetBeans component palette, either to an extant palette or to a user- or application-specific palette.
4. Use the new component in the creation of more complex enclosing visual components.

The process is repeated as many times as necessary, both forming many components out of the same selection of JavaBeans and continually enhancing the palette by the more deeply nested JavaBean composition. Thus a simple visual program is composed of a small selection of top-level JavaBeans and any wrapper or nonvisual helper classes that are required.

All the Usual Features

NetBeans offers all the usual and expected features of an IDE:

- A syntax-coloring editor aware not only of the Java language, but also XML, HTML, and many other languages
- Component inspector
- Object browser

 The NetBeans Object Browser has in the latest revisions of NetBeans moved out of the core to become an optional external module that you may install via the NetBeans Update Center if you so choose.

- Debugger
- Integrated source control support for
  — External Concurrent Versions System (CVS)
  — Built-in CVS
  — Most external source control systems of your choice
- In addition to its own internal build system and compiler, NetBeans offers integration with external compilers and an external build system, *http://jakarta.apache.org/ant/index.html*, Jakarta Ant, one that is rapidly becoming the dominant build tool in the Java/XML world and beyond
- "Wizard" dialogs to assist the user at choice points

It also has many other features and tools about which you will read about later in this book.

NetBeans as a Tools Platform

NetBeans is an extraordinarily versatile tools platform. We could say that NetBeans is like a Swiss army knife onto which new blades can be attached at any time.

NetBeans itself is written wholly in Java, which is why it runs on any platform that supports the JDK. Furthermore, the runtime configuration of NetBeans is described in XML. When the core of NetBeans loads, it configures and launches the rest of the system. The core reads the XML description and loads the appropriate *modules*, that is, components written in Java against the *NetBeans API*.

It is this modules concept that allows extension of NetBeans. Many or most of the important features of NetBeans are modules that can be detached from the system and upgraded as needed. And because NetBeans is open source software, you are free to modify and recompile any modules whose behavior you wish to change. Thus, NetBeans has a close relationship with the programs it is developing that most other IDEs do not possess. NetBeans itself is developed in NetBeans, and any NetBeans user who wishes to join in may be part of that process.

In fact, NetBeans is so attractive a platform for tool architects that over 80 organizations have specifically ported their tool applications to NetBeans modules to make it more convenient for developers to use their tools. Visit the *http://www.netbeans.org/third-party.html*, Who is building on top of NetBeans, page to browse the eclectic mix of target applications from business and industry that use NetBeans as their development front end or as glue to hold their application presentation together.

Beyond the usefulness of adding features by adding modules to NetBeans, understanding how the individual tools that make up the NetBeans experience interoperate is a beneficial exercise for understanding the integration of component-based software. Whatever applications you wish to develop using NetBeans, if you work diligently and are lucky, over time the programs you write will come to be as well architected as NetBeans itself.

NetBeans as an Open Source Community

Many "real programmers" are not well-disposed toward IDEs. An IDE is no substitute for knowing the fine details of a programming language and its toolchain. Some IDEs surreptitiously introduce into a program de jure dependencies on a vendor's libraries or de facto human dependency on the IDE for program maintenance. Worse, many IDEs obstruct the flow of creativity and impose their theories of software engineering upon the work flow in a fashion likely to clash with the programmer's creative muse.

NetBeans has none of these flaws to any great extent. It neither ties the user to proprietary libraries nor renders source unmaintainable to an ordinary editor. NetBeans is an IDE for the expert programmer, yet gentle and easy for the novice. It achieves this by being the product of a community of expert Java programmers who have labored to render their own Java practice more enjoyable and more productive. Such individuals have no doctrine to impose other than the doctrine of mutual assistance, free software, and coding that must bear the scrutiny of the public eye.

NetBeans is open. Modules may be added and, perhaps more importantly, subtracted from the NetBeans installation. NetBeans source can also be modified under NetBeans and then recompiled to the tastes of the user. The usefulness of NetBeans is that there is as little of NetBeans between the programmer and his or her program as the programmer wills.

Don't Be Cross that This Book Is Cross-Platform

As we have mentioned, unlike other IDEs for Java, NetBeans is coded in pure Java. This means that NetBeans runs on any platform that offers the minima, particularly in terms of the Java environment.

One easily anticipated result of this flexibility of NetBeans is that the various authors of this book are each working on different platforms and at different levels of this open source project. Therefore, illustrations in this book will be somewhat inconsistent because they are drawn from screenshots of NetBeans running in the Java environments for Linux, Solaris, Windows, and possibly other operating systems.

We could have standardized on one platform to present the illustrations, but why play favorites? You, our readers, will be running NetBeans on a variety of platforms. The model of NetBeans behavior is consistent and pervasive even if the shape and color of its scroll bars change from platform to platform.

 It is in the nature of open source projects such as NetBeans to change rapidly. The authors of this book are working with NetBeans 3.3.1 and are trying in this book to be as general as possible in describing the functionality and operation of NetBeans because by the time you read this, some bright idea unknown to us at the time of writing may have worked its way into the latest release. Please remember this point, especially when viewing the illustrations, and do not be surprised if the layout of some or many windows has changed. It's almost certain that this will have occurred, but generally in the direction of augmented functionality. Rarely does a feature disappear, but this too has been known to happen from release to release, when one feature is replaced by a more advanced feature or set of features. In such cases, reading through the release notes may help point the way to finding the desired feature in its new location or its replacement.

Contents of the Accompanying Sources

The accompanying source download contains the following things:

- The source code to all of the examples in the book.
- Any libraries or other code required by the examples in this book.
- NetBeans Module files for complete NetBeans modules demonstrated in the half of the book on writing your own extensions modules for NetBeans. These files can be easily loaded into NetBeans to install the modules: just select **Tools →
Update Center** and choose **Install Manually Downloaded Modules** when prompted.

The accompanying sources can be downloaded from *http://www.oreilly.com/catalog/ netbeans*.

Licensing of the Code Examples in This Book

All of the source code examples in this book are open source and licensed under the Sun Public License, and you may copy or reuse them or portions thereof under its terms.

Writing Conventions in This Book

The structure of NetBeans, both internally and to the user, is very hierarchical. Very often you will open a dialog from a menu, which will then display a tree structure that you will need to navigate. In the procedures in this book, these containers are named inline—for example, "select **Tools → Options → IDE Configuration → Look and Feel → Menu Bar → File**" refers to both menu items and entities within the tree in the dialog that appears. Literally this translates to: Click the **Options** item on the **Tools** menu. Expand the folder **IDE Configuration**, its subfolder **Look and Feel**, and that folder's subfolder **Menu Bar** in the resulting dialog, and select the tree node labeled **File**. This convention is also followed in the NetBeans documentation.

We use the term `$NB_HOME` to denote the base directory for an installed copy of Net-Beans. A similar convention of using Unix-style environment variables is used to denote other information that varies between systems, such as `nbuser$VERSION`.

For brevity, most code examples omit import statements and such—we want this book to be readable. All of the code examples in the book are included in full source form on the accompanying downloadable sources.

Code listed in the book is generally formatted for readability and so may differ in indentation and line breaks from the downloadable sources. Where it was unavoidable to break a long line in print, but this line *cannot* actually be broken without affecting meaning, a hooked arrow (↵) is used at the printed break point.

Comments and Questions

Please address comments and questions concerning this book to the publisher:

O'Reilly & Associates, Inc.
1005 Gravenstein Highway North
Sebastopol, CA 95472
(800) 998-9938 (in the United States or Canada)
(707) 829-0515 (international or local)
(707) 829-0104 (fax)

We have a web page for this book, where we list errata, examples, and any additional information. You can access this page at

http://www.oreilly.com/catalog/netbeans

To comment or ask technical questions about this book, send email to

bookquestions@oreilly.com

For more information about our books, conferences, Resource Centers, and the O'Reilly Network, see our web site at

http://www.oreilly.com

Acknowledgments

This book could not have been created without the guidance, encouragement, and deadlines from our O'Reilly editors. Mike Loukides has been with us from the start, keeping us on track and moving forward. Brett McLaughlin joined later to give the project its final push and polish.

Reviewers

All of the authors are grateful to the NetBeans open source community for giving us the motivation to create this book, and especially to the community members who provided crucial feedback while the book evolved from early drafts to, we hope, a much finer finished product. They include Kevin Anderson, Wendy Blatt, Baerrach bonDierne, Joseph Bowbeer, Vincent Brabant, Mike Braden, Steve Brown, Dan Byers, James W. Y. F. Chan, Maarten Coene, Nicolai Czempin, Joan Friedman, Meg Garrison, Richard Gregor, Tim Halloran, Jirka Hana, Kristen Howe, Mike Hulse, Ben Hutchison, Jan Chalupa, Allan Jacobs, Kyley Jex, Thomas Kellerer, Petr Kuzel, Michael Lam, Louis Luangkesorn, Fiona MacGill, Cal McPherson, Karsten Meier, Francis Perreault, Ignacio Moran Pozzi, John Pramod, Patil Prashant, John Richardson, Georg Riker, Rochelle Roccah, Roxie Rochat, Adrian Romanelli, Phil Sager, Brian Sanders, Scott Schram, Jack Schuster, Bill Seddon, Julian Sinai, Andrew

Stevens, Ray Tayek, Josef Templ, Jaroslav Tulach, Bryan Vold, Christopher Webster, and Michael Wever.

There were others whose comments did not go through the email feedback channel or whose names could not be discerned from their email addresses. Please be assured that we greatly appreciated your contributions, even though your name may not be included in this list.

Simeon Greene

Firstly, I would like to thank my wife, Nikki, who continually supported me through many late nights working on the book. She was there every step of the way, and this accomplishment would not have been possible without her being at my side.

I would also like to thank Tim Boudreau for coming up with the idea for this book and being a real driving force behind the idea becoming a reality.

While contributing to this book, I had the pleasure of meeting some wonderful people who have encouraged and inspired me in many ways. Of these, Vaughn Spurlin and Michael Loukides deserve special mention. They both have kept me writing.

Finally, I would like to thank my family, especially my mother, and friends, especially Eric Staudt, for their never-ending support of me and all my endeavors. Thanks also to God for the talents that he gave me.

Vaughn Spurlin

Thanks first to my wife, Myrna, whose support and encouragement made the difference between wishing I had time to take on a significant project and actually sitting down and making it happen.

Coauthor Tim Boudreau deserves special notice for getting the project off the ground with the original outline and has my sincere gratitude for inviting me to join.

Finally, thanks to my colleagues at Sun Microsystems for their patience and assistance while I learned about NetBeans and to Sun's management from Scott McNealy on down for their vision in making the NetBeans phenomenon possible.

Jack Woehr

Thanks to the ladies and gentlemen of Pure Matrix, Inc., (*http://www.purematrix.com/*), who were unstinting in their generous loan of network bandwidth, an important consideration for an author constantly downloading new subrevisions of the Java Development Kit and of NetBeans itself.

Thanks also to Jon Erickson, Editor in Chief of *Dr. Dobb's Journal*, (*http://www.ddj.com/*), who has offered guidance and support to my writing projects over the past 12 years.

And thanks to my mom and dad, Mindell S., and Dr. Harry J. Woehr, for their encouragement and support. Born in the Roaring 'Twenties, they understand not a line of my technical writing, but they always buy a copy anyway.

Jesse Glick

Thanks go to Sun Microsystems for tolerating my peregrinations during the writing of this book, and to Michael Loukides and Brett McLaughlin among other staff at O'Reilly for their amazing patience, competence, and all-around cheer.

I was tickled pink by the number of detailed and helpful comments we received during the public review cycle for this book. Several people sent lengthy and well-thought-out reviews of many consecutive chapters—quite a lot of work, and completely volunteer. We can only hope that whatever wisdom lives in this book in tandem with the Net-Beans community will pay them back threefold for their time.

Thank you to the tireless creators of Emacs, DocBook XSL, Xalan, the GIMP, CVS, Ant, and the many other free tools whose quiet reliability helped give this book a tangible form.

Nothing would have been written had it not been for the support of friends to distract me during fits of writer's block. You know who you are, but I will thank Kristy anyway.

I would finally like to thank my parents for paying my way through college and all that stuff. It wasn't wasted.

Tim Boudreau

First and foremost, I thank my coauthor, colleague, and dear friend Jesse Glick, the accidental linguist. He has definitely been guru and I apprentice through the arduous process of writing this book. How could one not enjoy working with a colleague who wrote a Java method, the name of which was a single character in Sanskrit, just to see if he could? And for educating me in the dangers of indoor acid rain. Also thanks to Danese Cooper, without whom this project would never been started, Mike Loukides and Brett from O'Reilly, my coauthors, and the many reviewers named above, whose feedback helped make this book what it is.

Further, in no particular order:

- *Jon Locke*—for introducing me to TRS-80 Basic in 1982, being my partner in crime as 13 year olds with a pre-Internet startup, with fond memories of selling 5 1/4-inch floppies in sandwich baggies, discovering 1K digital audio sampling through the cassette port, and arguing over printing the documentation in letter quality mode because it would take three days on the dot-matrix printer.

- *Kami Pazderniková*—for giving me the extra excuse I needed to move to a country I love.

- *Jarda Tulach*—for nearly killing me with drunken bicycling in the mountains— or was it when I stole your swimming cap? Regardless, it's rare and wonderful to have such friends.

- *Doug Finn and Todd Hebert and all the others in Western Mass*—for actually supporting my crazy decision to give up life as a well-compensated contractor and go pursue the crazy idea of working for a startup in the Czech Republic for almost no money. Maybe now we'll have some time to record some music...

- *Evan Adams*—for being a mentor and friend and providing a roadmap and sometimes unwelcome advice for an independent-minded and often unruly former contractor, on how to survive and thrive in Dilbert-land.

- *Ian Formánek*—for being a friend, fellow musician, and manager extraordinaire. You have a surfeit of taste! That is, however, curable with medication...

- *Harold Wolfe and the others at Helios Custom Training*—who gave me my first taste of the joys and horrors of doing jobs for huge corporations. The debt is mine; I learned more than I thought I was learning, and in return was far more of a pain in the ass than you deserved.

- And all of the other people who have been part of my life over the course of getting the book done: Mike Boyer, George Dvôrák, Mike Gisondi, Monika Mayová, Bill Moffitt, Dan Roberts, Katka Rychtariková, and my tolerant roommates Jan Kratochvil and Karel Zatloukal. Special thanks to Don Bruce and Tracy Feldstein for letting me squat in their home and be "office gnome" for most of April 2002! And finally, thanks to the NetBeans community and Sun Microsystems for making NetBeans a project worth participating in and writing about. And last, but certainly not least, to my parents, for everything.

## CHAPTER 1

Getting and Installing the IDE

Platforms and Requirements

NetBeans has a set of basic requirements that must be checked before attempting to run the IDE. This section details these requirements.

What Are the System Requirements to Run NetBeans?

Large and complex Java programs are demanding of memory and processor resources, and NetBeans is no exception. Furthermore, whereas some programs can anticipate approximately how much memory or CPU time they will need, NetBeans, which allows the user to design an arbitrarily complex project, can make no such a priori assessment.

The *absolute* minima for running NetBeans are much more modest than the *practical* minima. For instance you *can* run NetBeans on an AMD 5x86 at 166 MHz with 64 MB of RAM and a 640 × 480 screen resolution, but only if you have no real work to do in NetBeans or any other tasks to perform on the machine in question. We know because we have tried it.

That said, we list in Table 1-1 the *practical* minima for running NetBeans on several popular platforms. These are of necessity somewhat subjective. One rule of thumb is that serious developers should take our word on the minima, but you can get by with less machine than we recommend if you only plan to explore NetBeans lightly (preparatory to finding yourself a more satisfactory platform on which to do serious development).

Table 1-1. NetBeans minimum requirements on several popular platforms

Platform	Processor (MHz)	Memory (MB)	Disk (MB)	Screen resolution	Color palette
Linux on Intel	233	128	75	800 × 600	65535
Mac OS X	400	256	75	Any modern color display	Any modern color display
Solaris on Intel	330	256	75	1024 × 768	16 million

Table 1-1. NetBeans minimum requirements on several popular platforms (continued)

Platform	Processor (MHz)	Memory (MB)	Disk (MB)	Screen resolution	Color palette
Solaris on Sparc	UltraSparc II 300	512	75	1024 × 768	16 million
Windows on Intel	330	192	75	800 × 600	16 million

The README.HTML shipped with a recent cut (3.3 beta 2) of NetBeans indicated minimal requirements somewhat more relaxed those listed in the table. However, these requirements are overly optimistic, and you'll find yourself having trouble doing meaningful work without more horsepower behind NetBeans.

For instance, this chapter and its illustrations are being developed on a Sun Blade with a 500-MHz UltraSparc II and 640 MB of memory. A medium-sized project currently open in NetBeans is consuming about 184 MB of memory on this machine, with peaks noticeably higher while compiling. As with any advanced design tool, NetBeans will always cheerfully accept more hardware resources and perform better for having them. The bigger and the more complex your projects are, the more NetBeans will want.

Also, you must consider what else you will be running at the same time as NetBeans. Are you developing an EJB project and debugging by running either JBoss or WebLogic as an application server instance on your local machine? Give that Wintel/ Lintel machine a minimum of 512 MB physical RAM and your Solaris Sparc machine 640 MB to 1 GB.

 Hint: If you're going to spend a little to upgrade your system for Net-Beans, you'll generally get more satisfaction out of increasing memory size first before you try other improvements such as processor speed, disk space, and so on.

Getting and Installing a JDK

You need the JDK installed on your computer to run NetBeans.

The Java Development Kit

Sun Microsystems' JDK consists of:

- The runtime engine for the Java programming environment
- The compiler and other basic tools essential to Java development
- The fundamental Java class libraries that make Java usable

Relationship of JDK to JRE

The Java Runtime Environment (JRE) consists of:

- The runtime engine for the Java programming environment
- The fundamental Java class libraries that make Java usable

The JRE is a runtime for users. The JDK is the complete software development environment for Java. Sun and other Java implementors provide the JRE packaged independently of the JDK. Everything that is in the JRE is also in the JDK—the JDK is a pure superset of the JRE.

 You will need the full JDK to do NetBeans development. NetBeans uses the development tools in the JDK to do much of its work.

Obtaining the JDK

Many operating systems nowadays, such as Linux and Solaris, come with a JDK preinstalled. Even so, you may want to obtain a later version of the JDK. At the web site java.sun.com (*http://java.sun.com/*) you can obtain free of charge the JDK for the following operating environments:

- Linux
- Solaris (both for Sparc and x86 architectures)
- Microsoft Windows

Other JDKs exist for various platforms created by various other vendors and open source software organizations. Among them are:

- Blackdown (*http://www.blackdown.org*)
- FreeBSD (*http://www.freebsd.org/java/*)
- IBM (*http://www.ibm.com/developerworks/java/*)

What JVM flavors and version are known to be supported by the IDE?

You will need JDK 1.3 or above to run NetBeans. Consult the NetBeans JVM Frequently Asked Questions (FAQ) (*http://www.netbeans.org/ide/support/faqs/ installation.html*) for more information about obtaining the JDK and setting it up in your particular operating environment. You will also find pertinent information in the NetBeans HowTo (*http://www.netbeans.org/project/www/articles/howtos.html*).

Which IDE Distribution?

You have several choices when picking a distribution of the NetBeans IDE to download and run on your personal computer or workstation. Your choices are

- Download or order the current Sun ONE Studio 4 packaging of NetBeans from the Sun ONE Studio 4 web site (*http://wwws.sun.com/software/sundev/jde/index. html*).

Sun ONE Studio 4 is the product formerly known as Sun Forte for Java.

- Download the latest stable release of NetBeans from the NetBeans downloads page (*http://www.netbeans.org/downloads.html*).
- Download an earlier stable release of NetBeans from the NetBeans downloads page (*http://www.netbeans.org/downloads.html*).
- Download a reasonably stable beta release of NetBeans from the NetBeans downloads page (*http://www.netbeans.org/downloads.html*).
- Download the latest build of NetBeans from the NetBeans downloads page (*http://www.netbeans.org/downloads.html*).
- Download the Q-build of NetBeans from the NetBeans Q-Builds Program (*http://qa.netbeans.org/processes/q-builds-program.html*).

Your choice will balance the trade-off between stability, commonality of experience with a wide range of developers of all skill levels, and advanced technology, as summarized in Table 1-2.

Table 1-2. Summary of trade-offs between NetBeans releases

Release	Advantages	Disadvantages
Sun ONE Studio 4	Sun ONE Studio 4 cuts of the NetBeans IDE are the most stable and long-lived cuts. Patches are offered via the Update Center (see "The Update Center"). Sun attempts to see that their enterprise customers and less adventurous developers have a reliable environment for routine Java development, one that possesses a clearly defined relationship to the trusted name and service offerings of Sun Microsystems.	New NetBeans features make their way slowly into Sun ONE Studio 4 releases. You really only need be slightly more adventurous than the typical Sun ONE Studio 4 user to go with the latest stable NetBeans release.
Latest Stable NetBeans	This is the best choice if you are a strong developer who still wants stability. With a stable, numbered NetBeans release you get a well-tested and matured collection of code that is up to date.	You may wish to consider the greater stability of a Sun ONE Studio 4 release, the more completely characterized environment provided by a previous stable release, or the important advances of a more recent build.
Earlier Stable NetBeans	With an earlier stable build of NetBeans, you stick with a system that is well understood. Recently, several team members on an important project using NetBeans declined to upgrade to NetBeans 3.2 and stuck with NetBeans 3.1. Although 3.2 had desirable improvement in CVS support, it also possessed a troublesome bug in menu code generation.	NetBeans is improving at a rapid pace. If you stick with an earlier release of NetBeans, you miss important improvements and may even find yourself expending more effort to get the same results you could get with less effort using a later release.

Table 1-2. Summary of trade-offs between NetBeans releases (continued)

Release	Advantages	Disadvantages
NetBeans Beta	With a NetBeans beta, you can get the latest and most stable (as compared to the Q-Build) approach to some hurdle NetBeans is currently vaulting. Another beta advantage is that you can validate fixes you are expecting in NetBeans in response to a bug report.	A given beta release may not be applicable to your work environment or may only serve to divert your attention from your own coding issues into the entertaining sideline of helping along the progress of NetBeans itself.
NetBeans Lastest Build	This is the bleeding edge. You not only like NetBeans, you like to build NetBeans often. These releases are posted approximately daily. Go for it!	On the other hand, the latest build • May not work as expected • May not work at all • May not even build correctly
NetBeans Q-Build	This is a compromise between the bleeding edge and stability. It's a more recent build than the last stable release or Beta release, but it surely compiles and runs.	The downside of the Q-Build is that it may have unreported bugs and/or may present undocumented or poorly documented new or altered features.

 We've used the term "beta" in the table to characterize a prerelease or release candidate of NetBeans. Often these releases do not actually bear the term "beta" in their name.

There is another kind of distribution that you might be interested in: as mentioned in the Preface, various vendors of development and deployment environments make special releases of NetBeans that integrate these vendors' niche-specific tools with the NetBeans environment. Visit the Who is building on top of NetBeans (*http://www.netbeans.org/third-party.html*) page to browse the distributions available from vendors in industries ranging from software modeling to data mining that integrate NetBeans into their products.

Installing Binary Distributions

It's easy to install a binary distribution of NetBeans, whether it's the current stable release, a beta, or a Q-build.

- On Windows, the distribution archive is itself an executable file. Run the installation *.exe* which will:
  — Unpack all files from within itself
  — Install all required program objects and ancillary files
  — Create a shortcut to NetBeans on your desktop from which you may start the application
- On Unix, unpack the distribution archive and move the unpacked tree to an appropriate file system location.

- On all platforms, be sure to read any and all Readme files found with the distribution. These files give up-to-the-minute information on installation issues and runtime issues. This especially applies to less widely used platforms such as Macintosh and OpenVMS.

Building the IDE from Source (Simple Builds)

In this section we are going to build NetBeans from source. You can skip this section if you don't want to build NetBeans from its source code. However, it's easy to build NetBeans, so you might as well try it once just for fun.

We're going to do a simple, straightforward build, no special options, no personal changes to the source code. If you are intererested in modifying NetBeans and rebuilding it, adding modules of your own to NetBeans, and advanced options, you will want to read *Section II: Extending NetBeans*.

What You'll Need to Build the IDE

To get started with developing and building NetBeans, first visit NetBeans DevHome (*http://www.netbeans.org/devhome/*), which has explanations of how to download NetBeans source code and the latest information on builds.

To build the IDE you need several items:

- A correctly configured installation of the Java Development Kit
- The NetBeans source
- Certain binary-only objects (sometimes called the *extra binaries*) distributed without source required for a NetBeans build
- The Jakarta Ant build system from the Apache Project

 The NetBeans extra binaries include a version of Ant sufficient to build the IDE. It is not necessary to download Ant separately.

For special issues pertaining to building NetBeans under Mac OS X, please see the web page Using NetBeans on Mac OS X (*http://www. netbeans.org/ide/support/mac.html*).

Setting Up and Performing the Build

Assuming that you now have the NetBeans sources archive file (or have performed an anonymous CVS checkout from the NetBeans source server) and that you also have downloaded the extra binaries archive (each typically a *.tar.gz* GNU zipped tar file or a *.zip* Windows-style zip file) downloaded to your machine, proceed through the following steps to build NetBeans:

1. Create a directory in which to work (e.g., */usr/local/src/netbeans* on Unix or *C:\ NetBeansSource* on Windows).

2. Change directory to your new work directory and unpack the NetBeans sources archive. It will create its own directory hierarchy whose top directory is *netbeans-src* below the current directory.

3. Create in the current directory (your new work directory) a subdirectory called *nbextra* (this subdir is not created automatically in unpacking).

4. Change directory into *nbextra* and unpack the NetBeans extra binaries required for the build.

5. Follow the instructions in the sidebar "Installing and Configuring Ant" to make sure the Ant build system used to perform the NetBeans source build is in place and ready to run.

6. Change directory back to your work directory (e.g., if you are still in *nbextra* then cd ..).

7. Change directory to the *netbeans-src* directory that was created automatically when you unpacked the NetBeans sources.

8. Change directory to the *nbbuild* directory.

9. Enter the ant command.

Ant will now start to run and read the build file *build.xml* and construct NetBeans per the project description found therein. The build process will take a few minutes even on a fast machine. Late in the build process, the newly compiled instance of NetBeans may load itself to configure its extensions and then will exit by itself, so don't be surprised if NetBeans spontaneously appears on your computer screen and then disappears.

Where Did Everything Go?

Okay, you did the build. Now, where did the build go? It was built in the *netbeans-src/nbbuild/netbeans* directory. You can run the newly built IDE from *netbeans-src/nbbuild/netbeans/bin* in the manner described in the sidebar "Installing and Configuring Ant."

How Do I Install a Newly Built Version of NetBeans?

At the end of the build process, a .zip distribution archive was created analogous to the ones you download from the NetBeans web pages when you download a prebuilt version. This .zip file is found after a successful build in the *netbeans-src/nbbuild* directory and is called:

```
NetBeans-dev-yyyymmddhhmm.zip
```

where *yyyymmddhhmm* is the year, month, day, hour, and minute in which the build was accomplished. Simply unpack that .zip file in the directory wherein you wish NetBeans to be located and you can run NetBeans from there in the manner described in Table 1-2.

Installing and Configuring Ant

Jakarta Ant is a dynamic open source project in rapid flux. Therefore, source distributions of NetBeans contain (in *nbbuild/bin/*) their own prebuilt version of Ant to ensure that a version appropriate to the style of the NetBeans *build.xml* file is available. The instructions below are minimal, relating to the configuration of the provided Ant binaries for the purpose of building NetBeans. It is not necessary to perform any special configuration for using the supplied version of Ant *within* NetBeans. For further information on configuring an Ant installation for general usage independent of NetBeans, please consult the Ant manual which is distributed from the Jakarta Ant web site.

To configure the provided Ant distribution for use in building NetBeans:

1. Find where you have installed the *nbbuild* directory and the extra binaries distribution and add the *bin* directory beneath that directory to your system's executable search path:
   - For a Unix system, the command might be
     ```
     PATH=/usr/local/src/NetBeans/netbeans-src/nbbuild/bin:$PATH; export PATH
     ```
   - For Windows, the command might be
     ```
     SET PATH=C:\NetBeansSource\netbeans-src\nbbuild\bin;%PATH%
     ```
     or, alternatively, set this path extension systemwide by **MyComputer** → **Properties** → **Advanced** → **Environment**.

2. Ant resides in part in a *bin* directory and in part in a sibling directory (one that is at the same level as *bin*), *lib*. Set the environment variable
   ```
   ANT_HOME
   ```
   to point to the parent directory of these two siblings. For example,
   - For a Unix system, the command might be
     ```
     ANT_HOME=/usr/local/src/NetBeans/netbeans-src/nbbuild; export ANT_HOME
     ```
   - For a Windows system, the command might be
     ```
     SET ANT_HOME=C:\NetBeansSource\netbeans-src\nbbuild
     ```
     or, alternatively, you could once again use the **MyComputer** properties to set the environment globally.

3. Set the environment variable
   ```
   JAVA_HOME
   ```
   to the location of your Java Development Kit (JDK) installation. For example,
   - For a Unix system, the command might be
     ```
     JAVA_HOME=/usr/java; export JAVA_HOME
     ```
   - For a Windows system, the command might be
     ```
     SET JAVA_HOME=C:\jdk1.3
     ```
     or, alternatively, you could once again use the **MyComputer** properties to set the environment globally.

Running the IDE

By now you're about ready to run the NetBeans IDE. Let's take one last look at what's necessary to launch NetBeans.

Minimal Environment

Once the minimal hardware and software requirements are met, all you need to get ready to run NetBeans is to make sure the minimal environmental requirements are met. There's really only one: NetBeans must be able to find the Java Development Kit.

- On Unix installations, the variable

  ```
  JDK_HOME
  ```

  must be set to the root of your JDK installation, something like

  ```
  JDK_HOME=/usr/java; export JDK_HOME
  ```

- On Mac OS X, the JDK is found in */Library/Java/Home*. Open the command shell (**Finder** → **Applications** → **Utilities** → **Terminal**) from which you will launch NetBeans. The shell given you in the OS X Terminal application is, by default, *tcsh*. In *tcsh* issue the command:

  ```
  setenv JDK_HOME
          /Library/Java/Home
  ```

  If you are using a shell such as *bash* or *zsh*, the syntax will be as for Unix above,

  ```
  JDK_HOME=/Library/Java/Home; export JDK_HOME
  ```

   For special issues pertaining to launching NetBeans under Mac OS X, please see the web page Using NetBeans on Mac OS X (*http://www. netbeans.org/ide/support/mac.html*).

- On Windows, NetBeans expects to be able to find the Java executable in your

  ```
  PATH
  ```

  variable. Either set this variable in the current command line session, for example,

  ```
  SET PATH=C:\JDK1.3;%PATH%
  ```

  or use **MyComputer** → **Properties** → **Advanced** → **Environment** to set the path permanently for all sessions.

   If you used the self-installing archive to install NetBeans on your Windows machine, all necessary pathing will be handled automatically by the NetBeans shortcut installed on your desktop.

- Alternatively, rather than set environment variables, you may modify *bin/ide.cfg* to include -jdkhome JAVA_HOME.

How to Launch NetBeans

NetBeans is pure Java, so all you have to do to start NetBeans is invoke the Java interpreter on the correct class file, right? Well, not exactly. NetBeans, as a user application, operates within a rich context that is pretty complicated to enter at the command line. Therefore, NetBeans is usually started by all except the experts by one of two executable files provided with the NetBeans installation. These files are present whether you downloaded a binary release of NetBeans or downloaded source and built and installed it.

- For Unix operating systems, the file is a shell script called *runide.sh*.
- For Mac OS X, you can use the same *runide.sh* as Unix, having first set the *JDK_HOME* variable as shown above in the same Terminal window as the one from which you are now launching NetBeans.

 There is a desktop-based launcher for NetBeans on Mac OS X. Although you can install NetBeans from any of the distributions provided on the NetBeans web site (*http://www.netbeans.org*), the Mac OS X distribution includes this launcher. Alternatively, you can obtain the launcher source by checking out the NetBeans sources for the module *core*.

- For Windows operating systems, the file is either of two Windows executables:
  - *runide.exe*, which starts a command line session that launches NetBeans, thus allowing you to watch all logging output as NetBeans runs. Also, you may examine the *ide.log* file, which records the logging output of NetBeans as it launches and runs.
  - *runidew.exe*, which starts NetBeans through a windowing system call without opening a command line session. When you start NetBeans this way, there is one less window cluttering up your desktop, but if any "interesting" things happen that make you want the logging output, you will have to go to the directory where NetBeans stores your settings and look at the file *ide.log* for the output.

 The local settings directory in which the files we have discussed above are found is called *nbuser* or some slightly different name in a given release of NetBeans (e.g., *nbuser33* for release 3.3.x. or *nbdev* for a development release). It's typically found on Unix systems in the user's home directory, though it may appear elsewhere. For Windows, this directory is found wherever the user at first install of Net-Beans indicated the settings directory should be placed, as described below in the section "Multiple NetBeans Users."

Switches to the runide.sh script

The *runide.sh* shell script for launching NetBeans on systems with a Unix-like shell can be passed two switches on the command line:

- *-jdkhome fullpath* tells NetBeans where the JDK home directory is, overriding built-in defaults and variables set in the user's environment.
- *-userdir fullpath* tells NetBeans which directory to use in the user's settings directory. This is very helpful if you are "stuck in a crack" between releases and are using two versions of NetBeans, both of which want to use the same user settings directory. Employing the *-userdir* switch keeps one NetBeans version from altering the settings you are maintaining for the other version.

In both cases, *fullpath* is the fully qualified path to the directory in question.

Multiple NetBeans Users

NetBeans is engineered to take into account multiple users launching NetBeans from the same installation. NetBeans accommodates this by keeping each user's personal settings separate from the NetBeans code installation. This is handled correctly on both Windows and Unix systems. Also, NetBeans distinguishes between NetBeans versions. So if you have previously run NetBeans and upgrade to a later version, the first time the new version runs, it will offer to migrate your settings from the previous version to the version you are now running.

- On Unix systems, settings are kept in a local settings directory created in the user's home directory the first time NetBeans is run.
- On Windows, the first time NetBeans is run, NetBeans prompts the user for the name of a directory in which settings should be stored (see Figure 1-1). The directory chosen by the user is stored in a Windows Registry key *HKEY_CURRENT_USER/Software/netbeans.org/NetBeans IDE/$VERSION*, which is how NetBeans finds the user settings directory each time it runs. Some points:
  - If the Registry variable is not set, the user will be prompted for a settings directory.
  - If the specified directory does not exist, it will be created. As of the current writing, NetBeans creates its user settings directory structure specifically in the directory you specify rather than automatically creating a *netbeans* subdirectory of the specified directory.
  - If the specified directory exists but is empty, NetBeans will dialog with user to create or import initial settings.

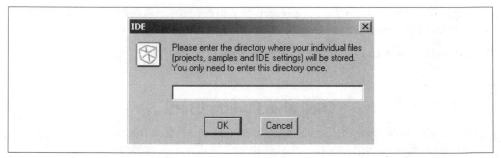

Figure 1-1. NetBeans running the first time on Windows prompts for a settings directory

Troubleshooting

Well, sometimes things do go wrong. Let's take a look at some of the things that can go wrong when you try to run NetBeans. Some of the problems mentioned below will probably only occur when you first try to run NetBeans; others can occur any time.

Launching

What do you do if NetBeans doesn't come up when you start it? Generally, there are only a few common things that can go wrong when launching NetBeans. Anything *uncommon* will probably leave some hint of the problem in the NetBeans *ide.log* file.

- Under Unix, this file is found at *$HOME/nbuser/system/ide.log*.
- Under Windows, this file will be found under the *system* directory located in the directory in which you told NetBeans (the first time it ran) to store your local settings file.

X Window System issues

This section applies only to those running NetBeans under the X Window System on a Unix-like operating system. There are primarily two problems relating to the X Window System that can prevent NetBeans from coming up on your local display:

1. Make sure that the *DISPLAY* variable for the session in which NetBeans is running is set to a meaningful value. For example, if NetBeans is running on *foo. mydomain.com* and your local box is *bar.mydomain.com*, you might execute something like the following in the command line session on *foo.mydomain.com* before issuing the command to launch NetBeans:

   ```
   DISPLAY=bar.mydomain.com:0.0 ; export DISPLAY
   ```

2. If you are running NetBeans on a remote Unix machine and using your local machine as an X Window System server (the X Window System uses the term *server* to mean the unit on which the display is rendered and *client* to mean the application that needs that display), remember to give the remote machine permission to draw on your local display or you will get a message about something like "can't open display."

SSH Tunnels X Window System

If you log in via the Secure Shell (SSH) into the machine on which NetBeans will run, you can tunnel X through the SSH connection by using the -X flag to the ssh command. In this case the DISPLAY variable gets set automatically to a "magic" value that SSH understands on both sides of the connection. See the documentation for your implementation of SSH.

Appearance once launched

Sometimes there are difficulties with the appearance of the NetBeans IDE once it is launched.

Screen resolution. As indicated previously, screen resolution can become an issue running NetBeans. NetBeans has a very "busy" display with a multitude of graphic indicators, icons, and badges that require screen real estate in which to communicate to you, the user.

If the display is at a minimum resolution, you will lose breadth of overview in favor of necessary detail. At 800 × 600 resolution it can be difficult to maintain your mental picure of the entire project you are working on because so many of the object names will have scrolled out of view in the NetBeans Explorer. At 1024 × 768 resolution the situation is acceptable if not ideal. You really will be much happier with at least a 17-inch display and a resolution above 1024 × 768. Sun Microsystems supports the development of NetBeans, so it's probably not entirely coincidental that the common Sun monitor resolution of 1152 × 900 is nearly ideal for NetBeans.

X Window System. Some X Window System servers (see above) seem not to cooperate perfectly with certain Java Swing widgets. For instance, on some X servers, the NetBeans main window, which should appear at NetBeans startup at the top of the useful display, will appear in the middle of the display. Usually resizing will clear up the problem. Try maximizing the NetBeans main window or minimize it and then maximize it.

SDI vs. MDI. NetBeans can either display its various tools as separate desktop windows (X Window System and OS/2 style, called *SDI* for *Single Document Interface*) or as a collection of child windows within a parent window (Windows style, called *MDI* for *Multiple Document Interface*). NetBeans by default allows the user to select one or the other of these modes the first time NetBeans is run. Whichever you choose, you can switch between SDI and MDI in any subsequent session.

Use the Options dialog (pull down **Tools** → **Options** → **Configuration** → **System** → **System Settings**) and change the **User Interface** property (which is a drop-down selector) to toggle between SDI and MDI interface.

The SDI interface allows you to

- Arrange NetBeans windows as you like
- Minimize individual windows
- Make an individual window full-screen

On the other hand, it's a bit more disorganized than MDI, as can be seen in Figure 1-2.

The MDI interface keeps all the NetBeans windows together and organized. On the other hand, it can get cluttered because generally no individual child window is full-screen. This interface is shown in Figure 1-3.

Summary regarding windowing issues. Windowing issues come up more frequently in NetBeans than in some other IDEs because NetBeans is so liberal in allowing modules to hook the window space of the IDE proper. If something is missing, look for it. If something is misdrawn, open and close it or resize it. If something has changed, read the README file. Post to the newsgroups (see Appendix D) when you have questions.

Updating the IDE Automatically

NetBeans can automatically upgrade its core and extension modules over the Internet.

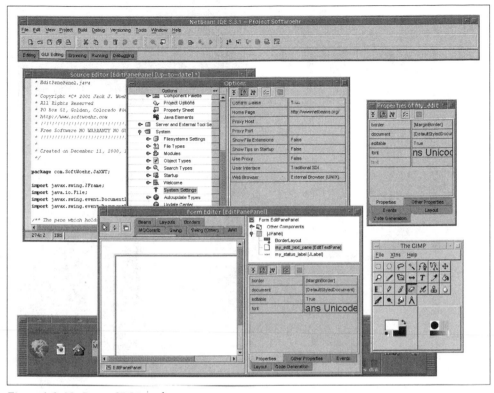

Figure 1-2. NetBeans SDI interface

The Update Center

NetBeans has a module that can run periodically on your behalf and check for updates to the revision of NetBeans which you are using. The *Update Center* also can download and install such upgrades on your behalf if you wish.

Configuring the Update Center

Use the Update Center Wizard to configure various factors for the Update Center, such as

- Update site
- Frequency of update checks
- Proxy usage

You can see these options in Figure 1-4.

You also use the Update Center to install optional modules and even experimental modules currently under development. Once the Update Center has loaded, explore the modules offered and try anything you like, such as the new XML Tree Editor.

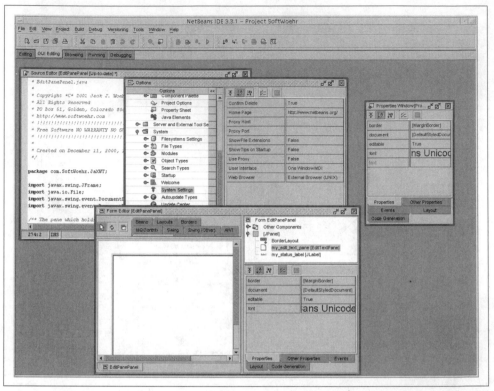

Figure 1-3. NetBeans MDI interface

Setup Wizard

Both changing between the MDI/SDI interface and controlling the Update Center can also be performed through the Setup Wizard (shown in Figure 1-5), along with installing and configuring NetBeans modules. Pull down **Tools → Setup Wizard** to launch the Setup Wizard, or just use it when it pops up automatically the first time you start NetBeans.

You're Now Running NetBeans

If you got this far in the book, you're now running NetBeans. You might wish at this point to simply run through the tutorial that is part of the NetBeans online help. Pull down **Help → Help Sets → Core IDE Help**. Pull down **Help → Contents** for the whole story.

And if you find yourself faced with problems not covered in this book, try NetBeans Frequently Asked Questions (*http://www.netbeans.org/ide/support/faqs*) on the web.

We hope you enjoy NetBeans.

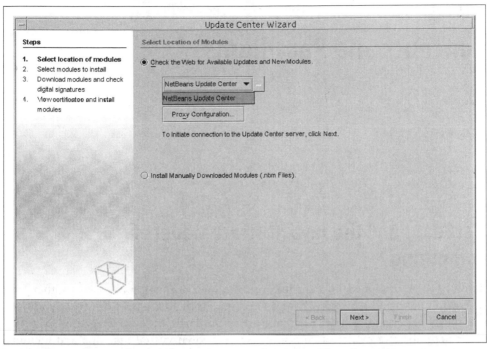

Figure 1-4. Configuring the Update Center using Update Center Wizard

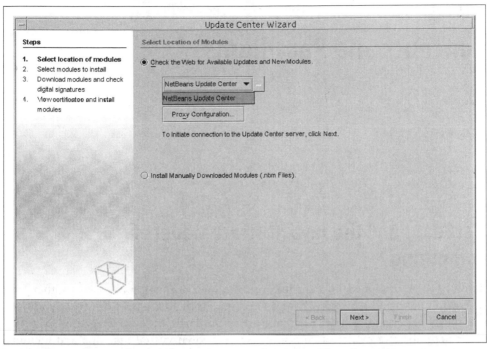

Figure 1-5. Configuring SDI/MDI using Setup Wizard

CHAPTER 2
Concepts and Paradigms

NetBeans and the Java Abstract Model of Computing

If you have programmed Java at the command line, or if you have used another Java IDE, you might find that many things are different in NetBeans from what you have previously experienced. The difference arises primarily because Java itself is a self-contained, abstract model of computing with its own virtual machine and memory model juxtaposed on the intent of the NetBeans designers to fulfill this model.

Java was at first intended to be an entire operating system; Sun and IBM even went a long way toward building a Java computer with a Java OS before Java retrenched and remained primarily a software virtual machine running under a host operating system. Java does not even presume the existence of a hosting hierarchical file system. Instead, it has its own hierarchy of nested packages that are Java's "native file system," as it were.

NetBeans goes a long way toward cooperating with Java's abstract model of computing. If Java really were the operating system of your computer, the GUI explorer you would use to navigate your system would look a lot like the NetBeans Explorer.

This is the essence of what is special about programming Java under NetBeans, as compared to programming Java at the command line. NetBeans leans toward presenting the Java computing universe to you from Java's point of view, not from the point of view of any particular hosting operating system.

Part of that Java view of computing is the familiar tight coupling of source objects with code objects emphasized by the package model of Java coding, including familiar details such as

- The rule of one public class per source file
- The hierarchical layout of packages and their applicable access rules
- Cross-object dependency checking carried out by the compiler

NetBeans closely adapts its visual presentation of Java coding to these conceptual models. You will be in a better position to appreciate this point after you have read in this chapter and the chapters to follow about the NetBeans Explorer, Source Editor, and Object Browser.

To commence our discussion of how NetBeans adapts itself to the conceptual models of Java, let's examine the correspondence between the NetBeans representation of your project and the host operating system's and host filesystem's representation of your project. This correspondence is not always obvious at first glance. In the next section, we'll discuss the NetBeans Explorer and

- The basics of how NetBeans represents your project
- How you navigate the NetBeans representation to
  — Create your NetBeans project
  — Edit the Java source for your NetBeans project
  — Compile the Java source of your NetBeans project
  — Run your NetBeans project
- The correspondence between what you see in NetBeans and what "really" exists at host operating system and file system layer.

Explorer

The user's primary tool in developing with NetBeans is the NetBeans Explorer.

Objects in the User Interface

The NetBeans Explorer is the NetBeans component that will become most familiar to you first. Explorer is your main interface to normal NetBeans operations on your files, objects, and projects.

NetBeans Explorer presents your project in the "explorer view," which has become a common visual metaphor in most graphical user interfaces (GUIs). All sorts of objects appear in that view, each represented as a *node* of the tree and having its own icon to indicate what sort of object the node represents. Representing objects as nodes allows NetBeans to construct various trees of nodes from different selection criteria. These trees offer you different collection views of the objects that make up your program and development environment.

One such view is of the objects and packages of your Java program. In this view objects and packages correspond roughly to files and folders in a typical Explorer view of a filesystem. However, each of the nodes in this type of NetBeans Explorer view represent not the individual files but rather all the files making up your class and its source lumped together. They are represented by one node; if you click on the node, it opens up into a subtree that contains more detail about the entity it represents.

Data Objects, Nodes, Actions, and Properties

NetBeans Explorer uses nodes to offer a view of your project as *objects*. Because the word "object" means different things in different contexts, let's make sure we know what we mean by "objects" in the context of NetBeans projects.

NetBeans Explorer nodes are representations of elements of your project as objects. An Explorer node represents, for instance, an entire class of your program as an object. This object has data members: fields and methods that belong to the class. The object has methods: actions that can be applied to the source or the byte code of the class. The object has properties: miscellaneous, generally simple aspects that can conveniently be manipulated at development time by the programmer under the familiar rubric of "properties."

IDE settings themselves are often expressed as properties and appear in a properties editor window, either standing alone or as a panel of some dialog. Wander around the Options window, which comes up when you choose **Tools → Options**, and you'll see lots and lots of properties.

 When you encounter properties sheets, the keyword for the property is to the left and the value is to the right. If the value can be edited, clicking in the region of the value will allow you to edit it in place.

- When a property can assume one of only a fixed set of possible values, clicking the gadget to the right of the value will pull down a list of the possible values.

- When a property consists of a long string or a list of values, clicking the gadget to the right of the value will open up an editing window.

When you create, author, and compile Java classes under NetBeans, a node appears for each class in the Explorer view. You can open that view up to a more detailed view by clicking on the little "switch" with the horizontal lever that appears in the Explorer next to the node. Then the lever points down and the view opens up. And if you double-click on any node representing a method or member of your class from within this expanded view, the NetBeans Source Editor opens on the source for that class on the very line where the method or member represented by the Explorer node is defined (shown in Figure 2-1).

This is a very convenient representation of a program element. Its data fields and methods appear as individual Explorer nodes as you expand the tree, as in Figure 2-1, an illustration of a visual Java class. You can explore properties of these individual objects represented by nodes by right-clicking the mouse and choosing Properties, as illustrated by Figure 2-2.

This concept of a Java class entity or its methods being Explorer objects, having default actions, and possessing something called "properties," is purely a NetBeans

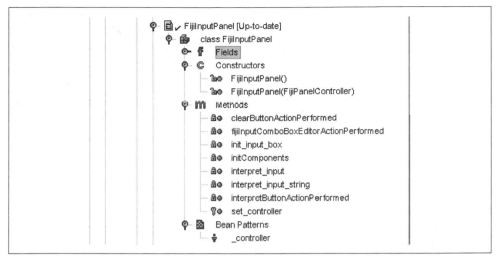

Figure 2-1. NetBeans Explorer expanded object view of a program element

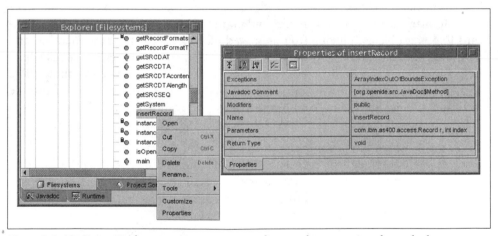

Figure 2-2. NetBeans Explorer opening a property editor on the properties of a method

construct, one that goes way beyond the definition of the Java programming language itself. It's just a viewpoint from which perspective the developer using Net-Beans is allowed to survey the taxonomy of a program element. This viewpoint allows development actions that in "classical" Java programming via a text editor would be regarded as different actions to be bundled together and presented under a unifying metaphor.

Here's an example of that bundling: when you "hop" to the appropriate editor(s) and specific line of source by double-clicking the mouse on a member or method node, from NetBeans Explorer's point of view, you are invoking the *default action* of that object. In the case of a method or member of a class being represented in an Explorer view, the default action is to open the source for the class in an appropriate editor. Because NetBeans Explorer represents many other program entities as Explorer nodes, you can guess that the default action for other objects might not be the same, and indeed it isn't. For instance, if you have an Ant build file in your source tree, the default action on a double-click is to run Ant on the build file.

Perhaps you want to edit either the source to a Java class or an Ant build file. Both these types of nodes offer you an "Open" selection. In the case of an Ant file, the Open operation is to open it in an appropriate editor, and that Open operation is not the default action (the double-click action). Open is, however, the default action for a Java class, and it results in opening an editor on the source.

Moreover, other Explorer objects might possess Open actions that are quite different from the Open action for an Ant build file or a Java class. It's all based on that idea of overloading a small set of action names that seem conceptually similar as a means of simplifying the IDE's user interface, the bundling together under a unifying metaphor we mentioned earlier.

Typical of this grouping together of disparate actions under a unifying metaphor is the concept that NetBeans Explorer nodes are pretty uniformly subject to some sort of "Customize" action. Customize is found on the context menus for all sorts of NetBeans Explorer objects, ranging from mounted filesystems to classes to methods and fields of classes. At each level that you encounter Customize it actually does something completely different from what it does at another level, yet somehow these varying Customize operations can be viewed as "the same kind of thing" from the practical developer viewpoint. And NetBeans, we will come to see, is always trying to group elements of our developer workflow together for practical simplification.

For instance, rather than open up the Source Editor on the Java source file for a class, it's sometimes convenient to edit the signature of a method by choosing the Customize option from the context menu for the method node as it appears in Explorer. This brings up a method signature editor, shown in Figure 2-3, which allows us to fill in the fields rather than wander around in the Source Editor.

The same Customize metaphor is also applied to other very different entities in NetBeans Explorer. You mount CVS source trees in the Explorer to make your source tree, and its corresponding repository appears as Explorer nodes. Once such a tree is mounted, it too is subject to a Customize action, one that allows you to change paths and repositories. It's quite a jump from the idea of Customize a method signature to Customize a mounted view of a source tree, but the conceptual similarity of the operations suggested to the creators of NetBeans the metaphor of overloading á la object-oriented programming a simple set of names and menu selections. Try clicking on various objects presented in the NetBeans Explorer and choosing **Customize** to see what's offered.

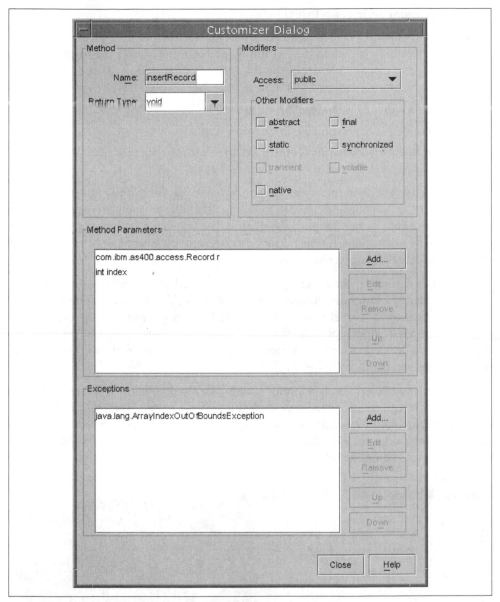

Figure 2-3. Customizing the signature of a method

There's also a lot more about customizing NetBeans in Chapter 6.

What has NetBeans Explorer got to hide?

In addition to showing you your classes in an expandable view, NetBeans Explorer also hides something from you that would be obvious in a simple file listing, that is, that the program element shown in the Explorer is composed of several files. In the illustration, the files represented by the Explorer object FijiInputPanel are threefold:

- The Java source file, *FijiInputPanel.java*
- The compiled Java class file *FijiInputPanel.class*
- The form file *FijiInputPanel.form* used by NetBeans to represent in XML the composition of visual classes

In other words, when you perform operations on an Explorer object that represents an element of your program, you are performing whatever operations on whatever file or files necessary to accomplish the goal of that operation. When you are editing a visual class in a NetBeans Form Editor, you are actually modifying both the source file *and* the form file that NetBeans uses internally.

When you design visual classes using NetBeans form editors, NetBeans *form files* are generated silently alongside the code for your classes. The form file (one per class) keeps information about elements of your design that require autogeneration of code. The shaded regions of code that the NetBeans editor won't let you edit and that you find in Java source files maintained by NetBeans form editors are the regions described by the form file for that class.

Figure 2-4 depicts a source file containing autogenerated code open in the NetBeans Source Editor with its protected regions shaded. Next to the NetBeans Source Editor, a plain text editor has the same file open, revealing metatags embedded in Java comments that indicate to the NetBeans editor where it shouldn't let you edit. (Hint: don't delete these comments.)

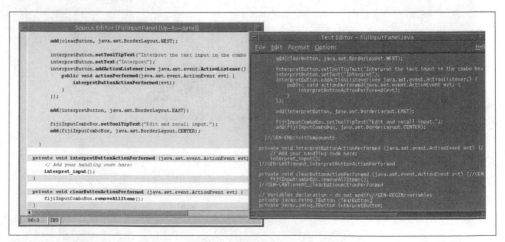

Figure 2-4. NetBeans Source Editor shades protected regions as a visual representation of the autogenerated code

The form file that NetBeans silently generates for the visual class always has the same name as the class but has an extension *.form* instead of *.java*. When you use the NetBeans Explorer to perform version control operations on your class, for example, to add the class to your CVS repository, the form file is automatically also added by NetBeans CVS support.

 Remember also to perform CVS operations on the form file if you perform manual CVS operations outside of NetBeans.

Although the NetBeans development model never requires you to edit the form file directly, the format is fairly intelligible to a casual reading. On occasion, the fastest way back to sanity after an accident with the form editor (either our mistake or the result of some subtle bug in an intermediate NetBeans release) has been to edit the form file manually. A portion of this file is shown in Example 2-1.

Example 2-1. A NetBeans form file

```
<Form version="1.0"
type="org.netbeans.modules.form.forminfo.JPanelFormInfo">
    <SyntheticProperties>
    </SyntheticProperties>

    <Layout
class="org.netbeans.modules.form.compat2.layouts.DesignBorderLayout"/>
    <SubComponents>
      <Component class="javax.swing.JButton" name="clearButton">
        <Properties>
          <Property name="toolTipText" type="java.lang.String"
            value="Clear entire history list of commands which you
entered at right."/>
          <Property name="text" type="java.lang.String" value="Clear"/>
        </Properties>
        <Events>
          <EventHandler event="actionPerformed"
listener="java.awt.event.ActionListener"
            parameters="java.awt.event.ActionEvent"
            handler="clearButtonActionPerformed"/>
        </Events>
        <Constraints>
          <Constraint

layoutClass="org.netbeans.modules.form.compat2.layouts.DesignBorderLayout"

value="org.netbeans.modules.form.compat2.layouts.DesignBorderLayout$Bord
erConstraintsDescription">
            <BorderConstraints direction="West"/>
          </Constraint>
        </Constraints>
      </Component>
```

Example 2-1. A NetBeans form file (continued)

```
    <Component class="javax.swing.JButton" name="interpretButton">
      <Properties>
        <Property name="toolTipText" type="java.lang.String"
          value="Interpret the text input in the combo box."/>
        <Property name="text" type="java.lang.String"
value="Interpret"/>
      </Properties>
      <Events>
        <EventHandler event="actionPerformed"
listener="java.awt.event.ActionListener"
          parameters="java.awt.event.ActionEvent"
          handler="interpretButtonActionPerformed"/>
      </Events>
      <Constraints>
        <Constraint

layoutClass="org.netbeans.modules.form.compat2.layouts.DesignBorderLayout"

value="org.netbeans.modules.form.compat2.layouts.DesignBorderLayout$Bord
erConstraintsDescription">
          <BorderConstraints direction="East"/>
        </Constraint>
      </Constraints>
    </Component>
    <Component class="com.SoftWoehr.FIJI.FijiInputComboBox"
name="fijiInputComboBox">
      <Properties>
        <Property name="toolTipText" type="java.lang.String"
          value="Edit and recall input."/>
      </Properties>
      <Constraints>
        <Constraint

layoutClass="org.netbeans.modules.form.compat2.layouts.DesignBorderLayout"

value="org.netbeans.modules.form.compat2.layouts.DesignBorderLayout$Bord
erConstraintsDescription">
          <BorderConstraints direction="Center"/>
        </Constraint>
      </Constraints>
    </Component>
  </SubComponents>
</Form>
```

However, it is probably safer to *always to use version control*, which in the context of the NetBeans Explorer, automatically adds your form files to the repository along with the Java files when you perform versioning operations on Explorer nodes. If you find that a form has changed in an untoward fashion, just exit the editor without saving or delete the problematic node and do a CVS update on the package to restore the file from your version repository. See Chapter 7 for more information.

Other file types

Files of a type NetBeans doesn't recognize actually cause the generation of another special-purpose file not saved in your versioning repository by NetBeans, the *.nbattrs* file. When a user clicks in the Explorer to open for editing or viewing a file of a type NetBeans does not recognize, NetBeans asks if the user wants to "convert the file to text." This is a bit misleading because *no conversion of the file takes place.* What really happens is that NetBeans writes an entry in that directory's *.nbattrs* file indicating what sort of file NetBeans is to assume the file is when NetBeans tries to display it. The *.nbattrs* file is just a reminder to NetBeans of which editor or viewer to use. (If you guessed that the format of the *.nbattrs* file conforms to yet another XML definition, you are correct.)

Tabs in the Explorer

The NetBeans Explorer presents views of your *project*. You can maintain multiple projects (see "Project Management" below) but only one is open at a time. Explorer views only the currently open project.

By default, the NetBeans Explorer offers four views of the currently opened project. These individual views are selected by tabs in the Explorer window. These four views are:

- Filesystems
- Project
- Javadoc
- Runtime

Two of these views deal with the main body of your project and are similar in appearance and purpose: the Filesystems and Project views. The other two views support ancillary tasks associated with your project.

So far we have been describing the NetBeans Explorer by drawing examples from the Filesystems view. We will now discuss all four views and their usage.

The Filesystems view

The Filesystems view is accessible through a tab near the bottom of the Explorer, as shown in Figure 2-5.

Figure 2-5. NetBeans Explorer Filesystems tab selected

The Filesystems view of the NetBeans Explorer is there to let you *mount* trees of code into the Explorer. Once they are mounted, you can expand the views of individual nodes (as we have already shown) and use contextual menus that pop up via a right mouse button click to perform all the necessary IDE operations on your code, such as edit, compile, run, and debug. You can see this view in action in Figure 2-6.

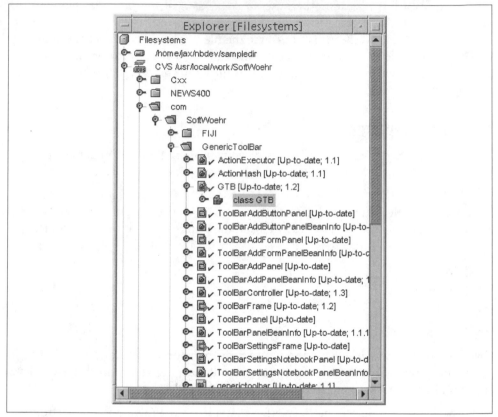

Figure 2-6. Illustration of NetBeans Explorer hierarchal expanding/collapsing list view

Mounting a filesystem means grafting onto the Filesystems view a tree of code. That tree always exists on disk storage; it may also be associated with a version control repository, as discussed later in this book in Chapter 7.

In other words, the NetBeans Explorer's Filesystems view represents a virtual filesystem built out of those pieces of your computer's native filesystem that you choose to mount in the Filesystems view. Furthermore, the classpath for the project consists, as we discuss later in this chapter, of the order in which these mounts appear in the Filesystems view. Archives of classes can also be mounted in the Filesystems view, in which case they are searched for classes in the order in which they appear in the view.

How to mount and unmount JARs and directories

- To mount a local directory into the Filesystems view, right-click on the Filesystems icon at the top of the Filesystems view and choose **Mount → Local Directory**. You will be presented with a file dialog that allows you to indicate the base directory of the hierarchy you want to graft into the Explorer Filesystems view.

- To mount a *.jar* or *.zip* archive that contains Java classes that you need for your project to have it found in the classpath search order during compiling and running, right-click on the Filesystems icon at the top of the Filesystems view and choose **Mount → Archive**. You will be presented with a file dialog allowing you to indicate the archive file you want to graft into the Explorer Filesystems view.

- For discussion of mounting a CVS repository along with the local directory into which files will be checked out, see Chapter 7.

Once you have mounted a tree or trees into the Filesystems view, you can operate on the program entities such as Java classes, build files, XML files, web applications, and so on, as described above and elsewhere in this book.

The Project view

The Project view is very similar to the Filesystems view in that it is a view of the hierarchical tree(s) of nodes representing your program objects. However, it is a second-order view derived mostly from the Filesystems view. Its purpose is to present a filtering of the Filesystems view to show more direct relevance to your workstyle. It's your own little project grove in a large project forest.

In Figures 2-7 and 2-8, the Filesystems view contains the mount of an entire CVS repository containing all sorts of code, including Rexx and C++ code along with Java code, as well as few *.jar* files necessary for compilation. In contrast, the "signal-to-noise" ratio of the corresponding Project view established by the Java programmer working on this tree is much higher, containing only a portion of the Filesystems view, a tree of Java code descending from the *com* folder.

To link a subset of your NetBeans Filesystems view mount(s) into the Project view, turn to the Project view tab, right-click on Project icon at the top of the view, and choose **Add Existing**.

You may also add Explorer nodes of various useful types to the Project view (though you cannot fully mount a tree from within Project view; go back to the Filesystems view to mount whole trees). To mount new individual folders and templated objects of various kinds, select the Project view tab, right-click on Project icon at the top of the view and choose **Add New**.

The Javadoc view

As you know, when you generate Javadoc documentation for your project from your source code, other bodies of code are referenced either implicitly or explicitly. The

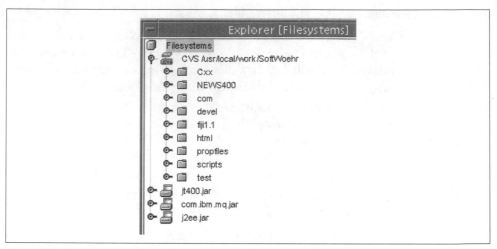

Figure 2-7. NetBeans Explorer Filesystems view of a big project

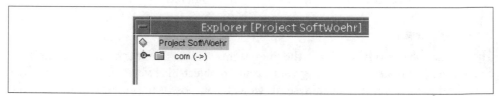

Figure 2-8. NetBeans Explorer Project view of a subset of a big project

Java's Javadoc documentation system likes to be able to cross-reference class documentation right back to the documentation for the universal Object superclass. The NetBeans Explorer keeps a list of all the places you tell it that Javadoc documentation germane to your project may be found while generating new Javadoc documentation. The Javadoc view (shown in Figure 2-9) maintains this search list and allows you to mount directories that contain Javadoc documentation the same way you mount source trees in the NetBeans Explorer Filesystem view.

By default, each project starts out with two Javadoc trees mounted, the Javadocs for the Ant build system and the directory in which NetBeans deposits all Javadocs that it generates on your behalf. You may at any time mount new directories, archives, or HTTP URLs in the Javadoc view to be searched while generating Javadocs. Simply right-click on the Javadoc icon at the top of the Javadoc view and choose either **Add Local Directory**, **Add Archive**, or **Add HTTP filesystem**, at which point you will be presented with a dialog analogous to the one that appears for mounting filesystems in the Filesystem view.

The Runtime view

The NetBeans Explorer Runtime view really might be called alternatively the What Happened? view. The Runtime view keeps track of various facilities available to your

Figure 2-9. Illustration of NetBeans Explorer Javadoc view

project and also operations that have been performed relative to your project. This is useful primarily when errors or problems occur, for example, if an RMI connection is being uncooperative or if there are difficulties encountered during version control operations. Expanding the view of an individual facility within the Runtime view yields a status view of that facility and a list of error messages from previous operations. The Runtime view is shown in Figure 2-10.

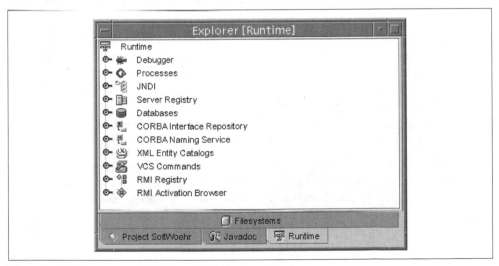

Figure 2-10. Illustration of NetBeans Explorer Runtime view

Node Paradigms

Node paradigms is a fancy way of saying How we operate on nodes represented by icons within the various NetBeans windows such as the Explorer and the Tools Options windows.

Explorer views of Java classes

NetBeans Explorer displays its nodes as icons in an expandable tree hierarchy matching the package structure of your program. Most of the icons are fairly intuitive. Java classes look like building blocks; the composite representation of the class and its source looks like a piece of paper with building blocks drawn on it. Filesystem mounts look like computer hard disk drives. There is a complete glossary of Explorer icons and their meanings in the online help for NetBeans. Do a search for "icon" and you will quickly find the relevant page.

Badges. NetBeans Explorer nodes are displayed as icons, but next to the icons are little subicons that in NetBeans parlance are called *badges*. Badges indicate something about the state of the object they sit next to in the Explorer view. There are badges to indicate such states as:

- The associated node needs compilation.
- The associated node is under version control and has been modified.
- The associated node has a syntactic error in its source code (NetBeans "live parses" your source as you edit it, so many errors can be caught by the IDE without even trying to compile the code).

There is a complete list of badges in the online help that comes with NetBeans. Do a search in the online help for "badges" and you will be shown pictures and explanations of the badges currently exhibited alongside to NetBeans objects.

Expanded view of classes. If you click the little horizontal lever to the left of one of Explorer's node icons that happens to represent Java source+class, the view will expand, as was illustrated in Figure 2-10.

When you start at the collapsed view of a Java class, you are seeing an object that, as has been noted, represents the class, its source, and pretty much everything about that class as one entity. The first click to expand this view shows you an object representation of the class itself (see Figure 2-11).

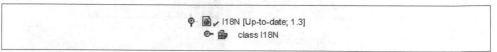

Figure 2-11. Explorer view of a class object expanded one level

If you again expand the view by clicking the little lever to the left, you get a view of fields, constructors, methods, and bean patterns, as shown in Figure 2-12.

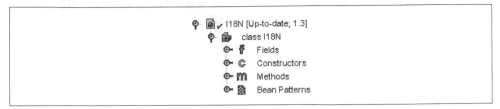

Figure 2-12. Explorer view of a class object expanded two levels

One more click on any of these entities opens up the individual fields, methods, constructors, or so on. The results of this additional click are detailed in Figure 2-13.

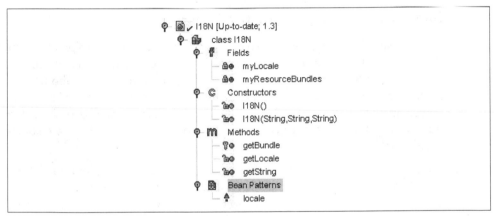

Figure 2-13. Explorer view of a class object expanded three levels

Furthermore, each representation has a pop-up menu associated with it by a right mouse click that allows you to customize and perform other operations on each element of your Java class. Wander around with the mouse and explore the Explorer.

Cut, copy, and paste subnodes

You can move portions of your project around the filesystem hierarchy using familiar GUI metaphors in the NetBeans Explorer. Just select a subnode (e.g., a folder), right-click and choose **Cut**, and move to another position on the tree view and choose **Paste** and the subnode and its descendants are moved.

Typically, if you cut a node it may not disappear until you try to paste it somewhere. And as regards a copy and paste operation, some objects, particularly nodes representing your Java classes, will offer the choice of a real copy operation or just inserting in the new location a link to the original object.

Be careful with cut. So much of what happens in the NetBeans Explorer (e.g., mounting/unmounting a file system) is virtual, it's easy to forget that cutting a file from a package is real and the file is indeed removed from its original location.

Tools actions

One of the submenu choices on the right-click context menu available for all objects visible in the NetBeans Explorer is **Tools**. This submenu contains tool operations appropriate to the type of object that was selected at the time the menu was pulled down. For instance, if the object is a folder, the selections offered by the Tools submenu might include **Update Parser Database** and **Generate Javadoc**, whereas if the object is a Java class, the selections would include operations like **Add to Component Palette** and **Set as Main Class**.

Sometimes Explorer Gets Behind the Times

As clever as it is, sometimes NetBeans Explorer gets a little confused. Explorer is not necessarily wrong. NetBeans is running in many threads, one of which is keeping an eye on your objects. Sometimes it can be a while until information about your project percolates through the system. NetBeans engineers sometimes view these delays as bugs and try to fix them. But the relative autonomy enjoyed by even the core modules of NetBeans ensures that interactions between the modules are somewhat loosely linked.

So here are comments on a few phenomena, mostly harmless but often confusing, that we have observed, along with tips how to shake the Explorer back to consciousness on those rare occasions when you suspect that Explorer has other things on its mind than the current and correct state of your project.

Does a file really need recompilation?

The NetBeans Explorer, as we've seen, annotates program objects visually using badges. Sometimes the needs recompilation badge is erroneously displayed next to an object that was either recently revealed to view in Explorer (either because the project changed or because you just opened its package) or was recently changed and recompiled. You can wait, and after a few seconds, NetBeans will usually update its view. If it doesn't, try opening, saving, and recompiling the object. If that doesn't work, and the object is under version control, try doing a CVS refresh on the object. Right-click on a parent folder of the package you are interested in to bring up the context menu and choose **CVS → Refresh Recursively**, and NetBeans Explorer will verify with the repository its view of the current state of all the objects and subpackages in the package.

Is a version really up to date? Is a file really local or is it already in the repository?

When a mounted tree is under version control, NetBeans Explorer indicates to the right of an object icon what the version level of an object is and whether it is up to date with respect to the repository. Explorer can sometimes end up momentarily out of sync with the versioning repository, indicating that a file that has been changed is up to date, or that a file that has been imported with an entire package into the repository is still local. Again, the solution is to do a recursive refresh on that branch of the mounted tree by right-clicking on the enclosing package and choosing **CVS Refresh Recursively**.

Summary

Perhaps these Explorer phenomema we have mentioned will be fixed in the version of NetBeans you are using. However, because they are artifacts of multithreading and the insoluble question of How often should NetBeans burn CPU cycles and network bandwidth to cross-check its view of the project?, it's likely something of the sort will occasionally pop up. The point is that unexpected albeit innocuous surprises can occur in NetBeans that require you to jiggle things around some to make sure you yourself are clear on the state of your project.

Filesystems and the CLASSPATH

The relationship between NetBeans Explorer's concept of mounted filesystems and classpath used by Java when compiling, debugging, and running your code is intricate. Here we attempt to untangle some of the mysteries involved.

How branches of the host filesystem manifest themselves in NetBeans

Any branch of the host filesystem might appear no times, one time, or any number of times in the same or in different projects. The view of any branch of the host file system is registered in the Explorer view by the process of mounting, discussed below.

How CLASSPATH is handled in the IDE

You already know how to compile a Java program and run it outside of NetBeans. Outside of NetBeans, you append to the CLASSPATH (typically a *shell environment variable*) the directory names or JAR filenames in which reside the package trees of any necessary supporting Java code, including the directory containing the packages of source for the code of your project. Then you compile and run.

Having this experience, you would easily guess that setting your CLASSPATH before running NetBeans would govern the CLASSPATH used by NetBeans to operate on your project. *But that guess is wrong.*

The CLASSPATH Shell Environment Variable

Let's refresh our memory on how one normally sets the CLASSPATH shell environment variable to compile or run Java applications at the command line.

- Under any Unix-like operating system, you set classpath in a shell command or a shell script with

  `CLASSPATH=$CLASSPATH:`*/some/path:/some/jar.jar:/some/path* ...

- Under Windows you either use the **MyComputer** → **Properties** → **Advanced** → **Environment** or using the command shell enter

  `SET CLASSPATH=%CLASSPATH%;`*\some\path;\some\jar.jar;\some\path* ...

  and use that same shell for your subsequent Java commands.

NetBeans *ignores* the CLASSPATH shell environment variable. NetBeans does this for two reasons:

1. NetBeans wants to make sure that for its own operation its own classes appear in the right order.

2. NetBeans allows the user to maintain multiple independent projects, each with its own CLASSPATH.

Instead of using your preset classpath, NetBeans assigns a per-project CLASSPATH that consists of a few hidden elements plus the order of mounts within the Filesystems view of the NetBeans Explorer for the project in question.

How to modify the IDE's CLASSPATH

As noted above, the IDE's CLASSPATH can be different for each project you are developing in NetBeans. When we say here "the IDE's CLASSPATH" we mean the classpath that NetBeans uses when analyzing, compiling, or running your project. We do not mean the classpath used when the IDE itself is launched: this latter issue is covered in the next section.

As noted above, controlling the classpath used by the IDE with regard to your project is very simple: The classpath used by the IDE consists of a few hidden elements plus the order of mounts within the Filesystems view of the NetBeans Explorer.

If you have a filesystem or filesystems mounted in a project but for some reason do not wish them to be used in the classpath (e.g., you have two versions of the same *.jar* file with which you are experimenting), you can edit the *capabilities* of that filesystem. Capabilities is one of the tabs of the properties editor for a filesystem. Right-click on the icon for the filesystem whose capabilities you wish to edit and choose **Properties** → **Capabilities**. All of this is shown in Figure 2-14.

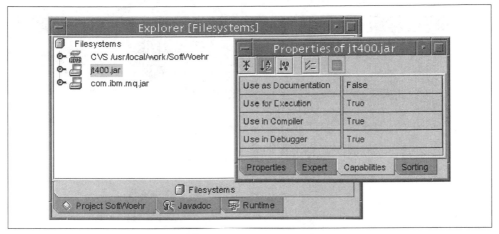

Figure 2-14. Editing filesystem capabilities

You can include or exclude a filesystem from the path for

- Documentation
- Execution
- Compilation
- Debugging

from the Capabilities tab of the Properties dialog.

By default, filesystems mounted in the NetBeans Explorer appear in the CLASS-PATH used by NetBeans to compile and run your code in the order in which they appear vertically in the NetBeans Explorer Filesystem view. To change the order of CLASSPATH evaluation change the vertical order in which they appear in the Net-Beans Explorer. Topmost elements appear foremost in the classpath.

In the NetBeans Explorer in the Filesystems view, right-click on Filesystems icon at the top and choose **Filesystems** → **Customize**. The Customizer Dialog appears. Right-click on the mount whose order you wish to change and choose Move up or Move down (see Figure 2-15).

Appending and prepending CLASSPATH to the IDE's CLASSPATH

You might be tempted to change the classpath that the IDE itself uses internally as it launches. Here's a hint: *Don't.* However, if you must, note that the IDE picks up its CLASSPATH from the script that launches it. If you're smart enough to know how to change the CLASSPATH of the IDE itself safely, you're smart enough to figure out everything you need to do from study of the launching script file.

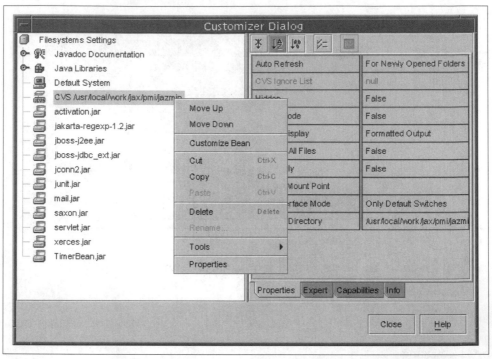

Figure 2-15. Using the Customizer Dialog to change NetBeans Explorer Filesystem mount order and thus the CLASSPATH for a project

Other CLASSPATH tricks

You can change the classpath associated with particular services such as compilation and execution. Choose **Tools → Options → Building → Compiler Types → External Compilation**. Then choose the Expert tab in the properties notebook, and you can change the classpath for external compilation in a number of different ways in the expert properties. In a similar fashion you can change the external execution classpath by choosing **Tools → Options → Debugging and Executing → Execution Types → External Execution**.

These settings are on a per-project basis: if you use the Project Manager to create multiple projects, each will have its own settings in this regard.

Creating Packages and Classes

To use an IDE to program Java, you have to be able to create packages of source code that you will subsequently compile.

Creating Packages

There are two ways to create packages in your NetBeans project:

1. You can step outside of NetBeans and create a package in your extant project. In this context, a package is just a filesystem directory. NetBeans will notice that the new package is there shortly after you create it, because NetBeans keeps an eye on the file trees grafted into its Explorer view of your project. NetBeans uses no special or hidden files to track the existence of packages, merely treating any subdirectory within a mounted tree as a package folder.

2. You can use the NetBeans Explorer to create the package. Right-click on the package under which you wish the new package to reside to bring up the context menu, choose **New** → **Java Package**, and the new package will be created.

 If the tree on which you are working is under version control, the new package still needs to be added to the repository. Right-click on the new package to bring up the context menu and choose: **CVS** → **Add**. This will allow you to enter any needed information in dialog boxes and then add the package to the CVS repository.

Creating Classes

You have a package to which to add Java classes. Okay, how do you add Java classes to the package? You could step outside the IDE and use a text editor to create new classes in the package, but you've already guessed there's an easier way in the IDE itself. You're right about that: NetBeans addresses creation of classes via *templates*.

Templates

In NetBeans IDE prototype Java classes and other source entities of all types (such as Ant build files, HTML documents, etc.) are saved as templates that can then be summoned up and instanced in your source tree as new files of the sort you want. Often the template contains macros.

Some of the macros expand to information from answers you give in the dialog that greets you when you invoke the template to create a new source node. You can create your own macros and then use them in new templates you create.

We'll discuss using templates, which is how you create new source files in NetBeans, and creating templates of your own to use to create new source files.

Using templates. To create a new source node in NetBeans, right-click on the package in which you wish to create the source node and choose **New**, which yields a submenu of the categories of templates from which you may choose (shown in Figure 2-16). Although many template categories are present in the default installation, the presence on the menu of certain categories depends on the modules you have chosen to install. For instance, in Figure 2-16, the XML and Document Type Definition (DTD) category of templates is present as a result of installing (via Update Center) optional modules extending NetBeans XML support.

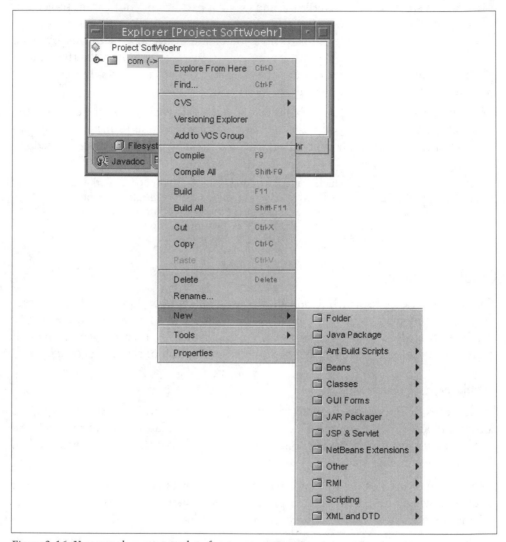

Figure 2-16. You can choose a template from many categories

When you choose a template, a dialog or series of dialogs allows you to fill in some information. The most important piece of information is the name of the new file to be created on the model of this template. In the case of Java files, more information is requested, such as in the case of creating a new "just plain class." For example, after choosing **New → Classes → Class**, the NetBeans New Wizard pops up to allow you to specify the derivation of the class. (The default superclass is, of course, *Object*.)

Other information that the New Wizard can use in creating your Java source file from a model template includes the names and types of data members you want to have present in the new class from the very start, if you choose to define such members in the New Wizard. This sort of information is, naturally, optional; you can add members and delete them at any time by editing the resulting source file, so it is not necessary to declare them at the time you create the new source file.

After you create your new source file, NetBeans immediately opens it in an appropriate editor. If it's a just plain class, it opens in the NetBeans Source Editor. If, instead, you create a visual form from a template, for instance, by choosing **New → GUI Forms → JFrame**, you will *not* be asked for derivation (the superclass is automatically *javax.swing.JFrame*), and after you are done specifying any other information about the new class, NetBeans will switch to the GUI editing workspace and open the NetBeans Form Editor.

Creating templates. You can create your own templates. There's nothing to it, at the simplest level. Edit a file, right-click on the representation of the file in the NetBeans Explorer, and choose **Save as Template**. A dialog asks for the category in which to place the template. If you want to create a new category for your own templates, choose **Tools → Options → Source Creation and Management** and right-click on the *Templates* folder and choose **New Folder**. Thereafter, that folder will show up in the Templates menu and as a choice in the categories to which you may add templates.

If you really want to get clever, you can use macros in the templates you create. These macros will be expanded each time the template is instanced as a source file. NetBeans has a number of preset macros, such as *__USER__*, which expands into the user's login name. You can insert *__USER__* anywhere in your own templates, as well as the other NetBeans preset macros such as *__DATE__*, *__TIME__*, and *__PACKAGE__*. A full list of the current set of preset macros is in the NetBeans online help. Do a search for "Creating Templates" and you will find this list.

Creating your own macros. You can create your own macros that will be expanded when found during instancing any template. To create a macro, choose **Tools → Options → Editing → Java Sources** and in the properties, open the String Table property and append your macro to the list of macros in the form:

```
__SOMEMACRO__=some expansion value
```

It will join the list of expansions undergone by templates at instancing time.

Services

NetBeans possesses a somewhat detached and detachable attitude toward the most basic functionality of an IDE, including compiling, executing, and debugging your program. These *services* can be provided by different modules. It's all under your control, including the behavior of the specific service-providing modules you choose, on a project-by-project basis. This section discusses using the provided NetBeans services for compiling, executing, and debugging your program and how they are chosen. More detail on the operation of the services themselves, especially debugging, will be provided in later chapters.

Compiler Services

Compiler services are how NetBeans refers to the cluster of functionality supporting the generation of object code from the sources of your project. NetBeans can use various different Java compilers, and the settings are there for you to change if you want.

Compiling your code

- To compile a Java source file, open the file in the Source Editor or select it in the NetBeans Explorer and either press **F9** or right-click and choose **Compile**. The source file will be compiled if necessary; if the object file is up to date with respect to the source, it will not be compiled.

- To force a source file to be compiled, even if the object is up to date, right-click on the file's representation in the NetBeans Explorer and choose **Build**.

- To compile a package, select the package in the NetBeans Explorer and right-click and choose **Compile**. All files whose objects are not up to date with respect to the source will be compiled.

- To force all source files in a package to be compiled, even if their objects are up to date, right-click on the package in the NetBeans Explorer and choose **Build**.

- To compile a package recursively including subpackages, select the package in the NetBeans Explorer, right-click, and choose **Compile All**. All files in the package and its subpackages whose objects are not up to date with respect to the source will be compiled.

- To force all source files in a package and all its subpackages to be compiled, even if their objects are up to date, right-click on the package in the NetBeans Explorer and choose **Build All**.

The Build and Compile operations are also available in the main NetBeans window under the **Build** menu.

Compiler settings

NetBeans allows you to:

- Choose a default compiler
- Associate a particular source file with a specific compiler type
- Associate source templates with specific compiler types

- Change the settings of various compilers
- Define new compiler types

Here's how to perform these operations, explained in brief. For a more thorough treatment of this topic, please see Chapter 5.

- To choose the default compiler, select **Tools → Options → Editing → Java Sources** and choose from the drop-down list for the property **Default Compiler**.

- To associate a particular source file with a specific compiler type, right-click on the file and choose **Properties**. In the Properties window, flip to the Execution tab and choose from the drop-down list for the property **Default Compiler**.

- To associate a template type with a compiler type, choose **Tools → Options → Source Creation and Management**, find the template you wish to modify, flip to the Execution tab, and choose from the drop-down list for the property **Default Compiler**.

- To change the settings of a compiler, choose **Tools → Options → Building → Compiler Types**, choose the compiler, and change the properties for the compiler.

- To define a new compiler type, choose **Tools → Options → Building**. Right-click on Compiler Types and choose **New → Compilation Service**. Edit the properties for the new type.

Execution Services

Execution services is what NetBeans calls the facilities for executing your program from within NetBeans. You can use execution services to execute your code under various Java Virtual Machines (JVMs) and to change the settings for those execution sessions. You can also associate templates or individual files with particular execution settings.

- To execute a Java class that has a *main()* method, select the class in the Explorer, or open it in the Source Editor, and press **F6** or right-click and choose **Execute**. If the file has not yet been compiled or is not up to date with respect to the source, it will be compiled before executing. NetBeans will then switch to the Running workspace and attempt to execute the *main()* method of the class. If there is any *System.out* or *System.err* output, or a request for input from *System. in*, an Input/Output window will open for that purpose to substitute for a command-line console. During the time the class is executing, the NetBeans Explorer Runtime tab will have information on the execution under its Processes node.

- To provide command-line arguments to the *main()* routine of your class when it executes, right-click on the class and choose **Properties**. Flip to the Execution tab and modify the **Arguments** property.

- To modify the settings for a particular execution type, choose **Tools → Options → Debugging and Executing → Execution Types**; then choose the execution type you wish to modify and modify its properties.

- To associate an execution type with an individual class, right-click on the class in the NetBeans Explorer and choose **Properties**. Flip to the Execution tab and modify the **Executor** property.

- To associate a template with an execution type, choose **Tools → Options → Source Creation and Management**, find the template you wish to modify, flip to the Execution tab, and choose from the drop-down list for the **Executor**.

 Several of these execution settings can also be manipulated by selecting the individual class and then pulling down the **Build** menu.

Debugging Services

Debugging services is what NetBeans calls the facilities for debugging your program from within NetBeans.

 Debugging your NetBeans project is covered in Chapter 4, which discusses how to run the debugger. Here we will just talk about debugger types and settings.

You can:

- Modify debugger settings
- Associate a debugger type with a template
- Associate a debugger type with a particular file

If you read and understood the previous sections on compilation and execution, you've probably already got the idea, but just for the record:

- To modify debugger settings, change properties for the debugger types—you'll find the properties in **Tools → Options → Debugging and Executing → Debugger Types**.

- To associate a debugger type with a template, it's back to **Tools → Options → Source Creation and Management**. Find the template you wish to modify, flip to the Execution tab, and choose from the drop-down list for the **Debugger**.

- To associate a debugger type with a particular class, you guessed it, right-click on the class in the NetBeans Explorer and choose **Properties**. Flip to the Execution tab and modify the **Debugger** property.

Workspaces

Workspaces are how NetBeans groups the user's work so that related tasks are associated with one another and disparate tasks can be hidden offscreen away from active tasks.

The NetBeans main window, shown in Figure 2-17, has several tabs on the bottom that tab into each of the NetBeans workspaces.

Figure 2-17. Main window workspace tabs

 It's possible to download a module via Autoupdate that will allow you to flip through your workspaces via a list box instead of using tabs.

Each workspace is a view of objects opened for manipulation in a different context. When one workspace is open, only the tools, forms editing instances, and runtime instances visible in that workspace are visible. The tools, forms, and editing and runtime instances associated with other workspaces become hidden.

Sometimes you tab back and forth between NetBeans workspaces. Sometimes NetBeans itself hops to a given workspace in response to your command for a specific tool action. For instance, if you start the NetBeans debugger, NetBeans hops to the Debugging workspace.

The various workspaces have names that explain the context of each workspace. The names of each of the workspaces follow, with a brief description of their contexts.

Editing

Editing is more or less the default workspace. NetBeans initially comes up with this workspace open and with the Explorer and a Properties browser open. If you use the NetBeans Explorer to open objects in your project for editing, and those objects were not composed as forms with the aid of those modules of NetBeans that support drag-and-drop composition of GUI forms, the Editor window pops up in this workspace.

GUI Editing

The GUI Editing workspace is where Form editors pop up. If you use the NetBeans Explorer to open objects in your project for editing, objects that were composed as forms with the aid of those modules of NetBeans that support drag-and-drop composition of GUI forms, the Editor window and associated Form editors pop up in this workspace.

GUI Editing is discussed fully in Chapter 8.

View Menu

Have you ever closed a window that you weren't using and then couldn't figure out how to get it back when you needed it? Look at the **View** menu in the main window. This menu allow you to open the IDE's most important windows in any workspace. Take any selection, and the window that it opens will remain available in the current workspace until you close it. This is the quickest way to customize the windows in your workspaces.

Browsing

The Browsing workspace is where object browsers open, because browsing objects by packages, classes, methods, and fields consumes much screen real estate.

Running

When you execute the main( ) of a Java class, NetBeans hops to the Running workspace to launch your class in a new thread. In the Running workspace, the output window and execution monitor(s) can pop up without cluttering your editing workspaces. The Running workspace is also used whenever NetBeans launches a thread to execute some Java code that can be viewed as conceptually external to NetBeans itself, as, for example, when Ant is invoked on a *build.xml* file.

Debugging

The NetBeans debugger, like object browsing, requires much screen real estate, so debugging runs go to their own Debugging workspace.

Persistence Across Sessions

The NetBeans workspaces are *persistent*. The persistent workspace is an IDE metaphor familiar since the early days of the Smalltalk programming environment. If you

---

have objects opened for editing in a workspace and you close NetBeans, when you next open NetBeans, generally the same objects will be open in that same workspace. However, that does not mean that debugging or execution sessions you were running before will be automatically started again.

Using Multiple Instances of Explorer

You can open the NetBeans Explorer in each workspace. Each instance of the Explorer is a separate instance, but all refer to the same project (the current project). This allows you to be focussed on a different part of your project in each workspace, as is often the case when you are editing both GUI and non-GUI components.

Using Multiple Instances of the Source Editor

You can open the NetBeans Source Editor in each workspace. Each workspace instance of the Editor is a different window, but files open in the Source Editor in any workspace are open in the Source Editor in all workspaces. This avoids a lot of confusion about what file was changed and/or saved in what workspace. The Form Editor portion of your edit session, however, only appears in the GUI Editing workspace.

Project Management

A project under NetBeans is a composite entity made up of:

- The project's package and class hierarchy
- The set of services for the project used to
  — Compile
  — Debug
  — Run
  — Perform version control
- Peripheral configuration, information, and logging relating to that project, such as:
  — Optional subtargets for build operations in the project
  — Results of previous build or version control operation
  — Elements to be added to the CLASSPATH when operating on the project

You might want to work on more than one project at once. So rather than leave all these matters to global preferences, NetBeans supports the concurrent maintenance of multiple projects, each with its own setup and its own set of persistent workspaces.

Managing Multiple Projects

If you are using NetBeans to work on one massive project, you may never bother with project management. When you launch NetBeans the first time, the default project is opened. You may continue to mount file hierarchies in the default project for as long as you like, provided there are no inherent conflicts in classpath requirements of the various subprojects you mount.

On the other hand, if you like or require a clear separation between projects, each with its own selection of filesystem mounts and archive mounts, multiple projects are well supported in NetBeans.

Pull down **Project** → **Project Manager**. You are presented with a simple dialog (see Figure 2-18) that allows you to create, open, and delete projects.

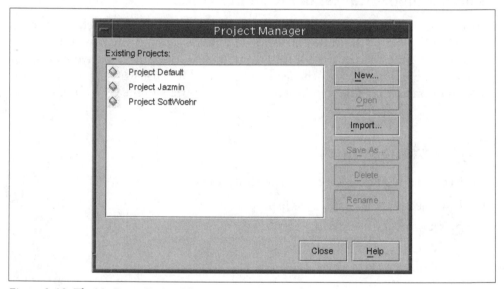

Figure 2-18. The NetBeans Project Manager

Each project has its own filesystem mounts, project choices, tools options, classpaths, and so on. To close a given project, simply use the Project Manager to open a different project. On orderly exit from NetBeans, your options are saved and the open project at the time of NetBeans exit is the one opened the next time you launch NetBeans. Of course, if you bomb out of NetBeans, for example, by a kill signal in the command window from which you launched NetBeans, some of the most recent changes to your project settings may be lost.

Managing Project Builds Using Ant

NetBeans IDE and Explorer offer useful support for Jakarta Ant. Ant is a build system intended to replace the traditional *make* utility, especially in building Java programs from source. A full introduction to Ant is beyond the scope of this book. Ant itself is included with NetBeans, and its HTML help files are packaged with NetBeans. Choose **Help → Help Sets → Ant Manual** for an introduction to the Ant build system.

The support for Ant in NetBeans consists of the following

1. An Ant build file is a known object type to the NetBeans Explorer (with its own cute little icon).

   - Right-clicking on an Ant build file will bring up a menu with appropriate options for that object type, topped by the Open selection, which opens the build file in an appropriate editor.

   - Double-clicking on an Ant build file performs the default action for an Ant build file, which is to invoke Ant on the build file. With a correctly written build file, it's just as easy to double-click on your Ant build file as it is to invoke compilation any other way in NetBeans and is much more configurable than other ways.

2. The NetBeans Source Editor knows about Ant build files.

3. The NetBeans Explorer offers a template Ant build file that can become the basis of your project-specific build file.

To use NetBeans support for creating Ant files, go to NetBeans Explorer and right-click in some folder of your choice from your mounts in either the Filesystem view or the Project view. Then choose **New → Ant → Build Scripts** and you will see the sub-menu shown in Figure 2-19.

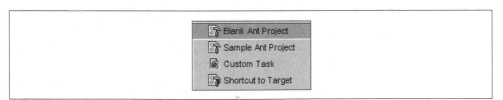

Figure 2-19. Ant template choices

The four options offered operate as follows:

1. Blank Ant Project brings up the NetBeans Source Editor on a new and empty Ant *build.xml* file.

2. Sample Ant Project brings up the NetBeans Source Editor on a template-derived new Ant *build.xml* file that probably will build your project well enough as-is but could use a great deal of customization.

3. Custom Task opens up the NetBeans Source Editor on a template-derived new Java file that, when compiled, will create a new Ant task. The new task can then be used in Ant *build.xml* files that have access to the compiled class. Ant's syntax is extensible and programmers can add functionality to Ant in this fashion. Consult the Ant manual in the appropriate Help set packaged with NetBeans for more information on custom Ant tasks.

4. Shortcut to Target allows you to create a *mini-script* and associate it as a short-cut to a specific target in an existing Ant *build.xml* file. Choosing this menu item brings up a wizard dialog that will walk you through the process of creating the mini-script and customizing the parameter(s) to the target(s) you choose.

Object Browser

The NetBeans Object Browser provides an object view that is a melding of the information available about your program objects from source inspection and object introspection. However, it has disappeared from the default distribution and become an optional module as of version 3.3.1, but it is still mentioned in the online help. To install the Object Browser, use the NetBeans Update Center (see Figure 2-20).

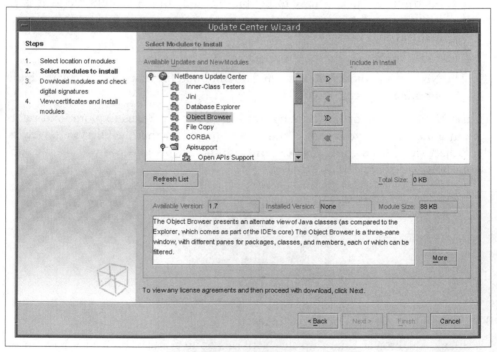

Figure 2-20. Using Update Center to install the Object Browser

The Object Browser metaphor occupies an important place in most Java IDEs. It always was important in NetBeans and has its own workspace tab once installed. It has moved off into "optional module land" in a typical open source fashion, that is:

1. The Object Browser was showing its age.
2. Another Object Browser-like analysis tool, the Freestyle Browser, is emerging from another open source project, and NetBeans plans to incorporate that one eventually in place of the Object Browser.

In this book we don't spend much time documenting optional IDE modules, but because object browsing is so fundamental to doing object programming in an IDE, we'll take a quick look at the classic NetBeans Object Browser, knowing that whatever replaces it eventually in NetBeans will be conceptually similar, albeit more modern and powerful.

Simply flipping to the workspace tab for Browsing invokes the Object Browser on the currently open project. The Browser windows open quickly and packages begin to appear incrementally (as seen in Figure 2-21) as the Object Browser takes a few moments to analyze your project when it first opens. Be patient.

Figure 2-21. The Object Browser open on a project

The Object Browser has three windows and is accompanied by an instance of the ubiquitous Properties window.

- The leftmost window is titled "Packages" and displays the Java packages found in your project.

- The next window to the right is titled "Objects" and displays the classes and interfaces defined in the package that is currently selected in the Package window.

- The next window to the right is titled "Members" and displays the data and method members of the class or interface selected in the Objects window.

- The Properties window displays the properties of the last entity you clicked in either of the three Object Browser window.

- You can right-click on entities in the three Object Browser windows to bring up menus of actions that you can perform on them from within the Object Browser, such as Customize, or Tools applications, such as Auto Comment.

- Double-click on any entity in any of the Object Browser windows to bring up the appropriate editor.

Both the NetBeans Object Browser and the newer Freestyle Browser exhibit a common deficiency: although they both can take you to the place in your code where you defined an object, they can't take you to the places where your objects are referenced. (The inability to find references of an object goes much deeper than the Object Browser and is not a direct goal of the Freestyle Browser. For this, a general, incrementally updated, automatic metadata cache of user data in the IDE would be needed. Open source contributors, take note.)

 In fact, open source contributors have already taken note. JRefactory (*http://jrefactory.sourceforge.net*) and Refactorit (an optional NetBeans module) are two interesting tools now available that are capable of finding references in your code.

Here are a couple of ways to find references to objects within your code:

1. Hop out to a command shell and do a recursive *grep* on your source tree.

 For more information on *grep*, see any textbook on Unix shell commands.

2. Use the NetBeans Find tool. Right-click on a Java package and choose **Find** and fill out the choices in the dialog to perform your recursive search. You can do full text searches, searches that are sensitive to Java context, or regular expression searches.

Summary

- NetBeans contains everything a good IDE should, and more. One difference from other IDEs is the broad flexibility provided by optional modules coded to the NetBeans open source APIs.

- Functionality not provided by the assortment of built-in modules that accompany NetBeans installation can often be found from an optional module or experimental module installable across the Net via the NetBeans Update Center.

- Functionality not provided either by core modules or by optional modules can be provided by your own or third-party modules.

- The authors of NetBeans and open source contributors to NetBeans are dedicated to the ideal of making NetBeans express the essence of Java development. So, look around, it's probably there somewhere.

## CHAPTER 3

Working with the Source Editor

Why Learn a New Editor?

Learning to use yet another source code editor was probably not high on your to-do list this year. However, the NetBeans syntax-coloring Source Editor, which is tightly integrated with the rest of the IDE, is *easy* to learn and is *indispensible* to your Net-Beans development work flow.

The reason it is easy to learn the NetBeans Source Editor is that its behavior is unsurprising to anyone who has ever used a modern GUI text editor, especially one coded in Java. Try to guess what key sequences are required to copy, cut, and paste highlighted text? If you guessed Control-C, Control-X, and Control-V, respectively, you were right. Control-S saves your changes, if any exist. Shift-Right Arrow selects text to the right, Shift-Control-Right Arrow selects text to the right a word at a time. Et cetera...no surprises here.

The reason that the NetBeans Source Editor is indispensible to your NetBeans development work flow is the level of integration provided between objects in the Net-Beans Explorer and Form Editor, code entities in your program, your actions within the editor, and the appearance of your code in the editor window.

Opening the Source Editor

There are two prinicipal ways to open a file in the NetBeans Source Editor:

1. From the NetBeans Main Window, pull down **File → Open** and use the file dialog to browse to the file you want to open.

2. From within the NetBeans Explorer, find the node representing your source, right-click on it, and choose **Edit** if that action is available or **Open** if there is no specific Edit action on the menu.

Actually, with Java sources and many other NetBeans Explorer nodes, you can just double-click on the node to open it in the NetBeans Source Editor. So why the rigamarole about Open and Edit?

Recall from our discussion of the NetBeans Explorer that a double-click invokes the default action of an Explorer node. If you double-click on an Explorer node representing a Java class, the default action is to open its source in the Source Editor. However, if you double-click on an Ant *build.xml* file, the default action is to switch to the Running workspace and invoke Ant on the build file.

Very well ... now what about Open versus Edit? There are special editing modes for things like Java properties files. If you double-click on a *.properties* file in the NetBeans Explorer, the default action is Open, which brings up a special editor oriented toward the user filling in key-and-value pairs in string gadgets. If you instead choose Edit from the menu, you get the good ol' NetBeans Source Editor open on the actual text of the *.properties* file.

All files opened in the Source Editor are opened in the same Source Editor frame. They are kept separate in tabbed notebook form. You flip between the files you have opened by clicking the tabs.

Whenever your code changes, an asterisk (*) appears by the filename when the file is being displayed in the Source Editor. **Control-S** then saves your changes. As a result of this save, your filenames will no longer have the asterisks (until the next change, of course).

Context Menus

When you right-click within the NetBeans Source Editor window, a contextual menu pops up. This menu has many of the selections that you would find when you right-click on the NetBeans Explorer node representation for the same entity. These selections include **CVS**, **Compile**, **Build**, and so on. Additionally, there are options on the menu relevant to the task of editing, such as **Cut**, **Copy**, and **Paste**.

Closing the Source Editor

When you click the close widget on the Source Editor window, the window closes, terminating all editing sessions. Alternatively, you may close an individual file by right-clicking on its editing window and choosing **Close**. In either case, if you have any unsaved changes, you will be offered the choice of saving the changes or abandoning the close operation. This choice is repeated for each unsaved, modified file until all files are closed.

Code Completion

Automated *code completion* is the NetBeans Source Editor's ability to supply the name of a partially entered package, class, interface, method, or member without your having to finish typing in all the characters of the name. NetBeans Source Editor keeps a database of Java classes and members and can present you with a list of candidate completions from which you select the actual completion. This wonderful labor-saving feature of the NetBeans Source Editor is useful, but it can at times be annoying.

Automated code completion is useful when you are whizzing through classes and methods the NetBeans Source Editor's database knows all about. Code completion saves typing when the editor knows what to expect.

Automated code completion is annoying when, after a predetermined timeout, the NetBeans Source Editor pops up the completion list window, obscuring your typing as you hesitate or as you try to enter something that NetBeans did not anticipate. But you can do something about that, as we'll find out below.

Using Code Completion

It's easy to turn NetBeans Source Editor code completion on and off according to your convenience.

Taking advantage of code completion

To use NetBeans Source Editor code completion, just start typing a package, class, member, or method name. At some point during your typing, NetBeans should attempt to complete the component name. If NetBeans doesn't automatically attempt to complete your code, type **Control-Space**. NetBeans Source Editor will then pop up the completion list window if it thinks it recognizes the incomplete syntax as the name of a class or member. (See Figure 3-1.)

Either scroll down to the desired entry and press **Enter** or continue typing in further letters of the desired member or method.

Avoiding code completion

There are three separate ways to avoid NetBeans Source Editor code completion:

1. One time: press Esc when the completion list window appears and it will go away.
2. As the default: disable (or slow down) automatic popup of the completion list window. The settings for code completion in the NetBeans Source Editor can be changed on a file-type basis. Just pull down **Tools → Options** and make the desired changes.

Figure 3-1. Code completion context window in the Source Editor

3. Finish typing quickly. Source completion only pops up while the cursor is within a lexical element containing no spaces. If you are past the end of the method or member name, you're in the clear as far as source completion is concerned.

As you can see in Figure 3-2, you can change the timeout before the code completion window pops up automatically, which is usually sufficient to diminish the resemblance of this useful NetBeans feature to a "talking paperclip."

Updating the Parser Database to Include New Classes

The *parser database* is the database that the NetBeans Source Editor references when performing code completion. If you attempt automatic code substitution where the correct substitution should be from your own classes but completion fails, it's time to update the parser database. This can be done by selecting the top of your tree or a particular package and using the **right** mouse button to invoke the NetBeans Explorer context menu.

The update applies to the package you selected and all subpackages of the selected package. Ergo, you'll usually do this at the top of your source tree. Be patient. On a large source tree this operation can take a while. A message box will keep you posted on the progress of the operation as the update executes.

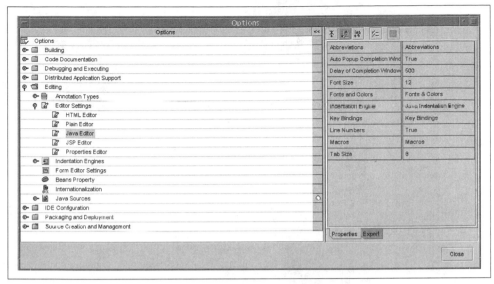

Figure 3-2. Changing the properties settings that govern code completion in the Source Editor

Abbreviations

You can assign abbreviations that the Source Editor expands. Just type the first few letters of the abbreviation and hit the **Spacebar**, and the Source Editor will expand the abbreviation.

The Source Editor keeps separate sets of abbreviations for each type of file you will be editing. That is, when you are editing Java files, there is one set, another for JSPs, and another for XML, and so on. You type a sequence of characters matching an abbreviation and press the spacebar, and the abbreviation will expand. To add a space without the Source Editor checking for abbreviations, press **Shift-Spacebar**.

To view or alter Source Editor abbreviations (there is a rather large set already established by default), choose **Tools → Options → Editing → Editor Settings → Java Editor** and in the properties view to the right, choose **Abbreviations**, clicking on the ellipsis to bring up the property editor for Source Editor abbreviations. (See Figures 3-3 and 3-4.)

Editor Colorings

Modules that support specific languages in NetBeans provide syntax highlighting support to the Source Editor. The colors used in the editor can be customized on a per-file-type basis. For example, to change the colors for Java source files, choose **Tools → Options → Editing → Editor Settings → Java Editor → Fonts and Colors**. There are additional color properties on the **Expert** tab of the **Java Editor** node to set things such as caret color and text-limit-line color.

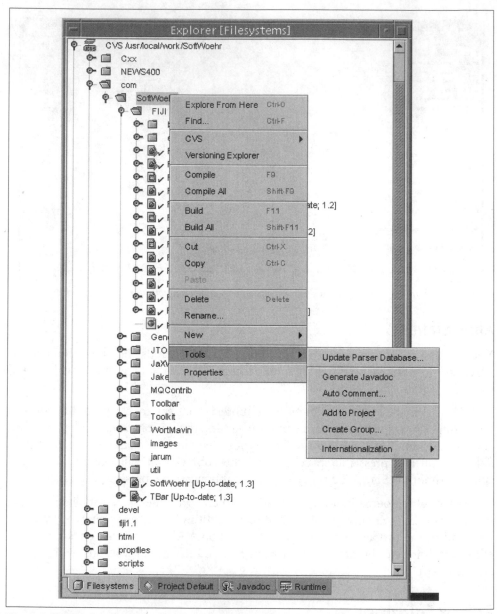

Figure 3-3. Asking NetBeans to update the parser database for a package

One highly useful but often ignored feature of the editor is the ability to highlight the line the text caret is on. By setting the color for **Highlight Insertion Point Row** in the **Fonts and Colors** dialog to a color only marginally different than the background color, you get a convenient and quick visual reference to find the text caret in the editor.

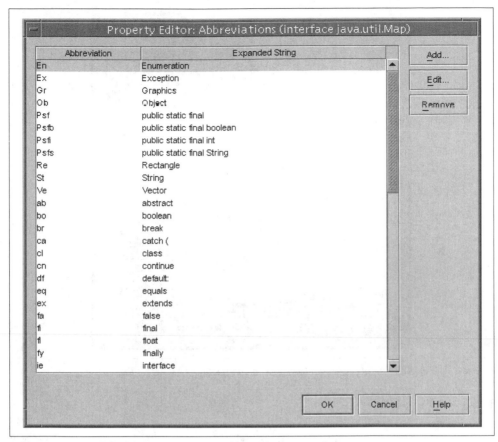

Figure 3-4. Some default NetBeans Source Editor abbreviations for Java

Note that if you want to completely customize the colors you see in the Source Editor, you will also want to modify settings underneath the **Annotation Types** subnode of **Editor Settings**. An "annotation" in NetBeans parlance is the marking of a single line of source code in the Source Editor. An example is the red background of a line indicating a compiler error can be changed here.

Shortcuts

You can create your own key bindings as shortcuts to editing operations. Editor operations have names, and a dialog exists by which you can edit the already existing shortcuts to these operations or establish new ones. Choose **Tools → Options → Editing → Editor Settings**, and click in the associated properties window to edit the **Key Bindings** property. (See Figure 3-5.)

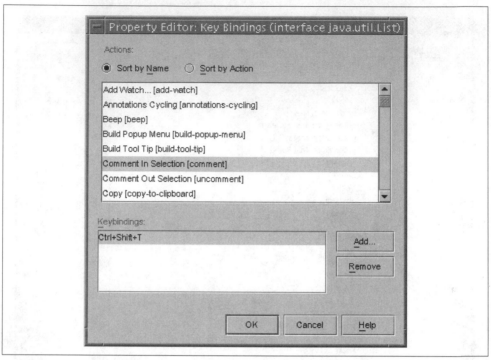

Figure 3-5. The Key Bindings dialog allows you to change Source Editor shortcuts

Word Matching

If you have already typed something once, why enter it again? Just enter the first few characters and type **Control-L** to search forward for text commencing with the same characters or **Control-K** to search similarly backward. If a match is found, a tentative completion will be inserted at the cursor point. If it's not the completion you want, keep typing **Control-L** or **Control-K** until the string you meant to locate for the completion is encountered. This is only a good idea if you are near where you have typed the word you want to complete. Often paging through an entire document to avoid typing "internationalization" wastes more time than simply typing the entire word manually.

Indentation Engines and Code Formatting

NetBeans Source Editor provides automatic code indentation by allowing modular indentation engines to associate themselves to object types. Invoke code indentation and reformatting by pressing **Shift-Control-F**. (See Figure 3-6.) After a while this key sequence becomes a NetBeans user's reflex action.

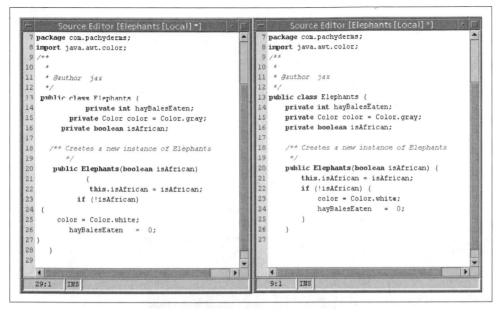

Figure 3-6. Text in the NetBeans Source Editor before and after reformatting

Of course you've guessed that a feature such as automatic indentation, which has uncanny power to touch the programmer's emotional hot buttons, will have settings you can modify. Select **Tools → Options → Editing → Indentation Options** and modify the appropriate properties.

Automatic Edits

Some features of NetBeans edit your source automatically and cause a "buffer changed" asterisk to appear in your source code's tab. Among these actions that edit your source are:

- Using the NetBeans Autocomment tool
- Using the Form Editor or a Properties dialog to make changes to your class
- Using wizard tools on your class

After such operations you must manually save your source via the context menu or **File** option for **Save** or via **Control-S**.

Regarding the latter, using wizard tools on your class, you can alter the signature of your class by right-clicking on the class in the NetBeans Explorer and choosing **Customize** or by expanding the view of the class in the Explorer, right-clicking on either **Fields**, **Constructors**, or **Methods**, and choosing **New** whichever. (See Figure 3-7.) You'll be presented a wizard dialog to create the new field, method, or member variable.

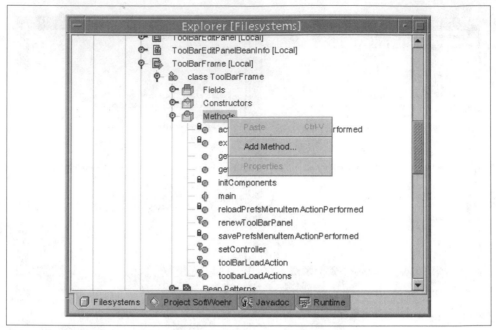

Figure 3-7. Invoking a wizard dialog to add a new method to a class

Other Editor Functionality

We have focussed here on editing Java via the Source Editor. However, the Net-Beans Source Editor also edits HTML, XML, Java Properties files, plain text, and other programming languages as NetBeans core developers and external open source contributors add modules to handle those languages. You can see the currently supported types by choosing **Tools → Options → Editing → Editor Settings**.

Sometimes the NetBeans Source Editor possesses an editing mode that works for a file type, but the Source Editor doesn't know about the filename extension. You can let the Source Editor know that a filename extension should be handled by a particular editing mode. You can add, for instance, *.wml* files to the list of files handled as XML by the Source Editor. Just choose **Tools → Options → IDE Configuration → System → ObjectTypes → XML** and add *wml* to the Extensions list in the properties. (See Figure 3-8.)

A Simple Example

Let's leave the realm of theory and turn to practice. We'll start from scratch now and use NetBeans and the Source Editor to build ourselves a little program and run it. Step-by-step instructions follow.

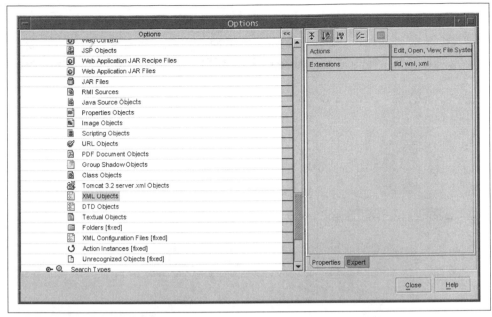

Figure 3-8. Adding a file type to XML editing

1. *Choose a package.* All NetBeans Java programming takes place in some package. Let's use the sample directory created and mounted for us in the Default project by NetBeans the first time we run it. We'll create a new package called *mysamples* in that sample directory. (If you have another project open and want to switch back to the Default project, use the Project Manager). Assuming that you currently have open the Default project, right-click on the topmost mounted directory (on my Unix system it's */home/jax/nbuser33/sampledir*) and choose **New → Java Package** and name the package *mysamples*.

2. *Create the source file.* Right-click on *mysamples* and choose **New → Classes → Class**, name the class *Hello*, and click **Finish**.

3. *Edit the code.* Here's a reasonable first program that, when its main( ) is run, will either say "Hello, you!" to standard output or, if provided at invocation with an argument, will say "Hello" to whatever name is input as an argument. (See Figure 3-9.)

```
/*
 * Hello.java
 *
 * Created on February 6, 2002, 12:21 PM
 */
package mysamples;

/**
 * This class, unsurprisingly, says Hello to you.
 *
 * @author  your_id
```

Figure 3-9. Commencing to edit our simple example

```
    */
public class Hello {
    private String toWhom;

    /** Creates a new instance of Hello */
    public Hello() {
        this("you");
    }

    public Hello(String name) {
        toWhom = name;
    }

    public void sayHello() {
        System.out.println("Hello, " + toWhom + "!");
    }

    public static void main(String [] args) {
        Hello hello;
        if (args.length >0) {
            hello = new Hello(args[0]);
        }
        else {
            hello = new Hello();
        }
        hello.sayHello();
    }
}
```

4. *Compile your code*. Either press the **F9** key or right-click in the Source Editor window and choose **Compile** to compile your code. If you committed any typographical errors that cause the compile to abort, click on the highlighted link in

the compiler's error output window to jump to the offending line in the source, correct the error, and recompile.

5. *Run your code.* Either press the **F6** key or right-click in the Source Editor window and choose **Execute** to run your code. Output, both standard out and standard error (*System.out* and *System.err* in Java), goes to the NetBeans Output window.

6. *The Output Window is tabbed.* Note that the Output Window is a tabbed notebook, so if many distinct NetBeans tasks produce output, you can click on an appropriate tab to see other program's output.

7. *You changed workspaces.* Note that you changed to the Running workspace when you executed your program. Choose the Editing tab of the NetBeans main window to get back to your work and continue our Source Editor exercise.

8. *Run your code providing a command-line argument.* Let's say hello to Ogden Nash, the poet who wrote about the man who wasn't there. In the NetBeans Explorer (not the Source Editor) right-click on the node representation of your Hello class and choose **Properties**, which brings up the NetBeans Properties Inspector on Hello. Click on the **Execution** tab and alter the **Arguments** property (by clicking to the right of the value and editing in the resulting window) to read "Ogden Nash" in quotes, just like that. (The quotes serve to make an argument of two words separated by a space be passed as one argument at runtime. If our main( ) function took two arguments, a first and a last name, we would leave out the quotes.)

Now click back into the Source Editor window and run your application again. There's no need to recompile; all that you changed were the arguments that will be passed to your class when NetBeans runs it on your behalf, and those are external to the class itself. (See Figure 3-10.)

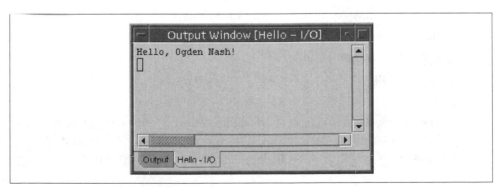

Figure 3-10. Running our simple example

9. *More on Customizing the Source Editor.* We have presented here a quick tour of the NetBeans Source Editor to give you enough to get started. There's more detail about customizing the NetBeans Source Editor in Chapter 6.

CHAPTER 4

Debugging

Debugger Types

Real programmers know that watching their applications run smoothly isn't nearly as much fun as just getting them to run in the first place. The best part is seeing what's going on under the hood. Don't you just love to watch the threads weaving around, and the values in one variable affecting another like a chain of dominos falling over? Well, the people at NetBeans understand, so they created some great debugging features. In the event that you make a programming error and can't immediately see what's wrong, you can use these debugging features to find out what's really going on. But I'm sure you're more careful than that, so just think of debugging as a fun diversion from writing code. Here are some of the ways you can play with the inner workings of your programs while they're running:

- Set breakpoints
- Watch values change for variables and expressions
- Examine and modify variable values
- Step through code, line by line
- Examine running threads, classes, and the callstack
- Run several debugging sessions at the same time

Actually, the same user interface supports a choice of backend debugging facilities. The Java Platform Debugger Architecture (JPDA) is the default. Be sure to specify the right debugger type for the object to be debugged; these types are delineated in Table 4-1.

Table 4-1. Debugger types that come with NetBeans 3.3

Debugger type	Remarks	Where to use it
Default	Based on JPDA	Use with ordinary Java applications
Applet	Based on JPDA	Required with applets

Table 4-1. Debugger types that come with NetBeans 3.3 (continued)

Debugger type	Remarks	Where to use it
JDK 1.1	Pre-JPDA, fewer features	Use only with pre-Java 2 applications
RMI	Based on JPDA	Use with RMI applications
J2EE server	Based on JPDA	Use with J2EE Server Integration

You can see the various debugger types for NetBeans in Figure 4-1.

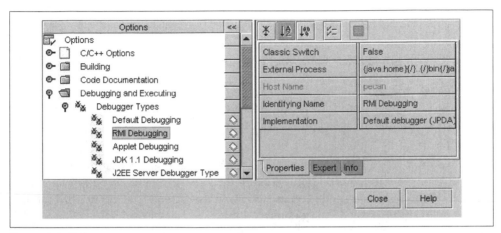

Figure 4-1. Debugger types

Breakpoint Types

Originally, setting a breakpoint simply told the debugger to stop execution at a specified source code line and to enter into an interactive debugging mode. But NetBeans (with JPDA) does much more than that. Setting a breakpoint now means responding to a variety of runtime events, listed in Table 4-2. The user can configure the response to each breakpoint to include either or both of the following actions:

- Suspend debugging pauses execution to allow the user to use the interactive debugging features.
- Print text displays a fully configurable message in the output window.

Table 4-2. Runtime events that can be used to trigger a breakpoint define the following breakpoint types

Breakpoint type	Runtime event	Options—specify when to activate breakpoint
Line	Execution reaches line in source	Condition—optional boolean expression
Method	Execution enters method	Apply also to anonymous inner classes, or to named classes only
		Apply to all methods of given classes, or only selected methods
		Condition—optional boolean expression

Table 4-2. Runtime events that can be used to trigger a breakpoint define the following breakpoint types (continued)

Breakpoint type	Runtime event	Options—specify when to activate breakpoint
Exception	Exception is thrown	Exception caught, uncaught, or both
		Condition—optional boolean expression
Variable	Variable is accessed or modified	All access to variable, or modification only
		Condition—optional boolean expression
Thread	Thread starts or dies	Thread start, thread death, or both
Class	Class is loaded or unloaded	Class loaded, unloaded, or both

The Condition option is probably the most interesting. You may enter a boolean expression as the Condition property in the dialogs for setting Line, Exception, Variable, and Method breakpoints. Start your application in debug mode, and it will ignore the breakpoints until the conditional expression evaluates to true. This saves lots of time, compared to stepping over breakpoints manually until you reach the conditions that you want to investigate.

There are some scope considerations in creating a breakpoint condition. With these considerations in mind, a breakpoint condition can be any valid Java expression that appears on the right side of the equals sign in an assignment statement with a boolean variable on the left side. Additionally:

- Variables and expressions in the Condition must be valid within the class, method, or line that the breakpoint is set in.
- "Import" statements are ignored, so external references must be fully qualified (e.g., use *java.lang.String*, instead of simply *String*).
- Outer class methods and variables are not directly accessible, so they also must be fully qualified (e.g., use *this.variableName* or *this$1.variableName*).

Adding and Removing Breakpoints

Let's have some fun and try out some of the debugging features. But first we need something to debug. Here's a little multithreaded class, shown in Example 4-1. Each thread simply displays a counter while counting to a limit. You may follow along with this example or use one of your own and do the same exercises. If you want to use this one, create a package named Debug under some working directory that you've mounted in the NetBeans Explorer. Download the source from the book's web site, or type it in manually.

Example 4-1. Multithreaded example for debugging demo—ThreadedCounter.java

```
package Debug;

/**
 * Multithreaded example for debugging demo.
```

Example 4-1. Multithreaded example for debugging demo—ThreadedCounter.java (continued)

```java
 *
 * @author   vaughn
 */
public class ThreadedCounter {

/** thread sleep delay interval for CountThread */
  private static long delay = 500;

/** number of iterations for 1st instance of CountThread */
  private static int maxcount = 20;

/** inner class object to run as a separate thread */
  private class CountThread implements Runnable {

/** number of iterations for CountThread */
    private int maxcount = 1000;

/** identifying name for instance of CountThread */
    private String countName;

/** iteration counter */
    private int count;

/** CountThread constructor */
    public CountThread(String name, int maxcount) {
      super();
      this.maxcount = maxcount;
      this.countName = name;
      new Thread(this).start();
    }

/** run method for thread */
    public void run() {
      for (count = 0; count < maxcount; count++) {
        try {
          Thread.sleep(delay);
        } catch (InterruptedException e) {}
        System.out.println(countName + " = " + count);
      }
    }
  }

/** ThreadedCounter constructor */
  public ThreadedCounter(String name, int limit) {
    System.out.println(name + " limit = " + limit);
    CountThread ct = new ThreadedCounter.CountThread(name, limit);
  }

  /**
   * @param args the command line arguments
   */
  public static void main (String args[]) {
    new ThreadedCounter("1st", maxcount);
```

```
    new ThreadedCounter("2nd", 10);
    }
}
```

Compile and execute `ThreadedCounter`, just to see what it does. Not much, but enough for our purposes. Both threads display the current count every half second. The second thread counts from 0 to 9 and then quits, whereas the first thread counts all the way to 19.

Now let's set some breakpoints. First, set breakpoint type Line at the line that starts with `System.out.println` in the `ThreadedCounter` constructor. As usual, there are several ways to do this. Open `ThreadedCounter` in the Source Editor, and put the cursor on the line with `System.out.println`. Right-click to get the context menu (shown in Figure 4-2), or open the **Debug** menu in the main window. Select **Toggle Breakpoint** from either menu. Or you could just put the cursor on the desired line and press **Shift-F8**. Notice that the line is highlighted in pink after the breakpoint has been set.

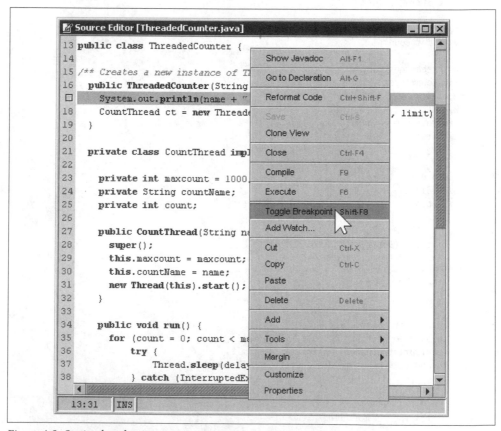

Figure 4-2. Setting breakpoints

To see something a bit more interesting let's set a breakpoint type Thread. Select **Add Breakpoint** from the **Debug** menu, or press **Control-Shift-F8** to pop up the **Add Breakpoint** dialog box (shown in Figure 4-3). Select **Breakpoint Type → Thread** and then change the **Set Breakpoint On** property to **Thread Start or Death**.

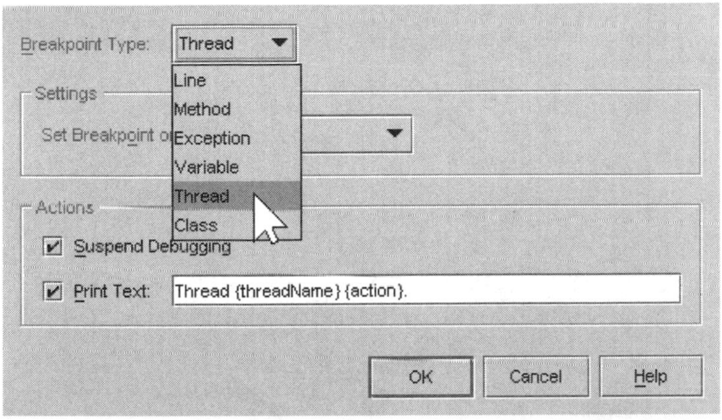

Figure 4-3. Add breakpoint dialog

Finally, let's set a breakpoint type Variable on the count variable in the CountThread inner class. This breakpoint type might be better named breakpoint type *Field*, because it only seems to work on variables with classwide scope. This author could not get it to work for variables with a narrower scope, such as internal to a for loop. That's why count in the code example is declared as a class member, instead of within the for loop. Click anywhere on the private int count; line and then press **Control-Shift-F8**. When the **Add Breakpoint** dialog box opens (illustrated in Figure 4-4), make sure **Breakpoint Type → Variable** and **Stop On Variable Modification** are selected. This time we'll also set a condition. Any valid boolean expression will work. Enter "count>14."

Setting Watches

Before running the Debugger, let's set watches on the count and countName variables in the CountThread inner class. A watch gives us a convenient way to see the current value in a variable while the application is running and the value keeps changing. Like setting breakpoints, you could start from the **Debug** menu or from the Source Editor with the mouse pointer positioned over the variable to be watched. For this example, put the pointer over count anywhere in the source, press **Control-Shift-F7**, then hit **OK** in the dialog box that pops up. Repeat with countName. That's all there is to it. Now, we're ready to debug.

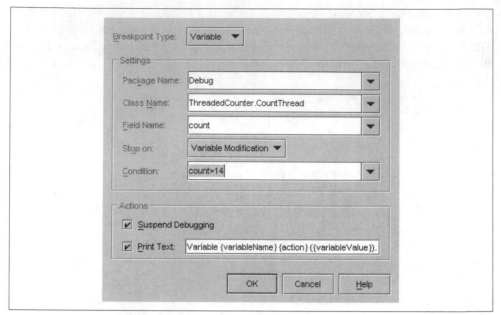

*Figure 4-4. Set breakpoint type **Variable***

Starting the Debugger

You can start the Debugger from the Editing, GUI Editing, or Debugging workspace. The source to be debugged must be open and selected in the Explorer or Source Editor, just as if you intended to Execute the class. Select **Start** from the **Debug** menu (as shown in Figure 4-5), or press **Alt-F5** to launch the Debugger. If you want the Debugger to pause at the first executable statement, press **F7** to start it. Once it starts, the IDE switches to the Debugging workspace.

When the Debugger starts, the class being debugged executes normally until it hits a breakpoint. Then it pauses with the Source Editor window open and the breakpoint line highlighted. If the program flow does not hit a breakpoint, you can always seize control by selecting **Pause** from the **Debug** menu. In our example we also set a breakpoint on **Thread Start or Death**, so there will not be a highlighted line at the first few pauses. Just press **Control-F5** to continue until it hits a breakpoint line. Then you can use **Step Over**, **Step Into**, and other standard debugger features to walk through the source. Table 4-3 is a summary of features available through the **Debug** menu.

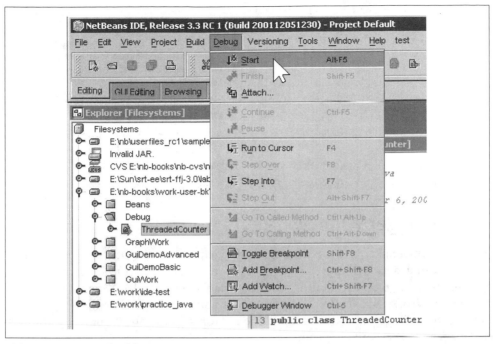

Figure 4-5. Starting the debugger

Table 4-3. Debug menu options

Debug menu	Shortcut keys	Debugger action
Start	Alt-F5	Start Debugger session and switch to Debugger workspace.
Finish	Shift-F5	End Debugger session.
Attach		Debug a remote process.
Continue	Control-F5	Resume execution until the next breakpoint.
Pause		Pause a running program that has not hit a breakpoint.
Run to Cursor	F4	Resume execution until the program pointer reaches the location of the cursor in the source.
Step Over	F8	Execute to next line in current method or constructor.
Step Into	F7	Same as Step Over (F8), unless current line is a method call. In that case, pauses at the first executable line in the method. This works to start a new debugger session and pause at the first line of the main method.
Step Out	Alt-Shift-F7	Same as Step Over (F8), unless current line is in a method. In that case, executes normally through return and pauses in the calling source at the line after the method call.
Go to Called Method	Control-Alt-Up	Move cursor in source to the current execution line in a called method. This only affects the cursor location, not the flow of execution.

Table 4-3. Debug menu options (continued)

Debug menu	Shortcut keys	Debugger action
Go to Calling Method	Control-Alt-Down	Move cursor in source to the point from which the current method was called. This only affects the cursor location, not the flow of execution.
Toggle Breakpoint	Shift-F8	If the cursor is on a line that does not have a breakpoint set, set a breakpoint. Otherwise, clear the breakpoint.
Add Breakpoint	Control-Shift-F8	Open dialog to add several breakpoint types—Line, Method, Exception, Variable, Thread, Class.
Add Watch	Control-Shift-F7	Add a watch on a variable or expression.
Debugger Window	Control-5	Open the Debugger window. (See next section for details.)

The Debugger Window

Remember my remark at the beginning of this chapter that the best part of programming is seeing what's going on under the hood? That's why the NetBeans people gave us the Debugger Window. So start a debugging session, let it switch you to the Debugging Workspace, and we'll look at what you can do with the Debugger Window. If the Debugger Window doesn't open automatically, press **Control-5** to open it. This window is shown in Figure 4-6.

The Debugger Window has three sections:

Toolbar
> Buttons to toggle View Panels and Property Sheet off and on

View Panels
> Up to seven views of what's going on under the hood of your programs

Property Sheet
> Property info on an object selected on a View Panel

The View Panels, which allow you to examine in depth the objects involved in running the object being debugged, include the following:

Sessions
> Shows all active debugging sessions. You can launch any number of simultaneous debugging sessions and switch back and forth among them.

Breakpoints
> Shows all breakpoints of every type set in all active sessions

Threads
> Shows all live threads in all active sessions

Call Stack
> Shows stack trace for each live thread in the currently selected session

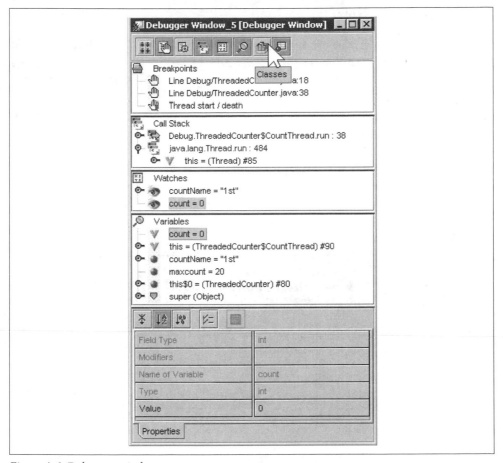

Figure 4-6. Debugger window

Watches

Shows all watches set on variables in all active sessions

Variables

Shows all variables visible within scope of currently selected thread

Classes

Shows classes visible in currently selected session

Use the debug functions for Continue, Step Into, and Step Over to slowly execute our ThreadedCounter example. Notice the values changing in the watches on the count and countName variables. Separately, the Output Window tracks execution progress by logging breakpoints that are hit. Open up nodes in the panels to look as deeply as you like. Inspecting the objects while they are running reveals what the JVM is doing with the classes that you're debugging.

The Variables View

Let's investigate the Variables view to see what's possible. You should have a Debugger Session running with ThreadedCounter, and the Debugger Window should be open with the Variables panel and the Property Sheet visible. If necessary, click the appropriate button in the Tool bar to make the panels visible.

Press **Control-F5** a few times to get past startup and into the main execution phase. Continue until the Watches or Variables panel shows count = 3. Click the value for count, click again to edit it, and change the value to count = 6. That's how easy it is to examine and modify the value of a variable during debugging. Try it with countName. Change the value to "3rd", or whatever you like. Or, as shown in Figure 4-7, open the nodes to expose the individual characters, and change them one by one.

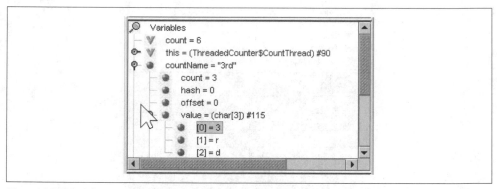

Figure 4-7. Modifying a variable

Remote Debugging in NetBeans

Any Java executable that can be run from the IDE can be debugged by it. This gives a developer the full range of NetBeans' debugging power for working with standalone applications, applets, and client applications that are based on a variety of technologies. The NetBeans debugger can also attach to a Java process already running in a separate JVM, either on the same computer or on a remote machine. This gives a developer the same power for debugging remote applications and components running in Java-based server containers.

Attaching to a remote JVM makes it possible to use breakpoints, conditionals, watches, and other debugging features with servlets, Enterprise JavaBeans, and RMI or CORBA server objects. Debugging remote objects without such features requires inserting a myriad of System.out.println() statements or other logging code. Using logging code for debugging is slow and inefficient, whereas using NetBeans is much more powerful.

Debugging Remotely

1. Start the JVM that you want to debug with the following switches:

```
java -Xint -Xdebug -Xnoagent -Xrunjdwp:transport=dt_socket,server=y,
    address=12999,suspend=n ...
```

-Xint

Turn off Hotspot optimizations. Although this is not strictly necessary, it does make the JVM far more stable while debugging.

-Xdebug

Turn on debug mode.

-Xnoagent

Disable the old sun.tools.debug.

-Xrunjdwp

Specify connection details:

- transport=dt_socket: tell the JVM to allow a remote debugger to connect via socket. Alternatively, transport=dt_shmem allows the remote debugger to connect over shared memory, which requires that the debugger be on the same machine as the JVM. As of NetBeans 3.2.1, it seems that only dt_socket is supported.

- server=y: tell the JVM to wait for a remote debugger to attach to it. Alternatively, server=n would cause the JVM to try to attach to a remote debugger.

- address=12999: specify port number to listen on. This can be any port that you have permissions to. Remember this port because you will need it to configure NetBeans later.

- suspend=n: if this is "y," it causes the JVM to suspend before the main class is loaded.

2. Start NetBeans.

3. Select **Debug → Attach** from the menus.

4. In the Attach window (shown in Figure 4-8) select the Default Debugger, the host you are connecting to, and the port on that machine that you specified when you started the JVM.

5. In your NetBeans output window, you will see Connecting to localhost:12999. You will be able to see your connection in the Sessions tab of the Debugger Window, shown in Figure 4-9.

6. Use the NetBeans Debugger just as you would a local debugging session.

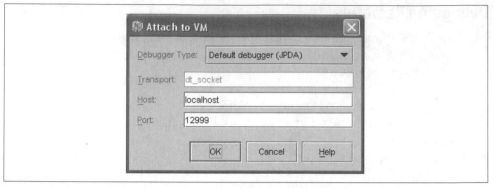

Figure 4-8. The Attach dialog box

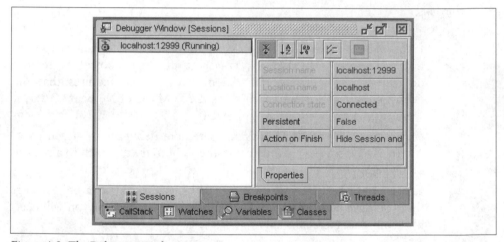

Figure 4-9. The Debugger window

Caveats

Connecting to a separate JVM, especially across a network to a remote machine, is significantly more complex behind the scenes and has more possibilities for problems. Nevertheless, the advanced debugging features more than make up for any extra patience and effort that the following issues may require.

- If you attach to debug a JVM and then disconnect, you will not be able to reconnect unless you restart your JVM. It seems that a given JVM will only accept one debugger connection while it is running.

- In Debug mode, your JVM may be much slower, because it needs to send a record of all method calls to the debugger.

- In Debug mode, your JVM will also be very unstable. Make sure that you have -Xint specified to disable Hotspot optimizations. You may also want to add -Djava.compiler=NONE to turn off the Just-In-Time (JIT) compiler.

- Conditional breakpoints with complex conditions may not work.

Advanced Features

If you have the source code of your server software, you can even debug into the server code. For example, open source projects such as JBoss, an Enterprise Java-Beans Container (found at *http://www.jboss.org*), and Tomcat, a Java Servlet engine (found at *http://jakarta.apache.org*), provide you with the source code of their servers. If you mount that code as a filesystem in NetBeans, you can debug into that code as well (you need not compile the code for this to work). Note that the version of the code must match exactly with that of the running software (i.e., trying to debug JBoss 2.4.0 with the source from JBoss 2.4.1 will not work).

Now that you have the tools for getting out of trouble, you're ready for more interesting ways to get into trouble. The chapters ahead will give you ample opportunity to get well acquainted with the NetBeans debugger as we look at increasingly sophisticated tools and technologies for building Java applications and components with NetBeans.

## CHAPTER 5

Compilation and Execution Services

Using Custom Compilation and Execution Services

The IDE uses Compilation and Execution services to compile and run Java programs. During setup, the IDE locates your Java Standard Development Kit (SDK) and sets up a Compilation service called the Internal Compilation Service that uses the standard javac tool as a compiler. You can customize this compiler from the IDE's Options dialog. In some cases, however, this compiler may not be desirable. In such cases, the IDE allows you to add your own Java compiler as an External Compilation Service. A good example of needing an External Compilation Service would be for compiling Java source code written for the Java 1.1 SDK or for using a third-party vendor's highly optimized compiler. Like Compilation services, Execution services are highly customizable in the IDE. Execution services use the Java interpreter to execute compiled classes in a given JVM. The current JVM is used by the Internal Execution Service, whereas additional JVMs can be configured using the External Execution Service (you can also have multiple configurations of the Internal Execution Service).

Creating and Customizing Internal Compilation Services

After installation, the IDE will configure a single default Internal Compilation Service. To configure the default Internal Compilation Service, select **Tools → Options**. In the Options window that appears, expand the nodes **Building → Compiler Types**. Select the **Internal Compilation** child node and you should see a Property Sheet appear in the right pane as shown in Figure 5-1.

The various configuration options for the Internal Configuration Service are described in Table 5-1; additionally, Figure 5-1 shows configurations for the service that are on the expert tab of the property sheet.

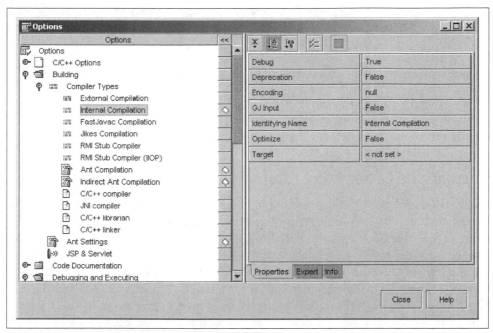

Figure 5-1. The Internal Compiler Service

Table 5-1. Configuration properties for the Internal Compilation Service

Property name	Description
Debug	When set to true, this property causes the compiler to produce debugging information in the compiled code.
Deprecation	When set to true, this property causes the compiler to treat deprecation warnings as errors.
Encoding	This property can be used to set the character encoding for the source file. The default value of null is used for the default character encoding.
GJInput	When set to true, this property causes the compiler to recognize generic types (parameterized types) in the source code.
Identifying name	The canonical name for this Internal Compiler Service
Optimize	When set to true, this property causes the compiler to generate optimized code.
Target	This property is used to set the target filesystem under which the generated class files will be stored.

Sometimes it is necessary to have different configurations of the same service for the sake of passing different compiler options to different files. For example, one Java source file may need to be compiled with debugging information whereas another, in the same project, does not. In this case you can create a new compiler service configuration. To create a new configuration, right-click on the **Compiler Types** node and select **New → Internal Compilation** from the context menu. Enter a name for the new compiler configuration and click the Finish button. Your new compiler should be added to the list of Compiler Types. Refer to Tables 5-1 and 5-2 to configure your new Internal Compiler Service as desired. Now you can associate Java source files with either the default service or the one you just created.

Table 5-2. Expert configuration properties for the Internal Compilation Service

Property name	Description
Boot Class Path	This property sets the boot CLASSPATH of your Java VM.
Class Path	This property is passed to the compiler and overrides your current CLASSPATH environment variable.

Creating and Customizing External Compilation Services

External Compilation Services allow you to use compilers other than the default one used by the Internal Compiler Service. For example, you might want to compile some Java source files using the JDK 1.1, some using JDK 1.4, and others using JDK 1.3. Because the Internal Compiler Service only allows you to customize one compiler, it cannot be used to accomplish this task. If you installed the IDE under 1.3 (the IDE cannot be installed under 1.1), the Internal Compiler will use the 1.3 javac. For the 1.4 and 1.1 JDKs, you can create custom configurations of the External Compiler Service. The External Compiler has a property that lets you specify which executable will be used as the javac tool. Other properties let you configure parameters that need to be passed to the tool as arguments. As an example of creating and customizing your own service, this section will show how to create a new JDK 1.1 External Compilation Service and configure it to compile source code written for the JDK 1.1 compiler. This example assumes that you have the JDK 1.1 installed. You can download the JDK from *http://java.sun.com/products/jdk/1.1*.

Creating a new JDK 1.1 External Compilation Service

To create a new JDK 1.1 External Compilation Service, right-click on the **Compiler Types** node and select **New → External Compilation**. Enter a name for the new service and click the Finish button. For this example we will use the name JDK 1.1 External Compilation Service. The newly created service should appear in the list of compiler types.

Configuring the new JDK 1.1 External Compilation Service. Select the newly created service and a tabbed property sheet should appear in the right pane as shown in Figure 5-2. External Compilation Services are far more configurable than Internal Compilation Services. There are standard properties for arguments that are passed to the compiler when it is called by the IDE. These arguments are referred to as tags and can be configured in the property sheets. For example, the argument (or tag) for debug optimization is usually -g. However, if you are using a third-party compiler, this option may be something like -d or -optimized. Using the property sheets you can set the value of this argument (true or false) and you can also change the name of the tag from -g to

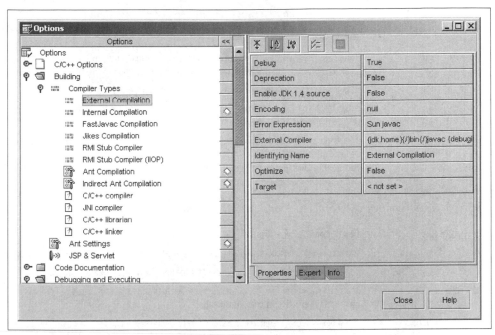

Figure 5-2. JDK 1.1 External Compilation Service

whatever you want. Most of the options that are expected by compilers are represented in the property sheets; however, you may need to add extra parameters for the compiler you are using or to remove some of the parameters that are not used. The IDE gives you maximum control of the external compiler by letting you format the actual command used to invoke the compilation process. This step is detailed in the next section. Figure 5-2 and Table 5-3 show the properties of the External Compiler Service configuration and Table 5-4 shows the expert properties for these services.. To add environment variables, click the **Expert** tab on the property sheet for a compilation service, then click the value field for its **Environment Variables** property. A specialized property editor dialog will pop up, as shown in Figure 5-3.

Table 5-3. Configuration properties for the External Compilation Service

Property name	Description
Debug	When this property is set to true, the IDE will send the debug flag to the compiler, causing it to produce debugging information in the compiled code.
Deprecation	When this property is set to true, the IDE will send the deprecation flag to the compiler, causing it to treat deprecated methods as errors.
Enable JDK 1.4 source	When this property is set to true, the IDE will send the "-source 1.4" flag to the compiler, enabling it to recognize JDK 1.4 assertions.
Encoding	This property sets the character encoding for the source code.
Error Expression	This property sets the format of error message output from the compiler using regular expression. It allows the IDE to identify error messages from different compilers.

Table 5-3. Configuration properties for the External Compilation Service (continued)

Property name	Description
External Compiler	This property allows you to configure the external process that is used by the IDE as the compiler executable. This property will be discussed in the next section.
Identifying Name	This property sets the canonical name for the External Compiler Service.
Optimize	When this property is set to true, the IDE will send the optimize flag to the compiler, causing it to generate optimized code.
Target	This property sets the target filesystem where the generated code should be created. This value of this property is sent to the compiler with the Output Dir tag. You should change the name of this tag in the expert tab of the property sheet if your compiler uses a different tag name than the default. (See Table 5-4).

Table 5-4. Expert configuration properties for the External Compilation Service

Property name	Description
Boot Class Path	This property sets the boot classpath where the compiler will find Java sources and extensions.
Boot Class Path Tag Replace	This property sets the tag name to be used for the Boot Class Path property.
Class Path	This property sets the Classpath that will be passed to the external compiler. It will replace the system classpath environment variable.
Debug Tag Replace	This property sets the tag name to be used for the Debug property.
Deprecation Tag Replace	This property sets the tag name to be used for the Deprecation property.
Environment Variables	This property sets a list of environment variables that will be made available to the external compiler. The environment variables should be added as name value pairs. For example, ENV_NAME=ENV_VALUE would set the environment variable ENV_NAME to ENV_VALUE. Use the Environment Variable property editor shown in Figure 5-3.
Filesystem Path	This read-only property shows the filesystem classpath that will be prepended to the classpath parameter sent to the external compiler.
Optimize Tag Replace	This property sets the tag name to be used for the Optimize property.
Output Dir Replace	This property sets the tag name to be used to replace the Target property.

Configuring the external process. External Compiler and Execution Services are called via an external process. The properties you set in the property sheets for configuring your service are passed to the external process as program arguments. For example, if you set the debug property to true in the property sheet for an External Compiler Service, the external process (in this case javac) will get an argument -d added to its argument list. Therefore the external process would look something like javac -d. It may be that the compiler you use has a different argument for the debug option than -d, let's say -debug. In this case you can change the substitution tag in the expert tab of the service's property sheet from -d to -debug. How does the IDE substitute the debug parameter, and what if there was no parameter (the debug property was set to false)? This is achieved by having a format of the execution command with substitution variables. The format is displayed as a string and stored as a property in the property sheet. For the External Compiler Service, it is the External Compiler property, and for External Execution Service, it is the External Executor property. These

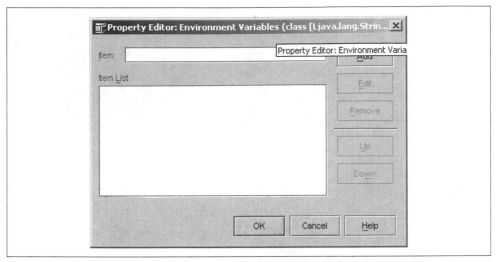

Figure 5-3. Environment variables property editor

properties allow you to configure the external process by modifiying the format of the execution command. A simple execution command might look like:

```
{jdk.home}{/}bin{/}javac {files}
```

This command calls javac on the files to be compiled. There are two parts to this command. A process, and the process arguments. In this example the process is {jdk.home}{/}bin{/}javac, and the only process argument is {files}. {jdk.home}, {/} and {files} are all examples of substitution variables. The IDE substitutes these variables with their respective values when the command is executed (i.e., when a file is compiled or executed using this service). Figure 5-4 shows the External Process Configuration dialog. To use this dialog, click on the External Compiler's (or, if you are configuring an External Execution Service, the External Executor's) property value in the property sheet and then click on the ellipsis button that appears. (For the rest of this section we will focus on the External Compiler Service for JDK 1.1).

The configuration dialog separates the process from its arguments. You can use the default process, because it uses substitution variables to find the compiler, or you can substitute this property with an absolute path to your compiler. For portability, the IDE offers the {/} substitution variable. This has the same effect as the Java variable File.separator in that it sets the correct file separator for file paths on your platform. For example, {/}jdk1.1.8{/}bin{/}javac becomes \jdk1.1.8\bin\javac on Windows and /jdk1.1.8/bin/javac on Unix systems. In the bottom section of the dialog, all the substitution variables are explained. To further explain how substitution variables are used, examine the argument line shown in Figure 5-4. Using this line, if the debug property was set to true, the -d argument would be passed to the process as the value of the substitution variable {debuginfo}.

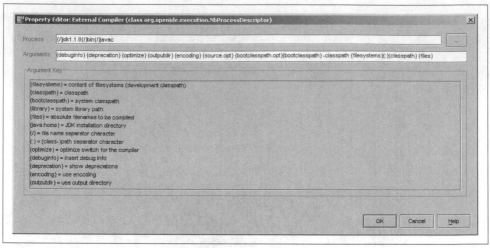

Figure 5-4. External Process configuration dialog

Because there is not a substitution variable for every possible process argument, what happens when we need to add more arguments to the process? In this case you can directly modify the process arguments line and insert constant arguments. For example, to add the -nowarn argument to the JDK 1.1 process, you can insert the -nowarn argument in the argument line. This is shown in Figure 5-5.

Be careful when placing constant arguments that they do not conflict with other arguments (for example, the nowarn argument must come before the {files} argument).

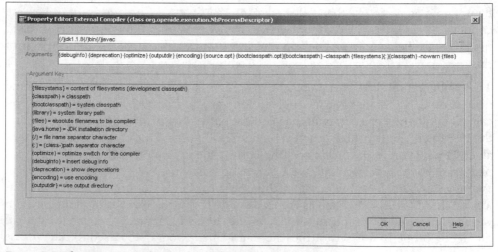

Figure 5-5. The JDK External Compiler with the nowarn argument

The Internal Execution Service

The IDE sets up one Internal Execution Service after install. This service is not very configurable and usually points to the current JVM pointed to by the JAVA_HOME environment variable. This service can be used to execute Java programs using the JVM with which the IDE was installed. To use different JVMs, you will need to configure an External Execution Service for each JVM you want to use.

Creating and Customizing External Execution Services

External Execution Services allow you to configure a custom JVM to run your Java classes. Like External Compiler Services they are configurable via property sheets. A good case for creating a new service of this type would be for executing code that needs to run in an older JVM version, such as JDK 1.1.

To create a new External Execution Service, select **Tools** → **Options** from the menu; right-click on the **Debugging and Executing Execution Types** node and select **New** → **External Execution** from the context menu. Enter a canonical name for your new service and click **OK**. Your newly created service should appear in the list of Execution Types.

To configure your service, select its node from the list and you should see its property sheet appear. If you don't see a property sheet, right-click on the node and select Properties from the context menu. The configuration properties for this type of service are described in Tables 5-5 and 5-6.

Table 5-5. Configuration properties for the External Execution Service

Property name	Description
External Process	This property is used to configure the external process called by the service.

Table 5-6. Expert configuration properties for the External Execution Service

Property name	Description
Append Environment Variables	When this property is set to true, the IDE will replace and append environment variables with the values supplied in the Environment Variables property.
Boot Class Path	This property sets the classpath used to locate the JVM and it's runtime classes
Class Path	This property sets the classpath that will be passed to the JVM. It will replace the system classpath environment variable.
Working Directory	This property sets the directory from which the JVM executable will be called.

Associating Services with Java Files

Now that you have learned to configure services, it will be useful to put those services into use by associating them with Java files in your project. You may choose to set up default services that get selected whenever you create a new Java file, or you may want to explicitly set services on files that need custom compilation or execution.

Setting Default Services for Java Files

To set a service as the default for all Java files, open the Options window and select **Editing → Java Sources**. In the right pane you can select the default execution from the drop-downs in the property sheet.

Setting Services for Specific Files

You can choose Compilation and Execution Services for each of the files in your project. If you compile the files in bulk, the IDE selects the compiler for each file and executes it in turn. To set a file's Compilation or Execution Service, right-click on the file and select **Properties** from the context menu. In the Properties dialog, select the **Execution** tab. Choose a Compilation Service from the Compiler drop-down, or choose an Execution Service from the Executor drop-down.

Building with Ant

Ant is a build tool much like GNU Make. Ant is implemented in Java and is driven by an XML build script—synonymous to a Make file—that defines targets for the tool to execute. This section is not intended to be a primer on Ant. You can learn more about Ant on the Apache's web site (*http://jakarta.apache.org/ant*).

The IDE incorporates Ant through the Ant module. The module allows you to run Ant scripts that can compile and execute your Java code. You can install the module through the AutoUpdate tool or download it from the NetBeans web site. Once installed, the module will add several Ant-related features to the IDE, notably Ant Execution and Compilation Services, Ant build script templates, and the ability to define targets, tasks, properties, and other Ant XML elements in the build script from the Explorer workspace.

Creating a Build Script

The build script that defines targets for Ant to execute is known as an Ant project. A project is simply a collection of targets. To create a new Ant project right-click on the folder in which you wish to add the build script and select **New → Ant Build Script → Blank Project** from the context menu. A new script should be added to the folder. The script is an XML file that can be edited by right-clicking on the script node and selecting **Open** from the context menu.

The IDE makes adding targets to the build script very easy by allowing you to add them from the Explorer workspace. To add a new target right-click on the script node and select **Add target** from the context menu. The new target will be added with the name "changeme." To see the newly added target you will have to expand the script node. Figure 5-6 shows an expanded build script node with the changeme target. You can change a target's name by right-clicking on it and selecting **Rename** from the context menu.

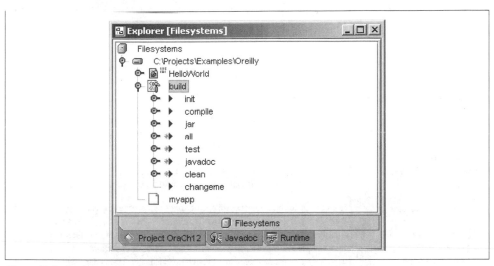

Figure 5-6. An Ant project build script

Finally you will want to add a task to the newly created target. To do this, right-click on the target's node and select **Add Task ...** from the context menu. You should see a dialog box like the one shown in Figure 5-7. The dialog box allows you to select a task from a list of valid Ant tasks. Click on the Help button for detailed help on the particular task.

Figure 5-7. Adding a new Ant task

Figure 5-8 shows help for the javac task.

You can add other elements to your build script from the Explorer. For each node, simply right-click and select Add from the context menu, and a list of valid tags should appear.

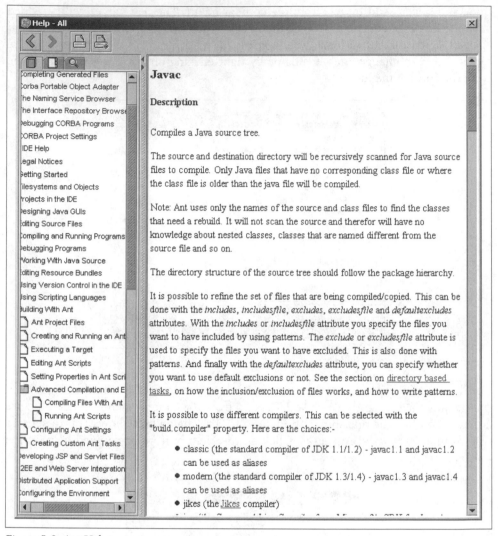

Figure 5-8. Ant Help page

Configuring the Ant Module

The Ant module is configurable via property sheets in the Options window, with global settings accessible at **Building → Ant Settings**. Table 5-7 explains the properties for the Ant settings node.

Table 5-7. Properties for Ant settings

Property name	Description
Default Compiler	This property sets the default compilation service for all Ant scripts (usually this property is set to "do not compile").
Default Executor	This property sets default execution service for all Ant scripts.
Properties	This property sets a list of Properties that will be passed in to Ant scripts when they are executed in the IDE.
Reuse Output Tag	This property causes all executing scripts to use the same output tab.
Save Files	When set to true, this property causes the IDE to save all modified files before executing Ant.
Verbosity Level	This property sets the level of output that Ant should display when executing targets.

The module also creates two Compilation Services and an Execution Service—Ant Script Compilation, Indirect Ant Compilation, and Ant Script Execution. All Compilation Services implement Build, Clean, and Compile actions. The Ant Compilation Services have properties that can be configured to define the actions by executing targets in an Ant build script. For example, in the Options window see **Building →️ Compiler Types →️ Ant Script Compilation**. Notice the **Build Target(s)** property. Its default setting is clean, all. The targets are executed from left to right. If a source object uses Ant Script Compilation, selecting the **Build** action from the object's context menu results in executing the clean target, followed by the all target in the Ant build script. See Table 5-8.

Table 5-8. Properties for the Ant compiler

Property name	Description
Build Target(s)	This property lists the targets that should be executed when the Build action (usually invoked from) is called on an Ant script. The targets will be executed in succession from left to right. Each target should be separated by a comma.
Clean Target(s)	This property lists the targets that should be executed when the Clean action (usually invoked from) is called on an Ant script. The targets will be executed in succession from left to right. Each target should be separated by a comma.
Compile Targets	This property lists the targets that should be executed when the Clean action (usually invoked from) is called on an Ant script. The targets will be executed in succession from left to right. Each target should be separated by a comma.

The Indirect Ant Compilation compiler service is useful when you want to call an Ant script while compiling another file. For example, it could be used to call the compile target in an Ant script when compiling a Java file. The Indirect Ant Compilation has the very same properties as the Ant Compiler with the addition of a property to specify the Ant script that defines the necessary targets to invoke.

The Ant Executor found in the Options window at **Debugging and Executing →️ Execution Types →️ Ant Script Execution** defines targets to run when an Ant script is executed. The default target of the Ant script is executed if no target is defined here.

Executing and Compiling with Ant Scripts

By default, double-clicking an Ant build script should run the default target of that script. To run a specific target, you can right-click on the target's node and select **Execute** from the context menu. The output from the Ant script should appear in the Output tab. There is usually no need to define compilation for Ant script because you can simply execute the compile target declared in the script. However, if you set the Compiler property to the Ant compiler service, you could select **Build** or **Compile** from the **Build** menu and the respective targets will be executed.

Why Use Ant?

NetBeans already has compilation and execution services for all the object types that are supported for development. Why not just use the services that are provided? The short answer is If you're happy without Ant, don't use it. If you only build and execute single classes or small projects, you probably don't need the flexibility that a build tool like Ant offers. But if you're involved in a large project, especially a project that has complex needs and unique actions to be performed many times during the course of development, look to Ant for a powerful, easy-to-use, easy-to-configure tool.

For example, this book was developed by several authors working remotely with Linux, Solaris, and Windows computers with shared access to a CVS repository for storing the drafts of chapters, source examples, and related material. The text was written in DocBook XML, which the authors and editors needed to validate and transform into HTML or PDF frequently. We created an Ant build script to perform the tasks. As the project progressed and the variety of tasks expanded, the build script grew to accommodate the needs. A simple CVS update automatically brought the enhanced build script into each author's environment. Without CVS and Ant, there would have been many more emails and phone calls asking how to do common tasks. With these tools, we have been able to keep our focus on the project goals.

## CHAPTER 6

Customizing the Environment

The NetBeans IDE offers a highly customizeable environment through wizards and options that can be serialized. In this chapter you will learn how to customize your IDE environment. We will look at the following areas of customization:

- Setup Wizard
- Toolbars
- Menus
- Editors
- Modules

The Setup Wizard

The Setup Wizards allows you to quickly configure your IDE with some general settings required for everyday use. It is especially useful after an initial install of the IDE and is usually launched the first time you run NetBeans. To use the Setup Wizard any time after the initial launch select **Tools**⟶**Setup Wizard** from the menu bar.

General NetBeans Settings

The first pane of the Setup Wizard, shown in Figure 6-1, allows you to configure a proxy server, a window mode, and an HTML browser.

The proxy server settings will be used for all the network and Internet needs of the IDE such as acquiring information for AutoUpdate from a remote Update Center. Your network administrator should be able to supply you with the server and port information of your proxy server. You will generally only need these settings if you are using the IDE behind a firewall.

The window mode setting is used to determine the type of windowing interface NetBeans should use. There are generally two types of interfaces: SDI and MDI. The main difference between the two interfaces is that in SDI mode, the IDE has no

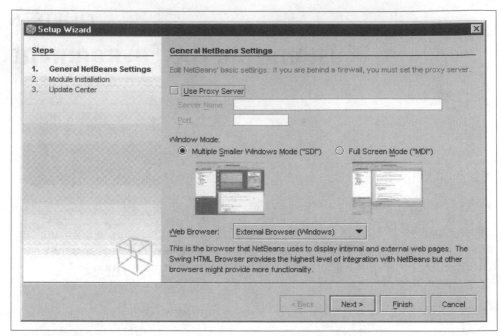

Figure 6-1. The first pane of the Setup Wizard

main window, and each workspace has its own window, whereas in MDI mode, all the windows are managed by a single window known as the main frame. Your choice of a window mode depends on your taste. They both have their advantages. In SDI mode the proliferation of windows for every document and workspace can be quite messy and annoying. The one benefit is that screen size per window can be maximized. In MDI mode there is one window and everything else is a child of that window. This makes window management very easy and agreeable for the programmer who already has 12 other applications opened. The one caveat is that because MDI child windows share space with a parent window, they cannot be maximized to take advantage of the entire screen area. This can be especially annoying with an editor window displaying Java source. It's often convenient to minimize scrolling by showing as much text as possible. Microsoft Windows users may favor MDI mode because many Windows applications are MDI, including the DevStudio IDE.

The differences between the two modes do not necessarily form a fork in the road, and neither of them can be considered "the road less traveled." This is because the IDE lets you have the best of both worlds. In NetBeans, windows can be docked into one another. Windows—also referred to as frames—can also be made into separate windows, regardless of the mode you chose. This is an advanced level of customization for the NetBeans IDE, but it remains simple to accomplish. For example, if you chose MDI mode from the Setup Wizard, but would like your editor to be displayed as a separate window so that you could take advantage of more screen real estate, simply open a Java file; once the editor is opened select **Window → Frame Resides → As Separate Window** from the menu bar. You should now see the editor in a separate window. Conversely, if you preferred to dock the editor window and back **Window → Frame Resides → As Separate Window** into the main frame, you would select **Window → Frame Resides → In IDE Desktop**. You can also chose to combine multiple windows via docking. For example, to add the filesystem explorer to the left side of an editor window, set the focus to the filesystem explorer, select **Window → Dock View Into → Source Editor → Left**. Figure 6-2 shows an editor window with a filesystem explorer docked on the left.

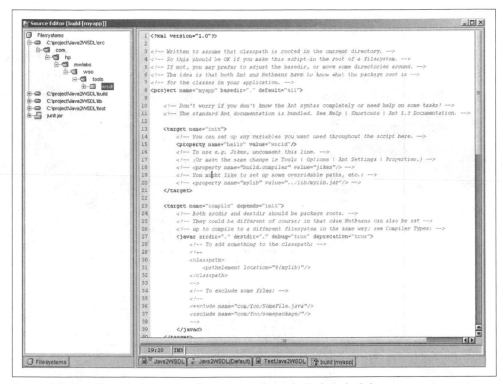

Figure 6-2. An editor window with a filesystem explorer docked on the left

The Web Browser selection is used for all the IDE's browsing needs such as javadoc searching and JavaServer Pages (JSP) previewing. NetBeans comes with the ICE Browser embedded. This will usually be sufficient for all your needs and provides the tightest integration with the IDE; however, it lacks the feature-rich capabilities of some commercial browsers, and in that case you may wish to select an external browser for default HTML browsing. If you choose an external browser, you will have to configure it later by selecting **Tools → Options** and then expand the Web Browser's node.

Module Installation

The second pane of the Setup Wizard (see Figure 6-3) allows you to configure which modules will be used by the IDE at runtime. The modules are shown in a table along with their enabled status (true\false), version number, and description. Upon start-up, the IDE will attempt to load each of the enabled modules. This process becomes slower with the number and complexity of the installed modules. Memory usage is also a consideration because all modules are issued their own classloader and run simultaneously in memory. For these reasons it may not be desirable to enable every possible module. To disable a module, simply select false under the enabled column of that module's entry.

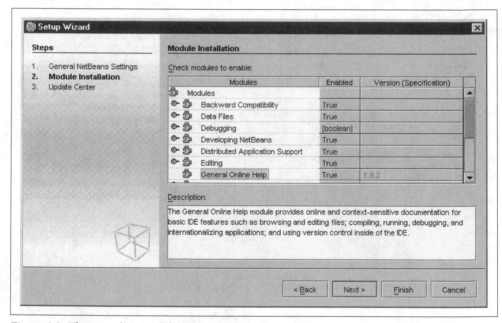

Figure 6-3. The second pane of the Setup Wizard

Update Center

The third pane of the Setup Wizard, shown in Figure 6-4, allows you to configure the Update Center connection for the IDE's Auto Update tool. The Auto Update tool connects to an Update Center to acquire modules and core components for installation. You can configure Auto Update to be automatically invoked on a recurring schedule, or you can manually invoke it any time by selecting **Tools → Update Center...** from the menu bar.

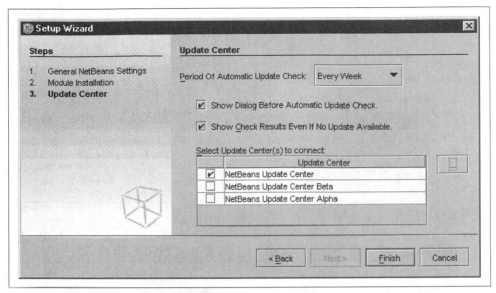

Figure 6-4. The third pane of the Setup Wizard

The Tools→Options Dialog

Most NetBeans global or project-level settings can be managed in the dialog invoked when you pull down **Tools → Options** dialog. The components in this dialog represent the vast array of configurable settings in the IDE. The components are organized in the left pane of this dialog in a tree of nodes. Each node represents a specific configuration component, and the folders represent categories by which the components are grouped.

When you select a component, its properties will appear in the left pane in a table that is known as the property sheet. Property sheets consist of two cells, a property name cell and a property value cell. Typically the property value cell is to the right of the property name cell. You can change a component's settings by changing the data in its property value cell.

Some property value cells allow you to enter plain text. Others, such as true/false properties, will have a combo box of valid entries. Some value cells may require data that is not easily entered as text and will prompt you to use a special property editor. When the option to use a property editor is available, an ellipsis (...) will appear in the rightmost end of the cell when you click on it. Clicking on this ellipsis will launch the property editor for that cell. Cells that require Color values frequently provide property editors that allow you to choose colors from a pallete.

You may want to change some settings globally. You may want to apply only other settings changes to the project you have open. Fortunately, NetBeans provides a means to specify the scope of a **Tools → Options** setting.

In Figure 6-5, we have circled a very small and important button. This button, which bears two left angle brackets, or "arrows" (<<) as its emblem, is called the Show Levels button. If you click it, a new panel "unfolds" into the options listing, and you are offered three choices for the level of settings persistence that can be applied on a per-setting basis, as shown in Figure 6-6.

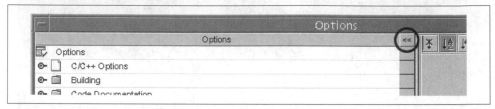

Figure 6-5. The Show Levels Button

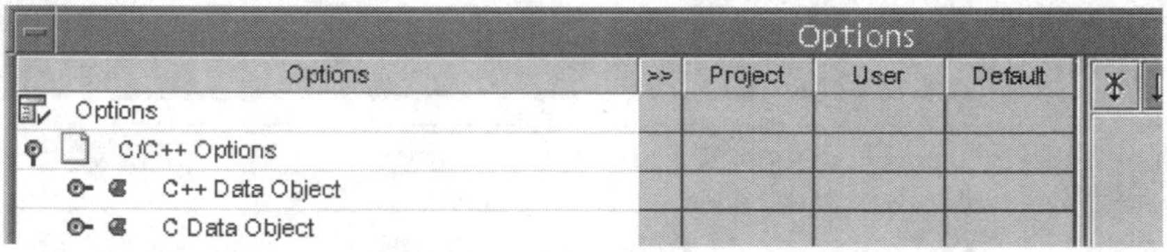

Figure 6-6. Show Levels opened

The three choices for settings persistence are as follows:

Default
> Keeps the default settings shipped with NetBeans; doesn't allow the user to apply any changes. Of course, if you change your mind, you can always remove this persistence to change the given setting. It's just a safety net.

Project
> Settings changes are applied to the current project only. Any other project will retain the settings it was left with until they are changed while that project is open.

User
> All changes apply to all projects for that user.

You can click the Show Levels button again to fold back this settings persistence panel so that it's out of your way.

Configuring Toolbars

Toolbars are similar to menus. They are panels consisting of image buttons that are mapped to a specific task. Each button on a toolbar will usually have a brief text description, commonly called a *tooltip*, and there may also be a sequence of keys associated with a button known as its shortcut key. The IDE comes preconfigured with several toolbars that would most likely be sufficient for everyday development tasks. If the preconfigured toolbars do not meet your needs, you can always modify them or create entirely new ones to perform your custom tasks.

In the NetBeans IDE, each toolbar button is tied to an action. You may think of an action as a task. For example Cut, Paste, and Copy are all actions. Most of the IDE's actions are prepackaged; others are provided by third-party modules. To begin configuring toolbars select **Tools → Options** and then go to **IDE Configuration → Look and Feel → Toolbars**. Figure 6-7 shows the toolbar options.

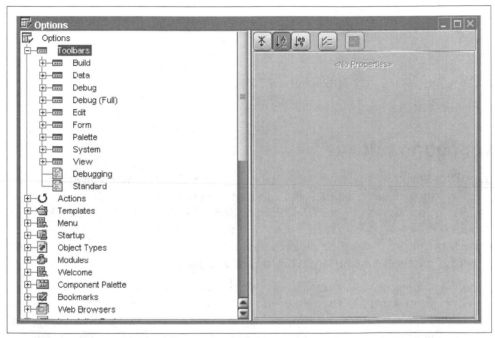

Figure 6-7. Toolbar options

These options allow you to edit and delete existing toolbars or create your own. You can add new buttons to an existing toolbar by copying and pasting actions. For example, to add a new button to the Build toolbar for compiling, you would perform the following steps:

1. Expand the **Build toolbar** node.
2. Expand **Actions → Build**, right-click on the **Compile** node, and select **Copy** from the context menu.
3. Right-click on the **Build** toolbar node and select **Paste → Copy** from the context menu.

You can also rearrange the ordering of toolbar buttons. To change the button order on a particular toolbar, right-click on its node and select **Change Order** from the context menu. You will be presented with the dialog box shown in Figure 6-8. Use the **Move Up** and **Move Down** buttons to reorder each toolbar button's position. The toolbar button at the top of the list will appear first from the left on the toolbar.

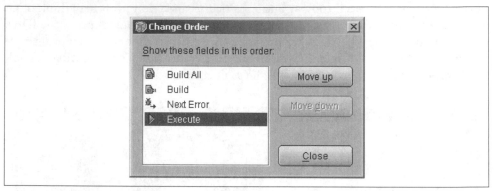

Figure 6-8. Changing toolbar button order

Configuring Menus

The IDE also allows you to edit and create menus in the same way you edit and create toolbars. To begin editing and creating menus open the options dialog box (**Tools** → **Options**) and go to **IDE Configuration** → **Look and Feel** → **Menu Bar**. You should see a list of nodes similar to the ones shown in Figure 6-9 that represent your current menu bar. By expanding each menu, you will see a list of menu items. An item can be either an action or a separator. Menus can also contain submenus.

To add a submenu to a menu, right-click on the menu node and select **New** → **Menu** from the context menu. The new menu is immediately viewable under the menu where you created it. Adding a menu item requires steps similar to the aforementioned toolbar button steps. After copying an action, right-click on the destination menu node and select **Paste** → **Copy** from the context menu. The reordering of menu items within menus is done exactly the same way toolbar buttons are reordered (right-click a menu node and select **Change Order...** from the context menu). You can also delete and rename menu items and menus in much the same way you would any node in the IDE. There is also an easy way for mapping shortcuts to menus. When supplying a name for the menu, type an ampersand (&) in front of the letter you want to map. For example, "&File" will be mapped to the shortcut Alt-F.

Configuring Editors

Of all the components in the IDE, the editor will most likely be the one involved in your day-to-day programming use. Therefore it makes sense that it is one of the most configurable of all the components in the IDE. Although it may seem that you are

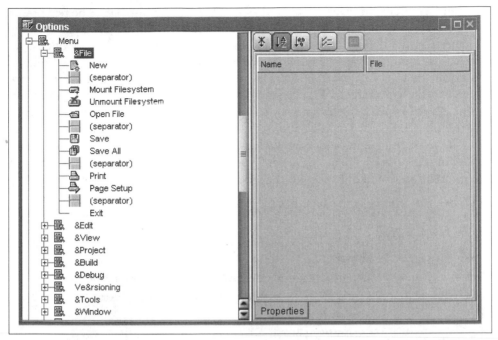

Figure 6-9. Creating and editing menus

always working with one editor, there are in fact different editors for different types of files. A file type is identified by its extension. The mapping of editor to file type is a one-to-many relationship. Although the content they handle may be different, editors share a common set of configurable attributes. Some editors may choose to disable some of these attributes because of the irrelevance to the particular implementation—for example, the Auto Popup Code Completion feature is disabled in the Plain editor. Editors for some object types may have multiple views; in such cases special menu items are provided for switching between views. For example, there is a specialized editor for modifying Properties files. That editor has two views: one provides a table for editing properties and values, and the other provides a plain text view. Selecting Open from the context menu for a Properties file results in the default view, which is the table view. To access the alternate plain text view, select Edit from the context menu.

Object Type Associations

As previously mentioned, editors are mapped to file and MIME types. In the IDE, a file is basically a type of object. The IDE uses Object Types to identify files based on their extensions. Object Types do not always map to files. Some are used internally as objects by modules. You can map several file extensions to a single Object Type, thereby associating the files with those extensions to a particular file type in the IDE. For example, adding java as an extension to the Java Source Object Type would make all files ending in *.java* recognized as Java file types in the IDE. The real power of Object Types comes in when you associate actions with an Object Type. Actions are objects in the IDE that are mapped to menu items and used to carry out a specific task on a target object. Compile is one example of an IDE action. The Compile action can be used on Java Object types to invoke a configured Compiler Service with a Java file as its target. Nothing stops you from adding the Compile action to an Image Object Type. If for example you had a special Compiler Service that converted GIF to JPEG, it would be useful to be able to right-click on a *.gif* file, select Compile from the menu, and have your file converted. Configuring Object Types makes all this possible. Usually Object Types come with preconfigured actions and extensions. You would only need to change these to add custom behavior.

Table 6-1 shows some common Object Types and their descriptions.

Table 6-1. Object Types

Object Type	Description
Form	Objects that refer to Java source files that have IDE-managed GUI code in them
NBM	Objects that refer to NetBeans Modules files that can be used to install modules
HTML	Objects that refer to HTML files
JSP	Objects that refer to JSP files
XML	Objects that refer to XML files
Java Source	Objects that refer to Java source files
Properties	Objects that refer to Properties files, which usually contain name/value pairs
Image	Objects that refer to IDE-supported images (ex. gif, jpeg)
Class	Objects that refer to compiled Java classes
Text	Objects that refer to arbitrary text files

Usually the only property of an Object Type you would configure would be the extensions. This is useful if you would like to add a new extension so that it is recognized by the IDE. For example, if you want the IDE to recognize files with the jad extensions as Java Source files, simply go to the Java Source Objects node and in the property sheet click on the pane to edit the Extensions and Mime Types. Click on the ellipsis that appears and you should see a dialog box like the one shown in Figure 6-10. Enter "jad" (you enter extensions without the dot prefix) in the input box and then click add. Close the dialog box. Any files in your mounted filesystems that have a jad extension should now appear with the icon denoted for Java source files. When you double-click the file, you should see the source code in the Java editor.

Editor Settings

At the heart of Editor configuration is the Editor Settings. The Editor Settings node can be found in the Options Dialog under **Editing → Editor Settings.** When you expand this node, you will see all the various editors in the IDE. Usually an editor's name will give you a good idea of the types of files it supports. Most of the editors have the same configuration parameters; however, you will be able to configure them separately and maintain your changes.

Global Key Bindings (shortcut keys)

Key bindings are the mapping of keys to predefined IDE actions. For example, the mapping of the Control key and the C key combination is to the Copy action. Many combinations can be mapped to a single action. Each mapping is known as a *binding* because the sequence of key strokes is bound to the particular action. Global Key Bindings are inherited by all the editors. Each editor also has its own specific bindings that can override global key bindings or provide their own mapping. Global key bindings are configured by selecting the **Editor Settings** node, clicking on the **Key Bindings** cell in the property sheet, and then clicking on the ellipsis (...) that appears. You should see a dialog box similar to the one shown in Figure 6-10. The predefined actions are shown in the List box and can be sorted by name or action (the internal action name). To add a new binding, first select an action from the list and then click on the **Add...** button. In the dialog box that appears, enter the key sequence that will cause the IDE to invoke the action. For meta keys such as Control and Alt, you will need to hold on the key while typing. So for binding the beep action to the Control key and B key combination, you would hold on the Control key while typing B in this dialog box. After clicking OK to close the dialog box, the new key binding should appear in the Keybindings list box.

You can modify an editor's local key bindings by selecting that editor from the list of nodes under **Editor Settings** and editing its Key Binding property. This behaves exactly like the global options except that these local options override any existing global key bindings for the specific editor with which the binding is associated.

Fonts and colors

Each editor has its own properties for fonts and colors. Color is divided into foreground and background and is individually configured for each syntax element of an editor. For example in the Java Editor, Java Keyword is a syntax element and it has its own foreground and background color properties. So for a keyword such as if the foreground and background color properties selected would be shown whenever it is typed. There is a default syntax element whose properties the other syntax elements can inherit or override. This allows you to set a consistent background color, for instance, and only chose different foreground colors for various elements. Fonts are also chosen independently for each syntax element and may be inherited from the default. To modify fonts or colors for a particular editor, select that editor from the nodes under **Editor Settings**, click the **Colors and Fonts** cell in the property sheet, and then click on the ellipsis that appears. You should see a dialog box that looks like Figure 6-11. Syntax elements are listed in the list box to the right.

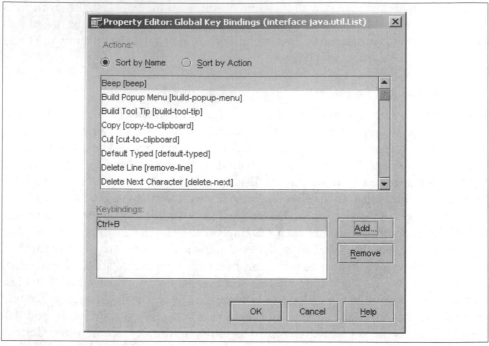

Figure 6-10 . Global key bindings

Click on an element to modify its font and color properties. The Default element should be at the top of the list. To change the background from the white default to a light yellow (the color of a sticky pad for instance), select the default syntax element, click on the button in the Background Color box, and then click on the ellipsis that appears. You should see a dialog box like the one shown in Figure 6-12. This is the color picker dialog box. Each tab shows a pallete from which you can chose colors. Use the first pallette to select the light shade of yellow. As an alternative, instead of clicking on the ellipsis and using the color picker, you could type in the RGB color code in the edit box. The RGB color code for this shade of yellow is 255,255,204.

Your default background color should now be set; however, some of the syntax elements may not choose to inherit this property. You will need to go through the elements and click the **Inherit** check box in the **Background Color**. This causes the background color chosen for the default syntax element to be applied to the current syntax element.

Choosing a font is just as easy as choosing colors. To modify the font for single-line comments in the Java Editor, changing it from plain italics to bold italics, click on the button in the Font box and then click on the ellipsis that appears. You should see a dialog box similar to the one shown in Figure 6-13. In the first list you select the Font name. The second list allows you to configure the syle of the font. For this example you would select Bold Italic from that list. The third list allows you to select the font size. Once you have configured the font settings, click **OK** to close the dialog box. The settings in this example should only affect single-line comments (comments that begin with //). Now every time you type a single-line comment, it will appear as a font with a bold-italic style.

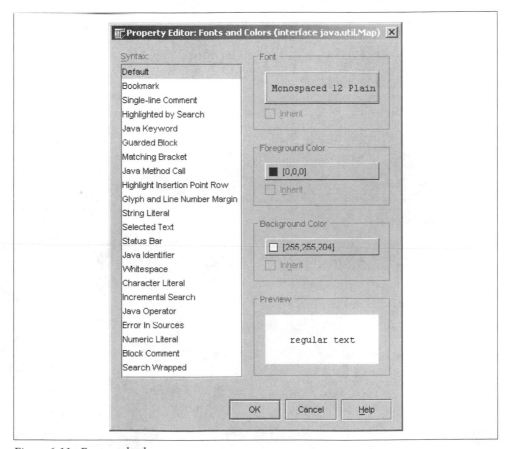

Figure 6-11 . Fonts and colors

Macros

In Chapter 2 you learned about macros in templates that were used for string expansion. In this section you will learn about a different macro used to execute a task on a particular editor. You can refer to these as editor macros. Editor macros can be recorded, saved, and executed. An editor macro can only be executed in the editor in which it was recorded and saved. Finally an editor macro is mapped to a shortcut key so that it can be easily invoked through convenient keystrokes.

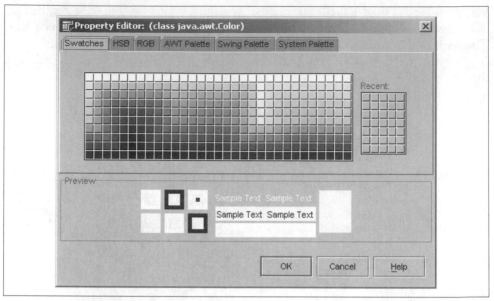

Figure 6-12. Color editor

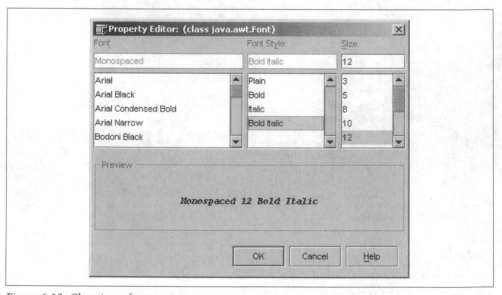

Figure 6-13. Choosing a font

Recording and saving macros. Let's say you were using a logging class that would emit messages to a log file when the log method was called with the classname and log message as parameters. The static method signature is:

```
Logger.logMessage(this.getClass(),"message");
```

Instead of having to type that every time you want to log a message, an editor macro can be created to type the entire method signature and then position the caret between the quotation marks so that a message can be typed.

To begin recording your macro, open a Java source file. This macro will be available for all source files opened with the Java editor. Start the macro recorder by typing Control-J and then S (hold Control key, type J, release Control key, type S). You should see the message "Recording" appear in the editor's status bar (the message goes away once you begin typing). Every keystroke beyond this point is recorded as part of the macro. Type the following code snippet:

```
Logger.logMessage(this.getClass(),"");
```

When finished typing, use the back arrow key to move the caret between the two quotation marks. Type Control-J and then E to end the macro recorder. A dialog box like the one shown in Figure 6-14 should appear. Type in a canonical name for the macro in the **Name** edit box and then click the **Add...** button. Another dialog should pop up, prompting you to enter a key binding for this macro. Type in a key sequence that you find convenient, for example Alt-Shift-0 (do not type in the plus sign or hyphen and remember to keep holding meta keys such as Alt while you type). Click **OK** and your new macro should be saved.

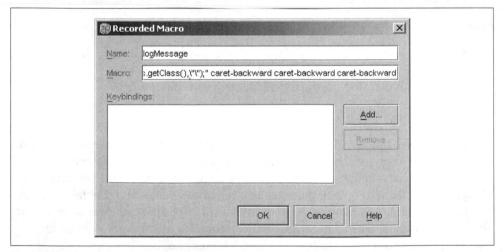

Figure 6-14. Recording a macro

 When recording macros, the IDE ignores mouse movements. Therefore avoid using the mouse while recording. You can use shortcut keys, however. This allows you to build complex actions, made up of several shortcut key sequences, and then assign the complex action to a single shortcut key sequence.

Editing and executing macros. After a macro is saved, it becomes one of the properties of the editor in which it was recorded. The macro we wrote in the previous section will be available to any source file opened with the Java editor. To modify the macro we can edit it through the macro property found in the property sheet for the particular editor. Click on the **Macros** cell to edit the property and click on the ellipsis. You should see a dialog box similar to that shown in Figure 6-15. Select the macro you want to edit from the table and click on the **Edit...** button to change the name or macro expansion.

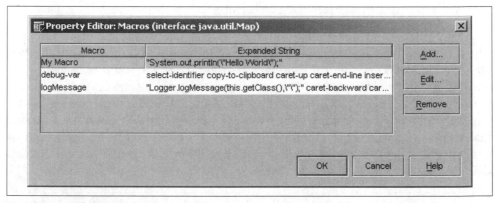

Figure 6-15. Editing a macro

To execute the macro, type the keyboard shortcut anywhere in the editor. For this example we used Control-Alt-0, so typing that will execute the macro and we should see the code with our caret positioned between the quotation marks.

Indentation engines

The IDE uses the concept of an indentation engine to format code in the Source Editor. Setting the width of tab spaces, adding a leading asterisk to comment lines, and placing spaces before parentheses are some examples of its use. You can create two types of engines, a Java Indentation Engine or a Simple Indentation Engine. The Java Indentation Engine has more options and is specific to formatting Java source code. Simple Indentation only allows you to configure the number of spaces for tab. Table 6-2 shows the properties of the Java Indentation Engine.

Table 6-2. Java Indentation Engine properties

Property	Description
Add Leading Star In Comment	If this property is set to true, the IDE will automatically add an asterisk (*) to the beginning of every line in a multiline comment (a comment starting with /* or /**).
Add Newline Before Brace	If this property is set to true, the IDE will start the brace for functions, classes, and other scopes, on the next line.

Table 6-2. Java Indentation Engine properties (continued)

Property	Description
Add Space Before Parenthesis	If this property is set to true, the IDE will add a single space before each opening parenthesis.
Expands Tab To Spaces	If this property is set to true, the IDE will add spaces (equal to the number of spaces per tab property) each time the tab key is pressed. Otherwise the IDE will advance the caret to the position necessary for the tab and insert the tab character (\t) into the file.
Number of Spaces Per Tab	This property sets the number of spaces that the caret should advance when the tab key is pressed.

You can associate an engine with any of the editors by selecting the editor from the list of nodes under **Editor Settings**, clicking on the Indentation Engine cell in the property editor, and then clicking on the ellipsis. You should see a dialog similar to the one shown in Figure 6-16, allowing you to select an Indentation Engine and configure it. Many editors can use the same engine. Changing the engine's settings will affect all the editors that reference it.

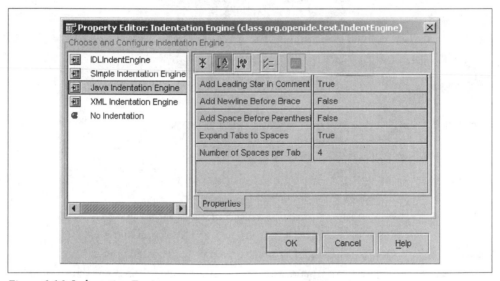

Figure 6-16. Indentation Engine

Command Line Options

The IDE can be run from the command line with arguments. At the command line type *runide.exe -help* (*runide.sh* on UNIX systems) and you will see a dialog box like the one shown in Figure 6-17 with the command line options.

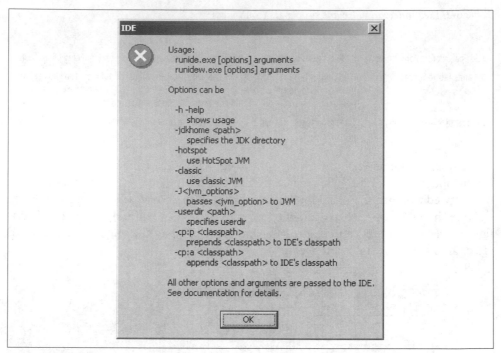

Figure 6-17. IDE options

These options are shown and described in Table 6-3.

Table 6-3. IDE command line arguments

Argument	Description
-h or -help	This argument displays the help dialog.
-jdkhome	This argument sets the directory where the IDE is to find the installed JDK.
-hotspot	If this argument is supplied, the IDE will use the hotspot JVM as opposed to classic.
-classic	If this argument is supplied, the IDE will use the classic JVM as opposed to hotspot.
-J<jvm_options>	This argument allows jvm options to be passed to the underlying JVM (i.e., the parameter is not used by the IDE). For example, setting the JVM stack size to 96 MB can be specified with -J-Xss96m.
-userdir	This argument specifies the user directory that the IDE will use to store project settings and user-specific information.
-cp:p <classpath>	This argument prepends the specified <classpath> to the IDE's classpath.
-cp:a <classpath>	This argument appends the specified <classpath> to the IDE's classpath.

Instead of typing the arguments at the command line each time you run the IDE, you can save your settings to a file that is read into the IDE as command line parameters. Your arguments need to be in the *ide.cfg* file found in the *bin* directory of your installation. For example, if you wanted to specify *xerces.jar* ahead of the IDE's classpath and set the maximum heap size to 256MB, your *ide.cfg* file will consist of a single line that looks like this:

```
-cp:pc:\xerces\lib\xerces.jar -J-Xmx256m
```

Modules

Modules are what make the NetBeans IDE extensible. The IDE consists of a thin layer known as the core on top of which are modules that provide most of the features you use. In the second part of this book you will learn how to create modules and build the IDE sources with minimal modules. This section gives you an introduction to modules and shows you how to install, uninstall and configure them in the IDE.

Installing Modules

The IDE allows you to install modules from NetBeans Update Centers (available through the web) or manually downloaded NBM files. Both of these methods are accomplished using the Auto Update Tool. To use Auto Update select **Tools** → **UpdateCenter**. You will see a dialog box like the one shown in Figure 6-18.

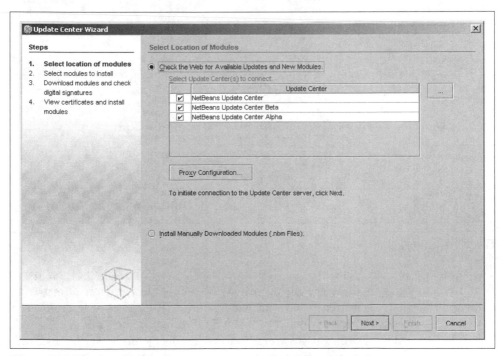

Figure 6-18. The Auto Update Center

If you are installing modules from the web, select the Update Centers you want to connect to from the list provided and click next. If you are behind a firewall, you will need to click on the **Proxy Configuration** button and supply the proxy server and port.

Installing from the Web

If you chose to install from the web and clicked the next button, you should see the next pane of the wizard as shown in Figure 6-19. If you do not see this pane, there may be something wrong with your Internet connection, or the Update Centers you chose were invalid or experiencing network problems. Another cause for problems could be your proxy settings. Check your settings, or consult with a systems administrator if you're using your company network, and try to connect again.

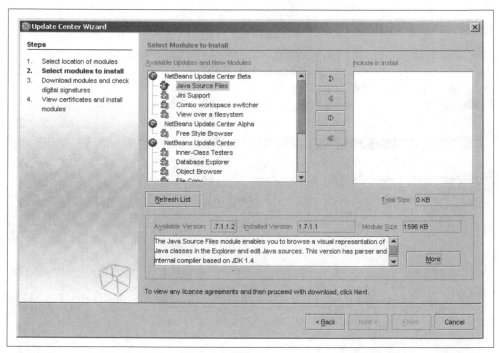

Figure 6-19. Installing modules via the Web

The modules are listed under each Update Center you selected in the first pane. When you select a module, the dialog displays the module's version information compared to what you currently have installed. The text box gives a description of the module and what it does. A web page giving more information about the module can be viewed by clicking on the **More** button. To select a module to be installed, select the module's node in the left list box and then click on the arrow pointing to the right or to the Include To Install list box. You can select multiple modules by holding the Control key while selecting and use the same arrow to chose those modules for installation. The other arrow button pointing to the right allows you to select all the modules for installation. Click the next button and you might see a license agreement. If you chose many modules, you might have to click **Accept** on each of the license agreement dialogs that pop up. After accepting the license agreement, the IDE will attempt to download the modules and check for any digital signatures. When the downloading is complete, click **Next** for the last pane.

This is the final pane. You should see a list of modules that were downloaded. If the module is digitally signed and has a valid certificate, it will appear with the word "Trusted" under it. You can select a module and click the View Certificate button to view its digital signature certificate. The checkbox to the left of a module indicates whether you want this module installed when you click the **Finish** button. Checking it means you would like it installed. The IDE must be restarted for a module to be utilized. You can choose to have the IDE restart immediately (don't worry, your files will be automatically saved first) or install immediately and restart later at your own convenience. Once you click the Finish button, the module will be installed.

Installing manually downloaded NBM files

If you chose to install manually, you should see a dialog box like the one shown in Figure 6-20 after clicking **Next** on the first pane. This pane allows you to add *.nbm* files. You can use the Browse button to find *.nbm* files on your local system or on the network. Once you click the Next button, the wizard will be the same as the previously explained web module installation.

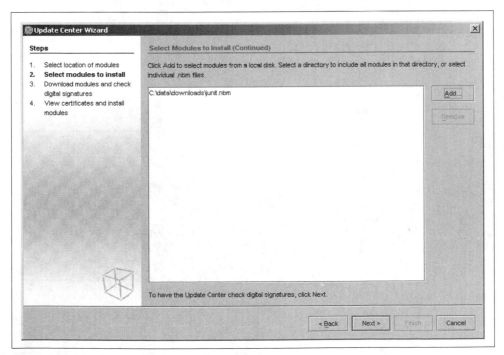

Figure 6-20. Installing modules manually

Enabling and Disabling Modules

By default, when a module is installed, it is enabled. To improve performance and startup time you might want to run with a minimum set of modules. In this case you need to disable the modules you won't be using. To disable a module, select **Tools →** **Options** under **IDE Configurations → System → Modules** and find the module category for your module. Usually third-party modules will create their own module category. You can chose to disable an entire module by selecting the category and chosing false for the enabled property in the property sheet. Under the category's node are the specific module features. These can be disabled as well by chosing false in the enabled property of the feature. By disabling the category, all module features are instantly removed from the IDE until the category is enabled by chosing true for the enabled property.

## CHAPTER 7

Using Source Control (CVS)

What Is CVS?

CVS is a system used by multiple developers to share a centralized source code repository from which they can all check out files, make changes to those files, and then check the modified files back in. Other developers may also concurrently work on the same files, with merges of overlapping changes being handled by CVS at check-in time.

Perhaps you have already used *revision control*. This is the software development process of checking code incrementally into some sort of automated repository. Doing this allows programmers to retrieve not only the latest revision but also previous revisions when they want to *revert*, that is, drop back to a previous revision, perhaps to recover some lost code. Also, automated revisioning systems allow development projects to *branch* code so that a current or past release can be maintained and have bugs fixed while the main line of the code continues to progress toward the next release. This avoids having the less-tested technology under development in the main line (or in another branch) injected into the stable release.

 The terms "version control" and "versioning" are used interchangeably with the term "revision control."

Conceptually (and often in implementation) CVS is a shell around and extension of the Revision Control System (RCS). RCS deals with storing revisions of single files under the effective control of a single developer. Whereas RCS deals with files, CVS deals with *source modules* (not to be confused with *NetBeans modules*, discussed elsewhere in this book). Source modules are collections of files. In CVS, a module consists of all the source files in a given directory and its subdirectories. Modules can also be aliases for a number of directory hierarchies to be checked out at one time.

Under CVS, source modules consisting of any depth of directories and files can be checked out by any number of developers concurrently. Whenever the modules are checked back in, CVS helps the developers, usually by managing automatically the merge of variants caused by concurrent revision and less frequently by pointing out differences that cannot be reconciled automatically. These differences must be reconciled manually by the developer who checks in the latest revision that caused the conflicts.

The relationship between RCS and CVS is summarized in Table 7-1.

Table 7-1. Summary of how CVS extends RCS

Concept	RCS	CVS
Concurrent developers	Single	Multiple
Scope of management	Individual files resident in a single directory	Contents of a CVS root directory and its entire subdirectory hierarchy
Repository location	Local subdirectory named RCS	Centralized shared repository with TCP/IP server support

If you want to study CVS itself, which is a good idea if you have read this far without ever having used it, you may read *http://www.cvshome.org/docs/manual/*, The CVS Info Manual.

NetBeans supports CVS in two ways:

1. Executing an external CVS application against an existing archive via host operating system commands
2. Performing CVS operations on an existing archive via NetBeans' own Java-coded module for CVS support

The name CVS is applied to more than one implementation of the CVS idea, notably the classic CVS (*http://www.cvshome.org/*) associated with the Free Software Foundation GNU Project (*http://www.gnu.org*). There are also other version control applications in the world of software development. In addition to supporting CVS, NetBeans allows you to use pretty much any other versioning system in place of either command-line or built-in CVS.

NetBeans allows you to use "real CVS" (either NetBeans' own built-in implementation or a command line version of CVS), or any generic version control system (VCS). You configure the two types of systems separately. But once configured, versioning operations except mounting a filesystem fall usually under the menu selection CVS and do not distinguish between CVS/VCS. In other words, in the context of everyday operations on a mounted versioned filesystem, it's all just called CVS. However, some VCS profiles, for instance, the ClearCase template, create a menu selection that identifies the specific VCS system.

NetBeans allows you to use any reasonable generic version control system, with specific support for the most popular systems, as we will see below. But because

1. CVS specifically is so well supported in NetBeans, and
2. If you are in a position to use a different versioning system, you probably know a good deal about such matters already,

our exposition here of versioning under NetBeans will mostly be expressed in terms of CVS, while still informing you of that which is necessary for successful use of any generic version control system.

The How, When, and Why of CVS in NetBeans

If you're a lone developer, you might wonder why and when you would want to use CVS. Isn't it just one more bureaucratic obstruction to your work flow?

When to Use CVS

You use CVS always. Always! It is a important for you as a developer to make sure you keep all your projects and even your little test programs in a source repository. The trouble it takes you to set up CVS (usually about 5 minutes) is more than amply repaid the first time you need to retrieve important code from an archived revision. CVS also allows you to collate the entire body of your work in what is effectively a neatly indexed source code database.

Where to Get a Client

CVS is available in both source code and binary form for any platform on which NetBeans will run. Offerings range from full CVS including the server to client-only implementations of varying degrees of completeness and GUI support. See Appendix C for links to sites offering CVS downloads.

For use with NetBeans, you generally don't need a CVS client. Net-Beans' CVS support module implements a CVS client in Java and is usually sufficient for your needs. However, if you plan on dealing with a shared source repository against which other members of your team are executing command-line CVS operations, you probably will also want to have at your disposal a CVS client for use from the command line.

NetBeans and CVS

Depending on how you set up your project,C NetBeans performs CVS operations in any of three ways:

1. Command-line CVS formulates CVS-specific command lines and passes these command lines to the operating system shell.

2. Built-in CVS uses a NetBeans module consisting of Java classes that mimic classic CVS operations.

3. Generic VCS formulates command lines based upon a user-supplied template and passes these command lines to the operating system shell.

In cases where command templates are used, the templates are parameterized; that is, the NetBeans logic concerned with CVS operations performs substitutions on special variables. This is so that the template does not need to contain, for instance, the name of every file the user might want to check in. When an operation is requested as a result of the user interacting with the Explorer, NetBeans substitutes the values of variables such as ${ROOTDIR} based on the current project.

Using Generic VCS

Using a generic VCS as an alternative to using CVS means that you can use pretty much any versioning system you please. Essentially, all that is required is that the versioning system provide a method of command-line invocation. NetBeans generic VCS support allows you to create a template of command-line strings subject to variable substitution that NetBeans can then invoke with appropriate instantiations of the variables to execute the high-level operations that you have requested via the NetBeans Explorer menu options for version control.

Don't worry too much about writing a template for your favorite versioning system. First of all, it's easy, and more importantly, most popular version control systems have already been tried with NetBeans and templates already exist for dealing with them. Many of these templates are shipped with NetBeans. Still others, which you may download and install into NetBeans generic VCS support, may be found at *http:// vcsgeneric.netbeans.org/profiles/index.html*.

Using Command-Line CVS Support

As mentioned above, NetBeans possesses two means of accessing CVS repositories:

1. An installable module that implements most of a CVS client in Java
2. A facility for issuing CVS commands via the operating system shell to an external CVS client implementation

Generally, CVS operations in NetBeans default to mounting via built-in CVS. This is as it should be, because the built-in CVS client is quite reliable and there's no reason that chasing down problems in versioning operations under NetBeans should be muddied by having to audit the behavior of your external CVS client. There are, however, a couple of reasons you might end up using command-line support via an external client for your CVS operations:

1. You want to customize your CVS operations to a greater degree than practical via the built-in CVS client.
2. Some feature in your external command-line CVS client isn't implemented in built-in CVS.

In any event, the NetBeans development team seems to be deprecating specific command-line support for CVS as opposed to treating command-line CVS as just one more instance of the support for generic VCS. We'll be showing you how to use the specific command-line support for CVS in NetBeans, but probably generic VCS and a CVS template is the future of command-line CVS in NetBeans.

CVS and NetBeans Projects

NetBeans Explorer presents a view of a project and its components. This view contains both more information than is available in a directory listing (such as methods and fields of classes) and less information (the Explorer doesn't show the form files NetBeans uses to describe visual components). CVS itself deals with files and directories, and understands none of the abstractions employed by the NetBeans Explorer to present its object-centric view of the project to the user.

When you use the NetBeans Explorer to create a new Java package, a directory is created in the filesystem. When you likewise create a new class, a *.java* file is added and later a *.class* file results from compiling the *.java* file. When you create a class from a Swing-based template, a *.form* file is created, which is an XML file describing the composition of the visual component that the user is creating. NetBeans Explorer displays the composition of the class in great detail but doesn't specifically reveal that there are often three files behind the Explorer's rendition—the *.java*, *.class*, and the *.form* files.

So when NetBeans prepares a CVS operation in the Explorer, NetBeans makes its own assumptions about what is to be saved. Adding a Java package to CVS means, to NetBeans, adding the directory and its *.java* and *.form* files. Additionally, if there are any files of a type that NetBeans either recognizes as significant, such as *.xml* and *.html* files, these files are added, along with any files of types NetBeans doesn't recognize, such as *.foo*, *.xyz*, or *.chocolate_malted_milk*. *NetBeans CVS support does not check in .class files*. You don't want these in your repository; you compile them while you are working on checked out source. *Nor does NetBeans CVS support check in .nbattrs* files. They're simply not terribly important and are regenerated when missing, if and when they are needed.

New Files and Packages

NetBeans does *not* automatically add new files and packages you create to the repository at the time you create them. Read on in this chapter to see how you add new files and packages to the repository.

CVS Outside of NetBeans

If you try to perform CVS operations on a source tree that is mounted in NetBeans, either at the command line or via some GUI tool other than NetBeans, it is best to close NetBeans while you are doing so.

To operate on your project outside of NetBeans CVS support:

1. Make sure that the *CVSROOT* environment variable is set to point to the repository where your project is kept and, optionally, that the type of repository and server name (in the case of external or password servers) is provided in the *CVSROOT* environment variable.

    • In the case of an external or password server, make sure you are logged in or otherwise prepared for authentication.

    • Alternatively, you can pass these options with the -d switch to CVS.

2. Change directory to the appropriate directory, usually the top level of your project.

3. Perform your CVS operations.

If you choose to perform CVS operations outside NetBeans on a file tree used by NetBeans, be sure that you take into account that which we mentioned earlier about the actions NetBeans CVS support performs on your behalf behind the facade of the NetBeans Explorer object representation of your project. For instance, *don't* forget to check in *.form* files and *do* forget to check in *.nbattrs* files.

Mounting CVS Sources

A source hierarchy that is backed by a CVS or other versioning system repository is mounted in a fashion similar to mounting any source hierarchy in the NetBeans Explorer. In the Filesystem view of your project, right-click on the Filesystems icon and choose either **Mount → Version Control → CVS** or **Mount → Version Control →**

Generic VCS. We'll discuss the details of the dialogs that are then presented a little later in this chapter.

After your hierarchy has been mounted, it appears like any other mounted source hierarchy. However, the icon at the top of the mounted versioned hierarchy is different to indicate that this is a tree under version control. Thereafter, you can not only perform all the normal operations pertaining to your development work flow on any tree, but you can also now right-click on a node of the tree and perform versioning operations such as checkin, checkout, update, and refresh on all or any part of the tree.

Exploring Versioned Sources

NetBeans Explorer offers a special mode for examing versioned sources. Right-click anywhere in the Explorer Filesystems view and select **CVS Versioning Explorer** and the Version Explorer will pop up in a new window (see Figure 7-1).

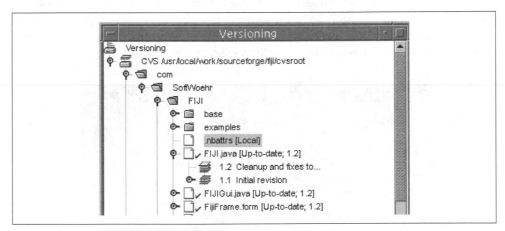

Figure 7-1. NetBeans Versioning Explorer

Versioning Explorer, unlike the regular NetBeans Explorer, represents *everything* as an object in the mounted hierarchy being explored. *.form* files are shown right along side *.java* files. If the file the object represents is not under version control, Versioning Explorer will indicate so.

If you click the little switch icon to the left of an object, the object will expand to show all its versions with the revision comment you entered at the time you committed the change. Right-clicking in the Versioning Explorer brings up various other menus, allowing you to do diffs, merges, and other normal CVS operations. Oddly enough, the little switch also appears to the left of objects not under version control, but once you click it and Versioning Explorer verifies that the object is not versioned, the switch will disappear.

Versioning Explorer is a good window to visit for sanity checks on the state of versioning in your project.

Common CVS Operations

NetBeans CVS operations can be performed on individual nodes or on several nodes at once. Either select a single entity in the NetBeans Explorer, or using **Shift-Left Click** to select a range of files or **Control-Left Click** to select multiple individual nodes.

The default mode of CVS operations in NetBeans is to use a default set of options issued behind the scenes to the CVS commands backing NetBeans CVS support. We recommend changing your CVS settings in NetBeans (which are kept on a project-by-project basis) to use the GUI Style operations, which present a dialog each time you perform a CVS operation. Choose **Tools** → **Options** → **Source Creation and Management** → **Version Control Settings** → **CVS Settings** and set User Interface Mode property to **GUI Style**. Thereafter, you'll get a dialog for most CVS operations that allows you to add options by checking boxes. Also, the dialog will show you what your checked options translate to in terms of switches to the operating systems shell *cvs* command. Figure 7-2 shows some useful options checked [prune empty directories, create new directories, reset all sticky (version number) flags] that are not default settings for the Update operation in NetBeans CVS support.

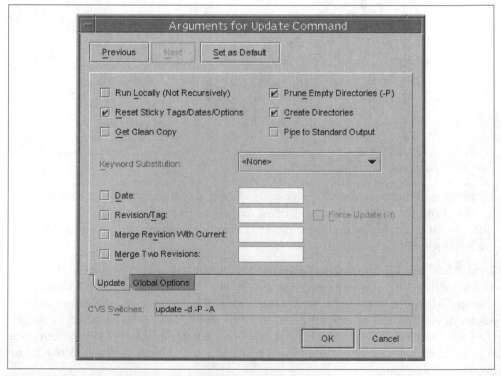

Figure 7-2. The GUI style CVS options dialog box for an update

Checkout/Get

Once you have your source tree mounted, it's easy to check out or get any level of it. Right-click on the node that you want to check out and choose **CVS → Checkout**.

At least as far as real CVS is concerned, a Checkout/Get performed on a tree that's already been checked out is the equivalent of a cvs update -D (update adding any new subdirectories that have appeared in the interim). Furthermore, any modified files will *not* be overwritten, and the CVS log will show that there were modified files. This implies that if there were concurrent changes entered in the repository, your local file was either:

- Not updated, or
- Was transformed by the update into a merge of the repository version and your local version, and that merged version has not been committed back to the repository.

In the latter case you will also see messages in the CVS log about a merge. If you need to review the messages issued by CVS, remember the NetBeans Explorer Runtime view, VCS Operations node.

Checkin and Commit

Checking in your source is the process of entering your changed files into the central source repository. To check in all sources in a package, select the package in the Net-Beans Explorer by single-clicking the mouse on its icon (not its name). This can start as high up in your source hierarchy as you like; you can start from your top-level package and commit all changed sources in that package and below it. Right-click on the package now and select **CVS → Commit**.

You will be offered a dialog that contains some options and a text entry box in which to enter your commit comment for the revision log of the file(s) being committed. The options offered by this dialog will vary depending on how you have set your NetBeans CVS options.

Add and Import

After you create a new folder, Java class, Ant build file, or other program object visible in the NetBeans Explorer, you can add it into your source repository so that upon checkout it appears in the same relative place in your source tree that it occupied at the time it was added. To add source or a folder or Java package, right-click on the object in the NetBeans Explorer and choose **CVS → Add**. The added entity will thereafter be annotated in the NetBeans Explorer as "Locally Added" until you commit it.

Remember two things about an add operation in CVS:

1. add is a marking of the entity for a later commit. Thus, you still must perform a commit to complete the entry of the new entity into the source repository. The

status window that pops up during an add has a button on it that you can click to complete the commit. Alternatively, you can right-click on the added entity at some later time and choose **CVS → Commit**.

2. add does not add the contents of a folder/project or any subfolder/project. It only adds the specific item you selected.

Apropos the second point, there is a similar but different CVS operation called import. A CVS import operation immediately adds a file, folder, or Java package to the repository, along with all its contents and subfolders/packages. It's like an item-by-item add with a subsequent commit. Right-click on the file or folder/package and choose **CVS → Import** to import many items at once.

 If any items in a folder to be imported need special handling (e.g., if they are binary and might not be recognized as such by NetBeans CVS support), you should instead add the containing folder and add individually its contents.

Log

You can browse a log of the version control activity relative to one or many objects. Right-click on the object and choose **CVS → Log** to see a GUI-formatted CVS log of your file. Clicking on an individual revision will expand the comments pertaining to that revision, as shown in Figure 7-3.

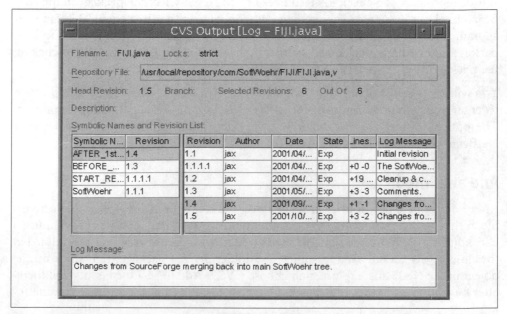

Figure 7-3. Browsing the CVS log of a source tree

Diff

You can invoke a textual or visual representation of all the differences between the version of a file that you are currently working on and the latest version in the repository (or between the current file and any version in the repository). Right-click on the object and choose **CVS → Diff → Textual** or **CVS → Diff → Graphical** to see either a textual or graphical difference report of the file or files selected. Figure 7-4 shows this in action.

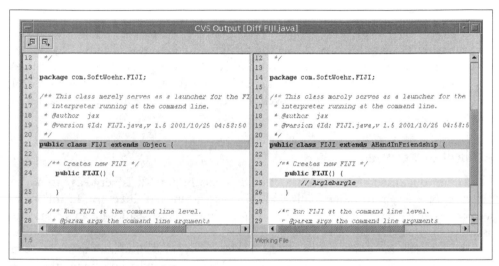

Figure 7-4. Performing a CVS diff operation

Update

For projects on which several developers are working, the source can change without you touching it. You can always update your tree safely to the latest version of a file or project without losing changes you yourself made. Right-click on the topmost node of your mount that you wish to update, and choose **CVS → Update**.

- If you have left NetBeans CVS settings at the default, the update will occur with default switches.
- If you are using CVS GUI Dialogs instead, you will be able to check boxes, and the switches formulated for your selections will be displayed toward the bottom of the dialog.

Unexpected Results

At times, you may find that the CVS support in NetBeans does something different from what you expected. Often, this is not a result of you making a mistake, but of a quirk associated with NetBeans or its built-in CVS client. To avoid getting tripped up by these quirks, several common ones are listed here for reference.

Spurious [Local] Designation

Sometimes NetBeans seems to think a folder or other object that is indeed under version control is a locally added folder that has recently been added to the filesystem. In such cases the [Local] designation appears to the right of the folder in the NetBeans Explorer.

Usually this is just a case of the multithreaded nature of NetBeans where the thread that refreshes the Explorer view is a little behind. Sometimes it is caused by operations performed on the file hierarchy outside NetBeans (e.g., at the command line) not being "noticed" by NetBeans. In any case, by right-clicking on a parent folder and choosing **CVS → Refresh Recursively** you can cause NetBeans Explorer to recalculate its view of things.

Adding Directories

Remember our discussion above about Add versus Import? It is very easy to add a directory and forget to individually add the files within that directory. In this case, *fewer* files have been added than you might think. This results in an erroneous assumption that all your files have been added to the CVS repository. In a similar manner, it is common to import a directory mistakenly, instead of adding it. This can result in *more* files being added than intended. Use caution when dealing with entire directories, and choose whether to add or import carefully.

Adding Binary Files

NetBeans is pretty smart about distinguishing between binary files, which must be added with the *-kb* option to prevent their content from being damaged by carriage return and line feed processing and keyword expansion. However, mistakes can occur when using only the default switches for NetBeans CVS support. Using these defaults, CVS does what you would usually want; however, in fringe cases, it doesn't ask you if you want something different.

One way to avoid this sort of problem is to change your CVS settings in NetBeans to use the GUI Style form of CVS commands as mentioned above.

If a file is somehow added mistakenly to a CVS repository without the binary options, it is best to fix matters before you check the binary object out and in again. It's easy to modify the relevant CVS options at the command line. Move to the directory in which the file is located. Let's say the file is *myfile.bin* and is in the current directory. Enter the command cvs admin -kb myfile.bin, and the repository will be modified to indicate that on this file no end-of-line processing and no CVS keyword expansion should take place.

Usually, NetBeans recognizes it is adding files of a binary type and formulates the correct switches. If you have any trouble with this automated support you can always choose **Versioning** → **Run CVS Command** from the main window and formulate all the switches manually.

> We've been bitten by the "CVS destroyed my binary object!" bug enough times that we wish to emphasize again the critical point of handling binary objects in CVS. (Again, by "binary objects" we mean files ending in extensions like *.jar*, *.zip*, *.exe*, *.jpg*, files that are not readable text.) The critical point to remember is that *they must be checked in from the start as binary* (i.e., using the -kb switch as applied to the add or import commands). Once you check them in the wrong way, they may be damaged. (The actual results of an error in this regard vary somewhat from CVS implementation to CVS implementation.)

Uncommon CVS Operations

Although we've covered the basics of CVS already, you may find that you need to perform some of the more advanced operations upon a CVS repository from within NetBeans. This section details these less-used, yet powerful, commands.

Branching, Merging, and Tagging

Branching and Merging of source paths are fully supported via your typical GUI dialogs under NetBeans. You can right-click on an object and choose **CVS** → **Branching and Tagging** for a submenu full of these options, each of which leads to dialogs. If you understand CVS branching, merging, and tagging, you will understand these dialogs without difficulty. If you do not understand CVS branching, merging, and tagging, we are not in a position to instruct you on this most complex aspect of CVS in the course of this volume.

NetBeans CVS and the Secure Shell (SSH)

Some remote CVS repositories only allow the user to log in via the SSH. This form of communication and authentication typically uses the *:ext:* style of CVS server (one with an external authentication mechanism). SourceForge is a good example of this type of CVS repository. Typically you will have to use *ssh-agent*, a part of the SSH suite, to handle the key exchange. However, once you have this running correctly on your operating system, and once your public key has been stored on the remote server in a fashion the administrator of the remote system will specify for you, NetBeans will correctly manage such a CVS mount. *If you have trouble connecting*, we find empirically that, despite the CVS mount in NetBeans having all the information about the repository, sometimes it helps to have launched NetBeans from a shell in which the CVSROOT variable is already set to the repository accessed via SSH. In other words, in

Unix, a command like `CVSROOT=:ext:someuser@someserver.foo:/usr/local/mydir;` `export CVSROOT; run-ide.sh` is a good way to start NetBeans if you are planning on accessing a remote server over SSH. (For links on obtaining more information about SSH and how it negotiates keys for login and encrypts your entire session, please see the Secure Shell resources section in the appendixes.)

Mounting a Generic Versioning System

Mounting a source tree backed by a generic version control system other than CVS is similar to mounting a CVS source tree. If the non-CVS versioning system is one of those supported by a NetBeans-supplied template, it is quite simple. If there is not a template provided for your particular versioning system, there are a few extra steps; specifically, you must provide the command lines that NetBeans will execute on your behalf to manipulate your source repository.

The first step in mounting a source tree backed by some generic versioning system is to pull down **Versioning → Mount Generic Version Control System** from the Net-Beans main window (as shown in Figure 7-5).

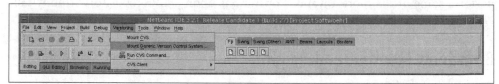

Figure 7-5. Pulling down the Versioning menu

This brings up the generic versioning system Customizer dialog box, shown in Figure 7-6. You can now choose from a supported template. More templates may be available at *http://vcsgeneric.netbeans.org/profiles/index.html*.

If you are able to use a template, you need only fill in Working Directory and Relative Mount Point fields in the customizer dialog. However, if no template suffices, you will have to proceed to the Advanced tab (see Figure 7-7).

Click on the **Edit Commands** button to bring up the generic versioning Command Editor (shown in Figure 7-8). The Command Editor will allow you to fill in the appropriate commands that NetBeans generic version control support will issue on your behalf when you afterward choose versioning actions in the Explorer. You can see that its layout is styled to reflect the menu presented in the Explorer for generic versioning.

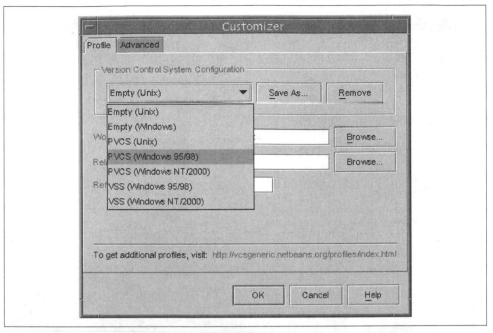

Figure 7-6. The generic versioning Customizer dialog box

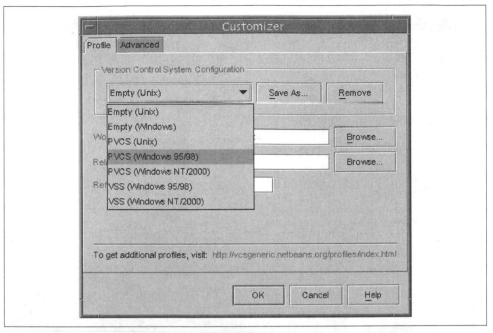

Figure 7-7. Advanced options for the CVS Versioning window

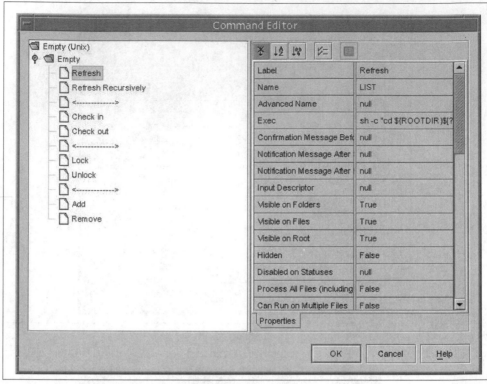

Figure 7-8. Editing the generic versioning commands

One Final Tip

When working on a large versioned tree, here's a good practice we've used for years with great success. Once every few days:

1. Exit from NetBeans

2. Rename the local directory you have been using to hold the checked-out sources

3. Recreate your working directory with its original name

4. Manually do a fresh checkout in this working directory

Then reload NetBeans and continue your development. This is a sort of sanity check. It does two things:

1. It makes sure you start your tree clean once in a while, which is one sure way of proving that you have remembered to add to version control all the new files you have added.

2. It gives you a local and recent backup of your working directory complete with revision control information (e.g., the *./CVS* subdirectories in each directory in the case of real CVS) ready to swap back into place if there's a problem in the new directory.

Admittedly, it's a belt-plus-suspenders approach, but it works because:

- When you get confused about the state of your sources, you verify against the repository.
- When you get confused about *both* the state of your sources *and* the state of the repository, you have the saved older working directory to swap in and compare to the repository via commands like diff.

You may scoff, yet there will almost certainly come a time when you are absolutely sure you performed every operation correctly, yet some recent work will seem to have vanished. This is known scientifically as the principle of *Stuff Happens* and is generally ascribed to neutrino beams emanating from Mars. It happens to every programmer at least once. Be prepared.

CHAPTER 8

GUI Building

The first contact that most users have with computers is through GUIs, and the primary means of accessing the most advanced applications by the most sophisticated users is also through GUIs. So it's natural that building GUIs is one of the first concerns of most new programmers and of many experienced programmers learning a new language like Java or a new tool like NetBeans.

Support for creating GUI applications and components has been essential in Net-Beans since its beginning, and it is among its most mature features. But GUI development in NetBeans continues to evolve in response to user requests and technological advances. For example, the serialized objects used in early versions of NetBeans for persistent storage of GUI design details have long since been replaced by XML files. NetBeans is an excellent choice for creating GUIs because its GUI development tools are mature and stable, its GUI development features are easily adaptable to individual preferences, and it has a history of quickly adapting to the needs of the user community.

Creating a GUI Frame or Panel

On the surface GUI building is quite straightforward. Start by creating a container from a template, drag and drop some visual components into it, and then adjust properties for the components as needed. Dig deeper, and you may find some pitfalls. For example, NetBeans translates visually designed forms into automatically generated read-only code, called *guarded code*. What if the read-only code doesn't quite do what you want? We'll talk about ways to make it behave later in this chapter and in the next.

Let's start by building a very simple GUI class. Our example GUI will concatenate strings in two textfields and then show the result in a third textfield. We won't build a complete application, but just enough to give you a good start for more complex forms. We'll start developing the example in this chapter, and then continue through the JavaBeans chapter that follows. Look at the source code example *GuiDemoBasic* to see the results through the end of this chapter.

First, start NetBeans running, open up a working directory, and create a package for the GUI demo that we're building:

1. Launch the IDE.

2. Click the **GUI Editing** tab in the main window to switch to the GUI workspace.

3. Decide what directory that you want use for building the source files. If the directory is already mounted, open up nodes in the Explorer window to expose it. If the directory isn't mounted, right-click the Filesystems top node, select **Mount Directory** from the context menu, and mount it. Or start in the main window **File** menu, select **Mount Filesystem**, and use the **Mount Filesystem** wizard. As usual, there's more than one way to accomplish anything you might want to do.

4. Right-click the containing directory, select **New** → **Java Package**. Name the new package *GuiDemoBasic*. This operation is shown in Figure 8-1.

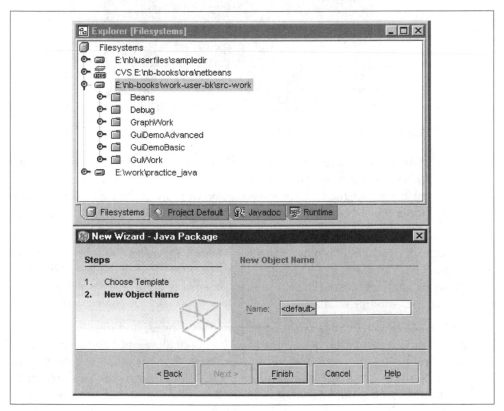

Figure 8-1. Creating the GuiDemoBasic package

Next, create the GUI container class from a template. We will choose JFrame for this example. The choices include an AWT Applet, Dialog, Frame, or Panel or a Swing JApplet, JDialog, JInternalFrame, JFrame, or JPanel.

1. Right-click the **GuiDemoBasic** package and then select **New → GUI Forms → JFrame** from the context menu. Or start in the main window **File** menu and then select **New** to launch the New Wizard.

2. Navigate to select the JFrame template. The New Wizard looks a little different, depending on which route you took, but it's nicely intuitive. Name your new JFrame object AddStrings, as shown in Figure 8-2 and then click **Finish**.

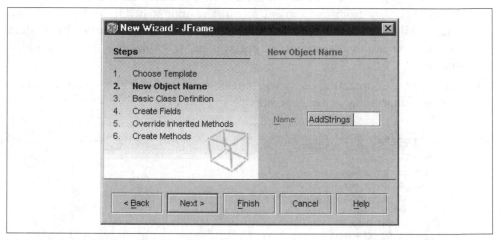

Figure 8-2. Creating the AddStrings JFrame

3. The IDE opens a Source Editor window with Java code for your new JFrame class. It also opens a *Form Editor* window, which includes the *Component Palette* panel at the top, the *Component Inspector* window at the right side, and the Form Editor panel below the Component Palette. We'll say more about these panels shortly.

Let's go outside the IDE for a moment to see what's happening. Look in your working directory with an external file browser. There's a *.java* file with the base name that you chose for your new JFrame class. The new *.java* file contains the Java code that is open in the IDE's Source Editor.

Java code created with NetBeans can be exported, compiled, and run outside of the IDE in any valid Java environment. And valid Java code developed elsewhere can be imported, modified, compiled, and run in NetBeans. Currently, there is no way to generate a NetBeans *.form* file from imported code. That means that imported code must be modified by hand, instead of with the Form Editor. Don't mess up a good *.form* file, or you'll be stuck with hand editing the Java code whenever you need to change the GUI.

Adding Components to a GUI Container

The Component Palette at the top of the Form Editor window (shown in Figure 8-3) looks like a large toolbar, but it contains more than action buttons. The tabs on the right of the Component Palette provide categories of components for building up GUI forms. The three buttons on the left are used to set the Form Editor's mode. We'll look at these buttons more closely as we progress. For now, make sure the *Selection Mode* button is pressed.

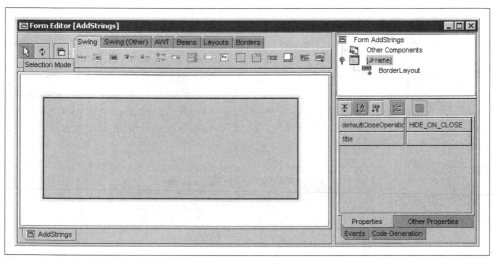

Figure 8-3. The NetBeans Form Editor

Click the Swing tab in the Component Palette to reveal a selection of basic Swing components. Click the JLabel button, which by default is the first component on the Swing tab. Hold down the shift key and then click three times in the Form Editor for our AddStrings GUI. This adds three JLabel components to the form. If you had not held down the Shift key while clicking in the Form Editor, only one JLabel would have been added. The default behavior is to only drop a component on the first click of the mouse; to have the selected component dropped for successive clicks, hold Shift while clicking in the Form Editor window.

If you're new to Java, but have had experience building GUIs with other languages, you may be startled to see that the components you drop into the form don't stay where you clicked to drop them. Component size and position is determined by a layout manager, not by the developer directly, and every Java GUI container has a layout manager. A novice will be tempted to fight the layout manager's apparent misbehavior. A Java guru knows how to use layout managers to handle the tedious work of GUI layout. We'll get deeper into layout managers soon. For now, don't be too concerned about component positioning.

We will use a slightly different procedure for adding the JTextField components. Right-click [JFrame] in the Component Inspector panel on the right. Select **Add From Palette** in the context menu to get a submenu that matches the Component Palette tabs. Select **Swing JTextField**. Do this three times, and notice that the components appear in both the Form Editor and Component Inspector panels. This way you don't need to remember the component icons or hover your mouse pointer to see their names in the tooltip. Once again, there are several ways to get the same result with NetBeans.

We have a quick and easy way to see what a GUI form will look like during actual execution. Check the tooltips to identify the **Test Form** button in the left end of the Component Palette. Click the button now to see what the form will look like in execution. When you use the Test Form feature, the layout manager works and the GUI components respond to mouse and keyboard activity just as they would during execution, but the components are not connected and event handling code is not executed. The Test Form feature enables you to fine tune your form without compiling it. This gives you a first look at AddStrings from a user's viewpoint. You should see a window much like that shown in Figure 8-4.

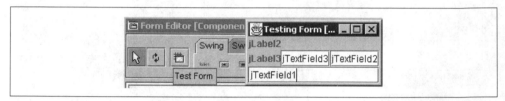

Figure 8-4. The GuiBasicDemo example being tested

So far so good, except that the layout looks terrible. The default layout manager for a JFrame is BorderLayout. Let's try FlowLayout. There are several ways to change the layout. We could go back to the Component Palette, click the Layouts tab, click the **Flow Layout** button, and click anywhere inside the JFrame border in the Form Editor. But let's do something different. Go to the Component Inspector and right-click the **JFrame** node. Select **Set Layout FlowLayout** from the context menu and then click the **Test Form** button again to see how it looks (see Figure 8-5). That's a little better. Now, at least we can see all the components. But it still isn't quite what we want. Let's see what else can be done in the Component Inspector.

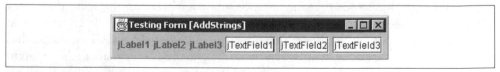

Figure 8-5. Testing the form with a FlowLayout

Configuring Components

Scroll the Source Editor to show the InitComponents() method of AddStrings. Notice that it's shaded light blue. That identifies guarded code. It's generated automatically and must not be modified directly. Keep this code visible so you can watch it while we work with the Component Inspector.

1. Setting Text

   In the Component Inspector select jLabel1. Click the Properties tab and then locate the text property. Change its value from jLabel1 to String A. Notice that the value also changes in the Form Editor and in the guarded code of the Source Editor. Now change the value of the text property for the other components as shown in Table 8-1. While you're in the properties window, turn off the editable property for jTextField3 because it needs to be a display only field.

Table 8-1. Text and editable property settings for AddStrings components

Component	Text	Editable
jLabel1	String A	N/A
jLabel2	String B	N/A
jLabel3	String A+B	N/A
jTextField1	A default	True
jTextField2	B default	True
jTextField3	result	False

2. Sizing Components

   Notice that our components changed their size to fit the amount of text. Click the **Other Properties** tab and then locate the preferredSize property. Change its value for all of our JLabel and JTextField components to [80,30]. Let's see how it looks so far. Go back to the main window and click the **Test Form** button in the Form toolbar. It's nice to see all the components at the same size, but it doesn't make sense for them all to be on one line. We'll fix that soon, when we change the layout manager.

3. Renaming Components

   Let's give more meaningful names to our components. In the Component Inspector right-click the **JLabel** and **JTextField** components and then select **Rename** from the context menu. Or just click to select the component, pause for the double-click interval to lapse, and then click again to open the name for editing. Rename the components as shown in Table 8-2.

Table 8-2. Names for AddStrings components

Original name	New name
jLabel1	lblA
jLabel2	lblB
jLabel3	lblSum
jTextField1	tfA
jTextField2	tfB
jTextField3	tfSum

4. Set Frame Title

Set the title property of **AddStrings [JFrame]** to AddStrings 1.0.

Building Menus

Now add a JMenuBar to your AddStrings form. You can select **JMenuBar** from the Swing component palette and then click anywhere in the Form Editor window to drop it in. Or you can navigate from the context menu for the JFrame component in the Component Inspector through the submenus to select **JMenuBar**. Initially, the menu bar will have one menu, but no menu items. You could also add a JPopupMenu through a similar procedure.

In the Component Inspector right-click your new **JMenuBar** and then select **Add JMenu** from the context menu. What good is a menu without selections? Right-click **jMenu1** and then select in the context menu **Add JMenuItem**. Notice the standard menu item types that are available: JMenuItem, JCheckBoxMenuItem, JRadioButtonMenuItem, JMenu (for submenus), and JSeparator. Move over to **jMenu2** and add another JMenuItem, a JSeparator, and a JMenuItem. Rename the JMenu and JMenuItem components, and modify their properties as shown in Table 8-3.

Table 8-3. Menu item properties for AddStrings

Original name	New name	Text	Tooltip text	Mnemonic
jMenu1	FileMenu	File	File	F
jMenuItem1	ExitItem	Exit	Exit	X
jMenu2	HelpMenu	Help	Help	H
jMenuItem2	ContentsItem	Contents	Contents	C
jMenuItem3	AboutItem	About	About	A

We have nice looking menus, but they don't do anything yet. We'll take care of that later in this chapter, when we look at event handlers. But first, let's fix the layout.

Changing a Container's Layout

We already know how to change the layout manager, because we changed it from the default `BorderLayout` to `FlowLayout`. That made it possible to set the size of the visual components, which was much more functional than the default. But we really want the three labels to line up neatly over the three textfields. To accomplish this, we'll change the layout manager again, this time to `GridLayout`. By now you know two ways to change a nonvisual component. Either select **GridLayout** on the Component Palette and then drop it onto the Form Editor, or right-click **JFrame** or **FlowLayout** in the Component Inspector and then select **GridLayout** from the context menu.

Now change the **Columns** property of your layout manager to 3 and the **Rows** property to 2. Finally, everything lines up correctly. But you lose some control over the size of the visual components. `GridLayout` makes every cell the same size, just large enough to accommodate the largest of the visual components. You can see this new layout in action in Figure 8-6.

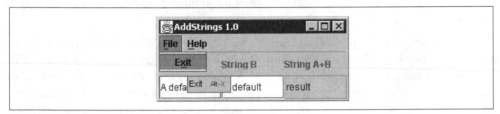

Figure 8-6. GuiDemoBasic using GridLayout

Working with Borders

We can add some class to our GUI design by applying a few finishing touches to the visual components. Select our result field `tfSum` in the Component Inspector and click the **Other Properties** tab. Notice that its **border** property defaults to [CompoundBorderUIResource]. Click the value side of the property to get the ... button and then click that button to get the **border** property editor. Select [BevelBorder], and a property sheet appears. Depending on the border type, you may be able to configure such properties as **Highlight Color**, **Bevel Type**, **Title**, and **Insets**. Compile and execute your modified form to see how it looks. It should be a bit nicer, with the result field standing out a bit.

Play around with the other components as well. Give each `JLabel` component a different border type and color, just to see what's possible. [CompoundBorder] gives you an inside border and an outside border. You can use different border types inside and outside a simple text field.

Accessibility

The following discussion about accessibility digresses somewhat from our main thread, using NetBeans for the GUI building tasks that most developers need. But this is the right time for the discussion, because building in the simplest accessibility features greatly benefits users who have limitations while significantly improving usability for ordinary users. Learn now what little is needed and make a habit of applying the techniques; ordinary users will benefit, users with limitations will be able to use your GUI, and you will meet legal requirements for certain kinds of usage.

Providing *accessibility* in a computer application means building in features that assistive technologies can use to enable persons with disabilities to use the application easily. For example, when a blind person moves a mouse pointer to a GUI component, an assistive device can generate speech that names and describes the component. Accessibility is required by law in the United States for most computer applications that are available to the public or used for government purposes. It's worth doing in all GUI applications worldwide, public or private, whether required by law or not.

Building accessibility into the GUI classes that you develop with NetBeans is surprisingly easy, thanks to the Java Accessibility Application Programming Interface (API) that is included with all releases of Java 2. When you know what's needed, you can write code with little extra effort that automatically provides most of what assistive technologies require. The IDE does not yet provide an accessibility testing tool, but that's under development and will be available soon. Meanwhile, see the following links for guidelines on providing accessibility manually:

Developing Accessible JFC Applications
> Clear explanation of why and how to make Swing classes accessible.
> (*http://www.sun.com/access/developers/developing-accessible-apps/*)

Java™ Accessibility Quick Tips
> Checklist for ensuring that your Swing classes are accessible.
> (*http://www.sun.com/access/developers/tips.html*)

All Java 2 Swing components implement the `Accessible` interface, which allows assistive technology devices to retrieve an instance of `AccessibleContext` with its **AccessibleName** and **AccessibleDescription** properties. Assistive devices use a variety of technologies, such as speech synthesis, to communicate the values of these properties, allowing disabled users to work with the GUI. If you just make sure every GUI component has a meaningful value for **AccessibleName**, you will meet the bare minimum to make your components available to assistive technologies. It's easy, because the value of **AccessibleName** defaults to the **text** property that labels, buttons, menu items, and other components normally show to the user. Always fill in meaningful text, and you will automatically meet the minimum for accessibility.

Sometimes one component identifies another; for example, a JLabel identifies a blank JTextField. In this case set the **JLabel.LabelFor** property, and the JTextField will set its **AccessibleName** from the JLabel that identifies it. In our AddStrings example the JLabel lblA identifies the JTextField tfA, so we would add the following:

```
lblA.setLabelFor(tfA);
```

If the component has a value set for its tooltip, **AccessibleDescription** defaults to the tooltip value. This is especially important if the **AccessibleName** does not adequately describe the component. Just make a habit of filling in the tooltip for every visible component, and you will make your application more usable for ordinary users while greatly enhancing its accessibility.

Now we'll get back to the main thread of GUI building. The sections that we just finished focus on the visual aspect of GUI building—putting the right components in place and setting their visible features correctly. The sections that follow focus more on the code behind the components—making them work the way you want in response to user actions.

Copying a Source Object

You can copy and paste objects in the Explorer window with ease. In fact, you can even copy class members—fields, constructors, methods, and bean patterns—between classes, and you can copy GUI components between forms. Let's start by copying the example class from the previous chapter:

1. Create a new package to contain the copy. Right-click the mounted filesystem, select **New Java Package**, and name the package *GuiDemoAdvanced*.

2. Right-click the **AddStrings** source object in the old *GuiDemoBasic* package and then select Copy from the context menu.

3. Right-click the *GuiDemoAdvanced* package and select **Paste Copy** from the context menus. Once again we have a context menu that provides every reasonable action for the copied object.

4. Double-click the copied AddStrings object to open it in the Source Editor and Form Editor windows. Notice that the package name was changed automatically to the new location.

5. Go to the Component Inspector and set the title property of **AddStrings[JFrame]** to AddStrings 2.0.

The Connection Wizard

We want the third JTextField, tfSum, to display the concatenation of the other two at all times. If either tfA or tfB fires an ActionEvent, the text property of tfSum must change to show the new result. The Connection Wizard helps us link events fired by one component to actions that belong to another component. The Connection Wizard is enabled by clicking the **Connection Mode** button in the Component Palette (shown in Figure 8-7), next to the **Selection Mode** button.

Figure 8-7. The Connection Mode button

Here are the specific steps to link up your events:

1. Click the **Connection Mode** button in the Component Palette.

2. In the Form Editor click the component that will send the ActionEvent. That's the JTextField named tfA, displaying text "A default."

3. Next, click the target component. That's the JTextField named tfSum, displaying text "result."

4. The Connection Wizard will launch. Open the action node, and select **actionPerformed**. Accept the default method name tfAActionPerformed, and click **Next**.

5. In the next pane of the Connection Wizard keep the default operation Set Property, select the property **text**, and click Next.

6. In the last pane specify Get Parameter From by pressing the **User Code** radiobutton. Enter the following in the User Code textfield and then click Finish:

        tfA.getText() + tfB.getText()

7. Look in the Source Editor window. Notice that a new method tfAActionPerformed was created to handle the ActionEvent fired by the tfA component.

8. Repeat the procedure for the other input textfield, tfB.

9. Compile and execute. Change the input textfields to verify that it works. The result textfield, tfSum, will show tfA concatenated with tfB, as illustrated in Figure 8-8.

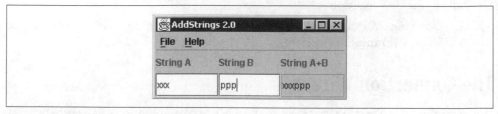

Figure 8-8. Testing after linking events

The GridBagLayout Customizer

What if you want more control over the size and placement of GUI components? Use `GridBagLayout`. You could use **Null Layout** (no layout manager), but that would reduce cross-platform portability. Or you could use `AbsoluteLayout`, a custom layout manager that is included with NetBeans. But that would add complexity to distribution and maintenance of your application. `GridBagLayout` is a standard Java layout manager that was designed for precise control over GUI components while preserving portability. However, there is a cost for this flexibility. `GridBagLayout` is complex to configure and tedious to modify. Many developers avoid `GridBagLayout` because configuring it by hand can take too much time.

But there's a better way. The *GridBagLayout Customizer* gives the full power of `GridBagLayout` to the developer in a visual tool. With the GridBagLayout Customizer you can visually adjust the size and placement of your components and then numerically fine tune them for maximum precision.

We used the `GridLayout` to divide our `AddStrings` example into a grid of equally sized rectangular cells. Each cell can hold one visual component. The `GridBagLayout` also defines a grid, but each component can occupy several cells in a rectangular subarray. Furthermore, the rows and columns in `GridBagLayout` are not required to be all the same height or width. You can see just such an example in Figure 8-9.

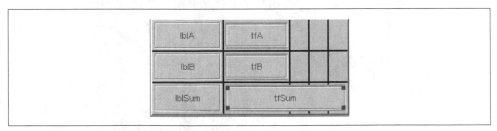

Figure 8-9. A GridBaglayout example, with three rows and five columns

Here's a general procedure for building a GUI with `GridBagLayout` in NetBeans. Let's follow the procedure with our `AddStrings` example.

1. The first step is to add visual components to a GUI container using any layout. In our example we have already done this step.

2. Change to `GridBagLayout`. Either drop `GridBagLayout` from the Component Palette onto the Form Editor or right-click the container node in the Component Inspector and select **Set Layout** from the context menu.

3. Start the Customizer. In the Component Inspector window right-click the **Grid-BagLayout** node and then select **Customize** from the context menu to open the **Customizer Dialog**.

4. Resize and move the components. Just drag their edges, corners, and centers as needed in the visual pane of the customizer. Create roughly the arrangement that you want. Make the JLabel and JTextField components in our AddStrings example match Figure 8-10.

- Place the JLabel components in the first column
- Place the JTextField components in the second column

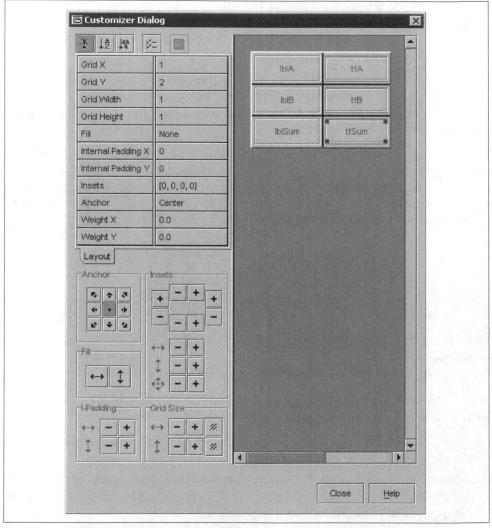

Figure 8-10. GridBagLayout Customizer Dialog

5. Fine tune the components. Click a component in the right pane to select it and then make the fine adjustments in the left panes. Either adjust the properties in the upper left, or adjust the visual controls in the lower left.

In our AddStrings example the only component we need to change is the tfSum JTextField. It should be about double the size of the input fields. Adjust its properties to match Table 8-4 and then close the Customizer, compile, and test.

Table 8-4. Customizer properties

Property	New value
Fill	Horizontal
Grid width	4
Internal padding X	60

6. You can also adjust layout properties without opening the Customizer. Just select any visual component node in the top pane of the Component Inspector and then click the Layout tab at the bottom. You can access the same properties that the Customizer shows.

What are all those properties in the GridBagLayout Customizer? They're the GridBagConstraints properties. Each visual component has its own set, which tells the GridBagLayout manager how to display the component. Here's a summary of the properties:

Anchor

Specifies where to place the component within the free space in the grid cells that it occupies. Values are Center, North, Northeast, and so on. Can also be set by **Anchor** buttons.

Fill

Specifies whether or not the component should fill all the horizontal and vertical space in the grid cells that it occupies. Can also be set by **Fill** buttons.

Grid Height and **Grid Width**

Component height as number of rows and width as number of columns. Can also be adjusted by **Grid Size** buttons in the lower left pane.

Grid X and **Grid Y**

Row and column location of the component in the grid. Can also be adjusted by dragging the component in the visual pane.

Insets

Each number specifies the minimum distance between the edge of the component and its grid cell boundary. Numbers denote pixels. The four numbers apply to the top, left side, bottom, and right side, respectively. Can also be adjusted by **Insets** buttons.

Internal Padding X and **Internal Padding Y**

Extends component width and height. Numbers denote pixels, not rows or columns. Can also be adjusted by **I-Padding** buttons.

Weight X and **Weight Y**

Specifies the distribution of available space among all the components in a row or column when the container is resized. Components with larger weights get more space. Weights are relative numbers, not pixels or cell counts.

Adding Event Handlers

Let's take a closer look at the code that the IDE generates to handle GUI events. It automatically creates an event handler method for the `windowClosing` event. The IDE also supports all possible events for other GUI components and will create a handler method for any event that the developer selects manually. The Connection Wizard includes a step for the developer to select an event and then creates a handler method for it. We will examine several different ways of creating event handler methods.

Locate the `exitForm` method in the Java source for our `AddStrings` class, usually just above the `main` method. This method is the code for the `windowClosing` event handler that was generated automatically when the initial `JFrame` container was created. Notice that the first and last lines of `exitForm` are guarded code (shaded light blue), but the body of the method is not. You are free to modify the body of this method as needed. This is the pattern for event handler methods that the IDE generates. By default the `exitForm` method for a `JFrame` contains only the following line, which you are free to replace or augment as needed:

```
System.exit(0);
```

Locate our **AddStrings** example in the Explorer window. If it isn't open already, double-click to open it. Then open its nodes all the way to **ExitItem**, as follows: **AddStrings → Form AddStrings → [JFrame] → jMenuBar1 → FileMenu → ExitItem**. Now let's give that menu item some action. Right-click **ExitItem→ Events→ Action → actionPerformed**. This action is shown in progress in Figure 8-11. Now, locate the `ExitItemActionPerformed` method. It's an empty method because there is no reasonable default. Copy (or retype) the `System.exit(0);` line from the `exitForm` method into `ExitItemActionPerformed` method.

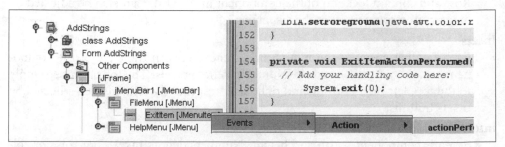

Figure 8-11. Generating an ExitItem event

Remember `tfAActionPerformed` and `tfBActionPerformed`? Those event handler methods were created when we used the Connection Wizard to connect actions in the `tfA` and `tfB` textfields to results in `tfSum`. As usual, they were created as empty methods, which we filled in to produce the results we want. However, the two methods have identical code. That's redundant, so let's fix it. Select `tfB` in the Component Inspector and then click the Events tab at the bottom of the window. Here we have yet another approach to creating event handlers, with possible events in the left column and any handler methods in the right. Click `tfBActionPerformed` at the top of the right column and then click the "..." button. This opens a window that allows you to specify the event handler methods for any event. Remove `tfBActionPerformed` and add `tfAActionPerformed`. Click **OK** to finish, and look at the source. Notice that `tfBActionPerformed` is no longer needed and has been deleted automatically. Now we have a cleaner, simpler program. This approach makes it easy to mix and match new or existing event handler methods with any number of events.

We'll finish this section with one more way to create event handlers. Right-click `lblA` in the Component Inspector. From the context menu select **Events → Mouse → mouseEntered**. This creates the `lblAMouseEntered( )` method. Insert the following line:

```
lblA.setForeground(java.awt.Color.red);
```

Next, right-click `lblA` in the Form Editor window. Again, select from the context menu **Events → Mouse → mouseExited** as shown in Figure 8-12 to create the `lblAMouseExited` method. Insert the following line:

```
lblA.setForeground(java.awt.Color.green);
```

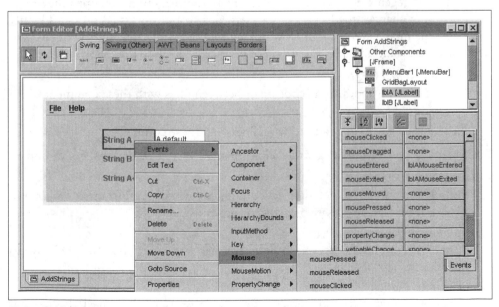

Figure 8-12. Selecting an event handler

Compile, test, and behold Figure 8-13. The label changes color when the mouse rolls over it. Also, the Exit selection in the File menu works as expected.

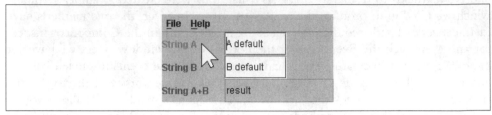

Figure 8-13. The AddStrings example running

Using the Code Generation Properties

In our earlier discussion about configuring components with the Component Inspector we mentioned guarded code, shaded light blue in the Source Editor. By now our AddStrings example has much more blue than white. Guarded code is automatically generated to reflect the GUI design in the Form Editor and property settings in the Component Inspector. The IDE will not allow you to directly modify guarded code in the Source Editor, but you can easily modify it indirectly through the Component Inspector.

It is possible to use an external editor to modify Java code that was created by the IDE, but this is not recommended. You must be very careful not to modify the guarded code. The IDE regenerates guarded code automatically every time you open the source object, so any changes made outside of NetBeans would be lost. You can identify guarded code in an external editor by looking for comments that start with //GEN-. If you insist on using an external editor to modify code, stick to the following rules:

//GEN-BEGIN: and GEN-END
Never externally modify any code on or between lines with these comments.

//GEN-FIRST: and GEN-LAST
Never externally modify any code on lines with these comments.

But you might need to modify guarded code for some very good reasons. For example:

Instantiation with parameters
Suppose you want to include a few arguments when you instantiate a component, but the IDE always invokes the default constructor.

Instantiation with factory objects
Suppose you want to recycle objects through a factory, but the IDE always instantiates new objects.

Complex initialization
Suppose you want to add elements to a JList or JTree, but the IDE does not fully support initialization of complex components.

The recommended safe way to modify guarded code is through the Code Generation properties in the Component Inspector. Go to the Component Inspector and select any component, visual or nonvisual, including menu items or the GUI container itself. Then click the Code Generation tab at the bottom of the window. This exposes properties that directly modify the guarded code that NetBeans generates. Play around with them to see what's affected. Pick any property that is initially empty, fill in a comment, and then look in the Source Editor to see what happened.

For example, select lblA. Modify its **Post-Creation Code** property by replacing the initially empty value with a comment, as seen in Figure 8-14. Look in the Source Editor window for the text of the comment, and you will see the following lines:

```
lblA = new javax.swing.JLabel();
/* post lblA create */
```

Notice that the code you inserted into the Post-Creation Code property appears immediately after the line that creates lblA. If you need to insert some logic immediately after a component is created, you can simply enter that logic into the Post-Creation Code property. In other words, just replace the sample comment that we entered with a snippet of source code to do whatever post-creation work that is necessary.

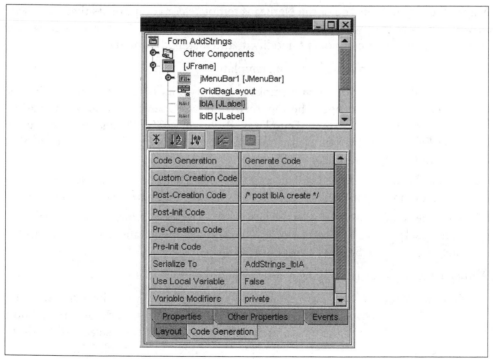

Figure 8-14. Adding post-creation code

The **Custom Creation Code** property is especially powerful. You can replace the default constructor for a component with any code that returns a suitable object. This is the place to use a custom component, recycle factory-managed objects, or add parameters to the default empty constructor.

Working Around Code Generation

What if there's a problem with the generated code? Maybe one of the NetBeans GUI templates or components has a bug, or maybe you want to use an obscure GUI property that NetBeans just doesn't expose. Here are some workarounds.

The quickest fix is through the Code Generation properties in the Component Inspector. Take a good look at all the properties, and you will probably find the right place to insert the code you need.

A quick and dirty workaround is to insert the code you want after the generated code that you don't like. You can use the **Post-Creation Code** and **Post-Init Code** Code Generation properties. Or you could avoid guarded code altogether by adding a few lines to your GUI class constructor, right after invoking `initComponents();`.

Maybe there's a bug in one of the NetBeans templates or components that you used, or you just want it to work differently. Then make your own. Start with a copy of a NetBeans template or component, modify it, and install it in the IDE.

Here are the steps for making a custom template:

1. Optionally, create your own template category. Start from the main window **Tools → Options** to open the Options window. Open nodes **Source Creation and Management** and then **Templates**. Right-click **GUI Forms** and then select **New Folder**. Finally, name this new folder and click Finish. The result of this operation is shown in Figure 8-15.

2. Create the source to use for your template. Start with one of the NetBeans templates and modify it to meet your needs, or create completely new source code.

3. Save the source as a template. Start in the Explorer window, right-click the source, select **Save as Template** from the context menu, and select the template category from the **Save As Template** dialog.

And here are the steps for making a custom GUI component:

1. Optionally, create your own Component Palette tab. From the main window select **Tools → Options**. Open nodes **IDE Configuration node** and then **Look and Feel**. Right-click the **Component Palette** node and then select **Add Palette Category** from context menu. Name the new category, and click **OK**.

2. Create or locate the new component. It's just a JavaBean. Use an existing bean, or write your own. See the next chapter for more on beans.

3. Add the new component to the Component Palette and then customize it.

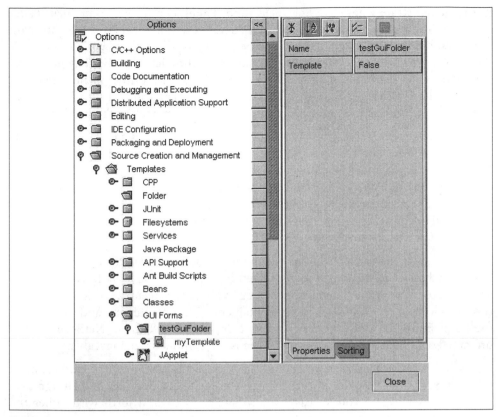

Figure 8-15. Creating a custom template category

We will take a closer look at adding components to the Component Palette in the next chapter, after creating our own JavaBean component.

Containers Within Containers

A JPanel can contain any number of components. Because a JPanel is itself a component, it can be contained within another JPanel, a JFrame, or any other GUI container. As we will see in the next section, this can be a powerful technique for building complex GUIs. But there's a potential editing problem with components in containers within containers. If all the components in all the containers were visible at the same time, it could become visually confusing and unmanageable. The Form Editor prevents such confusion by showing only one container with its components at a time and by enabling the developer to choose which container to show. Let's walk through a short demonstration to see how it works.

Notice the empty space in the upper right corner of our AddStrings example. Let's fill the space with a JPanel and then put a couple of GUI components into the JPanel just to demonstrate what's possible. Select the **JPanel** icon in the Component Pallet and then drop it into the empty corner of AddStrings in the Form Editor. It shows up as a small blue square, much too small to be useful. We'll fix that by using the Grid-Bag Customizer to adjust the space it occupies. Right-click **GridBagLayout** in the Component Inspector and then select **Customize** from the context menu. Select the **JPanel** in the Customizer Dialog window and then adjust GridWidth to 3 and Grid-Height to 2. Close the Customizer and turn your attention back to the Form Editor.

Where's our JPanel? The little blue square has vanished, and the space just looks blank in the Form Editor. No problem, the JPanel still there in the Component Inspector. Select it in the Component Inspector, and the blue square reappears. The JPanel was just hidden, and selecting it in the Component Inspector brought it to the fore in the Form Editor. Right-click the **JPanel** in the Component Inspector and then select **Design This Container** from the context menu. Now the JPanel takes over all the space, and the JFrame disappears.

Drop in a few components from the Component Palette—a JButton or two, maybe a JLabel—whatever you like just to get something visible in the JPanel. Then compile and execute to see what you've done. Not fancy, but it opens up a world of possibilities. By allowing the developer to put containers within containers, and by focusing the Form Editor on one container and its components at a time, NetBeans allows unlimited complexity in GUI design and keeps the complexity manageable.

Go back to the Form Editor, which has the JPanel visible. Right-click, and examine the context menu. Now the choices include **Design This Container** and **Design Top Container**. This gives you an easy way to switch back and forth with either the JFrame or JPanel in the foreground.

Building Complex GUIs

When you create a complex GUI with many components, it can be difficult to make them behave properly. Trying to control the size and placement of even a few components can be like herding cats; focus your attention on one, and the others run amok. As we have seen, GridBagLayout is often your best hope for managing multiple components in a single container. But there's another way. Instead of struggling with too many components in one container, use the containers within containers technique to build a GUI that's many layers deep with just a few components in each layer.

Create a container, say a JPanel, and then add just a few components to the container, few enough that you can easily control their size and placement. Use the container in constructing the next layer of your complex GUI. For greater flexibility in testing and reuse, and for a cleaner design, you may choose to turn the container with its components into a JavaBean. This is exactly where we're headed with the AddStrings example. We will place a manageable number of components into a JPanel container and then turn the JPanel into a Bean. We will add our new Bean to a JFrame container and use the Bean properties to configure it. Of course, if you're only creating a Bean as an intermediate component for one project, you won't need to do everything that will be done in the JavaBeans chapter—create a BeanInfo class, link it to an icon, and add it to your Component Palette. Giving your intermediate containers a few basic Bean features will be enough to greatly simplify your GUI building task.

By now our AddStrings example is looking good and running smoothly. But it's a standalone application. The only way other users could benefit from using the application would be to install it, launch it every time they wanted to use it, and then explicitly exit when they're done. If we convert the application into a component that other developers can include in larger applications, it can be used much more widely and easily. So, in the next chapter, we will build a JavaBean around the essential feature of AddStrings. Then anyone using Java to build a complex GUI can drop AddStrings into their form with just a few mouse clicks.

CHAPTER 9
JavaBeans

Why Should I Make Beans?

You should make JavaBeans to encourage reuse of your Java code. JavaBeans is the standard architecture for building reusable components in Java. Originally intended as visual components for building GUIs, now the JavaBeans are widely used in all Java environments, including JSP and EJB development. Like components in other object-oriented programming languages, JavaBeans have properties that can be set at design-time by visual design tools or at runtime by the containing program.

If you want other developers to use your code, if you want your components to snap together with ease, if you want to spend your time developing application logic instead of debugging interfaces, make JavaBeans. For a deeper understanding of the JavaBeans architecture, see Sun's JavaBeans Technology (*http://java.sun.com/beans*) page or read *Developing JavaBeans* by Robert Englander (O'Reilly).

Creating JavaBeans

We will continue with the AddStrings example from the last chapter to demonstrate NetBeans features for developing JavaBeans. It is *not* necessary to go through all this to create a Bean from scratch. Simply follow the procedure for creating a new Java object, and use the Bean template. We're taking the long route to show more ways that NetBeans can help. Here's the plan:

1. Create a GUI component from the AddStrings JFrame.
2. Convert the component into a proper Bean.
3. Add an event set to inform the container about changes to Bean properties.
4. Generate a BeanInfo class to support using the Bean in a visual design tool, such as NetBeans.
   - Generate the BeanInfo class.
   - Launch and use the BeanInfo Editor.
   - Add a design time Icon.

5. Add your own category to the NetBeans Component Palette.

6. Add the Bean to your Component Palette category.

7. Use the Bean in GUI construction.

Next, we will go through the steps for this plan in detail. With any application, the functional decomposition necessary to create usable components from the application's logic requires analytical skill and care. But once you've decided what to include in each component, the process of creating JavaBeans from application code is straightforward. We will go through the process more thoroughly than you may choose to do in actual practice, just to give a complete picture of what's possible.

Creating a GUI Component

A GUI component is an object that can be placed in a GUI container. A JFrame is a container, but it is not a component and cannot be placed in a container. A JPanel is both a container and a component, so it can contain other components, and it can be placed in a container. We based our original AddStrings example on a JFrame to make testing easy, because a JFrame is a top-level window that can be executed alone. But the JFrame version of AddStrings cannot be used as a component. Therefore, the first step in creating an AddStrings JavaBean is to create an AddStrings JPanel with the same components and logic as the original JFrame example from the previous chapter.

1. Let's keep the name AddStrings for the component we are creating. We need to avoid a name conflict between the new AddStrings JPanel and the old AddStrings JFrame. So our example uses a new package named *Beans*. You could also rename or move the old JFrame.

2. Create a JPanel named AddStrings in the new *Beans* package. Change the layout manager to GridBagLayout.

3. Open both the old and new AddStrings objects by double-clicking their nodes in the Explorer. Open the **Form AddStrings** node for both objects and then the **JPanel** and **JFrame** nodes to expose their components.

4. Select and copy the JLabel and JTextField components from the JFrame (see Figure 9-1). Don't bother with the JMenu components because they aren't needed for the Bean that we're creating.

5. Paste the components copied from the JFrame in the *GuiDemoAdvanced* package into the JPanel in the Beans package. You may close the old AddStrings JFrame.

6. In the new JPanel create ActionPerformed events for JTextFields tbA and tbB. Fill in the handling code for each event. While we're at it, let's extract the common code into a convenient method named updateTfSum, creating the code shown in Example 9-1. The new AddStrings JPanel isn't a Bean yet, but it is a component that we can use in GUI building.

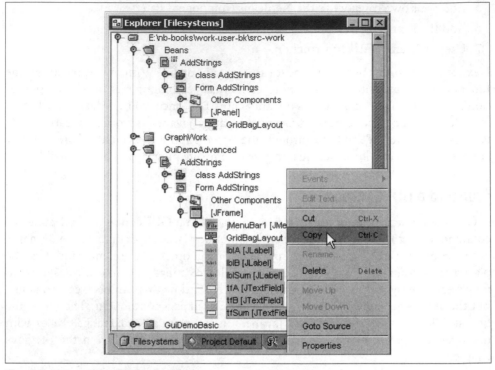

Figure 9-1. Copying AddStrings components

Example 9-1. Code in AddStrings JFrame needed for the new Bean

```
private void tfAActionPerformed(java.awt.event.ActionEvent evt) {
  // Add your handling code here:
  updateTfSum();
}

private void tfBActionPerformed(java.awt.event.ActionEvent evt) {
  // Add your handling code here:
  updateTfSum();
}

private void updateTfSum(){
  tfSum.setText(tfA.getText() + tfB.getText());
}
```

Compile and continue to the next step. Don't try to execute the compiled class because the JPanel doesn't have a main.

7. Let's test it. We'll add the JPanel component to a JFrame and execute the JFrame.

- Create a new JFrame named ASTest1.

- In the Explorer (not the Component Inspector) open the nodes of the JFrame to expose its components.

- Copy the JPanel to the system clipboard—right-click the highest level node of the new **AddStrings** JPanel and then select Copy from the context menu.

- Paste the JPanel into the JFrame—right-click the JFrame level of **ASTest1** and then select Paste from the context menu. This adds **AddStrings** as a component in **ASTest1**.

8. Compile and Execute ASTest1. You will see the AddStrings GUI, familiar from the previous chapter.

We will continue working with the same AddStrings source as we develop our example. For reference, the author has saved a copy named AddStrings_1 at this stage. To make it easy to follow the process of creating an AddStrings Bean, intermediate source has been saved at several stages and is available for download from the O'Reilly web site (*http://www.oreilly.com/catalog/netbeans*).

Converting a GUI Component into a Bean

A bare bones Bean doesn't need much. It needs to be serializable and have a no-argument constructor and at least one property with public getter and setter methods. Our Bean will be a bit more interesting, but we'll start by giving it the bare essentials.

1. A Bean must be serializable, so modify the AddStrings class declaration to be:

```
public class AddStrings extends javax.swing.JPanel
        implements java.io.Serializable {
```

2. AddStrings already has a no-argument constructor, so we don't need to do anything to meet that requirement.

3. Let's add some Bean properties. Open nodes in the Explorer from the top-level **AddStrings** object down through the **class AddStrings** node to **Bean Patterns**. We will add Bean properties that correspond to the text fields in AddStrings. Right-click **Bean Patterns**, select Add, and then select Property to launch the Bean Property wizard. Fill in the wizard properties as shown in Table 9-1. This requires using the wizard three times for the three text fields in AddStrings.

Table 9-1. Setting wizard properties for the AddStrings Bean

Wizard property	1st text field	2nd text field	3rd text field
Name	textA	textB	textSum
Type	String	String	String
Mode	Read/write	Read/write	Read only
Bound	Checked	Checked	Checked
Constrained	Unchecked	Unchecked	Unchecked
Generate Field	Checked	Checked	Unchecked
Generate Return Statement	Checked	Checked	Unchecked
Generate Set Statement	Checked	Checked	Unchecked
Generate Property Change Support	Unchecked	Unchecked	Unchecked

4. Now we have a valid Bean, but the properties aren't worth much because they aren't connected to anything. Modify the getter and setter methods as shown in Example 9-2. Just add the lines from the following code sample that have the comment /*connect property to field*/. Notice that the read-only property **textSum** does not store its value in a separate field. Its getter method just calculates the value when it's needed.

Example 9-2. Code needed in getter and setter methods for AddStrings Bean

```
/** Getter for property textA.
 * @return Value of property textA.
 */
public String getTextA() {
  return this.textA;
}

/** Setter for property textA.
 * @param textA New value of property textA.
 */
public void setTextA(String textA) {
this.textA = textA;
  tfA.setText(this.textA);/*connect property to field*/
  updateTfSum();/*connect property to field*/
}

/** Getter for property textB.
 * @return Value of property textB.
 */
public String getTextB() {
  return this.textB;
}

/** Setter for property textB.
 * @param textB New value of property textB.
 */
public void setTextB(String textB) {
this.textB = textB;
  tfB.setText(this.textB);/*connect property to field*/
  updateTfSum();/*connect property to field*/
}

/** Getter for property textSum.
 * @return Value of property textSum.
 */
public String getTextSum() {
  return tfSum.getText();/*connect property to field*/
}
```

Compile and continue to the next step.

5. Now that our component is a Bean, it's time to test it again. One quick way to test it is similar to the BeanBox that comes with the JavaBeans Development Kit (BDK) from Sun Microsystems. Right-click **AddStrings** in the Explorer and then

select **Customize Bean** from the context menu. Two windows will open—a Bean properties editor and a Bean test window. This should be sufficient for testing during normal development. The Customize Bean tool also provides a way to set property values and save the results as a serialized object.

But we will continue building test drivers to demonstrate the Bean in a more realistic context. Create a new JFrame named ASTest2. Open its nodes in the Explorer to expose the components in the JFrame. Right-click the highest level **AddStrings** node in the Explorer and then select Copy from the context menu. Right-click the JFrame level of **ASTest2** and then select Paste from the context menu.

So far it's like the previous test driver, ASTest1. Next, add two JTextField components and one JLabel. Be sure to add them to the JFrame and not to addStrings1. Keep the default names for the components and then use the Layout tab in the Component Inspector to set their Direction property in the default BorderLayout as shown in Table 9-2.

Table 9-2. Setting component directions

Component	Direction
jTextField1	West
jTextField2	Center
jLabel1	East
addStrings1	South

Use the Events tab in the Component Inspector to add ActionPerformed event handler methods for the two JTextFields. Add method body code as shown in Example 9-3. The added lines use the Bean's setter methods to modify its **TextA** and **TextB** properties.

Example 9-3. Event handler methods in AddStrings Bean

```
private void jTextField1ActionPerformed(java.awt.event.ActionEvent evt) {
    // Add your handling code here:
    addStrings1.setTextA(jTextField1.getText());
    jLabel1.setText(jTextField1.getText() + jTextField2.getText());
}

private void jTextField2ActionPerformed(java.awt.event.ActionEvent evt) {
    // Add your handling code here:
    addStrings1.setTextB(jTextField2.getText());
    jLabel1.setText(jTextField1.getText() + jTextField2.getText());
}
```

6. We aren't finished with AddStrings yet, but we've done enough to test it as a Bean. Compile and execute ASTest2. It should look like Figure 9-2.

   The lower part of the window shows the familiar AddStrings GUI. The text fields in the upper part allow us to test AddStrings as a Bean. When you change infor-

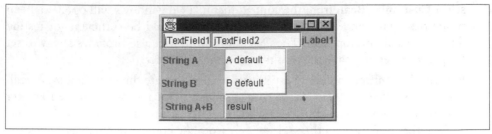

Figure 9-2. Testing the AddStrings Bean

mation in the upper text fields, the corresponding Bean properties and the associated `AddStrings` fields are also changed. But we're only half done because changing `AddStrings` fields should also change the upper `ASTest2` fields. As before, the author has saved a reference copy at this stage named `AddStrings_2` that is available for download from the O'Reilly website (*http://www.oreilly.com/catalog/netbeans*).

Adding an Event Set to a Bean

Next, we'll turn the Read/Write properties of `AddStrings` into *bound* properties. That means any change to a property will fire an event to inform listening objects about the change. We will use this to update the upper text fields in our test driver when the `AddStrings` fields are changed. This is only one way for our Bean to inform listeners about property changes. As you step through the process, you'll glimpse other options and get a sense of what's possible with NetBeans.

1. Again, open nodes in the Explorer from the top-level **AddStrings** object down through the **class AddStrings** node to **Bean Patterns**. Right-click **Bean Patterns**, select Add, and then select **Multicast Event Source** to launch the Event Set wizard. Fill in the wizard properties as shown in Table 9-3.

Table 9-3. Setting wizard properties for event listeners

Wizard property	Value
Type	java.beans.PropertyChangeListener
Implementation option	Generate EventListenerList Implementation
Generate event firing methods	Checked
Pass event as parameter	Checked

2. The event processing code that was added needs customization before it will do the job.

   a. Remove the following line from the `tfAActionPerformed` and `tfBActionPerformed` methods:

      ```
      updateTfSum();
      ```

b. Add the lines from Example 9-4 that have the comment /*needed for event*/.

Example 9-4. Code needed for events in AddStrings Bean

```java
private void tfAActionPerformed(java.awt.event.ActionEvent evt) {
  // Add your handling code here:
    setTextA(tfA.getText());/*needed for event*/
}

private void tfBActionPerformed(java.awt.event.ActionEvent evt) {
  // Add your handling code here:
    setTextB(tfB.getText());/*needed for event*/
}

private void updateTfSum(){
    tfSum.setText(tfA.getText() + tfB.getText());
}

/** Getter for property textA.
 * @return Value of property textA.
 */
public String getTextA() {
    return this.textA;
}

/** Setter for property textA.
 * @param textA New value of property textA.
 */
public void setTextA(String textA) {
    String oldTextA = this.textA;/*needed for event*/
    this.textA = textA;
    tfA.setText(this.textA);/*connect property to field*/
updateTfSum();/*connect property to field*/
  java.beans.PropertyChangeEvent event = /*needed for event*/
      new java.beans.PropertyChangeEvent(this, "textA", oldTextA, this.textA);
    firePropertyChangeListenerPropertyChange(event);/*needed for event*/
}

/** Getter for property textB.
 * @return Value of property textB.
 */
public String getTextB() {
    return this.textB;
}

/** Setter for property textB.
 * @param textB New value of property textB.
 */
public void setTextB(String textB) {
  String oldtextB = this.textB;/*needed for event*/
    this.textB = textB;
    tfB.setText(this.textB);/*connect property to field*/
```

Example 9-4. Code needed for events in AddStrings Bean (continued)

```
updateTfSum();/*connect property to field*/
java.beans.PropertyChangeEvent event = /*needed for event*/
   new java.beans.PropertyChangeEvent(this, "textB", oldtextB, this.textB);
firePropertyChangeListenerPropertyChange(event);/*needed for event*/
}
```

Compile and continue to the next step.

3. We're ready for the next test driver. Copy ASTest2, paste the copy into your working directory, and rename the copy ASTest3. Open it for editing, and change ASTest2 to ASTest3 globally.

4. AddStrings will fire PropertyChangeEvent, so ASTest3 must implement PropertyChangeListener and must be registered as a listener with AddStrings. Modify the ASTest3 class declaration and constructor as shown in Example 9-5. When you modify the class declaration, NetBeans launches a wizard that recommends adding a propertyChange method. Click **Process All** to accept the recommendation.

Example 9-5. Beginning of ASTest3

```
public class ASTest3 extends javax.swing.JFrame
  implements java.beans.PropertyChangeListener {

/** Creates new form ASTest3 */
  public ASTest3() {
      initComponents();
      addStrings1.addPropertyChangeListener(this);
  }
```

5. Implement the propertyChange method as shown in Example 9-6. This will update the editable text fields in ASTest3 with any changes to the corresponding text fields in the AddStrings Bean.

Example 9-6. propertyChange Method in ASTest3

```
public void propertyChange
      (java.beans.PropertyChangeEvent propertyChangeEvent) {
    if (propertyChangeEvent.getSource() == addStrings1) {
      String propertyName = propertyChangeEvent.getPropertyName();
      String propertyNewValue = (String)propertyChangeEvent.getNewValue();
      if (propertyName == "textA") {
        if (!(jTextField1.getText()).equals(propertyNewValue)) {
          jTextField1.setText(propertyNewValue);
        }
      }
      else if (propertyName == "textB") {
        if (!(jTextField2.getText()).equals(propertyNewValue)) {
          jTextField2.setText(propertyNewValue);
        }
      }
    }
```

Example 9-6. propertyChange Method in ASTest3 (continued)

```
    jLabel1.setText(addStrings1.getTextSum());
    }
}
```

6. Now that ASTest3 is listening for propertyChangeEvent, the propertyChange method will be called each time addStrings1.setTextA or addStrings1.setTextB is called. Because the propertyChange method updates jLabel1, we can optionally remove the commented lines in Example 9-7.

Example 9-7. ActionPerformed Event Handlers in ASTest3

```
private void jTextField1ActionPerformed(java.awt.event.ActionEvent evt) {
    // Add your handling code here:
    addStrings1.setTextA(jTextField1.getText());
    // jLabel1.setText(addStrings1.getTextSum());
}

private void jTextField2ActionPerformed(java.awt.event.ActionEvent evt) {
    // Add your handling code here:
    addStrings1.setTextB(jTextField2.getText());
    // jLabel1.setText(addStrings1.getTextSum());
}
```

7. Compile and execute ASTest3. Notice that the test driver fields and the Bean fields stay in sync with changes to either. Again, the author has saved a reference copy of the Bean at this stage, named AddStrings_3, that is available for download from the O'Reilly web site (*http://www.oreilly.com/catalog/netbeans*).

Generating a BeanInfo Class

A BeanInfo class is optional and provides additional information about its Bean. To be efficient, a Bean should only include features and information that are needed at runtime. A BeanInfo class provides features and information that support design-time activities. A visual design tool like NetBeans can use a BeanInfo class to configure a Bean property's default values.

NetBeans provides a powerful BeanInfo Editor for creating and modifying BeanInfo classes. The Editor uses introspection to determine the Bean's public runtime properties, methods, and event sources, whether inherited or declared. It displays all this information, plus some design-time properties that apply to the Bean and the BeanInfo classes. You, the developer, decide what to include in the BeanInfo class. The IDE generates BeanInfo source for the properties you chose. Much of the generated source is guarded code, which follows the same rules as guarded code for GUI forms. You must use the BeanInfo Editor to modify it. Let's create a BeanInfo class for the AddStrings Bean to see what's possible.

1. Launch the BeanInfo Editor. Open nodes in the Explorer from the top-level **AddStrings** object down through the **class AddStrings** node to **Bean Patterns**. Right-click **Bean Patterns** and select **BeanInfo Editor**. The dialog box (seen in Figure 9-3) displays nodes for the BeanInfo and the Bean, followed by a very long list of runtime properties, methods, and event sources (mostly inherited from superclasses) that could be included in the BeanInfo class.

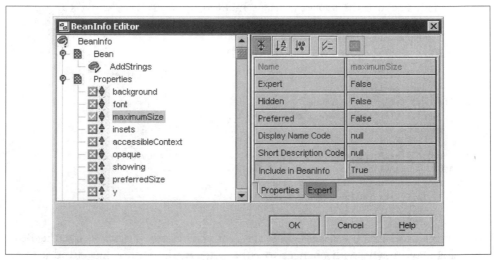

Figure 9-3. The BeanInfo Editor dialog box

2. Select Event Sources and Methods to include in the BeanInfo class. The Bean, Properties, Event Sources, and Methods nodes have a property named **Get From Introspection**. The default value is false, meaning the BeanInfo class will provide values for the design time properties for the subordinate nodes. Source code will be generated in the BeanInfo class to provide the information. We don't want this much code to be generated for our AddStrings example, so change the value of **Get From Introspection** to true for the **Event Sources** and **Methods** nodes. Notice that the lower nodes are grayed out when **Get From Introspection** is true.

3. Select Properties to include in the BeanInfo class. The lower nodes have a property named **Include in BeanInfo**. For example, under the **Properties** node click the **background** node. Set **Include in BeanInfo** to false for all the nodes under **Properties** except for **textA**, **textB**, and **textSum**. You can multiselect the unwanted nodes to change them all at once. Notice the red X icon next to the nodes that have **Include in BeanInfo** set to false.

4. Generate the BeanInfo class. Click the **OK** button in the BeanInfo Editor. A BeanInfo class named AddStringsBeanInfo will be created and opened in the Source Editor. Compile it.

When you install a Bean for use as a component in a GUI building tool, such as Net-Beans or any other full-featured IDE for Java development, the tool automatically uses the corresponding `BeanInfo` class if it exists. The `BeanInfo` class enables the GUI building tool to present Bean users with the view that the Bean developer intended. For example, only the properties that are appropriate for adjustment by a Bean user will be exposed, instead of all the properties inherited from the Bean's superclasses. We will see this in action in the next section, when we add our `AddStrings` Bean to the Component Palette.

Adding a Design-Time Icon

Let's give our `AddStrings` an icon to identify it in the Component Palette. It's optional, but it will give our component a nice finished look in the IDE. A 16 × 16 icon, *AddStrings.gif,* has been included with the source examples for this book. Figure 9-4 is an enlarged view.

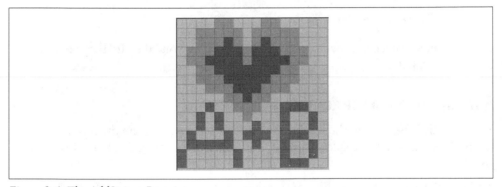

Figure 9-4. The AddStrings Bean icon

In the BeanInfo Editor select the topmost node, named simply **BeanInfo**. Fill in the **Icon 16x16 Color** property with the classpath to the icon. If you want help getting the classpath right, click the ellipsis button to open the Icon Property Editor, select its Classpath radiobutton, click the ellipsis button in its Name field, and browse through the Filesystems nodes to the *AddStrings.gif* file. When the classpath is correct, the icon appears in the space below the Name field. When you click OK to close the BeanInfo Editor, guarded code in `AddStringsBeanInfo` is modified, so be sure to recompile.

Component Palette

We need to make our Bean available within the IDE to fully appreciate its value as a component for GUI building. Let's add it to the Component Palette, but let's create our own Category in which to place the Bean. We could easily add the Bean to an existing category, but let's keep it separate from the NetBeans components.

Adding a Category to the Component Palette

It's surprisingly easy to create a new Component Palette Category. Just right-click the right spot in the Component Palette and then select **Create → New Category** from the context menu. What exactly is the right spot? Try the empty space to the right of the last tab for the existing categories. Or try a hairsbreadth above any existing tab, as seen in Figure 9-5.

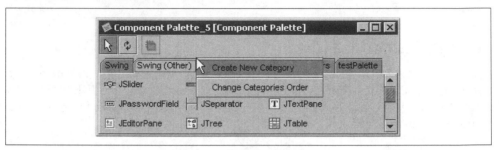

Figure 9-5. Creating a new component palette category

Create a new category now, and name it whatever you like. In the example it's named **testPalette**.

Adding a Bean to the Component Palette

You can add a Bean from the Explorer or from a JAR file, but the procedures are different. We will use the Explorer procedure because we haven't put our Bean into a JAR file.

Adding a Bean from the Explorer takes only a few seconds. Right-click the AddStrings class to pop up the context menu, then select **Tools → Add to Component Palette** to open the **Palette Category** dialog, and select the new category created above. There's our `AddStrings` Bean in the Component Palette with its icon, as Figure 9-6 illustrates.

Figure 9-6. The AddStrings Bean in the component palette

Now let's create one more test driver just to prove that `AddStrings` works in the Component Palette. Start by creating a new `JFrame` named `ASTest4` in your working directory. Then click **AddStrings** in the Component Palette, drop it into ASTest4, compile, and test. Works perfectly, doesn't it?

For the final test, let's set the Bean's properties. Double-click **ASTest4** in the Explorer to open it in the Component Inspector. Open the **JFrame** node in the Component Inspector to expose its components. Select **AddStrings** to expose its properties. Only **textA** and **textB** are available. They are the writeable properties that were selected to include in the BeanInfo class. Give them initial values, for example AAA and BBB, and initialization code is inserted into the initComponents method as shown in Example 9-8.

Example 9-8. initComponents method for ASTest4

```
private void initComponents() {
  addStrings1 = new Beans.AddStrings();

  addWindowListener(new java.awt.event.WindowAdapter() {
    public void windowClosing(java.awt.event.WindowEvent evt) {
      exitForm(evt);
    }
  });

  addStrings1.setTextB("BBB");
  addStrings1.setTextA("AAA");
  getContentPane().add(addStrings1, java.awt.BorderLayout.CENTER);

  pack();
}
```

Component Palette Problems

Of course, things can always go wrong. Perhaps your Bean disappeared from the Component Palette. Did you wipe out the compiled class file and reopen NetBeans? The component palette can't show a Bean that has no class file.

Does your Bean no longer have the icon you assigned it? Perhaps you generated a BeanInfo class for your Bean but didn't compile it. The BeanInfo class is the link from the icon to the IDE. The source examples with this book must be compiled before the BeanInfo class can do its job. When you configured the BeanInfo class with the icon's classpath, was the icon's image correct in the Icon Property Editor? The icon file must be a valid graphic type, and the classpath must be right. GIF, JPG, and PNG types should work, but don't count on ICO, BMP, or others.

This chapter demonstrated the features NetBeans provides for creating and managing JavaBeans, building a visual component as an example. Beans are perhaps the most commonly used design pattern in Java, used for far more than visual components. If it makes sense for a class to use properties for communicating with the outside world, it makes sense for the class to be a JavaBean or at least to have some Bean patterns, and it makes sense to use the Bean building features of NetBeans. ·

## CHAPTER 10

Using Javadoc

Javadoc Support in NetBeans

All programmers are familliar with code commenting. The Java language supports C-style code commenting (/* and */ for multiline comments and // for single-line comments) plus an additional commenting style called "doc comments." A doc comment in a Java source file begins with /** (note the double asteriks) and ends with */. These comments are viewed as regular comments by the compiler, but the javadoc tool can be used to parse them and produce an HTML document known as a Javadoc.

Because doc comments are used to produce HTML they can contain HTML markup tags. Typically these are HTML formatting tags such as <B> and <I>. There are also several special non-HTML tags that can be used. For more information on the javadoc tool and the Javadoc tags see The Javadoc Tools Homepage (*http://java.sun.com/ j2se/javadoc/*).

The javadoc tool has been fully integrated into the NetBeans IDE. Developers can search and browse Javadoc libraries (JAR files or folders containing Javadoc HTML files), get context-sensitive Javadocs, add and verify Javadoc tags to their code, and create Javadocs from their source code using the IDE's Javadoc features.

Mounting Javadocs

 The Javadoc Repository will be removed in NetBeans 3.4.

Before you can search and browse Javadocs, they must be mounted in the Javadoc repository. NetBeans maintains a separate repository for each project you create. The repository contains folders and JAR files that contain Javadocs in HTML format. To see a list of folders and JARs currently loaded in the repository, click on the Javadoc tab in the explorer. Figure 10-1 shows the Javadoc repository.

Figure 10-1. The Javadoc repository

You can add Javadocs to the repository by mounting the root folder or JAR file. Only folders and JAR files that contain a valid Javadoc file structure are allowed to be mounted in the repository. A valid Javadoc file structure is one that contains one of the following files in its root directory:

- *index-files*
- *api/index-files*
- *index-all.html*
- *api/index-all.html*

Once you have mounted a valid Javadoc folder or archive, its contents become immediately available for searching and browsing. Typically, there will be an index.HTML file in the root of each mounted Javadoc in the repository. Double-clicking on this file allows you to browse the Javadocs just as you would with a web browser.

The Javadoc Search Tool

The Javadoc Search Tool allows users to search and view Javadocs in HTML format. Figure 10-2 shows the Javadoc Search Tool in the IDE. To launch the tool from the IDE select **Javadoc Index Search** from the **View** menu, or hit Alt-F1. The buttons seen in the tool are listed and described in Table 10-1.

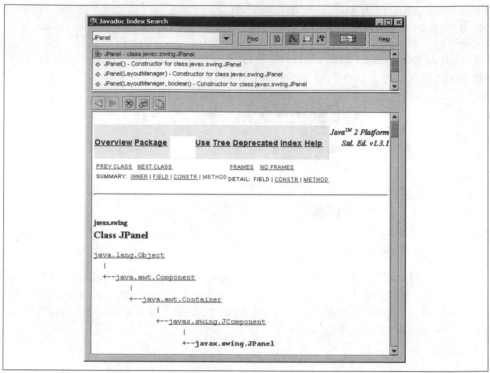

Figure 10-2. The Javadoc Search Tool

Table 10-1. Javadoc Search Tool buttons

Button name	Button image	Description
Show Source		Shows the source code for the current Javadoc comments if the source can be found in one of the mounted filesystems.
Sort Alphabetically		Sorts the Javadoc search results in descending alphabetical order.
Sort by Packages		Groups the Javadoc search results based on package names and then sorts the results in descending alphabetical order.
Sort by Type		Sorts the Javadoc search results based on their types (i.e., Class, Interface, Exception, Method, Field).
Toggle HTML		Toggles the HTML view of the search tool.
Back		Goes to the last page visited in the browser.
Forward		Goes forward to the next page visited by the browser.
Next		Stops the browser from completing loading of the current page.

Table 10-1. Javadoc Search Tool buttons (continued)

Button name	Button image	Description
Reload		Reloads the current page in the browser.
History		Shows a history of pages (with hyperlinks) viewed with the browser over a period of time. Pages in the history can be loaded in the browser again by clicking on their hyperlink.

The search tool is divided into three panes (these panes may be arranged differently in your distribution). The top section is used to enter a Javadoc query string. The query string need not be complete but must at least match the begining of a class, interface, exception, method, or field in the Javadoc repository. After entering the string and clicking on the Find button, the left pane of the tool is populated with a list of results matching the query. If no entry is found for the query, the message "No Documentation Found" is shown. If this occurs, you should check your spelling and make sure that you have all the necessary Javadoc archives mounted in the Javadoc repository (covered in the next section). Each entry in the list is associated with Javadoc comments that can be viewed in HTML format. The list can be sorted alphabetically or by type and can also be grouped by package names using the buttons found in the top section of the tool. Clicking on an entry in the list causes the right section of the tool to be populated with its Javadocs in HTML format. This pane acts as an HTML browser, so hyperlinks in the Javadocs can be further explored in this view. Double-clicking on an item in the left section launches a Web Browser to show the Javadocs for that item.

The search tool can also be launched from the editor to perform a context-sensitive search. The context of the search will be the currently selected text or the current word on which the cursor is positioned. For example, to perform a context-sensitive Javadoc search for a method named getString you would select the word "get-String" in the text editor and then hit Alt-F1. The search tool will be launched with getString as the query string and the results of the query showing in the list in the left section of the tool's window. This process is illustrated in Figures 10-3 and 10-4. The same effect is achieved by right-clicking on a word in the Source Editor and selecting **Tools → Show Javadoc** from the context menu.

```
19     /**
20      * @param args the command line arguments
21      */
22     public static void main (String args[])
23     {
24             ResourceBundle bundle = ResourceBundle.getBundle("JavaDocClass");
25             bundle.getString("Test");
26     }
```

Figure 10-3. Select the text to search for in Javadocs and hit Control-F1

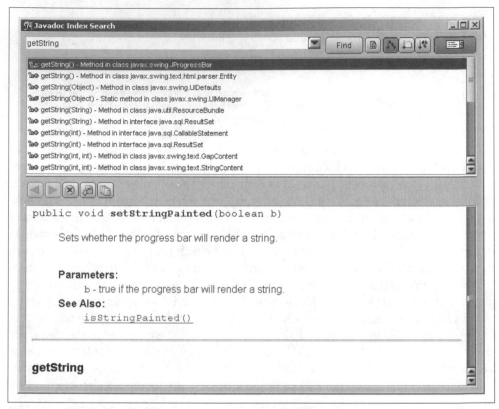

Figure 10-4. The search tool starts with your text and matching results.

Creating Javadoc

After using the Javadoc search tool and seeing how simple it is to add archives to the IDE's repository, you'll probably realize how convenient it would be to generate Javadocs for your own source code and distribute them to your cohorts to mount, query, and browse in their NetBeans environment. Before you go on to document generation heaven, however, you should make sure that your comments, specifically your Javadoc tags, are correct and according to standards. This can be a tedious task and is probably why many developers are not enthusiastic about producing Javadocs for their code. The NetBeans IDE comes to the rescue here with a saavy tool, the Javadoc Auto Commenting Tool, that allows you to easily create, edit, and manage Javadocs by focusing explicitly on the related comments.

The Auto Comment Tool

You may use the Auto Comment Tool at any point during development. It is also useful for nondevelopers; for example, an editor may use the tool to correct spelling and add formatting without contaminating the source code. The Auto Commenting Tool is shown in Figure 10-5.

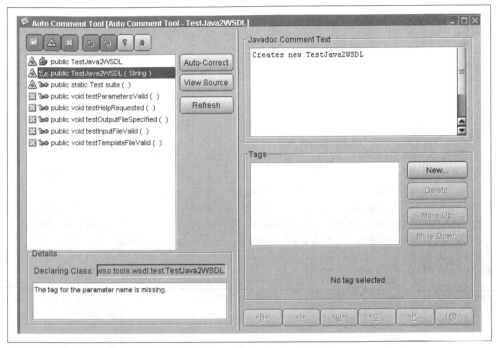

Figure 10-5. The Javadoc Auto-Commenting Tool

To launch the Auto Commenting Tool, open the Java source file in the editor, right-click on the opened file and select **Tools → Auto Comment**. You should now see a dialog box similar to the one shown in Figure 10-5. The tool lists all the classes, methods, and fields in the the Java file and allows you to view and correct the Javadoc comments. The tool also points out which of these elements have well-formed Javadoc comments and which do not. A class, method, or field element has a well-formed Javadoc comment if there are Javadoc tags for each part of the element as is necessary. For example, examine the following method:

```
/**
*
* This method prints a hello message
*/
public void sayHello(String sayHelloTo)
{
    ...
}
```

Although the fragment contains an informative comment, it does not have a well-formed Javadoc comment because the tag for documenting the sayHelloTo parameter is missing. The well-formed version of this method is

```
/**
 *
 * This method prints a hello message
 *
 *@param sayHelloTo The method will print a hello message using this
 parameter as the name.  Ex. "Hello Bob" if set to Bob.
 */
public void sayHello(String sayHelloTo)
{
    ...
}
```

Javadoc filtering

The Auto Comment Tool shows you which classes, methods, and fields are not well-formed and can even autocorrect the problem for you. You can control which of these elements needs correcting or viewing by using one of the seven filtering buttons provided by the tool. Each button is represented by an icon that indicates whether the Javadoc comments are correct or erroneous, or the element visibility (public, private, protected). Table 10-2 shows the filtering buttons.

Table 10-2. Method filtering buttons

Button	Description
	Displays all classes, methods, and fields that contain compliant (well-formed) Javadoc comments.
	Displays all classes, methods, and fields that have partial or erroneous Javadoc Comments. The tool can autofix some of these Javadoc errors by making assumptions based on the format of the methods. For example, parameter tags may be added for a method with parameters, but for a void method that returns nothing, it throws no exceptions and has no parameters. No assumptions can be made as to what Javadoc tags, if any, are needed, and so these cannot be autofixed. Simply adding arbitrary text to the comments can fix such problems.
	Displays all classes, methods, and fields that have no Javadoc comments. The tool can autofix some of these Javadoc errors by making assumptions based on the format of the methods.
	Displays all public classes, methods, and fields.
	Displays all protected classes, methods, and fields.
	Displays all package level classes, methods, and fields.
	Displays all private classes, methods, and fields.

Viewing, editing, and correcting Javadoc comments

Now that you've filtered the classes, methods, and fields that you would like to have Javadocs generated for, you'll want to make corrections as suggested by the Auto

Comment Tool. Correcting Javadocs typically involves adding comment text and Javadoc tags. When you press the filtering buttons, a list of filtered items gets displayed. Selecting any of the filtered items displays the related comment text and tags. The Details section of the tool's dialog box informs you of any Javadoc errors associated with the selected item. Based on the errors reported here, you can make the corrections by modifying text in the Javadoc Comment Text and the Tags sections.

Typing text in the Javadoc Comment Text section will update an element's Javadoc comments. You will typically write any informative blurb here that describes the class, method, or field to a perusing developer. This is also a good place for an editor to make grammatical and typographical corrections. You can add HTML tags to your text for formatting purposes. The tool includes six HTML formatting buttons that add tags to your text. These buttons are located just beneath the Tags section. Any formatting that is applied to your text will be seen in the HTML after it is generated by a Javadoc generation tool.

The Details section will inform you of any tags that may be missing from the currently selected item. You can modify an item's tags by using the buttons provided in the Tags section. For example, examine the following method signature:

```
public float getCurrentTemperature(boolean celsius) throws ThermometerException
```

After adding some documentation in the Javadoc Comment Text section, you would click the **New** button in the Tags section, select the radio box named **@param**, and click the **OK** button. You should see a combo box and a text box appear. Select the **celsius** parameter from the drop-down box, and type in a description of the parameter in the text box. You also have to add tags for the return value and the Exception. The steps for adding these are quite similar. For the return value you need to select the **@return** radio box, and for the exception you will need to select **@throws**. Once you've completed all editing, you can click the Refresh button to commit the changes and update the filtered item list.

After making corrections in the Auto Comment Tool, you will still need to save the Java source file to permanently commit your changes.

Javadoc Generation

You are now ready to generate your own Javadocs based on source files in your project. The IDE has an embedded, customizeable Documentation Engine that is used for this task. The documentation engine consists of the following customizeable options:

- Javadoc Search Types
- Javadoc Executors
- Doclets

These options are described in the following sections. To select the customized properties, you can set them as the default values for the Documentation Engine by selecting **Code Documentation → Documentation** from the Options dialog and selecting your Default Search Engine and Executor from the drop-down lists provided (doclets are selected in the property sheets for Javadoc Executors).

You may chose to generate Javadocs for a single class or for an entire package. If you choose to perform generation on a package and would like the process to be recursive, you must be sure to have the recursive property set to true on the Javadoc Executor option that the Documentation Engine is using (see Table 10-3). To begin generation, right-click on the folder (package) or file (in Explorer or in an opened editor) and select **Tools → Generate Javadoc** from the context menu. If generation is successful, you will be prompted to view the docs in an HTML browser. Click the Yes button to review your Javadocs.

Javadoc Search Types

NetBeans provides a mechanism for you to search internationalized Javadocs using Javadoc Search Types. Currently the IDE ships with a Javadoc Search Type for the Japanese locale in addition to the default English. By selecting this search type, you can browse Javadoc HTML documents generated for the Japanese locale. In the near future other locales may become available and can be added to your installation via the NetBeans Update Center.

Javadoc Executors

A Javadoc Executor is an Execution Service that processes source files in the IDE to produce Javadoc files. Like Java source file Execution Services, there is an External and Internal Execution Service for Javadocs. The External Service can be used to call a javadoc tool other than the one in the JVM used by the IDE (this is used by the Internal Service). Both executors are configurable in the Options dialog (**Tools → Options → Code Documentation**). Table 10-3 explains the properties for the External Javadoc Executor.

Table 10-3. External Javadoc Executor

Property	Description
1.1 styleDoclets	If this property is set to true, the executor will generate Javadocs in the JDK 1.1 style.
Doclets	This property specifies the doclet to use to format and generate the HTML page(s). Doclets are explained in the next section.
Encoding	This property specifies the character encoding for generation. For more information on character encoding support, see *http://java.sun.com/j2se/1.3/docs/guide/intl/encoding.doc.html*.
Extdirs	This property specifies additional directories that the executor will use to find source files or classes for Javadoc generation.

Table 10-3. External Javadoc Executor (continued)

Property	Description
External Executor Engine	This property allows you to configure the external process (usually the javadoc tool) that will be used to generate Javadoc for your source files. See Chapter 6 for information on configuring external processes.
Locale	This property allows you to set the locale to use during document generation. The locale consists of a lowercase language code and an uppercase country code. For example, en_US is used for English language in the United States. For valid language and country codes see *http://www-old.ics.uci.edu/pub/ietf/http/related/iso639.txt* (language codes) and *http://userpage.chemie.fu-berlin.de/diverse/doc/ISO_3166.html* (country codes).
Members	This property specifies which class members should appear in the generated documentation. The choices for this property are Java's visibility modifiers (public, package, protected, private). The choices work opposite to their meanings. For example, private will cause all class members to appear in the generated documentation, and public will only show members declared as public. The default is protected, which allows access to members declared as public, protected, or package.
Overview	This property specifies the name of the overview file (usually overview.html) used for the Javadoc Overview page.
Recursive	If this property is set to true, the generation engine will recurse through all the directories and generate Javadocs for all the source files found.
Verbose	If this property is set to true, the executor will output more detailed messages during the generation process.

When you choose to generate Javadocs for a given source file or package, a Javadoc executor is invoked that generates Javadoc HTML files in the specified directory. The executor will format the HTML files based on the preconfigured doclet that is specified in the Doclets property. Additional source files can be added to your generated Javadocs if you specify them in the Extdirs property. Any Java files found in these directories will be processed by the executor and the resulting HTML files copied to the specified output directory.

Doclets

Doclets are Java programs used to format and add content to the output of the javadoc tool. Java has a doclet API that all doclets must be written against. A doclet basically operates on the Javadoc tags. It can perform specific operations based on a given tag. For example, it will create a hyperlink in the HTML when it encounters the @link tag. By default, the javadoc tool uses a standard doclet. This doclet generates API documentation in HTML format. The doclet API allows you to extend the standard API or write your own doclets for maximum flexibility. Using your own doclet or an extension of the standard one is extremely useful when you want to introduce custom Javadoc tags. When using custom doclets with the javadoc tool, you must specify the classname of the doclet you are using:

```
javadoc -doclet ora.com.MyDoclet MyClass.java
```

For more on doclets and the doclet API go to *http://java.sun.com/products/jdk/1.2/docs/tooldocs/javadoc/overview.html*.

The IDE comes with a standard doclet that has customizeable properties. This doclet is the default for the Internal and External Javadoc Executors. You can create many versions of this doclet, each with its own customized properties. However, you cannot create your own custom doclet. You can create a new doclet (based on the standard doclet) by selecting Code **Documentation** → **Doclets,** right-clicking, and selecting **New** → **Standard Doclet** from the context menu. The newly created doclet can be configured via its property sheets. These properties are explained in the sections to follow.

Adding content. Doclet properties can be used to add additional content to each Java page produced in the generation process. Table 10-4 shows doclet properties that can be used to add content to generated Javadocs.

Table 10-4. External Javadoc Executor

Property	Description
Bottom	This property is used to add HTML text to the bottom of each generated page. You can add HTML markup such as copyright information here and it will appear at the bottom of each Javadoc page.
Doc Title	This property adds a title to the Overview page for your generated Javadocs.
Footer	This property is used to add HTML text in the footer area of each HTML file.
Header	This property is used to add HTML text in the header area of each HTML file.
Window Title	This property adds a title to the browser window for the generated HTML files.

Adding links. At times you may need to provide a link in the Javadocs of one class to the Javadoc of another using the @link tag. The IDE allows you to specify links to other generated Javadocs by using the doclet's Link and Link Offline properties. The difference between these properties is that the former requires a path to a directory where a package-list file can be found, and the latter does not require the package-list files to be existent at the time of generation.

To add links to your generation, click on the ellipsis button that appears when editing the Link or Link Offline property in the doclet property sheet. You should see a dialog box similar to the one shown in Figure 10-6. Type in the path to the directory containing the package-list file and use the **Add** button to add it to the list of links. The Up and Down buttons can be used to move links higher or lower in the search path.

Customizing the HTML format. Other properties are available to format the HTML produced by the generation process. The charset property is used to set the ISO character encoding for the HTML file, allowing it to be ported to other platforms. For maximum formatting, you can always specify a stylesheet file that can contain formatting rules for any HTML tag in the generated Javadocs. You specify the location of your stylesheet in the Style Sheet File property of the doclet.

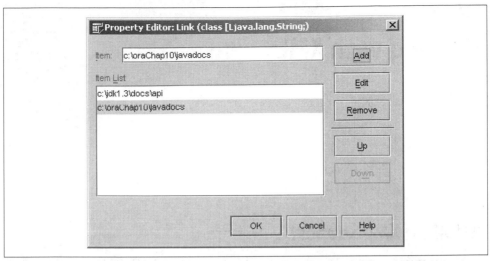

Figure 10-6. Adding Javadoc links

Additional properties. Additional doclet properties are described in Table 10-5.

Table 10-5. Additional doclet properties

Property	Description
Destination	This property sets the destination directory where the documentation engine will store the generated Javadoc files.
Help	This property specifies the location of a HTML file to be used as a link to help instead of the default-generated help-doc.html.
No Deprecated	If this property is set to true, no deprecated members will be added to the generated Javadocs.
No Deprecated List	If this property is set to true, the deprecated-list.html file that contains a list of deprecated APIs will not be created.
No Help	If this property is set to true, no help links are generated.
No Index	If this property is set to true, no index will be generated.
No Navbar	If this property is set to true, no navbar is created, which also means that the header and footer will also not be generated.
No Tree	If this property is set to true, no tree is generated to show the hierarchial structure of the classes and packages.
Split Index	If this property is set to true, the index is split up into files, one for each letter.
Use	If this property is set to true, a Use page will be created for each generated Javadoc. The Use page can be edited to describe the classes and members documented.
Version	If this property is set to true, the @version tag is processed and included in the text of the generated HTML files.

Working with XML

Installing XML Support

NetBeans provides extensive support for developing with XML.* But it isn't bundled with NetBeans 3.3.2, so you need to get it from the Update Center. Go to **Tools menu → Update Center** to launch the Update Center Wizard. Check the NetBeans Update Center. You will find several modules under the XML node, **CSS Support** through **XML Tree Editor** (see Figure 11-1). Install them all. After the IDE restarts, look at **Help menu → Help Sets → XML Support** for complete instructions on using all the features. In this chapter we'll mention the high points and then build some examples.

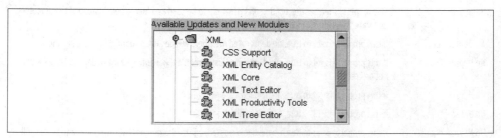

Figure 11-1. Installing modules for XML support

Overview

We'll spend the bulk of this chapter delving into the XML support available in NetBeans. Before getting into detail, though, you should get an idea of what is available and how it all fits together. You'll then be ready to dive into specific topics.

---

* To learn more about XML processing with Java, or to get an overview of XML- related technologies, see Java and XML (O'Reilly), by Brett McLaughlin.

Templates

NetBeans provides a variety of templates to get you started on creating the following XML documents:

- Plain XML
- XML with DTD included or referenced
- DTD alone
- Cascading Style Sheet (CSS)
- Extensible Style Sheet (XSL)
- OASIS Specification XML entity catalog

You can also mount existing XML catalogs that meet other specifications, but only the OASIS specification is explicitly supported for creating new catalogs.

Browsing and Editing

Once you've used a template to create a new XML-based document or mounted an existing document, you will want to browse and edit it. If the XML is well formed, you can open the document's nodes and browse it in the Explorer. NetBeans also provides both a text editor and a tree editor for modifying XML files or for closely examinining their contents. The tree editor gives a node view just like the Explorer view, and specialized property editors that change to match the object type of the currently selected node. Context menus help you keep XML source well formed and consistent with DTD during editing through the **Check XML** and **Validate XML** actions, both of which will be explained in later sections.

Generating Documentation

After working hard to create a DTD, you probably want to document it so others can share its value. It's as easy as generating a Javadoc for Java source. Right-click, select **Generate Documentation**, and it's done. You get an XHTML document that describes the content of the DTD, which you may augment with text describing the business meaning of the XML elements and attributes.

Accessing with Java

Of course, you'll want to access your XML documents with Java to take full advantage of XML's power. The first step is as easy as generating documentation. Right-click the DTD and select **Generate DOM Tree Scanner** or **SAX Document Handler Wizard** to generate source for Java classes to access the XML. Use a *DOM Tree Scanner* to modify XML documents, and use a lighter-weight *SAX Document Handler* if you only need to read the documents. We'll take a closer look at this throughout the rest of this chapter.

XML Schema Support

XML schema support is coming soon. NetBeans 3.4 will have several XML-related enhancements, including XML document validation by XML Schema. See XML—planned features for NetBeans 3.4 (*http://xml.netbeans.org/plans/features34.html*) for specifics. NetBeans 4.0 should get you even more excited. See XML—planned features index page (*http://xml.netbeans.org/plans/features.html*) for a look further ahead.

Of course, it's impossible for any set of development tools to keep completely up to date with advancing technologies. But NetBeans with its highly modular architecture does a remarkable job of bringing out new features quickly. If you want to speed up the process, learn how to build NetBeans modules from this book and start participating in the open source community.

XML Editors

Let's create an XML document with a DTD. We need a work area, so first create a new Java package named XMLWork. Right-click the package in the Explorer, select **New → XML and DTD → XML with DTD** to launch the New Wizard, and create a new XML document from a template. Name it *Inventory* and then click Finish. The document appears as a node in the Explorer and in a tree editor view of the Source Editor. Open the nodes in both the Explorer and the Source Editor, and you will see that both views are identical. When the top-level node is open, the name **Inventory** appears three times, first as the name of the entire document, next as DOCTYPE root element name in the DTD, and last as a top-level element name in the XML data (see Figure 11-2). Right-click the top-level node and select **Edit** to access the same information as plain text.

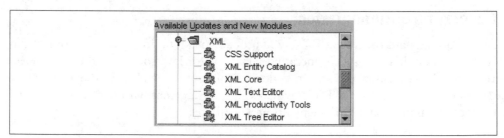

Figure 11-2. The XML tree editor and text editor

Any change made in the tree view is immediately applied to the text view. You can see this by clicking back and forth between the tree view and text view tabs at the bottom of the Source Editor. Let's undock the text view to make it easier to watch. Right-click the text view tab, select **Dock View Into → New Single Frame**, and you can see both views at the same time.

We need to add a few elements and attributes to make our document interesting. Our *Inventory* document will describe **Kit**s, which contain **Part**s; **Supplier**s, which produce the **Part**s; and **Part**s, which have **Size** and **Color**. Everything will have a **Description**.

Right-click (in either the Explorer or the Source Editor tree view) the **Inventory** element node, which is the last node named **Inventory**. Select from the context menu **Add Element**. Name it **Kit**, click **OK**, and notice that a new element is added inside the top-level **Inventory** element. Did you see all the choices when the context menu for Add was open? You could add anything from Attribute to Text, everything you need for complete XML data editing. So let's add an attribute. Right-click **Inventory** again; this time select **Add Attribute**. Name it **Description**, and give it the value Kit Inventory. It's often easier to add new attributes while creating an element. Just click the Add button while the Element wizard is open, instead of going directly to the OK button, and the little Add Attribute wizard will open. You can also get to the Add Attribute wizard from the specialized property editor that appears in the right panel of the tree editor whenever an element is selected in the left panel. To add some text to the **Part** element, right-click, select **Add Text** and then fill in Part A in Kit.

Continue using the tree view to add elements and attributes (as shown in Figure 11-3) until the text view of your XML document matches Example 11-1 (except for insignificant blank lines). You can copy and paste in the tree editor. We want all the **Part** elements to have the same **Description**, Part A. Once you've created the first Part A **Description**, you can just copy and paste into the other **Part** elements. Of course, you could simply paste Example 11-1 directly into the text editor. But the purpose of this exercise is to gain experience with the tree editor. With large, complex XML documents the tree editor is much easier to use because it automatically keeps the syntax correct. Moving nodes to restructure the data with copy, cut, and paste operations is quick and accurate.

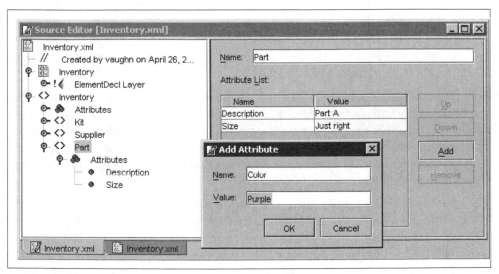

Figure 11-3. Adding a new attribute

Example 11-1. Inventory.xml after adding elements and attributes

```
<?xml version="1.0" encoding="UTF-8"?>
<!-- Created by vaughn on April 26, 2002, 6:07 PM -->
<!DOCTYPE Inventory [
    <!ELEMENT Inventory ANY>
]>
<Inventory Description="Kit Inventory">
    <Kit Description="The first kit">
        <Part Description="Part A">Part A in Kit</Part>

    </Kit>
    <Supplier Description="Our favorite supplier">
        <Part Description="Part A">Part A in Supplier</Part>
    </Supplier>
    <Part Description="Part A" Size="Just right" Color="Purple">Part A
    alone</Part>
</Inventory>
```

Our example is small, but it's enough to demonstrate what NetBeans can do with XML documents. We'll keep it small while creating DTD, CSS, and other files based on its content.

Beyond Editing XML

Let's look at the other features in addition to the editors that NetBeans provides for working with XML documents.

Checking and Validating XML

When an XML document is opened in the Explorer, it's automatically checked for syntax. If you change an XML document in the text editor, it's a good idea to run the syntax check manually. Right-click anywhere in the text editor or on the top-level node of an XML document in the Explorer or tree editor and then select **Check XML**. Any errors will be identified in the Output window.

You can also select **Validate XML** from the context menu. Validation verifies that the XML is fully and correctly described in a DTD. Do it now with our sample XML document. Right-click and select **Validate XML**. The output window will show lots of errors because the DTD section of our example is empty. Unfortunately, adding XML data elements does not generate corresponding DTD. More unfortunately, you can't use the tree editor to build your DTD.

If a suitable external DTD file exists, you can simply assign the external DTD to your XML document. We do not yet have such a file, but let's walk through the process for future reference. In the Explorer window right-click the node for the XML file that needs DTD. That's **Inventory** in our example. In the context menu select **Add Document Type** to open the **Add Document Type** dialog. If the DTD file is accessible remotely, enter its URL in the **Public ID:** text field. Or, if it's in the local filesystem, enter its name in the **System ID:** text field. Because we don't have either choice available yet, just click **Cancel**.

The only other choice is to type in the DTD information manually in the text editor. So you had better know what you're doing, and the Check XML feature will definitely come in handy. Replace the `<!DOCTYPE>` instruction of your sample XML document with the text in Example 11-2. Don't forget to Check XML and Validate XML.

Example 11-2. DTD text for Inventory.xml

```
<!DOCTYPE Inventory [
<!ELEMENT Inventory (Supplier|Kit|Part)*>
<!ATTLIST Inventory
    Description CDATA #IMPLIED
  >

<!ELEMENT Kit (Part)*>
<!ATTLIST Kit
    Description CDATA #IMPLIED
  >

<!ELEMENT Part ANY>
<!ATTLIST Part
    Description CDATA #IMPLIED
    Color CDATA #IMPLIED
    Size CDATA #IMPLIED
  >

<!ELEMENT Supplier (Part)*>
<!ATTLIST Supplier
    Description CDATA #IMPLIED
  >
]>
```

Setting the Node View

Now that you've added a valid DTD to the sample XML document, let's look at its node view. The Explorer window and the Source Editor tree view give exactly the same node view of an XML file, so it doesn't matter which one you work in. Open the top-level node of **Inventory** and then open the two nodes below, also named **Inventory**, one for the document's DTD, and one for its data. If you compare the tree view to the text view, you'll find the elements and attributes in the data section match up, one to one in the same order. But the DTD section is different. In the tree view all the elements are listed first under the **ElementDeclLayer** node, and the attributes are listed separately under **AttlistDeclLayer**. The difference is determined by the document's Node View setting. To access the Node View setting (as in Figure 11-4), Right-click the top **Inventory** node, select **Properties** from the context menu, and click the View tab.

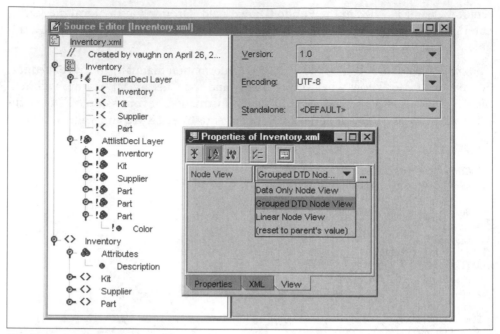

Figure 11-4. DTD and data nodes

Try out the different views. The Linear Node View shows DTD element and attribute declarations in the same order as the text document. The Data Only Node View has the same order but hides comments and processing instructions. You can set the node view at any level, from the topmost node to the lowest, to completely customize the overall view of a large XML document. Setting a node's view to (**reset to parent's value**) gives the view the same setting as the next higher level. For the top level, (**reset to parent's value**) applies the default, **Grouped DTD Node View**.

Generating a DTD

Several XML features require a DTD in a separate file, instead of an internal DTD. So there's a way to split an XML document with an internal DTD into a separate DTD file and a data-only XML document. Right-click the top-level **Inventory** node, and select **Generate DTD** from the context menu. A little dialog will pop up prompting you to name the new DTD file. Accept the default *Inventory_Inventory*, click **Yes** in the next dialog (Do you want to use generated DTD as external document type?), and the original XML with DTD document is split neatly in two (see Figure 11-5). Now, you can create as many XML data files as desired, all validated by the same single DTD file. And you have the DTD input needed to use the following features.

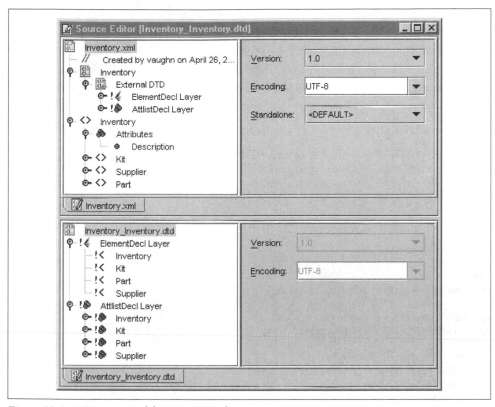

Figure 11-5. DTD separated from an XML document

Generating Documentation

Having a separate DTD file makes it possible for any number of XML documents to use it and for developers to design any number of applications to use the data that it describes. We need documentation that developers can read to help them build their applications. The IDE can generate an excellent HTML framework for building documentation. Just right-click the DTD file **Inventory_Inventory**, and select **Generate Documentation** from the context menu. Again a dialog pops up prompting you to name the new documentation file. Accept the default *Inventory_InventoryDocumentation*, and the HTML file shown in Example 11-3 is generated to document the DTD. Use the NetBeans editor or any HTML editor to enhance the documentation as needed.

Example 11-3. HTML documentation for Inventory.xml

```
<!DOCTYPE html PUBLIC "-//W3C//DTD XHTML 1.0 Strict//EN"
  "http://www.w3.org/TR/xhtml1/DTD/xhtml1-strict.dtd">
<html>
<head>
```

Example 11-3. HTML documentation for Inventory.xml (continued)

```
<title>DTD Grammar Documentation</title>
<meta http-equiv="Content-Type" content="text/xhtml; charset=UTF-8" />
</head>

<!-- Generated on May 11, 2002 by NetBeans XML module. -->
<body>

<hr />
<h2>Element Index</h2>
<ul><li><tt><a href="#Inventory">Inventory</a></tt></li>
<li><tt><a href="#Kit">Kit</a></tt></li>
<li><tt><a href="#Part">Part</a></tt></li>
<li><tt><a href="#Supplier">Supplier</a></tt></li>
</ul>

<hr />
<h2>Element Details</h2>

<hr />
<h2><a name="Inventory"></a>Inventory</h2>

<p><b>Declared Attributes</b></p>
<ul><li><tt>#IMPLIED CDATA Description</tt></li>
</ul>
<p><b>Element Content Model</b></p>
<p><tt>(<a href="#Supplier">Supplier</a> |
  <a href="#Kit">Kit</a> | <a href="#Part">Part</a>)*</tt></p>
<p><b>Referenced by</b></p>
<p><tt></tt></p>

<hr />
<h2><a name="Kit"></a>Kit</h2>

<p><b>Declared Attributes</b></p>
<ul><li><tt>#IMPLIED CDATA Description</tt></li>
</ul>
<p><b>Element Content Model</b></p>
<p><tt>(<a href="#Part">Part</a>)*</tt></p>
<p><b>Referenced by</b></p>
<p><tt><a href="#Inventory">Inventory</a></tt></p>

<hr />
<h2><a name="Part"></a>Part</h2>

<p><b>Declared Attributes</b></p>
<ul><li><tt>#IMPLIED CDATA Description</tt></li>
<li><tt>#IMPLIED CDATA Color</tt></li>
<li><tt>#IMPLIED CDATA Size</tt></li>
</ul>
<p><b>Element Content Model</b></p>
<p><tt>(#PCDATA)*</tt></p>
<p><b>Referenced by</b></p>
```

Example 11-3. HTML documentation for Inventory.xml (continued)

```
<p><tt><a href="#Inventory">Inventory</a>, <a href="#Kit">Kit</a>,
  <a href="#Supplier">Supplier</a></tt></p>

<hr />
<h2><a name="Supplier"></a>Supplier</h2>

<p><b>Declared Attributes</b></p>
<ul><li><tt>#IMPLIED CDATA Description</tt></li>
</ul>
<p><b>Element Content Model</b></p>
<p><tt>(<a href="#Part">Part</a>)*</tt></p>
<p><b>Referenced by</b></p>
<p><tt><a href="#Inventory">Inventory</a></tt></p>
</body></html>
```

Generating CSS

Similarly, you can easily generate a CSS document. Right-click the DTD file **Inventory_Inventory**, select **Generate CSS** from the context menu, accept the default name *Inventory_InventoryStylesheet*, and the CSS file shown in Example 11-4 is generated based on the DTD.

Example 11-4. Cascading Stylesheet for Inventory.xml

```
/* Cascade style sheet based on Inventory_Inventory.dtd DTD */
Inventory { display: block }
Kit { display: block }
Part { display: block }
Supplier { display: block }
```

Like the HTML file generated above, this CSS file is a framework that a developer can enhance as needed. The essential purpose of an XML document is to store information content in a standard format that is independant of any presentation appearance. Before the information can be viewed, it must be transformed into HTML, WML, or some other format that can be rendered by a browser, printer, or other presentation device. The essential purpose of a CSS document is to control the transformation process, making it possible to view information from an XML document in a comfortable format. The stylesheet information in Example 11-4 simply states that information from each element in *Inventory.xml* should be presented in a separate block of text. You could enhance the CSS file by adding specifications to give different font properties to each element type. For example, information from **Kit** elements could be big and green, and information from **Part** elements could be small and red.

Generating Java Classes

Here comes the best part (after all, we *are* Java programmers): generating Java source code to process XML documents. First, we'll create a SAX document handler to read through our sample XML document and extract its element and attribute values. This gives us serial read-only access, useful in applications that need to get the information in an XML document quickly with minimal memory requirements. Next, we'll create a DOM tree scanner, useful in applications that need to access the information from an XML document in random order, update it, and output a modified XML document.

Generating a SAX Document Handler

Our next example will be a basic Simple API for XML (SAX) parser that simply lists the attributes and text in our *Inventory.xml* XML document. First, we will use the **SAX Document Handler Wizard** to generate source for the Java classes that will parse *Inventory.xml*. We will add a few lines of code to invoke the parser and display the parsed information. Finally, we will configure the execution service parameters and run it.

To launch the Wizard, right-click the DTD file **Inventory_Inventory** and then select **SAX Document Handler Wizard** from the context menu. The wizard's frame 1 of 4 specifies the API versions to use in generating code. For our example, select JAXP 1.1, not JAXP 1.0. Select SAX 2.0, not 1.0. Check the checkbox **Propogate SAX Events to Generated Handler**. Frame 2 allows you to customize the handling of each element. Accept the defaults because no special handling is needed. Frame 3 allows you to specify converter methods in case the extracted data requires a format conversion. Accept the defaults because no conversion is needed. Frame 4 allows you to specify the output File Names. Accept defaults for the file names, but uncheck the checkbox **Save Customized Bindings**. When the wizard is finished, three Java files will be generated:

- *Inventory_InventoryHandler.java*: abstract class that declares callback methods for handling elements in *Inventory.xml*
- *Inventory_InventoryHandlerImpl.java*: implementation of call back methods
- *Inventory_InventoryParser.java*: logic to call SAX parser methods and then call handler methods to process the parsed data

After the files have been generated, a **Confirm Changes** dialog will pop up recommending changes in the implementation class to implement abstract methods. Check the **Perform synchronization without confirmation** radio button and click **Process All**.

Now that we have some source to work with, we need to make a few additions. First, add a main method to the parser classType or paste Example 11-5 into *Inventory_InventoryParser.java*.

Example 11-5. main method for Inventory_InventoryParser

```
public static void main(String[] args) throws Exception {
  Inventory_InventoryHandler handler =
```

Example 11-5. main method for Inventory_InventoryParser (continued)

```
        new Inventory_InventoryHandlerImpl();
    EntityResolver resolver = null;
    Inventory_InventoryParser parser =
        new Inventory_InventoryParser(handler, resolver);
    InputSource input = new InputSource(args[0]);
    parser.parse(input);
}
```

All we need now is some print logic in the handler class. We will enhance a couple of callback methods in *Inventory_InventoryHandlerImpl.java* to handle the parsed data. Replace the characters method in *Inventory_InventoryHandlerImpl.java* with Example 11-6.

Example 11-6. characters method for Inventory_InventoryHandlerImpl

```
public void characters(char[] values, int param, int param2)
    throws org.xml.sax.SAXException {
  System.out.println("  Element Data: " +
    new String(values, param, param2));
}
```

Replace the startElement method in *Inventory_InventoryHandlerImpl.java* with Example 11-7. That's all the source changes we need. Right-click the package, and select **Build All** from the context menu to compile the classes.

Example 11-7. startElement method for Inventory_InventoryHandlerImpl

```
public void startElement(String str, String str1, String str2,
    org.xml.sax.Attributes attributes) throws org.xml.sax.SAXException {
  System.out.println("Element: " + str2);
  for (int i=0; i<attributes.getLength(); i++){
    String name = attributes.getQName(i);
    String value = attributes.getValue(i);
    System.out.println("  Attribute: " + name + " = " + value);
  }
}
```

One more step, configuring execution parameters for the parser, and we'll be ready for a test. Open the Properties sheet for *Inventory_InventoryParser.java*. Click the Execution tab. Set the **Arguments** property to *Inventory.xml*. Invoke the Customizer dialog for the Executor property by clicking the value and then the ellipsis button. Click the Expert tab of the Customizer dialog to expose the **Working Directory** property. Set **Working Directory** to the directory that contains the *Inventory.xml* file, presumably the same as the source directory in which we've been working.

Finally, we're ready to test the completed SAX parser. Right-click **Inventory_InventoryParser.java** and select **Execute** from the context menu. If all goes well, the IDE will switch to the Running workspace, open an Output Window, and produce the results shown in Example 11-8.

Example 11-8. Output from Inventory_InventoryHandlerImpl

```
Element: Inventory
  Attribute: Description = Kit Inventory
Element: Kit
  Attribute: Description = The first kit
Element: Part
  Attribute: Description = Part A
  Element Data: Part A in Kit
Element: Supplier
  Attribute: Description = Our favorite supplier
Element: Part
  Attribute: Description = Part A
  Element Data: Part A in Supplier
Element: Part
  Attribute: Description = Part A
  Attribute: Size = Just right
  Attribute: Color = Purple
  Element Data: Part A alone
```

Generating a DOM Tree Scanner

And here we have the process for creating a basic Document Object Model (DOM) Tree Scanner. Like the SAX Document Handler above, it will list the attributes and text in our *Inventory.xml* document. But it will also make a small change to the attribute values to prove that the output is not exactly the same as the input. Our DOM Tree Scanner will change the input by prepending a coded abbreviation for each attribute's qualified name to the attribute's value. Finally, our DOM Tree Scanner will output XML data showing the modified attribute values.

We will start, just as with the SAX Document Handler, by generating the source, adding some code to display the input data, and running a test to verify the results. Then, we will code to output the attribute values and output the modified XML document. The output will be in the same format as the input but with slightly different data.

To generate the source, right-click the DTD file **Inventory_Inventory** and then select **Generate DOM Tree Scanner** from the context menu. Accept the default name *Inventory_InventoryScanner*. Add a main method. Type or paste Example 11-9 into *Inventory_InventoryScanner.java*. This code was adapted from the example in the comments near the top of the generated source, just after the package statement. Notice that similar comments are sprinkled throughout the source, code examples that could be uncommented to gain access to data parsed out of the XML input.

Example 11-9. main method for Inventory_InventoryScanner

```java
public static void main(String[] args) throws Exception {
  javax.xml.parsers.DocumentBuilderFactory builderFactory =
    javax.xml.parsers.DocumentBuilderFactory.newInstance();
  javax.xml.parsers.DocumentBuilder builder =
```

Example 11-9. main method for Inventory_InventoryScanner (continued)

```
    builderFactory.newDocumentBuilder();
  org.w3c.dom.Document document =
    builder.parse (new org.xml.sax.InputSource (args[0]));
  Inventory_InventoryScanner scanner =
    new Inventory_InventoryScanner (document);
  scanner.visitDocument();
}
```

The generated source includes a method to process each element in the XML document, and each method includes logic to process the element's attributes. Each method is different, but they all have a structure similar to visitElement_Part shown in Table 11-1. We will augment the generated source as instructed in the following text and tables.

We need to add logic to print the name of each element. Search the source for occurrences of the following commented line. This line is one of the comments sprinkled throughout the source that shows how to access the data parsed from the XML input.

```
    // element.getValue();
```

Add the print statements shown in Table 11-1 right after the commented lines that were found. Or replace the commented lines with the new statements, if you prefer.

Table 11-1. Printing element names in Inventory_InventoryScanner

Method	Print statement
visitElement_Inventory	System.out.println("Element: Inventory");
visitElement_Kit	System.out.println("Element: Kit");
visitElement_Part	System.out.println("Element: Part");
visitElement_Supplier	System.out.println("Element: Supplier");

We need to add logic to print the attribute names and values. Search the source for occurrences of the following commented line. Again, this is one of the comments sprinkled throughout the source that shows how to access the data parsed from the XML input:

```
    // attr.getValue();
```

Add the print statements shown in Table 11-2 right after the commented lines that were found. Or replace the commented lines with the new statements, if you prefer.

Table 11-2. Printing attribute values in Inventory_InventoryScanner

Method	Attribute	Print statement
visitElement_Inventory	Description	System.out.println(" Attribute: Description = " + attr.getValue());
visitElement_Kit	Description	System.out.println(" Attribute: Description = " + attr.getValue());

Method	Attribute	Print statement
visitElement_Part	Description	System.out.println(" Attribute: Description = " + attr.getValue());
visitElement_Part	Color	System.out.println(" Attribute: Color = " + attr.getValue());
visitElement_Part	Size	System.out.println(" Attribute: Size = " + attr.getValue());
visitElement_Supplier	Description	System.out.println(" Attribute: Description = " + attr.getValue());

Finally, we need to add logic to print the data for each element. This is easy in our example because only the **Part** element has data. Search the source for occurrences of the following commented line:

```
// ((org.w3c.dom.Text)node).getData();
```

Add the print statements shown in Table 11-3 right after the commented line that was found. Or replace the commented line with the new statement, if you prefer.

Table 11-3. Printing element data in Inventory_InventoryScanner

Method	Print statement
visitElement_Part	System.out.println(" Element Data: " + ((org.w3c.dom.Text)node).getData());

Now, configure execution parameters for the scanner, just as you did in the previous section for the parser. Open the Properties sheet for *Inventory_InventoryScanner. java*, click the Execution tab, and set the **Arguments** property to *Inventory.xml*. Invoke the Customizer dialog for the Executor property by clicking the value and then the **...** button, click the Expert tab of the Customizer dialog to expose the **Working Directory** property, and set **Working Directory** to the directory that contains the *Inventory.xml*, the same as the source directory. It's time to test. Compile and execute Inventory_InventoryScanner. The results should match Example 11-8.

Next, add code to make a slight modification to the data values, just enough to prove that they're different when the new XML is output later. Locate the statements that you added to print the attribute values. Before each statement that you located, add a new statement to change the value of the data. We want to prove that the data was changed when it's output again later. Add statements that invoke attr.setValue as shown in Table 11-3. For example, to see what visitElement_Part looks like with all changes in place, see Table 11-4.

Table 11-4. Modifying attribute values in Inventory_InventoryScanner

Method	Attribute	Statement to modify data
visitElement_Inventory	Description	attr.setValue("ID:" + attr.getValue());
visitElement_Kit	Description	attr.setValue("KD:" + attr.getValue());
visitElement_Part	Description	attr.setValue("PD:" + attr.getValue());
visitElement_Part	Color	attr.setValue("PC:" + attr.getValue());

Table 11-4. Modifying attribute values in Inventory_InventoryScanner (continued)

Method	Attribute	Statement to modify data
visitElement_Part	Size	attr.setValue("PS:" + attr.getValue());
visitElement_Supplier	Description	attr.setValue("SD:" + attr.getValue());

Near the end of the visitElement_Part method locate the statement that prints the value of data in a Part node. Before the print statement add a statement invoking node.setData to change the text data, as shown in Example 11-10. The entire method is given to show all the added code in context.

Example 11-10. visitElement_Part method with all changes applied

```java
/** Scan through org.w3c.dom.Element named Part. */
void visitElement_Part(org.w3c.dom.Element element) { // <Part>
  // element.getValue();
  System.out.println("Element: Part");
  org.w3c.dom.NamedNodeMap attrs = element.getAttributes();
  for (int i = 0; i < attrs.getLength(); i++) {
    org.w3c.dom.Attr attr = (org.w3c.dom.Attr)attrs.item(i);
    if (attr.getName().equals("Description")) { // <Part Description="???">
      // attr.getValue();
      attr.setValue("PD:" + attr.getValue());
      System.out.println(" Attribute: Description = " + attr.getValue());
    }
    if (attr.getName().equals("Color")) { // <Part Color="???">
      // attr.getValue();
      attr.setValue("PC:" + attr.getValue());
      System.out.println(" Attribute: Color = " + attr.getValue());
    }
    if (attr.getName().equals("Size")) { // <Part Size="???">
      // attr.getValue();
      attr.setValue("PS:" + attr.getValue());
      System.out.println(" Attribute: Size = " + attr.getValue());
    }
  }
  org.w3c.dom.NodeList nodes = element.getChildNodes();
  for (int i = 0; i < nodes.getLength(); i++) {
    org.w3c.dom.Node node = nodes.item(i);
    switch (node.getNodeType()) {
      case org.w3c.dom.Node.CDATA_SECTION_NODE:
        // ((org.w3c.dom.CDATASection)node).getData();
        break;
      case org.w3c.dom.Node.ELEMENT_NODE:
        org.w3c.dom.Element nodeElement = (org.w3c.dom.Element)node;
        if (nodeElement.getTagName().equals("Inventory")) {
          visitElement_Inventory(nodeElement);
        }
        if (nodeElement.getTagName().equals("Kit")) {
          visitElement_Kit(nodeElement);
        }
```

```
            if (nodeElement.getTagName().equals("Part")) {
              visitElement_Part(nodeElement);
            }
            if (nodeElement.getTagName().equals("Supplier")) {
              visitElement_Supplier(nodeElement);
            }
            break;
        case org.w3c.dom.Node.PROCESSING_INSTRUCTION_NODE:
            // ((org.w3c.dom.ProcessingInstruction)node).getTarget();
            // ((org.w3c.dom.ProcessingInstruction)node).getData();
            break;
        case org.w3c.dom.Node.TEXT_NODE:
            // ((org.w3c.dom.Text)node).getData();
            ((org.w3c.dom.Text)node).setData("PT:" +
                            ((org.w3c.dom.Text)node).getData());
            System.out.println(" Element Data: " +
                            ((org.w3c.dom.Text)node).getData());
            break;
        }
      }
    }
```

We're almost done. Let's take a moment to compile and test. The new output should show our modifications to the input data.

Finally, we'll add more code to output the modified XML data. We will use a `Transformer` object to copy the document with its modified data to an output stream. Add code to the `main` method so that it matches Example 11-11.

Example 11-11. main method with all changes applied

```
public static void main(String[] args) throws Exception {
  javax.xml.parsers.DocumentBuilderFactory builderFactory =
    javax.xml.parsers.DocumentBuilderFactory.newInstance();
  javax.xml.parsers.DocumentBuilder builder =
    builderFactory.newDocumentBuilder();
  org.w3c.dom.Document document =
    builder.parse (new org.xml.sax.InputSource (args[0]));
  Inventory_InventoryScanner scanner =
    new Inventory_InventoryScanner (document);
  scanner.visitDocument();

  // Output modified Inventory.xml
  TransformerFactory tranFact = TransformerFactory.newInstance();
  Transformer tran = tranFact.newTransformer();
  DOMSource DSource = new DOMSource(document);
  StreamResult SResult = new StreamResult(System.out);
  tran.transform(DSource, SResult);
}
```

Add the import statements in Example 11-12 after the package statement at the top.

Example 11-12. Import statements for Transformer references

```
import javax.xml.transform.*;
import javax.xml.transform.dom.*;
import javax.xml.transform.stream.*;
```

Compile and execute. Your output window should match Example 11-13 (except for a couple of line breaks added for readability). At the top is the data extracted and then modified from the input XML document. Next is the new XML document showing the modified data.

Example 11-13. Output from Inventory_InventoryScanner

```
Element: Inventory
  Attribute: Description = ID:Kit Inventory
Element: Kit
  Attribute: Description = KD:The first kit
Element: Part
  Attribute: Description = PD:Part A
  Element Data: PT:Part A in Kit
Element: Supplier
  Attribute: Description = SD:Our favorite supplier
Element: Part
  Attribute: Description = PD:Part A
  Element Data: PT:Part A in Supplier
Element: Part
  Attribute: Description = PD:Part A
  Attribute: Size = PS:Just right
  Attribute: Color = PC:Purple
  Element Data: PT:Part A alone

<!-- Created by vaughn on May 11, 2002, 9:01 PM -->
<Inventory Description="ID:Kit Inventory">
    <Kit Description="KD:The first kit">
        <Part Description="PD:Part A">PT:Part A in Kit</Part>

    </Kit>
    <Supplier Description="SD:Our favorite supplier">
        <Part Description="PD:Part A">PT:Part A in Supplier</Part></Supplier>
    <Part Description="PD:Part A" Size="PS:Just right"
                Color="PC:Purple">PT:Part A alone</Part>
</Inventory>
```

These examples give the basics of reading, modifying, and writing XML documents with Java classes. NetBeans makes it easy to access XML documents wherever you find them or to generate your own whenever you need to share data with other applications. Just remember to use a SAX document handler if serial read access is adequate, especially when speed and memory are critical. Use a DOM tree scanner if you need random access to the data elements in the XML document, if you need to update the data, or if you need to generate a new document. SAX document handlers are widely used in web applications, where resources are tight. Keep that in mind while you're reading the next chapter.

## CHAPTER 12

Developing Web Applications

Why the IDE Supports Web Application Development

Most basic IDEs associated with Java programming provide developers with the tools necessary to create, execute, and debug Java programs. These features have met requirements over the years because Java was traditionally associated with *.java* files and applications were traditionally developed as independent entities with local scope. With the emergence of the Java 2 Enterprise Edition platform, however, the Java language has been transformed, and a myriad of new standards and methodologies have been adopted. These changes have consequently upped the ante for development environments. The plain vanilla "write a Java applet or class file" IDE simply won't suffice in the modern Java world. Developers need an IDE that provides support for the new and emerging J2EE standards. This typically means supporting Web Application (JSPs and servlets) and Enterprise JavaBean development.

At the time of this writing, the NetBeans IDE has support for developing J2EE Web Applications with the JSP/Servlet module. EJB development is not currently supported in NetBeans. Sun ONE Studio 4, Enterprise Edition for Java (formerly Forte for Java), which is based on NetBeans, provides support for advanced EJB development.

How the IDE Provides Web Application Support

NetBeans provides support for web applications with the JSP/Servlet module. This module can be installed using the IDE's Auto Update feature, or you can download the associated JAR and manually install it. To see if the module is already installed, you can check the list of modules by expanding the Modules node found in **Tools →
Options**. The module is active if it appears in this list and its Enabled property is set to true.

The JSP/Servlet module allows you to develop J2EE web application components using the IDE and provides the Tomcat Application Server as a container for your components to be executed and debugged in. Table 12-1 shows a listing of some of the important features, configuration options, actions, and services that are added to the IDE by the module. These features will be described in detail throughout this chapter.

Table 12-1. Features added by the JSP/Servlet module

Feature	Location	Description
Templates	IDE Menu: File → New	A collection of templates that provide skeleton code for developing complete web application components such as JSPs, Servlets, HTML pages, and other web resources
JSP/Servlet Executor	IDE Menu: Tools → Options, Server Execution Options node.	Executes JSPs, Servlets, and web applications in the Tomcat Application Server
WAR Packager	IDE Menu: Tools → Export WAR File (while a Web Application node is selected in the project or filesystem view).	Provides a wizard for packaging a web application into a Web Archive (WAR) that can be deployed to another J2EE compliant application server.

Creating a Web Application

A web application is a collection of servlets, JSPs, HTML files, and other web-related resources (for example, image and audio files). Web applications are identified by their directory structure defined in the Java Servlet Specification version 2.2. The specification states that a valid directory structure must contain a subdirectory called *WEB-INF*, which may optionally contain two other directories called *lib* and *classes*. Furthermore, the *WEB-INF* directory must contain an XML file called *web.xml*. This file is known as the deployment descriptor and can be used to configure the web application.

In the IDE, a filesystem is identified as a web application if it conforms to the afore-mentioned directory structure. Therefore, any existing filesystem with a *WEB-INF* subdirectory containing a valid *web.xml* will be viewed as a web application in the IDE. If a filesystem does not conform to the specification, it can be easily converted to a web application and the necessary subdirectories will be created. The process of converting an existing filesystem into a web application is also known as creating a web module.

To create a web module, right-click on the root directory of a filesystem and select **Tools**. Select **Convert Filesystem into Web Module** from the submenu. You should then see a message box with the prompt **Convert this Filesystem into a J2EE Web Module?**. Click the **OK** button to continue. You will be presented with another message box with the message **Alternate view on web module installed in Project**. This message is informing you about the two views that the IDE maintains for web applications. More on these two views will be covered later in this section; for now click the **OK** button to continue.

If you expand the filesystem, you should see the *WEB-INF* directory that was created by the IDE. Expand the *WEB-INF* directory and you will see the *classes* and *lib* directories. Figure 12-1 shows this directory structure. These directories should be empty. Finally you should see the *web.xml* file in the *WEB-INF* directory. If you have the XML support module installed, you should be able to expand this file and view the elements of the deployment descriptor. These elements will be explained in more detail later in this section and used throughout this chapter.

Figure 12-1. A web application directory structure in Filesystems view

The IDE maintains two views of your web application—a Filesystems view and a Web Project view.

The Filesystems View

The Filesystems view allows you to see the files in your web application as you would if you were browsing them in a file browser such as Windows Explorer or Midnight Commander. JSPs, servlets, and other web-related files can be added in the same way that they are added to other mounted filesystems. In fact, web applications have no special distinction from other mounted filesystems in the Filesystems view. For J2EE web module-related features such as configuring the deployment descriptor, deploying your web application, and executing it in the Tomcat application server, you will need to work in the Web Project view, as shown in Figure 12-2.

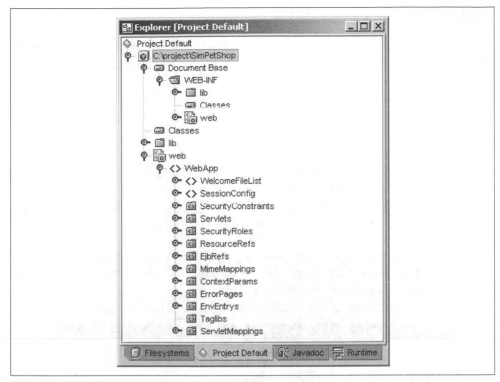

Figure 12-2. The Web Project view

The Web Project View

In the Web Project view, a web module is identified by a special icon and the name of it's root folder in the Filesystems view. A similar file listing is used except for the addition of a special folder called "Document Base." This folder represents the root folder for adding your application files and is simply a pointer to the file structure you saw in the Filesystems view. When you need to add files to your application from the Web Project view, you will right-click on this folder and proceed with adding the file as if you were using the Filesystems view. The folders *lib* and *classes* are also identified in this view. They are both pointers to the same directories found in the Filesystems view and also in the Document Base directory. The Web Project view allows you to do more with your application than merely add files. It provides you with the functionality to develop, deploy, debug, and manage a J2EE web application. It is recommended that you use this view as the primary Explorer view when developing J2EE web-related applications. To access the Web Project view, select the Project tab in the Explorer.

While developing in this view, you will have access to special actions specific to web application development. These actions are located in the Tools context menu when you right-click on the web module root (identified by the special icon). Throughout this chapter we will be working in the Web Project view to develop web applications.

Working with JSP and HTML Files

You are now ready to begin adding JSP and HTML files to your web application. New files are added using templates. The IDE provides several templates for creating new web application files. Table 12-2 shows the current set of web application templates available and a description of their intended purpose.

Table 12-2. Templates for creating web application files

Template name	Description
JSP	Allows you to create JSP files with JSP and HTML syntax coloring and code completion.
Servlet	Provides a template java file for servlets.
Web Module	A template for creating new web applications. Your project can contain several web applications that can be added to a server configuration module or run independently.

To add a new JSP page to the application click on the Document Base folder in the Project view to select it; then select **File → New** from the IDE menubar. You should see a dialog box similar to the one shown in Figure 12-3.

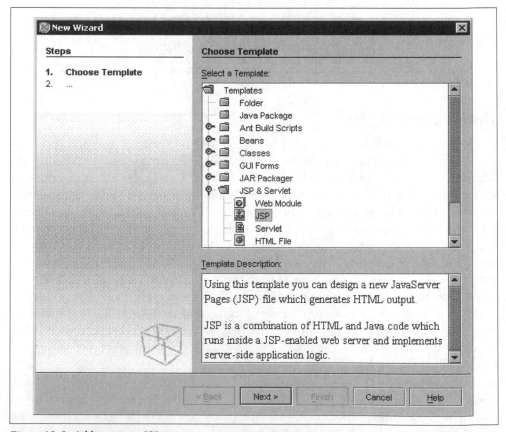

Figure 12-3. Adding a new JSP

This is the template chooser dialog. The template chooser contains all the templates that are available in the IDE and allows you to create new files.

Expand the JSP & Servlet node to view the templates available for common web application files.

Select JSP from the Template Chooser and click OK. Name the file *index* (.jsp will be added automatically) and click Finish in the New JSP file Wizard. The Source Editor should open, showing you the source of the *index.jsp* file. Because the file was created from the JSP template, it will contain the minimum source code for a valid HTML file. Modify your newly created JSP to match Example 12-1.

Example 12-1. Source listing for index.jsp

```
<%@page import="java.util.Date" contentType=
"text/html"%>
<html>
    <head>
        <title>Developed By NetBeans</title>
    </head>
    <body>
        <center><h1>A Trivial Welcome
        Page</h1></center>
        <%="Today's date is " + new Date() %>
    </body>
</html>
```

You can preview JSP files with an external web browser configured, to be launched by the IDE. Right-click on the file in either the Project or Filesystems view and select Execute from the context menu. If you entered the source code shown in Example 12-1, you should see output similar to that shown in Figure 12-4. To add HTML files, follow the same steps for adding JSP files. HTML templates, however, are found in the Other node of the Template Chooser.

Figure 12-4. JSP page in browser

Advanced Web Applications Features

In the previous section we added a simple JSP page to a web application and previewed it with an external browser. Creating and previewing JSPs are the most common tasks for web authors, and NetBeans is well suited for them. However, we have only scratched the surface in terms of the IDE's J2EE web development capabilities. This section includes some of the more advanced features of the IDE's web application development support.

Executing Web Applications

Previously you saw how to execute JSP files individually and preview the HTML with a web browser in the IDE. A web application consists of one or more JSP files (or servlets) and other web resources. The JSP files can be executed directly, or the application can be executed as an entity. The application's deployment descriptor determines what file to run when the web application is executed as an entity. For example, a JSP may be configured as a welcome file, or a servlet mapping may exist that maps the root folder / to a specific servlet that should be executed. To execute the web application go to the Project view; right-click on the web module (root folder) and select **Tools → Execute** from the context menu. You should see output similar to that shown in your IDE's configured web browser.

Working with Servlets

Servlets are an integral part of the J2EE web application specification. A servlet is basically a Java class that is loaded by an application server and is allowed to handle HTTP requests the same way traditional Common Gateway Interface scripts work. JSP technology is hinged on servlets because JSP files are translated to servlets at runtime. The IDE has a tight integration with the Tomcat Servlet Engine that provides support for servlets, the compilation of JSP pages to servlets, and JSP debugging.

Viewing JSPs as servlets

As previously mentioned, JSPs are compiled into servlets at runtime. You may, however, wish to see the servlet code generated for a JSP before running it. To view a JSP's servlet code, select the JSP file in the Explorer, right-click, and select **View as Servlet** from the context menu. The last compiled Java code for the JSP should appear in the current editor. Note that to view the servlet code your JSP must be compiled at least once. For every update of the JSP code you will need to recompile for the changes to be reflected in the corresponding servlet code. Compile the JSP by right-clicking and selecting **Compile** from the context menu.

Adding servlets

Because servlets are class files, they should be added to the *classes* subfolder of your web application. At runtime, the Servlet Engine will find these classes as part of the classpath for the application. Servlets may also be contained in JAR files, in which case the entire JAR file should be copied to the *lib* subfolder of the web application.

Adding a new servlet. To add a new servlet to your web application, right-click on the *classes* folder in the Project view and select **New** → **Servlet & JSP** → **Servlet** from the context menu. You should be see a dialog box similar to the one shown in Figure 12-5. The source window should then open, showing you the source code for your new servlet. The IDE will create a basic servlet with the necessary inheritance and methods.

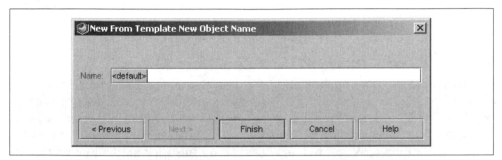

Figure 12-5. Creating a new servlet

Adding an existing servlet. For existing servlets, the task of adding them to your web application in the IDE is simply a matter of copying the class file or JAR file to the appropriate subfolder. Class files should be copied to the *classes* folder, whereas JAR files should be copied to the *lib* folder. Keep in mind that all dependencies of the servlet class, including runtime dependencies in the form of other JAR files and classes, must also be copied to appropriate folders in your web application project.

Executing servlets

Earlier in this chapter you learned how to execute web application and JSP files. Servlets can also be executed directly. The simplest way to run a servlet is to right-click on the servlet file in the Explorer window and select **Execute** from the context menu. The servlet output should be displayed in a browser window.

Passing request parameters

It is common in JSP and servlet development to pass request parameters in a URL. These parameters are often used by the JSP or servlet referenced by the URL to fill in values for variables. The list of request parameters begins after the filename in a URL and is indicated by a question mark followed by a set of name-value pairs, each separated by ampersands. An example URL with request parameters looks like *http://www.someserver.com/index.jsp?name=myName&age=28*. To set request parameters on a servlet or JSP, right-click on the file's node in the Explorer and select **Tools** → **Set Request Parameters**. In the dialog box that opens enter the list of parameters, omitting the question mark. When you execute the servlet or JSP file, the request parameters will be shown in the browser's address bar.

Packaging and Deploying Web Applications

After developing your web application, you'll want to package the files and deploy them to an application server of your choice. Web applications are packaged into WAR files. The IDE can export your web application files as a WAR file. To do so, select the Web Application Module or the root filesystem from the Explorer, right-click, and select **Tools → Export WAR File....** Enter a new filename for the WAR file and select OK.

Deploying Web Applications

The IDE can deploy web applications to a list of applicable servers in the Server Registry. As the NetBeans community grows, more and more application server vendors will be offering modules that will incorporate their servers into the Server Registry. To deploy to a server supplied by a vendor as a module you will have to set it as the default application server for web modules. To do this click on the Runtime tab of the explorer; expand **Server Registry → Default Servers**; right-click on the **Web Module/ Web Module Groups** node and select **Set Default Server** from the context menu. From the dialog box shown in Figure 12-6, select the application server you want to use as a default for web applications.

Once you have selected a default application server, you can deploy your web applications to it by right-clicking on a web module in the project view and selecting **Deploy** from the context menu.

Configuring Tomcat

The IDE contains a list of application servers in the Server Registry. The registry contains an area for default servers and a listing for all the servers currently installed. At the time of this writing the IDE only contains Tomcat as an installed application server.

 The ability to deploy directly to an application server is only available in NetBeans versions 3.3 and higher. If you do not see the windows and options mentioned in this section, you may need to upgrade your NetBeans distribution.

To configure Tomcat from the IDE, go to the runtime tab of the explorer, expand **Server Registry → Installed Servers**, and select the Tomcat 3.2 node (or whichever version of Tomcat is displayed). You should see a Properties pane appear; if not, right-click on the node and select Properties from the context menu. The settings allow you to set the various ports for HTTP and debugging. Figure 12-7 shows the configuration properties for the Tomcat Servlet Engine.

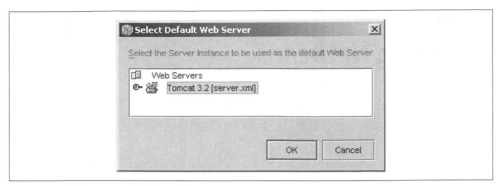

Figure 12-6. Selecting a default application server

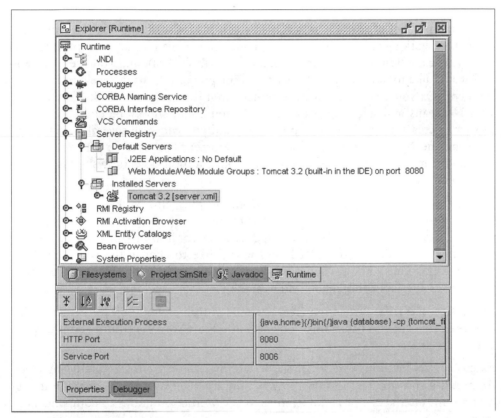

Figure 12-7. Configuring the Tomcat server

Tomcat maintains a configuration file (*server.xml*) that is also accessible via the IDE. To access and modify the configuration file, right-click on the Tomcat Server node and select Open from the context menu. You can then make whatever changes are needed to configure your Tomcat installation.

CHAPTER 13
Extending NetBeans

There any number of reasons to develop extensions to NetBeans. Perhaps you are a developer, working on a project that has some unique needs (such as deployment to a particular application server or use of a code analysis tool), and you use NetBeans and would like to have support for that tool integrated into your development environment. Or you could have a development tool that you would like to integrate with NetBeans and sell as an extension. Or you could simply be embarking on a project to create a large desktop application, and you can save several person-years by using the NetBeans core without its development-tool-specific functionality to handle the menus, windowing, file access, configuration, and browsing aspects of your application.

This half of the book is about writing *modules* to plug into NetBeans to extend its functionality. So it is of particular interest to people developing or using tools for software development, people developing desktop applications in Java, or anyone who simply uses the NetBeans IDE and would like to change the way something works. We assume you have some familiarity with NetBeans as a development tool and its user interface components and with the Java language.

The design of NetBeans is also a great example of well-crafted object-oriented architecture. Odds are good that this book will affect the way you think about how to build software.

Extensions to NetBeans are developed by writing Java code to the NetBeans *Open APIs*. API stands for Application Programming Interface and is the common industry term for interfaces a program exposes to allow other programs or components to interact with it.

Extensive documentation of the NetBeans APIs is available in Javadoc and prose format on the NetBeans web site. This book complements the Open APIs reference documentation; it isn't a replacement. Javadoc is a very good tool for explaining APIs using their package and class structures as its organizing principle, and the Javadoc set for NetBeans contains excellent overviews of each API that cover how to use them. But people do not necessarily think in terms of a class hierarchy structure—generally, they start with a problem to solve. With this book we intend to provide a task-oriented guide to using these APIs. We hope to leave you with a rich understanding of how NetBeans works and the philosophy guiding its design.

What's Different About NetBeans?

Most people know NetBeans as an integrated development environment (IDE) written in Java. Being written in Java, it should (and generally does) run on a Java 2 JVM, version 1.3 or higher. What makes NetBeans different from other development environments is its flexibility. While the first incarnation of it was a tool for Java programming, over three generations of its architecture, it was redesigned to be a generic tools platform to support development in any language, not just Java. The key is its modular design. A basic, generic application runtime that does not even know it is an IDE is implemented in the NetBeans core. Extensions to this framework in the form of modules are what actually make it an IDE. The code editor, the Java language support, and almost everything you see in NetBeans is implemented as a pluggable module.

This means that not only can NetBeans be used as a tool for Java development, people can use the NetBeans core with only modules they've written (and possibly some other NetBeans modules) installed to build a desktop application that might have nothing to do with software development. A number of companies and individuals have done this, and the result is (at the time of this writing) four commercial IDEs that are NetBeans plus some custom modules (Sun's Forte for Java, Compuware's OptimalJ, Compaq NetBeans, and Zucotto's Whiteboard) and applications running the gamut from a CAD tool for designing coal mines (ECSI Minex—*http://www.ecsi.com.au/*), to a tool for managing a hair salon (SalonTango), to a music composition and notation tool (Project XEMO—*http://www.xemo.org/*). By the time you read this, there will no doubt be many more. For an up-to-date list, see the *netbeans.org* third party page (*http://www.netbeans.org/about/third-party.html*).

Since all of the IDE-like behavior of NetBeans is implemented in the form of plug-in modules, you can use the NetBeans core to handle a lot of the grunt work involved in writing a desktop application. Most applications need access to files, need to provide menus and toolbars and windows, and need to store settings. Having the implementation of these things handled for you solidly by the NetBeans core can save a lot of development time and effort. NetBeans is to the desktop much what an application server is to a server computer—where an application server provides an execution context for arbitrary Enterprise JavaBeans, NetBeans provides an execution context for arbitrary modules. Both frameworks are designed to handle commonly needed tasks so you can concentrate on the actual logic.

The Core and the Open APIs

The architecture of NetBeans breaks down into two major sections: The *core* (also referred to as the *application runtime*) and the Open APIs. The core plus the Open APIs make up the NetBeans Platform. These are represented in the org.netbeans.core.* and org.openide.* Java packages, respectively, in the source code for NetBeans. Binary libraries of these packages are part of your installation of NetBeans in the files *$NB_HOME/lib/core.jar* and *$NB_HOME/lib/openide.jar*. The core implements many interfaces defined in the Open APIs and is NetBeans' runtime engine. The Open APIs are the toolset available to module authors who want to write modules to implement functionality that will run inside NetBeans. A module is a *.jar* (Java ARchive or *JAR*) file that contains the module's Java classes and a *manifest* file, which describes the module and how to install and uninstall it, to NetBeans' runtime.

As with any application, for an IDE such architecture has a number of advantages. First is the ability to support multiple languages. Another significant advantage is the ability to wrap the functionality of other development tools and present it within the IDE. The simplest example of this kind of wrapping is the way external compilers and Java virtual machines can be used for compilation and execution by defining services that launch an external process and parse and present the output of that process (for example, compiler error messages). A more complex example would be the integration of a preexisting UML tool to allow seamless interaction with it through Net-Beans' user interface.

A number of the elements of NetBeans, such as the Filesystems, Nodes, and Explorer APIs, can also be used as standalone libraries for client- and server-side Java applications outside NetBeans. In a sense, NetBeans *is* a set of libraries.*

A caveat to this type of design is that no module should call functionality that does not appear in the Open APIs—for example, getting an object with an interface declared in the Open APIs and then casting to a core implementation class to access some method that isn't defined in the APIs. The contract of an API is to provide access to functionality that will continue to work even if the underlying implementation is replaced. This means that there is no guarantee that anything not declared in the Open APIs documentation will be present in future versions of the IDE, and any code using the core implementation classes directly is liable to be broken in some future version of NetBeans. If you need to do something that is inconvenient or not possible with the APIs, on the NetBeans mailing lists (*http://www.netbeans.org/about/community/lists.html*), ask if there is a different approach you should take; if there is not, file an enhancement request in the bug tracking tool (*http://www.netbeans.org/issues/query.cgi*) on the *netbeans.org* web site.

---

* As this book is being written and NetBeans 3.4 is in development, one of the thrusts is to decompose the core into smaller, independent libraries implementing specific APIs. This work will further enable applications to use and distribute only the functionality needed.

The License

Licensing of software and source code determines what other people can and cannot do with that software. The source code to NetBeans is available under a license called the Sun Public License, which is very non-restrictive.

License Compatibility

There are a lot of religious arguments about software licenses, and this book is not going to take a position with regard to them. There are cases where software licenses are "encumbered"—a license places certain obligations on the author of any code using that license, the users of code written under that license, and in some cases, anyone who distributes code under more than one license as a single product. There are situations in which the licenses of two products, if distributed together, place contradictory demands on either the author or the user. These are termed incompatible licenses.

The GNU General Public License (GPL) is one such case—it requires that people distributing software under other licenses along with GPL software apply the GNU license to all software that is packaged with it (requiring them to give away the source code). There is a possibility of something called "dual licensing," which allows users and vendors to choose which license applies where, but this also lands in completely uncharted legal waters.

Because the GPL (requiring all source code to be "free") and the license NetBeans is under (which allows you to give away what you want and sell what you want) are not compatible, it is the requirement of Sun Microsystems' lawyers that incompatibly licensed software not be hosted on *netbeans.org*. Since Sun foots the bill for the site, this legal advice is taken seriously.

If you decide to contribute a module to *netbeans.org*, simply use the same license (*http://www.netbeans.org/about/os/license.html*) as the rest of the NetBeans sources.

Please bear in mind that the authors of this book *are not lawyers*, and none of the licensing-related text in this book should be construed as legal advice. If you are writing software and have questions about how to license it, consult qualified legal counsel.

This license allows you to do as follows:

- Use NetBeans to create commercial or non-commercial software
- Build modules that integrate with NetBeans and sell them or give them away
- Redistribute NetBeans either for free or for sale with your own branding and custom configuration, with additional modules you supply and with removal of any modules you don't want in your distribution.
- Use parts of NetBeans code (for example, the Filesystems library, or the core) in your own applications, commercial or non-commercial.

The Sun Public License (SPL) is a minor variant of the Mozilla Public License (MPL), the license Netscape created when it released the sources to its web browser. The only significant differences are that the word *Netscape* is replaced by *Sun Microsystems* and the license covers open-sourcing the documentation as well, which Netscape did not explicitly do. For the full details (including a diff with the MPL) see *http://www.netbeans.org/about/os/license.html*.

Open Source

NetBeans is an open source project hosted at *http://www.netbeans.org/*. This means that the source code for the entire IDE is available for download. A principle of open source is open communication, and design discussions happen on the public mailing lists at *netbeans.org*. The site is divided into various subproject sites (for example, *http://editor.netbeans.org/*) for the various modules that are part of NetBeans. Decisions are reached by consensus on the mailing lists (see Appendix E for an explanation of how this works in practice); there is a governance board consisting of two members chosen by the community on the mailing lists and one appointed by Sun Microsystems (which donated the code that started the project, employs many of the developers of NetBeans, and financially supports the site's infrastructure). In the event of an intractable dispute, the board exists to make decisions. In practice, issues of such magnitude are extremely rare.

Because it is an open source project, you can also get involved in the ongoing development of NetBeans. Code contributions, patches, and bug fixes are always welcome. To learn more about getting involved in the NetBeans project, see the contributions page (*http://www.netbeans.org/devhome/community/contribute.html*).

If you write a module for NetBeans that you do not intend to sell, but which would be generally useful to the community at large, you have the option of contributing that module to *netbeans.org*. Please do! Assuming a compatible license, the sources can be hosted in CVS, mailing lists set up for discussing the ongoing maintenance of that code and bug categories for the module you created. If you want to do this, send a proposal to the *nbdev@netbeans.org* mailing list about your module, and assuming the consensus is that your module would be a good addition to the NetBeans project, follow the contribution instructions on the web site. See Appendix E for details.

Note that contributing a module involves an ongoing commitment to maintain it—it is never a good idea to contribute a module as a way of abandoning it.

The netbeans.org Web Site

The main pages of the NetBeans web site can be found at *http://www.netbeans.org/*. They include overviews of NetBeans, news from the various subprojects on the site, documentation, bug tracking, and indexes of interesting documents from subprojects such as new feature proposals, how-to's, and FAQs.

The site, which uses an open source infrastructure called SourceCast, is hosted by a company called CollabNet, under contract to Sun Microsystems. As mentioned, NetBeans is modular—a lot of subprojects are part of NetBeans, and if they were all hosted on the top-level web site, the number of documents would quickly become unmanageable. Instead, a module or set of modules has its own web pages on a *virtual host*—a virtual web site with a different name, for example, *http://editor.netbeans.org/* for the pages relating to the code editor. Each module project may have its own mailing lists for development discussion, user questions, and such. Not all do—it is at the discretion of the maintainers of that particular project whether their project needs its own mailing lists. Most projects are small enough that discussion should simply happen on the top-level user and development mailing lists. There is a convention for posting messages of interest only to developers of a single module or topic of interest to a minority of members of a mailing list: Put the topic in square brackets, for example, [performance] Caught exceptions on startup.

There are also several "meta-projects," which are not really modules in their own right, but exist as jumping-off points for related modules that have their own virtual hosts. An example of this is *das.netbeans.org*; DAS stands for Distributed Application Support—the project is mainly a homepage for getting to modules such as CORBA and RMI support. These meta-projects serve to group related modules and keep the initial list of projects confronting visitors to the site from being intimidatingly large.

Additionally, there are a number of subprojects that are not specifically coding-related, such as the *http://qa.netbeans.org/* quality assurance subsite, which has graphs of the bug counts of recent builds, as well as other useful resources. Another interesting site of this type is *http://ui.netbeans.org/*, maintained by Sun's team of human interface engineers, who work to ensure that the user interface to NetBeans is usable and consistent, and do other work such as icon and interaction design.

Registration

While open source sites should and generally do have low barriers to entry, some functions of the site require you to register and get a login ID and password. These include filing bug reports, signing up for mailing lists, and, of course, CVS (Concurrent Versioning System, the tool for storing and accessing source code) and administrative access. One of the purposes for this mechanism is to give people who are the maintainers of a project access permissions to manage their own mailing lists and project subsite, and so that when you file a bug, you'll get an automated email if it's fixed or its status changes.

Bug tracking

Bugs are tracked using Issuezilla, an enhanced version of the Mozilla project's bug tracking tool Bugzilla. Issuezilla lacks some bells and whistles, and has a somewhat intimidating query interface, but is generally usable. Eventually, CollabNet plans to replace it with a new system, but the timetable for this is still undetermined at the time of this writing. Items in Issuezilla are categorized as defects, enhancement requests, or tasks.

A simple query interface is available at *http://www.netbeans.org/devhome/issues.html*. Anyone can anonymously query the bug database; to enter new items in Issuezilla, you will need to register and get a login ID.

Ways to participate

Open source is not just about writing code. There are many ways to participate in an open source community—the simplest is to download a copy of the software and join a mailing list. Open source is about people building software more efficiently by benefiting from each other's expertise. Filing enhancement requests and bug reports and asking and answering questions on mailing lists are as important as writing code. Along with reading this book, we encourage you to subscribe to the *nbdev@netbeans.org*, *dev@openide.netbeans.org*, or *nbusers@netbeans.org* mailing lists and get a sense of what the NetBeans community is like. See the NetBeans Mailing Lists page (*http://www.netbeans.org/devhome/community/mail-top.html*) to sign up.

The netbeans.org FAQs and mailing lists

The mailing lists on *netbeans.org* are particularly useful supplements to the contents of this book. Many subprojects have their own development mailing lists for discussion of development on that particular project (for example, *dev@editor.netbeans.org*).

Another useful resource to supplement this book is the *dev@openide.netbeans.org* mailing list. The *http://openide.netbeans.org/* project is where the ongoing evolution of the Open APIs takes place. If you have questions about how to do something, the use of a particular part of the Open APIs, the APIs documentation, or this book, that is the place to go. As with any mailing list of this type, please check the Frequently Asked Question (FAQ) pages at *http://www.netbeans.org/devhome/docs/index.html*. You may well find the answer to your question there.

You can also read and post to the *netbeans.org* mailing lists via a newsreader, by connecting to *news://news.netbeans.org*. Note that posts from unregistered email addresses are moderated—they need to be approved by someone. So, if you post via a newsreader or by using an email address in the From: field of your email other than the one you registered with, there may be a delay before your first post appears. An increasing amount of "spam" mail is being sent daily to the *netbeans.org* mailing lists—moderators make sure this unwanted email does not end up cluttering the mailboxes of everyone on the mailing lists, hence the need for this protection mechanism.

Another useful resource is the NetBeans weekly newsletter, which is run by volunteers and mailed every Monday to the *nbannounce@netbeans.org* mailing list. It contains summaries of what happened with NetBeans during the previous week, any new contributions, and links to web archives of interesting conversations from the public mailing lists.

For a listing of the top-level mailing lists and a form to allow you to subscribe to them, go to *http://www.netbeans.org/devhome/community/lists.html*. To subscribe to individual project mailing lists, follow the links from the home pages of the projects you are interested in. As with any set of community mailing lists, it pays to lurk a little while before posting, to get a feel for the community and a sense of what subjects are appropriate to each mailing list.

NetBeans for Bean Counters

At the time of this writing, the NetBeans open source project has been running for more than two years. Here are some interesting statistics about it:

- The oldest code in the codebase is from 1997, from NetBeans 2.0.
- The codebase is currently around 800,000 lines of code.
- There have been 386,300 downloads of NetBeans.
- There have been more than a million downloads of Sun Microsystems' distribution of NetBeans, Forte for Java.
- The average number of messages on all the top-level mailing lists combined is around 2,000 messages per-month.
- The combined subscribership count of all top-level mailing lists is about 2,000— of course, by the time you read this, many of these numbers will be even higher.

Getting and Installing the Open APIs Support Module

Not only are there tools to make general Java coding easier within NetBeans, but also there is a module that provides a substantial amount of help with building extensions to the IDE or building applications on the platform. This is the Open APIs Support module. It includes the following:

- Templates for various kinds of objects commonly subclassed in writing extensions, with helpful comments and examples.
- The NetBeans Open APIs Javadoc and prose reference documentation, installed in the IDE's Javadoc repository, so the documentation can be viewed and searched from within the IDE.
- Execution services for commonly used interface components—so instead of having to install a component you're creating into the IDE, you can simply execute the component to test it.
- The Bean Browser, which is rather like the traditional explorer tree, but allows you to browse objects within the internal hierarchy of objects in the IDE, which are not normally exposed by the user interface.
- Support for dynamically reloading modules for testing purposes—it would be awful to have to restart the IDE to test each revision to one's code.
- Structural editing of XML layers (a configuration file most modules use) and graphical access to components and attributes of modules under development in the **Explorer** tree.

You will need the Open APIs Support module to do many of the examples in this book. To get the module, follow these steps:

1. Make sure you have a working Internet connection to download the module.
2. Select **Tools** → **Update Center** off the main menu.

3. If you are behind a firewall, click the **Proxy Configuration** button and enter the proxy configuration information.

 If you are behind a SOCKS firewall, you will need to pass the proxy information to the JVM the IDE is running in. You need to do this when you start the IDE, for example, runide.sh -J-DsocksProxyPort=1080 -J-DsocksProxyHost=socksproxy.foo.com. Note that even if you are behind a SOCKS firewall, you should still be able to use a simple HTTP proxy if one is available—so this is seldom necessary. If you will need to use a SOCKS proxy every time you run NetBeans, create or edit the file called *ide.cfg* in *$NB_HOME/bin* to contain the preceding line switches.

4. Follow the instructions in the Update Center wizard and wait for it to check for new modules.

5. Soon you will see a wizard pane with a list of modules you can add. Select the **Open APIs Support** module and the **Open APIs Support with Ant** module from the list of available modules in the Extensions category, and click **Add**. Click **Next** and follow the instructions on the remaining panels of the wizard, and the module will be downloaded and installed.

For more information see the module's web page (*http://apisupport.netbeans.org/*).

Life Is Change

No piece of software is ever "finished," and this is certainly true of NetBeans. We began writing the book at the beginning of the NetBeans 3.2 release cycle; as this paragraph is being written, 3.3.2 is released, 3.4 is almost ready, and 4.0 looms on the horizon. There are ways to do things in NetBeans today that simplify things compared with the previous release, and there are ways of doing things that were recommended for 3.2 that are now deprecated (but, unless noted in the upgrade guide bundled with the Open APIs documentation, still function). This will be true of future releases as well. Where possible in this book, we project what changes are expected with 3.4 and higher. This book primarily covers NetBeans 3.3.x, though major changes in NetBeans 3.4 are noted where appropriate.

This shouldn't be cause for alarm—great effort is put into making NetBeans backward compatible. What it does mean is that since technical books, particularly about software, are quickly obsolete, it is worth checking the upgrade guides for module authors for versions subsequent to 3.3, and the published errata for this book. For details on the pending changes known at this time, and the general direction in which the NetBeans APIs are evolving, see Appendix D.

Source Code for the Examples

As noted in the preface and throughout the text, sources and compiled module *.nbm* files for the examples in this book can be found at *http://www.oreilly.com/netbeans*.

CHAPTER 14

Understanding the NetBeans APIs

You would think that in writing an IDE the first priority would be an editor—this is a thing that edits files, right? Then you write code for compilation, execution, and so on, and you have an IDE. This is a fine design for a small application. But what happens when you want to, say, integrate source code management with the tool? You find you have to rewrite a lot of your file access code. What about integrating access to databases? You'll need some way to make connections, browse databases, and so on. And interestingly, you'll find a lot of the user-interface code you're writing (select an object representing the database, get some information from it, present it), looks an awful lot like the code you're writing for browsing files...which looks like the code for managing user settings, and so on. Your codebase is growing rapidly (and getting less maintainable in the process), and a lot of it is code to do very similar things.

The team that created NetBeans went through this, as NetBeans 2.0 evolved. As a result, if you are building an application on top of the NetBeans core, you get to benefit from their experience. You can start writing your application with all the problems they encountered already solved for you.

Design Philosophy of NetBeans

NetBeans solves problems like those above through very heavy use of abstractions. For example, when you interact with a file, you will be using a `FileObject`, not an instance of `java.io.File`. When you deal with menu items and toolbar buttons, you will be developing subclasses of `org.openide.util.actions.SystemAction`, not directly interacting with menus and toolbars (though you can create custom components to use if you need them). The preceding problem is solved through an abstraction called *nodes*, which is explained in more detail later. In general, the NetBeans platform provides high-level abstractions to handle the common cases found in development, while allowing the flexibility needed to do something more low-level if the need arises.

There will be times when you may wonder why things are done the way they are. One of the goals of this part of the book is to familiarize you with the abstractions exposed by the Open APIs and how to use them—to start you thinking in terms of these abstractions and, ideally, using the patterns you encounter in NetBeans to create abstractions that solve your own problems.

Abstracting the Abstractions—the Open APIs

The Open APIs are the set of interfaces, defined in the package org.openide and its subpackages, and the specifications (such as for manifest files and XML layers) specified in the Open APIs Javadoc documentation. The Open APIs define how modules interface with NetBeans. The Javadoc (and the prose documentation that accompanies it) is the canonical documentation of the Open APIs. The NetBeans APIs can be broken down into a number of sections based on the roles they play, such as:

Filesystems
    Communication with persistent data storage

Datasystems
    Recognition and interpretation of different types of data

Actions
    User-invokable functionality

Nodes
    Useful hierarchical relationships between data or objects and some aspects of how they are presented to the user

Explorer
    Presentation of hierarchical data structures

Services/Lookup
    Locating objects or services provided by modules, which can be used by other modules or invoked by the user. Services are often used for performing complex operations on groups of objects, such as compilation, execution, or searching.

Window System
    Manipulating and configuring windows and visual components of the user interface

Modularity

Modularity is one of the primary defining design characteristics of NetBeans—the notion that functionality should be discrete and capable of being added and removed painlessly. There is a Modules API, which defines what a module is and how to install and uninstall modules.

Modules can also offer their own APIs so that other modules can use functionality they implement. For example, the XML modules offer basic support for XML documents that can be used by other modules designed to work with specific flavors of XML. For cases like this, there is a way to declare intermodule dependencies. The

NetBeans runtime will not allow a module to be installed if it requires another module that is not present; it will not allow a module to be disabled without also disabling those modules dependent on it.

Standards

One of the most striking aspects of the design and codebase of NetBeans is its use of *standards*. Wherever a standard for doing something existed, the developers of NetBeans opted to use it, rather than reinvent the wheel. For example, module manifest files are based on the Java Versioning Specification, Nodes are conceptually based on the JavaBeans BeanContext specification, and so on. Wherever there was an existing standard or a near match, it was used.

What this adherence to standards achieves is extensibility. As other pieces of code that work with the same standards are created, it is much less difficult to get them to interoperate with NetBeans. It requires greater discipline to adhere to standards than to reinvent the wheel, but doing so gets you maintainability and interoperability, as standards are, by definition, documented, and if something is a standard, others are using it as well.

Hierarchy, Files, and Nodes

In any large, extensible application, you need a way for components of the system to create objects and for other parts of the system to notice and work with them. Additionally, you need a way to present those objects to a user. Think of the example at the beginning of this chapter in which your database access UI looks a lot like your file management UI, which looks a lot like other parts of your UI. Most data formats are structured and have subcomponents, and it's useful to be able to both manipulate and present those subcomponents as contained entities belonging to a parent entity. A generic system is needed that can nonetheless provide data-type-specific functionality.

For the first problem, creating and working with arbitrary objects, there is a convenient and understandable paradigm that arises from operating systems: files. Applications running in an operating system create files on disk and then work with them. The operating system provides the low-level services of creating and accessing files and is not interested in the content of user-created files. Modules in NetBeans are fairly analogous to applications in an operating system, and files are the core metaphor used to manage persistent objects created by modules. NetBeans has a concept of a *filesystem* that, in its basic sense, means a storage area or namespace into which files may be written and from which they can be read. It also has semantics by which a "file" can be a factory for Java objects.

For the second problem, presentation and containment, NetBeans provides a content-agnostic abstraction, the *node*, which is used to handle hierarchical representation of data and presentation of that data in arbitrary ways through a user interface. A Node is not a container for data, so much as a pointer to data. Under the hood, bridging filesystems and nodes are *data objects*, which identify types of data and potentially aggregate multiple related files into a single entity.

Everything Is a File—Virtually

To understand filesystems in the NetBeans paradigm, you will need to stretch your concept of what a filesystem is. A filesystem in NetBeans is a place where you can hierarchically store and read files. But NetBeans does not require that a filesystem absolutely be files on a disk—only that it behave as if it were. This can be accomplished by implementing a set of interfaces defined in the Filesystems API. A filesystem need only satisfy the contract of conforming to those interfaces; how and where the data is physically stored is irrelevant and transparent to code that acts on the files.

A filesystem is effectively a hierarchical *namespace* for named entities that contain data or contain entities that contain data. There is a Service Provider Interface (SPI) for extending NetBeans with alternate types of file storage. As a concrete example (which will be important later in this chapter), NetBeans defines and internally uses XML filesystems which are, for all intents and purposes, analogous to physical files on disk. Additionally, there are extensions to support FTP, CVS, and other types of storage, available in separate modules that plug into NetBeans.

File Attributes

Most people are familiar with the notion of files having attributes, such as whether they are read-write and so on. NetBeans borrows a concept from IBM's OS/2 in allowing files to have arbitrary additional attributes, which can be added to or removed from. In the IDE, this mechanism is used to specify things such as whether a particular compilation or execution service has been specified for a given file. These attributes are stored, for local files, in *.nbattrs* files in the same directory as the files in question. Attributes are stored using XML and Java serialization, so potentially any Java object can be associated with a file attribute.

Once you have virtualized the concept of a filesystem, there are some other useful things you can do. If all you need to do to create a filesystem is to satisfy this contract, why not also have a virtual filesystem that owns a collection of subfilesystems and presents all of them in the same virtual namespace? NetBeans provides a concrete implementation of this in the class MultiFileSystem, part of the Filesystems API. This class allows you to construct a single namespace that merges a set of discrete subfilesystems called *layers* and acts as if the contents of all of them live in the same namespace (as shown in Figure 14-1). If two different layers contain a folder called */MyFolder/* with different contents, listing the contents of the MultiFileSystem's */MyFolder/* gets you the contents of both. For dealing with name collisions (for example, two layers contain different files with the same name and path), MultiFileSystem has a stacking order of *layers*. In the case of a conflict, whichever filesystem is on the top of the stack is the one whose file is returned. Changes written to a MultiFileSystem are written to one or another writable layer. There are also semantics for one filesystem to mask a file that exists in another layer so that it appears not to exist even though one of the merged filesystems underneath contains it. Furthermore, it is possible to insert and remove layers at runtime.

Figure 14-1. MultiFileSystem merging constituent filesystems

Mapping Files to Java Objects

NetBeans is a Java application; simply throwing around lots of files is not terribly useful. Java object instances, on the other hand, are. So NetBeans defines semantics for mapping files to Java as object instances. You can create a file with a name such as *com-mycom-MyClass.instance*. The Datasystems API contains a facility (implemented in a class called InstanceDataObject) to dereference a file with such a name and return an instance of the named class.

Using this infrastructure, files can be factories for Java objects. This infrastructure serves two primary purposes in NetBeans: First, it allows for modules to register objects with the system (for example, adding beans to the **Component Palette** or adding menu items to a menu). Second, it allows objects to be registered without the JVM actually loading the class in question unless it is actually needed, thus saving memory.

On top of this infrastructure is a facility called Lookup. Lookup adds a layer of indirection that allows module code to find objects registered via files in special folders (see Example 14-1) without dealing directly with filesystems.

As we just mentioned in the concept of an XML filesystem, the contents of the filesystem are actually represented in an XML document. In a NetBeans XML filesystem, the XML to add a Java class to a filesystem looks like Example 14-1.

Example 14-1. Adding a .instance to the System Filesystem

```
<filesystem>
  <folder name="Menu">
    <folder name="View">
      <file
        name="org-netbeans-examples-quickpanel-ShowQuickPanelAction.instance"/>
    </folder>
  </folder>
</filesystem>
```

The effect of the preceding example is that when the system creates the main menu, it creates an instance of `org.netbeans.examples.quickpanel.ShowQuickPanelAction`, which supplies the icon and display name for the action on the menu, whose `actionPerformed()` method will be called if the user selects the menu item.

The System Filesystem

Not only does NetBeans use the concept of virtual filesystems for managing user files, it also uses a special virtual filesystem that contains configuration information for NetBeans itself. This is called the system filesystem. Using the convention of *.instance* files and other similar mechanisms to represent Java objects, NetBeans stores a wide variety of information in the system filesystem. For example, the system filesystem contains a folder called */Menu* which contains subfolders with names such as *File* and *Edit*. Those subfolders in turn contain *.instance* files for Java classes which implement the actions that appear in the **File** and **Edit** menus. Modules are free to create their own folders in the system filesystem to store data interesting to them or add objects to folders that have defined meanings within NetBeans. One of the reasons for using the system filesystem is that it allows objects to be declared, but their classes are not actually loaded by the JVM until something needs to use them, thus saving memory. The system filesystem is the general registry for publicly accessible data and objects.

One important aspect of a NetBeans virtual filesystem is that it can fire events to notify the rest of the system when something in it changes. NetBeans listens for changes in the system filesystem, and if, for example, something creates a new *.instance* file in one of the menu folders, that new item will appear on the menu.

Module Layers

The primary way modules install their functionality into the runtime environment is via files—specifically via virtual files defined in the module's XML filesystem layer (or *module layer*). This is a small XML document in the module's JAR, conforming to the NetBeans filesystems DTD. It is declared in the module's JAR manifest. Since NetBeans' infrastructure allows files to actually map to Java class instances, what a module generally installs is class instances, using the *.instance* file convention just described. The files are put into folders in the system filesystem that have defined meanings to the system or to a module. The XML layer defines a hierarchy of files and folders which may or may not overlap with existing folders in the system filesystem. When a module is loaded, this small XML filesystem is merged with the system filesystem, shown in Figure 14-2.

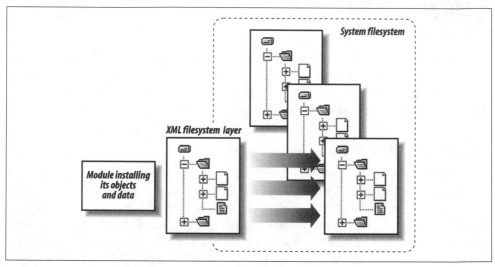

Figure 14-2. Module adding XML layer to the system filesystem

Often a module needs to install objects that should be available to the runtime (such as action classes that define menu items to appear on the main menu), or to other modules (for example, services such as Java compilation). The system filesystem provides a way to do this that allows loose coupling between the modules and the system—neither the runtime nor other modules need to have been coded to anticipate the presence of these specific objects.

When a module is removed, its XML layer is cleanly extracted from the system filesystem, and the objects, menu items, services and such that it contained simply disappear from the system. For a more detailed overview of the semantics and implementation details, see Chapter 15.

Layers in the System Filesystem

Earlier we mentioned a class called MultiFileSystem, which could present a set of filesystems as if they were one—indeed, we've already mentioned that this is how the merging of XML layers to create the system filesystem is accomplished. But there is more to it. The system filesystem is composed of three distinct layers, which determine where settings are stored.

The system filesystem is composed of three outer layers of MultiFileSystem as follows:

Default or Global

This is a MultiFileSystem that contains the contents of the *system/* subdirectory of the directory in which NetBeans is installed. The contents of this filesystem are merged with any XML filesystems from modules that are bundled with Net-Beans. Changes to this layer will propagate to all users using a shared copy of NetBeans.

Session or User

This is the content of the user's settings directory. On Unix systems this might be the *nbuserVERSION/system* or *nbdev/system* subdirectory of the user's home directory* (the folder name is *nbdev* or *nbuser* and a version number depending on whether the build is a development build or a stable release). On Windows systems, the *runide.exe* launcher prompts the user for this directory the first time NetBeans is run.† The session layer is where things such as window positions, editor colorings, and the like are stored—settings that are specific to one user and should not be applied globally.

Project

The project layer contains settings that apply to the current project (which comprises a set of files, window positions, and so forth). It is designed to store settings relating to a given project. At the time of this writing, project support is still evolving toward NetBeans 4.0. The current location of project files is *$HOME/ nbuserVERSION/Projects/PROJECT_NAME/system/*, but this is subject to change once sharable projects are available. As with the Session layer, the directory name may be called *nbuser* or *nbdev*, depending on the type of build, followed by the version.

Note that as of NetBeans 3.4, NetBeans user directories live in a *.netbeans* directory off the user's home directory, such as *$HOME/ .netbeans/3.4dev>*. For other differences likely to be found in Net-Beans 3.4 and later releases, see Appendix D.

The system filesystem is a MultiFileSystem containing other MultiFileSystems, as shown in Figure 14-3.

---

* On NetBeans 3.4 and later, these directories are placed inside a *.netbeans* directory in the user's home directory.

† On all systems, the location of this directory can be overridden on startup by adding the line switch -userdir some_directory/. NetBeans 3.4 changes the default locations somewhat, but you can always select a user directory with this switch.

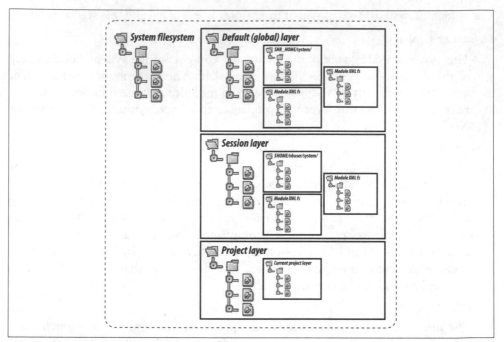

Figure 14-3. Structure of the system filesystem

Exploring the System Filesystem

To really get a sense of what lives in the system filesystem, you need to actually explore it. By default it is hidden from the **Filesystems** tab in **Explorer**. Try the following:

1. In the main **Explorer** window, go to the **Filesystems** tab, right-click the root filesystems node labeled **Filesystems** to bring up the context menu.

2. Select **Customize** from the pop-up menu. A dialog box will appear in which you can choose which filesystems are visible in the **Filesystems** tab of the **Explorer** window.

3. Find the node labeled **Default System** and click it to select it.

4. On the adjacent property sheet in the customizer dialog box, find the **Hidden** property and set it to False.

5. Close the dialog box and browse the system filesystem by opening folders within it in **Explorer** (see Figure 14-4).

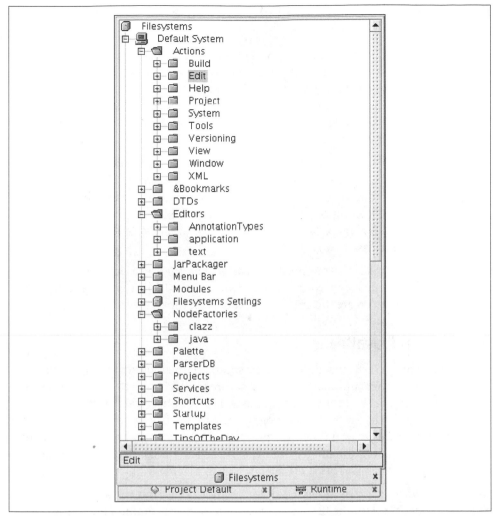

Figure 14-4. The system filesystem viewed from the Explorer window

 When you browse the system filesystem in the **Explorer** window, the names you see for folders and files are the *display names*. These can be localized, and are not necessarily the same as their programmatic names. If you want to add an object to the system filesystem, you need to use the programmatic name for the folder in which it should be placed. This programmatic name is easily seen in the property sheet: select the folder and look at the value of the **Name** property.

Data Objects—Wrappers for Persistent Data

The high-level view of NetBeans design is that it is a tool to edit and otherwise interact with *data objects*. An abstraction and Java class called DataObject exists to represent objects that contain modifiable data, and to provide ways to modify that data. DataObjects are part of the Datasystems API—modules register DataLoaders, which are responsible for creating DataObjects for files of a given type. Generally, your code will deal more with DataObjects that represent files (and provide structural programmatic access to their content), as opposed to working directly with files.

DataObjects provide the additional layer of indirection between files and Nodes; these objects identify what type of data a file contains (for example, Java source code, HTML, text, Java bytecode), and they provide ways to interact with that file appropriate to its data type. Additionally, a DataObject may be a wrapper for multiple files, such as a Java class file and a Java source file, which are in most cases more usefully treated as a single entity.

Modules install MIMEResolvers and DataLoaders. The MIMEResolvers identify a file's MIME type (file format, for example, text/plain). The MIME type determines what DataLoader is used to create the appropriate DataObject for a given file.

NetBeans and JavaBeans

The model behind NetBeans' design can be summed up as *everything is a bean*. JavaBeans have properties and methods—you can read or change their properties, and ask them to do things by calling their methods. If you've used the NetBeans IDE, you may have noticed that most of the objects you interact with (for example, in the **Explorer** tree, **Debugger** window, or **Options** dialog) have property sheets to manipulate them and actions (methods) that can be called on by right-clicking them to bring up a context menu. This is the bean model in action.

As we mentioned, there is the issue of hierarchy of containment and presentation. The file metaphor solves the first piece of the equation—a common infrastructure for storing both user data files and system and session settings internal to the IDE. A filesystem is hierarchical and employs a tree structure; however, it is not flexible enough for all of the presentation and containment issues a large application is likely to face. There are times when it is desirable to restrict the files or objects that are visible, such as when the user should select a folder but not be able to select files inside folders. It is often useful to present different views of a data object, appropriate to the task the user is performing. There are cases in which you might want to present the same object as being the child of different containers, depending on the task. The semantics of a filesystem are not flexible enough to address all of these issues, and while data objects aggregate files, they are not hierarchical.

What is needed is a generic hierarchical, tree-like containment paradigm that is agnostic as to what kinds of things it is representing, and that doesn't force any particular constraints on what can and can't be a parent. An abstraction called *nodes* solves this problem.

Nodes—the Application as Hierarchy

Both user data files and objects internal to the IDE are most often represented to the user via Nodes—tree structures. Nodes are what you see rendered in the **Explorer**, **Debugger**, and **Options** windows, to name a few places. Almost every object you interact with in the IDE is something represented by Nodes, even if the interface to that object is not a tree-based control. Nodes are similar to JavaBeans components in that they have properties and methods. Unlike ordinary JavaBeans components, the properties and methods can change dynamically at runtime. Also, Nodes can be cut, copied, and pasted and can support context-sensitive documentation.

A Node is an object that implements the interface org.openide.nodes.Node. Nodes provide the following features:

- A list of other Nodes that are its children—which live below it in the hierarchy.

- One or more sets of *properties*. Properties are arbitrarily named Java objects that represent attributes of the object (such as a file) that a Node represents. They are instances of the class Node.Property. Node properties are very much like the Java-Beans concept of properties, except that the set of properties can change dynamically at runtime.

- Other arbitrary Java objects that provide access to the data or object the Node represents are called *cookies* in the NetBeans paradigm. Code can ask for a Node instance if it possesses a Cookie of a particular class and then fetch that Cookie and cast it to the requested class.

  Cookies provide a dynamic multiple inheritance for Nodes and DataObjects (DataObjects also possess Cookies).

- A list of *actions* that can be performed upon the Node.

- Notification of changes in the available cookies, properties, or actions available on a Node.

In the course of writing your own functionality for NetBeans, you may need to create Node subclasses or instances. If the notion of writing a class that explicitly declares Node.Property objects for each property you want to expose sounds intimidating, consider using org.openide.nodes.BeanNode, a Node subclass that simply wraps any JavaBean class and presents its properties as Node.Property objects using introspection. You still have the option of a more complex implementation if that better serves your needs. Also available is org.openide.nodes.AbstractNode, an abstract base class that handles the localized display name and icon that should be exposed in the user interface. It also gives you complete flexibility with regard to implementing behavior, properties, children, and so on, while handling the more common cases with minimal required coding. The Open APIs contain many such base classes that can speed development.

An important distinction to remember is that Nodes are a *presentation layer*—a Node is more like a pointer to some other object, such as a DataObject representing a Java source file or a JavaBean whose properties are persistent settings the user may need to configure. A Node does not directly contain data, but exposes the properties of the underlying object and provides a way to locate interesting interfaces to interact with the data the Node represents (such as the logical structure of a Java file's source code or an interface with a method to open that file in the editor). Nodes are not visual components; as discussed in the next section, NetBeans also provides a flexible and generic visualization toolkit for presenting Nodes in the user interface with the Explorer API.

Presenting Nodes to the User—Explorer

Having a nonvisual tree structure is not useful without a way to represent it in a user interface. It is generally considered good programming practice to separate the presentation of data from the data, and NetBeans does this. Nodes provide the underlying structure, and NetBeans provides a toolkit for rendering Nodes on screen in the *Explorer API*. This API accomplishes two things:

- Provides visual components that display Nodes in a variety of ways (trees, lists, menus, combo boxes, and so on)
- Provides a concept of *context*—the notion that at any time, some Nodes will be active (selected), and the user interface should present functionality appropriate to what is active (for example, enabling or disabling compile or save actions in menus according to whether the active Node can be compiled or saved)

The visual classes in the Explorer API can be used as they are or subclassed to modify the way data is displayed.

The abstraction of *explorer views* sits at the heart of NetBeans' user interface. Many components you interact with in NetBeans are explorer views. An explorer view is a user interface component that is connected to a *root node* and visually renders it (and optionally its child Nodes). The window called **Explorer** that you see when you first start NetBeans is a window containing tabs that show explorer views rooted on different Nodes.

Many visual components in NetBeans are explorer views of one type or another—the package chooser in the **New** wizard, which is where you can choose to create new files; the list of breakpoints in the debugger window; and the **New** menu are only a few examples. Explorer views are not limited to the tree-style view you see in the main **Explorer** window—the Explorer API supplies a rich set of user interface components that module authors can use or subclass to display hierarchies of Nodes as menus, drop-down list components, lists, and more. Module authors can also create their own custom explorer view components, but more often it is possible to simply use the existing view components by creating custom Nodes.

For another example of the myriad uses of the Nodes and explorer views, right-click the tabs on the main window that allow you to switch workspaces. Choose **Customize Workspaces** from the context menu. The dialog box that pops up contains an explorer view window showing the hierarchy of workspaces. In fact, if you were to open **Tools → Options → IDE Configuration → Look and Feel**, you would notice a node called **Workspaces** with the same contents as the configuration window that just popped up—both are views of the same underlying Node.

MVC Architecture

The essence of this style of design is a paradigm called *Model-View-Controller*, which was first developed at Xerox's Palo Alto Research Center in the late 1970s, and first found its way into programming in the Smalltalk language. If you have worked with Swing components, you have seen a variant of this design style. The idea is that the most flexible design for user interfaces is that what the user interacts with should be made up of three components:

A model
> Encapsulates data or useful functionality or both. An example of this in NetBeans is a DataObject, which represents files that contain user-modifiable data, for example, source code.

A view
> A visual component that presents the contents of the model to the user. An example of this in NetBeans is any of the classes in the org.openide.explorer.view package, which are visual classes that can display an arbitrary subsection of the nodes hierarchy in one way or another.

A controller
> An object through which the view and model communicate. In NetBeans, this corresponds to nodes themselves—they are pointers to model-like objects, not containers for data in and of themselves, and an explorer view presents the underlying model to the user by presenting a hierarchy of nodes.

The result of such a design is that you get a huge amount of flexibility and code reuse. Any of the three components of MVC architecture can be replaced without the others needing to be reworked or redesigned. It is the MVC paradigm that forms the foundation of NetBeans' architecture, as shown in Figure 14-5.

User-Level Customization

You can do quite a bit of customization to NetBeans without writing any code. When you open **Tools → Options → IDE Configuration → Look and Feel** you are

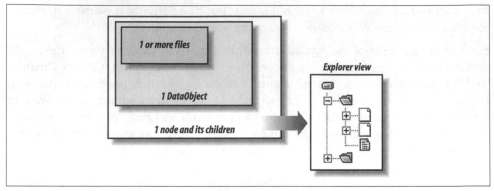

Figure 14-5. Architectural domains underlying nodes

presented with a tree view of a set of nodes in a window with an attached property sheet.[*] If you read the section discussing the system filesystem, you may have already guessed that these nodes literally represent folders, subfolders, and files in the system filesystem. Some of the subnodes in this tree are:

- Toolbars
- Menu Bar
- Actions
- Component Palette

If you expand the Menu Bar node, you will find child nodes named for all of the menus in the IDE—and these then contain child nodes for each item that appears on that menu. Recalling that Nodes are like JavaBeans components that can be cut and pasted, try the following:

1. Expand the **Menu Bar** → **Build** node. Here you see all of the items that occur on the **Build** menu in NetBeans.
2. Right-click the node for the menu item **Build** to bring up its context menu.
3. Choose **Copy** from the menu.
4. Right-click the node for the **File** menu to bring up its context menu.
5. Choose **Paste** → **Copy as Link**.
6. Click the **File** menu on the main window. Notice that there is now a menu item for **Build**. To visualize this, take a look at Figure 14-6 and Figure 14-7.

What you've done is to add an empty *.instance* file to the *system/Menu/File/* subfolder of your user directory. The *$NB_USER/system/* directory comprises the session layer in the system filesystem. Thus the new menu item will remain on the **File**

---

[*] In NetBeans 3.2, this was a large tree of option nodes. In NetBeans 3.3, these are grouped into category folders. If you are using 3.2, ignore the folders we tell you to navigate and look for the settings node we name.

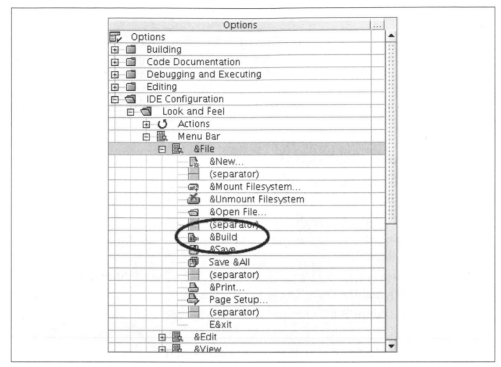

Figure 14-6. The menu configuration folders in the Options window

menu when you run NetBeans in the future, but since the modification is in the user directory, this customization will not be propagated to other users of the same copy of NetBeans. The customization will also remain even if you replace your NetBeans installation with a newer release.

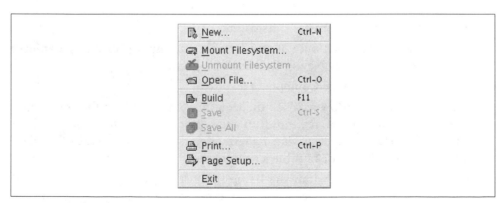

Figure 14-7. The File menu with the Build action added to it

Nodes in Action

Since NetBeans uses the nodes and bean model consistently throughout its user interface and its underlying infrastructure, you can do a surprising amount of customization without ever writing a line of code. Via the options hierarchy and the system filesystem, it is possible to substantially modify the NetBeans environment (including rendering it unusable, when it comes to the system filesystem—handle with care!).

Adding to the Component Palette using Paste Link

Let's try a more useful example—making additional components available on the **Component Palette**:

1. In **Explorer** → **Filesystems**, right-click a package and choose **New** → **GUI Forms** → **JPanel**. A dialog box will open and ask you for a class name and offer to let you override methods.

2. Name the class YellowPanel and click Finish. The **Code Editor** will open with your class in it, and the **Form Editor** will also open.

3. In the editor, add the following line to the constructor:

   ```
   setBackground(java.awt.Color.yellow);
   ```

4. Compile the YellowPanel class by clicking **Build Compile**.

5. Find the node in **Explorer** → **Filesystems** for your class. Right-click it and choose **Copy** from the context menu.

6. If it's not already open, open **Tools** → **Options**. The contents of the component palette are configured via a node of the tree you see in this dialog box.

7. Expand the **IDE Configuration** → **Look and Feel** → **Component Palette** → **Beans** node.

8. Right-click it and choose **Paste** → **Paste Link**.

9. Create a new form based on a JFrame by right-clicking a package in **Explorer Filesystems** and selecting **New** → **GUI Forms** → **JPanel**.

10. Click the **Beans** tab on the **Component Palette**.

11. Once the **Form Editor** opens, click the icon for YellowPanel on the component palette. Since we did not create an icon and a BeanInfo class for it, it will show up with the default icon displaying a question mark. You can be sure of its identity by hovering the mouse over the icon until the tool tip appears.

12. In the **Form Editor**, click within the JFrame you just created to add an instance of YellowPanel to the form. A yellow area appears—you have just added your own component to the component palette and dropped it on a form.

To remove YellowPanel from the Component Palette, simply right-click the YellowPanel node you pasted into Tools › Options › IDE Configuration › Look and Feel › Component Palette › Beans and choose Delete from its context menu.

That was a lot of steps! There actually is an easier way to accomplish the same thing: Right-click your YellowPanel class and choose **Tools → Add to Component Palette**. If you make a change to the component we created, such as changing its background color to blue, you don't have to delete it from the component palette and re-add it, although the class name would be misleading—just recompile it! Using **Tools → Add to Component Palette**, you will find that in *$USER_DIR/system/Palette/Beans*, there is now a file called *com-mybeans-panels-YellowPanel.instance*.

Rearranging actions/toolbar contents/menu contents

The folder in **Options** called **Actions** is where modules that are installed in the IDE add user-performable actions, which can live on menus, toolbars, or both. If you open the **Actions** node, you will see a large number of nodes for different actions, including some that don't even appear on a menu or toolbar (like **Garbage Collection**, which will attempt to invoke the garbage collector for the JVM the IDE is running in).

From here, you can freely copy and paste into the **Menus** and **Toolbars** folders to completely customize the menus and toolbars of the IDE. The **Actions** folder is what NetBeans' infrastructure for configuring keyboard shortcuts uses to find available actions.

Pasting a compiled class to a menu and executing it from there

To examine an even less common example, try the following:

1. Create a new executable Java class by choosing **New → Classes → Main** from the context menu of a package in **Explorer → Filesystems**.
2. Add the following line to its main() method:
   ```
   System.out.println("Hello!");
   ```
   Now compile it.
3. As in the previous examples, right-click the node for your class in the **Explorer** window.
4. Choose **Copy** from the context menu for your class's node in the **Explorer** window.
5. As you did earlier, paste it into the node for the **File** menu in the hierarchy under **Tools → Options → Paste-As-Link**.
6. Now click the **File** menu in the main window. Your class now appears in the list of choices (see Figure 14-8). Click the menu item for it.

At this point, if it isn't already open, the Output Window will appear, and the text Hello! will appear in it.

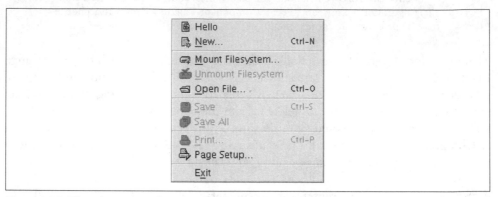

Figure 14-8. The File menu with a custom executable class added to it

Modules—Overview

We've already mentioned modules a couple of times. What are they? A module is a JAR file—a Java archive containing a set of class and other files that make up the module. What makes it a module is a set of special tags in the JAR manifest that mark it as a module and tell the IDE what to do to install it. If you look in *$NB_ HOME/modules/*, you will find quite a few JAR files. These are all of the modules that came with the IDE. The JAR files making up the modules that are part of a distribution of NetBeans physically reside in the *modules/* subdirectory underneath the directory it is installed in *($NB_HOME/modules)*. NetBeans has a concept of the *user directory*, which is where user-specific settings are stored. If you download a module using the update center, that module will be stored in the *modules/* subdirectory of your user directory—so a module you download won't suddenly appear to everyone else running that copy of NetBeans.

 It is possible for a module to require being installed globally, but this is not typically true of modules delivered by the NetBeans update center.

There is also the concept of the *project directory*, where shared settings belonging to multiple developers who are all working on the same project are stored. At the time of this writing, project support is undergoing a major rewrite, and precisely how this will be handled is not yet clear.

How Modules Add Functionality

A module literally provides additional classes that do something useful. Via its manifest, a module describes how to load these classes and use them in NetBeans. By and large, modules add functionality by adding entries to the system filesystem, just as pasting an element into the **Menu Bar** subfolder under **Tools → Options** creates an additional menu item. So, on encountering an unknown JAR file in the *modules* subdirectory on startup, NetBeans examines its manifest file, and looks for entries such as:

```
Manifest-Version: 1.0
OpenIDE-Module: org.netbeans.modules.autoupdate/1
OpenIDE-Module-Localizing-Bundle: org/netbeans/modules/autoupdate/
  Bundle.properties
OpenIDE-Module-Layer: org/netbeans/modules/autoupdate/
  resources/mf-layer.xml
OpenIDE-Module-Install: org/netbeans/modules/autoupdate/
  AutoUpdateModule.class
OpenIDE-Module-IDE-Dependencies: IDE/1 > 1.28
OpenIDE-Module-Module-Dependencies: org.netbeans.core/1 > 1.0
OpenIDE-Module-Specification-Version: 1.7
OpenIDE-Module-Implementation-Version: 200111231643

Name: org/netbeans/modules/autoupdate/NbmDataLoader.class
OpenIDE-Module-Class: Loader
```

to tell it what to do with the contents of this JAR file. For an explanation of the module manifest format, see Chapter 15.

A module actually does not have to have an installer class for the IDE to load it. A module's manifest can specify an XML layer file packaged inside it (in its JAR file), which declares what objects should be created, and where. Where possible, using layers is the preferred way to have your module install itself.

How Modules Install Virtual Filesystem Layers

This is actually quite simple—a module needs to include in its manifest a line such as

```
OpenIDE-Module-Layer: org/netbeans/modules/autoupdate/resources/mf-layer.xml
```

The path specified here is a path to the layer XML file within the module JAR file. NetBeans will extract the specified XML file when your module is loaded and merge it into the system filesystem. The syntax of a layer is fairly simple—the filesystem element contains a set of folder and file elements that make a small virtual filesystem. A top-level XML element called `filesystem` can contain the subelements `folder` and `file`, and `folder` elements can then contain additional `folder` and `file` elements. `folder` and `file` elements can have attributes and also can have either `CDATA` sections specifying their content, or have a URL property that points to what should appear to be the content of the file. The contents of the virtual filesystem, declared in XML, are the module's "layer."

What Modules Can Do

There is no fixed description for what a module can do. Part of the purpose and strength of a tools platform with generic APIs is to leave as much choice as possible up to the module author. Essentially, anything you can do in Java is possible, from building support for Perl with syntax highlighting and GUI design, to adding debuggers, tools for deploying classes to an application server, code profilers, UML tools, jargonizers, a Tetris game, or a full-blown office productivity suite!

So, in summary:

- A module is a JAR file.
- A module contains Java class files that interact with the IDE through the Open APIs.
- A module has a *META-INF/MANIFEST.MF* file that contains special tags that tell the IDE what to do with the classes in the JAR file.
- Modules included in a distribution of NetBeans reside in the *modules/* subdirectory of the NetBeans installation.
- Modules downloaded by the user live in the *modules/* subdirectory of that user's user directory.
- Modules contain XML filesystem layers, which add files to the system filesystem. In many cases these files are factories for Java class instances.

Disabling Modules

Modules can also be dynamically loaded and unloaded by disabling them in **Tools** → **Options** → **IDE Configuration** → **System** → **Modules**. For example, try the following:

1. Create a GUI form and open it by right-clicking a package in **Explorer** → **Filesystems** and choosing **New** → **GUI Forms** → **JPanel**. The **Form Editor** will open, with its associated component palette, on the **GUI Editing** workspace.
2. Open NetBeans' main configuration window in **Tools** → **Options**.
3. Find and expand the node called **Modules**.
4. Locate the node labeled **Form Editor** and click it to select it.
5. On the property sheet, set the **Enabled** property to False.

Notice that the **GUI Editing** workspace immediately disappears—and the **Form Editor** closes. Also notice, you now have two files listed in **Explorer**—one of them with the extension *.form* (the form editor stores GUI design data in this XML file and causes it to be hidden in the explorer). If you reenable the module, the **Form Editor** menu item will reappear in the **View** menu, and you will once again be able to work with forms.

Disabling or Deleting?

A common erroneous assumption people make about NetBeans is that disabling a module can't possibly save as much memory as deleting the module's JAR file. This is simply not true—if the module is marked as disabled, it *really* isn't looked at by the IDE again in any significant way. The memory saved by actually deleting modules is truly trivial, as is the performance impact. It is generally a better idea to simply disable a module, rather than completely deleting it.

What has actually happened is that the IDE has unloaded the classes provided by the module from memory, removed any objects the module specifies that the IDE should add to the system filesystem via its manifest, and called the module's `uninstalled()` method if the module specified an installer class in its manifest to perform any additional cleanup. The result is that the next time NetBeans is started, it will no longer use the module JAR file.

Deleting module files means that they do not get the chance to clean up after themselves. The result can be exceptions and unpredictable behavior. Also, bear in mind that there are cases of module interdependencies. NetBeans has built-in protection against disabling modules on which other modules have dependencies. Deleting modules short-circuits this protection. Don't do it! While future versions of NetBeans will have support for physically deleting modules, manually deleting their files is never a good idea.

An Illustration—NetBeans with No Modules

It's all well and good to talk about modules in the abstract; however, the following experiment will give you a tangible sense of just how modular the NetBeans IDE is:

1. Start with a clean, never-run installation of the IDE.
2. To be sure it won't use settings from your working copy or install modules you've downloaded, create an empty directory, for example, in */tmp/userdir*.
3. After installation, delete the entire contents of *$NB_HOME/modules/*. Also delete the contents of *$NB_HOME/system/Modules/*.
4. Now start the IDE from a command prompt, passing the argument `-userdir` `/tmp/userdir` on the command line, so the empty user directory will be used.

What comes up is an application with almost *no features*. You get an Explorer window with a tree view of files. Note that you now see both *.java* and *.class* files separately in Explorer, whereas, if the Java module were installed, they would be aggregated as a single node. With this instance of NetBeans, you can only cut and paste files—it is a glorified file browser, and little else.

While this is not the most useful way to run the NetBeans IDE, it truly makes the point of just how modular NetBeans is!

Interacting with the IDE

Executing anything in the IDE is accomplished via an abstraction called *Execution services*. An execution service takes an object that can be executed and performs some actions to execute it. The Java module provides two ways to execute Java files—*internal execution* and *external execution*. The former loads the class to be executed right into the same JVM the IDE is running in, and is quite fast. The latter calls the *java* executable on your system and passes the classpath argument with all of your mounted filesystems. It then parses any text output from your program and displays it in the Output Window. Additional external execution services can be created, so you can have a second execution service for running code on JDK 1.1 for testing applets, for example.

Internal execution is also a convenient way to interact with the running IDE. Since your code will be running in the same JVM, you can call any static method or constructor of any public class that is part of NetBeans. And the primary entry points to functionality within the IDE are static methods that allow you to locate objects of interest.

If you are going to interact with the IDE via internal execution, you will need to mount *openide.jar* from the *lib/* directory of your copy of NetBeans in **Explorer Filesystems**. If you have installed the Open APIs Support module, this is already done for you (it is hidden, but if you right-click the root **Filesystems** node and choose **Customize**, you will see it). If it is not mounted, the compiler will not find the classes your code needs to interact with.

To set a class to use internal execution:

1. Right-click the node for your Java class in **Filesystems**.
2. If you don't have the global properties window open, choose **Properties** from the context menu. A property sheet will appear.
3. Click the **Execution** tab on that property sheet.
4. Set the **Executor** property to **Internal Execution**.

When a class is run with internal execution, all of the internals of the IDE are visible to it, so it is possible to write code that will interact with the IDE.

Internal execution starts faster than external execution, since a new JVM does not have to be started. If you are reading this book, you probably are thinking about writing code that needs to run with internal execution, so it will be sensible to set this as the default. You can do this in **Tools** → **Options** → **Editing** → **Java Sources** → **Default Executor**.

At the same time, some things can interfere directly with NetBeans, such as adding global AWTEventListeners, and there are other ways for code to misbehave, so it is always safer to use external execution if you don't truly need to interact programmatically with NetBeans. For more on internal and external execution, refer to Chapter 2.

Setting the Status Bar Text

For a simple example of interacting directly with NetBeans' runtime via internal execution, let's try creating a small class which will write to the status bar in the main window. Create the class shown in Example 14-2.

Example 14-2. Writing to the status bar

```
import org.openide.TopManager;
public class StatusWriter {
  public static void main(String args[]) {
    TopManager.getDefault().setStatusText("Hello world!");
  }
}
```

Set the class to use Internal Execution and run it (press **F6**). You will see the text of the status bar change to Hello World!

Did you get a missing import error when you compiled the code? If so, *openide.jar* is not on your classpath (not mounted in **Filesystems Settings** in the **Options** window). The Open APIs Support module will mount it for you automatically.

Did you get a bunch of text in the output window that resembled what you see in a console window when you launch NetBeans? If so, then you ran the code with external execution. Set this class to internal execution as just described.

Note that the Open APIs Support module includes a template called "API Test Script," which will set internal execution by default and includes common imports needed when using the NetBeans Open APIs.

Setting the Current Workspace

Let us change this code to do something marginally more useful—change the current workspace in the running IDE. Edit the class file you created before and replace the line that prints Hello with the following:

```
TopManager.getDefault().getWindowManager().findWorkspace("Debugging").activate();
```

Recompile your class and execute it. The current set of windows disappears, and you have changed to the **Debugging** workspace (to get back to the editor, simply click the **Editing** tab at the bottom of the main IDE window).

As you can see, quite a bit is going on under the hood of NetBeans. For testing and experimentation, basic functionality can be accessed fairly simply using internal execution. NetBeans is a complex piece of software, but it provides well-defined contracts for adding components via the Open APIs. Next we will examine those APIs in detail, so that you can begin to understand how the various pieces that make up an application built on NetBeans interoperate.

## CHAPTER 15

The Open APIs

Part of the process of designing software is deciding what functionality needs to be abstracted and exposed for extensibility and what should be encapsulated and invisible to someone extending the system. One good example is Presenters. Presenters are NetBeans' abstraction for components such as menu items and toolbar buttons—usually the default implementation is sufficient, and you simply specify an icon and display name and the runtime takes care of actually creating a user-interface component for them, but you can override this behavior if necessary.

The simplest way to let someone extend menus and toolbars is to give them access to a JMenu and let them add components to it. However, this is unmaintainable—if five third-party modules all add items to the File menu, the resulting interface is not likely to be very usable. In such a situation different modules might do things to the menu that interfere with each other working correctly, because there is no contract for how they should behave.

The solution is, appropriately, an abstraction that wraps concepts such as presentation of functionality, and even the Action abstraction for user-invokable behaviors. The goal is to give someone the ability to add *functionality*, not menu items per se. So we have the **Actions**, **Menus**, and **Toolbars** hierarchies in **Tools** → **Options** → **IDE Configuration** → **Look and Feel**. As a result, it becomes possible to consistently integrate new functionality—the core takes care of presenting it to the user and managing the GUI components; you just specify where and how it should be presented. Net-Beans' APIs are divided into sets that cover various functions, such as user-invokable actions or data access.

Another advantage to this approach is that the thing that needs to be maintained is the public API—the underlying implementation can be replaced. As long as the new implementation reliably implements the same set of interfaces and methods that were public in the old implementation, all the modules that depend on that API will continue to work. This is, for example, why it was possible to add MDI* windowing support to the IDE. Because modules rely on the NetBeans Window System API (`org.openide.windows.*`), it was possible to rewrite almost the entire windowing system to support two radically different styles of window management. All of the modules remained compatible, because none of them depended on calling into `org.netbeans.core.windows.*`, the private implementation of the public window system APIs.

This does not mean that the Open APIs are not an evolving entity. New ways of doing things are sometimes introduced, old ways of doing things are deprecated. Please do read Appendix D to get a sense of the future directions of the Open APIs.

Nonetheless, for most of the APIs in this chapter, there are no large changes expected that will invalidate the information presented here. Deprecated means *inadvisable*, not *removed*, at least in the case of NetBeans. Surely some of the APIs and techniques in this book will be deprecated at some time, but the core architecture and concepts they demonstrate will remain valid over time. It is always advisable to check the current Open APIs documentation to learn what improvements time has brought. In general, examples presented here will continue to work well into the future.

APIs versus Core versus Modules

The separation of APIs and their implementation in NetBeans can be rendered as follows:

The Open APIs
> These are the public interfaces and classes available to module writers. They are divided into specific APIs for dealing with different types of functionality. The contents and behavior of the Java source packages `org.openide.*` and its subpackages, as specified in the Open APIs reference documentation, are the APIs.

The Core
> This is the implementation of the APIs, in the classes in `org.netbeans.core.*`.

Modules
> Sets of classes, delivered in JARs that conform to the Modules API, that add functionality to NetBeans and interact with the the runtime through the Open APIs.

Module APIs
> Modules can implement their own APIs to allow themselves to be extended. For example, the XML and Editor modules both offer APIs allowing other modules to work with them. If your module relies on code in another module, the dependency must be declared in your module's manifest. For examples of declaring intermodule dependencies in practice, see Chapter 27.

---

* MDI, or Multiple Document Interface, is a windowing style that originated on Microsoft Windows, in which a container window holds child windows belonging to a particular application. Support for this windowing style was added to NetBeans in the spring of 2000.

What if the APIs Don't Support Something I Need to Do?

It is possible to find a situation where you need to do something the APIs don't support. Having the source code to the core implementation of the APIs, you may find that you could call into the core to solve the problem. *Don't do it!* This is a great way to end up with difficult-to-maintain code, because there's no guarantee that the method or class you're calling will still exist next week. The public APIs are stable and will remain backward compatible. However, the implementation could easily be changed in a way that breaks your code if you rely on the implementation, rather than the API (in the form of an interface or public method calls). Furthermore, in NetBeans 3.4, the class loaders inside the NetBeans environment will explicitly prevent modules from accessing core code unless they declare a dependency on the core, producing NoClassDefFoundErrors if called.

One of the beautiful things about open source projects is that everyone has a voice. The right thing to do in this situation is to get on the *dev@openide.netbeans.org* mailing list and post your problem. It may be that there's another way to do what you need to do, or it may be that you have indeed turned up a weakness in the APIs that should be rectified.

It's worth noting that the APIs are not just sets of Java classes—for example, the Modules API defines manifest formats and XML DTDs, which are as much a part of the API as the classes therein. The contract between a module developer and the NetBeans environment is that the modules will use the public methods of classes in org.openide.* and other specifications associated with NetBeans as documented. If you do that, your module should continue to work with future releases of NetBeans. The entire set of specifications is included in the documentation installed by the Open APIs Support module.

Service Provider Interfaces and Client APIs

Another distinction is that, while we generally use the blanket term "APIs," they are divided into two flavors: *service provider interfaces* (SPIs) and client APIs.

Service provider interfaces are interfaces that allow you to enhance existing functionality. When you are writing to a service provider interface, you are not intending that your code be called directly; client code will access your functionality through the intermediary of an existing service in NetBeans. For example, if you write a Filesystems implementation that allows the IDE to see files via NFS (Network Filesystem), you are using the Filesystems subsystem's service provider interface. The classes you write will allow the common interface for file access in NetBeans to read and write files over a network using NFS protocol. Modules that manipulate files will simply use the common interface used for all file access in NetBeans to do the reading and writing. Other modules will never directly call your code, but the NetBeans environment has been significantly enhanced by your module.

Client APIs are the APIs other modules will use to access objects or services. A client API generally encapsulates services added via its service provider interface. An example of a call to a client interface is to get a reference to an object representing a file and retrieve the file's size.

Overview of the APIs and Their Purposes

The APIs can be broken down into the following general categories:

Finding/creating Java objects provided by other parts of NetBeans
> The Services API and its Lookup subsystem is particularly concerned with this, as are Cookies. For example, the Java module implements structural parsing of Java files. A module that provided UML diagramming needs a way to find the results of this parsing. These APIs allow modules to find Java objects created by other modules with which they need to interact, and do so in a way that allows them to be loosely coupled so functionality can be added to and removed from the system.

Presenting functionality to the user
> The Window System, Actions, Wizards and Explorer APIs are all concerned with the actual presentation of functionality in a GUI.

Managing access to data
> The Filesystems and Datasystems APIs provide the engine for representing stored data as Java objects in useful ways. Filesystems is concerned with the raw storage of data, and Datasystems with useful structural, programmatic access to parsed data.

Installing and uninstalling functionality
> The meat of the Modules API is in the specifications for manifests and XML layer files, and the ModuleInstall class, which allows a module to perform initialization and uninitialization operations.

Processing of data
> The Datasystems API, and some APIs that use the Services API, such as Compilation, Execution, and Debugger and search functionality.

Storing settings and state
> The Options API provides generic ways to store the state of user configurable settings in NetBeans when the environment is shut down, and restore them on restart. Modules can define SystemOptions, which are JavaBeans whose properties are exposed to the user in the Options window.

There is excellent Javadoc documentation covering the Open APIs in great detail, for which this chapter is no substitute. The Open APIs documentation consists of Javadoc for accessible API classes, plus extensive prose documentation explaining their purpose and use and giving additional specifications and hints. This prose documentation is packaged with the Open APIs Javadoc. For several APIs such as Modules and Window System, the prose documentation is more important than the Javadoc class documentation. What we *will* try to do here is sort the wheat from the chaff and point out some of the more commonly used classes and specifications. The Javadoc is included in the Open APIs Support module; if you have that installed, you should be able to find it on the **Javadoc** tab of your **Explorer** window. If so, you can access it via **Help → Local → Open APIs Documentation**.

Since it is better for this book to complement the APIs documentation in a task-oriented way, we won't go through it in minute detail here; instead, we will provide a guide to the more interesting classes and aspects of specific APIs.

Modules

`org.openide.modules.*`
> Defines the module abstraction, and in particular, `ModuleInstall`, a class that modules can use to do any work they need to do on startup, shutdown, installation, or removal.

`ModuleInstall`
> Should be implemented by a module's main class and identified in the manifest tag `OpenIDE-Module-Install`. This class contains methods you can implement if your module needs to do custom initialization or cleanup when it is installed, uninstalled, or when the IDE is started or shut down.
>
> Note that many modules will not need a `ModuleInstall` class. Most common things a module will need to do on install, uninstall, startup, and shutdown can be specified declaratively in XML.

Java classes are not the lion's share of the Modules API, but the specifications for module manifest files and XML layers, which define how modules register themselves with the system and install functionality declaratively.

Module manifests

The module manifest is the first thing that NetBeans looks at when it loads a module. Module manifests contain the following information:

Identification of the module
> With both a code name and a display name.

Versioning information about the module
> Identifies what version of the module the module JAR file contains, using the Java Package Versioning Specification (*http://java.sun.com/products/jdk/1.4/docs/guide/versioning/index.html*) in the form of a *specification version* and an *implementation version*.

Dependency information

Using the same versioning specification to specify other modules or components that need to be in the system in order for that module to function. NetBeans will not attempt to load a module whose dependencies are not satisfied.

Classpath entries required by this module

This is important! If your module installs a library in *modules/ext*, it needs to declare this dependency or you will encounter NoClassDefFoundExceptions. Your module has its own class loader, which can see the core Java APIs, the Open APIs, any libraries globally installed in NetBeans, and whatever it declares a dependency on. For details, see Figure 15-11 near the end of this chapter.

A localizing bundle

Provides localized names for attributes such as the display name of the module which can be specified in the manifest.

NetBeans-specific manifest sections

With the specification for XML layers being both more powerful and less memory intensive, a number of manifest sections are now deprecated. There are still a few cases where things must be installed via the manifest, but these are also planned to be replaced with XML module layer specifications in NetBeans 3.4 or 4.0.

As of NetBeans 3.3, DataLoaders, the classes responsible for loading files of known data types, still must be installed via the manifest, as are Nodes (for example, adding a Node to the **Runtime** tab in Explorer) and actions. This will probably be done declaratively with XML layers in NetBeans 3.4 or 4.0, though the manifest approach will continue to work. Other things, such as SystemOptions (user configuration settings) and filesystem storage providers can be installed either via the manifest or via the module's XML layer. Wherever there is a way to install via XML, this is the preferred way.

Let's examine the manifest of the Debugger Core module, shown in Example 15-1.

Example 15-1. Sample module manifest—the Debugger Core module

```
OpenIDE-Module: org.netbeans.modules.debugger.core/3
OpenIDE-Module-Localizing-Bundle: org/netbeans/modules/debugger/Bundle.properties
OpenIDE-Module-Install: org/netbeans/modules/debugger/multisession/EnterpriseModule.class
OpenIDE-Module-Layer: org/netbeans/modules/debugger/resources/mf-layer.xml
OpenIDE-Module-IDE-Dependencies: IDE/1 > 1.24
OpenIDE-Module-Specification-Version: 2.2
OpenIDE-Module-Implementation-Version: 200205011235

Name: org/netbeans/modules/debugger/multisession/EnterpriseDebugger.class
OpenIDE-Module-Class: Debugger

Name: org/netbeans/modules/debugger/support/nodes/DebuggerNode.class
OpenIDE-Module-Class: Node
Type: Environment
```

The first entry is the module's code name. The code name is used in the log file and is primarily useful to code that needs to identify a given module (for instance, to declare a dependency on it), or for support engineers who need to know precisely what modules a user has installed. Following this is a reference to a "localizing bundle" that will be used at runtime to supply internationalized text for the display name and description of the module itself. Note that objects installed from the module's layer refer to their own localizing bundle(s) independently, which need not be the same bundle as is referenced in OpenIDE-Module-Localizing-Bundle.

The next item identifies a Java class that is a subclass of org.openide.modules. ModuleInstall, and has methods that should be run to initialize or clean up on install, uninstall, start up, and shut down. Generally these are to be avoided where possible, as they can add to startup time, but there are cases where they are needed.* The OpenIDE-Module-Layer line identifies the path in the JAR file to the module's XML layer file. This is followed by a declared dependency on a specific minimum version of the APIs. Following this is versioning information used by NetBeans for dependency management and to determine if a version of a module available through the Update Center is really newer than this one and thus an update.

Following these attributes, after the blank line, are groups of lines that are the Net-Beans-specific *module sections*: The first section installs the debugger—unless you plan to write a wholesale replacement for NetBeans' debugger, you will probably never use this particular type of module section. This is followed by an entry for a Node—the one you can find in the **Runtime** tab of the **Explorer** window, which lists under it all of the running debugging sessions.

Several other types of module sections exist, such as for installing Nodes. The entire manifest specification is covered in the Modules API prose documentation. Note that the Open APIs Support module has support for automatic generation of the common entries in a module's manifest—to see this, create a new module JAR from template, and look on the **Module** properties tab of its property sheet. If you have the Open APIs Support module installed, many of the common manifest and layer entries can be created using cut and paste operations into the children of your module's node. For example, once you have created a module's layer file, simply copy and paste it into the **Layer** subnode of the module JAR in the **Explorer** window.

XML layers

XML layers are used to install data and factories for Java objects in the system file-system. The system filesystem contains a number of folders that are special because

---

* An example of this is the HTTP Server module. Imagine NetBeans has been restarted, but a browser window is left open and aimed at some Javadoc being served by the previous run of NetBeans. The right behavior is for the user to be able to still use that browser window. If the HTTP server were not started when NetBeans starts, and the user tries to browse the documentation that's already open, the result will be a 404 error—there will be no web server listening.

NetBeans uses them for a specific purpose. For example, menus, toolbars, and the settings UI are all created from folders and files inside the system filesystem. Persistent settings can be managed using *.settings* files, which are factories for Java objects, as are *.instance* files. These files differ only in that, when an instance is created from a *.settings* file, NetBeans will try to attach a PropertyChangeListener to it. If a PropertyChangeEvent is fired, the changes will be saved so that they will persist for future NetBeans sessions.

The primary use of XML layers is to place Java classes into folders in the system filesystem that have special functions, such as the registration of services or menu items. Many systems in NetBeans use this functionality. For example, there are extensible wizards which can have panels added to them by adding files to a particular folder. Modules can also define their own folders in the system filesystem and use them, which can be useful for ensuring lazy instantiation of objects and separating a module's configuration from its code. Declaring a Java class instance in a module layer is illustrated in Example 15-2.

Example 15-2. A simple XML layer declaring a Java instance

```
<!DOCTYPE filesystem PUBLIC
        "-//NetBeans//DTD Filesystem 1.1//EN"
        "http://www.netbeans.org/dtds/filesystem-1_1.dtd">
<filesystem>
  <folder name="Services">
    <folder name="Hidden">
      <file name="com-mymodule-MyClass.instance">
        <attr name="instanceOf" stringvalue="com.mymodule.MyClass"/>
      </file>
    </folder>
  </folder>
</filesystem>
```

By using the special *Services* folder of the system filesystem, this file entry is also automatically registered with the lookup subsystem. When some code calls Lookup. getDefault().lookup(com.mymodule.MyClass.class), the system will call the default constructor to create an instance of com.mymodule.MyClass and return it. Because the class name is specified in the XML, the JVM need not actually load the implementation class (taking up valuable memory and CPU cycles in the process) unless client code requests an instance. The mechanism underlying this is a class called InstanceDataObject—files with the extension *.instance* are represented by DataObjects that possess an InstanceCookie, as shown in Figure 15-2. The InstanceCookie interface has a method called instanceCreate() that will instantiate and weakly cache an instance of the class specified in the file's name or attributes. This mapping is shown in Figure 15-1.

XML layers allow you to define not only what class is instantiated, but also how it is instantiated. Perhaps you need to do some initialization and the default constructor

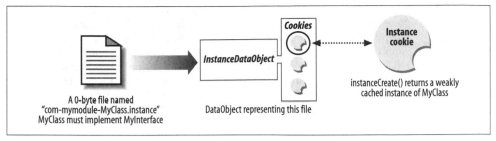

Figure 15-1. Mapping of files to Java class instances

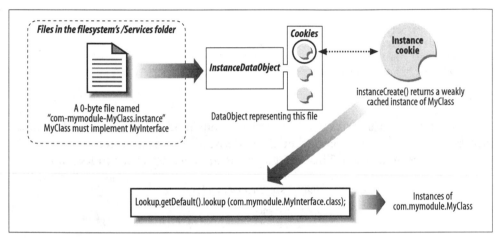

Figure 15-2. Mapping from files to InstanceDataObjects to lookup

is not appropriate. This is not a problem. Replace the file entry in Example 15-2 with the example in Example 15-3.

Example 15-3. Specifying a static factory method for instances in a module layer

```
<file name="com-mymodule-MyClass.instance">
  <attr name="instanceOf" stringvalue="com.mymodule.MyClass"/>
  <attr name="instanceCreate"
        methodvalue="com.mymodule.MyFactory.createMyInstance"/>
</file>
```

A file attribute has been added. `instanceCreate` specifies a factory method that should be called to do the work of creating and initializing the instance.

 File attribute names are case sensitive, just like Java identifiers. No warning message will generally be shown if you mistype a file attribute name, so check the spelling if you are having problems.

`com.mymodule.MyFactory.createMyInstance()` can be any static method on any class in your module. When the system requests your instance, this factory method will be called. The factory method could look like Example 15-4.

Note that it is encouraged, but not required, to use the `instanceOf` attribute; this is an optimization that avoids instantiating the class simply so that a query can determine if it is a match or not. The attribute must list every interesting interface or superclass implemented by the actual instance class; lookup queries on a class or interface that is not listed in `instanceOf` will *not* succeed. It is safe to omit the attribute—then lookup will *always* try to load your class and check if it really matches.

Example 15-4. Factory method to instantiate a class from a .instance file

```
package com.mymodule;
public class MyFactory {
  public static MyInterface createMyInstance() {
    // whatever constructor or initialization you need:
    return new MyClass("someParam", true);
  }
}
```

Encapsulation is an important thing. Perhaps your module specifies a public interface, and the implementation of that class is private. You need to return an instance of the interface in question. This is not a problem, as demonstrated in Example 15-5.

Example 15-5. Specifying the class that will be created in a layer

```
<file name="com-mymodule-my-instance.instance">
  <attr name="instanceClass" stringvalue="com.mymodule.MyClass"/>
  <attr name="instanceCreate"
        methodvalue="com.mymodule.MyFactory.createMyInstance"/>
  <attr name="instanceOf" stringvalue="com.mymodule.MyInterface"/>
</file>
```

Another file attribute has been added. `instanceClass` defines what class you want the returned instance to be. Consider the case where you define a public interface for which you want to produce an instance from the system filesystem (perhaps via Lookup). You don't want to expose the class that implements this interface, just an instance of that interface. `instanceClass` allows you to restrict what class appears to be returned when an instance is created from this file entry.

In NetBeans 3.4 `instanceClass` would be optional in this example: if omitted, the `instanceCreate` attribute is sufficient.

The filename has also ceased to matter, since the class to be instantiated is declared as an attribute of the file. So it is also now possible to have more than one instance of the same class in the same folder.

But that still might not be quite enough—you may want to specify some arguments to the factory method in order to use the same factory for differently configured instances. This is possible too; Example 15-6 is an example of this.

Example 15-6. Specifying initialization data for a Java instance declared in a layer

```
<file name="com-mymodule-my-instance.instance">
  <attr name="instanceClass" stringvalue="com.mymodule.MyClass"/>
  <attr name="instanceCreate"
        methodvalue="com.mymodule.MyFactory.createMyInstance"/>
  <attr name="instanceOf" stringvalue="com.mymodule.MyInterface"/>
  <attr name="myInitString" stringvalue="myValue"/>
</file>
```

A fourth attribute has been added: `myInitString`. This attribute does not have any special meaning to NetBeans' infrastructure. File attributes can be arbitrarily named strings. But the factory method that instantiates the class has access to file attributes. There are two possible signatures for the factory method; the first is shown in Example 15-7.

Example 15-7. Simple factory method for an XML layer instance

```
public static MyInterface createMyInstance() {
  return new MyClass(/* fixed arguments */);
}
```

Depending on the method signature of `createMyInstance()`, it can be passed the `FileObject` that is being used, utilizing the more complex method signature shown in Example 15-8.

Example 15-8. Complex factory method for an XML layer instance

```
public static MyInterface createMyInstance(FileObject fo) {
  String initString = (String)fo.getAttribute("myInitString");
  return new MyClass(initString);
}
```

With this second style, you can attach any sort of arbitrary initialization data you want to the file via its attributes. The result is that you have complete declarative control of how your class is instantiated, but there is no need for the JVM to actually load your class until something asks for it via lookup.

Supplying actual data in a module layer file is possible simply by providing an XML CDATA section between the opening and closing file tags in the XML. However, this technique is generally not recommended for reasons of memory performance, and can be tricky with respect to whitespace and non-ASCII characters. Instead, the preferred method is to use a URL pointing to the data the file should appear to contain, where the file referenced by the URL is inside the module JAR. The format for this is quite simple, and shown in Example 15-9.

Example 15-9. Declaring file contents using URLs in XML layers

```
<file name="MyTemplate.java"
      url="templates/MyTemplate.java.tmpl"/>
```

The URL is resolved relative to the root of the module JAR archive, and for client code that accesses the file, the contents of the file pointed to by the URL will appear to be its content.

Ordering files in XML layers

Given that files in XML layers are used to install things such as menu items, some means of establishing the order in which files appear is necessary. The Filesystems API does not specify the order in which files will occur in a folder—just as file order is not consistent when listing the same directory on Unix and Windows.

It is the Datasystems API that specifies ordering constraints for files. The ordering of the children of a `FileObject` is undefined; the ordering of children of a `DataFolder` can be specified.

Ordering of files in an XML filesystem is accomplished by adding attributes to the containing folder. The syntax is fairly simple. The name of the attribute specifies an ordering constraint for two files, separated by a slash, for example, `file.before/file.after`. Neither filename mentioned in the constraint need be a file supplied by the module installing the constraint (though in practice, at least one of them will be). The module author need know only the filenames in question. Example 15-10 shows what this looks like in practice, using the XML layer from the Form Editor module as a template.

Example 15-10. Ordering attributes in XML layers

```
<folder name="View">
  <attr name="org-netbeans-core-actions-HTMLViewAction.instance/org-netbeans-,↵
modules-form-actions-FormEditorAction.instance" boolvalue="true"/>
  <file name="org-netbeans-modules-form-actions-FormEditorAction.instance"/>
  <attr name="org-netbeans-modules-form-actions-FormEditorAction.instance/org-,↵
netbeans-modules-objectbrowser-ShowBrowserAction.instance" boolvalue="true"/>
</folder>
```

In Example 15-10, the Form Editor is installing a single menu item, yet it installs *two* constraints. NetBeans is an extensible system, and other modules may also want to include a menu item before or after the same element. For example, two modules might want to put a menu item after **Web Browser** (*org-netbeans-core-actions-HTMLViewAction.instance*). Without a second constraint, either one could end up following the web browser. If you are aware of the other module's desire to follow **Web Browser**, you can preempt that by declaring a second constraint that the file from the other module should follow yours.

The other curious thing you may have noticed in the preceding listing is the presence of `boolvalue="true"` for each constraint. Since all of the ordering information needed is contained in the attribute name, this looks superfluous. In a sense, it is, but the contract for `FileObject` specifies that attributes map names to Java objects. Thus, it is required that the value of an ordering constraint be `Boolean.TRUE`.

Lastly, note the order in which the attributes occur in the example. The ordering attribute that specifies the file occurring before the visible file is placed before the file in the listing. The attribute that specifies the file occurring after the visible file is placed after it. There is no technical requirement that files or attributes in an XML folder be declared in any particular order; however, it is a convention adopted in NetBeans sources to improve readability, and we encourage you to use it.

Lookup and the Services API

NetBeans contains a generic registration for *services*. A common use of services is to register a service that can perform some operation over a group of files, such as compilation or text searching. But services can be used for most any sort of functionality. NetBeans also contains an even more general registry of interesting objects, called *lookup*. Lookup is a system by which a module can place a query for a particular interface and get back pointers to all registered instances of it.

Lookup, .settings files, the system filesystem, and layers

Various packages in the APIs

Permits different kinds of functionality to be installed and queried in a general way. Services can be registered in the lookup system and then can be found by other modules. This allows a module to find and interact with objects produced by other modules. Modules can register objects with the lookup system very simply by declaring them in their XML layer inside the `Services/` folder. The Lookup API also provides a service provider interface that can be implemented by modules that provide factories for objects of potential interest to other modules. Those modules can then register their lookup implementation with the system-wide lookup system (`Lookup.getDefault()`) and thus be queried whenever any module queries the default lookup system.

Implementing lookup and registering your lookup provider with the system sounds like a lot of of work, but there is an easy way out. Say you have a class that is the entry point for the functionality of your module. You don't actually have to do anything except to define, in your module's XML layer, a *settings* file that dereferences a bean the same way *.instance* files do, and define it as living in the *Services* folder. The system filesystem defines two ways to instantiate objects. The first is *.instance* files, which specify that a class NetBeans should instantiate on demand via `InstanceCookie.createInstance()`. *.settings* files follow the same model, but are generally used for JavaBeans only and expand on the model in the following ways:

- Property change listeners will be added if and when your bean is created.
- Introspection will be used to detect the `addPropertyChangeListener()` method.
- If properties are changed, they are saved to the user or project layer of the system filesystem and will persist for future IDE sessions. In NetBeans 3.3, serialization is used for this purpose.

Commonly used or interesting classes in this package

`Lookup`

This class provides a very generic interface for looking up objects. Lookup provides a generic "NetBeans Yellow Pages." Callers can query a `Lookup` implementation for instances of a given interface. The system has a default lookup implementation available via `Lookup.getDefault()`. The default implementation allows other implementations to register themselves with it and be queried via this call. Thus, any module that makes objects available using `Lookup` can add itself to this central point for queries. Simple queries happen via the method `Lookup.lookup(Class clazz)`—note here the resemblance to `Node.getCookie(Class clazz)`, its logical precursor. This method will return an object of the desired class, or `null`. If there may be more than one result of your query, or the result might change over time, use the call `lookup(Lookup.Template template)`.

`Lookup.Template`

This class represents complex queries of the lookup subsystem. Queries can include a class, a specific instance, and/or an identifying string.

`Lookup.Result`

Represents the results of a query of the lookup system, including all available instances (not just the first). If it is desirable to listen for changes in the result of a query, it is possible to hold a reference to a `Result` and attach a listener to it.

`AbstractLookup`

This is a partial convenience implementation of `Lookup` that modules may subclass and register if it is useful for them to implement `Lookup`. If the set of items available in this lookup implementation will not change, an `AbstractLookup` instance can also be instantiated by passing its constructor an instance of `InstanceContent` that determines the contents.

`LookupListener`

A listener for changes that can be attached to an instance of `Lookup.Result` and be notified if the results of the lookup have changed.

`ProxyLookup`

An implementation of `Lookup` that can delegate the actual work of looking something up to a collection of other implementations of `Lookup`.

`FolderLookup`
> Though part of the Datasystems API by package, this very important class allows lookups on the contents of a folder (which may be a physical folder on disk, an XML filesystem installed by a module, or anything else handled by Filesystems). It is this mechanism that allows modules to register objects with the lookup system by simply declaring them as virtual files in their XML layers. Furthermore, if a `FolderLookup` finds an implementation of `Lookup` among the instance files in its folder, it will proxy to that `Lookup` instance. If a module needs to create one or more registries of objects that may change dynamically at runtime (for example, for an application broken out into domains with string IDs), this is a convenient tool.

Services

Services, or service types, are a slightly older idiom in the NetBeans world—originally NetBeans had separate compiler, debugger, and execution infrastructure. The generalization that all of these things are "services" was retrofitted to this several years ago; yet even this was not generic enough, so the more generic `Lookup` infrastructure was born. New kinds of services can be any JavaBeans, and no longer need to extend `ServiceType`.

The general aspects of services are:

Services are JavaBeans
> A service (whether extending `ServiceType` or not) must be configurable as a JavaBean. Its property management and user presentation is done through introspection.

A class of service is registered, and the environment can contain multiple discrete instances of that class with different configurations
> An example of this is the External Compilation service. You can copy and paste the **External Compilation** node to create a second instance of this service and then configure it to call a different compiler.

Individual instances of services can be looked up by name, for example:
```
ServiceType.Registry reg = TopManager.getDefault().getServices();
CompilerType type = (CompilerType)reg.find("External Compilation");
```

You can also find services in `Lookup` by matching on a superclass. `DataObjects` will often want to be associated with one or more services (for example, a Java file with a compiler and execution service), and there are standard support classes that make this easy, such as `ExecSupport` and `CompilerSupport`. You can read about the user aspect of this technique in Chapter 5.

Nodes

`org.openide.nodes.*`

Defines the Node interface. Nodes represent JavaBeans or other "property containers"—that is to say, objects with properties that potentially may be exposed to the user via the user interface. Nodes exist in a tree-like hierarchy, so any given node probably has a parent node and potentially a collection of child nodes, which in turn may have their own child nodes.

Nodes are used pervasively throughout the NetBeans user interface as presentation objects (despite the fact that Nodes are not visual components). For those familiar with the Model-View-Controller design model, a node is the *controller* object; the object it represents is the *model*, and the *view* is the Explorer component (an Explorer view, as detailed in Figure 15-3) being used to render the node in Net-Beans' user interface.

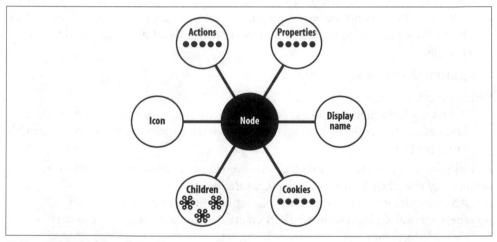

Figure 15-3. Anatomy of a node

Nodes are not containers for data themselves, but are more like pointers that aggregate a set of related objects (refer to Figure 15-3). For example, a subnode of a node representing a Java source file may represent a method within a class in that file. Modules can access the contents and structure of the method source code by asking the node for a cookie of the class SourceCookie. The node exposes properties of the method source code, such as the arguments passed to the method, via its properties. User-invokable actions are available via the Node.getActions() method, and so forth.

The inspiration for Nodes is the JavaBeans specification, but differs in several respects:

Hierarchy

Nodes live in a tree-like hierarchy; nodes can have a parent (containing) node and child nodes. These are supplied by an instance of the class `Children` owned by the node and retrieved via the method `someNodeInstance.getChildren()`.

Dynamic properties

In the JavaBeans spec, properties are determined at compile time, depending on method signatures. Properties of nodes are instances of `Node.Property` and can potentially change at runtime. If you want to represent a standard JavaBean as a node, this is quite easy using the `BeanNode` wrapper class.

Dynamic actions

A node has a set of actions that can be performed on it, which may vary depending on the state of the object it represents.

Cookies

A node has a set of cookies, which are objects that implement the `Node.Cookie` marker interface. A cookie is an arbitrary Java class instance that can provide access to objects relating to the node. A cookie can be any Java object that is useful to expose to other code that might interact with the `Node`. For example, a cookie may implement actions that can be performed on the `Node` by the user, or provide structural access to the data in the underlying `DataObject`. Cookies are retrieved by passing the `Class` object for the desired interface to `someNode.getCookie(Class clazz)` and casting the result (if non-null) to that interface.

For example, a node representing a file the user has opened in the **Editor** will provide an `EditorCookie`. The `EditorCookie` implementation that is returned provides both methods for opening the document in the editor and for accessing the document object the editor uses, finding all open editor panes that are editing this file, and other editing-related functionality.

Commonly used or interesting classes in this package

`AbstractNode`

An implementation of the `Node` interface that provides functionality common to most `Nodes`, such as icon and name handling. When creating your own `Node` implementations, you will usually want to subclass `AbstractNode`.

`BeanNode`

A wrapper for JavaBeans that can expose an existing JavaBean and its properties as a node. It also adopts a name and icon from the JavaBean if that information is available in its `BeanInfo`. BeanNode is essentially an adapter to allow you to represent and work with JavaBeans as `Nodes` with minimal coding.

`Children`

Nodes live in a hierarchy, so nodes can have, by definition, *children*—Nodes that live below them in the hierarchy. When you call `someNode.getChildren()`, you will be returned an `org.openide.nodes.Children` object, which you can query for the child nodes of someNode.

FilterNode

> This is a node that actually represents another node somewhere else in memory. It delegates some or all of its functionality to the original node, depending on its implementation. A common use is to provide a node that provides a different set of child nodes, properties, or cookies than the original.

Node.Cookie

> This is an empty marker interface for cookies. Node and DataObject instances both have a set of cookies that can change dynamically. You can listen for changes in the set of cookies available.

Node.Property

> An object representing a property of a node. Properties are arbitrary name-value pairs, as displayed in a Node's property sheet.

Node.PropertySet

> Yet another layer of indirection in the relationship between nodes and their properties. Node.Property objects are contained in one or more PropertySet objects owned by the Node. This allows Nodes to have different categories of properties, such as **Expert** properties that are occasionally useful to expose but that will not routinely be modified by the casual user. One Node.PropertySet corresponds to one tab of the Property Sheet window.

Datasystems

`org.openide.loaders.*`

Used to manage the loading and handling of DataObjects; this is largely the API used when support for a new data type is implemented.

DataObject

> An object that encapsulates one or several files. If the data it represents is structured, a common thing for a DataObject to do is to provide structural, programmatic representations of the data via its Cookies.

DataLoader

> Factories for DataObjects. When NetBeans encounters a new file, it figures out what type of data it is and invokes the DataLoader for that type of data to create a DataObject to represent it.

MultiDataObject

> Why is a layer between files and nodes needed? One of the most compelling reasons is that it may be desirable to present multiple files as a single object. In practice, almost all data objects extend MultiDataObject, even though only one file can be contained in the object.

DataFolder

A `DataObject` implementation that represents a folder that contains other `DataObjects`.

DataNode

A `Node` implementation that represents a `DataObject`.

UniFileLoader

Registers a set of extensions or MIME types and is responsible for loading data from files of these types.

MultiFileLoader

Similar to `UniFileLoader`, but responsible for loading data from multiple files that should be represented as a single entity within NetBeans (for example, a Java source file with an associated compiled class file and possibly an XML form file that defines the GUI layout). Almost all loaders extend `MultiFileLoader`.

OpenSupport

This class implements methods from `OpenCookie`, `ViewCookie`, and `CloseCookie`, but does not declare itself to implement any of these interfaces. To implement any of these cookies, simply subclass `OpenSupport` and declare your subclass to implement any of the interfaces it supports. `OpenSupport` provides generic support for opening documents. Depending on the type of editor(s) to be instantiated, this functionality may be better referred to as Viewing, Opening, or Editing.

FolderInstance

This class is particularly useful if you need to create a component that assembles itself from instances or subfolders in a folder. `FolderInstance` contains logic for accepting or rejecting instances contained in that folder, or for overriding the supplied instance (this is the mechanism by which it is possible to paste compiled classes into menus and toolbars). In particular, it is sensitive to the addition or deletion of files within the folder and can be used to rebuild the component in question with minimal coding on the part of the module author. For a good example of its usage, see the sources for `org.openide.awt.MenuBar`.

Explorer

`org.openide.explorer.*` and subpackages

The Explorer package contains tools for visually representing hierarchies of `Nodes` in a variety of ways, such as tree views, menus, and property sheets.

`org.openide.explorer.view.*`

Contains GUI components that can represent `Nodes` graphically, including tree, menu, drop-down, list, and table views. An Explorer view is created and is given a root node. Some views display the root node and its children (perhaps recursively). Others display nodes contained in the explored context (another parent node). Still others display the selected node (or nodes) only.

ExplorerManager

This interface is the entry point for communicating with Explorer views. An ExplorerManager tracks changes in the node selection, as well as the root node and explored context, for one or more Explorer views associated with it. To listen for changes on an open Explorer view, attach a listener to its manager.

ExplorerPanel

A very convenient visual class that you can use to create compound components that contain one or more Explorer views. ExplorerPanel extends org.openide. windows.TopComponent, the base class for dockable windows in NetBeans, and implements ExplorerManager.Provider (a way of finding ExplorerManagers). To associate an Explorer view with the ExplorerPanel so you can listen to it for changes in selection, and so on, simply add your view to the ExplorerPanel as a Swing component.

explorer.propertysheet.*

This package contains classes that are responsible for property sheets in Net-Beans. Property sheets and instances of the PropertyPanel class in this package provide one of the primary ways for users to adjust settings and attributes of objects in NetBeans. NetBeans contains some enhancements to the JavaBeans property editor infrastructure. Also present is the PropertySheetView visual class, an Explorer view that, when given a node selection from an explorer manager, displays the user-editable properties of that node (or set of nodes) as a familiar property sheet.

There are a variety of useful components in the subpackage org.openide.explorer. view. Explorer views are GUI components such as the **Filesystems** tree in the main Explorer window of NetBeans. A variety of components are provided which implement different styles of views. What these classes have in common is that they each can be managed by an ExplorerManager. The ExplorerManager connects an explorer component with the rest of NetBeans' infrastructure so that when the user selects a different node, NetBeans is aware of it (changes in the set of activated Nodes are fired and actions are enabled or disabled as appropriate, and so on.). Here are several of these views:

BeanTreeView

This is the standard tree view you see in the main Explorer window in the IDE, as shown in Figure 15-4.

ChoiceView

A drop-down list component that displays an Explorer tree to some fixed depth, as shown in Figure 15-5.

Figure 15-4. Explorer views—BeanTreeView

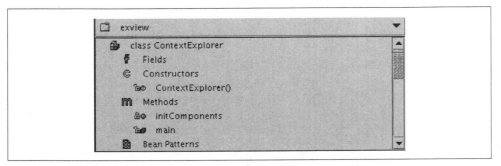

Figure 15-5. Explorer views—ChoiceView

IconView

A component that displays nodes as icons, reminiscent of the Microsoft Windows Explorer (see Figure 15-6). This class is not used in the current NetBeans distribution, but was part of the original **New** Wizard and is maintained as part of the APIs.

Figure 15-6. Explorer views—IconView

ListView

Displays the children of one Node in a flat list, without indentation, illustrated in Figure 15-7.

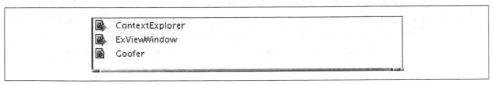

Figure 15-7. Explorer views—ListView

MenuView

> This view presents a set of Nodes in a menu, with submenus for nodes that have children (see Figure 15-8).

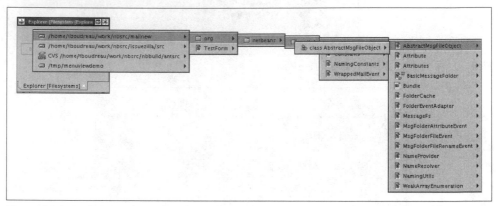

Figure 15-8. Explorer views—MenuView

ContextTreeView

> This looks the same as BeanTreeView, but there is a significant difference. When you select a node in this view, the ExplorerManager managing the Explorer views changes the explored context for all other Explorer views to the node you have selected in your ContextTreeView component. If you've used Windows, think of Windows Explorer here, with its left-hand pane to select the current directory and its right-hand pane to display that directory's contents. By changing the context for all other components managed by its manager, you can actually create a component very much like the Windows Explorer within NetBeans, as seen in Figure 15-9.

TreeTableView

> It is not uncommon in NetBeans to have a dialog box or window that displays a number of nodes, the purpose being to configure only a few properties of all of these nodes. An example of this is the panel for enabling and disabling modules in the **Setup Wizard**.

> This class provides a flexible way to display specific properties of a given set of Nodes in a table alongside a tree. A TreeTableView displays a tree view of nodes, and can be given one or more properties (if present) to display for each node in the tree. What is displayed in the view depends on the model supplied to the tree and the array of property names provided for the component to expose. Take a look at Figure 15-10 for an idea of this view.

Actions

org.openide.actions.*, org.openide.util.actions.*

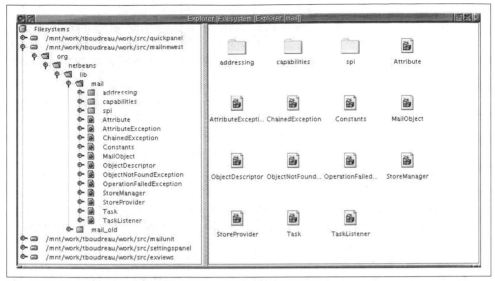

Figure 15-9. A "Pseudo-Windows Explorer" mock-up created using IconView and ContextTreeView

Modules		Enabled	Version (Specification)
Modules			
⊙	Backward Compatibility	False	
⊙	Data Files	[boolean]	
	Image	False	1.8
	Resource Bundles	True	1.8
	Text	True	1.8
⊙	Debugging	False	
⊙	Developing NetBeans	[boolean]	
⊙	Distributed Application Support	False	
⊙	Editing	True	
	Editor	True	1.9
	General Online Help	False	1.10

Figure 15-10. Explorer views—TreeTableView

Defines user-invokable behaviors. User-invokable actions in NetBeans take the form of subclasses of `org.openide.actions.SystemAction` which is an extension of the Swing Action API. `SystemAction` instances in the IDE should be *singletons*—all state information should be static. As of NetBeans 3.3, `javax.swing.Action`s (which need not be singletons) can also be used in some, but not all, circumstances.[*]

---

[*] This change precedes the move to fully declarative actions whose activation constraints are specified in the module XML layer, which do not require complementary action implementation classes.

An action is an abstraction for user-invokable behavior. An action has a display name and optionally an icon; if the action is added to the *Menu* or *Toolbars* folder of the system filesystem (by creating an empty file such as com-foo-MyAction.instance in the module's XML layer) a menu item or toolbar button will appear in the user interface to represent it.

Some actions are always enabled, such as those that bring up a wizard or window. Actions can also be context sensitive. An action may be enabled or disabled depending on whether the currently selected node (e.g., a file selected in the Explorer window when it has focus, or the file currently open in the editor when it has focus) can have that action performed on it.

SystemAction
> All actions in NetBeans subclass SystemAction, which is an extension to the Swing action API, extending the Open APIs class SharedClassObject and expecting to be a singleton.

CallableSystemAction
> A convenience base class for non-context-sensitive actions. Implementing a single abstract method allows your action to be invoked.

CallbackSystemAction
> An action which has a separate performer object associated with it that actually performs the action. The performer can be changed on the fly. This is typically used for actions whose meaning depends on the selected window. When no performer is present, the action is disabled.

NodeAction
> An action which can listen to what the currently selected node is, and set its enabled state accordingly.

CookieAction
> This very useful base class provides an action whose state is enabled or disabled depending on what Node.Cookie classes are held by the activated nodes.

Options

org.openide.options.*

The Options API is the API for user-modifiable configuration information and its storage. NetBeans has a set of singleton SystemOptions that are exposed to the user through the configuration window available via **Tools → Options**. You don't need to write code to do the dirty work of persistent storage of these settings if you use SystemOption and as long as your data is serializable (this is a requirement for persistent storage).

SystemOptions are user-configurable settings that may be installed by modules to configure the behavior of that module. Examples of SystemOption properties are the settings for which HTML browser to use when a user views an HTML file, or for whether to display the **Welcome** screen on startup. SystemOptions are singletons, and all configuration information that a user can modify should be stored by the class in static variables or its properties via the putProperty() and getProperty() methods. As with SystemAction, SystemOption is a subclass of org.openide.util.SharedClassObject, which provides infrastructure for creating singleton classes (which enforce the existence of only one instance per class). The getters and setters of a SystemOption should be non-static instance methods, despite the fact that the data storage is class-scope.

SystemOptions are not nodes, but are presented via nodes to the user. InstanceDataObjects can provide nodes that represent the object instance in question, but will not actually instantiate the object unless it is needed, for example when a property sheet must be displayed.

SystemOptions are installed via the module manifest or XML layer, which should contain a reference to your SystemOption class. To discover the properties of your SystemOption that should be saved, introspection is used. For greater control over the process, always create a BeanInfo class describing your SystemOption.

SystemOption
> An object that represents a group of related user-modifiable settings (exposed through the SystemOption subclass's bean properties).

ContextSystemOption
> A SystemOption that is a container for additional child SystemOptions.

Compiler

org.openide.compiler.*

Defines the compilation process, using the infrastructure of the Services API.

CompilerJob
> NetBeans does not assume compilation is a one-step process. A compiler job consists of a set of compilers with possible dependencies on one another. Compilation may proceed in one or more stages, each of which can run varied compilation procedures.

Compiler
> An object that represents one compilable file or other unit in a compiler group.

CompilerGroup
> An object that represents one step in a compiler job, perhaps compiling a cluster of similar files.

CompilerType
> A ServiceType that has a method for contributing to a compiler job.

CompilerSupport

A cookie implementation that, when present in a node's cookie set, indicates that the thing represented by the node can be compiled. Provides methods for adding a `DataObject` to a compiler job.

Editor

`org.openide.text.*`

The editing infrastructure of the IDE. This API covers both the infrastructure for clients to interact with editors that are installed in NetBeans (for example, opening a file in an editor, finding the selected region, and so on) and the SPI for integrating new editor kits.

The editor API uses the Swing `EditorKit` interface; it is possible to plug any editor into NetBeans that implements this interface. "Documents" are instances of `javax.swing.text.StyledDocument`.

CloneableEditorSupport

A base class that can provide implementations of the following `Cookie` interfaces as needed:

EditorCookie

A cookie class that supports opening documents in an editor window and finding instances of editors already editing a file. This cookie further permits nonblocking loads of documents and queries of document load status.

LineCookie

A cookie class that provides access to a document as a set of lines, represented as Java objects that can be held even if the document they reference is edited and line numbers change.

OpenCookie

A cookie class that provides a method for opening a document in the default editor for that document type.

EditCookie

A cookie very similar to `OpenCookie`, but used to emphasize that this is an editing operation on the object, whereas `OpenCookie` opens it graphically.

ViewCookie

Also similar to `OpenCookie`, but used to emphasize that the operation will not modify the object but only allow the user to view it.

PrintCookie

Supports printing of a document.

DataEditorSupport

A class that extends `CloneableEditorSupport` to support associating an editor with a `DataObject` representing the file or files to be edited.

NbDocument

This is a utility class with static methods and interfaces for handling NetBeans' document conventions.

Line

Represents one line in a document. If a reference to a Line object is held, it will continue to represent the same line of text, even if the document is altered so that its position in the document has changed.

Annotation

This is the base class for objects representing some user-presentable marker that applies to a line or part of a line within a document. The graphic displayed in the **Editor**'s line-number gutter and background color of a line in a Java file that has been set as a breakpoint is an example of an annotation. Another example is the highlighting that occurs when you click a compiler error in the **Output Window**.

Windowing System

org.openide.windows.*

NetBeans has a rich window management system that allows you to concentrate on the layout of those UI components you need to create without having to perform the grunt work of managing windows, window positioning, and so on. The windowing system provides base classes you can subclass, and using the Open APIs Support module, you can use the NetBeans Form Editor to design the GUI for your module.

Among the features of NetBeans' windowing system are:

Docking

UI components can be mixed inside a window, with tabs to access the different components. Components can also be docked into the sides, top, and bottom of windows that support this, such as the Editor window.

Workspaces

Support for discrete sets of windows organized by task.

MDI & SDI modes

SDI (single document interface) means you have multiple windows on the screen. MDI (multiple document interface) means that there is one large window with subwindows inside that window.

Workspace

A workspace is a set of open windows, their contents, positions, and frame styles. To get the current workspace, call TopManager().getDefault(). getWindowManager().getCurrentWorkspace(). Workspaces contain Modes.

Mode

An interface representing a window containing GUI components. Modes define *docking*. Windows may contain multiple components on a tabbed pane or components that are docked into the top, bottom, left, right, or the center of the window (using draggable splitters so the user can adjust the relative sizes). Generally, modules don't need to interact directly with the mechanics of modes; however, if there's a particular window, such as the Explorer or Editor windows, that you want your component to open in, you can locate that Mode by calling Mode mode = TopManager.getDefault().getWindowManager().findMode(String name) and add your TopComponent to it by calling the dockInto() method with your component as the argument.

Modes contain one or more TopComponents. This can also be done via XML layers, as explained at the end of this list.

TopComponent

This is the base class for all dockable window components in the IDE. A TopComponent is a generic GUI container component, subclassing javax.swing.JComponent. The difference is that it has the hooks to be connected to NetBeans' window management system (see Figure 15-11 for a big-picture view).

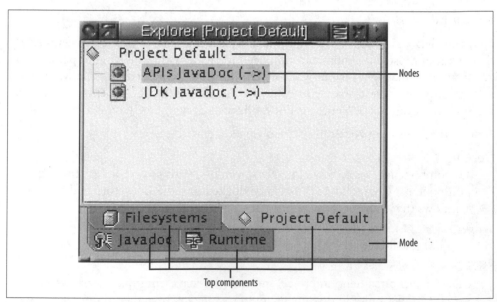

Figure 15-11. Modes, TopComponents, and Nodes—anatomy of the Explorer window

WindowManager

This is the class that actually handles the opening and closing of TopComponents and the docking behavior of Modes and that you can listen to for changes in the current workspace and available set of workspaces. To get the default instance, call TopManager.getDefault().getWindowManager().

`TopComponent.Registry`

> This is another singleton class; it has methods you can call to get the set of currently active nodes. All `TopComponents` instantiated in NetBeans are registered here. When a `TopComponent` gets input focus, it becomes the "active" `TopComponent` and gains control over what the active nodes are. The active nodes arc used in turn to enable or disable functionality (such as menu items) depending on what nodes the user has selected. To get this registry, call `TopManager.getDefault().getWindowManager().getRegistry()`.

`Modes`, `TopComponents`, and `Workspaces` can also be installed declaratively by modules, using XML layers. For an overview of interacting with the window system through the system filesystem, see Chapter 17. There are XML formats for files to define `Workspaces`, `Modes`, and their contents.

Cookies

`org.openide.cookies.*`

Cookies are a design pattern to allow the lookup of arbitrary Java objects. Any class that implements the empty `Node.Cookie` interface is a "cookie." All `Nodes` and `DataObjects` can hold cookies; for the convenience of subclasses, `AbstractNode` and `MultiDataObject` normally hold cookies in their protected `CookieSet`. A cookie can be retrieved by calling `someNode.getCookie(Class cookieClass)` or `someDataObject.getCookie(Class cookieClass)`. Generally one defines an interface that extends a `Cookie` and provides an implementation of it that can be fetched from a `DataObject` or `Node`. There are some useful basic implementations of common cookies in the Open APIs—generally these are classes whose names end with `Support`.

This package defines some cookie classes that apply broadly to NetBeans, specifying such common actions as printing, opening files in an editor, opening files in a viewer, saving, and so forth.

`OpenCookie`

> A cookie class that has a single method called `open()`, which tells NetBeans to open an object (normally in an editor, whether as text or graphically).

`EditorCookie`

> A cookie to allow access to a document object and the editor instances that have the document open and determine if the document is modified.

`SaveCookie`

> A cookie with a single method `save()` to instruct NetBeans to save an object.

`InstanceCookie`

> Some Nodes, such as JavaBeans on the **Form Editor**'s **Component Palette**, are able to create instances of some arbitrary object (for example, when you drop a `JButton` on a form). `InstanceCookie` provides support for creating this instance via its `instanceCreate()` method. Another powerful use of `InstanceCookie` is its

use to create a node that represents a Java class instance without NetBeans having to load that class unless something actually calls `instanceCreate()`.

SourceCookie

> Objects representing Java source files will have a `SourceCookie` providing access to a `SourceElement` object, which has methods such as `getClasses()` and `getImports()`, which give the caller structured access to the contents of that source file.

Cookies and supports

As just mentioned, the convention for `Cookies` is that the interface be distinct from the implementation. This helps to enforce a clean separation between an interface that is to be exposed to client modules and the implementation of the functionality. The implementation might be in a class implementing the interface that exposes members that client code should not manipulate. The following are support classes that provide implementations of various `Node.Cookies` within NetBeans, which you may subclass or use "as is" in your own code:

CloneableEditorSupport or the more concrete DataEditorSupport

> These classes can implement `EditorCookie`, `OpenCookie`, `ViewCookie`, `EditCookie`, `LineCookie`, `CloseCookie`, and `PrintCookie`, all representing functionality common to most text editing. `SaveCookie` is often implemented manually in conjunction with an editor support.

InstanceSupport

> Implements `InstanceCookie` and `InstanceCookie.Of`, providing support for dereferencing a JavaBean that is being represented by the cookie holder.

ExecSupport

> Implements `ArgumentsCookie`, `DebuggerCookie`, and `ExecCookie` to provide the ability to execute or debug a `DataObject`.

CompilerSupport

> Implements `CompilerCookie` and has inner classes for supporting compile, clean, and build operations on `DataObjects`.

Execution

`org.openide.execution.*`

Support for executing data objects. Many types of data in an IDE can be executed in one way or another. The Execution API provides generic support for execution. This API supports the preparation of an environment in which a program will be run, running it, and managing any output from that process. NetBeans has `Executors`, configured instances of execution services that can be associated with individual `DataObjects`, such as those representing Java or C++ classes, in order to override project-wide defaults. They are invoked against those objects to run them. For example, the NetBeans Java support module contains two such execution services, one for starting an external JVM and one for loading classes within the same JVM in which NetBeans is running. Modules can install additional execution services, and users can create additional instances of a given class of execution service with varying arguments (such as creating a special execution service for running code in a Java 1.1 VM to test applets). Execution may be as simple as running a Java class, or as complex as deploying code to a remote application server and running it there.

Executor

> A class that is able to launch an execution process via its execute(DataObject obj) method.

ProcessExecutor

> Launches an external process including passing command-line arguments.

ThreadExecutor

> Launches a process in a new thread in the VM in which NetBeans is running.

ScriptType

> NetBeans can support a variety of scripting languages, such as Jython, via the Scripting module. This class provides basic support for executing a script.

ExecSupport

> An implementation of ExecCookie and DebuggerCookie, which provide methods to execute and debug objects such as Java classes.

Java Hierarchy

org.openide.src.* and org.openide.src.nodes.*

The Java Hierarchy API provides classes that structurally represent Java sources and classes and the subcomponents that comprise them, such as methods, fields, inner classes, and so on, so they can be manipulated programmatically. The general structure is as follows:

SourceElement

> The top-level container representing an entire source file, which can be retrieved via SourceCookie. It contains ClassElements.

ClassElement

> Represents a Java class or interface. It contains MemberElements.

MemberElement

> Comprises the appropriately named ClassElement (for named inner classes), MethodElement, FieldElement, or ConstructorElement.

Using the preceding classes, it is possible to programmatically explore and modify source files in NetBeans.

Element

> A base class for structural elements of source files, such as fields, methods, classes, and so on.

`InitializerElement`
    A class to represent an initializer section in a Java file, for example:

```
public class MyClass {
  static {
    doSomething();
  }
}
```

`Import`
    Represents an import statement in a source file.

`Identifier`
    Represents an identifier, such as `String` or `com.foo.MyClass`.

Filesystems

`org.openide.filesystems.*`

The Filesystems API implements the concept of virtual filesystems and layered filesystems within NetBeans. It provides an abstraction on top of `java.io.File` that is not tied directly to files on disk; a file can be any data-containing entity that has a name and can live in a hierarchy. It is the concept of merged layers making up a single filesystem, or namespace, that allows modules to add functionality to NetBeans declaratively, without programmatic intervention.

The Filesystems API is divided into two sections—the public APIs and the service provider interface. A module written to the Filesystems SPI can add support to NetBeans for new ways of storing data. And all other code that references files through the Filesystems public API in all other modules will be able to use files transparently in this new data store without changes. To add support for a new storage medium, a module needs to include support for reading and writing data and for listening for changes on file objects within a data store. By implementing the `FileSystem` interface, such a module contracts with the rest of NetBeans that files in the store peculiar to that storage medium will be accessible via the interfaces defined in the Filesystems API. Without any modules, the NetBeans platform supports the following types of storage:

Local filesystems
    A provider to allow mounting of local directories.

JAR/ZIP filesystems
    Access to files within a JAR or ZIP archive.

XML filesystems
    Access to "files" that are really entries in an XML file in a predefined format.

The standard distribution of the IDE also contains modules to support the following additional forms of data storage:

JavaCVS filesystems

Allows for access to a remote CVS (Concurrent Versioning System) repository, and all the common operations done in CVS. The implementation is written entirely in Java, using the JavaCVS library (*http://javacvs.netbeans.org/library/index.html*).

Generic VCS filesystems

This module supports access to a variety of version control systems by defining commands that launch that system's utilities in a shell and parse the output of the external process.

Another interesting aspect of Filesystems is the concept of *layered filesystems*. One can create a MultiFileSystem that contains a set of other filesystems and presents them as a single filesystem with a common namespace. At the outset, this seems trivial, but taken in the context of being able to do the things listed here, you can begin to see the power of such a model:

- Define a filesystem as the contents of an XML document.

- Define Java objects within that filesystem by specifying a file whose name, contents, or attributes can be dereferenced to load a class and create an instance of that class via the default (no argument) JavaBean constructor.

- Merge multiple filesystems into a single namespace, as if the entire contents of the filesystem lived in a single namespace.

If a filesystem can be an XML file, can specify a set of Java classes to instantiate on demand, and can be merged with other similar filesystems, you have an infrastructure by which components can be arbitrarily added to an infrastructure and cleanly removed without dependencies on initially loading Java classes or on the contents of the virtual filesystem remaining static. Many components in NetBeans (some wizards, dialog boxes, and menus) assemble themselves from a folder containing *.instance* files and other folders that define their contents.

Additionally, it is possible to use the Filesystems API as a standalone library—it does not depend on other parts of NetBeans to do its work. For more information about how to do this, see the Filesystems Library (*http://openide.netbeans.org/fs/index.html*) page. This is also true of a number of other APIs and subsystems, notably Nodes and Explorer. More information can be found on the NetBeans web site under the **Platform** tab.

FileSystem

The abstract base class that all filesystems (such as local, ZIP/JAR, CVS) extend. FileSystem is the interface module that code will use to interact with any filesystem.

FileObject

An abstraction for a file. FileObjects also support annotations, which allow, for example, a version control system to expose the information that a file is out of date. FileObjects can have attributes that go beyond the typical operating system file attributes. Arbitrary Java objects may be added to a `FileObject` as named attributes.

`AbstractFileSystem`

This is a base class that makes implementing a new filesystem much easier than if you subclass `FileSystem` directly. It contains a few simple interfaces that, when implemented, will take care of most of the work of interfacing to a new kind of storage system.

`MIMEResolver`

Files in NetBeans are identified by their MIME type. When you write a `DataLoader` to load a new file type, you may need to create and register a `MIMEResolver`. When NetBeans encounters a new file type, it queries the pool of available resolvers. If a resolver recognizes the file type, it will provide an appropriate `DataLoader` for the file. There is a declarative syntax for defining `MIMEResolver`s in XML, described in the Open APIs documentation and covered in this book in Chapter 21.

Modules, JARs, and Class Loaders

Like many Java applications that actually host a number of independently written and distributed components, NetBeans tries to insulate modules from one another to some extent using class loaders. This strategy permits modules to act in some ways like independent programs and helps to enforce dependencies between modules.

There are several levels of class loading used in NetBeans. Each has at least one class loader in it. Each level *inherits* from the previous levels so that a class (or resource) loadable from one level is also loadable from the following ones, as shown by Figure 15-12.

1. The Java bootstrap class loader is created by the Java VM and is normally not touched by applications (NetBeans included). Assuming you are running the J2SDK needed for NetBeans, it typically loads from *jre/lib/rt.jar* (the JRE or Java Platform) as well as extensions in *jre/lib/ext/*.jar*.

   When NetBeans starts up, the full list of these JARs is printed in the log file, as of NetBeans 3.4. In NetBeans 3.3 or earlier, you can look at **Tools → Options → Debugging and Executing → Execution Types → External Execution → Expert → Boot Classpath**, and the other paths shown there may be useful to look at, too. Using the NetBeans APIs, you can also find the boot classpath using the call `org.openide.execution.NbClassPath.createBootClassPath()`.

2. The application class loader contains what is normally thought of as the "classpath." `ClassLoader.getSystemClassLoader()` retrieves this loader. In NetBeans, it is used for NetBeans core and API platform classes loaded from *lib/core.jar* and *lib/openide.jar*; any core patches in *lib/patches/*.jar* (these come at the front of the classpath); and any other basic libraries, such as XML parsers found in *lib/ext/*.jar*. It will also include *lib/tools.jar* from the J2SDK, which contains code for tools such as the `javac` compiler.

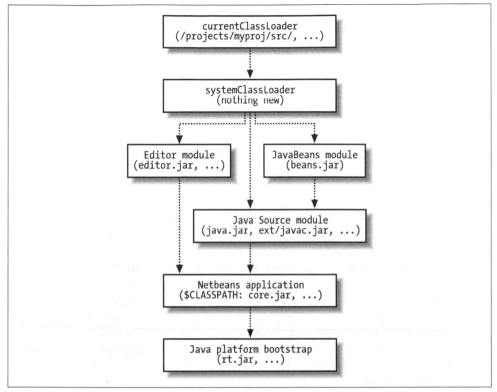

Figure 15-12. NetBeans class loaders (with three modules installed)

The NetBeans classpath is determined by its launch script. It normally does not include anything supplied by modules, only the platform, and except in special circumstances users should not try to modify this classpath. You can see your classpath in the log file using all versions of NetBeans. Programmatically, use NbClassPath.createClassPath().

3. Each NetBeans module has its own dedicated class loader. This class loader always loads from the module JAR itself in *modules/*, of course. (Some modules reside in *modules/autoload/*.jar* or *modules/eager/*.jar*, but that is not important for this discussion.)

It may also load from related JAR files. If a module manifest contains the attribute Class-Path, this points to other associated JAR files that the module owns. For example, the Java Source module (*modules/java.jar*) also uses a separate parser living in *modules/ext/javac.jar* and *modules/ext/java-gj.jar*. NetBeans opens these JARs and uses them automatically. Conventionally these live in the *modules/ext/* directory. Sometimes *modules/docs/* is also used to store online help archives. The Class-Path syntax is part of the JRE and is covered in the Extension Mechanism Architecture (*http://java.sun.com/j2se/1.4/docs/guide/extensions/spec.html#bundled*).

What Exactly Is a Class Loader?

If you are a Java programmer, you are probably aware that your compiled bytecode is loaded into the Java VM using a flexible mechanism called a *class loader*. But unless you are in the habit of writing dynamic code interpreters or EJB containers, the details may be a haze. Java takes care of creating a class loader to run your application (or applet, or J2EE component), and you just need to compile and run code.

The basic function of a class loader is to load a group of related classes into their own namespace. Most commonly these classes are loaded from a JAR file, but they could come from the network or even be generated on the fly.

Every class loader except for the very first one made in the VM has a *parent* class loader that it delegates to. The parent (or grandparent...) is searched first for a class name to load, then the child if the parent cannot load it. By creating multiple class loaders, you can break a big application into manageable pieces. Each piece can have its own list of available libraries, and even its own security domain. A piece of code loaded into a user-created class loader can be unloaded and reloaded without restarting the VM, making class loaders key to dynamically configurable applications like NetBeans.

An aspect of class loaders that many people are not aware of is the notion of the *defining* class loader of a class. Every class remembers the class loader that *actually* was able to load and define it, even if the request started from a child class loader. When compile-time references in a class to other classes are resolved, they must be available to the class loader that defined the original class. If they are not, you will see a `NoClassDefFoundError`.

Modules that have resources specific to several languages or national regions may also have some JAR files in *modules/locale/* that are loaded by NetBeans automatically, too. Each module might also have some patches applied to it. Classes are loaded from patch JARs before the module JAR itself is searched. These can reside in *modules/patches/the-module-name/*.jar* where the-module-name is the programmatic name of the module (determined by replacing the dashes in the filename with dots).[*]

In the current NetBeans APIs, there is not a simple way to find the list of all JAR files used by a particular module's class loader. The call `org.netbeans.core.modules.Module.getAllJars()` works but is in the core, not the public APIs, and so may not be used from module code. In the future, you will be able to see a module's "classpath" in the GUI.

---

[*] Patches for *autoload* and *eager* modules use a slightly different path: *modules/autoload/patches/the-module-name/*.jar or *modules/eager/patches/the-module-name/*.jar respectively. See Chapter 27 for details on these kinds of modules.

Besides being able to load from the module and extension JAR files and from the bootstrap and application class loaders, a module class loader can load from other module class loaders. This is possible whenever the module declares a dependency on those other modules. For example, the beans module declares a dependency on the java module, because the NetBeans JavaBeans support makes heavy use of the Java source code support. That means that classes in *modules/beans.jar* can directly refer to classes in *modules/java.jar*, if that is necessary. The reverse is *not* true: classes in *java.jar* cannot refer to classes in *beans.jar*. Unlike conventional Java class loaders, then, NetBeans module class loaders can have more than one parent and delegate to all of them.

Module class loaders are created when a module is turned on (perhaps during startup, perhaps later) and destroyed when it is turned off. If you mark the module as reloadable, you can turn off the module, change its JAR file, turn it back on, and immediately see the new code in action: there will be a fresh class loader for the new copy.

4. The NetBeans system class loader is a special class loader accessible via the API call `org.openide.TopManager.systemClassLoader()`. This class loader delegates to *all* module class loaders (as well as the bootstrap and application loaders). It does not add any JAR files: it exists only for delegation.

It is often used as a default class loader in the APIs, whenever a class needs to be loaded by name but might be present in any module. Throughout this section, you will see many examples of settings and configuration files that give class names and create Java objects as a result; the NetBeans platform code looks in the system class loader to find these classes.

The identity of the system class loader is left unchanged when modules are turned on, though as new modules are added, it becomes able to delegate to their class loaders dynamically. When modules are turned off, a fresh system class loader must be created, which will not delegate to the now-defunct module class loaders.

5. Finally, the current class loader (accessible via `TopManager.currentClassLoader()`) delegates to the system class loader and can also load classes or resources from the contents of all mounted filesystems (if they are marked by the user to be used during execution). See Chapter 2 for background.

While this class loader is not used very heavily, it is handy for some purposes. For example, Java classes run via "internal execution" can be loaded from this class loader or one like it. (See Chapter 14 for an example.) JavaBeans components added to the Form Editor's Component Palette are also loaded from this class loader. Its advantage is that a user can easily modify classes used in this class loader, and modules then get an easy way to let the user provide code to be run inside NetBeans.

The current class loader is supposed to always reflect the "current" state of code in mounted filesystems. For example, if a user makes changes to a Java source inside NetBeans and recompiles it, and this class was loaded by the current class loader in the past, it will be reset if requested again: the old class loader is discarded and a fresh one created. This feature is automatic, which means that when using internal execution, you can edit code and try again without restarting NetBeans.

Refer to the preceding list whenever you are unsure where a class is coming from, why you seem to be using an "old" version of a class you changed recently, and so on. The Java method call Class.getClassLoader() can be invaluable during debugging, too.

Reversed compile-time references are errors
If you are seeing mysterious NoClassDefFoundErrors coming from your module or customized NetBeans installation, usually this means you tried to make a compile-time reference going in the wrong direction: from a parent class loader to a child class loader. A typical mistake is placing a JAR in the application classpath (*lib/ext/*) and then expecting classes in it to be able to refer to classes in your module.

Overriding classes does not work
Another common mistake is thinking that classes in your module JAR will be able to override classes in a parent class loader. This will not work without some explicit class loader wizardry.

Splitting packages across JARs
The NetBeans module and system class loaders can have several parents; the order is arbitrary, and it is expected (for reasons of class loading speed) that a given Java package is *never* distributed across more than one class loader. So do not put part of a package in one module and use the same package name in another module that depends on it. If two independent modules use the same package name, a third module depending on *both* of them cannot safely load from this package; it could get either copy at random, since one class loader cannot load two versions of the same class.

Threading, Deadlocks, and How to Avoid Them

The power of multithreaded programming bears with it a requirement for a degree of discipline on the part of the programmer. A common source of difficult-to-trace showstopper bugs is careless use of threads, resulting in *deadlock*. A deadlock is the situation in which two threads are waiting for each other to complete their work—in which case, each is paralyzed by the other.

In Java GUI applications, a deadlock in the event thread is easy to recognize: all windows turn solid gray and are unresponsive to input. While on occasion this just means that some computation running in the VM has spun out of control and is preventing anything else from running, in most cases, the problem is that two or more threads have attempted to hold the same synchronization locks in different orders, and now none of them can continue. Since NetBeans is a multithreaded application, a carelessly written module can produce such a situation.

The most important debugging technique for deadlocks is the *thread dump*, which lets you analyze what threads were doing at the time the deadlock occurred. To get a thread dump from NetBeans, it is best to have run it from the command line: on Unix, typing `runide.sh` at a shell prompt; on Windows, using `runide.exe` rather than `runidew.exe`. Now you can press **Control-** on Unix or **Control-Break** on Windows to see a thread dump.

 On Windows it is useful to have already set the console window to have a large enough scroll-back buffer to contain a lengthy thread-dump.

On Unix, if you have run NetBeans in the background (for example, using a launcher icon under Gnome), find the Java process using `ps` and then signal it using `kill -QUIT process-ID`. You can then see the thread dump in the command's output log, for example *~/.gnomerc-errors*. JDK 1.3 gives usable information, but JDK 1.4 gives a richer dump including a list of locks held.

There are a number of scenarios in which deadlocks are likely in NetBeans:

- Synchronization locks are acquired in a haphazard order. Make sure you ask for locks in a well-defined sequence in all your code.

- Your event listener is called while an important operation, such as a file change, is in progress, and you try to do something complicated in the listener body. Try running your handling code *later* (asynchronously) so that the operation can complete before or while your code is run. `org.openide.util.RequestProcessor` is a good way to do this. When writing an event source that might fire changes to unknown listeners, carefully document what these listeners are permitted to do.

- One task (for example, using `RequestProcessor`) waits for another task to finish before it can continue. If the other task was posted to the same `RequestProcessor`, you will deadlock! Any calls to `Task.waitFinished()` should be examined carefully. When in doubt, use *private* `RequestProcessor` instances for each kind of functionality. NetBeans 3.4 makes this easier, but you can do it in NetBeans 3.3, too.

- You display a modal dialog box and wait for the result. Sometimes programmers do not even realize they are blocking until the dialog box closes. If the call is made from a sensitive thread, you could deadlock. Display a non-modal dialog box or make the call to `show()` from a fresh `Thread`. In NetBeans 3.4, use `RequestProcessor.getDefault().post()`.

- You try to do some kind of computation in code run inside the AWT/Swing event thread or other critical shared thread. If it takes too long, NetBeans may freeze. A common offender is XML parsing; be aware that parsing an XML document can make HTTP connections to resolve a DTD. While it may appear to work on your machine, if the user is not connected to the Internet, he or she will be very unhappy! Use an explicit `EntityResolver` to ensure that no network connections are made, or perform the parsing in another thread.

Detailed information on the threading models used in the NetBeans Open APIs is included in the API documentation. Choose the **Threading Models** link from the summary page of the APIs.

The Open APIs offer a powerful mechanism by which applications and extensions to the NetBeans IDE can be built. Having gone over them, in the next chapter, we will put them to use creating a simple module.

## CHAPTER 16

Developing Modules—the New Module Wizard

The HelloWorld Module

In this chapter, we will walk through creating and running a trivial module.

Creating a Module Using the New Module Wizard

The quickest way to make a new module is by using the *New Module Wizard* as shown here:

1. Select **File** → **New** and in the wizard that appears, select **Templates** → **NetBeans Extensions** → **IDE Plug-in Module**.

2. First you must choose a name for the module JAR (try helloworld) and a place to put it. The exact location is not very important. You will also be asked to choose a display name for the module that the user will see (try Hello World), and a location in which to put the classes and resources that will form a part of your new module. Choose a package name, such as com.mycompany. nbmodules.helloworld.

3. We will create a module with just one feature in it: it will add a new menu item to the IDE. So in the appropriate step of the wizard, ask to add a menu or toolbar item, but do not request a new file type.

4. Next you must choose where your new menu item will go. Pick some menu in the IDE, such as **File**. You can specify exact placement in the menu as well. For now it does not matter, so select any position in the menu. Give the menu item a name, such as Say Hello; you may also select an icon (in GIF format at 16 × 16 size) to use for the menu item, if you wish.

5. You will be prompted to provide a version number, category, and description for the module. These pieces of information are not important for now, so you can leave them blank.

6. When you are done, click **Finish** on the wizard to create the module.

The IDE's Explorer should show the new files it created, or if not just browse to the Java package you selected in the wizard. You can open the new source files in the Editor by double-clicking them.

7. Find the actual module JAR that is created with this icon:

   It should display with the JAR name and display name you configured, for example: **helloworld [Hello World]**. Click it and press **Execute**.

   The IDE should tell you it is installing your module, and in a few moments you should see your new menu item **Say Hello** in the **File** menu.

8. At this point, the menu item does not do anything when selected. But we can easily insert functionality. Open the action class in the Editor. It will be named **MyAction** or something similar. Find the performAction() method and insert some code, for example:

   ```
   NotifyDescriptor desc = new NotifyDescriptor.Message("Hello from a module!");
   TopManager.getDefault().notify(desc);
   ```

   Do not forget to import the right API packages, in this case just one:

   ```
   import org.openide.*;
   ```

   > You do not need to manually type this line. Just move the cursor to a class you wish to import and press **Alt-Shift-I** and accept the class name proffered in the dialog box.

   What does this code do? TopManager is a special class in the IDE's APIs that serves as an index for the implementations of other APIs. One of its functions is to ask the window system to display a dialog box or wizard with a standardized user interface. NotifyDescriptor is a simple dialog box, and NotifyDescriptor.Message is a dialog box that just displays a message but does not ask anything of the user. notify() displays the dialog and waits for the user to close it.

9. After inserting the code to show the dialog box, just click the module JAR in the Explorer window once again and press **Execute**. The IDE notices that you have made changes in the action class that implements the menu item, so it is automatically recompiled, the JAR recreated, and the module reinstalled in a few seconds. Again select **File → Say Hello** and this time a small dialog box should appear with a message in it. To test any further changes to the module, all you need do is click the JAR file after typing in code changes, press **Execute**, and you can see the effect at once.

The Source Files

Let's take a look at these new files and see how they fit together as a module. First, the action is shown in Example 16-1.

Example 16-1. MyAction.java for the Hello World module

```java
public class MyAction extends CallableSystemAction {
  public void performAction() {
    NotifyDescriptor desc =
      new NotifyDescriptor.Message("Hello from a module!");
    TopManager.getDefault().notify(desc);
  }
  public String getName() {
    return NbBundle.getMessage(MyAction.class, "LBL_Action");
  }
  protected String iconResource() {
    return "MyActionIcon.gif";
  }
  public HelpCtx getHelpCtx() {
    return HelpCtx.DEFAULT_HELP;
  }
}
```

In NetBeans, rather than directly creating Swing menu items, toolbar buttons, and so on, there is an abstract class named org.openide.util.actions.SystemAction that represents the action. The available action classes are covered in Chapter 15.

Here the Open APIs Support provides a basic action implementation using CallableSystemAction. This subclass of SystemAction is intended for simple actions that are always enabled. It implements several visual presenters. The presenter we will use here is org.openide.util.actions.Presenter.Menu, which provides a simple menu item using the display name and icon of the action (as supplied by the getName() and iconResource() methods).

When invoked (for example, when the user selects a menu item), the method performAction() will be called.

 performAction() will not be called in the AWT event thread. This means you must not directly manipulate GUI components in its body. But TopManager.notify() is fine to call. When in doubt, consult the document Threading Models included in the Open APIs reference documentation.

It is necessary to override one more method: getHelpCtx() can be used to link context-sensitive help to an action. Since this is only useful at production time, for testing we just use DEFAULT_HELP, which means no context help is available.

The next file created by the wizard, *MyActionIcon.gif*, is a simple GIF-format image that serves as the icon for the action and appears in the menu item.

The last file, *Bundle.properties*, is a Java resource bundle used to localize all human-visible text used by the module. This file is shown in Example 16-2.

Example 16-2. Bundle.properties for Hello World module

```
# MyAction
LBL_Action=Hello
```

NbBundle, used in `MyAction.getName()`, is a utility class in the Open APIs that simplifies the job of accessing internationalized resources and handles some class loader issues. More information on `NbBundle` is presented in Chapter 17.

Next comes the XML layer. We have to specify that the action should be installed into some part of the IDE's user interface by the module, and where in that UI it should go. In NetBeans, many parts of the IDE are configured by files that can represent GUI components, options, and many other things. In the case of menus, the system filesystem has a subdirectory *Menu* under which are subdirectories for each menu, and under these are files representing menu items. In our case, *.instance* files are used to represent instances of actions. This style of object installation is discussed in Chapter 14.

The module could manually create the *.instance* files in the system filesystem, and remove them when it is uninstalled. To simplify this process, the APIs permit you to install files into fixed locations using declarative XML layers, as discussed in previous chapters. So our module has a simple layer, as shown in Example 16-3.

Example 16-3. mf-layer.xml for Hello World module

```
<!DOCTYPE filesystem PUBLIC
          "-//NetBeans//DTD Filesystem 1.1//EN"
          "http://www.netbeans.org/dtds/filesystem-1_1.dtd">
<filesystem>
  <folder name="Menu">
    <folder name="File">
      <file name="com-somewhere-nbmodule-MyAction.instance"/>
    </folder>
  </folder>
</filesystem>
```

This layer says that an empty file named *com-somewhere-nbmodule-MyAction.instance* should be placed in the folder *Menu/File/* in the system filesystem. The IDE recognizes the *.instance* extension and associates an *instance* of your action class with the file. This is done behind the scenes with `InstanceCookie`, as described in Chapter 15. When it finds the instance in the **File** menu configuration area, it adds a menu item (in no particular order) to the menu.

To bring everything together and tell the IDE what kinds of things are available in the module, you need a manifest. The JAR manifest lists entry points into NetBeans for the module. The manifest for this sample module could look like Example 16-4.

Example 16-4. Manifest for Hello World module

```
OpenIDE-Module: com.mycompany.nbmodules.helloworld/1
OpenIDE-Module-Name: Test Module
OpenIDE-Module-Specification-Version: 0.1
OpenIDE-Module-Layer: com/mycompany/nbmodules/helloworld/mf-layer.xml
```

Here we specify the internal unique name for the module with the `OpenIDE-Module` tag, which the IDE also uses to tell if a JAR is really a module or not. `OpenIDE-Module-Name` gives it a display name. `OpenIDE-Module-Specification-Version` gives a version number; details on version numbers are given in Chapter 27. Finally, we use the `OpenIDE-Module-Layer` attribute to point to the XML layer inside the JAR, which in turn installs the menu item.

If you examine the contents of the module JAR file, for example using `jar tvf mymodule.jar`, you should see the files just mentioned:

```
META-INF/MANIFEST.MF
com/mycompany/nbmodules/helloworld/Bundle.properties
com/mycompany/nbmodules/helloworld/MyAction.class
com/mycompany/nbmodules/helloworld/MyActionIcon.gif
com/mycompany/nbmodules/helloworld/mf-layer.xml
```

This JAR file is a complete NetBeans module. You can install it into any copy of the IDE by dropping it into the *modules* directory before starting it, or while the IDE is running using **Tools → Options → Modules → New Module** and selecting the JAR.

That's all! You should now have a basic idea of what a module JAR looks like and how it is put together. With this foundation, you can begin experimenting with more complex modules. In the next chapter, we will delve more deeply into some aspects of the NetBeans architecture that will help you continue.

## CHAPTER 17

Internals of the Running IDE

Writing code to interact with a running application requires knowledge of what is going on behind the scenes in that application and what resources are available to you at runtime. This chapter will acquaint you with what is going on behind the scenes in NetBeans.

The Activated Node(s)

One of the reasons many user interface components in NetBeans are explorer views is that explorer views have a concept of a Node or set of Nodes being activated. At any time, only one window has input focus, meaning that it is responding to the keyboard. Many windows contain tabbed panes—the component comprising each individual pane is a TopComponent. Whichever tab is displayed in the window that has focus is the active TopComponent. Many TopComponents display Nodes in one way or another. Multiple Nodes in an explorer view can be selected (by Shift- or Control-left-clicking them). The Nodes that are selected in the active TopComponent are "activated." The *activated nodes* provide the context by which NetBeans decides what actions should be available, by enabling or disabling menu items and toolbar buttons. They also determine what properties should be shown in the global property sheet. For context-sensitive actions such as **Compile**, it is this context that determines if the action can be performed and what the target of that action is. Note that in the **Code Editor**, the selected node is determined by the cursor position. If you were to expand a Java class Node in **Explorer → Filesystems**, you would find a Node for the method you are editing. This *is* the selected Node if the cursor is within that method's body in the editor, and if you had edited the file since you last compiled it, the **Compile** action would be enabled. On the other hand, if you are changing the editor colors, and the selected Node is a Node representing settings for display colors in the Editor, the **Compile** action should not be enabled—that's not a thing you can compile.

In the case of multiple selection, the available actions are the intersection of the actions possessed in common by all of the activated Nodes. Each such action can decide for itself whether it will be enabled on the multiple selection—for example, **Compile** will work as easily on five Java sources as one, whereas **Customize Bean** works only on one class at a time and so will appear in the context menu but be disabled (grayed out). The global property sheet displays only properties shared by all the selected nodes. If all the nodes have the same value for a property, that value will be displayed, and otherwise you will see, for example, <Different Values>.

At any time, your code can find out what the activated Nodes are by calling TopManager.getDefault().getWindowManager().getRegistry().getActivatedNodes().

Cookies

A Node owns an arbitrary set of cookies. A cookie can be any Java class that implements the empty Node.Cookie marker interface. Cookies provide a generic way to look up arbitrary functionality associated with a node. If you know about a given subinterface of Node.Cookie that has a method you're interested in calling, you can ask any Node whether it can supply an instance of an implementation of this class by calling someNode.getCookie(SomeCookie.class). In this sense, Cookies are for anything you want to use them for. For example, if you had a Node that represented a C++ source file, you might want to create a cookie class that provided access to a structural, parsed analysis of that class.

Why Cookies?

According to Yarda Tulach, "The name 'cookie' was invented by us, and was meant as something special and sweet that is provided by an object, which you can ask for." NetBeans' cookies bear a fleeting resemblance to the concept as defined by web browsers, but only inasmuch as they are objects held by a provider object that is not expected to know much about what kinds of cookies it possesses. *Do not confuse NetBeans' concept of cookies with browser cookies.* The name probably contributes a little bit to Cookies being a stumbling block for people getting involved in coding for NetBeans.

Cookies in NetBeans are actually quite simple and solve several important problems. The first is that they allow for separation of data storage and business logic—an object representing some data is not required to also implement all functions pertaining to that data.

Secondly, they allow for the dynamic addition and removal of behavior, providing a sort of dynamic multiple inheritance at runtime.

Thirdly, since they are based on interfaces (or abstract classes), not concrete classes, they can hide the implementation details of the class that actually implements the Cookie.

Finally, another reason for cookies is reuse of implementation: There are a number of cookie implementations in the APIs (usually with class names such as SomeSupport) which module authors can subclass and customize. This provides convenience to module authors and reduces memory footprint—cookie authors need not reinvent the wheel.

One of the most common uses of Cookies is to implement actions. A brief look at some of the Node.Cookie implementations defined in the Open APIs gives a pretty good sense of common uses for Cookies: CloseCookie, ExecCookie, OpenCookie, PrintCookie, SaveCookie, EditCookie. So, if you press **F9** to compile, the decision tree is something like this:

1. What is the currently selected node?
2. Does it have a CompilerCookie?
3. If yes, compile, if not, beep.

Now let's take the case where you have an HTML file and a Java file selected in **Explorer**. The decision tree is only slightly different:

1. What are the currently selected nodes?
2. Does each one have a CompilerCookie? (No, you can't compile an HTML file.)
3. No, one of these Nodes does not have a compiler cookie. Beep.

In the next section, you will have the opportunity to browse some objects within the running IDE and see what Cookies they support.

A Peek under the Hood

Mount the directory *examples/extending-netbeans/sources/current-node-viewer/* from the downloadable sources associated with this book. In this directory in the util package is a small Java class called CurrentNodeViewer. Run this class with internal execution.[*] It displays a window that simply displays text information about whatever Node is selected. Now, with that window open, try selecting random nodes and components of the IDE with the mouse or keyboard—try options in the **Tools →
Options** window. Move the cursor around in the code in the **Editor** window and notice that the selected Node changes as you move from method to method. Spend five or ten minutes selecting other nodes and components in the IDE and observe the

---

[*] The directory includes an *.nbattrs* file with the attributes set correctly for NetBeans 3.3. If you are using a later version, and have any difficulties running it, copy sources to a new directory and compile and run it from there.

list of Cookies available, the node classes, and so on. You can begin to get a better sense of exactly what is going on under the hood as you interact with NetBeans.

In particular, open any source file in the editor. Place the cursor at the top of the file and type a character or two so that the file now needs to be saved. Notice that the list of Cookies available in the **CurrentNodeViewer** window has changed—a SaveCookie has been added to the list of available Cookies. If you press **Control-S** to save it, the SaveCookie will disappear from the list.

Touring NetBeans with the Bean Browser

The Bean Browser is another tree-based style of explorer view, but considerably more powerful in its ability to browse hierarchies of Nodes, using introspection to allow you to drill much deeper than just observing those objects that are exposed directly in the user interface, as you did with the previous example.

The Bean Browser is included in the Open APIs Support module. It allows you to browse and manipulate live nodes within the IDE and uses introspection to examine non-node objects surfaced as properties by nodes. To open the Bean Browser, right-click a Node in an explorer view, and choose **Tools → Bean Browse → Bean Browse Node**. A new Bean Browser window will open, rooted on that node. You can also browse starting from a set of common jumping-off points in NetBeans by choosing **Bean Browse Master** (see Figure 17-1).

When you open a Node in the Bean Browser, you may see a set of several Nodes underneath it that can include:

Properties
  Items this object exposes as properties according to its BeanInfo. Properties of primitive types, such as strings, are skipped.

Children
  Child Nodes of this node, which can be browsed as well by expanding them in the tree.

Instance of SomeClass
  If the Node gives you access (via an InstanceCookie—more on that in Chapter 15) to an instance of some object.

Cookies
  The Cookies the Node has in its cookie set—if you tried the CurrentNodeViewer example before, you may be beginning to get a sense of how Cookies are used inside NetBeans.

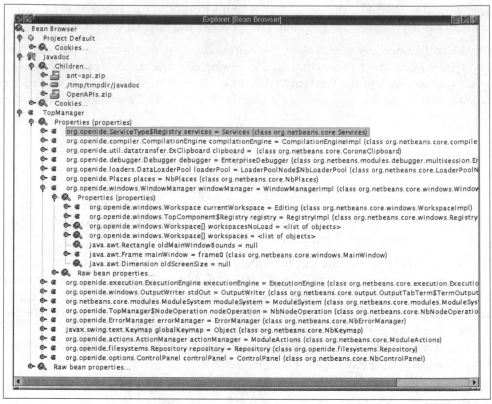

Figure 17-1. Bean Browser—master view

What you see is not necessarily the entire set of Cookies the Node has, but only those declared in the Open APIs and thus known to the **Bean Browser**. Since Cookies must be requested by class, there is no way to read the entire set of Cookies a Node or DataObject possesses. This is an API limitation. A module that defines a new kind of cookie can, however, register it with the Bean Browser so it will appear on nodes that hold it. See, for example, the downloadable sources for the Minicomposer example.

Raw Bean Properties

Properties of the object available simply by calling getter methods, and ignoring any declared BeanInfo. Properties of primitive types are exposed, and even properties with non-public getters are shown, so you can find out as much as possible about an object.

For a deeper sense of what lives under the hood in NetBeans, try the **Bean Browse Master** menu item mentioned above, and explore the Nodes you see there. The Bean Browser is a powerful tool for getting to know the internals of NetBeans, and quickly finding what Cookies and properties are available on an object your module needs to interact with.

The Bean Browser can also be used to test your own JavaBeans classes—there is an execution service the Open APIs Support module installs which will create an instance of a JavaBean (a class which has a no-argument constructor) and open a Bean Browser rooted on your JavaBean—so you can test non-visual classes visually using introspection, and also drill down through any JavaBeans your initial bean exposes as properties. To use this functionality, select your JavaBean class in Explorer, and, on the **Execution** tab of its property sheet, set the **Executor** property to **Test Beans**.

If you test a bean using this executor, the bean class must not be available in an enabled module. If it is, you will be testing the module's version of the class, rather than the version you are editing in **Filesystems**. For an explanation of why this is so, see Chapter 15.

Data Objects, Nodes, and Cookies

A common use of Nodes is to represent DataObjects. A DataObject is an object which owns some textual or binary content, such as a Java source file or an image. DataObject is NetBeans' abstraction for things that contain data. A DataLoader registers itself with the system as being able to load a particular file type. When a new file is found, all of the registered loaders are asked if they can recognize/load this file type, until one is found that can. DataLoaders are factories for DataObjects.

Like Nodes, DataObjects also support cookies. In fact, a DataNode, which is the standard Node implementation to represent DataObjects, by default uses the cookie set of the DataObject to provide cookies.

If you call someNode.getCookie(OpenCookie.class), you can find out whether an instance of org.openide.cookies.OpenCookie is in the set of cookies of the Node you're calling this method on, and therefore, whether the Open action can be performed (OpenCookie implements a method, open( ), for this purpose).

A good way to think of what you see in NetBeans when editing is that you have a Node which represents a DataObject which represents one or more FileObjects, such as a *.java* file and its associated *.class* file(s). In the **Editor**, in turn, you are looking at a Document which represents the data contained by the DataObject.

Filesystems and the Repository

When you deal with files in the IDE, you never are dealing with java.io.File. Net-Beans contains a virtual wrapper around files, org.openide.filesystems.FileObject. This abstraction is what allows NetBeans to do the following:

- Transparently support different sources of file-like objects, such as CVS, FTP-based filesystems, and JAR/ZIP archives so that module code does not have to care how or where the data is stored.

- Be extended to support other types of filesystems without affecting modules that will operate on those files.

The filesystems paradigm takes its cue from the filesystem model of the Unix operating system. On Unix systems, one "mounts" a device, such as a hard drive partition, or a directory on a remote server via NFS (Network File System). That device then appears to be just another subdirectory of the root filesystem. (Microsoft Windows takes a different approach, using letters to specify devices, for example, the C: drive.)

Filesystems work very much like UNIX mount points do; that is, the user "mounts" a directory, and thus adds it to the set of directories that can be seen and interacted with inside NetBeans. The mounted filesystem can be of any type that is supported in NetBeans, such as a local directory, a JAR or ZIP file, or a remote CVS repository. Since Filesystems can be extended, the mounts can use other types of storage, too, if there are providers installed for them. For example, there is an experimental module for mounting FTP (File Transfer Protocol) servers. If you have the remotefs module installed, you will be able to mount the contents of an FTP server as well. Once a filesystem is mounted, you can browse its files and subdirectories and read and write files in it.

The **Filesystems** hierarchy you see in the **Explorer** was originally labeled **Repository** in the GUI, and for backward compatibility reasons is still called that in the Open APIs. To retrieve the set of filesystems mounted in the IDE, call org.openide.filesystems.Repository.getDefault().

When you interact with files, you will be dealing with org.openide.filesystems.FileObject. For filesystems that somehow represent directories on disk, you can use a utility method FileUtil.toFile() to get the actual java.io.File represented by a file object. However, unless you absolutely must work with this object, it is preferable to use the methods of FileObject. The toFile() method returns null when given a file object that does not correspond to a file on disk, such as an entry in a JAR file.

Services

A lot of the things an IDE will need to do involve performing a series of operations on a file or set of files. NetBeans has an abstraction called ServiceType (shown in the browser in Figure 17-2) to deal with this.

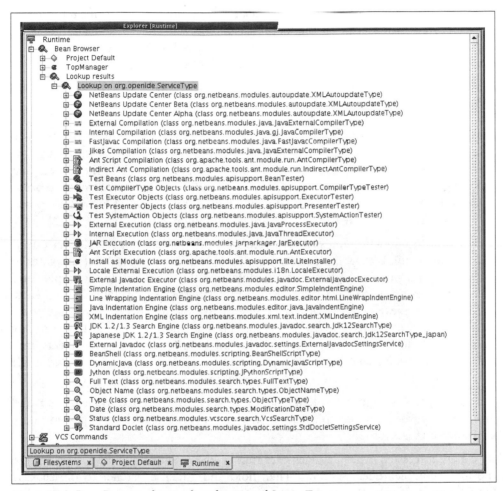

Figure 17-2. Bean Browser showing list of registered ServiceTypes

The following are the basics of services:

- Services are JavaBeans that perform a specific function registered as services inside NetBeans.

- Services are *not* singletons—multiple instances with different configurations can exist (for example, two instances of the **External Execution** service that pass different parameters to the JVMs they launch).

- A common usage of services is to implement processes that are launched and produce results in stages, such as compilation, execution, or text searches across files. This is not their only use, but typical of the needs of an IDE. If you are writing functionality that can have multiple standard sets of parameters that should coexist in the runtime simultaneously, services will probably be useful to you.

Instances of a service type can also be associated with individual files, if supported by the `DataObject` that represents the file. For example, you can set a default compilation service IDE-wide, but override this on a class-by-class basis in each file's property sheet. A reference to the service in question is stored in the file's attributes.

Lookup

Lookup is one of the newer APIs in the NetBeans paradigm. Its power is in its absolute genericness. It is exactly what its name implies—a way to look things up; the NetBeans yellow pages. You ask a lookup implementation for all of the objects that are assignable to a given Java class. There is a default implementation (`Lookup.getDefault()`), which is generally what you will use. Other types of queries are possible, such as string based keys, but these are less commonly used.

When you do a lookup, you get back zero or more objects that match that query. The global default `Lookup` implementation does nothing on its own, but delegates to lookup implementations registered by modules and the core. This fairly simple entry point provides a way to locate almost any interesting object available in NetBeans' JVM and provides a way to do so by interface. Modules need only make some objects of a given interface available via lookup, and they are then available to any module that knows the interface they implement. A simple way to make objects findable via the default `Lookup` (`Lookup.getDefault()`) is to simply add *.instance* file entries to the system filesystem's *Services/* folder for the objects in question.

`Lookup` supports two types of queries: simple queries, in which a `Class` is passed, and an object returned; and complex queries, where a `Lookup.Template` is passed and a `Lookup.Result` is returned.

If you are interested in the changes over time to the result of a lookup, you can use the more complex query method. Then hold and attach a listener to the `Lookup.Result` object. If new objects matching your query become available in the `Lookup` instance you queried, or old ones disappear, you will be notified.

Lookup has no UI of its own—it is entirely an under-the-hood technology. As of NetBeans 3.3, the Bean Browser provides a UI for querying and rendering the results of a lookup.

`Cookies`, `ServiceType.Registry` and other registry classes in the Open APIs are the historical precursors to `Lookup`, and the proliferation of such classes in the APIs for looking up various kinds of objects demonstrates the need for exactly the generic sort of infrastructure the Lookup API provides. If your module creates sets of objects that another module may need to locate and use, consider using lookups to achieve this.

Options

Options are JavaBeans whose properties are settings the user can modify, such as editor colors, abbreviations, compiler settings, and the like. The parent class for all options is org.openide.options.SystemOption. Options are not Nodes, although an option is generally represented in the UI using the node delegate from an InstanceDataObject, which gets its properties from the underlying JavaBean. For options such as Editor Settings, which has child options, there is the class org. openide.options.ContextSystemOption, which has a method SystemOption[ ] getOptions() that returns an array of suboptions.

Options are singletons—there should be only one instance of an option class in the NetBeans JVM at a time. Options support PropertyChangeListeners, which are notified when the user changes a property of an option. If you write code that needs to respond to changes in the options your module installs, simply look up the option instance that your module installed (this is specified in the module layer) and attach a listener to it, as in Example 17-1.

Example 17-1. Locating a SystemOption

```
MyOption opt = (MyOption)SharedClassObject.findObject(MyObject.class, true);
// Can equivalently write:
// opt = (MyOption)Lookup.getDefault().lookup(MyOption.class);
PropertyChangeListener listener = ...;
opt.addPropertyChangeListener(listener);
```

We've discussed the concept of layers with regard to Filesystems. Options take advantage of this infrastructure and are stored in the system filesystem. Depending on the type of option and user preferences, options may be stored in the default or project layers of the system filesystem (for a discussion of these layers, see Chapter 14). Options are stored to disk within seconds of a modification being written and are loaded on demand during a new session.

Options are installed via your module's XML layer, using *.settings* files, by putting them in one of the subfolders of *Services/*. Normally, you will also make a symbolic link (*.shadow* file) from some part of *UI/Services/* to the settings file, to cause the option to appear in the **Options** window. A symbolic link is represented by org. openide.loaders.DataShadow and consists of two lines of text: the relative path of the target file in its containing filesystem; then the unique name of that filesystem (FileSystem.getSystemName()), which for settings will always be SystemFileSystem.

UI Components

NetBeans provides a number of standard UI components and base classes for creating your own components that will interact well with the rest of the environment. Using them and letting NetBeans runtime do the work of managing them is one of the things that enhances productivity for developers using the NetBeans platform to create their own applications.

TopComponents, Modes, and Workspaces

Any large application probably has at least several windows—and often those windows will contain tabs or some other mechanism so that each window serves not one purpose, but several related purposes. A means of managing these windows and components is necessary. The requirements become even more extreme when the application is large and *extensible*—any module can add components to existing windows, create new windows, and so forth.

NetBeans solves this problem by providing a window and component management system. This system manages creating windows, managing components within windows, and storing their position and content on shutdown. It also provides a degree of user-level control over windows. The basics of NetBeans' windowing system are:

- The fundamental visual control module authors work with is the component, not the window. The system will take care of creating windows and putting components into them. The basic component module authors will use to create their own components is a subclass of `javax.swing.JComponent`, which can interact with NetBeans' window system. It is called `org.openide.windows. TopComponent`.

- Windows are almost exclusively tabbed containers. Windows can contain multiple components, and there is a switching mechanism available to the user to change between components. A component that is contained in a window is said to be *docked* into that window.

- The APIs completely encapsulate windows—there is minimal access to physical windows via the APIs. Module authors deal with the interface `org.openide. windows.Mode`, which represents windows on the user desktop and allows some superficial access to physical window properties such as position. Programmatically, you don't request that a given *window* be displayed, but rather that a given `TopComponent` be displayed. It will be displayed in whatever window currently contains it, or a new window if necessary.

- Windows live in *workspaces* (`org.openide.windows.Workspace`). A workspace is a set of windows and the components they contain, rather like a virtual desktop. Workspaces are user-switchable, and the current workspace can also be changed programmatically when the user changes tasks.

- There are some standard windows that modules can add components to, such as the Explorer window. Modules may also define their own workspaces and modes.

- Modules may define new Modes and dock TopComponents into them.

- There is an XML specification for defining workspaces and modes, by which workspaces, modes, and the components they contain exist as files in the system filesystem. The preferred way to install windows and workspaces is using this specification, rather than programmatically.

The name of the interface for windows, Mode, is a curious one—why would anyone think of a window as a mode? Mode is shorthand for *docking mode*. In other words, it is *really* not a window—it is a place components can be docked. A Mode is *not* a graphical component, it is a wrapper for one—a wrapper that hides almost all details of the underlying container component.

This all probably sounds rather draconian—NetBeans rules your components with an iron fist! What the design imparts is a huge amount of flexibility. Both MDI (multiple document interface—application windows live inside one big window) and SDI (single document interface—each window is a separate OS-level window) are supported, along with combinations thereof. That would never be possible if modules created and managed their own windows independently. As a module author, you don't have to be concerned about window management; you design your components, and, if necessary, specify where you'd like them to live, and you're done. It is this window management system that makes that possible: If too much about the physical containers components live in were exposed by the APIs, it would have encouraged module authors to make assumptions about the type of containers their components live in. As a result, MDI support could never have been retrofitted to the existing API.

The windowing system further allows users to configure their environment to suit their work style. A TopComponent in one window can be docked into (moved to) another window or be cloned to create a duplicate of the original. Users can create new workspaces and populate them with the components they want.

A component can be docked into a mode with constraints. For example, a Mode can be divided into regions such as north, south, east, west, and center. The window will have tabbed containers in each location divided by sliders.

Working with TopComponents, the fundamental GUI component of NetBeans' windowing system, is easy. Design a TopComponent as you would a window, with whatever contents you want. The simplest way to display a TopComponent is to call someTopComponent.open( ). Creating Modes is also easy, either programmatically or via XML. If your module creates a number of components for users to interact with, as does the Debugger module, it may make sense for your module to create its own Mode to contain these components and add it to the **View** Menu. If interacting with components it installs is a fundamentally different task from other activities within Net-Beans, your module may also create its own workspace.

Browsing the window system in the system filesystem

All components of the window system are browsable as folders and files within the system filesystem and can be manipulated via the system filesystem in the Explorer window. Open the *Windows/* folder. You will see two folders, *WindowManager/* and *Components/*. *WindowManager/* contains a set of folder representing workspaces. If you open one of the workspace folders, you will see folders for each Mode open on that workspace (see Figure 17-3). You can open those folders and see the components that live in each Mode. Each tab that a window contains shows up as a file inside a folder representing the Mode that contains it.

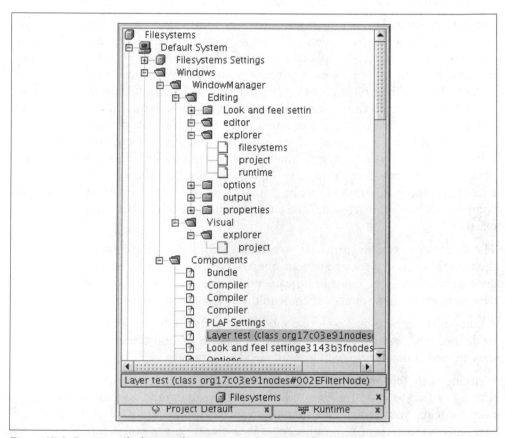

Figure 17-3. Browsing the live window system in the system filesystem

The second child folder of *Windows/* is called *Components/*. It exists because the same TopComponent may be open on one or more workspaces. It contains files representing all of the available TopComponents in the system. A TopComponent can be open only once on a given workspace, but may be shared across several workspaces.

To see the interface between the windows you see onscreen and this set of virtual files in action, try the following: If the global **Properties** window is not open, open it using **View → Properties**. Open the folder under *Windows/WindowManager/* that represents the workspace currently visible in NetBeans. Find the folder called *Properties/* and open it. You will see a file inside it, also called **Properties**. Delete this file. The open **Properties** window will disappear.

You can also use copying and pasting to rearrange your workspaces from within these folders. It is by installing files into these folders that modules can add items to the Explorer or Editor windows, create new workspaces, and otherwise manipulate the window system.

 When NetBeans is shut down, serialization is used to save the contents of the window system to disk. If you write your own TopComponents, they must be serializable. If you use the template provided by the Open APIs Support module, the skeleton code you will need is part of the template.

XML format for workspaces, modes, and components

Actually using XML to manipulate the window system is a bit less straightforward than programmatic calls, so we will try to clarify here how it works. The first thing that is not apparent from browsing the system filesystem is that each workspace is a pair of objects—a folder and an XML file that is not visible when you browse the system filesystem (although you can see most of its contents on the property sheet when you select a folder representing a workspace or mode). There are separate XML DTDs for the window manager, workspaces, modes, and references to TopComponents (see Table 17-1). Files using these DTDs also have their own specific extensions. New versions of these DTDs are sometimes published with minor revisions. Always check for the latest DTD applicable to your version of NetBeans.

Table 17-1. XML files controlling the window system in the system filesystem

Type of file	Defines	Extension	DTD	URL for DTD
reference	A unique ID that should be shared with a file representing the TopComponent in question in the folder identifying the mode it will be docked into. The ID will match the name (sans extension) of the instance file. Also defines the state (opened or closed) and docking constraints (such as "center"). These aspects can be defined separately for each window system style (MDI and SDI).	.wstcef	-//NetBeans//DTD Top Component in Mode Properties 1.0//EN	http://www.netbeans.org/dtds/tcref1_0.dtd
Mode	The mode's size (relative bounds), frame type (MDI/SDI), container type (for example, split), and the active mode.	.wsmode	-//NetBeans//DTD Mode Properties 1.0//EN	http://www.netbeans.org/dtds/modeproperties1_0.dtd
Workspace	Display name for the workspace, mode z-order as a comma-delimited list, the name of the toolbar configuration for this workspace, and the active mode.	.wswksp	-//NetBeans//DTD Workspace Properties 1.0//EN	http://www.netbeans.org/dtds/workspaceproperties1_0.dtd
Window Manager	Screen width and height (for use by the window system in positioning windows), global UI scheme (MDI or SDI), and which workspace is active.	.wswmgr	-//NetBeans//DTD Window Manager Properties 1.0//EN	http://www.netbeans.org/dtds/windowmanagerproperties1_0.dtd

Say that you have a module that needs to create a new workspace called **MyWorkspace**, create a new Mode on it called **MyMode** on it, and add some TopComponents defined in the module to it. You need to:

1. Add a folder called *MyWorkspace* to *Windows/WindowManager/* to represent the new workspace.

2. Add a matching *MyWorkspace.wswksp* XML file conforming to the workspace DTD, also to *Windows/WindowManager/*.

3. Add a folder called *MyMode* to *Windows/WindowManager/MyWorkspace/* to represent the new `Mode`.

4. Add a matching *MyMode.wsmode* XML file conforming to the mode DTD, also to *Windows/WindowManager/MyWorkspace/*.

5. Add *.instance* or *.settings* files for all of the `TopComponents` that should initially be docked into your `Mode` to *Windows/Components/*.

6. Add *.wstcref* files to the folder you created to represent your `Mode`, referring with their IDs to the names of the files you just added to *WindowManager/Components/*.

To add files with actual XML contents to the system filesystem, just create each of the preceding XML files somewhere in your module JAR. Then define them in your module layer, each file definition in the layer having a URL attribute that points to the actual XML file in the JAR:

```
<file name="MyFile.xml" url="MyFileData.xml"/>
```

For an example of defining a `Workspace`, `Mode`, and `TopComponents`, see Chapter 20. For further details on these formats, see the prose overview of the Window System API, available from the main overview page of the Open APIs Javadoc.

Note that it is easy to accomplish programmatically the same things we just described. The downside of this is that your module installer class will have to do these things when it is installed, and there is no guarantee that a user will use your workspace and components—yet they have now been lugged into memory. Also your workspace and components will not be removed automatically if your module is uninstalled. However, for testing purposes, it may be useful to show your windows quickly. The rough equivalent in Java code of the XML definitions will look like this:

```
Workspace w = TopManager.getDefault().getWindowManager().createWorkspace(
    "myworkspace",
    NbBundle.getBundle(MyTopComponent.class).getString("CTL_MyWorkspaceName"));
Mode m = w.createMode(
    "mymode",
    NbBundle.getBundle(MyTopComponent.class).getString("CTL_MyModeName"),
    new URL("nbresloc:/com/foo/mymodule/myMode.gif"));
TopComponent tc = new MyTopComponent();
m.dockInto(tc);
```

One limitation of the programmatic approach is that the APIs do not support docking with constraints—that is, you cannot dock into the left, right, top, or bottom of a

Mode, only into the center. The XML approach is the preferred approach for production code; the preceding Java code simply speeds testing and developing a module.

 If creating the necessary XML files seems intimidating, you can let NetBeans do the work for you. Simply write Java code to instantiate your UI components and run it with internal execution. Run your code and configure the UI components as you wish (positioning, docking, and so on). This will cause the Workspace, Mode, and TopComponent XML files to be created under the *Windows/* folder of the system filesystem. You can simply browse the system filesystem, copy the files into your module, and add the appropriate entries to the module layer to point at these files.

Some renaming may be necessary to make them agree with the definitions in your module (for example, a TopComponent that is opened with someTopComponent.open() will use the display name of the TopComponent for the mode and resulting filename), but this is a small task. You will probably want to manually tune the XML files a bit— for example, the XML lets you specify relative sizes of components (percentages), whereas automatically saved XML definitions might just use pixel-based absolute sizes.

Another easy way to make professional-looking window system XML files is to find a module in the NetBeans sources that installs a similar workspace or modes and components. Copy its XML definitions and adjust them to match your module.

Actions

When you want to add an item to a menu, what are you really trying to do? You are creating another *action* that users can perform. That is to say, the goal is the functionality, not the presentation of that functionality.

The basics of actions are:

- Actions have icon, display name, and enabled properties. If any of these change, the change is automatically propagated to all presenters (components such as menu buttons and toolbar buttons representing the action).

- There are a number of typical patterns for determining if an action should be enabled in NetBeans, such as the active Nodes or TopComponent. Classes such as NodeAction, CookieAction, and CallbackSystemAction can be subclassed, and come with built-in logic for managing enablement depending on the state of NetBeans.

- NetBeans action classes support context-based help, unlike the Swing action classes they subclass. For the details of this, see Chapter 27.

- Actions can be accessed via scripting, including passing arguments such as a specific node selection. For more details on scripting, see the scripting project (*http://scripting.netbeans.org/*) on the *netbeans.org* web site.

As with the preceding windowing system, NetBeans provides an abstraction (extending the standard in the Swing Actions API to work with NetBeans' action management system), which allows you to concentrate on the logic and not worry about the presentation unless you really want to.

It's generally accepted in computerdom that it's better design to separate the presentation of an action from its implementation, and that is what NetBeans does. If you look in **Tools → Options → IDE Configuration → Look and Feel → Actions**, you will find a hierarchy of Nodes representing different actions, such as **Save**. Also in the **Options** tree, you'll find folders for **Menus** and **Toolbars**. The Nodes in all these trees are produced by InstanceDataObjects representing the same SystemAction classes. Thus, you implement your action once, and how it is presented to the user can be independent of the implementation of the action itself. Actions and their counterparts in menus and toolbars can be installed declaratively in the XML layer specified by a module's manifest—so you don't even have to write Java code to add your action to a menu or toolbar.

And if you do need to control how your action is presented to the user, you have all the control you could want by using *presenters*.

Presenters

One of the few places it can be generally useful to instantiate your own UI components is for toolbar and menu presenters—components that exist in a menu or toolbar and represent actions. There are default implementations of these that will be usable in most cases: If you subclass org.openide.actions.CallableSystemAction to implement whatever you want to happen when a user invokes your action, all you need to do is supply an icon and display name for the action, and standard menu items and toolbar buttons will be created for you when needed automatically.

If you do want to install a custom component in a toolbar or menu, rather than using the default toolbar buttons and menu items, simply override getToolbarPresenter() or getMenuPresenter() in your action class and return appropriate Swing components from each of these methods.

Custom Property Editors

Occasionally, you may need to create a custom property editor component. For example, imagine you are writing a module that requires the user to set a URL. If the URL is badly formatted, the right thing to do is to tell the users this upfront and give them the chance to correct it. All settings within NetBeans are handled via property editors. The JavaBeans specification provides an infrastructure for registering property editors for different Java classes.

To create a custom property editor, simply write a `PropertyEditor` subclass that returns your component for `getCustomEditor()`, and register it as defined in the Java-Beans specification or return it from `Node.Property.getPropertyEditor()`.

Localization

NetBeans is fully internationalized, and the convention is for all user-visible strings to be stored in resource bundles (*.properties* files), so that they can be easily translated into other languages. NetBeans employs a utility class called `NbBundle` to simplify managing internationalized strings for module developers.

`NbBundle` is a utility class in the Open APIs that simplifies resource access and handles issues of multiple class loaders. It is based closely on Java's standard `ResourceBundle` utility. The mechanics of using it are fairly straightforward: Create a resource bundle called *Bundle.properties* in the same directory (package) as the class that will be referencing it. You will be passing a `Class` object along with the bundle key when asking for a value. The `Class` will allow `NbBundle` to locate the bundle file by looking in the same package.

In NetBeans programming, the name *Bundle.properties* is the default name for a bundle holding strings used in the same Java package. In your source code, you can use `NbBundle.getMessage()` to retrieve messages by key. To use Java message formats such as `Say {0} to user`, just pass additional arguments to `getMessage()`. Creating versions of your module for different languages or regions becomes much easier this way. Just add a new file, for example, *Bundle_cs.properties*:

```
# MyAction
LBL_Action=Ahoj
```

Since some text that is visible to the user in NetBeans is specified in XML files and manifest files, there are methods for localizing these as well as using resource bundles. For a detailed discussion, see Chapter 27.

One reason to use `NbBundle` in preference to the JRE's own `ResourceBundle` is that it supports a special technique called *branding* (see Chapter 28): if you are using `NbBundle`, someone else can just include a branded variant of your bundle in the IDE and use it to customize your text easily.

Wizards

Wizards are multi-step modal dialog boxes that allow the user to perform a complex operation that is better divided into steps. Wizards aim to be user-friendly and convenient; on the left, they list the steps involved in the process, so the user knows where they are and where they are going. A wizard is represented by a `WizardDescriptor` and is made up of `WizardDescriptor.Panels` containing UI components, including instructions on each step. The wizard is managed by a

`WizardDescriptor.Iterator`, which instantiates the panels of the wizard and manages their order. If you need the user to perform a complex operation, consider using a wizard instead of (or in addition to) the property sheet.

Each panel in a wizard has an `isValid()` method that determines if the **Next** or **Finish** buttons should be enabled. The **Finish** button will be enabled in addition to **Next** if the panel is a subclass of `WizardDescriptor.FinishPanel`—use that for panels the user can exit from early. If there is data for the user to fill out, you can fire change events when the user changes the data. In `isValid()`, evaluate the data to see if it is complete, and the user can continue to the next panel (or finish).

 The interface `WizardDescriptor.Panel` has a method called `isValid()`. Unfortunately `java.awt.Component` also has an `isValid()` that will collide with the method declared in `WizardDescriptor.Panel`. Therefore, it is not a good idea to have `Component` subclasses directly implement `WizardDescriptor.Panel`.

Panels can also be dynamically added to and removed from wizards as it is in use. You can see this in the **New** wizard. In its first panel, you choose a type of object. If it is a Java class, there may be additional panels to set up what class you inherit from, and so on. If it is an HTML file, then the second panel where you specify the file is the last one. The iterator can fire change events when the list of panels changes.

Finally, wizard panels can also be created declaratively in a module's XML layer—a folder will represent a wizard, and *.instance* files within that folder will represent its panels. An example of this is the **Setup Wizard**—modules can add panels to this wizard simply by adding them to the XML. The class that accomplishes this is called `WizardFolder`. It is not currently part of the Open APIs; modules providing wizards that need to be extended are quite rare. If you need to do this, provisionally copy the implementation from `org.netbeans.core.ui.WizardFolder` and propose on *nbdev@netbeans.org* that it be moved into a shared location.

Jumping-off Places

We've talked about a number of object types your code will likely interact with inside the IDE. So how do you find live instances of them? How do you programmatically access them?

As we move toward NetBeans 3.4, the primary way to find objects of interest given a known interface is by using the Lookup API:

```
Lookup.getDefault().lookup(some.interesting.Interface.class)
```

However, there are a number of older methods that are also useful. If you tried the Bean Browser earlier in this chapter, you may have noticed that one of the items in the Bean Browser window was called `TopManager.org.openide.TopManager` is a singleton class, and a static method called getDefault() gives you the default instance of this class.

TopManager has non-static methods that allow you to access various objects within NetBeans, such as SystemOptions, services, Nodes, Workspaces, and so on.

Many of the objects you will be looking for are accessible via the Places API, which can be accessed via the methods TopManager.getDefault().getPlaces().folders() and TopManager.getDefault().getPlaces().nodes(). These get you instances of the classes Places.Folders and Places.Nodes, which in turn have methods for getting commonly needed objects or sets of objects. For example, to get the **Actions** folder (visible in **Tools → Options → IDE Configuration → Look & Feel**), you would call:

```
DataFolder actions = TopManager.getDefault().getPlaces().folders().actions();
```

More generally, get the system filesystem (an instance of org.openide.filesystems. FileSystem) this way:

```
FileSystem sfs = Repository.getDefault().getDefaultFileSystem();
```

Now you can reference any folders directly by name as follows:

```
DataFolder actions = DataFolder.findFolder(sfs.findResource("Actions"));
```

Special Folders in the System Filesystem

In Chapter 14 we asked you to browse the system filesystem to get a sense of what it is used for. Here we will identify some of the folders that have specific meanings, in which your modules may need to install files.

You will see a myriad of different folders and subfolders in the system filesystem. Some folders are defined by the NetBeans Open APIs; others are used by certain modules or the core for their own purposes. It is impossible to enumerate every folder you might find, since any module can add to the list. However, there are a number of folders that figure prominently in NetBeans module development that you should know about. Try looking through these folders in your own NetBeans installation and examine some of the files in them. You can always use the Bean Browser to get more information on a file, such as its (data object's) cookies, using **Tools → Bean Browse → Bean Browse Node**.

There are many other folders defined and used by the NetBeans core and various modules, but the preceding list should help you become familiar with the most important ones and the basic style of defining objects in the system filesystem. Particular APIs and modules that use a folder for a public purpose should document the name of the folder and its interpretation.

Actions/ (and subfolders)
   The "actions pool." All actions defined by modules should be placed in this area, organized by subfolders, as instance files. Since the pool is read-only for users, it

can serve to hold rarely-used actions that might be needed in menus, toolbars, or keyboard shortcut bindings. In the future, this pool might be replaced by *Templates/Actions/*; see Appendix D for more details.

Editors/ (and subfolders)

Information about installed editor kits. See Appendix A for information on extensibility of text editing. *Editors/AnnotationTypes/* is defined by the NetBeans Open APIs for adding kinds of visual annotations to documents, for example error markings or breakpoints. *Editors/TYPE/*, where TYPE is a MIME type such as text/x-java, contains several files, such as the kit instance, editor settings, toolbar and context menu configurations, and more.

Menu/ (and subfolders)

The menu bar of the NetBeans main window. Each subfolder, for example *Menu/File/*, represents one menu; instance files and sub-subfolders represents menu items or submenus.

Modules/

Contains XML files describing the status of known modules, both enabled and disabled. Read about a common use of this folder in Chapter 28.

Mount/ (and subfolders)

Contains instance files representing mounted filesystems. The default org.openide.filesystems.Repository is constructed from all FileSystem instances in this folder and its subfolders. In Chapter 27 you can see an example of mounting a filesystem using this folder.

Palette/ (and subfolders)

The **Component Palette** as used by the NetBeans Form Editor. See an example of this folder's use in Chapter 27.

ParserDB/

Parser database files used by the Source Editor to implement Java language code completion and other features. Discussed in Chapter 27.

Projects/ (and subfolders)

Each subfolder holds one user project. Beneath a project folder is a *Files/* subfolder containing files and symbolic links (*.shadow*) used in the project, as they appear in the **Project Name** tab in the Explorer window. A project will also have a *system/* subfolder that holds project-specific settings. This mechanism was discussed in Chapter 14.

Services/ (and subfolders)

Instances of many types of objects that should appear in lookup, as detailed in Chapter 15. Subfolders are used to group objects by type in many cases.

Shortcuts/

Contains instances of actions, where the name of the file indicates a keyboard shortcut to which the action should be bound.

Templates/ (and subfolders)

Templates for new kinds of files and other objects that might be created by the user. Most subfolders represent templates for normal user files, such as Java sources or text files. Other subfolders mirror folders in the system filesystem and permit the corresponding type of object to be made—for example, *Templates/Mount/* for types of mountable filesystem, or *Templates/Services/CompilerType/* for prototypes of configurable compiler services.

Toolbars/ (and subfolders)

Similar to *Menu/*, subfolders of this folder contain action instances used to construct the toolbars in NetBeans' main window.

UI/ (and subfolders)

User-visible hierarchies that modules may add to. *UI/Services/* comprises the displayed nodes in the **Options** window. In NetBeans 3.4, *UI/Runtime/* forms the **Runtime** tab of the Explorer window.

Windows/ (and subfolders)

The complete configuration of the window system—workspaces, positions, and styles of windows, and the exact configuration of each window and tab.

xml/ (and subfolders)

Special kinds of functionality associated with XML public IDs ("DOCTYPEs"). *xml/entities/* serves as an entity catalog inside NetBeans to find local copies of important DTDs. *xml/lookups/* maps public IDs to Java classes called *processors* that can interpret the XML formats and create live objects from the XML data.

The NetBeans runtime is a powerful engine for applications, at the heart of which are some simple paradigms: Files can be virtual, can represent Java class instances, and the system will notice changes in those files; Nodes allow you to aggregate related objects in a way suitable for presentation; Nodes provide a concept of selection or context for determining what functionality should be available; and DataObjects provide an abstraction layer for aggregating related data.

With this background, we are ready to try creating a somewhat more sophisticated module in the next chapter.

## CHAPTER 18

Creating the QuickPanel Module

Now that we've walked through the basic mechanics of creating a module, let's move on to a more advanced example that involves more interaction with the Open APIs. The *quickpanel* module will create a graphical TopComponent (we'll actually be subclassing a TopComponent subclass called ExplorerPanel) that can be docked into the editor window and contains a drop-down list containing all of the files available in the current project, including subfolders, allowing you to quickly navigate between files. Then we will add a second drop-down list that will allow you to navigate quickly among all of the methods in the currently opened source file.

So where to start? We know we need:

A combo box to display the contents of the current project
> An existing explorer view is such a component and can be rooted on an arbitrary node—org.openide.explorer.views.ChoiceView.

A container component for our combo boxes
> The Explorer API also provides the convenient visual org.openide.explorer. ExplorerPanel class that contains the hooks to talk to an explorer view residing inside it.

An action so the user can display the panel
> The basic, non-context-sensitive action class org.openide.actions. CallableSystemAction can be subclassed to do this.

A way of filtering out children of nodes we don't want
> We won't want to see **Classes**, **Methods**, and **Fields** subnodes of Java class files in our explorer view, just the nodes that represent folders or files. We will solve this by subclassing org.openide.nodes.FilterNode.Children.

A way of listening to selection changes in our drop-down list and responding to them
> By attaching a PropertyChangeListener to the ExplorerManager.

Abstractions Covered in This Chapter

This chapter will detail a number of abstractions in the NetBeans architecture:

Nodes
> The hierarchy of presentation objects inside the running IDE.

Explorer views
> An explorer view is a GUI component that presents a hierarchy of Nodes.

ExplorerManager
> There may be many different explorer views open at the same time in the IDE. When you create an explorer view component, you don't directly interact with it or listen for changes on it; you interact with its manager, which can tell you what Node is selected in it.

The active TopComponent
> TopComponents are GUI containers (descendants of javax.swing.JComponent). At any moment in the running IDE, one TopComponent has input focus, and is therefore the "active" one.

The activated nodes
> The set of nodes that are selected in the active TopComponent and that form the context for available actions and properties.

Children
> A Node can have a Children object that provides a list of Nodes that are its children.

FilterNodes
> A FilterNode is a Node that actually represents another node and delegates some or all of its presentation to the original Node. FilterNodes can be constructed including an alternate Children object that adds or filters out some of the children of the original Node. They can also do this with any other aspect of a Node, such as properties, Cookies, or actions.

SourceElements
> A SourceElement is an abstraction for an entity that contains Java language source code.

ClassElements
> A ClassElement is an object representing an individual Java class, with methods allowing you to retrieve information about the structure and source contents of that class.

Cookies: OpenCookie *and* SourceCookie
> Cookies are a way of looking up interfaces that relate to the thing a given node represents. A Node can be asked if it holds a cookie by requesting a particular interface from it, such as OpenCookie, and will either return an instance or null.

Note that there are a number of tasks in this chapter that could be somewhat simplified by using the **Form Editor** and templates provided by the Open APIs Support module. For the most part, these tools are intentionally neglected in this chapter, in order to present a hands-on understanding of the mechanics of building a simple module.

Creating the Project Files Drop-Down

We need a drop-down (combo box) full of nodes. The first instinct when writing a component such as this might be to subclass javax.swing.JComboBox. This is not actually the right approach—the APIs already provide very flexible pre-built components for this. A variety of different UI classes are provided in the org.openide. explorer.views package for various GUI components that are explorer views (things which can display Nodes). We will use a drop-down view called ChoiceView. It is actually not necessary to write any non-trivial rendering or user-interface presentation code to solve this problem—we simply need to use a canned explorer view component, but have it present a hierarchy of Nodes (effectively, the data model for the component) that only exposes the things we want to expose.

The secret is to use Nodes in conjunction with a GUI container that implements org.openide.explorer.ExplorerManager.Finder, such as org.openide.explorer. ExplorerPanel (a subclass of TopComponent). This interface lets a component supply an ExplorerManager. For any Explorer view (or set of views), the ExplorerManager can monitor the state, selected Nodes, and so on, and fire events as appropriate. So what we will actually do is create our view using the stock ChoiceView component and add it to the ExplorerPanel. We will control the content by controlling the nodes rendered by the ChoiceView component. All interaction with the ChoiceView component itself, beyond basic initialization, will happen through the ExplorerManager that comes built into the ExplorerPanel container. This goes as shown in Example 18-1.

> While there is a TopComponent template supplied by the Open APIs Support module, the examples in this chapter are designed to be entered completely by hand. It may be more useful to simply start with **File → New → Classes → Class**. The TopComponent template will open the form editor, which is not needed in this case.

Example 18-1. QuickPanel: FileSelector.java

```
package org.netbeans.examples.quickpanel;
import org.openide.explorer.view.*;
import org.openide.nodes.*;
import org.openide.explorer.*;
import org.openide.cookies.*;
import java.beans.*;
import org.openide.*;
public class FileSelector extends ExplorerPanel {
  private PropertyChangeListener selectListener;
```

Example 18-1. QuickPanel: FileSelector.java (continued)

```
public FileSelector() {
  setName("File Selector");
  // create a new ChoiceView Explorer view UI component
  ChoiceView fileDropDown = new ChoiceView();
  // set the depth of the tree that should be shown
  NodeListModel model = ((NodeListModel)fileDropDown.getModel());
  model.setDepth(50);
  add(fileDropDown, java.awt.BorderLayout.CENTER);
  // create a label
  add(new javax.swing.JLabel("Project files: "), java.awt.BorderLayout.WEST);
  // create the listener that will listen to this panel's ExplorerManager instance for
  // selected node changes.  Defer actually attaching it to the addNotify() method
  // so we don't attach it unnecessarily
  selectListener = new PropertyChangeListener() {
    public void propertyChange(PropertyChangeEvent e) {
      // if the selected node is what changed
      if (e.getPropertyName().equals(ExplorerManager.PROP_SELECTED_NODES)) {
        // call openCurrent to open the currently selected node if it has an OpenCookie
        openCurrent();
      }
    }
  };
}

public void addNotify() {
  super.addNotify();
  // add the property change listener when the component is added to a visual form
  getExplorerManager().addPropertyChangeListener(selectListener);
  // get the Project node (the same as is displayed in the Project tab in Explorer)
  Node projectRoot = TopManager.getDefault().getPlaces().nodes().projectDesktop();
  // Tell ExplorerManager that this is the root of the context for our drop-down
  getExplorerManager().setRootContext(projectRoot);
}

public void removeNotify() {
  // remove the listener if component no longer has a visible parent
  getExplorerManager().removePropertyChangeListener(selectListener);
  super.removeNotify();
}
```

This code gets us a ChoiceView component that is rooted on the same Project node that appears on the **Project** tab of the **Explorer** window. We really don't interact with the ChoiceView component, with the exception of setting the depth property to determine how many levels of hierarchy it should display. Instead, we interact with the ExplorerManager object that is managing our explorer view.

Now we need to write the code that gets called when the item is selected—an implementation of the openCurrent() method called inside our listener. Here is where we begin to deal with *cookies*. As mentioned earlier, Cookies are a way of looking up functionality. Cookies provide a generic mechanism for looking up arbitrary information relating to an object. The usage pattern for Cookies is:

```
SomeCookie cookie = (SomeCookie)SomeNode.getCookie(SomeCookie.class);
if (cookie != null) {
  cookie.doSomething();
}
```

In our particular case, we want to be dealing with org.openide.cookies.OpenCookie. This class has one method, open(), which, when called, asks the IDE to open the underlying DataObject in the Source Editor. Note that the method, field, and constructor subnodes of a Java source Node also supply an OpenCookie, which will open the file if it is not already open and place the text caret at the appropriate point in the source code for that particular item. In particular, notice the simplicity of the OpenCookie interface—the code we write here does not have to be concerned with how or in what window or with what kind of editor the file is opened, only that it is opened. Our module code need only be concerned with presenting its piece of logic, presenting the contents of the project in a different way, because the concept of bringing up a file in the Source Editor is handled through the abstraction of *open*. And because OpenCookie is a Cookie, we do not even need to know what kind of object is represented by a Node when we're asking it for an OpenCookie. We only need to be concerned with whether the cookie is present.

Note that since there are explorer views that allow multiple selection, the selected Nodes are returned as an array, although with a combo box, only one can be selected at a time. When the listener notices that the activated (selected) Nodes have changed, we want to open the currently activated node; add this method to your FileSelector source code:

```
/** Called by the selectListener's <code>propertyChange()</code>
 * method, this method contains code responsible for opening the
 * selected file by getting an <code>OpenCookie</code> for it
 * (if available) and calling its <code>open()</code> method.
 */
public void openCurrent() {
    // get the selected node array.  Since combo boxes are single-selection, we only care
    // about the first (and presumably only) element in the array
    Node[] sel = getExplorerManager().getSelectedNodes();
    if ((sel != null) && (sel.length > 0)) {
      // try to get an OpenCookie for this object
      OpenCookie oc = (OpenCookie)sel[0].getCookie(OpenCookie.class);
      if (oc != null) {
        // if there is one, perform the Open action
        oc.open();
      } else {
        // if an open cookie is not available, look for an edit cookie
        EditCookie ec = (EditCookie)sel[0].getCookie(EditCookie.class);
        if (ec != null) {
          ec.edit();
        }
      }
    }
  }
}
```

The result is, when an object is selected, if it has an OpenCookie, it will be opened in the editor. We can now add a main() method to the class and run it with internal execution to be sure it works:

1. Add the following method to the class:

   ```
   public static void main(String args[]) {
     new FileSelector().open();
   }
   ```

2. If the Project tab in Explorer does not have any files in it, select some Java files and packages and add them to the current project by right-clicking and choosing **Tools → Add to Project**.

3. Right-click the Node for the FileSelector class in Explorer and choose Properties from the context menu to display the property sheet for your class.

4. Click the Execution tab to display the execution options for the class.

5. Set the Execution property to Internal Execution, so the class will be run inside the IDE's JVM.

6. Click in the Editor window and press F6 to compile and execute the class.

Momentarily a window should pop up containing the FileSelector component. As you select different files in this drop-down list box, they will be opened in the editor.[*]

 If you have large source packages included in your project, running this example may result in a *very* long delay as the IDE parses each file in each folder of your project! In this case, you may want to remove some of the mounted folders before running this example. Since a ChoiceView component displays the expanded Project tree, all included packages and components thereof will be parsed when the component is instantiated. Figure 18-1 shows the example running in its current form.

If you are using NetBeans 3.4, the component will appear inside a single Explorer tab. As of NetBeans 3.4, a Mode will show a tab for a component, even if it is alone in the container. To get rid of the tab, add the following code to the component class's constructor:

```
putClientProperty("TabPolicy", "HideWhenAlone");
```

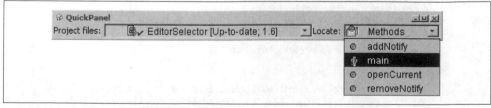

Figure 18-1. The FileSelector component

---

[*] Note that the window created by calling someTopComponent.open() does not respect the preferred size of the contained TopComponent. If the window initially appears too small, you may want to manually set the size of the component in the code.

FilterNode—Filtering Which Children of a Node Are Displayed

If you tried the preceding example, you may have noticed that you got not only all of the files that are part of your project, but also a tree including the methods, fields, and constructors subnodes you see when you expand a class Node in the Explorer tree. Since we're just interested in files here, we ought to filter non-file Nodes out.

The way to accomplish this is by using another very useful class, org.openide.nodes. FilterNode. A FilterNode is a Node that acts as a proxy for another Node—you pass the original Node in the FilterNode's constructor. FilterNode will handle keeping in sync with the original node, in terms of cookies, actions, and children; but subclasses can choose to offer subsets or supersets of the children, actions, and properties of the original node.

Nodes provide an org.openide.nodes.Children object via their getChildren() method. The Children object in turn has a getNodes() method that returns an array of the child Nodes. There is a constructor for FilterNode that takes arguments for both the original Node and an alternate Children object. It is through this Children object that we will limit the children displayed in our combo box—rather than root the component on the original node, we will create a new Node that represents the original, but restricts the displayed child Nodes to those that represent files or folders, and produces child Nodes using the same filtered children so that the effect is recursive. We will root our explorer view on this Node rather than the original.

To accomplish this, we will need to write an implementation of FilterNode.Children that only exposes child Nodes that represent folders; this implementation code is shown in Example 18-2. It will expose those children as new FilterNodes that in turn will return instances of our FilterNode.Children subclass, so the filtering is done recursively for the entire directory tree. Since there is a FilterNode constructor that can be passed a Children instance as an argument, this is quite painless.

Example 18-2. QuickPanel: FilesOnlyChildren.java

```
package org.netbeans.examples.quickpanel;
import org.openide.nodes.*;
import org.openide.cookies.*;
import org.openide.loaders.*;
class FilesOnlyChildren extends FilterNode.Children {
  public FilesOnlyChildren(Node orig) {
    super(orig);
  }

  protected Node[] createNodes(Object key) {
    // keys for FilterNode.Children will be the original nodes,
    // so cast as such
    Node child = (Node)key;
    // first see if it is a child of the project root node
```

Example 18-2. QuickPanel: FilesOnlyChildren.java (continued)

```
      boolean isValid = child.getParentNode().equals(
      org.openide.TopManager.getDefault().getPlaces().nodes().projectDesktop()
      );
      // if not, see if it is a folder
      if (!isValid) {
        isValid = child.getCookie(DataFolder.class) != null;
      }
      // if not, see if its parent is a folder - if so, it must be a file
      if (!isValid) {
        isValid = child.getParentNode().getCookie(DataFolder.class) != null;
      }
      if (isValid) {
        // Return a filtered set of child nodes
        return new Node[] {
          new FilterNode(child, new FilesOnlyChildren(child))
        };
      } else {
        // or else return an empty array
        return new Node[] {};
      }
    }
  }
}
```

Note that we don't actually subclass `FilterNode`—the `Children` object acts as a factory for child nodes, so the effect is recursive.

The interesting part of the preceding code is the `createNodes()` method, which guarantees that all children of the `Node` will also have a `FilesOnlyChildren` object for their child list. The logic in `createNodes()` is applied recursively to all children. It rejects any `Nodes` that are not either direct children of the root node or children of a node representing a folder. This effectively filters out nodes that do not represent files. The result is that we have a near-clone of the original node, but with limits on which children are displayed. Since we root our explorer view on our `FilterNode` pseudo-clone, our view will only show the child `Nodes` it exposes.

To make this actually work, there is one last step, which is to modify the `addNotify()` method in the preceding `FileSelector` class so that it will use our `FilterNode` instead:

```
public void addNotify() {
  super.addNotify();
  // add the property change listener when the component is added to a visual form
  getExplorerManager().addPropertyChangeListener(selectListener);
  // get the Project node (the same as is displayed in the Project tab in Explorer)
  Node projectRoot = TopManager.getDefault().getPlaces().nodes().projectDesktop();
  // create a new FilterNode which won't expose non-file children, mapped to
  // the project root
  Node workingRoot = new FilterNode(projectRoot, new FilesOnlyChildren(projectRoot));
  // Tell explorermanager that this is the root of the context for our drop-down
  getExplorerManager().setRootContext(workingRoot);
}
```

To see the improvement, compile and execute the FileSelector class again. The modified output is shown in Figure 18-2.

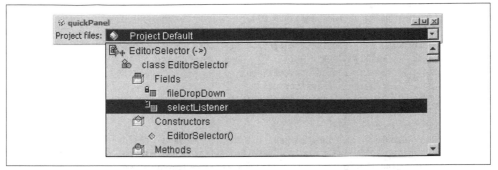

Figure 18-2. The improved FileSelector component

Creating the Methods Drop-Down

To further explore Nodes and their presentation options, let's create a second drop-down that only displays the methods of the class currently open in the Source Editor, so that the drop-down stays in sync with the editor or whatever you have selected in the Explorer window. This will mean finding the **Methods** subnode of the currently active Node (if it exists, as it does when the editor has focus and you are editing a Java source file).

We can start by copying all of the source code to our FileSelector class into a new class called MethodSelector. In the constructor, we want to add some code to create a second listener that will listen for changes in the active TopComponent; this new source is shown in Example 18-3 (for a complete listing of the MethodSelector source code, see Example 18-4).

Example 18-3. QuickPanel: MethodSelector.java—creating a listener to monitor the active TopComponent

```
activateListener = new PropertyChangeListener() {
  public void propertyChange(PropertyChangeEvent e) {
    if (e.getPropertyName().equals(TopComponent.Registry.PROP_ACTIVATED)) {
      // if the active TopComponent has changed, pass this info to
      // topComponentChanged() to rebuild the list of methods
      topComponentChanged((TopComponent)e.getNewValue());
    }
  }
};
```

We'll also need to create a private field activateListener. We will then need to implement the topComponentChanged() method, which will respond to changes in the active TopComponent, find out what the activated Nodes are, and update the Explorer view appropriately:

```
private void topComponentChanged(TopComponent tc) {
  // get the activated nodes in the current TopComponent
  if (tc == null) return;
  Node[] nds = tc.getActivatedNodes();
  if ((nds != null) && (nds.length > 0)) {
    // find a source cookie pointing to a SourceElement object
    SourceCookie sc = (SourceCookie)nds[0].getCookie(SourceCookie.class);
    if (sc != null) {
      // get the represented SourceElement
      SourceElement se = sc.getSource();
      // get an array of ClassElement objects for this SourceElement
      ClassElement[] ce = se.getAllClasses();
      if (ce.length > 0) {
        // create a new ClassNode and return its "Methods" child.  For
        // simplicity, we're only interested in the first element of the array
        // DefaultFactory creates nodes for source elements.  We will
        // create a node for the class, and find its child called
        // "methods"
        Node newNode = (
          new DefaultFactory(false)).createClassNode(
            ce[0]).getChildren().findChild("Methods");
        // tell the ExplorerManager managing the drop-down that the newly
        // created node is now the root node for the component
        getExplorerManager().setRootContext(newNode);
      }
    }
  }
}
```

What we're doing here is getting a SourceCookie from the first selected Node, if available, and then using that to retrieve a org.openide.src.SourceElement object, which in turn allows us to access an array of objects representing all of the contained classes in that element. We then create a new Node representing the first contained class, find its **Methods** child node, and change the root of our explorer view to that.

Lastly, we will need to add code to attach and detach the new listener in the addNotify() and removeNotify() methods. Insert this code in addNotify():

```
TopComponent.getRegistry().addPropertyChangeListener(activateListener);
```

Add the following code in removeNotify():

```
TopComponent.getRegistry().removePropertyChangeListener(activateListener);
```

We'll also need to remove the code copied from FileSelector that sets the root to the project node, since the root will now be set dynamically via the listener.

By adding a main() method, you can test this class as with the FileSelector component. For a full listing of this class and the rest of the code in this chapter, see the org.netbeans.examples.quickpanel package in the *examples/extending-netbeans/sources/quickpanel/* directory of the accompanying sources.

Improving the Methods Drop-Down

There's only one thing wrong with the preceding methods drop-down: it's fragile. The reason is, it is depending on the programmatic name methods to find the methods child of a class node. This *should* work in future releases, but that code name is not part of any API and could just as easily change. Fortunately, there is a safe, maintainable way to do this that is slightly more complex but that uses programmatic ways to create nodes for all of the methods.

In the topComponentChanged() method, replace the contents of the if clause if (ce. length > 0) { with the following:

```
// create a new ClassNode and return its "Methods" child.  For
// simplicity, we're only interested in the first element of the array
MethodElement[] me = ce[0].getMethods();
// create an array to hold nodes for each method
Node[] methodNodes = new Node[me.length];
// DefaultFactory is what creates nodes for source elements
DefaultFactory def = new DefaultFactory (false);
// Iterate the methods array and populate our nodes array
for (int i = 0; i < me.length; i++) {
  methodNodes[i] = def.createMethodNode(me[i]);
}
// Create an empty children object
Children.Array children = new Children.Array();
// Add our method nodes
children.add(methodNodes);
// Create a dummy abstract node
Node newNode = new AbstractNode (children);
// Give it a display name - note in production code, this
// would be internationalized!
newNode.setDisplayName ("Methods");
// tell the ExplorerManager managing the drop-down that the newly
// found node is now the root node for the component
getExplorerManager().setRootContext(newNode);
```

We now have a component that will stand the test of time.

Example 18-4. QuickPanel: MethodSelector.java—full listing

```
package org.netbeans.examples.quickpanel;
import org.openide.src.nodes.DefaultFactory;
import org.openide.explorer.view.*;
import org.openide.src.*;
import org.openide.windows.*;
import org.openide.nodes.*;
import org.openide.explorer.*;
import org.openide.cookies.*;
import java.beans.*;
import org.openide.windows.TopComponent;
/** An panel containing a drop-down listing all of the methods available on
 *  the currently open file
 *
```

Example 18-4. QuickPanel: MethodSelector.java—full listing (continued)

```java
 * @author   Tim Boudreau
 * @version 1.0
 */
public class MethodSelector extends ExplorerPanel {
  private PropertyChangeListener selectListener;
  private PropertyChangeListener activateListener;

  public MethodSelector() {
    setName("Method Selector");
    // create a new ChoiceView Explorer view UI component
    ChoiceView methodDropDown = new ChoiceView();
    // set the depth of the tree that should be shown
    NodeListModel model = ((NodeListModel) methodDropDown.getModel());
    model.setDepth(1);
    add(methodDropDown, java.awt.BorderLayout.CENTER);
    // create a label - for production code this should use a Java resource
    // bundle for internationalization
    add(new javax.swing.JLabel("Methods: "), java.awt.BorderLayout.WEST);
    // create the listener that will listen to this panel's ExplorerManager
    // instance for selected node changes
    selectListener = new PropertyChangeListener() {
      public void propertyChange(PropertyChangeEvent e) {
        // if the selected node is what changed
        if (e.getPropertyName().equals(ExplorerManager.PROP_SELECTED_NODES)) {
          // call openCurrent to open the currently selected node if it has an
          // OpenCookie
          openCurrent();
        }
      }
    };
    // create the listener that will listen to TopComponent.Registry to track
    // the currently active TopComponent
    activateListener = new PropertyChangeListener() {
      public void propertyChange(PropertyChangeEvent e) {
        if (e.getPropertyName().equals(TopComponent.Registry.PROP_ACTIVATED)) {
          // if the active TopComponent has changed, pass this info to
          // topComponentChanged() to rebuild the list of methods
          topComponentChanged((TopComponent) e.getNewValue());
        }
      }
    };
  }

  public void addNotify() {
    super.addNotify();
    // add the property change listener for selection changes
    // when the component is added to a visual form
    getExplorerManager().addPropertyChangeListener(selectListener);
    // add the property change listener that listens to the changes in the
    // selected TopComponent and rebuilds the method list as appropriate
    TopComponent.getRegistry().addPropertyChangeListener(activateListener);
    // set the root node for the ChoiceView component, via the ExplorerManager
```

Example 18-4. QuickPanel: MethodSelector.java—full listing (continued)

```java
    topComponentChanged(TopComponent.getRegistry().getActivated());
  }

  public void removeNotify() {
    // remove the listeners if component no longer has a visible parent
    getExplorerManager().removePropertyChangeListener(selectListener);
    TopComponent.getRegistry().removePropertyChangeListener(activateListener);
    super.removeNotify();
  }

  public void openCurrent() {
    // get the selected node array.  Since combo boxes are single-selection, we
    // only care about the first (and presumably only) element in the array
    Node[] sel = getExplorerManager().getSelectedNodes();
    if ((sel != null) && (sel.length > 0)) {
      // try to get an OpenCookie for this object
      OpenCookie oc = (OpenCookie)sel[0].getCookie(OpenCookie.class);
      if (oc != null) {
        // if there is one, perform the Open action
        oc.open();
      }
    }
  }
}

/*
  //Below is the initial version of TopComponentChanged from the text:
  private void topComponentChanged(TopComponent tc) {
    // get the activated nodes in the current TopComponent
    if (tc==null) return;
    Node[] nds = tc.getActivatedNodes();
    if ((nds != null) && (nds.length > 0)) {
      // find a source cookie pointing to a SourceElement object
      SourceCookie sc = (SourceCookie) nds[0].getCookie(SourceCookie.class);
      if (sc != null) {
        // get the represented SourceElement
        SourceElement se = sc.getSource();
        // get an array of ClassElement objects for this SourceElement
        ClassElement[] ce = se.getAllClasses();
        if (ce.length > 0) {
          // create a new ClassNode and return its "Methods" child.  For
          // simplicity, we're only interested in the first element of the array
          // DefaultFactory creates nodes for source elements.  We will
          // create a node for the class, and find its child called
          // "methods"
          Node newNode = (
            new DefaultFactory(false)).createClassNode(
              ce[0]).getChildren().findChild("Methods");
          // tell the ExplorerManager managing the drop-down that the newly
          // created node is now the root node for the component
          getExplorerManager().setRootContext(newNode);
        }
      }
```

Example 18-4. QuickPanel: MethodSelector.java—full listing (continued)

```
    }
  }
*/


  private void topComponentChanged(TopComponent tc) {
    // get the activated nodes in the current TopComponent
    if (tc == null) return;
    Node[] nds = tc.getActivatedNodes();
    if ((nds != null) && (nds.length > 0)) {
      // find a source cookie pointing to a SourceElement object
      SourceCookie sc = (SourceCookie)nds[0].getCookie(SourceCookie.class);
      if (sc != null) {
        // get the represented SourceElement
        SourceElement se = sc.getSource();
        // get an array of ClassElement objects for this SourceElement
        ClassElement[] ce = se.getAllClasses();
        if (ce.length > 0) {
          // create a new ClassNode and return its "Methods" child.  For
          // simplicity, we're only interested in the first element of the array
          MethodElement[] me = ce[0].getMethods();
          // create an array to hold nodes for each method
          Node[] methodNodes = new Node[me.length];
          // DefaultFactory is what creates nodes for source elements
          DefaultFactory def = new DefaultFactory(false);
          // Iterate the methods array and populate our nodes array
          for (int i = 0; i < me.length; i++) {
            methodNodes[i] = def.createMethodNode(me[i]);
          }
          // Create an empty children object
          Children.Array children = new Children.Array();
          // Add our method nodes
          children.add(methodNodes);
          // Create a dummy abstract node
          Node newNode = new AbstractNode(children);
          // Give it a display name - note in production code, this
          // would be internationalized!
          newNode.setDisplayName("Methods");
          // tell the ExplorerManager managing the drop-down that the newly
          // created node is now the root node for the component
          getExplorerManager().setRootContext(newNode);
        }
      }
    }
  }


  /** Main method for test execution */
  public static void main(String args[]) {
    new MethodSelector().open();
  }
}
```

Creating the Module

Now that we have these two UI components, the last step is to create a common visual container for them, create an action to display them, and then build a module JAR containing the results.

Creating a Container GUI Component

The visual container will simply be a `TopComponent` that contains instances of `MethodSelector` and `FileSelector`, and is shown in Example 18-5.

Example 18-5. QuickPanel: QuickPanel.java

```
package org.netbeans.examples.quickpanel;
import org.openide.windows.*;
public class QuickPanel extends TopComponent  {
  public QuickPanel() {
    setLayout(new java.awt.BorderLayout());
    // Display name of this component:
    setName("Quick Panel");
    // Create the FileSelector component to display Filesystems
    add(new FileSelector(), java.awt.BorderLayout.CENTER);
    // create the MethodSelector component to display methods
    add(new MethodSelector(), java.awt.BorderLayout.EAST);
  }
}
```

Once again, if you wish to try this combined component, you can simply add a test main method, as with the other examples. If you cut and paste from one of the other examples, make sure you remember to change the name of the class you want to instantiate and open.

Creating the ShowQuickPanelAction

We also need to create an `SystemAction` to display on the View menu and toolbar, which will instruct the IDE to display a `QuickPanel` instance. To do this, we will subclass the abstract convenience class `CallableSystemAction` and override its `performAction()` method to create and display a `QuickPanel` instance, as shown in Example 18-6.

Example 18-6. QuickPanel: ShowQuickPanelAction.java

```
package org.netbeans.examples.quickpanel;
import org.openide.util.actions.CallableSystemAction;
import org.openide.util.HelpCtx;
public class ShowQuickPanelAction extends CallableSystemAction {
  public void performAction() {
    // Create and instantiate a new TopComponent when action is performed
    new QuickPanel().open();
  }
```

Example 18-6. QuickPanel: ShowQuickPanelAction.java (continued)

```
  public String getName() {
    // return the display name for the action
    // in production code this should be internationalized
    return "Quick Panel";
  }

  protected String iconResource() {
    // return the icon for the action in menus and toolbars
    return "ShowQuickPanelActionIcon.gif";
  }

  public org.openide.util.HelpCtx getHelpCtx() {
    return HelpCtx.DEFAULT_HELP;
  }
}
```

You need to make sure there is a *ShowQuickPanelActionIcon.gif* in the same Java package, of course. The Open APIs Support module template for `CallableSystemAction` supplies such an icon for you.

Creating the XML Filesystem Layer

The next step is to create the module's XML layer—this is where you will specify locations where it should install the `ShowQuickPanelAction`, such as menus and toolbars. Right-click the package containing the module sources, choose **New → NetBeans Extensions → Modules API → XML Layer (Empty)**, and in the New wizard, specify the name of the layer.

We can now edit the new *layer.xml* file to look like Example 18-7.

Example 18-7. QuickPanel: layer.xml—creating the QuickPanel module's XML layer

```
<!DOCTYPE filesystem PUBLIC "-//NetBeans//DTD Filesystem 1.1//EN"
            "http://www.netbeans.org/dtds/filesystem-1_1.dtd">
<filesystem>
<folder name="Actions">
  <folder name="View">
    <file name="org-netbeans-examples-quickpanel-ShowQuickPanelAction.instance"/>
  </folder>
</folder>
<folder name="Menu">
  <folder name="View">
    <file name="org-netbeans-examples-quickpanel-ShowQuickPanelAction.instance"/>
  </folder>
</folder>
<folder name="Toolbars">
  <folder name="View">
    <file name="org-netbeans-examples-quickpanel-ShowQuickPanelAction.instance"/>
  </folder>
</folder>
</filesystem>
```

Note that the folder hierarchy represented in the *layer.xml* file exactly maps to the hierarchy you see in **Tools → Options → IDE Configuration → System → Modules**. What you are doing is literally specifying instances of your action class to be added to the system filesystem. It is these folders in the system filesystem that are represented by the Nodes hierarchy in the Actions, Menu, and Toolbars folders in the Options dialog box. The *.instance* filename extension is the convention for telling NetBeans that it should convert the dashes (-) to periods (.) and create an instance of the named class.

And having done this exercise, it's worth noting that the **New** menu you see when you right-click a folder node in Explorer *is an Explorer view*. It presents the same folder you see under **Tools → Options → Source Creation and Management → Templates** using menu items instead of a tree or a drop-down—it is an instance of org.openide.explorer.view.MenuView.

Creating and Populating the Module JAR

The last step is to create and build the module JAR file. Choose a mounted directory, right-click it in **Explorer**, choose **New → NetBeans Extensions → Modules API → Module JAR**, and give it the name quickpanel in the **New** wizard. When the new module JAR appears in the **Explorer** window, select it and open the Properties window for it. Find the **Content** property and bring up the custom property editor for it (click the **...** button that appears when you give focus to it in the property sheet). Here you get a dialog box that allows you to add content to the JAR file. Navigate to the sources; select the source code; bundle, layer and icon files; and click **Add** to add them to the content of the module JAR.

After closing the content dialog box, bring up the custom property editor for the **Manifest** property. Edit the manifest to appear as shown in Example 18-8.

Example 18-8. QuickPanel: MANIFEST.MF—the QuickPanel module's manifest

```
Manifest-Version: 1.0
Created-By: NetBeans
OpenIDE-Module: org.netbeans.examples.quickpanel
OpenIDE-Module-Layer: org/netbeans/examples/quickpanel/layer.xml
OpenIDE-Module-Name: QuickPanel
```

The OpenIDE-Module-Layer tag allows the IDE to find the *layer.xml* file in the module JAR. This is the module's XML layer. When the module is loaded, NetBeans' runtime will merge it with the existing virtual filesystem, allowing NetBeans to create an instance of the ShowQuickPanelAction class when it is needed.

Building and Testing the Module

We're now ready to test the module—right-click the module JAR file, choose Compile to update the JAR's contents with your classes and files, then right-click it again and choose Execute to install your module. You will see a message in the output window notifying you that your module has been installed, and the new **Quick Panel** item will appear in the View menu. Note that if you wish to make changes to the module and recompile and reload it, all you need to do is make your modifications and reexecute the module JAR file to cause it to be dynamically unloaded and reloaded with your changes made. This final version is shown in Figure 18-3.

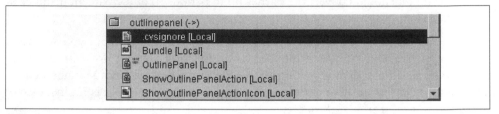

Figure 18-3. The final version of the QuickPanel component

A Little Homework

One of the best ways to get up to speed on an architecture is to modify existing code that interacts with that architecture. Here are a few things you can do with this example to increase your knowledge and comfort with what we've covered here.

 If you make modifications to the components in this chapter and then attempt to test them using the main( ) methods added to them for testing and get a warning in the status bar that the class has an invalid class loader, you still have the QuickPanel module installed. In order to again use internal execution on these classes, you need to disable the module via the modules list in **Tools → Options**.

- Modify the methods drop-down example to also show methods of inner classes of the currently selected source file.
- Modify both drop-downs so that they track what the user does—that is, if the active Node changes (for example, when the user moves the editor cursor into the body of another method or switches to a new source file), the item presented in the drop-down changes to match.
- Modify the MethodSelector drop-down to include fields and constructors.

## CHAPTER 19

A Mail-Based Filesystem

"Every program attempts to expand until it can read mail. Those programs which cannot so expand are replaced by ones which can." (See the on-line hacker Jargon File, version 4.3.1, 29 JUN 2001: Zawinski's Law (*http://www.tuxedo.org/~esr/jargon/ html/entry/Zawinski's-Law.html*).) The NetBeans IDE is no exception. Probably it will not replace your existing mail reader any time soon, but we *can* showcase how mail messages, including attachments, can be displayed inside the IDE. This chapter will show how to display an IMAP (Internet Message Access Protocol) mail server as a NetBeans filesystem.

Building a Mail Reader in the NetBeans Paradigm

To form the basic bones of our NetBeans mail reader, we start at the lowest level in the Open APIs hierarchy—the Filesystems API. All communication of the module with the mail server will happen via a filesystem that we define.

Why do our long examples start with the Filesystems API? This API is relatively self-contained (it can, in fact, be used independently of the rest of the NetBeans application) and so can be understood in its essentials within one chapter. Nonetheless, it provides a good summary of the basic programming style that characterizes the Net-Beans APIs.

In Chapter 17 we touched on the importance of this API to the IDE and gave some examples of why the abstraction of filesystems could be used to advantage within the application. In the mail reader module, we will show how other subsystems of the IDE, such as data objects and nodes, can work on top of our abstraction of an IMAP server to recognize structured objects and let the user work with them.

One extra step we will take in the construction of the filesystem is to separate the dependence on JavaMail into a separable interface so that we could use other Java-based mail interfaces with a minimum of work. The implementation of the generic mail interface using JavaMail will not be covered in this book as it would not be of interest to most readers; rather, we will focus on the NetBeans-specific filesystems code.

Implementing MailFileSystem Using AbstractFileSystem and JavaMail

We will start by making a skeleton of the code needed for a filesystem implementation. All filesystems in NetBeans must extend the abstract base class FileSystem. It is possible to extend this class directly, but doing so correctly requires a great deal of work. The Filesystems API specifies various services that a filesystem ought to provide, such as application-level file locking and change notification; implementation of these things from scratch involves tedious and error-prone data structure manipulation including thread synchronization and so on. Furthermore, the Filesystems API requires the filesystem to create FileObjects that are matched to the filesystem.

We will instead extend AbstractFileSystem. (In the NetBeans APIs, Abstract at the beginning of a class name often means "partial convenience implementation of.") This class provides many of the more difficult pieces of a filesystem implementation, including complete handling of file objects, file locking, event notification, refreshing, and so on. The minimum work needed to create a filesystem this way is to provide implementations of four easy-to-understand interfaces that are inner classes of AbstractFileSystem:

- Info asks you to provide basic data about the files, including access to the contents.
- List is used to list the contents of folders.
- Change methods are called when files are created, moved, or deleted.
- Attr provides access to *file attributes*, or arbitrary name-value pairs used by many parts of the IDE to keep metainformation associated with files.

All of these inner interfaces are part of the service provider interface to the Filesystems API; no client code should ever call methods in these interfaces, or even know if they are being used. Rather, AbstractFileSystem will call methods in these interfaces automatically, whenever it needs to, to implement its own FileSystem contract. Client code only calls FileSystem and FileObject methods.

Our example filesystem will be read-only: the user will not be able to make changes to the mail server from within NetBeans. Supporting filesystem modifications is not difficult from the NetBeans API perspective—and it will be pointed out in the following example code what can be changed to do so. It *is* complex from the IMAP side, however. A mail server imposes a number of restrictions on how messages can be moved and where. So to keep the example simpler, we will only consider reading from, not writing to, the server. Likewise, this filesystem will not listen for changes made on the server by another client, but doing so would be straightforward from the NetBeans side.

Creating a New AbstractFileSystem Implementation

It is easy to get started working on a filesystem using AbstractFileSystem, because the Open APIs Support provides a template for this purpose: **Templates** → **NetBeans** → **Extensions** → **Filesystems API** → **Local Filesystem**. Try selecting this template and take a look at the code that is generated. Select Test as the name for the filesystem, and browse through the class TestFileSystem when it is created.

As we go along, pieces of the MailFileSystem class will be presented showing how a real implementation works. Interested readers should consult the actual source code of the example (see *http://www.oreilly.com/catalog/netbeans*), as in some places uninteresting error-handling code has been simplified or omitted for brevity.

Let us look at the private inner classes that can be used to implement each of the four interfaces of AbstractFileSystem. Actually, the template shows you only three implementations; rather than implementing Attr directly, many filesystems prefer to use the standard concrete implementation DefaultAttributes (which takes the other three implementations as parameters). In this example we will not use DefaultAttributes because it is designed for filesystems that do not provide a special means of storing attributes, but use the XML-format *.nbattrs* files you may have seen on disk after using NetBeans. Since mail messages already have a system of MIME headers that can store attributes and IMAP provides access to them, we will use these directly instead of relying on *.nbattrs* files.

The instance variable mgr is used in these code segments as a handle to the mail server implementation. Its important methods should be clear from context.

Mail Filesystem: AbstractFileSystem.Info

Example 19-1 shows the implementation of the Info interface for *MailFileSystem.java*.

Example 19-1. InfoImpl implementation inside MailFileSystem.java

```
private class InfoImpl implements Info {
  private static final long serialVersionUID = 27698769845762L;
  public boolean folder(String name) {
    ObjectDescriptor od = null;
    try {
      od = mgr.getDescriptor(prefix(name));
    } catch (OperationFailedException ofe) {}
    if (od != null) {
      return od == ObjectDescriptor.DIRECTORY
          || od == ObjectDescriptor.MAILBOX
          || od == ObjectDescriptor.MULTIPART_MESSAGE
          || od == ObjectDescriptor.MULTIPART_SUBPART;
```

```
      } else {
        return false;
      }
    }
    public String mimeType(String name) {
      return (String)attr.readAttribute(name, "Content-Type");
    }
    public boolean readOnly(String name) {
      return true;
    }
    public Date lastModified(String name) {
      Date d = (Date)attr.readAttribute(name, Constants.A_SENTDATE);
      if (d != null) {
        return d;
      } else {
        return new Date();
      }
    }
    public long size(String name) {
      Content cp = null;
      try {
        cp = mgr.getContent(prefix(name));
      } catch (OperationFailedException e) {}
      return cp != null ? cp.getSize() : 0L;
    }
    public InputStream inputStream(String name) throws FileNotFoundException {
      Content cp = null;
      try {
        cp = mgr.getContent(prefix(name));
      } catch (OperationFailedException ofe) {}
      if (cp == null) throw new FileNotFoundException(name);
      try {
        return cp.getInputStream();
      } catch (IOException ioe) {
        throw new FileNotFoundException(ioe.toString());
      }
    }
    public OutputStream outputStream(String name) throws IOException {
      throw new IOException();
    }
    public void lock(String name) throws IOException {
      throw new IOException();
    }
    public void unlock(String name) {}
    public void markUnimportant(String name) {}
}
```

The first interface is Info and represents information about, and access to, a single
file or folder. You will notice that all the methods take a string argument name that
specifies the file. This is always given as a *resource name* according to Java conventions. For example, *com/hello/There.java* would be the name supplied for a Java

source file for the class `com.hello.There` (the forward slash is always used, even on Windows). We will always call `prefix()` on this resource name before actually passing it to the mail server, which permits the filesystem to prefix the path with some user-determined string. This has the effect of restricting the filesystem to some subfolder of the mail server rather than to the entire range of folders associated with the mail account.

Methods `folder()` and `mimeType()` provide basic information about whether a given path is a folder or a regular file, and, if a file, what type of data it contains. Most filesystems would simply return `null` from `mimeType` to let the IDE use built-in heuristics, but in our case we really know the MIME type because mail messages will usually have a `Content-Type` header. There are actually several types of objects on the mail server that will be represented as folders rather than as files to NetBeans. These are covered in "Creating Folder Objects for Attachments."

`readOnly()`, `lastModified()`, and `size()` should be self-explanatory—we can implement these easily. If the filesystem notices that such attributes change in the data source, it can fire events notifying the rest of the IDE of the change.

JavaMail supports listening to changes on the server, so when a notification arrives that some mail folder or message changed on the server, it could be passed on using the Filesystems API. `AbstractFileSystem` makes notification very easy: you need only call `refreshResource()` and mention the changed file and set expected to `false`; the filesystem will automatically construct an appropriate `FileEvent` and fire it to listeners. Other filesystem implementations may not have a good way of listening to changes directly. Instead, they can *poll* for changes (check periodically whether anything has changed). `AbstractFileSystem` makes this easy as well. You just need to call `setRefreshTime()` (as in the template), and the filesystem will begin polling for changes according to the specified period, transparently to the filesystem implementor.

`inputStream()` and `outputStream()` provide read and write access to file contents. For a mail message, we will first want to parse out headers and handle any message encodings, so that a client of this filesystem will see the natural file contents (when using the JavaMail API, this is handled by the API). `lock()` and `unlock()` can be used to match NetBeans' file locking to an external locking facility; we will assume that the mail server does not provide an explicit locking mechanism, and leave these methods blank.

`markUnimportant()` can tell a filesystem which files are important to users and should be preserved (such as Java sources) as opposed to transient or disposable files like class files. For a mail filesystem, we can assume that all files are important. A filesystem that is tied to a version control system would pay attention to this hint, perhaps by excluding the unimportant files from the shared repository by default.

Mail Filesystem: AbstractFileSystem.List

Example 19-2 shows the implementation of the ListImpl interface for our mail filesystem.

Example 19-2. ListImpl implementation inside MailFileSystem.java

```
private class ListImpl implements List {
  private static final long serialVersionUID = 72968756439298673L;
  public String[] children(String name) {
    try {
      String[] result = mgr.childrenOf(prefix(name));
      if (result == null) return new String[] {};
      int idx;
      for (int i = 0; i < result.length; i++) {
        idx = result[i].lastIndexOf("/");
        if (idx != -1) {
          result[i] = result[i].substring(idx + 1);
        }
      }
      return result;
    } catch (OperationFailedException ofe) {
      return new String[] {};
    }
  }
}
```

List is a simple interface that permits the filesystem to provide a hierarchy of files and subfolders. Its one method, children(), is given the name of a folder, and should produce a list of names of files and folders contained in that folder. In the case of an IMAP server, we would list the names of messages or subfolders. Again, AbstractFileSystem will handle firing changes if different results are returned from two successive calls to this method, so most filesystems need not do any more than compute the children list when requested.

Mail Filesystem: AbstractFileSystem.Change

Since we are implementing our mail system as read-only, implementing the Change interface is simple. This implementation is shown in Example 19-3.

Example 19-3. ChangeImpl implementation inside MailFileSystem.java

```
private class ChangeImpl implements Change {
  private static final long serialVersionUID = 87656723962265L;
  public void createFolder(String name) throws IOException {
    throw new IOException();
  }
  public void createData(String name) throws IOException {
    throw new IOException();
  }
  public void rename(String oldName, String newName) throws IOException {
```

```
    throw new IOException();
  }
  public void delete(String name) throws IOException {
    throw new IOException();
  }
}
```

Change provides simplified calls for the four basic operations that affect the hierarchy of files: creating subfolders, creating new (empty) files in folders, changing file (or folder) names, and deleting files (or folders, recursively). All of these could be mapped into IMAP folder and message operations, but we will avoid this complexity for purposes of this example.

Some filesystems may want to support moving a file between folders directly, rather than by deleting it and creating a copy in the new location. For example, IMAP servers generally permit such an atomic operation. To support this optimization, we could provide an implementation of the optional interface Transfer using IMAP operations to move messages between mail folders efficiently.

Mail Filesystem: AbstractFileSystem.Attr

Example 19-4 shows the implementation of the Attr interface.

Example 19-4. AttrImpl implementation inside MailFileSystem.java

```
private class AttrImpl implements Attr {
  private static final long serialVersionUID = 7694827698764524L;
  public Enumeration attributes(String name) {
    Attributes att = null;
    try {
      att - mgr.gctAttributes(prefix(name));
    } catch (OperationFailedException ofe) {}
    if (att == null) return EmptyEnumeration.EMPTY;
    return att.getNames();
  }
  public Object readAttribute(String name, String attrName) {
    Attributes att = null;
    try {
      att = mgr.getAttributes(prefix(name));
      if (att != null) {
        return att.get(attrName);
      }
    } catch (OperationFailedException ofe) {}
    return null;
  }
  public void writeAttribute(String name, String attrName, Object value)
      throws IOException {
    throw new IOException();
  }
```

```
    public void deleteAttributes(String name) {}
    public void renameAttributes(String oldName, String newName) {}
}
```

Since we chose not to use DefaultAttributes to store file attributes in *.nbattrs* files, we need to create an implementation of Attr. The methods attributes() and readAttribute() will scan the message headers and return their values. writeAttribute() could correspondingly store new or modified message headers for an existing message, but as the filesystem is read-only, we will not support this operation. Attributes could be deleted using the filesystem interface as well: the value null means to delete the named header. Even if implementing file copies and moves on the server, we will continue to leave deleteAttributes() and renameAttributes() blank; the IMAP server will keep message headers associated with the right message without needing NetBeans to copy them explicitly.

Other Parts of AbstractFileSystem

With this handful of interfaces implemented to delegate to the underlying mail server storage, our basic filesystem is mostly written. Only a few methods pertaining to the filesystem as a whole (rather than particular files) remain. The completed version is shown in Example 19-5.

Example 19-5. Mail filesystem: MailFileSystem implementation as a whole

```
public class MailFileSystem extends AbstractFileSystem {
  private static final long serialVersionUID = 762436798762L;
  private String server, root;
  private transient String password;
  private transient StoreManager mgr;
  public MailFileSystem() throws IOException {
    this("imap://username:PASSWORD@host/", null, "Mail");
  }
  public MailFileSystem(String server, String password, String root)
      throws IOException {
    this.server = server;
    this.password = password;
    this.root = root;
    info = new InfoImpl();
    change = new ChangeImpl();
    attr = new AttrImpl();
    list = new ListImpl();
    try {
      setSystemName(server + root);
    } catch (PropertyVetoException pve) {
      throw new IOException(pve.toString());
    }
    FileSystemCapability.Bean cap = new FileSystemCapability.Bean();
    cap.setCompile(false);
    cap.setDebug(false);
```

Example 19-5. Mail filesystem: MailFileSystem implementation as a whole (continued)

```
        cap.setDoc(false);
        cap.setExecute(false);
        setCapability(cap);
        init();
    }
    private void init() throws IOException {
        if (mgr == null) {
            // This is the only place where the JavaMail implementation is selected:
            try {
                mgr = StoreProvider.getDefault().get(loadPassword(server));
            } catch (IOException ioe) {
                throw ioe;
            } catch (Exception e) {
                throw new IOException(e.toString());
            }
        }
    }
    private void readObject(ObjectInputStream in)
            throws ClassNotFoundException, IOException {
        in.defaultReadObject();
        init();
    }
    // Bean accessors:
    public void setServer(String s) throws PropertyVetoException {
        setSystemName(s + root);
        server = s;
        password = null;
        try {
            init();
        } catch (IOException ioe) {
            TopManager.getDefault().getErrorManager().notify(ioe);
        }
        changeRoot();
    }
    public String getServer() {
        return server;
    }
    public String getRootFolder() {
        return root;
    }
    public void setRootFolder(String r) throws PropertyVetoException {
        if (r.endsWith("/")) {
            r = r.substring(0, r.length() - 1);
        }
        setSystemName(server + r);
        root = r;
        changeRoot();
    }
    // General methods:
    public String getDisplayName() {
        String s = server;
        String tok1 = "imap://";
```

```
      String tok2 = ":PASSWORD@";
      String tok3 = "/";
      if (s.startsWith(tok1) && s.endsWith(tok3)) {
        String inner = s.substring(tok1.length(), s.length() - tok3.length());
        int i = inner.indexOf(tok2);
        if (i != -1) {
          s = inner.substring(0, i) + "@" + inner.substring(i + tok2.length());
        }
      }
      return NbBundle.getMessage(MailFileSystem.class, "mail_fs_display_name", s);
    }
    public boolean isReadOnly() {
      return true;
    }
    // Helper methods:
    private void changeRoot() {
      mgr.setURL(loadPassword(server));
      firePropertyChange(PROP_ROOT, null, refreshRoot());
    }
    private String loadPassword(String url) {
      String token = ":PASSWORD@";
      int idx = url.indexOf(token);
      if (idx != -1) {
        if (password == null) {
          String title = NbBundle.getMessage(MailFileSystem.class,
                                          "Enter_Password_for_Mail_Server");
          JPanel p = new JPanel();
          JLabel l = new JLabel(NbBundle.getMessage(MailFileSystem.class,
                                          "Password_for_url", url));
          p.add(l);
          JPasswordField pf = new JPasswordField(20);
          l.setLabelFor(pf);
          KeyStroke enter = KeyStroke.getKeyStroke(KeyEvent.VK_ENTER, 0);
          pf.getKeymap().removeKeyStrokeBinding(enter);
          p.add(pf);
          NotifyDescriptor d = new NotifyDescriptor(p, title,
            NotifyDescriptor.OK_CANCEL_OPTION, NotifyDescriptor.PLAIN_MESSAGE,
            null, null);
          if (TopManager.getDefault().notify(d) == NotifyDescriptor.OK_OPTION) {
            password = new String(pf.getPassword());
          }
        }
        if (password != null) {
          url = url.substring(0, idx) + ":" + password + "@" +
                url.substring(idx + token.length());
        }
      }
      return url;
    }
    // this method is shared by the inner interfaces:
    private String prefix(String name) {
      if (root.length() == 0) {
        return name;
```

```
    } else {
      return root + "/" + name;
    }
  }
  // InfoImpl, ListImpl, ChangeImpl, AttrImpl as above...
}
```

First, we can provide getters and setters for various properties that the user should be able to configure on the filesystem; in NetBeans, filesystems are JavaBeans that can be created, configured, and saved. Every setter must use firePropertyChange() to notify listeners that the property has changed. The BeanInfo for the filesystem can provide niceties like localized display names and property editors for these properties, to simplify configuration from a GUI like the IDE. We will also provide a wizard that makes it easy for the user to completely configure the filesystem from the beginning. This wizard will use the helpful second constructor rather than the first (no-argument) constructor required of all beans.

Some properties are very basic and control the actual contents of the filesystem. In our case, these are server location (that is, IMAP URL, including the server hostname, possibly port, username, and password) and the top-level mail folder to open. When setters for these properties are called, it is possible to instruct AbstractFileSystem that the entire contents of the filesystem should be rechecked by firing a change of PROP_ROOT and passing the new root folder as obtained by refreshRoot().

We should also change the *system name* of the filesystem; this is a unique code string, such as a URL, which identifies the filesystem among others. For example, the IDE prevents you from mounting two filesystems with the same system name, as they would be considered duplicates. The system name is also used when serializing file object references. We will use a system name based on both the IMAP URL and the root folder, so any setters that change its value will also call setSystemName() to update it. If the user reconfigures either of these properties when the filesystem is already mounted, its entire contents will be rescanned.

Note that the IMAP password is not kept literally in the URL by default. The magic string PASSWORD is used as a placeholder. NetBeans will write out the regular instance fields to disk when serializing the filesystem configuration, which permits the application to remember the mount after a restart. We will ensure that this filesystem keeps the password only in a transient variable. It will be kept in memory, and the user will be prompted for it after a restart using a simple dialog box.

Finally, some miscellaneous methods remain. We will implement isReadOnly() according to whether the user (or any other part of the IDE) is permitted to change files on this filesystem; since our filesystem does not support modifications, this will always be true. getDisplayName() provides a human-friendly name for the filesystem, for example, to be displayed in the **Filesystems** tab of the Explorer.

Creating Folder Objects for Attachments

One difficulty with building a filesystem based on IMAP is that a mail server is not designed to hold arbitrary files. It is constrained to store messages. So we will need a mapping between mail concepts and file concepts.

There are several different sorts of objects on the mail server that we will wish to represent using the Filesystems API.

General folder

> Some folders are designed only to hold other folders, rather than messages directly. These are used for grouping your mail account. In the filesystem, these will be ordinary file folders: FileObjects for which isFolder() is true.

Message folder

> Other folders specifically hold messages and cannot hold subfolders. In the filesystem, these will again be file folders. They can be distinguished from general folders by a special file attribute, org.netbeans.lib.mail.Constants.A_HOLDSMSGS, available using the regular method call FileObject.getAttribute(), which will call our implementation in Info.readAttribute().*

Simple message

> Simple messages (with only one part, usually a plain text body) are represented as simple files (FileObjects for which isData() holds true). The body of the message is the content of the file, and headers are represented as file attributes. The filename will end in *.msg*, and the name without this extension will be arbitrary (based on the message ID or an internal server ID, for example).

Multipart message

> Other messages contain several parts, for example, one main body (typically plain text), and some MIME attachments. More details of the MIME system are given in Chapter 21, but for now it is enough to know that most modern mail agents create and read attachments using this standard. The message *as a whole* is represented by a file folder, with the master headers (including the sender, subject, and so on) represented as file attributes. The content type will be multipart/mixed, and the message folder will again have a name ending in *.msg*.

Attachments

> Attached files, such as GIF-format images attached to an email message, are represented as simple files within the multipart message folder. These will have some headers (such as attachment name, content type, and so on). The main body of a multipart message falls into this category; so do forwarded simple messages (the MIME type text/rfc822 distinguishes these). Attachments with no

---

* Some IMAP servers actually do support mixed-mode folders with both messages and subfolders, and this is addressed by JavaMail. However, for simplicity, the current mail access library does not support such folders.

specific filename given in the message are represented to NetBeans as a file whose name ends in *.part*.

Subordinate MIME containers

A cross between the previous two sorts of objects, multipart messages may themselves contain sub-containers. For example, a forwarded multipart message is nested inside the forwarding message, or some attachments can be *presented* in multiple ways according to the ability of the mail reader, using mime/ alternative. Again, these sub-containers are represented as file folders and will have some number of headers represented as file attributes.

Using FileSystem.Status Annotations to Mark Unread Messages

One interesting ability given to filesystems is that of *annotating* objects stored on them as far as display name and icon are concerned. Remember that *data objects* are the higher-level view of files that, after being wrapped in nodes, are displayed in the Explorer window. These objects have a displayable name (usually taken from the filename) and an icon (usually determined by file type).

Some filesystems want to expose some additional clues to the user about how the system is storing files. For example, filesystems that are backed by version-control systems like CVS typically have a notion of *file status*. For example, "Needs Update" means that a local copy of a file is unmodified and that there is a newer version on the CVS server that the user should retrieve sooner or later. These statuses can be very important to the user's work and need to be presented in the GUI somehow.

Since the statuses are determined by the filesystem and are orthogonal to object type—for example, both Java sources and HTML files could need a CVS update or not—the NetBeans APIs permit the filesystem to add this information, with the cooperation of the data object.* The concept of data objects is discussed in Chapter 17: each file or file group, such as the Java source or HTML file, is represented by an object that encapsulates the behavior appropriate to that type of file.

Currently two kinds of annotation are defined. A filesystem may annotate the display name of the node in the Explorer so that a Java source *Print.java* might be displayed as **Print** [**Needs Update**]. Instead or in addition, it may annotate the icon of a node so that a Java source that normally looks like: 🔹 might look like this when the filesystem needs to draw attention to it: 🔹

---

* Data objects cooperate in using annotations by subclassing DataNode for their node delegates. DataNode checks to see if the filesystem wishes to add any annotations when constructing its display name and icon.

The API method `Utilities.mergeImages()` is often used by filesystems to place such badges on top of existing object icons. The NetBeans *http://ui.netbeans.org/docs/badging/badging.html* UI guidelines for badging have more information on this subject.

For the mail filesystem, we will implement a simple icon badging system to demonstrate the technique. Folders containing unread messages, as well as the unread messages themselves, will be marked with a red cross: ⁺

Example 19-6 adds status annotations to the mail system.

Example 19-6. Mail filesystem: MailFileSystem.java added inner class to support status

```java
private transient Status status;
public Status getStatus() {
  if (status == null) {
    status = new StatusImpl();
  }
  return status;
}
private class StatusImpl implements Status, FileChangeListener {
  private final Set monitoredFiles = new WeakSet(); // Set<FileObject>
  public Image annotateIcon(Image icon, int iconType, Set files) {
    FileObject fo = (FileObject)files.iterator().next();
    boolean unread = false;
    if (fo.isFolder()) {
      Integer i = (Integer)fo.getAttribute(Constants.A_UNREADMESSAGECOUNT);
      unread = i != null && i.intValue() > 0;
    } else {
      Boolean b = (Boolean)fo.getAttribute(Constants.F_SEEN);
      unread = b == null || !b.booleanValue();
    }
    if (unread) {
      Image badge =
        Utilities.loadImage("org/netbeans/modules/mailclient/unread.gif");
      icon = Utilities.mergeImages(icon, badge, 16, 0);
    }
    if (monitoredFiles.add(fo)) {
      fo.addFileChangeListener(WeakListener.fileChange(this, fo));
    }
    return icon;
  }
  public String annotateName(String name, Set files) {
    // Do not annotate names.
    return name;
  }
  public void fileAttributeChanged(FileAttributeEvent fe) {
    String attr = fe.getName();
    if (attr == null || attr.equals(Constants.A_UNREADMESSAGECOUNT) ||
                        attr.equals(Constants.F_SEEN)) {
      fireFileStatusChanged(
        new FileStatusEvent(MailFileSystem.this, fe.getFile(), true, false));
    }
  }
}
```

```
    public void fileChanged(FileEvent fe) {}
    public void fileDataCreated(FileEvent fe) {}
    public void fileDeleted(FileEvent fe) {}
    public void fileFolderCreated(FileEvent fe) {}
    public void fileRenamed(FileRenameEvent fe) {}
}
```

To provide annotations from a filesystem is not difficult. All that is necessary is to implement the FileSystem.Status interface and return this implementation from FileSystem.getStatus(). Our MailFileSystem.StatusImpl leaves the display name alone—it just returns the same name as was suggested by the data node—but implements annotateIcon() to add the "unread" badge to certain nodes.

The annotation methods actually receive a *set* of files, not just one; this permits the filesystem to decide what to do when several files it controls are grouped into a single object. For example, a CVS filesystem might version *Panel.java* and *Panel.form*, but the form object *Panel* groups these (as well as *Panel.class*). The two versioned files might have the same status, or not; the filesystem decides how to handle any mismatches. In the case of messages, we know that the message is by itself in a data object, so annotateIcon() just pays attention to the first supplied file (always the primary file).

Our status example will also demonstrate how to listen to changes in the read/unread state of the file and refire such changes as an icon change. Although the IMAP filesystem as implemented will not provide notification from the server of this kind of change in the file, we can see the NetBeans-specific code that would be required. If the status of a file changes after it is first queried, the user should see the new updated status immediately. For this, a filesystem may use the fireFileStatusChanged() method, which will notify listeners (normally just the object's node). The mail filesystem bases its annotations on the unread flags of messages and folders, so, after computing any annotation, we attach a file change listener to the file object in case it is later marked read or unread. The set monitoredFiles is used to make sure a listener is attached only once to a given file. If a file attribute named A_UNREADMESSAGECOUNT or F_SEEN is changed by the server, we know that the icon annotation needs to be updated, so a FileStatusEvent is fired that encapsulates the file (message), filesystem, and the knowledge that just the icon (and not the display name) needs to be recomputed.

BeanInfo—Displaying Filesystem Properties

As part of creating a FileSystem implementation in NetBeans, as with most Java-Beans made visible to the user, we will want to create a BeanInfo to make the filesystem properties look more pleasant, including the use of localized text strings. The required code is shown in Example 19-7.

Example 19-7. Mail filesystem: MailFileSystemBeanInfo.java

```java
public class MailFileSystemBeanInfo extends SimpleBeanInfo {
  public BeanInfo[] getAdditionalBeanInfo() {
    try {
      return new BeanInfo[] {Introspector.getBeanInfo(FileSystem.class)};
    } catch (IntrospectionException ie) {
      TopManager.getDefault().getErrorManager().notify(ie);
      return null;
    }
  }
  public PropertyDescriptor[] getPropertyDescriptors() {
    try {
      PropertyDescriptor server =
        new PropertyDescriptor("server", MailFileSystem.class);
      server.setDisplayName(NbBundle.getMessage(
        MailFileSystemBeanInfo.class, "Server_URL"));
      server.setShortDescription(NbBundle.getMessage(
        MailFileSystemBeanInfo.class, "Server_URL_hint"));
      PropertyDescriptor root =
        new PropertyDescriptor("rootFolder", MailFileSystem.class);
      root.setDisplayName(NbBundle.getMessage(
        MailFileSystemBeanInfo.class, "Root_Folder"));
      root.setShortDescription(NbBundle.getMessage(
        MailFileSystemBeanInfo.class, "Root_Folder_hint"));
      return new PropertyDescriptor[] {server, root};
    } catch (IntrospectionException ie) {
      TopManager.getDefault().getErrorManager().notify(ie);
      return null;
    }
  }
  public Image getIcon(int type) {
    if (type == BeanInfo.ICON_COLOR_16x16 || type == BeanInfo.ICON_MONO_16x16) {
      return Utilities.loadImage(
        "org/netbeans/modules/mailclient/resources/message.gif");
    } else {
      return null;
    }
  }
}
```

The getAdditionalBeanInfo() method ensures that any properties common to *all* filesystems are reasonably displayed, as implemented by the NetBeans core. getPropertyDescriptors() adds our two bean properties: server and rootFolder. getIcon() provides a distinctive icon for the filesystem, visible both in the Explorer window in the Filesystems tab and also in **Filesystems Settings** in the Options window (see Figure 19-1).

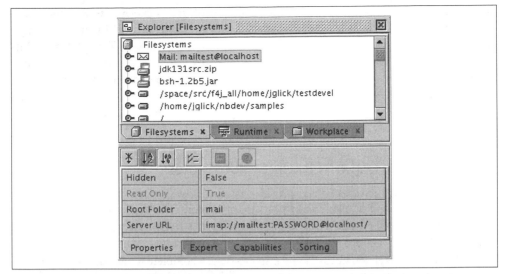

Figure 19-1. Mail filesystem: BeanInfo

Using the Wizard Framework to Set Up Mail Accounts

Without special support, novice users will not find it very pleasant to create a new mail filesystem. The standard IDE method of creating a new filesystem is used to start the process: **File → Mount...** and select a type of filesystem. However, by default, a user is forced to configure each aspect of the filesystem separately using the property sheet, with no indication of what should be configured first or which properties are required.

NetBeans, like most modern applications, provides wizards to help guide a user through various procedures that are either difficult to get a handhold on or that have such a regular order of operation that it is simplest to present all the steps in their natural sequence. We can use the wizard framework to help the user set up a filesystem corresponding to a mail account.

The *entry point* for creating the filesystem will be the **New** wizard as launched by **File → Mount Filesystem...** , which lets the user select a kind of new filesystem to create, configure, and mount.

Creating Wizard Classes

Making a new wizard does not need to be difficult, although the result can look like it was! You can use the API Support templates to get the basics right. Making a wizard from scratch means creating a `WizardDescriptor` that specifies the panels in the wizard, their sequencing, data held in the wizard between panels, labels for steps, and other details. If you select the template **Templates → NetBeans Extensions → Window System API → Wizard**, you can make a functional wizard by customizing a small amount of code in the template. You also need at least one **Templates → NetBeans Extensions → Window System API → Wizard Panel** to display; the API Support template lets you develop the panel visually in the Form Editor. The wizard infrastructure displays standard buttons along the bottom of the wizard dialog, a list of steps in the left column, and more. See Chapter 17 for background.

Why Use WizardDescriptor?

What does using `WizardDescriptor` provide? You can always create a dialog with arbitrary contents using a plain `DialogDescriptor`, which is in fact the superclass of `WizardDescriptor`. `DialogDescriptor` is better to use than the raw Swing `JOptionPane` as it interacts more cleanly with NetBeans' window system.

For one thing, it is generally easier and faster to write a complete wizard using this class than by constructing it manually, as many parts of the GUI are supplied for you: for example, the **Next**, **Previous**, **Finish**, **Help**, and **Cancel** buttons; the list of steps in the left pane; and the title header for each panel. It also simplifies storing state (user-entered data) between panels and handling the logic of turning buttons on and off.

Beyond that, `WizardDescriptor` enables the IDE to enforce a certain level of UI consistency in various details, so your wizard looks good alongside other NetBeans wizards. There have also been discussions of letting wizards built with the standard framework be accessible to command-line or remote users of NetBeans, though this goal has yet to be realized.

For this example the procedure is a bit different, since we are inserting panels into the **New** wizard. The NetBeans core already supplies some of the infrastructure for this wizard, including the `TemplateWizard` (a special kind of `WizardDescriptor`) and the first panel. The fixed first panel permits a template to be chosen. Normally this template is for a new data object, but when mounting a filesystem, it is a template for a new filesystem, such as Local Directory or Archive File. The remaining panels (if any) can be controlled by the template, using a `TemplateWizard.Iterator` implementation. Again **Templates → NetBeans Extensions → Window System API → Template Wizard** provides skeleton code for a `TemplateWizard.Iterator` to which you can add as many wizard panels as you like. The iterator specifies the sequence of steps and handles the final mounting of the filesystem; each panel defines the appearance and behavior of one step.

The IMAP Mail Server Template Wizard

Now let us look at the wizard implementation for adding a new mail server. For an IMAP filesystem, the first step must be to specify the IMAP server (hostname), and at the same time we can ask for a login, too (username and password). With this con-

---

nection info established, we can then try to connect to the server and ask it for available folders; the user may wish to select a particular root folder for the filesystem. Example 19-8 takes care of this first step, and the visual result is shown in Figure 19-2.

Example 19-8. Mail filesystem: SelectServerPanel.java

```java
public class SelectServerPanel extends JPanel
                            implements WizardDescriptor.Panel {
  private JTextField nameField, serverField;
  private JPasswordField passField;
  public SelectServerPanel() {
    // GUI initialization omitted...
  }
  public Component getComponent() {
    return this;
  }
  public HelpCtx getHelp() {
    return HelpCtx.DEFAULT_HELP;
  }
  public boolean isValid() {
    return true;
  }
  public void addChangeListener(ChangeListener l) {}
  public void removeChangeListener(ChangeListener l) {}
  public void readSettings(Object settings) {}
  public void storeSettings(Object settings) {
    WizardDescriptor wiz = (WizardDescriptor)settings;
    String url = "imap://" + nameField.getText() + ":PASSWORD@" +
                        serverField.getText() + "/";
    wiz.putProperty(ConnectionWizardIterator.PROP_SERVER, url);
    wiz.putProperty(ConnectionWizardIterator.PROP_PASSWORD,
                new String(passField.getPassword()));
  }
}
```

The first panel permits the user to select an IMAP server and enter a username and password. `WizardDescriptor.Panel.getComponent()` returns the actual Swing component displayed in the wizard, which is `SelectServerPanel` itself. `getHelp()` could provide a topic for the **Help** button if we wished. `isValid()` indicates whether the **Next** button should be enabled at any point. This simple example leaves the **Next** button on from the start, but to validate user input, `isValid()` could check whether all fields are populated, and we could fire a `ChangeEvent` when the panel is complete.

`readSettings()` is used to load data from previous panels. Since this is the first panel, we can leave it empty. `storeSettings()`, however, will be called when **Next** is pressed to save the data entered by the user; the best way to do this is by using name-value pairs in the associated `WizardDescriptor`, actually a `TemplateWizard`.

The second panel, `SelectRootFolderPanel`, is fairly similar, and is shown in Example 19-9. One difference is that `readSettings()` now picks up the server loca-

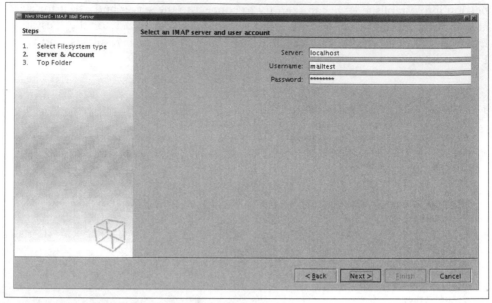

Figure 19-2. Mail filesystem: SelectServerPanel

tion, username, and password from the previous panel. It uses this information to actually connect to the mail server in order to retrieve a list of IMAP folders available for the account. Using the Explorer API, we display a MailFolderNode (discussed next) in a tree view, visually added to the explorer panel panel. storeSettings() again records the choice of root folder in the account.

Example 19-9. Mail filesystem: SelectRootFolderPanel.java (panel implementation)

```java
public class SelectRootFolderPanel extends JPanel
    implements WizardDescriptor.Panel, VetoableChangeListener {
  private ExplorerPanel panel;
  private ExplorerManager explorer;
  public SelectRootFolderPanel() {
    // GUI initialization omitted...
    explorer = panel.getExplorerManager();
  }
  public Component getComponent() {
    return this;
  }
  public HelpCtx getHelp() {
    return HelpCtx.DEFAULT_HELP;
  }
  public boolean isValid() {
    return true;
  }
  public final void addChangeListener(ChangeListener l) {}
  public final void removeChangeListener(ChangeListener l) {}
  public void readSettings(Object settings) {
```

Example 19-9. Mail filesystem: SelectRootFolderPanel.java (panel implementation) (continued)

```
    WizardDescriptor wiz = (WizardDescriptor)settings;
    String url = (String)wiz.getProperty(ConnectionWizardIterator.PROP_SERVER);
    String token = ":PASSWORD@";
    int idx = url.indexOf(token);
    if (idx != -1) {
      String pw =
        (String)wiz.getProperty(ConnectionWizardIterator.PROP_PASSWORD);
      if (pw != null) {
        url = url.substring(0, idx) + ":" + pw + "@" +
              url.substring(idx + token.length());
      }
    }
    try {
      StoreManager mgr = StoreProvider.getDefault().get(url);
      Node n = new MailFolderNode(mgr, "");
      explorer.setRootContext(n);
      try {
        explorer.setSelectedNodes(new Node[] { n });
      } catch (PropertyVetoException pve) {
        TopManager.getDefault().getErrorManager().notify(pve);
      }
    } catch (Exception e) {
      TopManager.getDefault().getErrorManager().notify(e);
    }
    explorer.addVetoableChangeListener(this);
  }
  public void storeSettings(Object settings) {
    WizardDescriptor wiz = (WizardDescriptor)settings;
    String path = ((MailFolderNode)explorer.getSelectedNodes()[0]).getPath();
    wiz.putProperty(ConnectionWizardIterator.PROP_ROOT, path);
  }
  public void vetoableChange(PropertyChangeEvent evt)
      throws PropertyVetoException {
    if (ExplorerManager.PROP_SELECTED_NODES.equals(evt.getPropertyName())) {
      Node[] nodes = (Node[])evt.getNewValue();
      if (nodes == null || nodes.length != 1) {
        throw new PropertyVetoException("Selection of != 1 node", evt);
      }
    }
  }
}
```

The explorer manager explorer handles the node selection. We attach a veto listener to the node selection: the user is prevented from selecting more than one root folder at once. This can also be accomplished by subclassing the GUI component BeanTreeView and overriding protected boolean selectionAccept(Node[ ]), or in NetBeans 3.4 by simply calling setSelectionMode(SINGLE_TREE_SELECTION) on the tree view.

You'll also need an inner class to handle display of the folders, as shown in Example 19-10.

Example 19-10. Mail filesystem: SelectRootFolderPanel.java
(MailFolderNode inner class)

```java
private static final class MailFolderNode extends AbstractNode {
  private final String path;
  public MailFolderNode(StoreManager mgr, String path) {
    super(new MailFolderChildren(mgr, path));
    this.path = path;
    setName(path);
    if (path.length() == 0) {
      setDisplayName(NbBundle.getMessage(SelectRootFolderPanel.class,
                                         "(Root)"));
    } else {
      int idx = path.lastIndexOf('/');
      if (idx == -1) {
        setDisplayName(path);
      } else {
        setDisplayName(path.substring(idx + 1));
      }
    }
  }
  public String getPath() {
    return path;
  }
  // Key type: String (relative name of child)
  private static final class MailFolderChildren extends Children.Keys {
    private final StoreManager mgr;
    private final String path;
    public MailFolderChildren(StoreManager mgr, String path) {
      this.mgr = mgr;
      this.path = path;
    }
    protected void addNotify() {
      try {
        String[] kids = mgr.childrenOf(path);
        if ((kids != null) && (kids.length > 0))
          setKeys(kids);
      } catch (OperationFailedException ofe) {
        setKeys(Collections.EMPTY_SET);
      }
    }
    protected void removeNotify() {
      setKeys(Collections.EMPTY_SET);
    }
    protected Node[] createNodes(Object key) {
      String name = (String)key;
      if (name.startsWith("~//")) {
        name = name.substring(3);
      }
      if (name.endsWith("/")) {
        name = name.substring(0, name.length() - 1);
      }
      try {
        ObjectDescriptor od = mgr.getDescriptor(path);
        if (od != null) {
```

```
            if (od.isDataChildren() || od.isFolderChildren()) {
              return new Node[] {new MailFolderNode(mgr, name)};
            }
          }
        } catch (OperationFailedException ofe) {
          TopManager.getDefault().getErrorManager().notify(ofe);
        }
        return null;
      }
    }
  }
}
```

The inner class `MailFolderNode` produces the node hierarchy to display in the tree view. It is more or less a direct mapping of the folders on the server, though some massaging of folder names is done in order to provide an intuitive display for the user, rather than the internal IMAP names. The use of `Children.Keys` to create a `Node` view of structured data is covered in detail in Chapter 25, so we will not go deeply into this subject here. The method `MailFolderNode.getPath()` returns the raw IMAP folder prefix corresponding to a node; it is used by `SelectRootFolderNode.storeSettings()` to determine the user's choice of a root folder.

The completed panel is shown as it appears in the wizard in Figure 19-3.

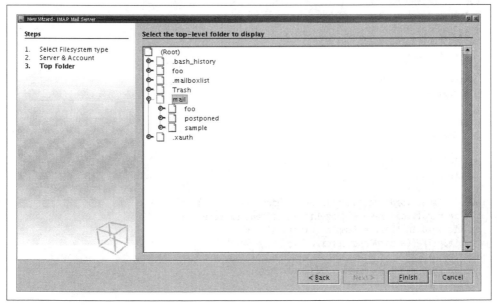

Figure 19-3. Mail filesystem: SelectRootFolderPanel

Example 19-11. Mail filesystem: ConnectionWizardIterator.java

```java
public class ConnectionWizardIterator implements TemplateWizard.Iterator {
  private static final long serialVersionUID = 8653597691208560L;
  static final String PROP_SERVER = "connection.server";
  static final String PROP_ROOT = "connection.root";
  static final String PROP_PASSWORD = "connection.password";
  private transient WizardDescriptor wiz = null;
  private transient int index = 0;
  private transient WizardDescriptor.Panel[] panels = null;
  private transient String[] steps = null;
  protected WizardDescriptor.Panel[] createPanels() {
    return new WizardDescriptor.Panel[] {
      new SelectServerPanel(),
      new SelectRootFolderPanel(),
    };
  }
  protected String[] createSteps() {
    return new String[] {
      NbBundle.getMessage(ConnectionWizardIterator.class, "Server_&_Account"),
      NbBundle.getMessage(ConnectionWizardIterator.class, "Top_Folder"),
    };
  }
  public String name() {
    return NbBundle.getMessage(ConnectionWizardIterator.class, "x_of_y",
      new Integer(index+1), new Integer(panels.length));
  }
  public boolean hasNext() {
    return index < panels.length - 1;
  }
  public boolean hasPrevious() {
    return index > 0;
  }
  public void nextPanel() {
    index++;
  }
  public void previousPanel() {
    index--;
  }
  public WizardDescriptor.Panel current() {
    return panels[index];
  }
  public final void addChangeListener(ChangeListener l) {}
  public final void removeChangeListener(ChangeListener l) {}
  public void initialize(TemplateWizard wiz) {
    initialize((WizardDescriptor)wiz);
  }
  public void initialize(WizardDescriptor wiz) {
    this.wiz = wiz;
    index = 0;
    panels = createPanels();
    String[] steps = createSteps();
    for (int i = 0; i < panels.length; i++) {
      JComponent jc = (JComponent)panels[i].getComponent();
```

Example 19-11. Mail filesystem: ConnectionWizardIterator.java (continued)

```
      jc.putClientProperty("WizardPanel_contentSelectedIndex", new Integer(i));
      jc.putClientProperty("WizardPanel_contentData", steps);
    }
  }
  public void uninitialize(TemplateWizard wiz) {
    wiz = null;
    panels = null;
  }
  public Set instantiate(TemplateWizard wiz) throws IOException {
    return instantiate((WizardDescriptor)wiz);
  }
  public Set instantiate(WizardDescriptor wiz) throws IOException {
    MailFileSystem fs = new MailFileSystem(
      (String)wiz.getProperty(PROP_SERVER),
      (String)wiz.getProperty(PROP_PASSWORD),
      (String)wiz.getProperty(PROP_ROOT));
    Repository.getDefault().addFileSystem(fs);
    return Collections.EMPTY_SET;
  }
}
```

ConnectionWizardIterator, shown in Example 19-11, manages the sequence of panels and controls the behavior when the wizard is finished. The constants such as PROP_SERVER are keys with which the wizard's data is stored in the TemplateWizard objects. These keys correspond to the **New** dialog box. createPanels() cooperates with hasNext(), hasPrevious(), nextPanel(), and previousPanel() to create the panel components and order them. initialize() is called when the **IMAP Mail Server** is selected, to permit the panels to be initialized, and uninitialize() permits the iterator to clean up in case the user changes his or her mind and selects a different kind of filesystem instead. createSteps() is a helper method used by initialize() to label each step of the wizard; these labels will appear in the left margin and help orient the user. name() is used to set the wizard title.

instantiate() is called if and when Finish is pressed. We read the stored data entered in the two wizard panels. A new MailFileSystem is constructed based on this information and mounted to the repository (the **Filesystems** tab in the Explorer window). The return value is a set of objects created by the wizard; this information is mostly useful for creating files (**File → New...**), but for mounting filesystems, we need not return anything.

The last step is to register the wizard as an available type of filesystem. NetBeans keeps templates for new filesystems to mount in the folder *Templates/Mount/* in the system filesystem. We therefore make an XML layer, as seen in Example 19-12, and reference it in the module manifest (Example 19-13).

Example 19-12. Mail filesystem: initial layer.xml

```xml
<!DOCTYPE filesystem PUBLIC
          "-//NetBeans//DTD Filesystem 1.1//EN"
          "http://www.netbeans.org/dtds/filesystem-1_1.dtd">
<filesystem>
  <folder name="Templates">
    <folder name="Mount">
      <file name="org-netbeans-modules-mailclient-new.xml" url="new.xml">
        <attr name="SystemFileSystem.localizingBundle"
              stringvalue="org.netbeans.modules.mailclient.resources.Bundle"/>
        <attr name="SystemFileSystem.icon" urlvalue=
            "nbresloc:/org/netbeans/modules/mailclient/resources/message.gif"/>
        <attr boolvalue="true" name="template"/>
        <attr name="templateWizardIterator"
        newvalue="org.netbeans.modules.mailclient.fs.ConnectionWizardIterator"/>
        <attr name="templateWizardURL" urlvalue=
            "nbresloc:/org/netbeans/modules/mailclient/resources/new-desc.html"/>
      </file>
    </folder>
  </folder>
</filesystem>
```

Example 19-13. Mail filesystem: initial module JAR manifest

```
Manifest-Version: 1.0
OpenIDE-Module: org.netbeans.modules.mailclient
OpenIDE-Module-Specification-Version: 0.2
OpenIDE-Module-Layer: org/netbeans/modules/mailclient/resources/layer.xml
OpenIDE-Module-Localizing-Bundle:
  org/netbeans/modules/mailclient/resources/Bundle.properties
Class-Path: ext/mail.jar ext/activation.jar
```

SystemFileSystem.localizingBundle and SystemFileSystem.icon control the physical appearance of the template in the first panel of the **New** wizard, and templateWizardURL provides a descriptive HTML blurb to guide the user. The attribute template is mandatory, as it indicates that this file is really a template and not just sitting in the folder incidentally. templateWizardIterator is the interesting attribute: its value will be a fresh instance of our TemplateWizard.Iterator implementation, permitting the **New** wizard to plug in our panels when the template is selected. Example 19-14 shows the simple bundle properties for this module.

Example 19-14. Mail filesystem: initial Bundle.properties

```
OpenIDE-Module-Name: Mail Client
OpenIDE-Module-Short-Description: Access messages on an IMAP mail server.
Templates/Mount/org-netbeans-modules-mailclient-new.xml=IMAP Mail Server
```

The file contents are mostly irrelevant, as the wizard does the work. However, we will use the settings file *new.xml* (shown in Example 19-15) just in case the wizard is bypassed somehow and the template instantiated directly: this settings file represents an unconfigured default instance of MailFileSystem.

Example 19-15. Mail filesystem: new.xml

```
<!DOCTYPE settings PUBLIC
          "-//NetBeans//DTD Session settings 1.0//EN"
          "http://www.netbeans.org/dtds/sessionsettings-1_0.dtd">
<settings version="1.0">
  <instanceof class="org.openide.filesystems.FileSystem"/>
  <instance class="org.netbeans.modules.mailclient.resources.MailFileSystem"/>
</settings>
```

The completed IMAP template is shown in Figure 19-4.

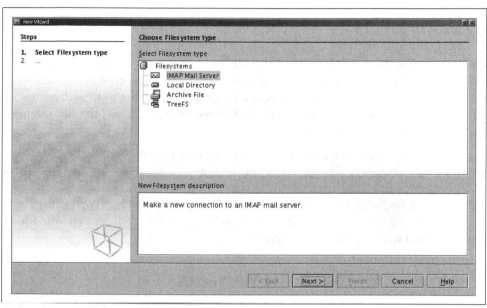

Figure 19-4. Mail filesystem: IMAP Mail Server template

In the next chapter we will focus less on infrastructure and more on the user interface, to see how to make the mail client look better to a user.

CHAPTER 20

Creating the User Interface for the Mail Client

Creating a filesystem to represent mail folders and messages takes care of the basic storage and fundamental interactions between a user and mail server. But it is a terrible user interface—users wish to see messages presented as in a normal email client for the most part, so we need to provide additional layers on top of the filesystem to make it a more plausible application.

We will start by displaying some special mail-specific information to the user when he or she is looking at a message and ensuring that text messages can be viewed and edited in the Source Editor window. But the most interesting UI addition will be to create special nodes to represent messages, folders, and threads, which can be displayed in the Explorer and provide a more refined model. A dedicated workspace will be created to focus the user's attention.

Creating a DataLoader for Messages

It is fine and good to cause messages to appear as files in the IMAP filesystem, but message "files" may typically be named arbitrarily (for example, by message ID) and might normally appear in the Explorer as blank icons, like this: ☐

Additionally, such "unrecognized objects" are not permitted to be opened in the editor (since the IDE does not know whether they are really textual, or binary) and we do not have much control over them.

 You will find a **Convert to Text** action on the context menu for such objects, which allows you to subsequently open such files.

So to make messages appear to the user as real objects that are supposed to be there, we define a *data loader* for them. This means that the IDE delegates some control over the appearance of these files to the mail module. There will actually be two loaders: one to recognize simple mail messages as well as files attached using the MIME system, and one to recognize multipart messages (containing several attachments).

Registration of the data loaders will be simple, using the module manifest shown in Example 20-1.

Example 20-1. Mail filesystem: module JAR manifest including data loaders

```
Manifest-Version: 1.0
OpenIDE-Module: org.netbeans.modules.mailclient
OpenIDE-Module-Name: Mail Client
OpenIDE-Module-Package-Dependencies: org.apache.regexp[RE]
OpenIDE-Module-Specification-Version: 0.2
OpenIDE-Module-Layer: org/netbeans/modules/mailclient/resources/layer.xml
Class-Path: ext/mail.jar ext/activation.jar

Name: org/netbeans/modules/mailclient/loaders/MailDataLoader.class
OpenIDE-Module-Class: Loader
Install-Before: org.netbeans.modules.text.TXTDataObject

Name: org/netbeans/modules/mailclient/loaders/MultipartMessageDataLoader.class
OpenIDE-Module-Class: Loader
Install-Before: org.openide.loaders.DataFolder
```

Displaying and Editing Simple Messages and Unnamed Attachments

The data loader shown in Example 20-2 recognizes any files with the *.msg* extension (simple text messages) or *.part* extension (unnamed textual MIME attachments). Named MIME attachments, such as HTML files and images, will be handled automatically by other NetBeans modules: the mail filesystem will provide as the name of such a FileObject the name given to the attachment by the sender, for example *some-picture.gif*.

Example 20-2. Mail filesystem: MailDataLoader.java

```java
public class MailDataLoader extends UniFileLoader {
  private static final long serialVersionUID = 769872698764545L;
  static final String MESSAGE_EXT = "msg";
  static final String PART_EXT = "part";
  public MailDataLoader() {
    super("org.netbeans.modules.mailclient.loaders.MailDataObject");
  }
  protected String defaultDisplayName() {
    return NbBundle.getMessage(MailDataLoader.class,
                        "Simple_Messages_and_Attachments");
  }
  protected SystemAction[] defaultActions() {
    return new SystemAction[] {
      SystemAction.get(OpenAction.class),
      SystemAction.get(FileSystemAction.class),
      null,
      SystemAction.get(SaveAsTemplateAction.class),
      null,
```

Example 20-2. Mail filesystem: MailDataLoader.java (continued)

```
      SystemAction.get(ToolsAction.class),
      SystemAction.get(PropertiesAction.class),
    };
  }
  protected void initialize() {
    super.initialize();
    ExtensionList exts = new ExtensionList();
    exts.addExtension(MESSAGE_EXT);
    exts.addExtension(PART_EXT);
    setExtensions(exts);
  }
  protected MultiDataObject createMultiObject(FileObject primaryFile)
  throws DataObjectExistsException, IOException {
    return new MailDataObject(primaryFile, this);
  }
}
```

The downloadable example sources also include a *MailDataLoaderBeanInfo.java* to configure some display aspects of the loader in the NetBeans Object Types settings node. Since this BeanInfo is unremarkable, it is not covered here.

The data object to handle such messages and anonymous attachments is rather simple, and is shown in Example 20-3. Its only distinguishing feature is that it adds an editor support to permit the message to be opened in the Source Editor window. addSaveCookie( ) and removeSaveCookie( ) are used by this editor support.

Example 20-3. Mail filesystem: MailDataObject.java

```
public class MailDataObject extends MultiDataObject {
  public MailDataObject(FileObject pf, MailDataLoader loader)
      throws DataObjectExistsException {
    super(pf, loader);
    getCookieSet().add(new MessageBodyEditorSupport(this));
  }
  public HelpCtx getHelpCtx() {
    return HelpCtx.DEFAULT_HELP;
  }
  protected Node createNodeDelegate() {
    return new MailDataNode(this);
  }
  final void addSaveCookie(SaveCookie save) {
    getCookieSet().add(save);
  }
  final void removeSaveCookie(SaveCookie save) {
    getCookieSet().remove(save);
  }
}
```

The editor support contains some simple modifications from the skeleton code that you can generate using **Templates → NetBeans Extensions → Editor API → Editor Support**. These modifications are shown in Example 20-4.

Example 20-4. Mail filesystem: MessageBodyEditorSupport.java

```java
public class MessageBodyEditorSupport extends DataEditorSupport
    implements EditorCookie, OpenCookie, LineCookie, CloseCookie, PrintCookie {
  public MessageBodyEditorSupport(MailDataObject obj) {
    super(obj, new MessageBodyEnv(obj));
    setMIMEType("text/plain");
  }
  protected String messageName() {
    String subject = (String)getDataObject().getPrimaryFile().
      getAttribute(Constants.A_SUBJECT);
    if (subject != null) {
      return subject;
    } else {
      return NbBundle.getMessage(MessageBodyEditorSupport.class,
                                 "<no_subject>");
    }
  }
  protected String messageToolTip() {
    return NbBundle.getMessage(MessageBodyEditorSupport.class,
      "Folder_tip", getDataObject().getPrimaryFile().getParent());
  }
  protected boolean notifyModified() {
    if (!super.notifyModified()) {
      return false;
    }
    MailDataObject obj = (MailDataObject)getDataObject();
    if (obj.getCookie(SaveCookie.class) == null) {
      obj.addSaveCookie(new Save());
      obj.setModified(true);
    }
    return true;
  }
  protected void notifyUnmodified() {
    super.notifyUnmodified();
    MailDataObject obj = (MailDataObject)getDataObject();
    SaveCookie save = (SaveCookie)obj.getCookie(SaveCookie.class);
    if (save != null) {
      obj.removeSaveCookie(save);
      obj.setModified(false);
    }
  }
  private class Save implements SaveCookie {
    public void save() throws IOException {
      saveDocument();
      getDataObject().setModified(false);
    }
  }
  private static class MessageBodyEnv extends DataEditorSupport.Env {
    private static final long serialVersionUID = 856398629567196L;
    public MessageBodyEnv(MailDataObject obj) {
      super(obj);
    }
```

Example 20-4. Mail filesystem: MessageBodyEditorSupport.java (continued)

```
    protected FileObject getFile() {
      return getDataObject().getPrimaryFile();
    }
    protected FileLock takeLock() throws IOException {
      return ((MailDataObject)getDataObject()).getPrimaryEntry().takeLock();
    }
    public CloneableOpenSupport findCloneableOpenSupport() {
      return (MessageBodyEditorSupport)getDataObject().
        getCookie(MessageBodyEditorSupport.class);
    }
  }
}
```

messageName() is overridden to display the subject header of the message, rather than the data object name. This subject will be displayed in the Source Editor tab when the message is opened. messageToolTip() shows the position of the message in its folder; this information is available as a tool tip on the editor tab.

A more advanced email application might want to provide a ViewCookie on messages that it determined to be of type text/html according to the server's MIME headers. Rather than using an editor support to open the message as text, it could use the API utility method TopManager.showUrl() to display the HTML attachment in the user's preferred web browser. The ViewCookie implementation could be exposed by including ViewAction in the context menu defined in MailDataLoader.defaultActions().

The data node implementation, as seen in Example 20-3 adds some special UI features. Mail messages are given a special icon, ✉ and so are anonymous attachments, ✐.

Example 20-5. Mail filesystem: MailDataNode.java

```
public class MailDataNode extends DataNode {
  public MailDataNode(MailDataObject obj) {
    super(obj, Children.LEAF);
    if (obj.getPrimaryFile().hasExt(MailDataLoader.MESSAGE_EXT)) {
      setIconBase("org/netbeans/modules/mailclient/resources/message");
    } else {
      setIconBase("org/netbeans/modules/mailclient/resources/attachment");
    }
  }
  protected Sheet createSheet() {
    Sheet sheet = super.createSheet();
    addToSheet(sheet, getDataObject().getPrimaryFile());
    return sheet;
  }
  static void addToSheet(Sheet s, FileObject fo) {
    if (fo.hasExt(MailDataLoader.PART_EXT)) {
      if (fo.getAttribute("From") == null) {
        // Random attachment, not a real message.
        return;
      }
```

Example 20-5. Mail filesystem: MailDataNode.java (continued)

```
    }
    Sheet.Set ss = new Sheet.Set();
    ss.setName("message");
    ss.setDisplayName(NbBundle.getMessage(MailDataNode.class, "Message"));
    ss.setShortDescription(NbBundle.getMessage(MailDataNode.class,
                                    "Message_headers."));
    ss.put(new HeaderProperty("From", fo));
    ss.put(new HeaderProperty("To", fo));
    ss.put(new HeaderProperty("Subject", fo));
    ss.put(new HeaderProperty("CC", fo));
    ss.put(new HeaderProperty("Date", fo));
    ss.put(new HeaderProperty("Content-Type", fo));
    s.put(ss);
  }
  private static final class HeaderProperty extends PropertySupport.ReadOnly {
    private final FileObject fo;
    public HeaderProperty(String header, FileObject fo) {
      super(header, String.class, header, header);
      this.fo = fo;
    }
    public Object getValue()
        throws IllegalAccessException, InvocationTargetException {
      Object o = fo.getAttribute(getName());
      if (o == null) {
        return "";
      } else {
        return o.toString();
      }
    }
  }
}
```

The property sheet for a mail message is augmented with a new tab **Message** containing information specific to reading mail: the sender, recipient, subject, and so on. All of this information is available from the filesystem as FileObject attributes, according to the standard MIME header names. The sheet, as it stands at this point, is shown in Figure 20-1.

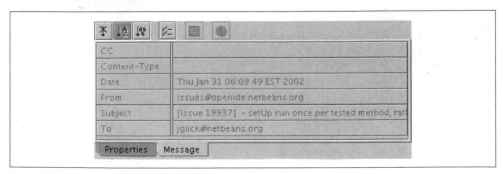

Figure 20-1. Mail filesystem: property sheet of a message

Handling Multipart Messages

Multipart messages are represented in the filesystem as folders containing some message bodies and attachments. We want to display such folders specially, to make them appear like other messages, but with subnodes in the Explorer window. To do this, it is enough to recognize them as a special kind of DataFolder; this is accomplished with the code shown in Example 20-6.

Example 20-6. Mail filesystem: MultipartMessageDataLoader.java

```java
public class MultipartMessageDataLoader extends UniFileLoader {
  private static final long serialVersionUID = 76987698762435245L;
  public MultipartMessageDataLoader() {
    super("org.netbeans.modules.mailclient.loaders.MultipartMessageDataObject");
  }
  protected String defaultDisplayName() {
    return NbBundle.getMessage(MultipartMessageDataLoader.class,
                               "Multipart_Messages");
  }
  protected SystemAction[] defaultActions() {
    return new SystemAction[] {
      SystemAction.get(OpenLocalExplorerAction.class),
      SystemAction.get(FileSystemAction.class),
      null,
      SystemAction.get(SaveAsTemplateAction.class),
      null,
      SystemAction.get(ToolsAction.class),
      SystemAction.get(PropertiesAction.class),
    };
  }
  protected FileObject findPrimaryFile(FileObject fo) {
    if (fo.isFolder() && fo.hasExt(MailDataLoader.MESSAGE_EXT)) {
      return fo;
    } else {
      return null;
    }
  }
  protected MultiDataObject.Entry createPrimaryEntry(MultiDataObject obj,
                                                     FileObject primaryFile) {
    return new FileEntry.Folder(obj, primaryFile);
  }
  protected MultiDataObject createMultiObject(FileObject primaryFile)
      throws DataObjectExistsException, IOException {
    return new MultipartMessageDataObject(primaryFile, this);
  }
}
```

The data loader simply recognizes any FileObjects that happen to be folders but have the *.msg* extension. Again, readers interested in *MultipartMessageDataLoaderBeanInfo.java* should consult the downloadable sources.

The data object (Example 20-7) and data node (Example 20-8) are unremarkable; the node adds the same message-oriented headers to the property sheet as we saw in MailDataNode. Readers who have not worked heavily with inner classes ought not be scared by the call to obj.super(): this rather obscure syntax invokes the default constructor of the non-static inner class DataFolder.FolderNode, using obj as the this reference.

Example 20-7. Mail filesystem: MultipartMessageDataObject.java

```
public class MultipartMessageDataObject extends DataFolder {
  public MultipartMessageDataObject(FileObject pf,
      MultipartMessageDataLoader loader) throws DataObjectExistsException {
    super(pf, loader);
  }
  public HelpCtx getHelpCtx() {
    return HelpCtx.DEFAULT_HELP;
  }
  protected Node createNodeDelegate() {
    return new MultipartMessageDataNode(this);
  }
}
```

Example 20-8. Mail filesystem: MultipartMessageDataNode.java

```
public class MultipartMessageDataNode extends DataFolder.FolderNode {
  public MultipartMessageDataNode(MultipartMessageDataObject obj) {
    ((DataFolder)obj).super();
    setIconBase("org/netbeans/modules/mailclient/resources/message");
  }
  protected Sheet createSheet() {
    Sheet sheet = super.createSheet();
    MailDataNode.addToSheet(sheet, getDataObject().getPrimaryFile());
    return sheet;
  }
}
```

Creating a Threaded Mail View Using Filter Nodes

After having defined data loaders for messages and status annotations for unread messages, we are still left with an unsatisfactory user interface (take a look at Figure 20-2). The user must browse mail servers in the **Filesystems** tab of the Explorer window, where they will be mixed with more normal development directories; messages are displayed in raw IMAP folders, essentially unsorted; context menus include many actions not suited to messages; node display names are based on the file they represent, whereas the user really wants to see the message subject.

We can solve all of these problems using a custom-built node hierarchy. Rather than create the nodes from scratch, we will delegate to the basic data nodes provided by

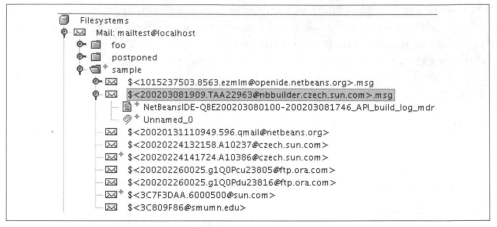

Figure 20-2. Mail filesystem: raw Filesystems view of a mail server

the loaders, but with some modifications. The technique used for this kind of incremental modification in the NetBeans APIs is to write `FilterNodes`. You have already seen the basic idea in action in Chapter 18.

Making a Basic Mail View

Our basic mail view will display all mounted IMAP servers and within a mail folder will display all messages sorted by date. Each message will be displayed in the Explorer window according to the sender and subject. We start with the root node, shown in Example 20-9, which is similar to the root node of the **Filesystems** tab.

Example 20-9. Mail filesystem: MessageFileSystemsNode.java

```java
public class MessageFileSystemsNode extends AbstractNode {
  public MessageFileSystemsNode() {
    super(new MessageFileSystemsChildren(
      TopManager.getDefault().getPlaces().nodes().repository()));
    setDisplayName(NbBundle.getMessage(MessageFileSystemsNode.class,
                                       "Message_Servers"));
    setShortDescription(NbBundle.getMessage(MessageFileSystemsNode.class,
                                            "Message_Servers_hint"));
    setIconBase("org/netbeans/modules/mailclient/resources/messageFolder");
  }
  protected SystemAction[] createActions() {
    return new SystemAction[] {
      SystemAction.get(OpenLocalExplorerAction.class),
      null,
      SystemAction.get(NewAction.class),
      null,
      SystemAction.get(PropertiesAction.class)
    };
  }
```

Example 20-9. Mail filesystem: MessageFileSystemsNode.java (continued)

```java
  public Node cloneNode() {
    return new MessageFileSystemsNode();
  }
  public Node.Handle getHandle() {
    return new MessageFileSystemsHandle();
  }
  private static class MessageFileSystemsHandle implements Node.Handle {
    private static final long serialVersionUID = 967519842663L;
    public MessageFileSystemsHandle() {}
    public Node getNode() throws IOException {
      return new MessageFileSystemsNode();
    }
  }
  public NewType[] getNewTypes() {
    return new NewType[] {new NewMailServer()};
  }
  private static final class NewMailServer extends NewType {
    public String getName() {
      return NbBundle.getMessage(MessageFileSystemsNode.class, "Mail_Server");
    }
    public void create() throws IOException {
      ConnectionWizardIterator it = new ConnectionWizardIterator();
      WizardDescriptor wiz = new WizardDescriptor(it);
      wiz.putProperty("WizardPanel_autoWizardStyle", Boolean.TRUE);
      wiz.putProperty("WizardPanel_contentDisplayed", Boolean.TRUE);
      wiz.putProperty("WizardPanel_contentNumbered", Boolean.TRUE);
      wiz.setTitle(NbBundle.getMessage(MessageFileSystemsNode.class,
                                "Add_New_Mail_Server"));
      it.initialize(wiz);
      TopManager.getDefault().createDialog(wiz).show();
      if (wiz.getValue() == WizardDescriptor.FINISH_OPTION) {
        it.instantiate(wiz);
      }
    }
  }
}
```

The root node must first declare its children. The child nodes will represent mail servers. The root node is given a pleasant display name, icon, and tool tip, followed by a few useful context-menu items in createActions(). cloneNode() permits this root node to be efficiently cloned if desired, and getHandle() permits it to be serialized. This will enable the user's node selection in the Explorer window to be persisted across NetBeans sessions.

getNewTypes() can provide a list of zero or more items to display in the **New…** submenu of the node's context menu. We are only providing one NewType, so in fact the submenu will be suppressed and just the menu item **Add Mail Server** will appear. The NewMailServer new-type specifies a display name for the context menu and what to do when the menu item is selected. We reuse the wizard classes developed in the previous chapter for inclusion in the **File → Mount Filesystem…** mounting wizard.

This time, however, we create the complete WizardDescriptor needed to make a dialog of our iterator and two panels. The three optional properties ensure that the wizard displays a list of steps and similar GUI niceties. If the user selects **Finish**, we ask the wizard iterator to proceed in creating and mounting the new filesystem. Functionally, there is no difference between displaying this wizard and displaying the **New** wizard with the **IMAP Mail Server** template selected, but providing the menu item here serves as a shortcut and makes the functionality easier to find.

MessageFileSystemsChildren, shown in Example 20-10, filters the children of the root node. All such children should be the root folders of various filesystems. We look for any children corresponding to MailFileSystems and discard the others. The mail root folder nodes are displayed as is, but their children are in turn filtered using GeneralFolderHierarchyChildren (Example 20-11).

Example 20-10. Mail filesystem: MessageFileSystemsChildren.java

```java
public class MessageFileSystemsChildren extends FilterNode.Children {
  public MessageFileSystemsChildren(Node orig) {
    super(orig);
  }
  public Object clone() {
    return new MessageFileSystemsChildren(original);
  }
  protected Node[] createNodes(Object key) {
    Node child = (Node)key;
    DataFolder f = (DataFolder)child.getCookie(DataFolder.class);
    if (f != null) {
      try {
        FileSystem fs = f.getPrimaryFile().getFileSystem();
        if (fs instanceof MailFileSystem) {
          return new Node[] {
            new FilterNode(child, new GeneralFolderHierarchyChildren(child))
          };
        }
      } catch (FileStateInvalidException fsie) {
        TopManager.getDefault().getErrorManager().
          notify(ErrorManager.INFORMATIONAL, fsie);
      }
    }
    return null;
  }
}
```

Example 20-11. Mail filesystem: GeneralFolderHierarchyChildren.java

```java
public class GeneralFolderHierarchyChildren extends FilterNode.Children {
  public GeneralFolderHierarchyChildren(Node orig) {
    super(orig);
  }
  public Object clone() {
    return new GeneralFolderHierarchyChildren(original);
  }
```

```java
  protected Node copyNode(Node child) {
    DataObject o = (DataObject)child.getCookie(DataObject.class);
    if (o != null) {
      FileObject f = o.getPrimaryFile();
      if ((o instanceof DataFolder) &&
          Boolean.TRUE.equals(f.getAttribute(Constants.A_HOLDSMSGS))) {
        return new FilterNode(child,
          new MessageFolderHierarchyChildren((DataFolder)o));
      }
    }
    return new FilterNode(child, new GeneralFolderHierarchyChildren(child));
  }
}
```

Many interior nodes have their children filtered using `GeneralFolderHierarchyChildren`.
This filtering makes no change to the appearance of the node tree until it descends
to the level of mail folders—folders on the server that directly contain messages,
rather than just subfolders. For these mail folders, the real work begins with
`MessageFolderHierarchyChildren`. The source for this class is shown in
Example 20-12.

Example 20-12. Mail filesystem: Initial MessageFolderHierarchyChildren.java

```java
public class MessageFolderHierarchyChildren extends Children.Keys
    implements Comparator {
  private final DataFolder folder;
  public MessageFolderHierarchyChildren(DataFolder folder) {
    this.folder = folder;
  }
  public Object clone() {
    return new MessageFolderHierarchyChildren(folder);
  }
  protected void addNotify() {
    updateKeys();
  }
  private void updateKeys() {
    keys = new TreeSet(this);
    keys.addAll(Arrays.asList(folder.getChildren()));
    setKeys(keys);
  }
  protected void removeNotify() {
    setKeys(Collections.EMPTY_SET);
  }
  protected Node[] createNodes(Object key) {
    DataObject o = (DataObject)key;
    return new Node[] {new MessageNode(o)};
  }
  public int compare(Object o1, Object o2) {
    Date d1 = (Date)((DataObject)o1).getPrimaryFile().
      getAttribute(Constants.A_SENTDATE);
    Date d2 = (Date)((DataObject)o2).getPrimaryFile().
```

```
      getAttribute(Constants.A_SENTDATE);
    if (d1 == null) {
      if (d2 == null) {
        // No dates, so arbitrary.
        return System.identityHashCode(o1) - System.identityHashCode(o2);
      } else {
        return 1;
      }
    } else {
      if (d2 == null) {
        return -1;
      } else {
        // Reverse sorting:
        return -d1.compareTo(d2);
      }
    }
  }
 }
}
```

We are no longer filtering existing node `Children` here, but creating the children directly, so we use `Children.Keys`. This important class in the Nodes API is covered in detail in Chapter 25. For now it is only necessary to understand that each key, here a `DataObject`, serves to represent one child node. `addNotify()` creates the keys needed, by finding all messages in the folder and sorting them by date (available from the server as a MIME header via file attributes). `createNodes()` will produce the actual child node corresponding to a key: a `MessageNode` (see Example 20-13).

If it were desirable to track changes in the messages present on the server, that is to say the result of `folder.getChildren()`, then `MessageFolderHierarchyChildren` would attach some sort of listener to the folder and call `setKeys()` whenever there was a change. For our simple example, we assume the mail server is both read-only and unchanging.

Example 20-13. Mail filesystem: MessageNode.java

```
public class MessageNode extends FilterNode {
  private final DataObject o;
  public MessageNode(DataObject o) {
    super(o.getNodeDelegate());
    this.o = o;
  }
  public String getDisplayName() {
    FileObject f = o.getPrimaryFile();
    String from = (String)f.getAttribute(Constants.A_FROM);
    if (from != null && from.length() == 0) from = null;
    String subject = (String)f.getAttribute(Constants.A_SUBJECT);
    if (subject != null && subject.length() == 0) subject = null;
    if (from != null) {
      if (subject != null) {
        return NbBundle.getMessage(MessageNode.class, "from_subject",
```

Example 20-13. Mail filesystem: MessageNode.java (continued)

```
                                  cleanupFrom(from), subject);
      } else {
        return cleanupFrom(from);
      }
    } else {
      if (subject != null) {
        return subject;
      } else {
        return NbBundle.getMessage(MessageNode.class, "<mystery_message>");
      }
    }
  }
  private String cleanupFrom(String from) {
    int idx = from.indexOf(',');
    if (idx != -1) {
      from = from.substring(0, idx);
    }
    idx = from.indexOf('<');
    if (idx != -1) {
      from = from.substring(0, idx);
    }
    return from.trim();
  }
  public Node.PropertySet[] getPropertySets() {
    Node.PropertySet[] pss = super.getPropertySets();
    List l = new ArrayList(1);
    for (int i = 0; i < pss.length; i++) {
      String name = pss[i].getName();
      if (!name.equals(Sheet.PROPERTIES) && !name.equals("sorting")) {
        l.add(pss[i]);
      }
    }
    return (Node.PropertySet[])l.toArray(new Node.PropertySet[l.size()]);
  }
  public SystemAction[] getActions() {
    return cleanActions(super.getActions());
  }
  public SystemAction[] getContextActions() {
    return cleanActions(super.getContextActions());
  }
  private static SystemAction[] cleanActions(SystemAction[] as) {
    List l = new ArrayList(10);
    for (int i = 0; i < as.length; i++) {
      if (as[i] != SystemAction.get(SaveAsTemplateAction.class) &&
          as[i] != SystemAction.get(ToolsAction.class)) {
        l.add(as[i]);
      }
    }
    return (SystemAction[])l.toArray(new SystemAction[l.size()]);
  }
}
```

MessageNode is again a filter node, based on the message data object's node delegate, and this time its children are not touched: by using the super constructor accepting only a Node and no Children, we leave any subnodes untouched.

getDisplayName() is overridden to display the sender and subject of a message, rather than its raw filename. Again, both of these pieces of information are available as MIME headers via file attributes. cleanupFrom() just removes some garbage from the email address of the sender to make it more displayable. For example, Bob <bob@nowhere.net> becomes just Bob.

getPropertySets() is also overridden to suppress a couple of tabs on the property sheet for the message node: Properties, which generally will just display a raw file name or similarly undesirable properties; and Sorting on multipart messages, which we have no need for. Other property sheet tabs, such as the Message tab we added in our data loader, are kept intact.

Finally, we ensure that getActions(), used to build a context menu for the node, excludes a couple of actions that are more likely to be distracting than useful on mail messages. getContextActions() is rarely used except in a few explorer views described in Chapter 15, but we override it just to be sure.

Now that the hierarchy of nodes for a sort-by-date view is complete, all we need to do is display it somewhere. The most natural place to put it is in the Runtime tab of the Explorer window, conventionally used to list external servers or transient run-time information. You should update your manifest to match Example 20-14.

Example 20-14. Mail filesystem: Module JAR Manifest with Node Registration

```
Manifest-Version: 1.0
OpenIDE-Module: org.netbeans.modules.mailclient
OpenIDE-Module-Name: Mail Client
OpenIDE-Module-Package-Dependencies: org.apache.regexp[RE]
OpenIDE-Module-Specification-Version: 0.2
OpenIDE-Module-Layer: org/netbeans/modules/mailclient/resources/layer.xml
Class-Path: ext/mail.jar ext/activation.jar

Name: org/netbeans/modules/mailclient/loaders/MailDataLoader.class
OpenIDE-Module-Class: Loader
Install-Before: org.netbeans.modules.text.TXTDataObject

Name: org/netbeans/modules/mailclient/loaders/MultipartMessageDataLoader.class
OpenIDE-Module-Class: Loader
Install-Before: org.openide.loaders.DataFolder

Name: org/netbeans/modules/mailclient/view/MessageFileSystemsNode.class
OpenIDE-Module-Class: Node
Type: Environment
```

Since MessageFileSystemsNode has a default constructor, it will now be displayed in the UI (see Figure 20-3).

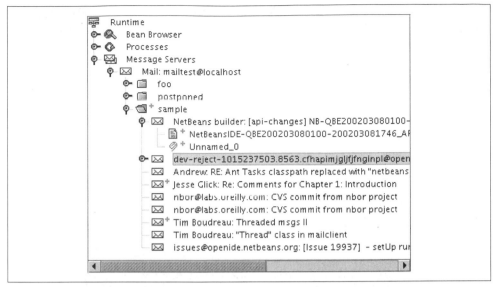

Figure 20-3. Mail filesystem: Message Servers in the Runtime tab

Making a Threaded Mail View as an Alternative

Now that we have done the work of preparing FilterNodes for message folders, modifying details of the view is not difficult. As an example, we will permit the user to choose a threaded view of messages rather than sorting by date. Let us start with the choice itself, which we will in fact persist to disk as a setting, using the Options API. This is handled by ViewTypeOptions, as shown in Example 20-15.

Example 20-15. Mail filesystem: ViewTypeOption.java

```
public class ViewTypeOption extends SystemOption {
  public static final String PROP_VIEW_TYPE = "viewType";
  public static final int VIEW_TYPE_THREADED = 0;
  public static final int VIEW_TYPE_BY_DATE = 1;
  private static final long serialVersionUID = 627896984756L;
  public static ViewTypeOption getDefault() {
    return (ViewTypeOption)SharedClassObject.findObject(ViewTypeOption.class,
                                                        true);
  }
  protected void initialize() {
    super.initialize();
    putProperty(PROP_VIEW_TYPE, new Integer(VIEW_TYPE_THREADED), false);
  }
  public int getViewType() {
    return ((Integer)getProperty(PROP_VIEW_TYPE)).intValue();
  }
  public void setViewType(int x) {
    putProperty(PROP_VIEW_TYPE, new Integer(x), true);
  }
```

Example 20-15. Mail filesystem: ViewTypeOption.java (continued)

```
public String displayName() {
  return "Mail View Type";
}
}
```

You should also make the following addition to your *layer.xml* to include this new option:

```
<folder name="Services">
  <file name="org-netbeans-modules-mailclient-view-type-option.settings"
        url="view-type-option.xml"/>
</folder>
```

You should also add the XML in Example 20-16 to your fileset for this module.

Example 20-16. Mail filesystem: view-type-option.xml

```
<!DOCTYPE settings PUBLIC
          "-//NetBeans//DTD Session settings 1.0//EN"
          "http://www.netbeans.org/dtds/sessionsettings-1_0.dtd">
<settings version="1.0">
  <module name="org.netbeans.modules.mailclient"/>
  <instanceof class="org.openide.options.SystemOption"/>
  <instanceof class="org.netbeans.modules.mailclient.view.ViewTypeOption"/>
  <instance class="org.netbeans.modules.mailclient.view.ViewTypeOption"/>
</settings>
```

ViewTypeOption is a standard system option whose state will be persisted once set, but it is never displayed directly to the user: there is no link to it in the system filesystem under *UI/Services/*. We will see how its one property is specially exposed in the GUI in a moment. The sole property, viewType, can take on the value VIEW_TYPE_ THREADED (the default) or VIEW_TYPE_BY_DATE. displayName() is really only needed for debugging since the option is never displayed as a whole, so the string does not need to be localized with NbBundle. For the same reason, we don't need to provide a BeanInfo to prettify the option.

You should also make some changes to MessageHolderHierarchyChildren for supporting the threaded view; these changes are detailed in Example 20-17.

Example 20-17. Mail filesystem: MessageFolderHierarchyChildren—threaded view

```
public class MessageFolderHierarchyChildren extends Children.Keys
    implements PropertyChangeListener, Comparator {
  // fields and constructor as before...
  protected void addNotify() {
    updateKeys();
    ViewTypeOption.getDefault().addPropertyChangeListener(this);
  }
  private void updateKeys() {
    switch (ViewTypeOption.getDefault().getViewType()) {
    case ViewTypeOption.VIEW_TYPE_THREADED:
```

```
        SortedSet keys = new TreeSet();
        DataObject[] kids = folder.getChildren();
        for (int i = 0; i < kids.length; i++) {
          String subject =
            (String)kids[i].getPrimaryFile().getAttribute(Constants.A_SUBJECT);
          keys.add(new MessageThread(subject, folder));
        }
        setKeys(keys);
        break;
      case ViewTypeOption.VIEW_TYPE_BY_DATE:
        keys = new TreeSet(this);
        keys.addAll(Arrays.asList(folder.getChildren()));
        setKeys(keys);
        break;
      default:
        throw new IllegalStateException();
    }
  }
  protected void removeNotify() {
    ViewTypeOption.getDefault().removePropertyChangeListener(this);
    setKeys(Collections.EMPTY_SET);
  }
  protected Node[] createNodes(Object key) {
    if (key instanceof MessageThread) {
      MessageThread thr = (MessageThread)key;
      AbstractNode n = new AbstractNode(new ThreadChildren(thr));
      if (thr.getNormalizedSubject() != null) {
        n.setName(thr.getNormalizedSubject());
        n.setDisplayName(thr.getPrettySubject());
      } else {
        n.setDisplayName(NbBundle.getMessage(MessageFolderHierarchyChildren.class,
                                    "<no_subject>"));
      }
      n.setIconBase("org/netbeans/modules/mailclient/resources/messageFolder");
      return new Node[] {n};
    } else {
      DataObject o = (DataObject)key;
      return new Node[] {new MessageNode(o)};
    }
  }
  public void propertyChange(PropertyChangeEvent evt) {
    if (evt.getPropertyName().equals(ViewTypeOption.PROP_VIEW_TYPE)) {
      updateKeys();
    }
  }
  // other methods as before...
}
```

The new child class is just a little more complicated. When the view type is set to Threaded, the children are not messages, but intermediary nodes, each corresponding to one thread: a common subject header, more or less. The threads are sorted alphabetically. If the view type changes after the message folder has been expanded, the view should update immediately—so we attach a property change listener to ViewTypeOption and call setKeys() again if PROP_VIEW_TYPE is fired from the option.

The class in Example 20-18 is a helper class that will support the threaded view.

Example 20-18. Mail filesystem: signature of MessageThread.java

```java
public final class MessageThread implements Comparable {
  /** Create a thread from a raw subject header and message folder. */
  public MessageThread(String subject, DataFolder folder);
  /** Get the raw subject header. */
  public String getSubject();
  /** Get a normalized (canonical) subject used for comparisons. */
  public String getNormalizedSubject();
  /** Get a user-friendly, displayable subject line. */
  public String getPrettySubject();
  /** Get the message folder. */
  public DataFolder getFolder();
  /** Get messages in the folder matching this thread. */
  public DataObject[] getItems();
  /** Compare to another thread object by normalized subject. */
  public boolean equals(Object o);
  /** Hash code based on normalized subject. */
  public int hashCode();
  /** Compare threads alphabetically. */
  public int compareTo(Object o);
}
```

The MessageThread helper class contains a number of tricks for processing subject lines with regular expressions to remove inessential components and help them thread better. Rather than examining the code in detail, it suffices to see the public signatures of the class's methods.

The simple Children implementation shown in Example 20-19 is used to supply the children of an intermediary thread node beneath a message folder node. Each child, a MessageNode as seen in the previous section, is represented by a DataObject. All messages in the folder matching the assigned thread can be gotten using thr.getItems().

Example 20-19. Mail filesystem: ThreadChildren.java

```java
public class ThreadChildren extends Children.Keys {
  private final MessageThread thr;
  public ThreadChildren(MessageThread thr) {
    this.thr = thr;
  }
  public Object clone() {
    return new ThreadChildren(thr);
  }
  protected void addNotify() {
    setKeys(thr.getItems());
  }
```

Example 20-19. Mail filesystem: ThreadChildren.java (continued)

```
  protected void removeNotify() {
    setKeys(Collections.EMPTY_SET);
  }
  protected Node[] createNodes(Object key) {
    DataObject o = (DataObject)key;
    return new Node[] {new MessageNode(o)};
  }
}
```

To help you keep track of all these nodes, what they represent, and what their children are, Figure 20-4 displays the basic relationships.

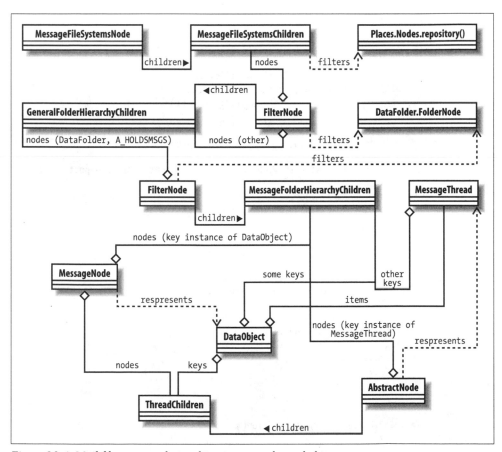

Figure 20-4. Mail filesystem: relationships among nodes and objects

All that remains is to activate the threaded/by date GUI switch. For simplicity, let us assume this switch is global (applies to all mounted IMAP servers at once) and so can be visually displayed on the property sheet for the **Message Servers** node. Make the changes shown here to the MessageFileSystemsNode class:

```java
protected Sheet createSheet() {
  Sheet s = new Sheet();
  Sheet.Set ss = Sheet.createPropertiesSet();
  ss.put(new ViewTypeProp());
  s.put(ss);
  return s;
}
private static final class ViewTypeProp extends PropertySupport.ReadWrite {
  public ViewTypeProp() {
    super("viewType", Integer.TYPE,
      NbBundle.getMessage(MessageFileSystemsNode.class, "View_Type"),
      NbBundle.getMessage(MessageFileSystemsNode.class,
                          "How_to_arrange_messages."));
  }
  public Object getValue()
      throws IllegalAccessException, InvocationTargetException {
    return new Integer(ViewTypeOption.getDefault().getViewType());
  }
  public void setValue(Object val) throws IllegalAccessException,
      IllegalArgumentException, InvocationTargetException {
    ViewTypeOption.getDefault().setViewType(((Integer)val).intValue());
  }
  public PropertyEditor getPropertyEditor() {
    return new ViewTypeEditor();
  }
  private static final class ViewTypeEditor extends PropertyEditorSupport {
    private static final String[] NAMES = {
      NbBundle.getMessage(MessageFileSystemsNode.class, "Threaded"),
      NbBundle.getMessage(MessageFileSystemsNode.class, "By_Date"),
    };
    public String[] getTags() {
      return NAMES;
    }
    public String getAsText() {
      int v = ((Integer)getValue()).intValue();
      return NAMES[v];
    }
    public void setAsText(String t) {
      for (int i = 0; i < NAMES.length; i++) {
        if (t.equals(NAMES[i])) {
          setValue(new Integer(i));
          return;
        }
      }
      throw new IllegalArgumentException();
    }
  }
}
```

This straightforward Node.Property implementation provides a UI for the ViewTypeOption.
viewType property. Since the option is of type int, we need to use a custom
PropertyEditor (defined in the JavaBeans specification) to make a polished drop-
down list with the values "Threaded" and "By Date."

The new threaded mail viewer is shown in Figure 20-5.

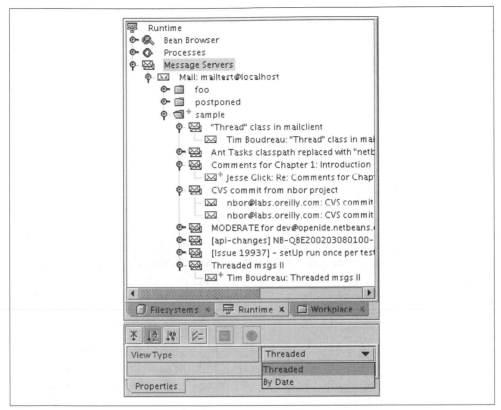

Figure 20-5. Mail filesystem: threaded view

Creating a Mail Workspace

Our last task for the mail client is to create a specialized *workspace* in the window system dedicated to browsing and reading messages. The preferred way to create such a workspace is to express almost all of it declaratively in XML files. General information about these formats was given in Chapter 17.

We will create only one new GUI TopComponent in Java code, which will simply be a tree view showing just the **Message Servers** node. The design is similar to that used by the Debugger Core module, which makes runtime information about the debugger available under the **Runtime** tab of the Explorer window, but also creates a dedicated workspace optimized for the debugging work flow (see Example 20-20).

Example 20-20. Mail filesystem: MessagesExplorer.java

```
public class MessagesExplorer extends ExplorerPanel {
  public static TopComponent create() {
```

Example 20-20. Mail filesystem: MessagesExplorer.java (continued)

```
    MessagesExplorer p = new MessagesExplorer();
    p.init();
    return p;
  }
  public MessagesExplorer() {
    setLayout(new BorderLayout());
    add(new BeanTreeView(), BorderLayout.CENTER);
  }
  private void init() {
    ExplorerManager m = getExplorerManager();
    Node n = new MessageFileSystemsNode();
    m.setRootContext(n);
    try {
      m.setSelectedNodes(new Node[] {n});
    } catch (PropertyVetoException pve) {
      pve.printStackTrace();
    }
  }
  protected void updateTitle() {
    setName(getExplorerManager().getRootContext().getDisplayName());
  }
  public Image getIcon() {
    return Utilities.loadImage(
      "org/netbeans/modules/mailclient/resources/messageFolder.gif");
  }
}
```

This `TopComponent` just contains a tree view, rooted with the same `MessageFileSystemsNode` we display in the Runtime tab. The `create()` factory method will be used from the module's XML layer, as you will see shortly.

The constructor initializes just the GUI layout of the component. The configuration of the root node is done only in the `init()` method called from the factory: when NetBeans is shut down and restarted, it will deserialize the `Externalizable` top component, first calling the constructor. All `ExplorerPanel`s automatically persist their root node, explorer context, and node selection, so we do not need to set the root node during deserialization. If the user changes the node selection in this tree view, the new selection will be automatically persisted as part of the component's state.

`updateTitle()` is called to set the window title of the component when it is created and whenever the selection changes. For our purposes, we can just inherit the title from the display name of the root node, Message Servers. `getIcon()` provides a window icon for the component, used sometimes in MDI mode, as well as in SDI mode on platforms that support setting a window icon from Java.

Make some new additions to your *layer.xml* now:

```
    <folder name="Windows">
      <folder name="WindowManager">
        <attr name="Editing/mail" boolvalue="true"/>
```

```
            <attr name="Visual/mail" boolvalue="true"/>
            <file name="mail.wswksp" url="windowmanager/mail.xml"/>
            <folder name="mail">
              <file name="explorer.wsmode" url="windowmanager/mail/explorer.xml"/>
              <folder name="explorer">
                <file name="messages.wstcref"
                      url="windowmanager/mail/explorer/messages.xml"/>
                <file name="properties.wstcref"
                      url="windowmanager/mail/explorer/properties.xml"/>
              </folder>
              <file name="properties.wsmode" url="windowmanager/mail/properties.xml"/>
              <folder name="properties">
                <file name="properties.wstcref"
                      url="windowmanager/mail/properties/properties.xml"/>
              </folder>
              <file name="editor.wsmode" url="windowmanager/mail/editor.xml"/>
              <folder name="editor"/>
            </folder>
            <attr name="mail/Running" boolvalue="true"/>
          </folder>
          <folder name="Components">
            <file name="messages.settings" url="windowmanager/messages-def.xml"/>
          </folder>
        </folder>
```

The layer adds a *.wswksp* file to *Windows/WindowManager/* that defines the work-space generally. Beneath that are definitions of modes: the Explorer mode, which in MDI also holds the global Property Sheet; the Properties mode, a separate window under SDI; and the Source Editor mode, which will hold messages opened as text. We leave this last mode empty: there are no initially defined components in it, but any editor support will open into this mode automatically based on the code name editor. Finally, in *Windows/Components/* we define the custom TopComponent.

Following are a few of the more interesting XML files defined in this layer. Other files are very similar to the ones shown, and interested readers can consult the downloadable sources for full details.

Example 20-21. Mail filesystem: mail.xml

```
<!DOCTYPE workspace PUBLIC
          "-//NetBeans//DTD Workspace Properties 1.0//EN"
          "http://www.netbeans.org/dtds/workspace-properties1_0.dtd">
<workspace version="1.0">
    <name unique="mail" display="CTL_mail" from-bundle="true"
          bundle="org.netbeans.modules.mailclient.resources.Bundle"/>
    <description display="CTL_mail_description"
                 bundle="org.netbeans.modules.mailclient.resources.Bundle"/>
    <module name="org.netbeans.modules.mailclient"/>
    <ui-type type="any">
        <cascade origin-x="0" origin-y="0" step-x="20" step-y="20" count="0"
                 current-x="0" current-y="147"/>
        <active mode="explorer"/>
```

Example 20-21. Mail filesystem: mail.xml (continued)

```
        <mode z-order="explorer,editor,properties"/>
        <toolbar configuration="Standard"/>
    </ui-type>
    <ui-type type="mdi">
        <cascade origin-x="0" origin-y="0" step-x="20" step-y="20" count="0"
                 current-x="0" current-y="0"/>
        <active mode="explorer"/>
        <mode z-order="explorer,editor"/>
        <toolbar configuration="Standard"/>
    </ui-type>
</workspace>
```

Make some additions to the *Bundle.properties* for workspace support:

```
CTL_mail=Mail
CTL_mail_description=Mail messages in IMAP.
```

The workspace definition specifies a few things of interest, besides the display name and accessible description of the workspace. (See Chapter 27 for more on accessibility.) The <<module>> tag indicates that the workspace is supplied by the mail module and should be removed if this module is uninstalled. The different <<ui-type>> tags permit the visual layout to be configured separately for MDI and SDI mode. They specify the mode (window) that should initially be selected. If the mail module has any special set of actions that we want to display, it is possible to create a custom toolbar configuration showing selected actions, active only on the mail workspace. The actual modes present in the workspace are determined by the presence of mode configuration files beneath the *Windows/WindowManager/mail/* folder.

Example 20-22. Mail filesystem: explorer.xml

```
<!DOCTYPE mode PUBLIC
          "-//NetBeans//DTD Mode Properties 1.0//EN"
          "http://www.netbeans.org/dtds/mode-properties1_0.dtd">
<mode version="1.0">
    <name unique="explorer" display="CTL_ExplorerWindow" from-bundle="true"
          bundle="org.netbeans.core.windows.Bundle"/>
    <description display="CTL_ExplorerWindowDescription"
                 bundle="org.netbeans.core.windows.Bundle"/>
    <ui-type type="any">
        <relative-bounds x="0" y="0" width="35" height="60"/>
        <frame type="window" constraints="left" state="normal"/>
        <container type="split" active-tc="messages"/>
        <icon url="nbresboot:/org/netbeans/core/resources/frames/explorer.gif"/>
        <other defined-by="module" mode-state="visible"/>
    </ui-type>
    <ui-type type="mdi">
        <relative-bounds x="0" y="0" width="35" height="100"/>
        <frame type="desktop" constraints="left" state="normal"/>
        <container type="split" active-tc="messages">
            <area constraint="center" relative-x="0" relative-y="0"
                  relative-width="98" relative-height="63"/>
```

Example 20-22. Mail filesystem: explorer.xml (continued)

```
        <area constraint="bottom" relative-x="0" relative-y="63"
            relative-width="98" relative-height="33"/>
    </container>
    <icon url="nbresboot:/org/netbeans/core/resources/frames/explorer.gif"/>
    <other defined-by="module" mode-state="visible"/>
  </ui-type>
</mode>
```

The mode definition for Explorer in our workspace (shown in Example 20-22) is based closely on that used in the regular NetBeans Editing workspace, except that the active component is defined to be the TopComponent with the reference name messages. In MDI mode, the window is split in half vertically in order to contain the Property Sheet in the bottom half.

Now add the XML document shown in Example 20-23 to your fileset and save it as *messages.xml*.

Example 20-23. Mail filesystem: messages.xml

```
<?xml version="1.0" encoding="UTF-8"?>
<!DOCTYPE tc-ref PUBLIC
        "-//NetBeans//DTD Top Component in Mode Properties 1.0//EN"
        "http://www.netbeans.org/dtds/tc-ref1_0.dtd">
<tc-ref version="1.0" id="messages">
    <ui-type type="any" state="opened" constraint="center" selected="true"/>
</tc-ref>
```

This XML file defines a reference to one TopComponent, our tree view of messages. It refers to the actual stored component state by a unique ID, messages. The window system will then look for an instance of TopComponent in the file *Windows/Components/messages.settings*. The extra layer of indirection permits a single component to be shared across several workspaces, storing its configuration in only one place.

Finally we see the definition of the custom top component (Example 20-24). The instance is produced by calling the factory method MessagesExplorer.create(). If the user makes any change to the configuration of the component—for example, changing the node selection—such changes will be serialized back to a file with the same name as this XML file, in the user directory in order to persist the change.

Example 20-24. Mail filesystem: messages-def.xml

```
<?xml version="1.0"?>
<!DOCTYPE settings PUBLIC
        "-//NetBeans//DTD Session settings 1.0//EN"
        "http://www.netbeans.org/dtds/sessionsettings-1_0.dtd">
<settings version="1.0">
    <instanceof class="org.openide.windows.TopComponent"/>
    <instance class="org.netbeans.modules.mailclient.view.MessagesExplorer"
            method="create"/>
</settings>
```

With these layer additions in place, NetBeans will display a custom workspace dedicated to our mail reader. This is shown in Figure 20-6.

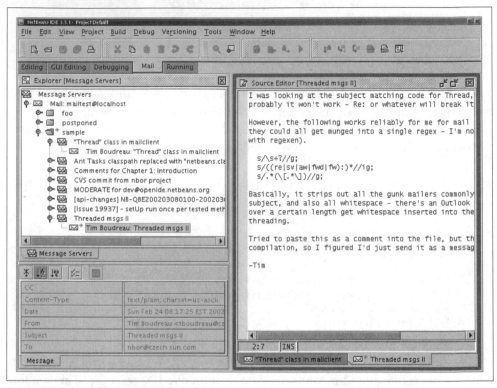

Figure 20-6. Mail filesystem: mail workspace

In the next five chapters, we will move on to a new module, the Minicomposer, which will showcase many of the advanced programming techniques used in real NetBeans modules.

## CHAPTER 21

Score File Support

For much of the rest of this book, we will be concerned with creating the *Minicomposer* module. This module will allow you to enter a series of musical notes into a "score file," "compile" them down to an audio file, and "execute" that audio file in the sense of playing it via the JavaSound API.

While no serious musician would find this module very useful, it is possible to explore a broad range of the NetBeans Open APIs in its implementation. Most importantly, you will learn how to use the different APIs in concert. (Excuse the pun!) Many real, complex modules follow the patterns shown in these chapters.

Overview—Functionality to be Implemented

The work flow for using the Minicomposer module should be familiar to you if you have used the NetBeans IDE. Its basic functionality is to support *score files*: an intentionally simple, artificial text format listing notes and durations. You have the choice of editing a score file in the text editor as a list of notes and values, or in a custom score editor component (GUI). A score file and its associated *.au* file will appear as a single node in the Explorer. Changes in the GUI editor will be synchronized with changes in the text editor. Score files will expose a set of editable properties and subnodes in the Explorer, and editing actions will be available from the context menu.

Samples of the code involved are given as we go. The complete source code for this example is available in the downloadable sources for this book. A snapshot of the module at the end of each chapter is available as well.

Creating the Minicomposer Module

We will start by creating the framework for our module—including the manifest, XML layer, JAR file, and a bundle for visible strings.

Creating the Manifest

Every module must have a manifest that describes at a high level what is in it; this is shown for the Minicomposer in Example 21-1. To start out, only the XML layer will be mentioned. Later we will add a few lines, called a *section*, to the manifest in order to install a data loader.

Example 21-1. Minicomposer: initial minicomposer.mf

```
Manifest-Version: 1.0
OpenIDE-Module: org.netbeans.examples.modules.minicomposer
OpenIDE-Module-Localizing-Bundle:
  org/netbeans/examples/modules/minicomposer/Bundle.properties
OpenIDE-Module-Specification-Version: 0.2
OpenIDE-Module-IDE-Dependencies: IDE/1 > 1.33
OpenIDE-Module-Layer: org/netbeans/examples/modules/minicomposer/layer.xml
```

The manifest specifies the code name of the module. For the code name, we give the name of the package that its Java sources use. `OpenIDE-Module-Localizing-Bundle` instructs the IDE where in the JAR to look for the human-visible strings, such as the module's display name. We give a version number for the module, and also state that the IDE running it must support at least version 1.33 of the APIs. You can find out more about version numbers and dependencies in Chapter 27. The last non-blank line points to the layer, which later on will install most of the objects provided by the module. Remember that the manifest should end with a blank line (two line-feeds) to ensure proper parsing.

We will keep all human-visible strings in a bundle to make it easy to internationalize everything. To start, our bundle can be very simple, and is shown in Example 21-2.

Example 21-2. Minicomposer: initial src/org/netbeans/examples/modules/minicomposer/Bundle. properties

```
OpenIDE-Module-Name: Mini-Composer
OpenIDE-Module-Display-Category: Data Files
OpenIDE-Module-Short-Description: Edit simple musical scores.
OpenIDE-Module-Long-Description: Permits graphical or textual editing \
  of musical scores; compiling to *.au audio files; and playing using \
  either internal or execution players.
```

Note that the backslash at the end of a line signifies a continuation onto the next line; leading spaces on the next line are then ignored. The spaces before the backslashes are significant and so form breaks between words.

Creating the Layer

The next basic file needed by the module is the XML layer. To begin, our layer will be empty, as shown in Example 21-3. Later, some things will be added to it as we need them.

Example 21-3. Minicomposer: initial src/org/netbeans/examples/modules/minicomposer/layer.xml

```
<!DOCTYPE filesystem PUBLIC
        "-//NetBeans//DTD Filesystem 1.1//EN"
        "http://www.netbeans.org/dtds/filesystem-1_1.dtd">
<filesystem>
</filesystem>
```

Creating a JAR File Using Ant

To make it easy to develop the module inside the NetBeans IDE, we will create a simple Ant script that both builds it (shown in Example 21-4) and loads it in testing mode so that it can be played with.

Example 21-4. Minicomposer: build.xml

```
<project name="minicomposer" default="reload" basedir=".">
  <!-- The following path will need to be overridden: -->
  <property name="openide.jar"
          location="/your/nb/installation/lib/openide.jar"/>
  <target name="build" description="Build minicomposer for testing purposes.">
    <javac srcdir="src" destdir="src">
      <classpath>
        <pathelement location="${openide.jar}"/>
      </classpath>
      <include name="org/netbeans/examples/modules/minicomposer/"/>
    </javac>
    <mkdir dir="reload"/>
    <jar jarfile="reload/minicomposer.jar" manifest="minicomposer.mf"
        compress="false">
      <fileset dir="src">
        <include name="org/netbeans/examples/modules/minicomposer/"/>
      </fileset>
    </jar>
  </target>
  <target name="reload" depends="build"
          description="Try installing minicomposer into running IDE.">
    <nbinstaller action="reinstall" module="reload/minicomposer.jar"/>
  </target>
</project>
```

The build target is the first target (executable block) in the Ant script. It creates the file *minicomposer.jar*, which is a complete module. The reload target first builds the JAR (if needed) and then loads it into the IDE, replacing any former version. This second target can only be run inside the IDE using the built-in Ant support.

To prepare the script for your own computer, you will first need to make sure the property *openide.jar* is set to the correct path with which to compile Java sources. Either modify the build script where indicated or add a property to **Tools → Options → Building → Ant Settings → Properties**, for example: openide.jar=/my/actual/nb/ installation/lib/openide.jar. You can find more information on using Ant inside NetBeans in Chapter 5.

Now you can try running the script. Double-click the script in the Explorer. You should see some text in the Output Window indicating that the script is building the JAR file and installing it. Now check **Tools → Options → Modules → Data Files**, and you should see the new module **Mini-Composer** with a test icon: 🐢.

Creating a UniFileLoader and MultiDataObject for *.score Files

Now that the infrastructure of the Minicomposer module is ready, we will begin to make it really do something.

The first order of business is to recognize *.score* files as meaningful in the IDE. While most of this is "boilerplate" code, several classes and setting files are involved, and it is worth examining each of them because we will need to understand and customize the code later on.

The basic hook the module adds to the IDE is a data loader that is tuned to notice score files and provide data objects that the IDE can interact with. We will make this data loader sensitive to file MIME type, rather than directly looking for a particular file extension. The first step is to define a MIME type for score files, meaning that the IDE understands that the files are in a certain format distinct from other text or binary files. The score file format is invented for this example and there is not a standard MIME type for it, so we will create one, text/x-minicomposer-score.

Ultimate responsibility for assigning a MIME type in the IDE lies with the filesystem on which the file resides. However, since the score format is our invention and we are defining the score MIME type ourselves, it cannot be expected that an existing filesystem would know about it. For this reason, the Filesystems API permits registration of a MIME resolver that filesystems may use to try to guess at the MIME type of a file in the absence of other information. A resolver could be written as a Java class that calculates the MIME type from a supplied file if it extends org.openide.filesystems.MIMEResolver, but for typical purposes this is unnecessary. You can use a declarative XML file to add resolvers using the most common decision logic, as shown in Example 21-5.

Example 21-5. Minicomposer: initial src/org/netbeans/examples/modules/minicomposer/mime-resolver.xml

```
<!DOCTYPE MIME-resolver PUBLIC
          "-//NetBeans//DTD MIME Resolver 1.0//EN"
          "http://www.netbeans.org/dtds/mime-resolver-1_0.dtd">
<MIME-resolver>
  <file>
    <ext name="score"/>
    <resolver mime="text/x-minicomposer-score"/>
  </file>
</MIME-resolver>
```

The file element defines just one rule for now (later on there will be another one). ext instructs the Filesystems API to match files ending in the *.score* extension. The resolver then declares that such files will be treated as having the MIME type text/x-minicomposer-score, unless some other resolver with higher priority overrides this type.

This declarative resolver must be placed in the IDE's services area in order to be useful. Normally resolvers are placed in the system filesystem under *Services/MIMEResolver/*. We can do this by inserting a file into the module's layer (*layer.xml*):

```xml
<folder name="Services">
  <folder name="MIMEResolver">
    <file name="org-netbeans-examples-modules-minicomposer-resolver.xml"
          url="mime-resolver.xml">
      <attr name="SystemFileSystem.localizingBundle"
            stringvalue="org.netbeans.examples.modules.minicomposer.Bundle"/>
      <attr name="SystemFileSystem.icon" urlvalue=
      "nbresloc:/org/netbeans/examples/modules/minicomposer/ScoreDataIcon.gif"/>
    </file>
  </folder>
</folder>
```

Since MIME resolvers can be presented to the user as configurable settings, we also make it appear attractive, with a customized display name and icon. For the display name, add to the bundle:

```
Services/MIMEResolver/org-netbeans-examples-modules-minicomposer-resolver.xml=Mini-
Composer Scores
```

Now that the MIME type has been defined, creating a loader to work with it is easy. We can use UniFileLoader, which permits single files to be recognized as objects. The score-specific extension of this is shown in Example 21-6.

Example 21-6. Minicomposer: initial src/org/netbeans/examples/modules/minicomposer/ ScoreDataLoader.java

```java
public class ScoreDataLoader extends UniFileLoader {
  public static final String SCORE_MIME = "text/x-minicomposer-score";
  private static final long serialVersionUID = 6424491892249774122L;
  public ScoreDataLoader() {
    super("org.netbeans.examples.modules.minicomposer.ScoreDataObject");
  }
  protected void initialize() {
    super.initialize();
    getExtensions().addMimeType(SCORE_MIME);
  }
  protected String defaultDisplayName() {
    return NbBundle.getMessage(ScoreDataLoader.class, "LBL_loaderName");
  }
  // Supplies actions for the data node's context menu:
  protected SystemAction[] defaultActions() {
    return new SystemAction[] {
      SystemAction.get(FileSystemAction.class),
```

```
            null, // this is a separator
            SystemAction.get(CutAction.class),
            SystemAction.get(CopyAction.class),
            null,
            SystemAction.get(DeleteAction.class),
            SystemAction.get(RenameAction.class),
            null,
            SystemAction.get(SaveAsTemplateAction.class),
            null,
            SystemAction.get(ToolsAction.class),
            SystemAction.get(PropertiesAction.class),
        };
    }
    protected MultiDataObject createMultiObject(FileObject primaryFile)
        throws DataObjectExistsException, IOException {
        return new ScoreDataObject(primaryFile, this);
    }
}
```

You should now add the following line to your *Bundle.properties*:

```
    LBL_loaderName=Mini-Composer Scores
```

This is all boilerplate code. A data object, data node, and data loader bean info are also needed; these can all be made just as easily using the API Support's template for a simple data loader, which creates all of these things. Later on the data object and node will do more interesting things and we will examine them in detail.

All that remains to be done is register the data loader in the module manifest:

```
    Manifest-Version: 1.0
    OpenIDE-Module: org.netbeans.examples.modules.minicomposer
    OpenIDE-Module-Localizing-Bundle:
      org/netbeans/examples/modules/minicomposer/Bundle.properties
    OpenIDE-Module-Specification-Version: 0.2
    OpenIDE-Module-IDE-Dependencies: IDE/1 > 1.33
    OpenIDE-Module-Layer: org/netbeans/examples/modules/minicomposer/layer.xml

    Name: org/netbeans/examples/modules/minicomposer/ScoreDataLoader.class
    OpenIDE-Module-Class: Loader
```

Now the module should be capable of recognizing score files, and they should appear in the Explorer with the score icon ♯.

The user cannot yet do anything useful with the score files beyond perhaps renaming or deleting them.

Creating an Editor Support for Scores

The first useful thing that a user might want to do with scores is edit them textually in the Source Editor window. This is easily done by adding an editor support to the data object (shown in Example 21-7). While there is a great deal of potential flexibility in how to make editing support work, for now we will use an essentially boilerplate editor support, according to the Open APIs Support template. Later on some minor additions will be required, but most of the support can be left as created by the template.

Example 21-7. Minicomposer: initial src/org/netbeans/examples/modules/minicomposer/ ScoreEditorSupport.java

```java
public class ScoreEditorSupport extends DataEditorSupport
    implements EditorCookie, EditCookie, PrintCookie, CloseCookie {
  public ScoreEditorSupport(ScoreDataObject obj) {
    super(obj, new ScoreEnv(obj));
  }
  protected boolean notifyModified() {
    if (!super.notifyModified()) {
      return false;
    }
    ScoreDataObject obj = (ScoreDataObject)getDataObject();
    if (obj.getCookie(SaveCookie.class) == null) {
      obj.addSaveCookie(new Save());
      obj.setModified(true);
    }
    return true;
  }
  protected void notifyUnmodified() {
    super.notifyUnmodified();
    ScoreDataObject obj = (ScoreDataObject)getDataObject();
    SaveCookie save = (SaveCookie)obj.getCookie(SaveCookie.class);
    if (save != null) {
      obj.removeSaveCookie(save);
      obj.setModified(false);
    }
  }
  private class Save implements SaveCookie {
    public void save() throws IOException {
      saveDocument();
      getDataObject().setModified(false);
    }
  }
  private static class ScoreEnv extends DataEditorSupport.Env {
    private static final long serialVersionUID = 85639662675875L;
    public ScoreEnv(ScoreDataObject obj) {
      super(obj);
    }
    protected FileObject getFile() {
      return getDataObject().getPrimaryFile();
    }
    protected FileLock takeLock() throws IOException {
      return ((ScoreDataObject)getDataObject()).getPrimaryEntry().takeLock();
    }
    public CloneableOpenSupport findCloneableOpenSupport() {
      return (ScoreEditorSupport)getDataObject().getCookie(
        ScoreEditorSupport.class);
    }
  }
}
```

The `ScoreEnv` and `Save` inner classes as well as the `notifyModified()` and `notifyUnmodified()` methods can be customized to control exactly what happens when the file is first modified, and then when it is saved. We will not need to make such customizations. The data object will now create an editor support and attach it to itself, as shown in Example 21-8.

Example 21-8. Minicomposer: src/org/netbeans/examples/modules/minicomposer/
ScoreDataObject.java with editor support

```java
public class ScoreDataObject extends MultiDataObject {
  private static final long serialVersionUID = 5776214949118746290L;
  public ScoreDataObject(FileObject pf, ScoreDataLoader loader)
      throws DataObjectExistsException {
    super(pf, loader);
    CookieSet cookies = getCookieSet();
    cookies.add(new ScoreEditorSupport(this));
  }
  protected Node createNodeDelegate() {
    return new ScoreDataNode(this);
  }
  void addSaveCookie(SaveCookie save) {
    getCookieSet().add(save);
  }
  void removeSaveCookie(SaveCookie save) {
    getCookieSet().remove(save);
  }
}
```

The data object is boilerplate except for the addition of the `ScoreEditorSupport` to its cookie set in the constructor and the `addSaveCookie()` and `removeSaveCookie()` methods. These methods are accessible to the editor support and permit it to decide when the object is modified and needs to be saved—`getCookieSet()` is protected in `MultiDataObject`, so the data object must give the editor support permission to add or remove cookies. Only the editor support will control the save cookie; we make the two methods package-private to prevent outside code from trying to manipulate the save cookie without going through the editor support, which could result in data loss or corruption.

Now that the object supports editing as text programmatically, we should make sure that the option to do this appears in the node's context menu. This can be done by customizing the data loader's `defaultActions()`:

```java
protected SystemAction[] defaultActions() {
  return new SystemAction[] {
    SystemAction.get(EditAction.class),
    SystemAction.get(FileSystemAction.class),
    null,
    // ...
  };
}
```

Now choosing Edit on the context menu of a score node should open it in the Editor as a plain text file (see Figure 21-1). Just double-clicking the node will work, too: the first listed context menu item is used as a default for what to do when a data node is double-clicked.

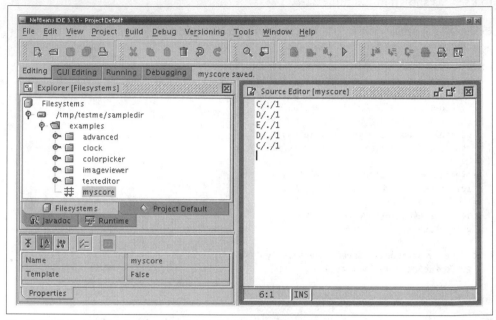

Figure 21-1. Score files displayed in the Explorer

As written, the Editor will show scores as simple text files without any fancy features. While we will not discuss it here, you could also create an editor kit for the text/x-minicomposer-score MIME type and add it to NetBeans. Such a kit could provide syntax highlighting, smart completion, special keyboard shortcuts, and other aids to editing scores textually. You can learn more about these capabilities in Appendix A.

Creating a Fixed ExecCookie to Play Scores

We can let the user play a score once it is written, but first it is necessary to know how to parse the score file. We will start by assuming a simple class that holds the structure of the score and includes facilities for parsing it as well as generating the text from the structure. Later on it will be used for structure editing of the score files. The details of the parsing are straightforward and do not involve NetBeans at all, so Example 21-9 is just a skeleton of the class.

Example 21-9. Minicomposer: public signature of src/org/netbeans/examples/modules/ minicomposer/Score.java

```java
public final class Score implements Serializable {
  public static final String[] TONES_SHORT = {"-", "C", "C#", /* ... */};
  // These are actually localized, see full example sources:
  public static final String[] TONES_LONG = {"Rest", "C", "C Sharp", /* ... */};
  public static final int DEFAULT_TONE1 = 1; // index of sample tone: C
  public static final String[] OCTAVES_SHORT = {"--", "-", ".", "+", "++"};
  public static final String[] OCTAVES_LONG = {"low", /* ... */};
  public static final int DEFAULT_OCTAVE = 2; // index of middle octave
  public static final float MIDDLE_C_HERTZ = 440.0f;
  public static final int WHERE_IS_C_TONE = 1; // index of C in tone list
  public static final int WHERE_IS_MIDDLE_OCTAVE = 2;
  public static final float HALF_STEP = (float)Math.pow(2.0, 1.0 / 12.0);
  public static final String[] DURATIONS_SHORT = {"1", "2", "4"};
  public static final String[] DURATIONS_LONG = {"Quarter", "Half", "Full"};
  public static final float[] DURATION_SECONDS = {0.25f, 0.5f, 1.0f};
  public static final int DEFAULT_DURATION = 0; // index of quarter duration
  /** Parse a score from a text stream. */
  public static Score parse(Reader r) throws IOException;
  /** Write a score to a text stream. */
  public static void generate(Score s, Writer w) throws IOException;
  /** One note (or rest) in a score. */
  public static final class Note implements Serializable, Cloneable {
    public Note(int tone, int octave, int duration);
    public int getTone();
    public int getOctave();
    public int getDuration();
    public Note cloneNote();
  }
  /** Create a new score programmatically.
   * Specify the tone, octave, and duration of each note. */
  public Score(List notes);
  /** Number of notes (and rests) in the score. */
  public int getSize();
  /** Get the note (or rest) at a given position. */
  public Note getNote(int pos);
  public boolean equals(Object o);
  public int hashCode();
}
```

We also need some support for turning a score structure into a waveform understandable by JavaSound. Such a waveform can be saved to an audio file or played directly. Again, the details are not important here, so we will just look at the signature of the support class in Example 21-10, as it will be called from NetBeans-specific classes.

Example 21-10. Minicomposer: public signature of src/org/netbeans/examples/modules/ minicomposer/LineInFromScore.java

```java
/** An implementation of JavaSound&rsquo;s TargetDataLine,
 * generating the waveform from a Score.
 */
```

Example 21-10. Minicomposer: public signature of src/org/netbeans/examples/modules/
minicomposer/LineInFromScore.java (continued)

```java
public class LineInFromScore implements TargetDataLine {
  /** An audio input stream based on the line in.
   * Computes the frame length based on some sampling rate.
   */
  public static class ScoreAudioInputStream extends AudioInputStream {
    public ScoreAudioInputStream(LineInFromScore line, float sampleRate);
  }
  public LineInFromScore(Score s);
  // ...
}
```

With these two utility classes in hand, code to play a score is fairly straightforward. First, we make an implementation of the NetBeans ExecCookie that represents something that can be run (later on we will reimplement this system to be somewhat more flexible). This is shown in Example 21-11.

Example 21-11. Minicomposer: src/org/netbeans/examples/modules/minicomposer/
ScoreExec.java

```java
public class ScoreExec implements ExecCookie {
  private final DataObject obj;
  public ScoreExec(DataObject obj) {
    this.obj = obj;
  }
  public void start() {
    try {
      Score score;
      InputStream is = obj.getPrimaryFile().getInputStream();
      try {
        score = Score.parse(new InputStreamReader(is));
      } finally {
        is.close();
      }
      LineInFromScore line = new LineInFromScore(score);
      AudioInputStream ais =
        new LineInFromScore.ScoreAudioInputStream(line, 24000.0f);
      AudioFormat format = ais.getFormat();
      DataLine.Info dlinfo = new DataLine.Info(Clip.class, ais.getFormat());
      Clip clip = (Clip)AudioSystem.getLine(dlinfo);
      clip.open(ais);
      clip.start();
      while (clip.isActive()) {
        Thread.sleep(1000);
      }
      clip.stop();
      clip.close();
    } catch (Exception e) {
      TopManager.getDefault().getErrorManager().notify(e);
    }
  }
}
```

This execution support is easily attached by adding it to the object's cookie set. Additionally the data loader should be told to include **Execute** in the context menu of score nodes. Here's the modified code that you should have in your `ScoreDataObject` constructor:

```
public ScoreDataObject(FileObject pf, ScoreDataLoader loader)
    throws DataObjectExistsException {
  super(pf, loader);
  CookieSet cookies = getCookieSet();
  cookies.add(new ScoreEditorSupport(this));
  cookies.add(new ScoreExec(this));
}
```

Additionally, you need to update the `defaultActions()` method of your `ScoreDataLoader` class as follows:

```
protected SystemAction[] defaultActions() {
  return new SystemAction[] {
    SystemAction.get(EditAction.class),
    SystemAction.get(FileSystemAction.class),
    null,
    SystemAction.get(ExecuteAction.class),
    null,
    // ...
  };
}
```

This simple support will only work if the user saves the file before running it, because it reads from the file object even if the editor support is modified.

With these changes, you can play the current score by pressing **Execute** with the score file selected. Before adding the `ExecCookie` implementation, the Execute action was disabled whenever a score file was selected.

Creating a Simple Template

It is easy to make a simple template for a score file. Without a template, the user would be forced to create a *.score* file manually in the operating system and then edit it in NetBeans—which would not be very friendly! So a template gives an initial score file that can be copied and used as a starting point.

In this example it makes sense for the template to be empty—start with no notes—because an empty score is still syntactically valid. Objects newly created from template ought never start with errors in them. A good example is provided by Java source files, which, when created from template, at least start with the mandatory package declaration and usually a class declaration, too.

All that is necessary to make a new template is to write it and place it wherever you like underneath the system filesystem's *Templates/* folder. You can make a new template subfolder or use an existing one. For this example it is enough to reuse the existing **Other** category, which, in the NetBeans IDE, holds templates for text files, HTML files, and other simple file types. You should make the following addition to your *layer.xml* to support this template:

```
<folder name="Templates">
  <folder name="Other">
    <file name="musical_score.score">
      <attr name="template" boolvalue="true"/>
      <attr name="SystemFileSystem.localizingBundle"
            stringvalue="org.netbeans.examples.modules.minicomposer.Bundle"/>
      <attr name="SystemFileSystem.icon" urlvalue=
    "nbresloc:/org/netbeans/examples/modules/minicomposer/ScoreDataIcon.gif"/>
      <attr name="templateWizardURL" urlvalue=
  "nbresloc:/org/netbeans/examples/modules/minicomposer/DescForTemplate.html"/>
    </file>
  </folder>
</folder>
```

This template is empty (it has no notes). If we wanted to provide a non-empty score template, the `file` element would be given a `url` attribute pointing to a file in the module JAR with the template contents.

Templates can be presented to the user quite prominently and should always be given an appropriate display name and icon.[*] Add this line to your *Bundle.properties* to take care of the display name:

```
Templates/Other/musical_score.score=Musical Score
```

The file attribute `templateWizardURL` is specific to templates and can point to a small HTML page that will be displayed to the user in the **New** wizard. Example 21-12 is a simple version of this sort of HTML.

Example 21-12. Minicomposer: src/org/netbeans/examples/modules/minicomposer/ DescForTemplate.html

```
<html><body>
A simple musical score.
<p>This template is empty, you must add notes to it.
</body></html>
```

With these changes to the layer and bundle in place and the added HTML file, the user can now go to **File → New** and see the choice **Templates → Other → Musical Score**. The result is the output shown in Figure 21-2.

When selected, this should prompt for the name of the new empty score file. After the user clicks **Finish**, NetBeans creates the new score file. It also opens the score in the Editor—if a file type has a default action that is run when it is double-clicked

---

[*] In this case the icon could be skipped because score files according to the data node already have a nice icon, but later on this icon will be marked with information about the current status of the file—so for now make sure it is the unadorned icon.

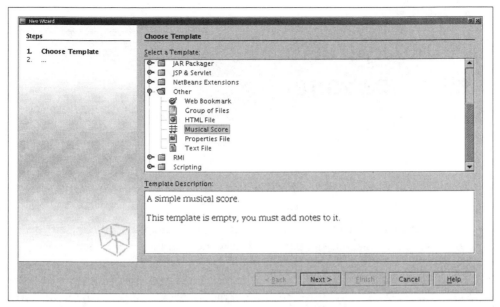

Figure 21-2. Minicomposer: using the Musical Score template

in the Explorer, this action is also run for convenience when a new file is created from template.

Now that we are able to provide basic support for score files, it is time to make Net-Beans more than a text editor for them—the IDE will understand the structure of scores.

## CHAPTER 22

Creating a Structural View of the Score

So far the user is able to edit score files as text and play them. But of course the purpose of an IDE is to make it easier for you to work with files in a variety of ways—editing as text is perhaps the most important, but the other ways generally involve working with the file structurally. For example, when you are working with Java sources in the IDE, you can see the structure of the source file mirrored in the Explorer (and can make edits there if you wish). Furthermore, many tools manipulate Java sources in the IDE—some, like the import management wizard, are provided by the Java module itself; some may be provided by other modules or even integrated applications such as UML modeling. Having the structural definition of the source enables these tools to cooperate, rather than all having to work with raw textual sources.

For our support for score files, we will travel a similar route. Rather than building different tools that each need to understand the score file text format, there will be a programmatic description of the structure of a score; the data object representing the score will have the responsibility of maintaining this alternate view of the score.

Creating a ScoreCookie to Represent a Sequence of Notes

To expose this new capability to clients, we will need a cookie that describes it and an implementation of which will be attached to the score object. Let us take a look at this Cookie (in Example 22-1), which like most cookies is an interface.

Example 22-1. Minicomposer: src/org/netbeans/examples/modules/minicomposer/ScoreCookie.java

```
public interface ScoreCookie extends Node.Cookie {
  public Score getScore() throws IOException;
  public void setScore(Score) throws IOException;
  public Task prepare();
  public boolean isValid();
  public void addChangeListener(ChangeListener);
  public void removeChangeListener(ChangeListener);
}
```

The most important methods are of course getScore() and setScore(). Together, these provide the essential two-way editing capability we wish to expose. getScore() parses the current text file (if it has not been already) and returns the structural view of the score that it finds there. If the file cannot be opened or contains syntax errors preventing parsing, then an exception will be thrown instead. setScore() replaces the current contents of the file with the supplied score structure. This means it generates a textual representation of the score and stores it in the file. It throws an exception if the file cannot be written to (is read only, or for some other reason). isValid() simply tests whether the file is currently valid—whether it is parsable or contains a syntax error.

The other methods manage the lifecycle of the cookie and the file itself. Since parsing the score may take some time, it is sometimes desirable to do this asynchronously. For example, many parts of the IDE that interact with Swing and GUI system are run in the AWT event thread. This Java thread is used solely for handling GUI display, and it is generally forbidden to use it for anything that might take time. Opening a large score file hosted on a remote file server and parsing could take a visible amount of time—a second, say—and it would be bad for the user if the entire IDE froze up during this time. Additionally, it is normal for the user to type something into the text file that is syntactically invalid with the expectation of correcting it in a moment. The IDE must understand the difference. Situations such as this are common sources of deadlocks—if you have not already, please read Chapter 15 for more help.

prepare() begins loading and parsing of the score file in another thread; it returns immediately with a org.openide.util.Task, which is a handle for some piece of work that may be completed later (you can be notified when it finishes or wait for it). If the file is already parsed and ready, this method still returns a task, but the task is already finished. Either way, you can safely call prepare() knowing that the current thread will not block as a result.

The final two methods permit clients of the cookie to attach ChangeListeners to the cookie. When something of interest happens—the score is changed in text or via setScore(), or it becomes invalid due to a textual change introducing a syntax error, or becomes valid again due to a textual change correcting an error—the stateChanged() method is called on all listeners to notify them that they may need to update something based on the new state of the score cookie.

Examples of State-Based Supports

The pattern we are following for ScoreCookie is a fairly common one; a similar technique is used in other places in the NetBeans Open APIs and in module APIs to handle preparation of an object and changes in its state. It is instructive to take a brief look at these. One example is org.openide.cookies.EditorCookie (shown in Example 22-2), which controls opening of a text document.

Example 22-2. Synopsis of EditorCookie

```
public interface EditorCookie extends LineCookie {
  public void open();
  public boolean close();
  public Task prepareDocument();
  public StyledDocument openDocument() throws IOException;
  public StyledDocument getDocument();
  public void saveDocument() throws IOException;
  public boolean isModified();
  public JEditorPane[] getOpenedPanes();
  // From LineCookie:
  public Line.Set getLineSet();
}
```

The details are not too important here, but you can see some of the same patterns: especially, getDocument() retrieves the document if it has already been loaded (otherwise it returns null); openDocument() also retrieves the document but blocks if necessary while opening it; and prepareDocument() can be used to initiate loading of the document asynchronously.

Even closer is SourceElement (shown in Example 22-3), which represents a source document (typically a Java language source) and provides the ability to control its parsing.

Example 22-3. Synopsis of selected methods in SourceElement

```
public class SourceElement extends Element {
  public static final int STATUS_NOT;
  public static final int STATUS_ERROR;
  public static final int STATUS_PARTIAL;
  public static final int STATUS_OK;
  public int getStatus();
  public Task prepare();
  public void runAtomic(Runnable);
  public void runAtomicAsUser(Runnable) throws SourceException;
  // many methods manipulating the source structure omitted ...
  // From Element:
  public void addPropertyChangeListener(PropertyChangeListener);
  public void removePropertyChangeListener(PropertyChangeListener);
  public static final String PROP_STATUS;
}
```

The source file can be in one of four states according to getStatus(): unparsed, completely erroneous, erroneous but otherwise parsable, and cleanly parsable. Clients can listen to changes in the state with a property change listener. prepare() begins parsing of the source if it is still unparsed and proceeds asynchronously. runAtomic() and runAtomicAsUser() provide a write mutex that can be used to safely perform a series of actions on the source tree. The SourceElement implementation provides the "two-way engineering" between textual Java source and its structured in-memory representation.

Creating a ScoreSupport

Having defined the ScoreCookie that permits clients to work with the score structurally, we will now proceed to implement it.

Why a Document Is Used

Comfortable two-way editing support requires that all views of the source be kept in sync with one another, as much as possible. It would not be hard to (for example) reparse the score every time the document was saved, but this would require the user to save frequently in order to check his work, and the resulting module would not feel as well "integrated" into the development environment: it would feel more like a standalone "score tool" needing manual refreshes. So it is best to update the structural view of the score as the user types.

This requirement means that the score should be parsed from the in-memory document whenever necessary. NetBeans uses the Swing Text API as a basis for implementing its text editor. This means that the javax.swing.text.Document, which holds the score text in memory, should be used as one view of the score. When the user begins typing into the Source Editor, this document is modified, and when the file is saved, the contents of the document are written to disk. NetBeans also handles a few details such as reloading the document when the file is changed on disk (by some external tool), so the Document is a convenient starting point.

Conversely, if the score is updated structurally, it would be one option to just write new file contents. But these new contents might conflict with textual edits the user had made since opening the file. So, again, it is better to regenerate the text after a structure edit into the document, not the file. NetBeans will automatically mark the file modified, save the results if requested, or undo the change if **Edit → Undo** (Control-Z) is invoked with the editor selected.

For all these reasons, we will require that the ScoreSupport implementation of the score cookie be driven by a Document, which we can obtain from an EditorCookie.

Implementation of ScoreSupport

The score support will be a class implementing ScoreCookie. Since this class is somewhat complex, we will step through it one piece at a time, beginning in Example 22-4. A few pieces of the code that contribute only robustness (checking for logic errors) or detailed error handling are omitted for brevity, but interested readers can, of course, refer to the full source of the example in the downloadable sources.

Example 22-4. Minicomposer: src/org/netbeans/examples/modules/minicomposer/
ScoreSupport.java (Text → Structure)

```
public class ScoreSupport implements ScoreCookie, Runnable, DocumentListener,
ChangeListener {
  private final DataObject obj;
```

```java
private final EditorCookie edit;
private Task prepareTask = null;
private Score score = null;
private IOException parseException = null;
private boolean addedEditorListener = false;
private Reference lastUsedDocument = null;
public ScoreSupport(DataObject obj, EditorCookie edit) {
  this.obj = obj;
  this.edit = edit;
}
public Score getScore() throws IOException {
  prepare().waitFinished();
  synchronized (this) {
    if (score != null && (parseException == null || obj.isModified())) {
      return score;
    } else {
      throw parseException;
    }
  }
}
public boolean isValid() {
  return parseException == null;
}
public synchronized Task prepare() {
  if (prepareTask == null)
    prepareTask = RequestProcessor.postRequest(this);
  return prepareTask;
}
public void run() {
  if (!obj.isValid()) {/* stop now, dead file */}
  edit.prepareDocument().waitFinished();
  final Document doc = edit.getDocument();
  if (!addedEditorListener) {
    addedEditorListener = true;
    if (edit instanceof CloneableEditorSupport) {
      ((CloneableEditorSupport)edit).addChangeListener(
        WeakListener.change(this, edit));
    }
  }
  doc.render(new Runnable() {
    public void run() {
      try {
        setScoreAndParseException(parse(doc), null);
      } catch (IOException ioe) {
        setScoreAndParseException(score, ioe);
      } catch (BadLocationException ble) {
        // similar...
      }
    }
  });
  Document lastDoc = null;
```

```
    if (lastUsedDocument != null) {
      lastDoc = (Document)lastUsedDocument.get();
    }
    if (lastDoc != doc) {
      if (lastDoc != null) {
        lastDoc.removeDocumentListener(this);
      }
      doc.addDocumentListener(this);
      lastUsedDocument = new WeakReference(doc);
    }
  }
  private synchronized void setScoreAndParseException(Score s, IOException e) {
    score = s;
    parseException = e;
    fireChange();
  }
  protected Score parse(Document doc) throws IOException, BadLocationException {
    String text = doc.getText(0, doc.getLength());
    return Score.parse(new StringReader(text));
  }
  // additional methods discussed later...
}
```

In the first part of the implementation, the three ScoreCookie methods that provide access to the structure of the score are given. First of all, the constructor for ScoreSupport principally accepts an EditorCookie from which the score is parsed; it also asks for a DataObject that is used for a few miscellaneous purposes (checking for modification and continued existence of the file).

getScore() and isValid() are fairly simple in this implementation; the real work is done in the parsing task started by prepare(). getScore() waits for parsing to finish (if it was not already finished) and then throws the saved parse exception if there was one, or returns the parsed score. Note the special logic in the if-clause: in case there was at one time a valid score, and an error was introduced by textual editing, getScore() will continue to return the old valid score until the error is corrected, as this is convenient for structure editing. But if the file is saved without the error being first corrected, then the support is more aggressive and refuses to return the now-obsolete parse. If the document was erroneous to begin with, there will be no parse at all and the error will be thrown. isValid() simply checks whether any error is currently known; it does not initiate a parse on its own, since isValid() may be called early on by the score node (more on this later), and we want to avoid parsing until the result is really needed.

prepare() keeps a cached parsing task on hand. The first time it is called, an asynchronous parse is initiated; subsequent calls give back a handle to the same task. Note that it is harmless to call prepare() after the parse is completed; the returned Task will already be *finished*.

The task itself is posted into the RequestProcessor, which is a commonly-used Net-Beans utility class for asynchronous computation. It accepts a Runnable, in this case the ScoreSupport itself, to implement the computation, and returns a Task handle that can be used to monitor progress. The run method then begins by checking that the data object has not already been invalidated; usually this would happen right after a score file has been deleted, in which case the score support is no longer needed and just accidentally in the request processor.

Before any parsing can take place, it is necessary to ensure that the document is completely loaded into memory. Otherwise, an early call to prepare() on an unopened file could fail—note that it is common in NetBeans for a Document to be loaded even without the file being visible in the Source Editor, just because the document provides such a convenient buffer for reading and manipulating the file textually. So the prepareDocument() method on the editor cookie is first called, and the score parsing task blocks on the task this returns, which loads the document. Additionally, the support attaches itself as a *listener* to the editor cookie; more on that in the next section.*

The parsing should happen atomically with respect to the document—we do not wish to have any race conditions caused by the user typing in the middle of a parse—so Document.render() is used. The utility method parse() actually retrieves the current document text and passes it to the parser in Score; if there are any parse errors, they are recorded in the support, else the newly parsed score is retained for later. Finally, a listener is attached to the document (if we did not already attach a listener to this document) in case it is modified by the user later:

```
private final Set listeners = new HashSet();
public synchronized void addChangeListener(ChangeListener l) {
  listeners.add(l);
}
public synchronized void removeChangeListener(ChangeListener l) {
  listeners.remove(l);
}
protected synchronized void fireChange() {
  final ChangeListener[] ls = (ChangeListener[])
    listeners.toArray(new ChangeListener[listeners.size()]);
  if (ls.length == 0) return;
  final ChangeEvent ev = new ChangeEvent(this);
  SwingUtilities.invokeLater(new Runnable() {
    public void run() {
      for (int i = 0; i < ls.length; i++) {
        ls[i].stateChanged(ev);
      }
    }
  });
```

---

* Currently the APIs do not permit listening to state changes in the general EditorCookie, so we cast to CloneableEditorSupport, which does permit this. Since the editor support created in Chapter 21 is in fact a CloneableEditorSupport (subclass), this is not a real problem.

```
    }
    public void stateChanged(ChangeEvent ev) {
      invalidate();
    }
    public void insertUpdate(DocumentEvent ev) {
      invalidate();
    }
    public void removeUpdate(DocumentEvent ev) {
      invalidate();
    }
    public void changedUpdate(DocumentEvent ev) {
    }
    protected synchronized void invalidate() {
      if (prepareTask != null) {
        prepareTask = null;
        fireChange();
      }
    }
  }
```

Many pieces of code outside the score support will need to know when the score has been changed. So the support will keep a Swing-style event set based on javax. swing.event.ChangeListener. Outside code will register its interest using addChangeListener() and removeChangeListener(); the fireChange() method is for the use of the support to send off the change events. (Note that we fire the events asynchronously to avoid possible deadlocks.) A more sophisticated support would probably fire finer-grained events.

stateChanged() will be called on the support itself (as opposed to its listeners) when the state of the editor support changes (recall that earlier we added this as a listener to the editor support). Typically, such a change means that the document has been opened and loaded, or that it has been closed, or the underlying file has been changed on disk or deleted. In such cases we let any users of the score cookie know that the score may have changed as a result; the invalidate() helper method clears the old parsing task (forcing the next call to prepare() to restart it) and forwards the announcement of the change to score listeners.

Similarly, any textual edit by the user to the score file may change the score. So, when any character is *inserted or deleted* into the document, the support gets an insertUpdate() or removeUpdate() from the Document (because it is a DocumentListener) and again marks the current parse as invalid and fires a change.

The third segment of the support permits the score to be set structurally from outside code, with the text being regenerated to match:

```
  public synchronized void setScore(final Score s) throws IOException {
    final Score oldScore = score;
    if (s.equals(oldScore)) {
      return;
    }
    prepareTask = Task.EMPTY;
    score = s;
```

```
    parseException = null;
    final StyledDocument doc = edit.openDocument();
    // also handles BadLocationException here...
    NbDocument.runAtomic(doc, new Runnable() {
      public void run() {
        doc.removeDocumentListener(ScoreSupport.this);
        try {
          generate(s, oldScore, doc);
        } finally {
          doc.addDocumentListener(ScoreSupport.this);
        }
      }
    });
    fireChange();
}
protected void generate(Score s, Score oldScore, Document doc)
    throws BadLocationException {
  CharArrayWriter wr = new CharArrayWriter();
  try {
    Score.generate(s, wr);
  } catch (IOException ioe) {
    // handle...
  }
  doc.remove(0, doc.getLength());
  doc.insertString(0, wr.toString(), null);
}
```

setScore() first ensures that the new score really differs from the old; otherwise, there is nothing to be done. prepareTask is set to a dummy task. Unless and until the score is changed textually, there is no further need to reparse. Both score and parseException are set according to the new structure.

The second half of the method regenerates the text. NbDocument.runAtomic() runs its body within a write lock on the document, preventing user edits from being attempted while the regeneration is in progress, as well as preventing readers from seeing a half-written document. The document listener is also temporarily suspended, since the support should not receive document change events from what it is writing. After rewriting the textual score, a change is fired to listeners to let them know the next call to getScore() will give a different result.

generate() is the actual implementation of the rewrite, with the document lock held. This simple implementation just removes the entire existing file and re-creates it. A more clever subclass could use the oldScore argument to detect small, local changes to the score (a change in just one note, for example) and rewrite only the relevant portion of the document.

Lifecycle of the Score

To more easily grasp the possible different states the score cookie can be in, see the state diagram in Figure 22-1. Note that the top half of the main state, **in use**, covers the parsed state of the score, while the bottom half covers the orthogonal modification state of the score file.

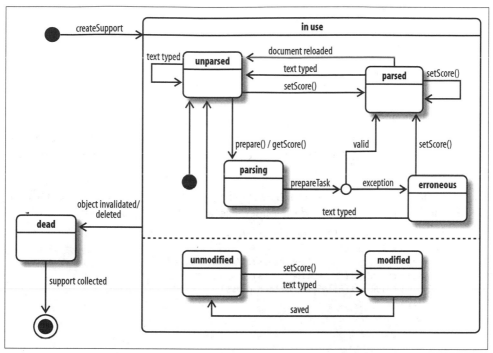

Figure 22-1. UML of the ScoreSupport lifecycle

A couple of details have been omitted here: the loading of the editor document is a part of the parsing process initially and after a document reload, but not in other situations. Additionally, the textual and visual views (windows) may be opened separately, all of which interacts with the document opening and saving cycle.

An OpenSupport

Our first application of the structural view of the score will be a GUI display. This can coexist alongside the textual display. Our textual `ScoreEditorSupport` implemented `EditCookie`, which permitted the `EditAction` to be used on it. To permit a GUI display, we will use the similar but distinct `OpenCookie`, which by convention is used for opening files visually, whereas `EditCookie` opens them textually. This new cookie support will permit `OpenAction` to be used on the score data object.

Creating an OpenCookie Implementation

First, we will look at the code to associate the open cookie with the data object; add the following method to `ScoreDataObject`:

```
public ScoreDataObject(FileObject pf, ScoreDataLoader loader)
    throws DataObjectExistsException {
  super(pf, loader);
  CookieSet cookies = getCookieSet();
  cookies.add(new ScoreExec(this));
  EditorCookie ed = new ScoreEditorSupport(this);
  cookies.add(ed);
  // Newly added:
  cookies.add(new ScoreSupport(this, ed));
  cookies.add(new ScoreOpenSupport(getPrimaryEntry()));
}
```

Here three cookies are being added to the data object: the editor cookie (handles
both the simple EditCookie and the document-oriented EditorCookie); a ScoreCookie
implementation; and an OpenCookie implementation (which will assume there is a
ScoreCookie available).

To make the Open menu item actually appear in the context menu of score nodes, a
one-line addition is made to the data loader's defaultActions() method:

```
protected SystemAction[] defaultActions() {
  return new SystemAction[] {
    SystemAction.get(OpenAction.class), // newly added
    SystemAction.get(EditAction.class),
    SystemAction.get(FileSystemAction.class),
    null,
    // ...
  };
}
```

Making OpenAction first in the list ensures that it will be the default
action to be run when the user double-clicks a score node.

The ScoreOpenSupport (shown in Example 22-5) is based on the common superclass
OpenSupport, which handles the standard behavior of opening and closing views of a
data object. Our implementation is customized a little to make sure GUI views are
saved before closing (unless a textual view is still open in which case this will ensure
the user saves before closing).

Example 22-5. Minicomposer: src/org/netbeans/examples/modules/minicomposer/
ScoreOpenSupport.java

```
public class ScoreOpenSupport extends OpenSupport
    implements OpenCookie, CloseCookie {
  public ScoreOpenSupport(MultiDataObject.Entry entry) {
    super(entry);
  }
  protected CloneableTopComponent createCloneableTopComponent() {
    return new ScorePanel(entry);
  }
```

```
  protected boolean canClose() {
    if (!super.canClose()) {
      return false;
    }
    DataObject dob = entry.getDataObject();
    if (!dob.isModified()) {
      return true;
    }
    ScoreEditorSupport ses = (ScoreEditorSupport)dob.getCookie(
      ScoreEditorSupport.class);
    if (ses.getOpenedPanes() != null) {
      return true;
    }
    boolean sesCanClose = ses.superCanClose();
    if (sesCanClose) ses.close();
    return sesCanClose;
  }
  boolean isOpen() {
    return !allEditors.isEmpty();
  }
}
```

Subclassers of OpenSupport need to explicitly implement such cookie interfaces as they wish to use. Here we use OpenCookie to open the view, and CloseCookie to permit it to be closed (though rarely used). ViewCookie could also be used; it is very similar to OpenCookie and EditCookie, but is conventionally used for read-only views of a file.

The constructor accepts a *data object entry*, essentially a binding between the data object and a particular file in it (in our case, the primary *.score* file). The only required method is createCloneableTopComponent(), which creates the actual GUI panel.

canClose() in an OpenSupport indicates the support's willingness to let the last *clone sister* or opened window associated with the support to be closed (there can be more than one if you select **Window → Clone View** on one such window). As a rule such methods check for unsaved changes. This support always permits closing if the score is unmodified; if it is modified, it first finds the editor support. If there are some open text panes, the GUI is closed without prompting (the user would still be prompted upon closing the last text pane). If the GUI is the last open view of the score of either kind, then the editor support is asked to take responsibility for actually handling the save: this includes displaying a prompt to save, possibly saving the document, and then proceeding to close (unless the dialog box was canceled).

isOpen() is an accessor method for the editor support, to take care of the other half of this cooperation between the two supports: when the last editor is being closed, it needs to know whether there is still an open GUI view that will take responsibility for any modifications to the score. isOpen() permits this information to be made available to the ScoreEditorSupport, which is then augmented with two methods:

```
protected boolean canClose() {
    ScoreOpenSupport sos = (ScoreOpenSupport)getDataObject().getCookie(
      ScoreOpenSupport.class);
    if (sos != null && sos.isOpen() && !getDataObject().isModified()) {
      sos.close();
      return true;
    } else {
      return superCanClose();
    }
}
boolean superCanClose() {
    return super.canClose();
}
```

Again, canClose() checks with the open support before closing, and superCanClose() is made available as an accessor method to ScoreOpenSupport.

Showing a GUI View of the ScoreCookie

All that is left to do is actually create the GUI panel. This will be a CloneableTopComponent, or Swing panel for which the NetBeans window system can form a container (and which can be cloned should the user wish to see more than one part of the same score at once). As this is again a somewhat lengthy class, it will be taken in pieces, and sections that are solely Swing presentation code will be omitted. Take a look at Example 22-6.

Example 22-6. Minicomposer: src/org/netbeans/examples/modules/minicomposer/ScorePanel.java (Creation and Persistence)

```
public class ScorePanel extends CloneableTopComponent {
  private static final long serialVersionUID = 7204432764586558961L;
  private MultiDataObject.Entry entry;
  private ScoreCookie cookie;
  private ScoreOpenSupport support;
  private Score score;
  private NodeListener listener;
  public ScorePanel(MultiDataObject.Entry entry) {
    super(entry.getDataObject());
    this.entry = entry;
    init();
  }
  public void open(Workspace ws) {
    if (ws == null) ws = TopManager.getDefault().getWindowManager()
                                      .getCurrentWorkspace();
    Mode mode = ws.findMode(CloneableEditorSupport.EDITOR_MODE);
    if (mode != null) mode.dockInto(this);
    super.open(ws);
  }
  protected CloneableTopComponent createClonedObject() {
```

```
    return new ScorePanel(entry);
  }
  protected boolean closeLast() {
    return support.canClose();
  }
  public void writeExternal(ObjectOutput oo) throws IOException {
    super.writeExternal(oo);
    oo.writeObject(entry);
  }
  public ScorePanel() {
  }
  public void readExternal(ObjectInput oi)
      throws IOException, ClassNotFoundException {
    super.readExternal(oi);
    entry = (MultiDataObject.Entry)oi.readObject();
    init();
  }
}
```

The score panel is initialized with the `MultiDataObject.Entry`, which in this class is used only for its handle to the `ScoreDataObject` and thus the `ScoreCookie`.

`open()` is called when the panel is actually being displayed. `ScorePanel` overrides this method in order to ensure that it is docked into the IDE's standard editor mode, which is the multi-tabbed window normally used for the Source Editor. `createClonedObject()` is used to create a copy of the panel displaying the same data. `closeLast()` checks with the open support to make sure the panel is really permitted to close (here "last" refers to "last clone on any workspace," as users sometimes keep the same file open in more than one workspace at once).

The Java Externalization methods here (`writeExternal()` and `readExternal()`) are used to ensure that after a restart of the IDE or project switch, any open score panels will be remembered. A default (no-argument) constructor is needed for externalization to work properly; `readExternal()` does the actual initialization. The only reason for storing the data object entry is to be able to restore the panels later. The `serialVersionUID` field is arbitrary but signals to the JVM that externalized panels from old user window settings should be considered compatible, so long as the magic number is not changed.

Here is the GUI initialization code:

```
private void init() {
  if (!SwingUtilities.isEventDispatchThread()) {
    SwingUtilities.invokeLater(new Runnable() {
      public void run() {
        init();
      }
    });
    return;
```

```
      }
      putClientProperty("PersistenceType", "OnlyOpened");
      final DataObject o = entry.getDataObject();
      final Node n = o.getNodeDelegate();
      updateNameAndIcon(o, n);
      listener = new NodeAdapter() {
        public void propertyChange(PropertyChangeEvent ev) {
          String prop = ev.getPropertyName();
          if (prop == null ||
              prop.equals(Node.PROP_DISPLAY_NAME) ||
              prop.equals(Node.PROP_ICON) ||
              prop.equals(DataObject.PROP_MODIFIED)) {
            updateNameAndIcon(o, n);
          }
        }
      };
      n.addNodeListener(WeakListener.node(listener, n));
      o.addPropertyChangeListener(WeakListener.propertyChange(listener, o));
      cookie = (ScoreCookie)entry.getDataObject().getCookie(ScoreCookie.class);
      Task t = cookie.prepare();
      class DeferredRun implements TaskListener, Runnable {
        public void taskFinished(Task t2) {
          SwingUtilities.invokeLater(this);
        }
        public void run() {
          init2();
        }
      }
      t.addTaskListener(new DeferredRun());
      score = new Score(Collections.EMPTY_LIST);
      support = (ScoreOpenSupport)entry.getDataObject().getCookie(
        ScoreOpenSupport.class);
      // also adds temporary JLabel "Loading..." here...
    }
    protected void updateNameAndIcon(DataObject o, Node n) {
      String displayName = n.getDisplayName();
      if (o.isModified()) {
        setName(NbBundle.getMessage(ScorePanel.class, "LBL_modified_name",
                                    displayName));
      } else {
        setName(displayName);
      }
      setIcon(n.getIcon(BeanInfo.ICON_COLOR_16x16));
    }
    private void init2() {
      try {
        score = cookie.getScore();
      } catch (IOException ioe) {
        TopManager.getDefault().getErrorManager().notify(ioe);
        return;
      }
      // GUI initialization including table = new JTable(new Model()) ...
      JButton add = new JButton(/* ... */);
      add.addActionListener(new ActionListener() {
```

```
        public void actionPerformed(ActionEvent ev) {
            addRow();
        }
    });
    JButton del = new JButton(/* ... */);
    del.addActionListener(new ActionListener() {
        public void actionPerformed(ActionEvent ev) {
            delRows(table.getSelectedRows());
        }
    });
    // more GUI initialization...
}
```

The init() method does the first pass of initialization of the panel, before the score file has necessarily been parsed. First, it ensures that it is run in the Swing event dispatch thread; since it manipulates live GUI components, such as a temporary **Loading** label, this is mandatory. The Swing ad-hoc client property PersistenceType can (as of NetBeans 3.3) be used to give hints to the NetBeans window system; here the value OnlyOpened restrains the window system from trying to save the panel's state unless it is open—windows by default can be reopened in the same position they were last closed, but we do not need or want this capability. It then matches the name and icon of the panel to those of the score node. The panel also attaches a listener to the node to check for changes in the name or icon, as well as listening to whether the data object is modified or unmodified (when modified, an asterisk (*) will appear after the name).

More importantly, the ScoreCookie is retrieved from the ScoreDataObject, and parsing of it is begun. (If it was already parsed, this will take no time to finish.) Rather than blocking the event thread—and thus the user's GUI work—while the score is parsed, it requests parsing to proceed in the background. When finished, the TaskListener is notified, and initialization continues with a second pass.

This pass, handled by init2(), gets the finished score parse (or thrown exception), and prepares the real GUI appearance (discarding the placeholder **Loading...** label). The GUI consists of a table of notes and two buttons to add or remove rows (notes).

Once the panel has been initialized, GUI handling is fairly straightforward. The addRow() and delRows() button action handlers just compute new scores structurally and store them in the score support. A table model maps the Score structure to a format understandable by JTable, so reads and writes of table cells are synchronized with the score. The model listens to external (for example textual) changes to the score and updates the table when this happens (a more sophisticated cookie and table model could fire changes in only those parts of the data that actually changed). Here is the relevant code:

```
private void addRow() {
    Score nue = /* copy of score but with one extra row */;
    try {
        cookie.setScore(nue);
    } catch (IOException ioe) {
```

```
      TopManager.getDefault().getErrorManager().notify(ioe);
    }
  }
  private void delRows(int[] rows) {
    Score nue = /* copy of score but with those rows missing */;
    try {
      cookie.setScore(nue);
    } catch (IOException ioe) {
      TopManager.getDefault().getErrorManager().notify(ioe);
    }
  }
  private class Model extends AbstractTableModel implements ChangeListener {
    public Model() {
      cookie.addChangeListener(WeakListener.change(this, cookie));
    }
    public void stateChanged(ChangeEvent ev) {
      try {
        score = cookie.getScore();
        fireTableDataChanged();
      } catch (IOException ioe) {
        // keep previous Score object instead
        if (entry.getDataObject().isValid()) {
          TopManager.getDefault().getErrorManager().notify(ioe);
        }
      }
    }
    public boolean isCellEditable(int row, int col) {
      return true;
    }
    public int getRowCount() {
      return score.getSize();
    }
    public int getColumnCount() {
      return 3;
    }
    public Object getValueAt(int row, int column) {
      if (column == 0)
        return new Integer(score.getNote(row).getTone());
      else if (column == 1)
        return new Integer(score.getNote(row).getOctave());
      else if (column == 2)
        return new Integer(score.getNote(row).getDuration());
      else
        throw new ArrayIndexOutOfBoundsException();
    }
    public void setValueAt(Object val, int row, int col) {
      Score nue = /* copy of score except with above change */;
      try {
        cookie.setScore(nue);
      } catch (IOException ioe) {
        TopManager.getDefault().getErrorManager().notify(ioe);
      }
    }
  }
}
```

In Figure 22-2, you can see a view of a simple score opened in both GUI and text modes at once, in an MDI split window.

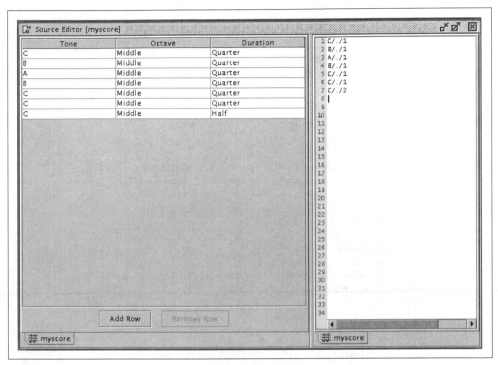

Figure 22-2. Minicomposer: two-way editing of score files

Indicating Parse Errors on the Node

Now that score files can be edited as text and will be parsed, it is a good idea to give the text-loving user some visual feedback when his text input is in error. It is easy to do this on the data node by attaching an error badge to the icon when the file is misparsed, so the resulting icon will look like this: ⌗.

To date we have not examined the data node in detail because it was just boilerplate code that could be gotten from any template. Now we are adding some interesting logic to it, so it is worth looking at the complete class in Example 22-7.

Example 22-7. Minicomposer: src/org/netbeans/examples/modules/minicomposer/ScoreDataNode. java with Parse Support

```
public class ScoreDataNode extends DataNode implements ChangeListener {
  private boolean inUse = false;
  public ScoreDataNode(ScoreDataObject obj) {
    super(obj, Children.LEAF);
    ScoreCookie score = (ScoreCookie)getCookie(ScoreCookie.class);
    if (score != null) {
```

```java
    score.addChangeListener(WeakListener.change(this, score));
  }
  EditorCookie ed = (EditorCookie)getCookie(EditorCookie.class);
  if (ed != null && (ed instanceof CloneableEditorSupport)) {
    ((CloneableEditorSupport)ed).addChangeListener(
      WeakListener.change(this, ed));
  }
}
public Image getIcon(int type) {
  if (type == BeanInfo.ICON_COLOR_16x16 ||
      type == BeanInfo.ICON_MONO_16x16) {
    Image icon = Utilities.loadImage(
      "org/netbeans/examples/modules/minicomposer/ScoreDataIcon.gif");
    ScoreCookie cookie = (ScoreCookie)getCookie(ScoreCookie.class);
    if (cookie != null) {
      if (inUse) {
        cookie.prepare();
      }
      if (!cookie.isValid()) {
        Image badge = Utilities.loadImage(
          "org/netbeans/examples/modules/minicomposer/error-badge.gif");
        icon = Utilities.mergeImages(icon, badge, 8, 8);
      }
    }
    try {
      DataObject obj = getDataObject();
      icon = obj.getPrimaryFile().getFileSystem().getStatus().
        annotateIcon(icon, type, obj.files());
    } catch (FileStateInvalidException fsie) {
      TopManager.getDefault().getErrorManager().
        notify(ErrorManager.INFORMATIONAL, fsie);
    }
    return icon;
  } else {
    return null;
  }
}
public Image getOpenedIcon(int type) {
  return getIcon(type);
}
public void stateChanged(ChangeEvent ev) {
  Object src = ev.getSource();
  if (!inUse && (src instanceof EditorCookie)) {
    inUse = true;
    fireIconChange();
  }
  if (src instanceof ScoreCookie) {
    fireIconChange();
  }
}
}
```

First, note the private flag inUse. When a folder containing some scores is first opened, it is quite possible that the user is not seriously interested in all or even any of the scores. While it would be technically correct (and in fact simpler to implement) to parse each and every one of them, just in case some of them were invalid on disk and should have an error badge, in practice this is a waste of processor power (and memory to hold the cached parses). The error badge is most useful when the user is actively editing a score. So unless and until the user actually opens a score file in the text editor, we will avoid asking for a parse of the score. Thus inUse is initially false. If the score is opened textually, it will be turned on (and kept on), so the node will then reflect the current validity of the text.

When the score node is constructed, it begins listening to possible changes in both the editor support and the score support. If the score support changes state, this might mean that it is now erroneous, or no longer erroneous. So stateChanged() when invoked because of a ScoreCookie *fires an icon change* to indicate to the Explorer displaying the node that the icon should be redisplayed.

getIcon() (and the similar getOpenedIcon() in case the node is expanded) is overridden to return either the plain icon or the icon with error badge. First, it loads the plain icon. (Utilities.loadImage() loads an image from the module class loader and caches it for a while, so there is no need to do your own caching.) If the score cookie is invalid—there was some sort of parse exception—then an additional error badge is loaded. This is an 8×8 transparent GIF. It is overlaid on the 16×16 base icon using Utilities.mergeImages() (which again does its own caching) in the lower-right quadrant.

The call to FileSystem.Status.annotateIcon() is present in the default DataNode implementation of getIcon(). It ensures that if the data object is present on a version-controlled filesystem (for example), that filesystem will have the opportunity to add its own badges. For example, CVS filesystems add a check mark (✓) to icons where the corresponding file is known to be up to date in the repository. Since we are overriding getIcon(), this feature does not come "for free," so we need to implement it ourselves.

Now back to the editor support. The node is listening to state changes in the editor support. If the score file is opened textually, an event will be fired after it is opened. The node catches this in stateChanged() and, if the inUse flag was not yet turned on, it is turned on now—and an icon change fired, in case the score was invalid on disk, in which case it should be parsed at once to show this.

When inUse is on, all calls to getIcon() call ScoreCookie.prepare() to ensure that a parse is at least started. If the score is already parsed, this has no effect. If it was not already parsed (either because the file was freshly opened or it was recently invalidated, then this call to getIcon() might not be correct, as the parsing proceeds in the background. However, when the parse is finished shortly afterwards, the score cookie will fire a state change, and getIcon() will be called again—this time correctly displaying the badged or plain icon.

Yours Is Not the Only Module

A common mistake among people first writing a NetBeans module is to forget about the rest of the world and the modules others may write or have written. If you are creating a custom distribution of the IDE with just your module and a limited or controlled set of other modules (see Chapter 22 for more), it might make sense for your module to occupy a dominant position in the IDE. However, modules that are used freely in conjunction with other modules should not be a burden to the others when they are left on. (Users can turn your module off of course, but it's better to not have to.)

There are a few facets to this:

- Avoid adding bulky GUI components when the module is not actively in use. These can include menu items or toolbar buttons, and especially entire menus and toolbars. If it is desirable to have plenty of toolbar GUI (context menus and buttons local to "top component" windows are not enough), consider making a special workspace to hold these toolbars and whatever GUI layout you want. The IDE can switch to this workspace when major functionality of your module is in use. Consider the NetBeans Form Editor, which has a special workspace and keeps the Component Palette attached to the forms themselves to avoid cluttering the global toolbar.

- Avoid doing any significant amount of work when the IDE is starting up. It will make startup slower (and consume more memory) for all users, whether your module is being used or not. See Appendix D for tips.

- Just because a data object and node of your custom object type are created does not mean the user is about to do anything with them. Such an object may just be sitting in a folder alongside other files the user is really working with. So creating a data object should be fast. Creating a data node should be fast. Querying a data object for standard cookies such as CompilerCookie should be fast.

- Permanent objects of your module, especially data loaders, should avoid doing any expensive work. Imagine that no object of your custom type is present in the IDE at all. How much overhead is your loader going to add to find this out? It should be very marginal.

How does the score module stack up? It adds no globally visible GUI components. It does no work during startup (besides what the IDE does when opening its JAR and installing its XML layer, which is unavoidable). Its MIME resolvers might add a bit of overhead, but the amortized cost is not much since there are usually several MIME resolvers active in the IDE and they can share information such as file headers. The data loader does little work unless it really gets a score file. Settings are not loaded until they are used. The data object adds some cookies when it is created—this could be optimized out using CookieSet.Factory, but most of these cookie implementations are not expensive to create. And as discussed here, the score node will not initiate a parse until it is really important to do so. So it is reasonable for a user who is only occasionally interested in score editing, to leave this module enabled just in case.

Note that icon changes in the node are propagated also to the `ScorePanel` and to the editor component created by `ScoreEditorSupport`. This means that when a score is opened either textually or visually, invalid textual changes will display an error badge in the Editor window's tab, too.

The following two chapters will delve into the Compiler and Execution APIs and show how they can enrich a real module.

CHAPTER 23

Compiling Scores

Until now, the score support has permitted you to write score files and play them directly from the IDE—the score is interpreted on the fly and fed directly to the Java-Sound sound driver. However, there is an obvious drawback to this for people looking to use their scores outside the IDE: there must be an "export format" for the music. A simple solution is to let the user create audio files in a standard audio format from the score. Such audio files can be played with standard player tools, added to web pages, and so on.

To support this from the NetBeans module, we could just make a special action, **Save as Audio**. But in general the user may be doing a number of such transformations as part of her project, and it would be cumbersome for them all to have separate actions with no integrated UI. So NetBeans supports an abstract notion of *compilation*. In the simplest cases, this could mean compiling Java sources to byte-code. But it can also apply to any situation where one set of files is generated mechanically from some source files, under the control of the IDE. The standard UI provides the Compile action that invokes the proper type of compilation on the selected object.

Compile All compiles a whole folder or folders of objects at once. Build (and Build All) forces rebuilds, and Clean (and Clean All) removes generated compilation products. So using the standard API not only simplifies the UI but permits these recursive actions to work with audio file generation, too. Another example of a benefit is using the JAR Packager. Creating a JAR of files is itself considered compilation, and it runs the compilation procedures for all included files first—so a JAR mentioning a score file will automatically create the audio file as needed when the JAR is built.

Creating the Compilers

The first step is to make a set of compilers that can transform score files into audio files. The sources will be gone over in detail, but remember that the Open APIs Support module provides templates that generate the boilerplate code you would need.

There will really be two separate compilers: one generates audio from score files; the other removes generated audio files when cleaning sources. Each kind of compiler has an associated compiler group. While a compiler object typically represents a single file or object to be compiled, a group represents a cluster of similar compilers that can be run together. For example, hundreds of Java sources can be compiled with a single command, if they use the same compiler flags, so there would be hundreds of compiler objects but only one group for all of them. If some of them needed to be compiled with debugging information turned on and others not, there would be two groups. For our example, any number of compilers will always form a single group.

Example 23-1 is the principal compiler, which holds the information about a single score file that should be turned into an audio file.

Example 23-1. Minicomposer: src/org/netbeans/examples/modules/minicomposer/
SampledAudioCompiler.java

```java
public class SampledAudioCompiler extends Compiler {
  private final FileObject scoreFile;
  private final boolean build;
  public SampledAudioCompiler(FileObject scoreFile, boolean build) {
    this.scoreFile = scoreFile;
    this.build = build;
  }
  public boolean equals(Object o) {
    if (o == null || !(o instanceof SampledAudioCompiler)) return false;
    return scoreFile.equals(((SampledAudioCompiler)o).scoreFile) &&
      build == ((SampledAudioCompiler)o).build;
  }
  public int hashCode() {
    return SampledAudioCompiler.class.hashCode() ^
      scoreFile.hashCode() ^
      (build ? 23 : 111);
  }
  public Class compilerGroupClass() {
    return SampledAudioCompilerGroup.class;
  }
  protected boolean isUpToDate() {
    if (build) return false;
    FileObject au = FileUtil.findBrother(scoreFile,
                                  ScoreDataLoader.STANDARD_AU_EXT);
    if (au == null) return false;
    return au.lastModified().after(scoreFile.lastModified());
  }
  public FileObject getScoreFile() {
    return scoreFile;
  }
}
```

The compiler is constructed with a file object representing the *.score* file, which is its primary piece of information. It also permits you to specify a flag build: if true, the compilation will be run unconditionally, but if false, it will be skipped in case some audio file already exists and is at least as new as the score file. Normally, users would run Compile, which will pass `false`, so only new and recently modified score files will have audio generated for them; the rest are assumed to be up-to-date already. If the user is making a "production run" of the scores, however, or just wants to be absolutely sure that everything is correct, he can choose Build, which will pass `true` here and force every audio file to be recreated using current score files.

`isUpToDate()` is the basic method called by the NetBeans compilation system to analyze which compilers really need to be run. First of all, if `build` was set, the compiler always requests that it be run. Otherwise, it looks for an audio file matching the score file (`FileUtil.findBrother()` is a convenience method to look for similarly-named files with different extensions in the same folder). If there is no audio file yet, then the compiler needs to run. If there is an audio file with the right name, it needs to be run only if the modification time on disk of the audio file is older than that of the score.

 Note that we are also adding one line to *ScoreDataLoader.java*, which we use to state the expected file extension of the audio files:

```
public static final String STANDARD_AU_EXT = "au";
```

Sometimes in the course of a complex build, a single object is asked several times to supply a compiler for itself. Of course only one compiler should really be run. So the Compiler API requires that compilers be comparable to one another using `equals()` and `hashCode()`—if several compilers are found to be interchangeable, all but one is discarded. `SampledAudioCompiler` (shown in Example 23-2) implements these methods in a straightforward way according to its fields, `scoreFile` and `build`.

`compilerGroupClass()` tells the Compiler API what kind of group this compiler should belong to. All `SampledAudioCompilers` being compiled at a time will be placed in a single `SampledAudioCompilerGroup`. If we wanted to split them up into several groups, it would be necessary to override the method `compilerGroupKey()`. You can consult the Javadoc for this method for more detail.

`getScoreFile()` is intended for the use of the compiler group, described next, and enables the essential information about the compiler to be used there.

Example 23-2. Minicomposer: src/org/netbeans/examples/modules/minicomposer/
SampledAudioCompilerGroup.java

```
public class SampledAudioCompilerGroup extends CompilerGroup {
  private final Set compilers = new HashSet(); // Set<SampledAudioCompiler>
  public void add(Compiler c) {
    compilers.add((SampledAudioCompiler)c);
  }
  public boolean start() {
    boolean ok = true;
    Iterator it = compilers.iterator();
```

Example 23-2. Minicomposer: src/org/netbeans/examples/modules/minicomposer/
SampledAudioCompilerGroup.java (continued)

```java
    while (it.hasNext()) {
      SampledAudioCompiler c = (SampledAudioCompiler)it.next();
      FileObject score = c.getScoreFile();
      FileObject au = FileUtil.findBrother(score,
                                           ScoreDataLoader.STANDARD_AU_EXT);
      try {
        if (au == null) {
          au = score.getParent().createData(score.getName(),
                                            ScoreDataLoader.STANDARD_AU_EXT);
        }
      } catch (IOException ioe) {
        TopManager.getDefault().getErrorManager().
          notify(ErrorManager.INFORMATIONAL, ioe);
        fireErrorEvent(new ErrorEvent(this, score, 0, 0, ioe.toString(), ""));
        ok = false;
        continue;
      }
      try {
        InputStream is = score.getInputStream();
        try {
          FileLock lock = au.lock();
          try {
            OutputStream os = au.getOutputStream(lock);
            try {
              fireProgressEvent(new ProgressEvent(this, au,
                                                  ProgressEvent.TASK_WRITING));
              LineInFromScore line =
                new LineInFromScore(Score.parse(new InputStreamReader(is)));
              AudioInputStream ais =
                new LineInFromScore.ScoreAudioInputStream(line, 24000.0f);
              AudioSystem.write(ais, AudioFileFormat.Type.AU, os);
            } finally {
              os.close();
            }
          } finally {
            lock.releaseLock();
          }
        } finally {
          is.close();
        }
      } catch (IOException ioe) {
        TopManager.getDefault().getErrorManager().
          notify(ErrorManager.INFORMATIONAL, ioe);
        fireErrorEvent(new ErrorEvent(this, au, 0, 0, ioe.toString(), ""));
        ok = false;
      }
    }
    return ok;
  }
}
```

The compiler group needs to implement two methods. The first, add( ), is trivial. It is simply used to pass in the compilers that should form the group, after the group has been created. (It must have a public default constructor to be created, since the compiler just gives the class.)

start( ) actually runs the compilation and is expected to indicate whether it finished normally or in error. Like many compiler groups, this one just iterates over all of its compilers and does a single action for each. Other groups might collect information from them to form a single command or action, where that is more efficient.

First the *.score* file is retrieved, and then a matching *.au* is either found or created.

If any problems arise during compilation, fireErrorEvent( ) prints a line in the Output Window's Compiler tab alerting the user, with an optional hyperlink to a guilty file—see the Javadoc for the exact options. We also send the details to the IDE's log file using ErrorManager in case further diagnostics are needed.

The audio file is written (or overwritten) using AudioSystem.write( ), a utility method from JavaSound. The audio content is created using LineInFromScore, discussed in Chapter 21. 24000 is the sampling rate for the audio data—later on we will show how to let the user customize this number, but this is a reasonable default for medium-quality audio (in this case in "AU" format, a widespread simple format).

Before starting to write the file, a ProgressEvent is fired from the compiler group, which the compilation engine in the IDE might use to display a brief message in the status line (so the user knows something is happening). Again, if writing the audio file fails, an error is reported to the output window. The compiler group is considered to have succeeded only if every audio file compilation proceeded normally.

For cleaning the disposable audio files and leaving the "pristine source" of the score files, a separate compiler and group are used. In Example 23-3, we make the group an inner class since both are fairly short.

Example 23-3. Minicomposer: src/org/netbeans/examples/modules/minicomposer/
SampledAudioCleaner.java

```java
public class SampledAudioCleaner extends Compiler {
  private FileObject scoreFile;
  public SampledAudioCleaner(FileObject scoreFile) {
    this.scoreFile = scoreFile;
  }
  public boolean equals(Object o) {
    if (o == null || !(o instanceof SampledAudioCleaner)) return false;
    return scoreFile.equals(((SampledAudioCleaner)o).scoreFile);
  }
  public int hashCode() {
    return SampledAudioCleaner.class.hashCode() ^ scoreFile.hashCode();
  }
}
```

```java
  public Class compilerGroupClass() {
    return Group.class;
  }
  protected boolean isUpToDate() {
    return FileUtil.findBrother(scoreFile,
                          ScoreDataLoader.STANDARD_AU_EXT) == null;
  }
  public FileObject getScoreFile() {
    return scoreFile;
  }
  public static class Group extends CompilerGroup {
    private Set compilers = new HashSet(); // Set<SampledAudioCleaner>
    public void add(Compiler c) {
      compilers.add((SampledAudioCleaner)c);
    }
    public boolean start() {
      boolean ok = true;
      Iterator it = compilers.iterator();
      while (it.hasNext()) {
        SampledAudioCleaner c = (SampledAudioCleaner)it.next();
        FileObject fo = c.getScoreFile();
        FileObject toClean = FileUtil.findBrother(fo,
                          ScoreDataLoader.STANDARD_AU_EXT);
        if (toClean != null) {
          try {
            fireProgressEvent(new ProgressEvent(this, toClean,
                                      ProgressEvent.TASK_CLEANING));
            toClean.delete();
          } catch (IOException ioe) {
            TopManager.getDefault().getErrorManager().
              notify(ErrorManager.INFORMATIONAL, ioe);
            fireErrorEvent(new ErrorEvent(this, toClean, 0, 0,
                                      ioe.toString(), ""));
            ok = false;
          }
        }
      }
      return ok;
    }
  }
}
```

The details of this compiler and group are almost the same, with only a few differences. The up-to-date check is reversed in a sense: the clean compiler must be run only if the audio file *does* exist (modification time is irrelevant). The compiler group simply iterates through all the score files, finds any existing audio files corresponding to them, and deletes the audio files.

Creating and Using the Compiler Cookie

In order to actually associate the ability to compile with a data object, the compiler cookie must be implemented and served from the object. There are actually three cookies: one for compiling, one for building, and one for cleaning.

The responsibility of the cookie is to create any compilers that are needed and then add them to the current compiler job. A job is created in response to a user action such as selecting **Compile** and tracks every compiler that must be run, including the set of groups and any mutual dependencies between compilers.

Our compiler cookie implementation is not very complicated, and is shown in Example 23-4.

Example 23-4. Minicomposer: src/org/netbeans/examples/modules/minicomposer/ ScoreCompilerSupport.java

```java
public abstract class ScoreCompilerSupport implements CompilerCookie {
  private final ScoreDataObject obj;
  protected ScoreCompilerSupport(ScoreDataObject obj) {
    this.obj = obj;
  }
  protected FileObject getPrimaryFile() {
    return obj.getPrimaryFile();
  }
  protected boolean saveFirst() {
    if (obj.isModified()) {
      SaveCookie save = (SaveCookie)obj.getCookie(SaveCookie.class);
      if (save != null) {
        try {
          save.save();
        } catch (IOException ioe) {
          TopManager.getDefault().getErrorManager().notify(ioe);
          return false;
        }
      }
    }
    return true;
  }
  public boolean isDepthSupported(Compiler.Depth depth) {
    return depth == Compiler.DEPTH_ONE;
  }
  public abstract void addToJob(CompilerJob job, Compiler.Depth depth);
  public static class Compile extends ScoreCompilerSupport
      implements CompilerCookie.Compile {
    public Compile(ScoreDataObject obj) {
      super(obj);
    }
    public void addToJob(CompilerJob job, Compiler.Depth depth) {
      if (this.saveFirst())
        job.add(new SampledAudioCompiler(getPrimaryFile(), false));
    }
```

```
  }
  public static class Build extends ScoreCompilerSupport
      implements CompilerCookie.Build {
    public Build(ScoreDataObject obj) {
      super(obj);
    }
    public void addToJob(CompilerJob job, Compiler.Depth depth) {
      if (this.saveFirst())
        job.add(new SampledAudioCompiler(getPrimaryFile(), true));
    }
  }
  public static class Clean extends ScoreCompilerSupport
      implements CompilerCookie.Clean {
    public Clean(ScoreDataObject obj) {
      super(obj);
    }
    public void addToJob(CompilerJob job, Compiler.Depth depth) {
      job.add(new SampledAudioCleaner(getPrimaryFile()));
    }
  }
}
```

isDepthSupported( ) is used by the compilation system to distinguish between recursive (folder) compilation and simple (file) compilation; we need not be concerned with it. addToJob( ) does the work; it is given a compiler job that should be added to and a recursion depth, which we will ignore.

Each inner class implements one of the compiler cookie variants. Compile and Build both first check whether the score file needs to be saved; the compilation is done with the file on disk only, so it would be misleading to compile a file with unsaved modifications. Each cookie implementation just creates a single compiler of the appropriate type and adds it to the pool of compilers in the job. More complex compiler supports sometimes create multiple compilers, often specifying cross-dependencies between them as well.

To attach the compiler cookies requires only a small change to the data object (*ScoreDataObject.java*):

```
public ScoreDataObject(FileObject pf, ScoreDataLoader loader)
    throws DataObjectExistsException {
  super(pf, loader);
  CookieSet cookies = getCookieSet();
  cookies.add(new ScoreExec(this));
  EditorCookie ed = new ScoreEditorSupport(this);
  cookies.add(ed);
  cookies.add(new ScoreSupport(this, ed));
  cookies.add(new ScoreOpenSupport(getPrimaryEntry()));
  // Newly added:
  cookies.add(new ScoreCompilerSupport.Compile(this));
```

```
      cookies.add(new ScoreCompilerSupport.Build(this));
      cookies.add(new ScoreCompilerSupport.Clean(this));
   }
```

Two changes need to be made to the data loader to match. First, the Compile and
Build actions should be added to the context menu for score files to remind the user
that they can be compiled. Second, the score loader should recognize *.au* files as secondary entries. If the loader handled only the score files but audio files were generated during compilation, extra nodes with blank icons ▭ for the audio files will
appear in the Explorer and be a distraction.

Here then is the revised loader:

```
public class ScoreDataLoader extends /* new superclass */ MultiFileLoader {
   public static final String SCORE_MIME = "text/x-minicomposer-score";
   public static final String AU_MIME = "audio/basic"; // newly added
   private static final long serialVersionUID = 6424491892249774122L;
   public ScoreDataLoader() {
      super("org.netbeans.examples.modules.minicomposer.ScoreDataObject");
   }
   protected String defaultDisplayName() {
      return NbBundle.getMessage(ScoreDataLoader.class, "LBL_loaderName");
   }
   protected SystemAction[] defaultActions() {
      return new SystemAction[] {
         SystemAction.get(OpenAction.class),
         SystemAction.get(EditAction.class),
         SystemAction.get(FileSystemAction.class),
         null,
         SystemAction.get(CompileAction.class), // newly added
         null,
         SystemAction.get(BuildAction.class), // newly added
         null,
         SystemAction.get(ExecuteAction.class),
         null,
         SystemAction.get(CutAction.class),
         SystemAction.get(CopyAction.class),
         null,
         SystemAction.get(DeleteAction.class),
         SystemAction.get(RenameAction.class),
         null,
         SystemAction.get(SaveAsTemplateAction.class),
         null,
         SystemAction.get(ToolsAction.class),
         SystemAction.get(PropertiesAction.class),
      };
   }
   protected FileObject findPrimaryFile(FileObject fo) { // newly added
      if (fo.getMIMEType().equals(SCORE_MIME)) {
         return fo;
      } else if (fo.getMIMEType().equals(AU_MIME) && !fo.isRoot()) {
         // Find a sibling with the MIME type for scores.
         Enumeration e = fo.getParent().getData(false);
         while (e.hasMoreElements()) {
```

```
        FileObject fo2 = (FileObject)e.nextElement();
        if (fo2.getMIMEType().equals(SCORE_MIME) &&
            fo2.getName().equals(fo.getName())) {
          return fo2;
        }
      }
      // This is an audio file but there is no score file to match.
      return null;
    } else {
      // Unrelated file.
      return null;
    }
  }
  protected MultiDataObject createMultiObject(FileObject primaryFile)
      throws DataObjectExistsException, IOException {
    return new ScoreDataObject(primaryFile, this);
  }
  protected MultiDataObject.Entry createPrimaryEntry(
      MultiDataObject obj, FileObject primaryFile) { // newly added
    return new FileEntry(obj, primaryFile);
  }
  protected MultiDataObject.Entry createSecondaryEntry(
      MultiDataObject obj, FileObject secondaryFile) { // newly added
    secondaryFile.setImportant(false);
    return new FileEntry.Numb(obj, secondaryFile);
  }
}
```

The main difference from the previous version of the loader is that it is now a
MultiFileLoader. There is no more extension list; the recognition logic must be done
explicitly. findPrimaryFile() is responsible for grouping files and specifying the primary files for the groups. Score files (SCORE_MIME) are always considered primary files,
while audio files (AU_MIME) are not. If a folder containing a score file also contains an
audio file whose name is the same as that of the score file, they are considered to
form a data object together; the score file is returned when the audio file is tested by
findPrimaryFile().

MultiFileLoader also permits and requires extra control over creation of the file
entries. createPrimaryEntry() is passed a ScoreDataObject and its primary score file.
It creates a FileEntry as the entry, which tells the data object to consider this file pre-
cious during significant operations: copy the score file when the score data object is
copied, rename it during a rename, and so on. createSecondaryEntry() is passed an
audio file. The implementation first marks the file unimportant on the filesystem; a
version-control filesystem might use this information to skip creation of backups or
guess that the file should not be committed to a repository. The file entry it makes,
FileEntry.Numb, indicates that the audio file is disposable; for example, when copying the score object, just delete the audio file. It can easily be re-created later.

To support the new AU_MIME requires a modification to the declarative MIME resolver
too. Edit your *mime-resolver.xml* to match Example 23-5.

Example 23-5. Minicomposer: mime-resolver.xml with compiler support

```
<!DOCTYPE MIME-resolver PUBLIC
        "-//NetBeans//DTD MIME Resolver 1.0//EN"
        "http://www.netbeans.org/dtds/mime-resolver-1_0.dtd">
<MIME-resolver>
  <file>
    <ext name="score"/>
    <resolver mime="text/x-minicomposer-score"/>
  </file>
  <file> <!-- newly added -->
    <!-- Either one of these: -->
    <ext name="au"/>
    <!-- ASCII: ".snd" -->
    <magic hex="2E736E64"/>
    <resolver mime="audio/basic"/>
  </file>
</MIME-resolver>
```

The added clause sets the MIME type audio/basic for any files ending in the *.au* extension, as well as any files beginning with the bytes *.snd* (which conventionally marks simple audio files, regardless of their names).

Displaying an Out-of-Date Badge on Score Icons

Since compiling a score can now result in the creation of an additional audio file, but these audio files are "hidden" inside the same ScoreDataNode as the score files, it is desirable to give the user a hint as to whether the audio files are there. More precisely, what is most likely to be of interest to a user is whether the score is *up to date*—whether an audio file both exists and was generated from the current score.

There is a standard GUI for this type of information in the IDE—the *out-of-date badge*. When the audio file is missing or too old, the Explorer will display this icon: ⌗▥

To do this requires some changes to the data node:

```
public class ScoreDataNode extends DataNode
    implements ChangeListener, PropertyChangeListener, FileChangeListener {
                    // ^  note new interfaces  ^
    // inUse as before
    // added field:
    private final Set listenedFiles = Collections.synchronizedSet(new WeakSet());
    public ScoreDataNode(ScoreDataObject obj) {
        // ...as before but also:
        obj.addPropertyChangeListener(WeakListener.propertyChange(this, obj));
        updateFileListeners();
    }
    public Image getIcon(int type) {
        // ...load base image as before, maybe add error badge, then:
        DataObject obj = getDataObject();
```

```
    if (obj.isModified() || outOfDate(obj)) {
      Image badge = Utilities.loadImage(
        "org/netbeans/examples/modules/minicomposer/out-of-date-badge.gif");
      icon = Utilities.mergeImages(icon, badge, 16, 0);
    }
    // annotate by filesystem as before and return...
  }
  // getOpenedIcon as before...
  // added methods:
  private static boolean outOfDate(DataObject obj) {
    CompilerCookie.Compile cookie =
      (CompilerCookie.Compile)obj.getCookie(CompilerCookie.Compile.class);
    if (cookie == null) return true;
    CompilerJob job = new CompilerJob(Compiler.DEPTH_ZERO);
    cookie.addToJob(job, Compiler.DEPTH_ZERO);
    return !job.isUpToDate();
  }
  public void propertyChange(PropertyChangeEvent ev) {
    String prop = ev.getPropertyName();
    if (prop == null ||
        prop.equals(DataObject.PROP_FILES) ||
        prop.equals(DataObject.PROP_MODIFIED)) {
      updateFileListeners();
      fireIconChange();
    }
  }
  private void updateFileListeners() {
    Iterator it = getDataObject().files().iterator();
    while (it.hasNext()) {
      FileObject fo = (FileObject)it.next();
      if (listenedFiles.add(fo)) {
        fo.addFileChangeListener(WeakListener.fileChange(this, fo));
      }
    }
  }
  public void fileRenamed(FileRenameEvent fe) {
    fireIconChange();
  }
  public void fileChanged(FileEvent fe) {
    fireIconChange();
  }
  public void fileDeleted(FileEvent fe) {
    fireIconChange();
  }
  public void fileAttributeChanged(FileAttributeEvent fe) {
  }
  public void fileFolderCreated(FileEvent fe) {
  }
  public void fileDataCreated(FileEvent fe) {
  }
}
```

First, getIcon() is enhanced to check for out-of-date status. If the score is modified in memory, certainly the audio file cannot be up to date (compilation always saves to disk first). If it is not modified, method outOfDate() probes the compiler for the audio file status. While we could have directly tested FileObject presence and time-stamps here, it is more modular to delegate this to the compiler that already knows how to do this well (and will permit us to plug in different compilers later with no modifications to ScoreDataNode). The compiler cookie is gotten from the data object, a new compiler job is created and prepared with that compiler cookie (which will add our SampledAudioCompiler to the job), and the job is tested for up-to-date status (which will just delegate to the one compiler in it).

If the score should be considered out of date, an out-of-date badge is loaded and overlaid on the base icon. It is an 8 × 8 GIF and is added to the upper extended quadrant of the icon, forming a 24 × 16 GIF. The NetBeans Explorer reserves space for 24 × 16 icons since many objects add an annotation to this extra 8 × 16 badge area; version-control filesystems often use the lower extended quadrant (the Net-Beans UI web site (*http://ui.netbeans.org/docs/badging/badging.html*) has a badging document which explains more).

Note that error and out-of-date badges can coexist, like this: 拷

Using Utilities.mergeImages() makes this easy; there is no need to construct every possible combination of badges in an icon editor.

The new badge needs to reflect the current state of the object, too. In the node constructor, we attach a listener to the data object. If PROP_MODIFIED is fired, then getIcon() will behave differently, so we fire an icon change. Similarly, if PROP_FILES is fired, this means the set of files in the data object changed—probably an audio file being added or removed—so again fire an icon change in case this affects the out-of-date badge.

The up-to-date status is also affected by the timestamp of the score and audio files. We should listen to changes in this, too; saving a modified score should mark it as out of date, but recompiling it should mark it up to date again. So the constructor calls updateFileListeners() to listen to changes in each file object (by being a FileListener). Renames and deletions of files are significant, as are changes of content (which affect timestamp). In addition, PROP_FILES might indicate a new secondary audio file, so we need to begin listening to that as well. The set of listenedFiles ensures that the listener is never added twice to the same file object.

If an IDE is defined by the edit-compile-run cycle, we have covered only two-thirds of its basic abilities. The next chapter will show how NetBeans helps a user configure how objects are run.

## CHAPTER 24

Executing Scores

In Chapter 21, we explored how to support execution of scores in a simple fashion: by directly interpreting the textual stream of the score using the Score class and converting it to a JavaSound audio stream to be played immediately.

However, since then we have added the ability to compile scores into standard audio files. These could be played instead of the score file itself. One way of playing these audio files is similar to what we did before: the audio file can be opened as a byte stream by the IDE when Execute is selected by the user, and this stream fed to a sound channel to be played.

There is another possibility. Most operating systems that support sound output include some kind of player that can play sound files when run as a command. The common AU format that our compiler produces is generally understood by such players. For example, on Windows 2000, the *mplayer2.exe* command can be passed an audio file; on many Linux systems, play does the same.

Which kind of player a user should use—*internal*, using JavaSound, or *external*, using an operating-system-dependent executable—is the user's choice. Some platforms may have good JavaSound support but no installed executable player. Others may have a great player with looping and pause support and a graphic equalizer, and JavaSound may not provide the best option (even if the score support module were to implement such features). So this chapter will demonstrate how to let the user decide, in general as well as for specific scores, exactly how to play sound files.

The NetBeans APIs have a general system whereby modules may define *service types*, which are Java classes that implement some general interface providing a kind of service to the system and that may be installed, configured, ordered, selected, and persisted. In the case of execution, the standard service type interface is Executor, an abstract class in the Execution API. We will define two such executors. The actual ExecCookie will not play the audio file, but will instead find the executor selected by the user and delegate work to it.

Creating the .au Player Executor

Here we will define two subclasses of Executor in turn. The implementations will look quite different, as the NetBeans Execution API has direct support for making external execution convenient, while internal execution is more free-form.

The Internal Player

To make an internal audio file player, we will directly extend Executor, as shown in Example 24-1.

Example 24-1. Minicomposer: src/org/netbeans/examples/modules/minicomposer/
InternalPlayer.java

```
public class InternalPlayer extends Executor {
  public ExecutorTask execute(DataObject obj) throws IOException {
    if (!(obj instanceof ScoreDataObject)) {
      IOException ioe = new IOException("Wrong type: " + obj);
      TopManager.getDefault().getErrorManager().annotate(ioe,
        NbBundle.getMessage(InternalPlayer.class, "EXC_wrong_type",
                            obj.getLoader().getDisplayName()));
      throw ioe;
    }
    FileObject fo = ScoreDataLoader.findAudioFile((ScoreDataObject)obj);
    if (fo == null) // throw another IOException with localized message...
    final File f = FileUtil.toFile(fo);
    if (f == null) // throw yet another IOException...
    class Job implements Runnable {
      public void run() {
        try {
          AudioInputStream ais = AudioSystem.getAudioInputStream(f);
          AudioFormat format = ais.getFormat();
          DataLine.Info dlinfo = new DataLine.Info(Clip.class, ais.getFormat());
          Clip clip = (Clip)AudioSystem.getLine(dlinfo);
          clip.open(ais);
          clip.start();
          try {
            while (clip.isActive()) {
              Thread.sleep(1000);
            }
          } catch (InterruptedException ie) {
            // ignore - job stopped
          }
          clip.stop();
          clip.close();
        } catch (Exception e) {
          // Will appear in Output Window.
          e.printStackTrace();
        }
      }
    }
    return TopManager.getDefault().getExecutionEngine().execute(
```

```
      NbBundle.getMessage(ScoreExecSupport.class, "LBL_audio_play_process"),
      new Job(), null);
  }
  private static final long serialVersionUID = -3129235161777547136L;
  public ExecutorTask execute(ExecInfo info) throws IOException {
    throw new IllegalStateException("not called");
  }
  public HelpCtx getHelpCtx() {
    return new HelpCtx("org.netbeans.examples.modules.minicomposer");
  }
}
```

The worker method is execute(DataObject). This is given an object to execute in
some fashion and is expected to provide a task it has started, which permits clients to
listen to completion of the task asynchronously and query its status.

The first steps involve sanity-checking of the data object argument. If something
other than a score object was passed in, this is a user error; the user may have inad-
vertently associated the internal player with a Java source file, for example. So an
IOException is thrown. It is made more pleasant, however, with a localized annotation. This is a bit of friendly and localizable text that gives the exception meaning to
the user, ideally explaining how the problem could be corrected. In this case the bundle file reads as follows:

```
# {0} - display name of type of strange object
EXC_wrong_type=Cannot "play" an object of type {0} as a sound file
```

The comment is a hint for future translators when constructing alternate wordings.
When ErrorManager (which is discussed in more detail in Chapter 27) is asked to add
a localized annotation to an exception, it remembers that phrase; later when the
exception is actually notified again using ErrorManager (in this case by ExecSupport,
which is calling the executor), a polite dialog box is displayed to the user giving the
localized message and prompting him to select an alternate executor.

In the same fashion, the executor looks for the audio file within the score support.
This is handled by a utility method we will add to the ScoreDataLoader class:

```
public static FileObject findAudioFile(ScoreDataObject obj) {
  Set seconds = obj.secondaryEntries(); // Set<MultiDataObject.Entry>
  if (seconds.isEmpty()) return null;
  MultiDataObject.Entry entry =
    (MultiDataObject.Entry)seconds.iterator().next();
  return entry.getFile();
}
```

If the audio file is not found, another exception is thrown with a different localized
message (not shown for brevity). This might happen if the user turned off **Run Compilation** in **Execution Settings** and the score file was not compiled at all.

We also try to find the disk file represented by the score. Recall that a FileObject might be an entry in a JAR, or even something more exotic like a file on a remote FTP server. We can get input streams from any file object, but some uses of Java-Sound require a stream from a file on disk, with a known length and seekable. So we explicitly prevent non-local audio files from being played. FileUtil.toFile() translates a file object to a disk file if it can, otherwise returning null—in which case we throw our third localized exception.

The Job local class actually plays the audio file now given by f. The details are vanilla JavaSound. To run the job and produce a task representing its status and completion, we use the system's execution engine as specified in the Execution API. This is a singleton service provided by the IDE that manages concurrent execution of processes. The NetBeans standard implementation can run jobs in private thread groups for maximum isolation, optionally displays a list of running processes in the Execution window, and supports terminating runaway processes by the user (in this same window).

We give the execution engine three parameters when starting the job. First, a display name for the process that will be run; since it is not null, the process will be displayed in the Execution window. Second, the runnable job itself. The third parameter is optional and is an InputOutput, or a handle to a tab in the Output Window; by default a fresh tab is created, labeled according to the supplied display name.

You can suppress any output if you want; here we permit the tab to appear. If some problem arises while playing the file and an exception is thrown—this can happen if JavaSound is incorrectly configured and cannot find a sound driver, for example—it is caught in Job.run() and printed to standard error. The execution engine automatically reroutes uses of standard I/O streams occurring within jobs it is executing, binding them to the Output Window. Otherwise, such messages would appear on the IDE's own console (or log file). It also traps calls to System.exit() and terminates the executed process rather than the whole IDE, though that does not concern us here.

Finally some miscellanea: The line defining serialVersionUID indicates our willingness to retain compatibility of serialized InternalPlayers across releases of the module. execute(ExecInfo) is an older method in Execute more suited to executing Java classes than arbitrary objects. So long as the newer execute(DataObject) is overridden, it will not be called by the system. getHelpCtx() is used to associate JavaHelp with the executor; help contexts will be discussed later in Chapter 27.

In addition to the player, it is usual to provide a BeanInfo. In general, services can be customized by the user—this one cannot, but it will be displayed alongside others that can. The BeanInfo can control the display name, tool tip, icon, help associations of the service, and more importantly properties and graphical customizers. This class is shown in Example 24-2.

Example 24-2. Minicomposer: src/org/netbeans/examples/modules/minicomposer/InternalPlayerBeanInfo.java

```java
public class InternalPlayerBeanInfo extends SimpleBeanInfo {
  public BeanInfo[] getAdditionalBeanInfo() {
    try {
      return new BeanInfo[] {Introspector.getBeanInfo(Executor.class)};
    } catch (IntrospectionException ie) {
      TopManager.getDefault().getErrorManager().notify(ie);
      return null;
    }
  }
  public BeanDescriptor getBeanDescriptor() {
    BeanDescriptor desc = new BeanDescriptor(InternalPlayer.class);
    desc.setDisplayName(NbBundle.getMessage(InternalPlayerBeanInfo.class,
                                    "LBL_InternalPlayer"));
    desc.setShortDescription(NbBundle.getMessage(InternalPlayerBeanInfo.class,
                                    "HINT_InternalPlayer"));
    return desc;
  }
  public Image getIcon(int type) {
    if (type == BeanInfo.ICON_COLOR_16x16 || type == BeanInfo.ICON_MONO_16x16) {
      return Utilities.loadImage(
        "org/netbeans/examples/modules/minicomposer/InternalPlayerIcon.gif");
    } else {
      return null;
    }
  }
}
```

We first explicitly inherit any info provided by the superclass, Executor; Executor has no interesting properties so this means just the Identifying Name property permitting the user to rename services. The bean descriptor can set a display name and tool tip for the service—though as we will see shortly, the XML layer provides a quicker way of specifying this information, which does not require the InternalPlayerBeanInfo to be loaded in many cases. getIcon() provides a 16 × 16 icon for the service: ◀

Recall that Utilities.loadImage() loads images from module JARs and does caching.

The External Player

The external player will be implemented differently. Extending the convenience base class ProcessExecutor (as shown in Example 24-3), the player will not directly handle the running of the process. Direct manipulation of external processes can become rather complicated: creating a customizable command line, launching it using Java's execution APIs, proxying I/O streams, and controlling termination. By extending ProcessExecutor, we can instead just supply a template for the command line to run, and the rest is automatic. The user can then edit this command line if necessary.

Example 24-3. Minicomposer: src/org/netbeans/examples/modules/minicomposer/
ExternalPlayer.java

```java
public class ExternalPlayer extends ProcessExecutor {
  private static final NbProcessDescriptor DEFAULT = new NbProcessDescriptor(
    Utilities.isWindows() ?
      "\"C:\\Program Files\\Windows Media Player\\mplayer2.exe\"" :
      "play",
    (Utilities.isWindows() ? "/Play " : "") +
      "{" + MyFormat.TAG_AUFILE + "}",
    NbBundle.getMessage(ExternalPlayer.class, "MSG_format_hint")
  );
  public ExternalPlayer() {
    setExternalExecutor(DEFAULT);
  }
  protected Process createProcess(DataObject obj) throws IOException {
    if (!(obj instanceof ScoreDataObject)) {
      // throw localized IOException as before...
    }
    FileObject fo = ScoreDataLoader.findAudioFile((ScoreDataObject)obj);
    if (fo == null) // again as before...
    final File f = FileUtil.toFile(fo);
    if (f == null) // once again as before...
    return getExternalExecutor().exec(new MyFormat(f));
  }
  private static final long serialVersionUID = -4397529002559509129L;
  protected Process createProcess(ExecInfo info) throws IOException {
    throw new IllegalStateException("Should not be called");
  }
  public HelpCtx getHelpCtx() {
    return new HelpCtx("org.netbeans.examples.modules.minicomposer");
  }
  private static class MyFormat extends MapFormat {
    static final String TAG_AUFILE = "aufile";
    private static final long serialVersionUID = 6980703950237286310L;
    MyFormat(File aufile) {
      super(new HashMap(1));
      getMap().put(TAG_AUFILE, aufile.getAbsolutePath());
    }
  }
}
```

Our first job is to specify the default command line that will be run to play the audio file. NbProcessDescriptor is a data structure holding the name of an executable program (file), as well as a string containing its arguments, and a legend for substitutions that can be made. The constructor sets this process descriptor as the default initial value for the executor.

The first parameter we pass when creating the DEFAULT descriptor is the executable. Here we test for the Windows operating system, and if so, use mplayer2.exe; otherwise, play is used, a common command on Linux. Of course this list of defaults could be expanded to cover more operating systems, though the user can always correct a bad guess.

The next parameter is the list of arguments. Actually, they are all given as a single string, as if ready to pass into a command shell such as the Unix Bourne shell (NbProcessDescriptor is responsible for handling platform-specific quoting conventions). mplayer2.exe requires a /Play switch; otherwise, we can just pass the file name. Rather than hard-code the audio filename here, we use the key {aufile} that will be substituted at runtime (more on this in a moment).

The legend for the process descriptor is displayed to the user when editing command lines based on it in a customizer dialog box. Normally this provides an explanation of any keys that may be used in the command line. Thus our bundle file contains

```
MSG_format_hint={aufile} = full path to AU file to play
```

createProcess(DataObject) is called when executing the object, to provide a Java handle for an external process. As with the internal player, createProcess(ExecInfo) is only used if you do not override this method. Again we start by doing some sanity checking on the input and throw localized IOExceptions if there is anything wrong, to help the user correct the problem. The actual creation of the external process is done by the exec() method on the configured process descriptor.

exec() normally takes a format for substituting keys in the process descriptor. It can also take a working directory and several other parameters covered in the Javadoc. This format is a general Java text format; it is applied to both the process name and arguments and is expected to result in the final command line. When applied to NbProcessDescriptors, the normal format to use is a MapFormat (a utility class in org.openide.util). MapFormat permits flexible substitution of named keys via a translation map. Our subclass MyFormat defines just one key, TAG_AUFILE, expected to map to the absolute path of the audio file. When such a format is made, the file path is specified by the executor and added to its (otherwise empty) map.

Again we provide a BeanInfo describing the executor; see Example 24-4.

Example 24-4. Minicomposer: src/org/netbeans/examples/modules/minicomposer/
ExternalPlayerBeanInfo.java

```java
public class ExternalPlayerBeanInfo extends SimpleBeanInfo {
  public BeanInfo[] getAdditionalBeanInfo() {
    try {
      return new BeanInfo[] {Introspector.getBeanInfo(ProcessExecutor.class)};
    } catch (IntrospectionException ie) {
      TopManager.getDefault().getErrorManager().notify(ie);
      return null;
    }
  }
  public BeanDescriptor getBeanDescriptor() {
    BeanDescriptor desc = new BeanDescriptor(ExternalPlayer.class);
```

```java
      desc.setDisplayName(NbBundle.getMessage(ExternalPlayerBeanInfo.class,
                                     "LBL_ExternalPlayer"));
      desc.setShortDescription(NbBundle.getMessage(ExternalPlayerBeanInfo.class,
                                     "HINT_ExternalPlayer"));
      return desc;
    }
    public PropertyDescriptor[] getPropertyDescriptors() {
      try {
        PropertyDescriptor classPath =
          new PropertyDescriptor("classPath", ProcessExecutor.class);
        classPath.setHidden(true);
        PropertyDescriptor bootClassPath =
          new PropertyDescriptor("bootClassPath", ProcessExecutor.class);
        bootClassPath.setHidden(true);
        PropertyDescriptor repositoryPath =
          new PropertyDescriptor("repositoryPath", ProcessExecutor.class,
                              "getRepositoryPath", null);
        repositoryPath.setHidden(true);
        PropertyDescriptor libraryPath =
          new PropertyDescriptor("libraryPath", ProcessExecutor.class,
                              "getLibraryPath", null);
        libraryPath.setHidden(true);
        PropertyDescriptor environmentVariables =
          new PropertyDescriptor("environmentVariables", ProcessExecutor.class);
        environmentVariables.setHidden(true);
        PropertyDescriptor workingDirectory =
          new PropertyDescriptor("workingDirectory", ProcessExecutor.class);
        workingDirectory.setHidden(true);
        PropertyDescriptor appendEnvironmentVariables =
          new PropertyDescriptor("appendEnvironmentVariables",
                              ProcessExecutor.class);
        appendEnvironmentVariables.setHidden(true);
        return new PropertyDescriptor[] {
          classPath, bootClassPath, repositoryPath, libraryPath,
          environmentVariables, workingDirectory, appendEnvironmentVariables
        };
      } catch (IntrospectionException ie) {
        TopManager.getDefault().getErrorManager().notify(ie);
        return null;
      }
    }
    public Image getIcon(int type) {
      if (type == BeanInfo.ICON_COLOR_16x16 || type == BeanInfo.ICON_MONO_16x16) {
        return Utilities.loadImage(
          "org/netbeans/examples/modules/minicomposer/ExternalPlayerIcon.gif");
      } else {
        return null;
      }
    }
  }
}
```

The additional bean info, bean descriptor, and icon are similar to the internal player's bean info. For the property descriptors, we need do a little more work—the ProcessExecutor superclass, which was originally designed with a Java IDE in mind, includes a number of parameters, such as classpath, that make sense only for Java execution and that we wish to suppress, as well as a few more general parameters such as working directory that we also do not have any use for. PropertyDescriptor. setHidden() is used to ensure that these properties do not appear to the user. We leave untouched the inherited externalExecutor property that *should* appear. An alternate approach would be to specify no inherited bean info and just provide the externalExecutor property and the name property inherited from ServiceType.

Registering the Players as Services

Now that the audio players have been created, they need to be registered so that the IDE can find them when requested. An older method of registration involves simply listing them in the module manifest. This is easy to do. However, it is also inefficient during startup of the IDE—every such service needs to be loaded into memory, including its BeanInfo, typically also loading a network of related classes, which contributes to bloating of the virtual machine with possibly unused classes and objects. Instead, we register XML files into the module's XML layer indicating the presence of such services and let them be loaded if and when they are needed. Make the following changes to your *layer.xml* document:

```
<folder name="Services">
  <folder name="Executor">
    <folder name="org-netbeans-examples-modules-minicomposer">
      <attr name="SystemFileSystem.localizingBundle"
            stringvalue="org.netbeans.examples.modules.minicomposer.Bundle"/>
      <attr name="SystemFileSystem.icon" urlvalue=
      "nbresloc:/org/netbeans/examples/modules/minicomposer/ScoreDataIcon.gif"/>
      <file name="internal-player.settings" url="internal-player.xml">
        <attr name="SystemFileSystem.localizingBundle"
              stringvalue="org.netbeans.examples.modules.minicomposer.Bundle"/>
        <attr name="SystemFileSystem.icon" urlvalue=
  "nbresloc:/org/netbeans/examples/modules/minicomposer/InternalPlayerIcon.gif"/>
        <attr name="SystemFileSystem.layer" stringvalue="project"/>
      </file>
      <file name="external-player.settings" url="external-player.xml">
        <attr name="SystemFileSystem.localizingBundle"
              stringvalue="org.netbeans.examples.modules.minicomposer.Bundle"/>
        <attr name="SystemFileSystem.icon" urlvalue=
  "nbresloc:/org/netbeans/examples/modules/minicomposer/ExternalPlayerIcon.gif"/>
        <attr name="SystemFileSystem.layer" stringvalue="project"/>
      </file>
    </folder>
  </folder>
</folder>
<folder name="Templates">
  <folder name="Services">
```

```
    <folder name="Executor">
      <folder name="org-netbeans-examples-modules-minicomposer">
        <attr name="SystemFileSystem.localizingBundle"
              stringvalue="org.netbeans.examples.modules.minicomposer.Bundle"/>
        <attr name="SystemFileSystem.icon" urlvalue=
     "nbresloc:/org/netbeans/examples/modules/minicomposer/ScoreDataIcon.gif"/>
        <file name="external-player.settings" url="external-player.xml">
          <attr name="SystemFileSystem.localizingBundle"
                stringvalue="org.netbeans.examples.modules.minicomposer.Bundle"/>
          <attr name="SystemFileSystem.icon" urlvalue=
     "nbresloc:/org/netbeans/examples/modules/minicomposer/ExternalPlayerIcon.gif"/>
          <attr name="template" boolvalue="true"/>
        </file>
      </folder>
    </folder>
  </folder>
</folder>
```

You also need to add these lines to your *Bundle.properties* file:

```
Templates/Services/Executor/org-netbeans-examples-modules-minicomposer=\
    Audio Players
Templates/Services/Executor/org-netbeans-examples-modules-minicomposer/\
    external-player.settings=External AU Player
Services/Executor/org-netbeans-examples-modules-minicomposer=\
    Audio Players
Services/Executor/org-netbeans-examples-modules-minicomposer/\
    external-player.settings=External AU Player
Services/Executor/org-netbeans-examples-modules-minicomposer/\
    internal-player.settings=Internal AU Player
```

Now create XML documents for the internal and external players. *internal-player.xml* is shown in Example 24-5, and *external-player.xml* is shown in Example 24-6.

Example 24-5. Minicomposer: src/org/netbeans/examples/modules/minicomposer/internal-player.xml

```
<!DOCTYPE settings PUBLIC
        "-//NetBeans//DTD Session settings 1.0//EN"
        "http://www.netbeans.org/dtds/sessionsettings-1_0.dtd">
<settings version="1.0">
  <module name="org.netbeans.examples.modules.minicomposer"/>
  <instanceof class="org.openide.execution.Executor"/>
  <instanceof
    class="org.netbeans.examples.modules.minicomposer.InternalPlayer"/>
  <instance class="org.netbeans.examples.modules.minicomposer.InternalPlayer"/>
</settings>
```

Example 24-6. Minicomposer: src/org/netbeans/examples/modules/minicomposer/external-player.xml

```
<!DOCTYPE settings PUBLIC
        "-//NetBeans//DTD Session settings 1.0//EN"
        "http://www.netbeans.org/dtds/sessionsettings-1_0.dtd">
```

Example 24-6. Minicomposer: src/org/netbeans/examples/modules/minicomposer/
external-player.xml (continued)

```
<settings version="1.0">
  <module name="org.netbeans.examples.modules.minicomposer"/>
  <instanceof class="org.openide.execution.Executor"/>
  <instanceof
    class="org.netbeans.examples.modules.minicomposer.ExternalPlayer"/>
  <instance class="org.netbeans.examples.modules.minicomposer.ExternalPlayer"/>
</settings>
```

First, we need to register the players as services. While they could in principle be placed anywhere in the *Services/* folder and be found, in order to appear in the UI of the **Options** window, they should be placed beneath *Services/Executor/* alongside other executors. In fact, we created a subfolder *org-netbeans-examples-modules-minicomposer* to hold the players, to better group them in the UI.

Each service is represented by one *.settings* file, a simple XML format that declares the class of the service, as well as its important superclasses (or interfaces).

Here we name the physical sources that will be put in the module JAR *.xml* since the contents are in an XML format and common source editors will recognize that extension and treat the file as XML. Nonetheless, the virtual file in the system filesystem must be named *.settings*, wherever the contents come from. Thus we have layer entries such as

```
<file name="external-player.settings" url="external-player.
xml">...</file>
```

Anyone asking the Lookup API for an Executor will be offered both services. Anyone asking for an ExternalPlayer will be offered the external player only (Lookup was discussed in Chapter 17). User customizations to the service will be written out in the same *.settings* file, but on disk in the user directory. The module element ensures that settings are uninstalled cleanly with the module, even if there is a modified *.settings* file on disk.

The addition of SystemFileSystem.localizingBundle and SystemFileSystem.icon control the display name and icon of the subfolder and services. If you use manifest-based registration, these are automatic for the services, because the BeanInfo is loaded; we wish to avoid that, so these are specified as attributes of the settings XML files. Thus the services can be pleasantly displayed without even loading the classes involved, until the Properties window needs to display per-service properties.

We also add some entries under *Templates/Services/* in a folder structure mirroring that under *Services/*. This causes the external player to be listed as a template that the user can construct more of. Perhaps the operating system has several audio players which are usable: by creating additional external player services from a template, it is possible for the user to make a service for each such program, and switch between them quickly. We make no template for the internal player, because it has no user-configurable properties, so there is no purpose in having more than one instance of it.

Figure 24-1 is the result when the user opens the Options window looking for players.

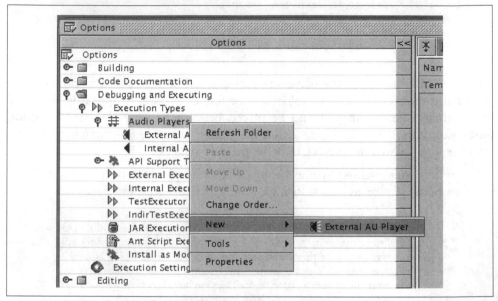

Figure 24-1. Minicomposer: audio players in Options window

Creating Player Configuration Support

It is fairly straightforward to replace the original fixed ExecCookie implementation with a switchable executor, as shown in Example 24-7. org.openide.loaders.ExecSupport provides a standardized way of binding a user-configurable execution service to a data object. It also handles debugger types as an implementation of DebuggerCookie, though we will not use this ability, and the very similar CompilerSupport provides a switchable implementation of the CompilerCookie subinterfaces.

Example 24-7. Minicomposer: src/org/netbeans/examples/modules/minicomposer/
ScoreExecSupport.java

```
public class ScoreExecSupport extends ExecSupport {
  public ScoreExecSupport(MultiDataObject.Entry entry) {
    super(entry);
  }
  protected Executor defaultExecutor() {
    return ComposerSettings.getDefault().getPlayer();
  }
}
```

You then need to add the following lines to your `ScoreDataObject`'s constructor:

```java
public ScoreDataObject(FileObject pf, ScoreDataLoader loader)
    throws DataObjectExistsException {
  super(pf, loader);
  CookieSet cookies = getCookieSet();
  EditorCookie ed = new ScoreEditorSupport(this);
  cookies.add(ed);
  cookies.add(new ScoreSupport(this, ed));
  cookies.add(new ScoreOpenSupport(getPrimaryEntry()));
  cookies.add(new ScoreCompilerSupport.Compile(this));
  cookies.add(new ScoreCompilerSupport.Build(this));
  cookies.add(new ScoreCompilerSupport.Clean(this));
  // ScoreExec replaced by:
  cookies.add(new ScoreExecSupport(getPrimaryEntry()));
}
```

The `ScoreExecSupport` is a simple subclass of the base class, which is initialized via the primary entry from the object (a representation of the *.score* file, in this case). All it must do is override `defaultExecutor()` to provide a default for the score's player where none has been explicitly configured by the user.

Using the `ExecSupport` class only guarantees that an `ExecCookie` will be available on the data object and that it will look for an explicit choice of executor (player). It does this lookup based on a file attribute of the data object's primary file: `NetBeansAttrExecutor`, which should be set to a `ServiceType.Handle`, a lightweight serializable handle for services that stores the *identifying name* (usually display name) and class of the service. Actually providing a UI for the user to configure the executor requires a second step, in `ScoreDataNode`:

```java
protected Sheet createSheet() {
  Sheet sheet = super.createSheet();
  ExecSupport support = (ExecSupport)getCookie(ExecSupport.class);
  Sheet.Set set = new Sheet.Set();
  set.setName("execution");
  set.setDisplayName(NbBundle.getMessage(ScoreDataNode.class,
                          "LBL_Execution"));
  set.setShortDescription(NbBundle.getMessage(ScoreDataNode.class,
                          "HINT_Execution"));
  support.addProperties(set);
  set.remove(ExecSupport.PROP_DEBUGGER_TYPE);
  set.remove(ExecSupport.PROP_FILE_PARAMS);
  sheet.put(set);
  return sheet;
}
```

We create an additional tab in the property sheet for score data nodes, labeled Execution, and use `ExecSupport.addProperties()` to include several properties in it that the support knows how to bind to the primary file using attributes. In fact `addProperties()` includes more properties than we need—Debugger and Arguments— so we simply remove the extraneous ones, as there is no expectation of a score being "debuggable" nor requiring additional per-score arguments to be played.

Figure 24-2 is a score file showing the ability to change its player, and Figure 24-3 is the custom Property Editor that permits detailed configuration, including selection of the process itself (in Figure 24-4).

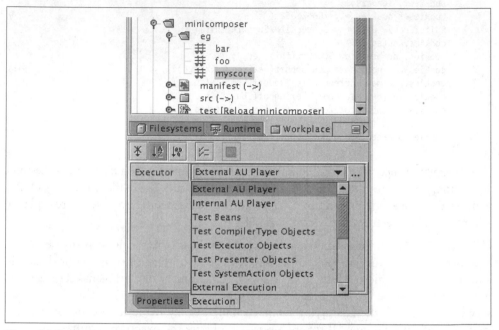

Figure 24-2. Minicomposer: choosing to use an external audio player

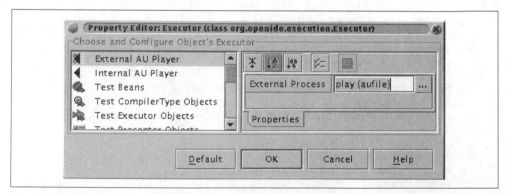

Figure 24-3. Minicomposer: configuring an external audio player

Creating a SystemOption for the Default Executor

In the previous section, we saw how to permit the user to select a player for a particular score. More commonly, a user will select a certain player as the default for *all*

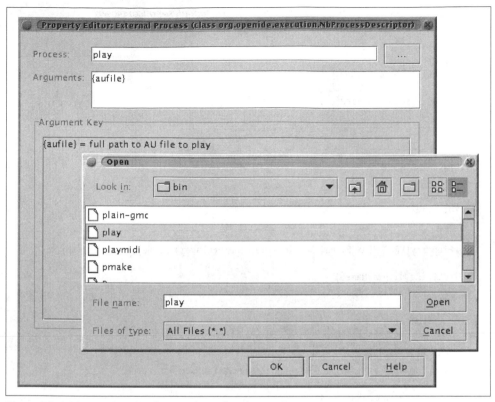

Figure 24-4. Minicomposer: selecting the audio player process

score files. The ScoreExecSupport can supply a default player where none is explicitly given, that is, where the primary *.score file has no NetBeansAttrExecutor file attribute. Now we need a GUI for the user to select this default and persist that choice.

This can be done using a *system option* (see Example 24-8), the standard means in the NetBeans APIs of storing a single property or cluster of them and providing a matching GUI. While we are making an option with a default player property, we will also introduce an additional property for the sample rate to use when compiling scores to audio files—this was previously hard-coded in Chapter 23.

Example 24-8. Minicomposer: src/org/netbeans/examples/modules/minicomposer/ ComposerSettings.java

```java
public class ComposerSettings extends SystemOption {
  public static final String PROP_PLAYER = "player";
  public static final String PROP_SAMPLE_RATE = "sampleRate";
  private static final long serialVersionUID = -1247005365478408406L;
  public Executor getPlayer() {
    ServiceType.Handle val = (ServiceType.Handle)getProperty(PROP_PLAYER);
    Executor exec = null;
    if (val != null) {
      exec = (Executor)val.getServiceType();
```

```
        }
    if (exec == null) {
        if (Utilities.isWindows() ||
            Utilities.getOperatingSystem() == Utilities.OS_SOLARIS) {
            exec = Executor.find(InternalPlayer.class);
        } else {
            exec = Executor.find(ExternalPlayer.class);
        }
    }
    if (exec == null) {
        exec = new InternalPlayer();
    }
    return exec;
}
public void setPlayer(Executor player) {
    putProperty(PROP_PLAYER, new ServiceType.Handle(player), true);
}
public String displayName() {
    return NbBundle.getMessage(ComposerSettings.class, "LBL_ComposerSettings");
}
public HelpCtx getHelpCtx() {
    return new HelpCtx("org.netbeans.examples.modules.minicomposer");
}
public static final ComposerSettings getDefault() {
    return (ComposerSettings)findObject(ComposerSettings.class, true);
}
public float getSampleRate() {
    Float val = (Float)getProperty(PROP_SAMPLE_RATE);
    if (val != null) {
        return val.floatValue();
    } else {
        return 24000.0f;
    }
}
public void setSampleRate(float sampleRate) {
    putProperty(PROP_SAMPLE_RATE, new Float(sampleRate), true);
}
}
```

Properties stored in system options are given as bean properties—this controls both
the serialization of the option, which is automatically done one property at a time for
robustness in case of deserialization failures, and the display of the properties in the
Options window.

getPlayer() looks up the current setting for the player property. This system option
uses the key-value storage available to every SharedClassObject (of which
SystemOption is a subclass) to actually store the properties. getProperty() gets a
value by name. Here the option actually stores ServiceType.Handles, which as previously mentioned retain the name and class name of the service—the actual instance

fields of the service are thus stored only in the pool of services, and the handle points to a member of the pool. In case the value has never been set, we make the internal player the default on Windows and Solaris machines, whereas others (for example, Linux) get an external player by default. Note that `Executor.find()` could return `null` in case the user has for some reason deleted every instance of a service class, so for safety the last fallback is to create a fresh internal player.

`setPlayer()`, the setter method corresponding to `getPlayer()`, stores a handle to the executor. The final argument `true` to `putProperty()` requests that a property change event also be fired from the system option (here with property name `PROP_PLAYER`), which is necessary for GUI updates and any code that might be listening for a change in the default.

`displayName()` and `getHelpCtx()` provide a display name for the option and a link to JavaHelp, respectively. `getDefault()` is a convenience method for client code to find the singleton instance of the option. Recall that `ScoreExecSupport` used this method to get the option instance, followed by `getPlayer()` to find a default player to use.

We also define an additional property with the name `PROP_SAMPLE_RATE` and default value 24000 (samples per second). For this to be used, it is only necessary to replace the line in `SampledAudioCompilerGroup`:

```
AudioInputStream ais =
    new LineInFromScore.ScoreAudioInputStream(line, 24000.0f);
```

This can be changed to the following:

```
AudioInputStream ais =
    new LineInFromScore.ScoreAudioInputStream(line,
        ComposerSettings.getDefault().getSampleRate());
```

A similar change can be made in the `LineInFromScore(Score)` constructor to not hard-code the sample rate. *LineInFromScore.java* is not listed here, so check the downloadable sources for the example if you are interested.

If the option is left without a bean info, it will be usable but unattractive to the user: the internal unlocalized property names `player` and `sampleRate` will be visible. So we give it a simple bean info, shown in Example 24-9.

Example 24-9. Minicomposer: src/org/netbeans/examples/modules/minicomposer/ ComposerSettingsBeanInfo.java

```
public class ComposerSettingsBeanInfo extends SimpleBeanInfo {
  public PropertyDescriptor[] getPropertyDescriptors() {
    ResourceBundle bundle = NbBundle.getBundle(ComposerSettingsBeanInfo.class);
    try {
      PropertyDescriptor player =
        new PropertyDescriptor("player", ComposerSettings.class);
      player.setDisplayName(bundle.getString("PROP_player"));
      player.setShortDescription(bundle.getString("HINT_player"));
      PropertyDescriptor sampleRate =
        new PropertyDescriptor("sampleRate", ComposerSettings.class);
      sampleRate.setDisplayName(bundle.getString("PROP_sampleRate"));
```

```java
      sampleRate.setShortDescription(bundle.getString("HINT_sampleRate"));
      sampleRate.setExpert(true);
      sampleRate.setPropertyEditorClass(SampleRateEd.class);
      return new PropertyDescriptor[] {player, sampleRate};
    } catch (IntrospectionException ie) {
      TopManager.getDefault().getErrorManager().notify(ie);
      return null;
    }
  }
  public Image getIcon(int type) {
    if (type == BeanInfo.ICON_COLOR_16x16 || type == BeanInfo.ICON_MONO_16x16) {
      return Utilities.loadImage(
        "org/netbeans/examples/modules/minicomposer/ScoreDataIcon.gif");
    } else {
      return null;
    }
  }
  public static class SampleRateEd extends PropertyEditorSupport {
    private static final float[] rates = new float[] {
      12000.0f, 24000.0f, 48000.0f
    };
    private static final String[] tags = new String[rates.length];
    static {
      NumberFormat format = new DecimalFormat();
      for (int i = 0; i < rates.length; i++) {
        tags[i] = format.format(rates[i]);
      }
    }
    public String[] getTags() {
      return tags;
    }
    public String getAsText() {
      float value = ((Float)getValue()).floatValue();
      for (int i = 0; i < rates.length; i++) {
        if (rates[i] == value) {
          return tags[i];
        }
      }
      return "???";
    }
    public void setAsText(String text) throws IllegalArgumentException {
      for (int i = 0; i < tags.length; i++) {
        if (tags[i].equals(text)) {
          setValue(new Float(rates[i]));
          return;
        }
      }
      throw new IllegalArgumentException();
    }
  }
}
```

The bean info is uninteresting except for the custom property editor attached to the sampleRate property. This editor supplies three standard sample rates common in audio files and permits one of them to be selected via a drop-down list. Note that the NetBeans infrastructure automatically supplies a property editor for the player property, as it is of type Executor—many commonly used types have standard property editors, which are listed in the Explorer API documentation. The Executor editor permits an existing executor to be selected from a drop-down list, and detailed properties of that editor can be configured from a custom editor dialog box.

To install the system option, we will eschew the older method of adding a line to the manifest, which is too eager to load its class, and instead install it via the XML layer (giving more control over UI as well). Add this fragment to your *layer.xml* document:

```
<folder name="Services">
  <file name="org-netbeans-examples-modules-minicomposer-option.settings"
        url="option.xml">
    <attr name="SystemFileSystem.localizingBundle"
          stringvalue="org.netbeans.examples.modules.minicomposer.Bundle"/>
    <attr name="SystemFileSystem.icon" urlvalue=
          "nbresloc:/org/netbeans/examples/modules/minicomposer/ScoreDataIcon.gif"/>
  </file>
</folder>
<folder name="UI">
  <folder name="Services">
    <folder name="IDEConfiguration">
      <folder name="ServerAndExternalToolSettings">
        <!-- Note: line break in file contents necessary: -->
        <file name="org-netbeans-examples-modules-minicomposer-option.shadow">
      <![CDATA[Services/org-netbeans-examples-modules-minicomposer-option.settings
SystemFileSystem
]]>
        </file>
      </folder>
    </folder>
  </folder>
</folder>
```

You will also need a settings file for the option, seen in Example 24-10.

Example 24-10. Minicomposer: src/org/netbeans/examples/modules/minicomposer/option.xml

```
<!DOCTYPE settings PUBLIC
          "-//NetBeans//DTD Session settings 1.0//EN"
          "http://www.netbeans.org/dtds/sessionsettings-1_0.dtd">
<settings version="1.0">
  <module name="org.netbeans.examples.modules.minicomposer"/>
  <instanceof class="org.openide.options.SystemOption"/>
  <instanceof
    class="org.netbeans.examples.modules.minicomposer.ComposerSettings"/>
  <instance
    class="org.netbeans.examples.modules.minicomposer.ComposerSettings"/>
</settings>
```

As with the players, we register the option as a *.settings* file in *Services/* (no particular subfolder is needed). It is again given a localized name and icon; the resource bundle should contain this line:

```
Services/org-netbeans-examples-modules-minicomposer-option.settings=\
    Mini-Composer Settings
```

By default objects in the top-level *Services/* folder are not visible in the GUI. Certain subfolders like *Executor/* are explicitly made visible by NetBeans' GUI configuration, for example, under the node **Execution Types** in the Options dialog box, but system options are not normally placed in such folders. To make the option appear, we choose a GUI category for it and create a *data shadow* pointing to its settings file (akin to a Unix symbolic link or Windows shortcut).

A shadow is a special kind of data object, `org.openide.loaders.DataShadow`, which delegates much of its appearance and behavior to its target. It has the *.shadow* extension and consists of two text lines: the first giving a resource path in a mounted filesystem, the second giving the programmatic system name of that filesystem.[*] The special filesystem controlling NetBeans configuration into which module XML layers are merged has the name `SystemFileSystem`, and the resource path matches what you see in the layer. We place this shadow beneath *UI/Services/*, which is the folder whose structure and contents directly generate the view seen in the Options window. *Services/* has a program-friendly structure that must be kept stable between module versions in order for user-customized settings to continue to override module-supplied defaults. By contrast, *UI/Services/* contains no real information except for the user-oriented GUI categories you see, and this structure can be freely rearranged between module or IDE releases.

The resulting option in the Options window looks like Figure 24-5. Although not displayed in the screenshot, the Expert tab holds the Sample Rate property.

The basic services of the Minicomposer are now complete. But since the NetBeans GUI is based heavily on the Explorer, we will next show how to fit scores naturally into the Explorer's UI model.

---

[*] NetBeans 3.4 also permits a simpler format for *.shadow* files based on file attributes.

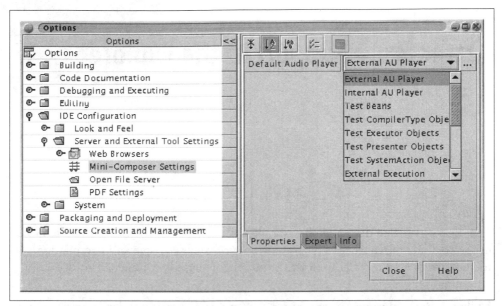

Figure 24-5. Minicomposer: settings displayed in Options window

## CHAPTER 25

Better Score Support in the Explorer

Until now, the score data node has shown the existence of a score, and its icon has displayed some miscellaneous bits of information such as parse and compilation status, but we have not really used the Explorer for what it is designed to do: display structure.

While it is fine to provide Swing-based GUI views of structural data, for many purposes some display of data in the Explorer tree and property sheet is an appropriate UI (as well as a textual view where applicable, of course). Additionally, Explorer nodes and properties tend to be more uniformly scriptable in a GUI-less environment, usable with only a keyboard and no mouse, and generally more amenable to alternate forms of presentation. Using the NetBeans scripting module you can access the Explorer via the Telnet protocol, and HTTP access through a web browser is easy, too! Exposure of functionality through nodes opens up user interaction modes you are not even aware of yet and helps to shape your thinking about what a module can do. So it is a good idea to provide full access to your module's capabilities through this medium.

In this chapter we will extend the score UI to include full manipulation of notes from the Explorer. To get warmed up, we will show how to add a property to the data node displaying information about the compiled audio file.

The Clip Length Property

In Chapter 24 we added an Executor property to the score node to permit the audio player to be configured by the user. But since the property was supplied by the ExecSupport, there was no chance to see how it really worked. Now we will add a custom node property to the score data node.

The property will display to the user the length (in seconds) of the audio file the score has been compiled into. If there is no compiled audio file yet, it will just show 0.0. Node properties must inherit from the class Node.Property; since this property is only for viewing and not for editing, we can subclass it indirectly using PropertySupport.ReadOnly, as seen in Example 25-1.

Example 25-1. Minicomposer: src/org/netbeans/examples/modules/minicomposer/ ClipLengthProperty.java

```java
public class ClipLengthProperty extends PropertySupport.ReadOnly
    implements PropertyChangeListener, FileChangeListener {
  private final ScoreDataObject obj;
  private final ScoreDataNode node;
  private Float value = null;
  public ClipLengthProperty(ScoreDataObject o, ScoreDataNode n) {
    super("clipLength", Float.TYPE,
          NbBundle.getMessage(ClipLengthProperty.class, "PROP_clipLength"),
          NbBundle.getMessage(ClipLengthProperty.class, "HINT_clipLength"));
    obj = o;
    node = n;
    obj.addPropertyChangeListener(WeakListener.propertyChange(this, obj));
    updateFileListeners();
  }
  public synchronized Object getValue()
      throws IllegalAccessException, InvocationTargetException {
    if (value == null) {
      FileObject fo = ScoreDataLoader.findAudioFile(obj);
      if (fo != null) {
        File f = FileUtil.toFile(fo);
        if (f != null) {
          try {
            AudioInputStream ais = AudioSystem.getAudioInputStream(f);
            try {
              value = new Float(ais.getFrameLength() /
                                ais.getFormat().getFrameRate());
            } finally {
              ais.close();
            }
          } catch (Exception e) {
            throw new InvocationTargetException(e);
          }
        } else {
          value = new Float(0.0f);
        }
      } else {
        value = new Float(0.0f);
      }
    }
    return value;
  }
  private void updateFileListeners() {
    FileObject fo = ScoreDataLoader.findAudioFile(obj);
    if (fo != null) {
      fo.addFileChangeListener(WeakListener.fileChange(this, fo));
    }
  }
```

```
  private void change() {
    value = null;
    node.fireClipLengthChange();
  }
  public void propertyChange(PropertyChangeEvent evt) {
    String prop = evt.getPropertyName();
    if (prop == null || prop.equals(DataObject.PROP_FILES)) {
      change();
      updateFileListeners();
    }
  }
  public void fileChanged(FileEvent fe) {
    change();
  }
  public void fileDeleted(FileEvent fe) {}
  public void fileFolderCreated(FileEvent fe) {}
  public void fileDataCreated(FileEvent fe) {}
  public void fileAttributeChanged(FileAttributeEvent fe) {}
  public void fileRenamed(FileRenameEvent fe) {}
}
```

The constructor for the property initializes its basic parameters in the super( ) call. The first argument, clipLength, is an arbitrary code name for the property that should identify it among all the properties of the node; we will use it later to fire changes. The second argument is the type of the property; it could be a regular Class object, but here we use the special Float.TYPE that indicates that the property will be of the primitive type float (though in fact the value will be manipulated as a wrapper Float). The third and fourth arguments are a display name and tool tip for the property to control its appearance in the property sheet; the bundle reads:

```
    PROP_clipLength=Clip Length
    HINT_clipLength=Length of the audio file in seconds, or 0 if none.
```

The constructor also keeps track of the data object and node that the property is bound to. We will come back to the listener additions in a moment.

getValue( ) is the principal method to implement to retrieve the current value. Here we keep the last-computed value in the variable value, or null to indicate that it is unknown. While it would be possible to compute the clip length every time the property is accessed, it is better to cache it, since the computation involves file I/O and might be a bit slow. (getValue( ) could be called whenever the user selects the node in the Explorer or switches property tabs, so it ought to be a quickly-executing method.) Recall that though the property is of type float, we will really return a Float wrapper because getValue( ) must return an Object.

ScoreDataLoader.findAudioFile( ) was discussed in Chapter 24. It finds the compiled audio file, if any, within a score object. If it exists, and is a real file on disk (otherwise, JavaSound may have difficulty working with it), we create a temporary audio stream and compute the length of the sound based on its audio parameters. The value is cached and returned. If there is any problem loading the audio stream (UnsupportedAudioFileException or IOException), the standard JavaBeans throwable wrapper InvocationTargetException is used to report it.

Clearing the Cache and Firing Changes

So far so good. But since we are caching the value for speed, we also have to know when to clear the cache. Also if the clip length changes while the property is displayed (for example, if a score is compiled for the first time or recompiled with a different length), we will want to update the display immediately. To force a redisplay, the helper method change() is used here to both clear the cache and inform listeners on the node (such as the NetBeans property sheet) that they should ask for a new value. This is done with an access method that we add to ScoreDataNode:

```
void fireClipLengthChange() {
  firePropertyChange("clipLength", null, null);
}
```

firePropertyChange() is a common source of confusion among new users of the Nodes API. A node can use a variety of protected methods such as fireDisplayNameChange(), fireIconChange(), and so on to tell listeners about changes in its inherent properties (its display name, its icon), and these changes can be listened to by attaching a NodeListener to the node with addNodeListener(). NodeListener is a PropertyChangeListener for properties such as Node.PROP_DISPLAY_NAME or Node.PROP_ICON, as well as having additional event delivery methods for changes in children and deletion of the node. *Independently of this*, a node may have some attached properties (displayed in the property sheet). Clients can listen to changes in these properties via addPropertyChangeListener(), which only receives events relating to these properties; changes are fired using firePropertyChange(). Here we fire such a change. The property name for the event, clipLength, must match the property name given in the Node.Property constructor; or null as a property name indicates a possible change in all attached properties, *not including* inherent properties.

Now it remains to find out when to clear this value cache and fire the change. In the constructor we attach two listeners, both implemented on the property itself, though inner classes could also be used. First, we add a listener to the data object and in propertyChange() check just for changes in DataObject.PROP_FILES. Such a change means that the set of files included in the data object has changed: for example, if an audio file is added after a compilation or removed after cleaning. If this happens, the value may need to be recomputed.

updateFileListeners() is also used from the constructor to attach a listener to the audio file in the object, if any. A change in PROP_FILES could also mean we have to update this listener, so we do: the FileChangeListener needs to be added to the new primary file.

For simplicity the listener is left on the old primary file. In practice if PROP_FILES is fired, it is likely that the old file has now been deleted anyway, as the score was moved to a new folder. Even if the old file continues to exist and the old listener receives a file change event, at worst the property will refire an spurious event from the node, which is harmless.

If the contents of the file change, fileChanged() will be called, and we can again force a recalculation of the clip length. Other changes in the audio file are not relevant—except fileDeleted(), but this would have already caused the data object to fire PROP_FILES.

Adding the Property to the Property Sheet

Attaching the property to the node is not difficult. createSheet() (in ScoreDataNode) just needs to be modified to include the new properties in the Properties tab:

```
protected Sheet createSheet() {
  Sheet sheet = super.createSheet();
  Sheet.Set properties = sheet.get(Sheet.PROPERTIES);
  // adding this line:
  properties.put(
    new ClipLengthProperty((ScoreDataObject)getDataObject(), this));
  // ...as before with ExecSupport...
  return sheet;
}
```

Now selecting an uncompiled score in the Explorer will show in the property sheet a grayed-out (read-only) Clip Length with value 0.0. After pressing Compile, it will change to the actual clip length in seconds, for example 3.25. After adding more notes and recompiling, it will change again.

Representing Notes as Subnodes Using Children.Keys

The fun is in the nodes. A score is logically composed of some number of notes (Score.Notes), so the score node should show one node per contained note when it is expanded in the Explorer using the tree view's expand handle. In the NetBeans Nodes API, for clarity and ease of composition, the set of children of a node is stored as a separate object from the node, assignable to Children. While in principle you could subclass Children directly to do what you need, in practice this is for gurus only! Rather, there is a variety of different Children subclasses available, each one suited to a certain style of representing the child nodes. The most popular and powerful is Children.Keys, which makes it easy to map a data abstraction into a node hierarchy.

Using Keys to Model Children

Before using this class, you need to decide on a key type. Each key should be drawn from a natural collection of objects in the data model, preferably ones that would already exist without any nodes to display them. A key can map to zero or more nodes, but usually exactly one, which represents that piece of data. Characteristics of good keys include small size and quick construction, intuitive membership in the data model, and a well-defined notion of equality. For the score example, we will use Score.Note as the key class. Each Note object will produce one NoteNode. Be sure to choose your key type carefully, for it is the most important step in creating key children.

Choosing a Key Type for Children

In deciding what kind of key to use for your Children.Keys implementation, it may be helpful to follow examples from the NetBeans source code.

- Folder nodes can be seen in the Filesystems tab of the Explorer window with this icon:
  They use DataObjects as keys for their children.

- The **Methods** node below a Java source file shows all methods present in the class. Each subnode is represented by a key of type MethodElement, from the Java Hierarchy API.

- The **Object Types** node visible in the Options window represents all object types in the system—which is to say, all registered data loaders in the loader pool. Therefore it uses DataLoader as the key type.

- The version control support modules provide a Versioning view that shows raw files (not data objects) together with information such as revision number, checkout status, and history. The vcscore module internally uses a class called RevisionItem to represent each version of a file. In the custom view, each file has subnodes corresponding to its historical versions. These are represented by RevisionItem keys.

Let us take a look at the children implementation in its basic form (see Example 25-2). Most Children.Keys subclasses share the same idiomatic structure. Though the class is short, it is important to understand how and why it works, as this pattern is central to using the Nodes API.

Example 25-2. Minicomposer: src/org/netbeans/examples/modules/minicomposer/ScoreChildren.java

```
public class ScoreChildren extends Children.Keys
    implements ChangeListener, TaskListener {
  private final ScoreCookie cookie;
  private boolean added = false;
```

Example 25-2. Minicomposer: src/org/netbeans/examples/modules/minicomposer/
ScoreChildren.java (continued)

```java
  public ScoreChildren(ScoreCookie cookie) {
    this.cookie = cookie;
  }
  protected Node[] createNodes(Object key) {
    Score.Note n = (Score.Note)key;
    return new Node[] {new NoteNode(n)};
  }
  protected void addNotify() {
    cookie.addChangeListener(this);
    added = true;
    stateChanged(null);
  }
  protected void removeNotify() {
    cookie.removeChangeListener(this);
    added = false;
    setKeys(Collections.EMPTY_SET);
  }
  public void stateChanged(ChangeEvent e) {
    if (added) {
      cookie.prepare().addTaskListener(this);
    }
  }
  public void taskFinished(Task task) {
    if (cookie.isValid()) {
      try {
        Score s = cookie.getScore();
        int c = s.getSize();
        Score.Note[] notes = new Score.Note[c];
        for (int i = 0; i < c; i++) {
          notes[i] = s.getNote(i);
        }
        setKeys(notes);
      } catch (IOException ioe) {}
    }
  }
}
```

As we did earlier with the GUI view of the score in ScorePanel, we again use the ScoreCookie as a central point of communication in this module by routing all structural reads and writes through the cookie. The essential method in Children.Keys is createNodes(), which is called when nodes are needed. The implementation is handed a key and must supply some nodes to represent it. Our keys are Notes, so we cast to this, and make a new NoteNode (discussed later) to represent it. Figure 25-1 shows the relationships between these classes.

Initially a Children.Keys object has no keys. The superclass actually stores the current keys and completely manages the subnodes. As a subclasser you can just give it a fresh list of keys whenever you need to. Call setKeys() with an array or collection of Object keys. (Such arrays or collections will be immediately copied, so it will have

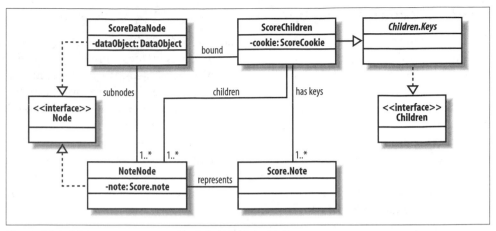

Figure 25-1. Minicomposer: parent and child nodes with keys

no effect to change elements later.) If the children object sees some keys that it did not have before (according to `Object.equals()`), subnodes will be created and added. If some keys are missing relative to the last call to `setKeys()`, the corresponding subnodes will be destroyed and removed from the children. If some keys are reordered, the matching nodes will be kept intact but reordered.

Once in a while you may want to change the node generated from a particular key. `refreshKey()` can be used to do this. However, think carefully before using this, as it may mean your original choice of key type was not prudent. If the nodes do not follow naturally from the keys, should you choose a key that better reflects what you want to show?

Modify the Keys, the Nodes Will Follow

It is important to remember that the keys come from your data model, and you should perform operations only on this model; the nodes will be quietly adjusted to match this, and you do not need to manipulate them directly. Some people notice that there are methods in superclasses of `Children.Keys` that let you directly add or remove nodes. These typically appear at the beginning or end of the children, in addition to key-based nodes.

While there are occasionally practical reasons for doing this (when subclassing some children implementations that do not expose their keys cleanly), in general you will just make trouble for yourself trying. In almost all cases, manipulation of the keys (data model) is the correct approach. This advice applies throughout the Nodes API, as we will see when working with deletion, node properties, and more. Keep a clear separation in your mind between model and view.

Being Lazy and Cleaning Up

Two important methods to understand are `addNotify()` and `removeNotify()`, common to all children. Remember that a `Children` object is created immediately with a node. Since most nodes with children are never expanded by the user in the Explorer, it would be senseless to compute the child nodes before the user asks for them. So a `Children` object should do little work in its constructor. When the expand handle is first expanded, `addNotify()` will be called, and the `Children` object may prepare its children for use. If the expand handle is collapsed and the node left untouched for a while, `removeNotify()` will be called to clean up for the time being (save memory and detach listeners). `Children.Keys` can be especially efficient because invisible nodes can be garbage collected freely while keys (typically lighter weight or already in the data model) remain in place.

In `ScoreChildren`, as is common, we do not start to make keys until `addNotify()` is called. At that time a flag `added` is set indicating that the `Children` object is "active," and we start to listen for changes in the score cookie that would mean a change in the list of notes. If any part of the system changes the score, `stateChanged()`, which is responsible for updating the note keys, will be called. `addNotify()` needs to do this once to install the initial set of keys. `removeNotify()` reverses the process and also clears the list of keys. Clearing the keys is not very important for this example, but it is a good habit, since it might permit the keys to be garbage-collected quickly as well as the nodes.

Many `Children.Keys` implementations would directly calculate the keys in a "refresh" method, which we here call `stateChanged()`. That style is fine if getting the keys is a cheap operation. For `ScoreChildren`, we prefer not to block the calling thread waiting for the score parse to complete from within `addNotify()`. This method can be called from the AWT event thread and ought not block. Instead, we just make sure parsing is initiated, and listen for it to finish asynchronously. If the score is changed by anyone later on, a textual change will trigger a reparse and later call `taskFinished()` on the children; a structural change (`setScore()`) will cause `taskFinished()` to be called right away since the new `Score` is already available.

Note that in case of a parse failure in the score, we leave the keys alone. This is for the user's benefit: when typing a line into a score one letter at a time, the parse is invalid until the line is complete, and it would be disconcerting to have the notes in the Explorer disappear and reappear during this interval.

Figure 25-2 is the state diagram for the `ScoreChildren` lifecycle.

Creating the Subnodes

Example 25-3 is a first revision of the node to represent the note. For now it will not do anything too exciting.

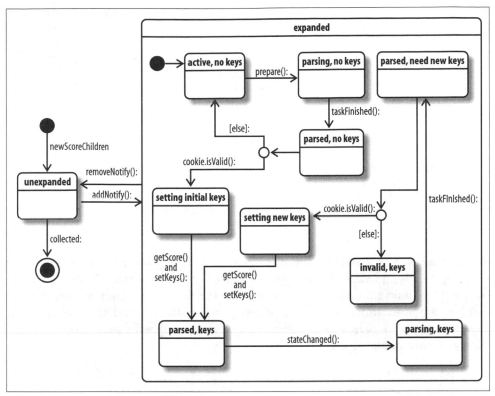

Figure 25-2. Minicomposer: ScoreChildren lifecycle state diagram

Example 25-3. Minicomposer: src/org/netbeans/examples/modules/minicomposer/
NoteNode.java in Basic Form

```java
public class NoteNode extends AbstractNode implements NodeListener {
  private final Score.Note note;
  private boolean addedCookieListener;
  public NoteNode(Score.Note note) {
    super(Children.LEAF);
    this.note = note;
    setName(Score.TONES_SHORT[note.getTone()]);
    setShortDescription(NbBundle.getMessage(NoteNode.class, "HINT_note_node",
                        Score.TONES_LONG[note.getTone()],
                        Score.OCTAVES_LONG[note.getOctave()],
                        Score.DURATIONS_LONG[note.getDuration()]));
    setIconBase("org/netbeans/examples/modules/minicomposer/NoteIcon");
  }
  public Node.Cookie getCookie(Class c) {
    Node parent = getParentNode();
    if (parent == null) return null;
    if (!addedCookieListener) {
      addedCookieListener = true;
      parent.addNodeListener(WeakListener.node(this, parent));
    }
    Node.Cookie cookie = parent.getCookie(c);
```

```
      return cookie;
    }
    public void propertyChange(PropertyChangeEvent evt) {
      if (Node.PROP_COOKIE.equals(evt.getPropertyName())) {
        fireCookieChange();
      }
    }
    public void childrenRemoved(NodeMemberEvent ev) {}
    public void childrenReordered(NodeReorderEvent ev) {}
    public void childrenAdded(NodeMemberEvent ev) {}
    public void nodeDestroyed(NodeEvent ev) {}
    public HelpCtx getHelpCtx() {
      return new HelpCtx("org.netbeans.examples.modules.minicomposer");
    }
}
```

We keep a `Score.Note` data structure associated with every node and pass it in to the constructor. Using `Children.LEAF` as the `Children` object indicates that the node will be a leaf (have no subnodes itself). We can set the node name (and, hence, also the display name) according to the tone it represents in the musical scale, as it would appear in textual scores. It is also easy to supply a tool tip with some more information, as shown in the bundle:

```
# {0} - tone
# {1} - octave
# {2} - duration
HINT_note_node={0} in {1} for {2}
```

We also set an icon for the node, in this case a fixed note icon: ♩

NoteNodes are not expected to carry any cookies of their own. However, it is convenient to delegate cookie requests to the parent node. A user who has a note selected in the Explorer can then press Save, Compile, and so on as if the score node were selected. To implement the delegation, `getCookie()` simply checks the parent node for the corresponding cookie and returns it.

We also want to listen to changes in the parent node's cookies. Consider clicking a note in a modified score in the Explorer window and choosing **File → Save**. This action will save the score and remove the `SaveCookie` from the `ScoreDataNode`. Without propagating cookie changes to the `NoteNode`, the Save menu item and toolbar button will continue to be enabled even after the score has been saved!

 If the user clicks elsewhere and clicks back on the note, Save will now be off, because `getCookie()` is called again.

By propagating the change, we can force `SaveAction` to turn off immediately. So a node listener is also added (once only) to the parent, and cookie changes are refired.

`childrenRemoved()`, `childrenReordered()`, `childrenAdded()`, and `nodeDestroyed()` are unused additional `NodeListener` methods.

Attaching the Children to the Parent

With the children and subnodes created, all that remains to do is attach the children to the `ScoreDataNode`. So we will change its constructor as follows:

```
public ScoreDataNode(ScoreDataObject obj) {
  this(obj, (ScoreCookie)obj.getCookie(ScoreCookie.class));
}
// adding new helper constructor so 'score' is accessible in super call:
private ScoreDataNode(ScoreDataObject obj, ScoreCookie score) {
  super(obj, new ScoreChildren(score)); // no longer Children.LEAF
  score.addChangeListener(WeakListener.change(this, score));
  // ...as before
}
```

Now a score will show its nodes in a substructure, as shown in Figure 25-3.

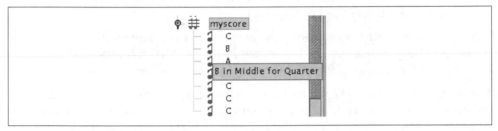

Figure 25-3. Minicomposer: score file with note subnodes

Permitting Subnodes to Be Renamed or Deleted

Two basic operations we want to permit on the note nodes are renaming and deletion. Let us start with deletion, since it is rather simple to implement.

Deletion of Notes

You can support deletion by adding the following code to your `NoteNode` class:

```
public boolean canDestroy() {
  return true;
}
public void destroy() throws IOException {
  ScoreCookie cookie = (ScoreCookie)getCookie(ScoreCookie.class);
  Score s = cookie.getScore();
  int size = s.getSize();
  List notes = new ArrayList(Math.max(size - 1, 1));
  for (int i = 0; i < size; i++) {
```

```
      Score.Note n = s.getNote(i);
      if (n != note) {
        notes.add(n);
      }
    }
    cookie.setScore(new Score(notes));
  }
  protected SystemAction[] createActions() {
    return new SystemAction[] {
      SystemAction.get(DeleteAction.class),
      null,
      SystemAction.get(ToolsAction.class),
    };
  }
```

`Node.canDestroy()` indicates a node's willingness to be deleted; the actual deletion is done by `Node.destroy()`. The first step is to get the score cookie. Recall that we are delegating cookie requests to the parent node, so `this.getCookie()` will find it. The current score is retrieved; note that it is assumed the score is valid, or else an `IOException` would be thrown. A new score identical to the old one but skipping this node's note is constructed and committed to the cookie.

Here we are not explicitly destroying the note node or removing it from its parent! It is only necessary to change the score to not include it. `Children.Keys` will automatically remove the node (and fire `nodeDestroyed()` to any listeners).

Implementing `canDestroy()` and `destroy()` as just shown is enough to make the node deletable via the **Delete** key, toolbar button, or menu item. We can also add `DeleteAction` to the context menu by overriding `createActions()`. `ToolsAction` is a generic action that should be included in the context menus of most nodes.

Renaming of Notes

Permitting a node to be renamed is conceptually similar. Make these additions to *NoteNode.java*:

```
public boolean canRename() {
  return true;
}
public void setName(String nue) throws IllegalArgumentException {
  if (nue.equals(getName())) return;
  int v;
  for (v = 0; v < Score.TONES_SHORT.length; v++) {
    if (nue.equals(Score.TONES_SHORT[v])) break;
  }
  if (v == Score.TONES_SHORT.length) {
    IllegalArgumentException iae =
      new IllegalArgumentException("bad tone: " + nue);
    TopManager.getDefault().getErrorManager().annotate(
      iae, ErrorManager.WARNING, null,
      NbBundle.getMessage(NoteNode.class, "EXC_bad_tone", nue), null, null);
    throw iae;
```

```
      }
      ScoreCookie cookie = (ScoreCookie)getCookie(ScoreCookie.class);
      try {
        Score s = cookie.getScore();
        int size = s.getSize();
        List notes = new ArrayList(Math.max(size, 1));
        for (int i = 0; i < size; i++) {
          Score.Note n = s.getNote(i);
          if (n == note) {
            n = new Score.Note(v, n.getOctave(), n.getDuration());
          }
          notes.add(n);
        }
        cookie.setScore(new Score(notes));
      } catch (IOException ioe) {
        TopManager.getDefault().getErrorManager().notify(ioe);
      }
    }
  }
  protected SystemAction[] createActions() {
    return new SystemAction[] {
      SystemAction.get(DeleteAction.class),
      SystemAction.get(RenameAction.class), // newly added
      null,
      SystemAction.get(ToolsAction.class),
    };
  }
```

Again canRename() indicates a willingness to be renamed and setName() actually handles it. For this example, the display name of the node matches the code name—both are the short name of the tone in the scale. This is often best; if the display name is different, the user by renaming the node changes the code name (which usually affects the display name, too). The new name should be a short tone name. If it is not a recognized name, we can throw an IllegalArgumentException to stop the rename. However, since this is only a case of "operator error," it should be polite. So we mark it as a WARNING-level exception and give it a localized exception message:

```
# {0} - attempted tone to rename to
EXC_bad_tone=Unrecognized tone: {0}
```

An attempt to choose an improper tone name results in a simple dialog box (shown in Figure 25-4), not a frightening exception dialog box.

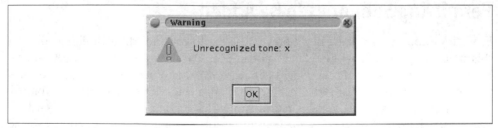

Figure 25-4. Minicomposer: unrecognized tone dialog

If the tone is valid, the variable v in setName() holds its index in the list of tones; again we replace the score with one identical to the previous score but with a substitution in this one note. ScoreChildren replaces this note node with a new one displaying the newly selected note.

Again RenameAction is added to the context menu to remind the user that renaming the node is an expected operation. It could also be renamed by clicking it in the Explorer while already selected, initiating an in-place rename, as seen in Figure 25-5.

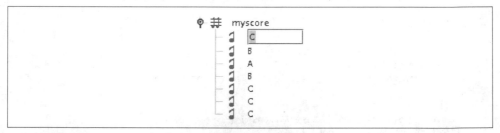

Figure 25-5. Minicomposer: in-place rename

If you try the in-place rename, you may notice that the new (renamed) node is no longer selected. This is because the old node was actually removed and replaced by a new note node. We can see here a (minor) weakness of the Score and ScoreCookie design: it permits the set of notes to be replaced, but has no notion of a change in a fixed note. That is, Score.Note is immutable (as is Score), and cookie changes are simple replacements of the entire score.

Many data models (such as the Java Hierarchy API in org.openide.src.*) have a finer-grained notion of object identity and change. The result is that an isolated node can be meaningfully renamed and still display the same object (which now has a new name). You can try this by doing an in-place rename on a method node beneath **Methods** in a Java source. The node will stay selected, because the org.openide.src.MethodElement is still the same object with a new name property. In that case setName() changes the name property, and a listener in the node refires changes in MethodElement.PROP_NAME as changes in Node.PROP_NAME. Take a look at NetBeans sources under *openide/src/org/ openide/src/nodes/* to see examples of these techniques in action.

Permitting Subnodes to Be Added

Providing support for adding new notes in the Explorer is not difficult either, though this time the modifications will take place in ScoreDataNode rather than in NoteNode. User-controlled creation of new objects beneath existing objects commonly proceeds in one of two ways in the NetBeans system. One is the creation of objects (typically data objects, that is to say, objects representing files on disk) via the **New** wizard. In most cases these new objects are made from existing templates that are copied to the destination folder. But opening a wizard just to add one note is too cumbersome.

The Nodes API provides a simple class NewType that enables the user to create a new object. A node can have one or more NewTypes associated with it. NewAction works with such nodes and runs one of the NewTypes. (Do not confuse NewAction with NewTemplateAction, which opens the **New** wizard!)

We will introduce a new utility class, NoteTransfer (shown in Example 25-4). It will hold the NewType, and we will use it more extensively later when working with clipboard operations. It just serves as a way to avoid bloat in the node classes.

Example 25-4. Minicomposer: src/org/netbeans/examples/modules/minicomposer/ NoteTransfer.java with NewType

```java
public final class NoteTransfer {
  public NoteTransfer() {}
  public static class NewNote extends NewType {
    private final ScoreCookie cookie;
    public NewNote(ScoreCookie cookie) {
      this.cookie = cookie;
    }
    public String getName() {
      return NbBundle.getMessage(NoteTransfer.class, "LBL_new_note");
    }
    public HelpCtx getHelpCtx() {
      return new HelpCtx("org.netbeans.examples.modules.minicomposer");
    }
    public void create() throws IOException {
      Score s = cookie.getScore();
      Score.Note n = requestNote();
      if (n == null) return;
      int c = s.getSize();
      List l = new ArrayList(c + 1);
      for (int i = 0; i < c; i++) {
        l.add(s.getNote(i));
      }
      l.add(n);
      cookie.setScore(new Score(l));
    }
    private Score.Note requestNote() {
      JPanel panel = new JPanel();
      // ...GUI setup omitted...
      DialogDescriptor d = new DialogDescriptor(panel,
        NbBundle.getMessage(NoteTransfer.class, "TITLE_add_note"));
      d.setModal(true);
      d.setHelpCtx(getHelpCtx());
      d.setMessageType(NotifyDescriptor.QUESTION_MESSAGE);
      d.setOptionType(NotifyDescriptor.OK_CANCEL_OPTION);
      Dialog dlg = TopManager.getDefault().createDialog(d);
      dlg.pack();
      dlg.show();
      if (d.getValue() == NotifyDescriptor.OK_OPTION) {
        // tone, octave, duration are JComboBox's
        return new Score.Note(tone.getSelectedIndex(),
                              octave.getSelectedIndex(),
```

```
                              duration.getSelectedIndex());
      } else {
        return null;
      }
    }
  }
}
```

`NewNote` will be the `NewType` that, when run, prompts the user for information about a new note and adds it to the score cookie passed to the `NewNote` constructor.

`getName()` and `getHelpCtx()` are used for presentation purposes. `NewAction` will display the provided name in its own menu item. It may also display menu items in a submenu, in case there is more than one `NewType` for the same node.

`create()` is called when the context menu item is selected. This simple implementation just requests a note from the user in a dialog box and sets a new score including this note at the end. As usual, just changing the score cookie triggers the listener in `ScoreChildren`, which changes the list of `Score.Note` keys, which results in a new node for the added note being appended to the children list.

`requestNote()` is a straightforward use of the NetBeans standardized dialog boxes. It creates a `JPanel` containing three combo boxes (for tone, octave, and duration), and displays it in a small modal dialog box with an OK button that adds the note, a Cancel button (returning `null` from the method), and a Help button in case everything is not clear.

Attaching the `NewType` to the score node is easy and is shown in this code fragment you should add to *ScoreDataNode.java*:

```
public NewType[] getNewTypes() {
  return new NewType[] {
    new NoteTransfer.NewNote((ScoreCookie)getCookie(ScoreCookie.class)),
  };
}
```

Of course the context menu for the score node must also include **Add...** for the new type to have any effect; make this change to `ScoreDataLoader`:

```
protected SystemAction[] defaultActions() {
  return new SystemAction[] {
    // as before...
    SystemAction.get(ExecuteAction.class),
    null,
    SystemAction.get(NewAction.class), // newly added
    null,
    SystemAction.get(CutAction.class),
    // ...as before
  };
}
```

Figure 25-6 shows the new context menu item **Add New Note...** in use.

Figure 25-6. Minicomposer: add new note dialog

Making Read/Write Properties on Subnodes

Since each note has three obvious properties—tone within the octave, octave, and duration—it makes sense to reflect these in the property sheet of a node as well. Providing read access to a note property is straightforward, and write access follows the same model as was already used to support renaming of note nodes. We will begin with a property class capable of representing all three properties according to a parameter, shown in Example 25-5.

Example 25-5. Minicomposer: src/org/netbeans/examples/modules/minicomposer/
NoteProperty.java

```
public class NoteProperty extends PropertySupport.ReadWrite {
  private final ScoreCookie cookie;
  private final Score.Note note;
  private final int type;
  public NoteProperty(ScoreCookie cookie, Score.Note note, int type) {
    super("noteProperty" + type, Integer.TYPE,
        NbBundle.getMessage(NoteProperty.class, "PROP_note_" + type),
        NbBundle.getMessage(NoteProperty.class, "HINT_note_" + type));
    this.cookie = cookie;
    this.note = note;
    this.type = type;
  }
  public Object getValue() {
    switch (type) {
    case 0:
      return new Integer(note.getTone());
    case 1:
      return new Integer(note.getOctave());
    default:
      return new Integer(note.getDuration());
    }
  }
  public void setValue(Object val)
      throws IllegalArgumentException, InvocationTargetException {
    int v = ((Integer)val).intValue();
```

```
    try {
      Score s = cookie.getScore();
      int size = s.getSize();
      List notes = new ArrayList(Math.max(size, 1));
      for (int i = 0; i < size; i++) {
        Score.Note n = s.getNote(i);
        if (n == note) {
          switch (type) {
          case 0:
            n = new Score.Note(v, n.getOctave(), n.getDuration());
            break;
          case 1:
            n = new Score.Note(n.getTone(), v, n.getDuration());
            break;
          default:
            n = new Score.Note(n.getTone(), n.getOctave(), v);
            break;
          }
        }
        notes.add(n);
      }
      cookie.setScore(new Score(notes));
    } catch (IOException ioe) {
      throw new InvocationTargetException(ioe);
    }
  }
  public PropertyEditor getPropertyEditor() {
    return new NotePropertyEditor(type);
  }
  private static final class NotePropertyEditor extends PropertyEditorSupport {
    private final int type;
    public NotePropertyEditor(int type) {
      this.type = type;
    }
    public String[] getTags() {
      switch (type) {
      case 0:
        return Score.TONES_LONG;
      case 1:
        return Score.OCTAVES_LONG;
      default:
        return Score.DURATIONS_LONG;
      }
    }
    public String getAsText() {
      int v = ((Integer)NotePropertyEditor.this.getValue()).intValue();
      return getTags()[v];
    }
    public void setAsText(String text) throws IllegalArgumentException {
      String[] tags = getTags();
      for (int i = 0; i < tags.length; i++) {
        if (tags[i].equals(text)) {
```

```
            NotePropertyEditor.this.setValue(new Integer(i));
            return;
          }
        }
      throw new IllegalArgumentException();
    }
  }
}
```

As with `ClipLengthProperty` earlier in the chapter, we extend a `PropertySupport` inner class, now `ReadWrite`, to make the property editable. `getValue()` is straightforward. It returns the tone, octave, or duration of the represented note, according to which of three properties this is.

`setValue()` is a little more complex, but the basic pattern follows that of `NodeNote`. `setName()` earlier. A new score is constructed matching the previous one except in one property of one note and is set to the score cookie. As with renaming note nodes, in trying these properties you may notice that after setting a new value, the affected node is actually deleted and immediately replaced by a new one with the altered property. Again this can be avoided only by making an individual note mutable and keeping the same node to represent it; in such a case the node will want to run code resembling the following fragment whenever a property changed, to force a refresh in the property sheet:

```
if (octaveChanged) {
    firePropertyChange("noteProperty1", null, null);
}
```

`getPropertyEditor()` can be used in a property to request a specific JavaBeans-style property editor, which actually controls the presentation of the property in its row in the property sheet: whether and how it can be edited as text, with an in-place graphical editor, with a custom dialog box, and so on. Here we provide a simple editor, `NotePropertyEditor`, which displays a drop-down list of valid values (in a reasonable display format, not the integer used internally) and does not permit other forms of editing.

To attach the three properties to `NoteNode`, we just add them in `createSheet()`. It is also desirable to include `PropertiesAction` in the context menu in case the global property sheet is not showing and the user wishes to see the node properties:

```
    protected Sheet createSheet() {
        Sheet s = super.createSheet();
        Sheet.Set ss = Sheet.createPropertiesSet();
        ScoreCookie cookie = (ScoreCookie)getCookie(ScoreCookie.class);
        ss.put(new NoteProperty(cookie, note, 0));
        ss.put(new NoteProperty(cookie, note, 1));
        ss.put(new NoteProperty(cookie, note, 2));
        s.put(ss);
        return s;
    }
```

```
    protected SystemAction[] createActions() {
        return new SystemAction[] {
            SystemAction.get(DeleteAction.class),
            SystemAction.get(RenameAction.class),
            null,
            SystemAction.get(PropertiesAction.class), // newly added
            SystemAction.get(ToolsAction.class),
        };
    }
```

The result looks like Figure 25-7.

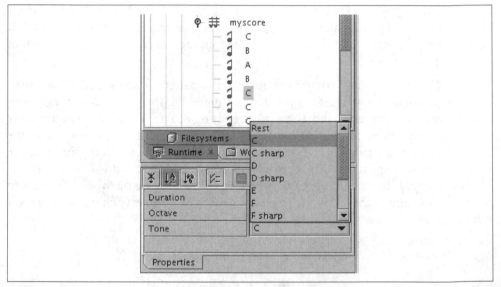

Figure 25-7. Minicomposer: property sheet for a note

Reordering Subnodes

The next order of business is reordering. Having added a number of nodes to a score, the user might wish to move some of them around. The Nodes API supports this directly using a special cookie, Index, which is the only major cookie defined in the Open APIs that is intended to operate specifically on nodes, rather than the things nodes represent.* Index specifies methods for retrieving those subnodes of a node that are reorderable—usually *all* the node's subnodes, but occasionally a subset; moving some nodes into different positions via permutations; and invoking a cus-

---

* ElementCookie and FilterCookie, as well as perhaps ConnectionCookie, can also be considered node-oriented cookies. However, they are probably on their way out in favor of the upcoming Looks and Metadata APIs, so they will not be treated in this book.

tomizer (generally a dialog box provided by the Nodes API) for visually reorganizing the nodes.

Reordering is normally handled by the children; it requires specific knowledge of the existing nodes in order to work, though we will make the actual order change via the data model. Make these additions to your ScoreChildren class:

```
public Index getIndex() {
  return new IndexImpl();
}
private class IndexImpl extends Index.Support {
  public Node[] getNodes() {
    return ScoreChildren.this.getNodes();
  }
  public int getNodesCount() {
    return getNodes().length;
  }
  public void reorder(int[] perm) {
    try {
      Score s = cookie.getScore();
      Score.Note[] notes = new Score.Note[perm.length];
      for (int i = 0; i < perm.length; i++) {
        notes[perm[i]] = s.getNote(i);
      }
      cookie.setScore(new Score(Arrays.asList(notes)));
      fireChangeEvent(new ChangeEvent(IndexImpl.this));
    } catch (IOException ioe) {
      TopManager.getDefault().getErrorManager().notify(ioe);
    }
  }
}
```

Index.Support implements some of the methods required by Index, leaving only straightforward ones. getNodes() and getNodesCount() are usually implemented to provide all the nodes available in the Children object; if you have some nodes that are "fixed" and cannot be moved but some that can, you return only the movable nodes (and permutations will refer only to these).

reorder() is the basic work method. It is given a permutation of nodes. For example, {1,2,0} applied to three nodes will rotate them down. Although the Index knows only about Nodes, we translate the permutation into an operation on the corresponding Notes by assuming they are in the same order, as they should be.

 It might be a little safer and cleaner to query each node for its position in the children and apply the permutation on that basis. However, with the simple Score data model we have, Notes do not "know" where in a Score they are, so this would be complicated.

When the new score is set, the Children.Keys infrastructure will notice that the same set of Notes as before is available in the keys list, but in a different order; and it will reorder the existing nodes. You will be able to see that in this example, unlike with renaming, a node will stay selected after it is moved: its identity is not changed, only its position.

`fireChangeEvent()` is technically required of `Index` implementations in order to inform possible listeners that the node order has changed.

To attach the `Index` cookie implementation to the score node, we just add it to the cookie set:

```
public ScoreDataNode(ScoreDataObject obj) {
  this(obj, (ScoreCookie)obj.getCookie(ScoreCookie.class));
}
private ScoreDataNode(ScoreDataObject obj, ScoreCookie score) {
  this(obj, score, new ScoreChildren(score));
}
// yet another helper constructor, so we keep a ref to the ScoreChildren obj:
private ScoreDataNode(ScoreDataObject obj, ScoreCookie score, ScoreChildren
children) {
    super(obj, children);
    getCookieSet().add(children.getIndex()); // newly added
    score.addChangeListener(WeakListener.change(this, score));
    // ...as before
}
```

The default NetBeans GUI configuration does not include any visible toolbar button or menu item to change node order, so it is necessary to include the correct actions in the appropriate context menus, using the `ScoreDataLoader`'s `defaultActions()` method:

```
protected SystemAction[] defaultActions() {
  return new SystemAction[] {
    // ...as before
    SystemAction.get(ExecuteAction.class),
    null,
    SystemAction.get(NewAction.class),
    SystemAction.get(ReorderAction.class), // newly added
    null,
    SystemAction.get(CutAction.class),
    // as before...
  };
}
```

You will also need to modify the `createActions()` method in `NoteNode`:

```
protected SystemAction[] createActions() {
  return new SystemAction[] {
    SystemAction.get(MoveUpAction.class), // newly added
    SystemAction.get(MoveDownAction.class), // newly added
    null,
    SystemAction.get(DeleteAction.class),
    SystemAction.get(RenameAction.class),
    null,
    SystemAction.get(PropertiesAction.class),
```

```
        SystemAction.get(ToolsAction.class),
    };
}
```

Note that the parent node—the one that actually has the Index cookie—should be given ReorderAction, which when run invokes a reordering dialog box permitting a number of nodes to be rearranged at once, as shown in Figure 25-8 and Figure 25-9.

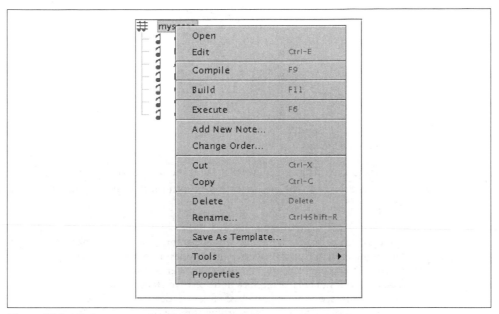

Figure 25-8. Minicomposer: the Change Order option

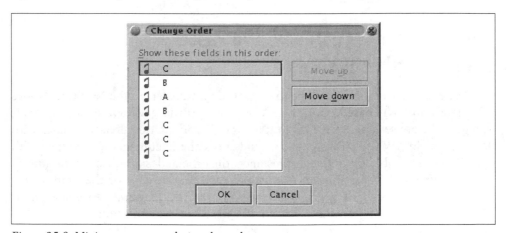

Figure 25-9. Minicomposer: reordering the nodes

Each child node should be given MoveUpAction and MoveDownAction, which move that node up or down one position in the list (see Figure 25-10).

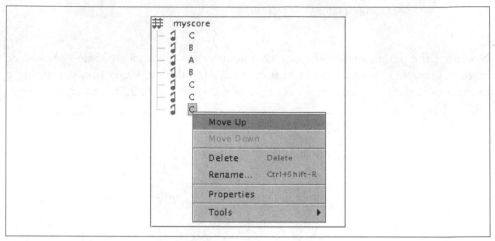

Figure 25-10. Minicomposer: moving a note up

Sometimes both a node and its parent support the Index cookie, in which case all three actions can be present on the node, but this situation does not occur in the Minicomposer example.

 If you are struggling to figure out why a parent node has an enabled context menu item **Reorder** but the child nodes do not have **Move Up** or **Move Down** enabled, use the Bean Browser to inspect the actual displayed nodes (**Tools → Explore node… → Itself as a bean**). Probably you will see some specialized filter nodes there. Check the FilterNode Javadoc for caveats regarding the use of index cookies and how to make it work.

Data Transfer—Cut, Copy, and Paste of Notes and Sequences

Our last exercise with nodes will be to support data transfer. In the NetBeans Nodes API, data transfer is based upon the AWT/Swing API in java.awt.datatransfer.*, though there are several extensions to it as well. If you are not already familiar with data transfer in AWT and Swing, you should check the documentation shipped with your JDK or read about it online: for instance, the official design specification (*http://java.sun.com/j2se/1.3/docs/guide/awt/designspec/datatransfer.html*) or the Transferring Data (*http://developer.java.sun.com/developer/Books/MasteringJava/Ch16/index.html*) chapter from *Mastering Java 2*. You should at least understand terms such as clipboard, transferable, data flavor, and transfer data.

An important extension that will *not* be covered here is the generalized transfer of nodes visible in org.openide.nodes.NodeTransfer, which permits a node or node selection to be moved to other nodes, where the transferable can directly access the

Nodes involved (or their cookies). The score module will support transfer of notes using a special data flavor, rather than this more general mechanism; on the other hand, it will demonstrate interoperation with clipboard operations on plain text using a clipboard convertor, as well as use of the NetBeans multi-transfer extension and other interesting topics.

Overview of the Transferables

The Swing API for data transfer is already subtle if logical, and the NetBeans extensions add some additional aspects. Now is a good time to make some coffee. While it brews, take a look at the Open APIs Support module's **Bean Browser** node in the Runtime tab of the Explorer. You can look at the NetBeans clipboard in detail this way.

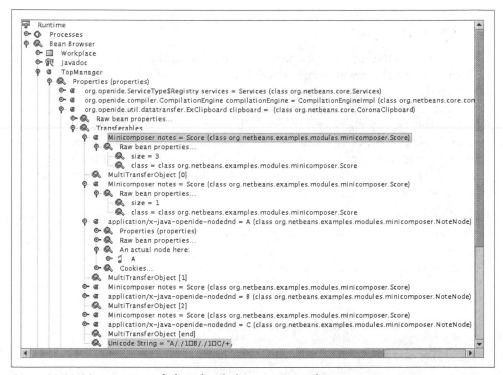

Figure 25-11. Minicomposer: clipboard with three notes copied

Figure 25-11 displays the clipboard after having pressed Copy on three note nodes (**A**, **B**, and **C**) inside a score, with the data transfer support we will explain in this section. Beneath Transferables you can see that there are three data flavors in the clipboard. We will define the first displayed flavor (selected); it provides a Score with three notes as the data. The second flavor, provided as a data transfer extension by the NetBeans APIs, actually has as its data a cluster of three normal transferables, which the Bean Browser displays broken out. Each sub-transferable comes from one copied node. It supports the score flavor (but with only one note). It also supports a general Node transfer flavor defined by the Nodes API, so you can see here the note node **A** that could be transferred by it. The third flavor available in the clipboard (also selected) is the regular AWT text selection flavor; the text is the fragment of textual score those represents those three notes in a row:

```
A/./1
B/./1
C/+/1
```

Were you to copy the score node rather than its note subnodes, you would see the same score flavor containing several notes, the same Nodes API flavor containing the score node, the AWT string flavor with the contents of the *.score* file, and additionally a Datasystems API flavor for transferring DataObjects.

Cutting and Copying

Let us begin with the copy or cut operation. If the CopyAction is run in NetBeans and the Explorer has focus with some selected nodes all of which indicate using Node. canCopy() that they can be copied, then Node.clipboardCopy() is called to produce a Transferable from each. In case there was just one node, this transferable is directly placed in the system clipboard; if more than one node, an ExTransferable.Multi transferable is created (this is defined by the NetBeans APIs) that is a sort of meta-transferable: it supports the special flavor ExTransferable.multiFlavor, and the transfer data is a MultiTransferObject that holds several other Transferables. CutAction is almost the same, but uses Node.canCut() and Node.clipboardCut().

We will first define a new data flavor that represents a Score (one or more notes) to be transferred; add the following lines to your *NoteTransfer.java* source file:

```
public static final DataFlavor SCORE_FLAVOR = new DataFlavor(Score.class,
    NbBundle.getMessage(NoteTransfer.class, "LBL_note_flavor"));
```

This flavor will expect to have instances of Score as its transfer data.

Note that although Score is serializable, transferring scores between Java VMs might not work even if both are running NetBeans, unless Score is accessible in the class loader found by AWT in the target VM. As of NetBeans 3.3, module-supplied classes are not accessible to inter-VM transfer.

If it were desirable to support not only inter-VM but perhaps Java-to-native transfer, assuming the text/x-minicomposer-score format were standardized and used for other applications, a more powerful approach might be to define the data flavor using this MIME type and java.io.InputStream as the representation class. Then even non-Java applications could read or send scores as byte streams.

Technically all data flavors are supposed to have a localized display name, though this is generally only used for Drag and Drop, so we provide one.

Now both individual notes and score nodes should permit copying to the clipboard using this data flavor. Note nodes will also support cutting to the clipboard with this data flavor, but score nodes will not, for reasons we will discuss below. First, these methods need to be added to NoteNode:

```
public boolean canCopy() {
  return true;
}
public boolean canCut() {
  return true;
}
public Transferable clipboardCopy() throws IOException {
  Transferable deflt = super.clipboardCopy();
  ExTransferable enriched = ExTransferable.create(deflt);
  enriched.put(new ExTransferable.Single(NoteTransfer.SCORE_FLAVOR) {
    protected Object getData() {
      return new Score(Collections.singletonList(note));
    }
  });
  return enriched;
}
public Transferable clipboardCut() throws IOException {
  destroy();
  return clipboardCopy();
}
```

You will also need an addition to ScoreDataNode:

```
public Transferable clipboardCopy() throws IOException {
  Transferable deflt = super.clipboardCopy();
  ExTransferable enriched = ExTransferable.create(deflt);
  enriched.put(new ExTransferable.Single(NoteTransfer.SCORE_FLAVOR) {
    protected Object getData() throws IOException {
      return ((ScoreCookie)getCookie(ScoreCookie.class)).getScore();
    }
  });
  return enriched;
}
```

In NoteNode we declare that both Copy and Cut should be supported. In the case of copy, the copied note is not affected. First AbstractNode.clipboardCopy() is called, which will create the Nodes API-supported transferable representing the Node in the clipboard, as mentioned earlier. We do not want to exclude this data flavor from the clipboard; we just want to add the score flavor to it. ExTransferable.create() provides a convenient way to create a new transferable covering all the data flavors of the old one, but to which you may add further flavors in the form of ExTransferable. Singles, which are simple transferables with only one flavor. So we add the SCORE_FLAVOR; if the data from this flavor is ever requested, getData() will be called, and we will make a new Score consisting of just the one note.

ScoreDataNode's `clipboardCopy()` follows the same pattern. Here the super call is actually to `DataNode.clipboardCopy()`, meaning that two flavors are already supported by default: copying the node itself and copying its `ScoreDataObject`. If the transfer data is requested, we just take the complete score from the `ScoreCookie`.

`NoteNode.clipboardCut()` produces the same transferable as `NoteNode.clipboardCopy()` but first deletes the node (thus, its associated note). The reason we do not make an analogous fourth method `ScoreDataNode.clipboardCut()` is that it would not behave consistently with other data nodes. In NetBeans, data nodes when cut are *not* immediately deleted—by default this is true of all nodes, though we overrode it for `NoteNode`. Rather, a reference to the node and data object is placed in the clipboard (using special data flavors that distinguish these from copy-transferables of nodes and data objects). If and when the result is ever pasted to a folder (or other suitable container), the actual move of the node (and perhaps data object) occurs.

This is because in general deleting a data object might not be reversible: consider "cutting" a 30 MB folder. Where would it go while it waits to be pasted? Furthermore if the user changes his mind and pastes it back where it came from to cancel the cut, the folder probably will be slightly different (corrupted file timestamps and so on).

Since cutting a data node does not normally delete it immediately, it would be surprising for Cut to do so for score nodes. Worse, the default node and data object transferables could not be placed in the clipboard after deleting it, since an attempt to paste from the clipboard to a new folder would fail when the cut `ScoreDataObject` no longer existed anywhere. We could implement `ScoreDataNode.clipboardCut()` to work like `clipboardCopy()` as far as the score flavor, but this would be senseless since Copy already works. Therefore, the method is left as implemented in `DataNode` and will not produce any score flavor.*

Pasting

We can now make an initial attempt at letting scores in the clipboard be Pasted to some destination. For the minicomposer, we want to paste the transferred score's list of notes at a place in the target score determined by the user. This might be the beginning, middle, or end of the target score. To make it simple, the user will be able to either select Paste on the score node—in which case the new notes will be added to the *beginning* of the score before any existing ones—or on an existing note node—in which case the new notes will be added *after* that node.

---

* The only way to make it work would be for there to be a "copy" score flavor and a "cut" score flavor, but this would also not work as expected when cutting and then pasting as text unless only the copy flavor were convertible to text—as text editors and so on would see only the AWT-defined string selection and not know to delete the `ScoreDataNode` at the same time. So it is simplest to not make any attempt to support cutting score nodes with a score flavor being left in the clipboard.

Again NoteTransfer can serve as a common place for the two similar operations:

```
public static PasteType createNotePasteType(
    Transferable t, ScoreCookie cookie, Score.Note after) {
  if (t.isDataFlavorSupported(SCORE_FLAVOR)) {
    return new NotePaste(t, cookie, after);
  } else {
    return null;
  }
}
private static final class NotePaste extends PasteType {
  private final Transferable t;
  private final ScoreCookie cookie;
  private final Score.Note after;
  public NotePaste(Transferable t, ScoreCookie cookie, Score.Note after) {
    this.t = t;
    this.cookie = cookie;
    this.after = after;
  }
  public String getName() {
    if (after != null) {
      return NbBundle.getMessage(NoteTransfer.class, "LBL_note_paste_after");
    } else {
      return NbBundle.getMessage(NoteTransfer.class, "LBL_note_paste");
    }
  }
  public HelpCtx getHelpCtx() {
    return new HelpCtx("org.netbeans.examples.modules.minicomposer");
  }
  public Transferable paste() throws IOException {
    Score s = cookie.getScore();
    int c = s.getSize();
    List notes = new ArrayList(c + 100);
    boolean pasted = false;
    if (after == null) {
      append(notes);
      pasted = true;
    }
    for (int i = 0; i < c; i++) {
      Score.Note n = s.getNote(i);
      notes.add(n);
      if (!pasted && after == n) {
        append(notes);
        pasted = true;
      }
    }
    cookie.setScore(new Score(notes));
    return null;
  }
  private void append(List notes) throws IOException {
    try {
      Score pasted = (Score)t.getTransferData(SCORE_FLAVOR);
      int size = pasted.getSize();
```

```
      for (int i = 0; i < size; i++) {
        notes.add(pasted.getNote(i).cloneNote());
      }
    } catch (UnsupportedFlavorException ufe) {/* should not happen */}
  }
}
```

The utility method NoteTransfer.createNotePasteType() can be used to create a score-related paste type. In the Nodes API, PasteType represents one kind of pasting that can be done on a given target node with a given transferable. If the clipboard supports the score data flavor, we create such a paste type, else null is returned.

NotePaste is configured with the transferable (expected to support SCORE_FLAVOR), a score cookie that the new notes are to be pasted into, and an optional note already in that cookie to paste after—if null, pasting is done at the beginning. getName() and getHelpCtx(), as with NewTypes, can assist the user in selecting a type of paste to perform when there is a choice.

paste() is called if and when the Paste operation is performed. We retrieve the existing score, find the position to paste in (at the beginning or after the indicated note), and insert the new notes there. The helper method append() retrieves the score from the clipboard and adds it to the growing list of notes.* Finally, the new score is saved to the cookie to perform the update. Returning null from paste() signals that the clipboard should be left untouched by the operation; it is possible to return a transferable that will replace the pasted transferable (usually this is ExTransferable.EMPTY, which effectively clears the clipboard).

Now making the paste types available from both kinds of nodes is straightforward. As a convenience to the user, Cut, Copy, and Paste should also be made available in the context menus on all nodes. Score nodes already had Cut and Copy because they are normal operations for all data nodes. Make this change in ScoreDataNode to support pasting:

```
protected void createPasteTypes(Transferable t, List s) {
  super.createPasteTypes(t, s);
  PasteType p = NoteTransfer.createNotePasteType(t,
    (ScoreCookie)getCookie(ScoreCookie.class), null);
  if (p != null) {
    s.add(p);
  }
}
```

---

* The reason for cloning the notes from the clipboard before pasting them into the target score is that otherwise a user might copy a note and then paste it back into the same score, resulting in two identical Score. Note keys in the children list. ScoreChildren can handle this perfectly well—two nodes will be displayed—but certain other pieces of logic in the module, such as the technique used in NoteNode.delete() to remove a note from the score, will be confused by the duplication. So it is safer to create clones of the Score.Note objects we paste.

The change in NoteNode is equally simple:

```
protected void createPasteTypes(Transferable t, List s) {
  super.createPasteTypes(t, s);
  PasteType p = NoteTransfer.createNotePasteType(t,
    (ScoreCookie)getCookie(ScoreCookie.class), note);
  if (p != null) {
    s.add(p);
  }
}
protected SystemAction[] createActions() {
  return new SystemAction[] {
    SystemAction.get(MoveUpAction.class),
    SystemAction.get(MoveDownAction.class),
    null,
    // adding this block:
    SystemAction.get(CutAction.class),
    SystemAction.get(CopyAction.class),
    SystemAction.get(PasteAction.class),
    null,
    SystemAction.get(DeleteAction.class),
    SystemAction.get(RenameAction.class),
    null,
    SystemAction.get(PropertiesAction.class),
    SystemAction.get(ToolsAction.class),
  };
}
```

Finally, you will need to add one item to ScoreDataLoader's defaultActions() method:

```
protected SystemAction[] defaultActions() {
  return new SystemAction[] {
    // ... as before
    SystemAction.get(ReorderAction.class),
    null,
    SystemAction.get(CutAction.class),
    SystemAction.get(CopyAction.class),
    SystemAction.get(PasteAction.class), // newly added
    null,
    SystemAction.get(DeleteAction.class),
    // as before...
  };
}
```

Now the user can Copy a score node and Paste onto any score or note node to insert the notes into the target, or Copy a note node and Paste on some target to make a copy of the note, or Cut a note node and Paste on a target to move the note there.

Drag & Drop

We have only discussed how to implement "traditional" cut, copy, and paste operations. However, NetBeans is also evolving to support Drag & Drop (D&D), meaning that data can be transferred interactively with the mouse.

While the NetBeans Nodes API does provide some special support for D&D, we will not need to use any of these special features. In fact, the data transfer support we have already written will work *automatically* when D&D is enabled. In NetBeans 3.4, D&D will be available when using JDK 1.4. Then notes can be dragged around inside a score or between scores. As of this writing, you can preview this functionality in a NetBeans development build.

Converting Score → Text, Text →Score, Several Scores → One

You may recall that when CopyAction (or similarly CutAction) processes a selection consisting of multiple nodes, it cannot simply place all the transferables directly in the clipboard because a clipboard holds only one transferable at a time. So an ExTransferable.Multi is created instead as a container for the cluster of regular transferables.

If the user copies one note node (or score note), the clipboard will directly contain a transferable supporting SCORE_FLAVOR, and our NotePaste.append retrieves the score and pastes it. But what happens if several notes are copied at once? The system clipboard's transferable does *not* in this case support SCORE_FLAVOR, and the initial call to createNotePasteType() will fail and return null! In fact the code works so far—you can paste the block of notes into a score—but only because of a bit of cleverness in PasteAction. It notices that the clipboard transferable is really a multi-transferable and that the target node did not understand it, so it breaks up the multi-transferable and checks whether the individual sub-transferables are accepted. Since the sub-transferables all provide SCORE_FLAVOR, they are accepted for pasting one by one (Node.getPasteTypes() returns at least one type). PasteAction then performs each paste in isolation, with the result that the complete list of notes is pasted onto the target.

While this works, it is clumsy: NotePaste.paste() is called once per pasted node, which is inefficient, and in a more complex application might even give semantically wrong results. What we really want is for all the individual note nodes' score transferables to be coalesced into one big score, which will then be pasted as a unit.

One way of achieving this is to check for the existence of ExTransferable. multiFlavor in NotePaste.paste(). And this will work. However, there is another feature we might like to implement while solving the multiple-paste problem, *conversion to and from text*. If a score is copied, it might be useful to have the clipboard also know about the textual representation of that score (sequence of notes) in the textual score format (that we defined as text/x-minicomposer-score) so that notes, passages, or entire scores can be copied in the Explorer and directly pasted into text files of various sorts. Or, after copying the textual representation of a passage embedded in an HTML document, you can paste the corresponding nodes directly into place in the Explorer.

To support such conversion of clipboard contents, we need to use a clipboard convertor. The NetBeans APIs include a little-used but powerful class, ExClipboard. Convertor, which if registered into the system's pool of services will be asked to massage whatever transferables come through the clipboard: typically adding derivative data flavors for the benefit of targets that do not understand the flavors produced by the source.

Our convertor will work in four basic modes, depending on what it sees in the clipboard (see Figure 25-12 for the complete picture):

1. If the clipboard contains just a string selection, add the score flavor to it. The transfer data will be a Score generated by parsing the string like a score file.

2. If the clipboard contains the score flavor, add a string selection. If requested, the transferred string will be the textual representation of the score as if saved to a file.

3. If the clipboard is a multi-transferable and each child transferable contains the score flavor, then add the score flavor to the master transferable with the data being a long score (all the child scores concatenated); also add the string flavor, with the text being the textual form of all the scores laid end to end.

4. If the transferable in the clipboard does not match any of the preceding criteria, do nothing.

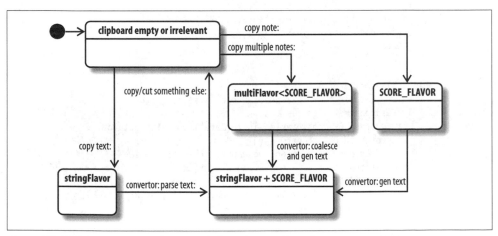

Figure 25-12. Minicomposer: changing clipboard contents with convertor active

We will make NoteTransfer implement the convertor interface just to save classes:

```
public final class NoteTransfer implements ExClipboard.Convertor {
                                    // ^ newly implemented interface
  public Transferable convert(final Transferable t) {
    boolean supportsString = t.isDataFlavorSupported(DataFlavor.stringFlavor);
    boolean supportsScore = t.isDataFlavorSupported(SCORE_FLAVOR);
    if (supportsString && !supportsScore) {
      ExTransferable t2 = ExTransferable.create(t);
      t2.put(new ExTransferable.Single(SCORE_FLAVOR) {
        protected Object getData()
            throws IOException, UnsupportedFlavorException {
          String text = (String)t.getTransferData(DataFlavor.stringFlavor);
          return Score.parse(new StringReader(text));
        }
      });
      return t2;
    } else if (!supportsString && supportsScore) {
      ExTransferable t2 = ExTransferable.create(t);
      t2.put(new ExTransferable.Single(DataFlavor.stringFlavor) {
        protected Object getData()
            throws IOException, UnsupportedFlavorException {
          Score s = (Score)t.getTransferData(SCORE_FLAVOR);
          StringWriter wr = new StringWriter();
          Score.generate(s, wr);
          return wr.toString();
        }
      });
      return t2;
    } else if (t.isDataFlavorSupported(ExTransferable.multiFlavor)) {
      try {
        final MultiTransferObject mto =
          (MultiTransferObject)t.getTransferData(ExTransferable.multiFlavor);
        boolean allSupportScore = true;
        for (int i = 0; i < mto.getCount(); i++) {
          if (!mto.isDataFlavorSupported(i, SCORE_FLAVOR)) {
            allSupportScore = false;
            break;
          }
        }
        if (allSupportScore) {
          ExTransferable t2 = ExTransferable.create(t);
          if (!supportsString) {
            t2.put(new ExTransferable.Single(DataFlavor.stringFlavor) {
              protected Object getData()
                  throws IOException, UnsupportedFlavorException {
                StringWriter wr = new StringWriter();
                for (int i = 0; i < mto.getCount(); i++) {
                  Score s = (Score)mto.getTransferData(i, SCORE_FLAVOR);
                  Score.generate(s, wr);
                }
                return wr.toString();
              }
            });
```

```
            }
            if (!supportsScore) {
               t2.put(new ExTransferable.Single(SCORE_FLAVOR) {
                  protected Object getData()
                        throws IOException, UnsupportedFlavorException {
                     List notes = new ArrayList();
                     for (int i = 0; i < mto.getCount(); i++) {
                        Score s = (Score)mto.getTransferData(i, SCORE_FLAVOR);
                        int size = s.getSize();
                        for (int j = 0; j < size; j++) {
                           notes.add(s.getNote(j));
                        }
                     }
                     return new Score(notes);
                  }
               });
            }
            return t2;
         } // end if allSupportScore
      } catch (Exception e) {/* should not happen */}
   } // end if string, score, or multi flavors supported
   return t;
}
// other static constants, methods, and inner classes as before...
}
```

The logic of the worker method convert() essentially follows the preceding four possibilities. The final line returns the original transferable in case none of the first three conditions matched (or in case there was a problem with the multi-transferable). As we did with the clipboardCopy() methods earlier, ExTransferable and ExTransferable. Single are used to create an enriched transferable supporting more flavors than it did before.

Before touching the incoming transferable, the convertor ensures that the flavor it intends to add is not already present in the transferable by some chance; otherwise, the original transfer data will be overridden with a generated flavor, which is probably not wanted.

Registering the convertor to the system is straightforward using the Services API. We just need to add an instance of NoteTransfer to the default lookup pool using *layer.xml*:

```
<filesystem>
  <folder name="Services">
    <folder name="Hidden">
      <file
        name="org-netbeans-examples-modules-minicomposer-NoteTransfer.instance"/>
    </folder>
  </folder>
</filesystem>
```

We place the instance in the *Hidden/* subfolder of *Services/* because it is not intended to ever be seen or manipulated by the user directly.

With the convertor in place, several kinds of data transfer can be done:

- Copy or cut a note or several notes and paste them onto another note to append them. Paste them onto a score to insert them at the beginning.
- Copy or cut a note or several notes and paste them in a text buffer.
- Copy a score and paste it in a text buffer, at the beginning of another score, or in the middle of another score.
- Copy or cut a few lines of well-formed score from a text buffer and paste them at the beginning of a score in the Explorer or after some note in it.
- Copy or cut textual lines and paste them into another textual buffer—of course, this is possible with no score module as well.
- Having made a new blank score, copy several other score nodes at once and paste them into the new long score.

Congratulations! You should now understand many of the mechanics of making a sophisticated NetBeans module. Now, to be good citizens of the NetBeans module universe, you need to learn how to make your own modules fast and lightweight.

## CHAPTER 26

Tuning Modules for Performance & Memory Footprint

NetBeans is, by definition, a large application, with a significant memory footprint. It is incumbent on anyone writing modules to write them responsibly, so that the user experience is not degraded. This chapter will outline some ways to do this in the context of NetBeans. For general optimization of Java code, we refer you to some of the excellent articles and books on the subject, such as *Java 2 Performance and Idiom Guide* by Craig Larman and Rhett Guthrie.

The limiting factor in NetBeans' performance is memory. As objects are created in memory and then are no longer referenced, the memory footprint grows until garbage collection is run in the JVM. This means three things:

- Modules should not create objects until they are about to be used.
- Care should be taken not to hold references to objects that may not be used again or for a long time.
- Once created, do my objects need to exist until NetBeans is shut down, or can they be disposed of sooner? What can I softly cache?*

NetBeans has a number of coding conventions and utility classes to optimize for memory footprint, which will be outlined throughout this chapter. Use them and your modules will run will in any reasonable environment. Some of the advice about use of threads is dependent on the target platform. But unless you're far better than the authors at predicting the future, you probably want your code to work in any environment in which it might be deployed. This chapter is your guide to common pitfalls and how to avoid them when coding for NetBeans.

---

* Soft caching is a means of holding a reference to an object, but still allowing it to be garbage collected by the JVM if memory is required. In that case it will need to be re-created on demand if requested again.

Startup Performance vs. Runtime Performance

Clearly you don't want to add any more to startup time than absolutely necessary. One of the reasons for the declarative XML syntax in module layers for instantiating objects is that, in addition to the flexibility it offers, it means that classes referenced in XML will not even be loaded into the JVM unless something requests an instance of the class referred to.

Loading classes into a Java VM is typically expensive. A trivial class takes at least 1K of memory, and the process of resolving a class, loading it, linking it and running static initializers takes time. A large chunk of NetBeans startup time is traceable directly to class loading. Most of the performance tricks in NetBeans are focused on letting a module avoid loading classes until they're actually going to be used. You can easily check how you're doing by running the VM in verbose class loading mode or using a profiler.

That being said, there will be times when doing some initialization on startup is the right thing to do. They are rare, but an example is when the Code Editor aggressively loads some of its configuration because the alternative would be an unacceptable delay the first time the user tries to edit a file. For most cases, and probably for your module, this is not going to be the case.

Operating Principles

While there are many places performance optimizations can be made, the following sections highlight a few ways of thinking and places to pay attention to that will assist you.

"Nobody Will Ever Use My Module"

Okay, that's a depressing thought. You wouldn't be writing a module if you didn't want people to use it! But it's also a good way to think about things when you're writing a module. If you've written fantastic Intercal (*http://www.tuxedo.org/~esr/intercal/*) support for NetBeans, you still probably don't want to assume that editing Intercal programs is the only thing the user is likely to be doing with NetBeans. This is doubly true for modules implementing a limited set of functionality (however difficult to implement) such as profiling or UML diagramming. The common activity in NetBeans is likely to be editing code, and no matter how revolutionary any module is, it needs to be a good citizen and stay out of the way when the user is not paying attention to it. Code on the assumption that the user is *not* using your module, and you will write a module that behaves well both when it is and when it is not being used.

For evidence of this, consider modules such as CORBA or RMI. How often do you use them? For some people it may be quite a bit, but even though most users of NetBeans will have these modules loaded they will rarely, if ever, use them. It is certainly the inappropriate choice for someone to have to disable a module to improve performance; the module should load nothing except, ideally, a few XML entries that will allow NetBeans to bootstrap the classes that are needed on demand and let the module go to work.

What Does My Module Really Need to Do on Startup?

It is tempting to bring your module to an initialized state when it is first loaded. But the real question is what you actually need to initialize. Anything done when a module is first loaded is going to add to startup time, and while this is in some ways less important than performing well at runtime, bear in mind that in a sense, the model for NetBeans modules is one of cooperative multitasking. The number of other modules your module will need to coexist cannot be determined, but any module can potentially degrade the performance of others. Therefore, it is important that each module be a good citizen of the NetBeans runtime, or everyone can suffer, and this applies equally to startup time and runtime performance. For better or worse, startup time is the user's first experience with an application. If you're building a module that runs inside NetBeans or an entire application based on NetBeans, you want the user to have a good first experience and a satisfying ongoing experience with your code.

There are cases where the time at which an object will be demanded cannot be determined. The HTTP Server module is an example of this, since on startup there may be an existing external HTTP client that expects to be able to interact with it. But these cases are few and far between, and even in these cases, there is the possibility for optimization (such as a dummy HTTP server that, when a connection is attempted, starts the real HTTP server and forwards the request).

What Are the Critical Paths?

Beyond startup performance, there are critical paths through the code where it is absolutely critical to optimize for performance. This applies mainly to commonly used API-specified objects. The constructor for any object is the most basic example of a critical path through the code. Constructors should not make any assumptions that the object being created will actually be used or that it will be used in the near term, and thus should do no more work than is absolutely necessary. Ideally, a constructor should simply instantiate an uninitialized object that will initialize itself when something tries to use it.

One particularly important example is Nodes. Nodes must be very inexpensive to create. One of the principal reasons a Node does not directly create its child nodes, but delegates this to a `Children` object, is to delay the creation of additional nodes until the last possible moment. This is done on the assumption that if the user doesn't actually expand the node, the child `Nodes` should never come into being. This principle of lazy instantiation is a good idea almost everywhere, but it is particularly critical in the case of `Nodes`, since creating `Nodes` is something that happens very frequently within the NetBeans environment. Note that this means you should avoid using `Children.Array`, since that class requires that the children be created when the `Node` is.

`DataLoaders` need to be able to recognize files *fast*. Your `DataLoader` is going to be called for every file in the system. This process must be optimized so that the negative test is as fast as possible, and your recognition code will return false at the earliest possible moment. If you're simply recognizing files by extension, this should already be fast. Register a `MIMEResolver` that can assign files relevant to your code to your `DataLoader`.

For identifying XML files by DTD, create a specialized MIME type such as `text/x-mytype+xml`. Your `MIMEResolver` will resolve the MIME type. You could accomplish this by subclassing `MIMEResolver`, but it is more efficient to use an XML MIME resolver in your module layer, as the Minicomposer example does. (For an example, see Chapter 21.) This allows you to declare a set of standard rules that will determine if a file is a match using magic byte sequence, extension, XML DOCTYPE, or root element. Then the optimization worries are those of NetBeans, and you can rest assured that recognition of your document type will be as optimized as possible. Another advantage of declaring your `MIMEResolver` in XML is that as of NetBeans 4.0 a `DataLoader` will never be loaded into the JVM until a file needing to be represented by it is encountered.

Cookie creation in `Nodes` and `DataObjects` should happen on demand. If the presence or absence of a given cookie depends on the state of the object the `Node` represents, override `getCookie()` to create the cookie and do the state calculations on demand. There is also a helper class `CookieSet.Factory` that can be used for this purpose.

Techniques

A number of best practices for performance have evolved over the course of NetBeans lifespan. Indeed, as the size and complexity of the NetBeans IDE has grown, sometimes what was once the best practice (such as aggressively loading classes for responsiveness at startup) can become a very bad practice later. By and large, these guidelines travel on the assumption that the application is a large one, and are geared toward conserving memory and performing work on demand rather than in anticipation of demand.

Lazy Initialization

This simple approach is a good coding practice in almost any application. When writing a class, don't create objects until something actually tries to use them. In its simplest form, this adds up to the difference between:

```
public class Foo extends Object {
  Bar myBar = new Bar();
  public void doSomething() {
    myBar.doSomething();
  }
}
```

and this code, which will load faster and potentially consume less memory:

```
public class Foo extends Object {
  Bar myBar;
  public void doSomething() {
    getBar().doSomething();
  }
  private Bar getBar() {
    if (myBar == null) {
      myBar = new Bar();
    }
    return myBar;
  }
}
```

This approach is nothing revolutionary, and there are more reasons than just optimization to take it. If you've ever been coding and had an insight that you actually ought to do one more piece of work when you initialize something like the Bar object above, you probably know the pain of going through your code and replacing the references to the variable for your object with a method call. Even with the niftiest refactoring support in the world, it's work that could have been avoided in the first place.

Avoid Static Initializers

Similar to the preceding example, it is generally preferable to avoid static initializer sections in your code, such as this:

```
public class Foo extends Object {
  protected static Bar[] myConstants;
  static {
    for (int i = 0; i < 200; i++) {
      myConstants[i] = new Bar(i);
    }
  }
}
```

This is true for several reasons: first, as soon as the Foo class is loaded, Bar is also yanked into memory; second, your code is assuming that at some point the user is going to do something that makes use of this array. *You don't know that!* Depending on how you write your code, it may be that your Foo class is referenced directly by a SystemAction that your module installs as a menu item. This means that as soon as NetBeans creates its main menu, Foo gets loaded, which in turn drags in Bar and creates 200 instances of it.

Avoid ModuleInstall Classes—Use XML Layers Instead

Another piece of the lazy initialization puzzle is avoiding ModuleInstall classes. This is a class that can be specified in a module's manifest, which has methods that will be run when the module is installed, uninstalled, restored (for example, NetBeans is restarted) or shut down. NetBeans offers XML layers as a way to specifically avoid doing unnecessary work during startup. There is an older infrastructure that allows these same things to be specified in the module manifest. This older infrastructure will cause classes to be loaded on startup and should be avoided any place it is possible to use XML instead. For the details of doing this, see Chapter 15.

As of NetBeans 3.3, only three kinds of sections must still be handled via the manifest: actions, data loaders, and nodes. In NetBeans 3.4, nodes will be taken off this list, and in NetBeans 4.0, it will be possible to handle actions and loaders declaratively in XML as well, effectively eliminating the need for any classes from a module to be loaded on startup. The specification for doing this is not crystallized at the time of this writing. Check the APIs for your version of NetBeans to find out how to do this.

.settings files

There is an extension to the Lookup mechanism: *.settings* files.

One advantage to using XML layers is that no work needs to be done to deregister your objects and clean up if your module is disabled—your module's XML layer is simply cleanly removed from the system. A well-behaved module will offer its services to the system via XML layers.

.settings files are similar to *.instance* files, except that when an instance is created, a PropertyChangeListener is also added to the object by the system. If any properties of the object are changed, those changes are written to disk and will be reflected in instances created from this *.settings* file in the future. This gets you persistent objects and storage for free, while retaining the advantage that an instance of your class that provides settings will never becomes instantiated and begin taking up memory unless the user or module code demands it.

Batching results of expensive operations

There is no getting around it—some operations occasionally take quite a bit of time. Some kinds of Nodes will require intensive calculation to instantiate their children (such as parsing a large document). The same is true of properties of objects. Sometimes delaying instantiation until the last possible moment results in an unacceptably long delay for the user. This is a bad thing for two reasons: first, the user can't do any other work while they wait for NetBeans to finish chewing; second, it simply creates a bad impression that makes people want to find a faster solution, one that may not involve your module or NetBeans.

Fortunately, such situations have at least a partial solution. In most cases you can do a partial calculation in a background thread, return the results and continue the work, while the user remains able to interact with NetBeans. The basic technique is this: if you are creating a Node with many children or properties, create a threshold number of them (for example, enough properties to fill most of a property sheet or subnodes in a typical Explorer tree view). Return those, and in the background create the rest in batched sets, firing events along the way to notify the system that the children or properties have changed and the UI should be updated.

Partial Loading Considerations—InstanceCookie and InstanceDataObject

If someone opens the Options window, they see a large number of Nodes that represent user-settable settings. The last thing anybody wants is to cause classes from every module that installs a settings Node to get dragged into memory, simply because the user is being presented with a dialog. After all, the user most likely wants to change one or two things when opening the settings dialog box. So it's practically guaranteed that most elements in the Options tree will not be touched in a given invocation of the dialog box.

NetBeans contains infrastructure for name-based lookup and loading of classes. By using XML layers and InstanceDataObject, you can know the name of the class you want to get and have the appropriate icon and localized display name for it, without actually forcing it to be loaded unless the class needs to do some work, such as displaying its properties. Use this pattern in your own classes for greater efficiency.

Use URLs Instead of CDATA Sections in XML Layers

The specification for XML layers includes the ability to include file data within <<file>> tags in XML. However, this imposes a memory penalty, since the string representation of that data will be held in memory. It is equally possible to provide a URL in the XML layer that points to the actual content as a path inside your module JAR. This is the better approach, since no memory is taken up by data that might not be used (except for the URL string) and the file on the other end of that URL will be provided as the content of that file if the data is actually needed by the system.

Additionally, pointing to external content using a URL makes it simpler to work with non-ASCII characters or binary files and avoids possible confusion about whitespace surrounding the content.

Reduce the Number of Classes You Create

Current JVMs are still a bit inefficient when loading classes. Where possible, aggregate. For example, if your class attaches property change listeners to several types of objects, it is more efficient to test for the source of the change event and handle it accordingly than to create several anonymous inner property change listeners to do the job.

Another example is the case where you need to start a thread and Runnable listen for completion. One typically thinks of the listener as pretty distinct from the thread being run, but the following code is actually more efficient:

```
Task t = cookie.prepare();
class MyRun implements TaskListener, Runnable {
  public void taskFinished(Task t2) {
    SwingUtilities.invokeLater(this);
  }
  public void run() {
    // do the work...
  }
}
t.addTaskListener(new MyRun());
```

GUI Components—Wait for addNotify()

When creating GUI components, there is a temptation to create all the subcomponents of a component in the constructor. This is, however, a comparatively expensive process. Your component cannot guarantee it is going to be displayed until it appears onscreen. java.awt.Component and its descendants provide a convenient method to hook into the operation of displaying and hiding a component in the methods addNotify() and removeNotify(). If you need to do significant work with adding and initializing components, do this in addNotify() and release any resources you can in removeNotify(). Remember that you *must* call the super method when overriding addNotify() and removeNotify(), or bizarre bugs may result.

Using the addNotify() and removeNotify() Pattern Where Exposed by Non-GUI Classes

Nodes mirror the addNotify() and removeNotify() pattern found in java.awt. Component. When a Node is first expanded, addNotify() is called on the children, which indicates that its children are soon to be required and that it needs to calculate the keys or whatever initial data is needed so it can provide them. If the Node is closed, removeNotify() will eventually be called, at which time your Node should dispose of its keys and return to its uninitialized state. This way objects created by expanding it can be garbage collected if the JVM is low on memory.

SystemActions also have addNotify() and removeNotify() methods (implemented in the SharedClassObject ancestor class). These methods are called based on the presence of listeners on the action. The presence of listeners implies that some component is presenting the action to the user. Then all code involving your action attaching listeners to other objects or other initialization can be postponed until listeners are attached *to it.* If it is not being presented to the user, an action should not incur any overhead in the system. For most SystemAction subclasses, however, you will not be directly implementing SystemAction, but one of the convenience subclasses for context-sensitive actions such as NodeAction, CookieAction, or CallbackSystemAction, which handle this logic for you. If you are implementing addNotify() and removeNotify() to do something particularly clever with your action, it's worth putting in some debug code that logs output using ErrorManager on calls to these methods and make sure you're not doing excessive work here.

While DataObjects lack the addNotify()/removeNotify() pattern, with a little care you can nonetheless defer any expensive operations with the data object. Most commonly, the real functionality is available from some cookie served by the object. Do not initiate work such as parsing unless and until this cookie is actually requested.

Use Weak and Soft References for Objects

The java.lang.ref package contains a number of helper classes that can help you save memory by not forcing a hard reference to an object. In Java, an object is retained in memory as long as it is referenced by another object. Objects that are not known to any other object in the system are no longer needed, and their memory can be reclaimed. When garbage collection starts, it does a pass through all objects in an area of memory and marks those that are not reachable as eligible to be collected. Then it takes a second pass to free up the memory they're consuming. One of the primary sources of memory leaks in Java code is holding references to objects that will never be touched, or probably won't be touched again but that can be created if needed.

A weak reference is a reference that the garbage collector will not count in deciding whether an object is still referenced. If an object is only weakly reachable, it will generally be garbage collected soon, like a completely unreachable object. This is possible because the object that is only weakly reachable is wrapped in a java.lang.ref. WeakReference object that holds a reference to the object. WeakReference classes have a method Object get() that returns the object referenced, or null if it was garbage collected.

If you are creating an object that may or may not be needed or used for long periods of time, use either java.lang.ref.WeakReference or java.lang.ref.SoftReference to hold these objects, and provide a getter method that dereferences and returns the weakly referenced object. As long as some other code is using your object, it can't be garbage collected because there will be a hard reference to it. If there are no hard references, it can safely be garbage collected, and your getter can re-create it on demand.

To show this in action, let's look at some examples:

```java
public class MySingletonObject {
  public MySingletonObject defaultInstance =
    new MySingletonObject();
}
```

The preceding example is what you absolutely don't want to do—force creation of your object when the class is first loaded, whether or not it will be used! The following example is slightly better:

```java
public class MySingletonObject {
  private MySingletonObject defaultInstance = null;
  public MySingletonObject getDefault() {
    if (defaultInstance == null) {
      defaultInstance = new MySingletonObject();
    }
    return defaultInstance;
  }
}
```

But this is still not ideal—what if your object were used only once in an entire session of running NetBeans? Your object would spend the rest of its life taking up memory and waiting for the phone to ring. This is where weak references come in:

```java
public class MySingletonObject {
  private static Reference defaultInstance = null;
  public static synchronized MySingletonObject getDefault() {
    MySingletonObject obj;
    if (defaultInstance != null) {
      obj = (MySingletonObject)defaultInstance.get();
    } else {
      obj = null;
    }
    if (obj == null) {
      obj = new MySingletonObject();
      defaultInstance = new WeakReference(obj);
    }
    return obj;
  }
}
```

This example gets your singleton, but without requiring it to remain in memory if it's not actually being used.

If your object is something that may live longer but that can be re-created, use `java.lang.ref.SoftReference` instead. It is functionally similar to `WeakReference` but might not be collected even if there is no one holding a strong reference until JVM memory becomes very low. In some situations use of weak references is logical, and in other situations you should use soft references—they are not usually interchangeable.

Note that *overuse* of weak references can hurt performance in some circumstances by causing excessive object re-creation. Soft references do not suffer from this problem, but might consume memory for a long time holding objects no one will ask for. Always use a profiler and/or logging code to examine how often your object is really disposed and re-created.

Utility classes that can help

The Open APIs contain several helper classes that can assist you. Particularly of interest may be org.openide.util.WeakSet, which is a Set implementation whose members can disappear on garbage collection if they are not referenced elsewhere. If you need to keep a list of all instances of a class, use WeakSet to do so. The Java platform class java.util.WeakHashMap can also be helpful.

Use WeakListener

org.openide.util.WeakListener is probably the most commonly used helper class for saving memory in NetBeans. Say that you have a long-lived object such as a data model that holds a structural representation of some document you've parsed. A common situation is that you also want to attach a listener to it from a more peripheral piece of code, such as a GUI component, so that that component can update its state if the model is changed. The chances are that the model will outlive the GUI component, which the user may close. If the GUI component directly attaches a listener to the model, you've introduced a memory leak of sorts: The GUI component can never be garbage collected unless the model is as well because the model is still holding a reference to it—the listener. The model could end up holding references to many defunct objects this way. Worse, it is still firing changes to them.

WeakListener is the solution to this problem. It allows you to attach a listener that is only weakly referenced by the object to which it is attached, so events can still be fired, but the object that is listening can be garbage collected if nothing else references it anymore. The WeakListener class has inner classes that implement a number of the standard JDK and NetBeans listener classes, such as EventListener, PropertyChangeListener, and so forth. Static methods are on the WeakListener class to attach all of these listeners, by basically creating a proxy listener that holds a weak reference to the real listener. To attach a PropertyChangeListener to the data model we just discussed, the code will look like this (assuming our short-lived GUI component implements PropertyChangeListener):

```
model.addPropertyChangeListener(WeakListener.propertyChange(this, model));
```

If the GUI component in question gets garbage collected, the WeakListener removes itself from the model. If you need to implement a custom listener WeakListener does not support, you can subclass WeakListener to accomplish this.

If you have a listening object with addNotify() and removeNotify() methods (for example, Children or Component), you do not need to use WeakListener. It is simpler and more efficient to attach a listener directly in addNotify() and detach it in removeNotify().

Avoid Excessive Event Firing

You never know what may be listening to your objects and possibly champing at the bit to do time- and memory-consuming work just because a property of your object changed. A practical example is a Node that can be renamed by the user. It is not difficult for a user to click and hover the mouse too long over the in-place editor in the Explorer window, which means it is opened and closed, even though the name of the object that was clicked was not actually changed. Confirm that the property has actually changed the name before firing changes that could galvanize ponderous parsing processes into action.

Avoid Overuse of Threads

Overuse of threads can be a problem on some operating systems and not on others. Since you (presumably) want your code to run smoothly and cleanly on as many platforms as possible, it's always a good practice to optimize. On Windows this does not present a tremendous problem; on Linux overuse of threads causes a minor performance hit; on Solaris the effect can be severe.

In practice two pieces of advice will help: Avoid switching between threads more than is absolutely necessary, and if you need to do something in a different thread, create it and do as much work as you can in a single pass. Entering a thread, synchronizing it, and running it is expensive in Java.

The utility `org.openide.util.RequestProcessor.postRequest()` provides a convenient technique for creating a new runnable and dumping it on a queue to be run later. This is useful in many parts of NetBeans programming where you need to do something but doing so at the present time would be dangerous (for example, if you're holding a lock and you're in an arbitrary thread and need to change the GUI). You can also use `SwingUtilities.invokeLater()` for similar purposes, and the advice is the same. A common mistake is to post too many `Runnables` for trivial purposes. The next section covers one of the primary causes of this.

Note that for NetBeans 3.4, it is deprecated to post requests into the singleton public request processor instance, as such requests are run serially and can deadlock one another unless written carefully to avoid this. In NetBeans 3.3 you can create a private request processor to ensure that such deadlocks do not occur as a result of your code, but the price is the creation of a dedicated thread; in 3.4 creating a private request processor is lightweight and recommended more broadly.

Another thing to avoid is too much synchronization when using threads. Wherever possible, use a single lock or mutex (the class `org.openide.util.Mutex` exists to help with this). Synchronization is expensive!

Batching Events

A typical mistake is to have a class that may have hundreds of instances, all listening to the same object. It is a far better practice to batch the changes. One way to accomplish this is to maintain a WeakSet with all instances of your class. In the case of a change they will need to be notified of, iterate through that set and notify the necessary objects. This is particularly important in cases where each notification could involve thread creation.

Another case in which you will want to batch events is where a change that will have large effects on subsidiary objects is being made. Filesystem operations are typical of this class of event. If you're in the NetBeans IDE and you rename or move a Java package, this has a ripple effect on all of the DataObjects in the system that represent Java sources in that package. And you definitely don't want the effects of the rename to start to cause cascading events of their own before the renaming work is complete. FileSystem.runAtomic() exists for this reason. If you need to do a large number of file operations at once, it is best to run them as an atomic block. This avoids some synchronization costs and fires changes only once, at the end of the operation. All changes are queued and duplicates are pruned.

Swing Performance

Excellent resources are available on Swing performance, so we won't cover this topic in great detail. Most of the preceding advice is applicable to Swing programming as well, along with such advice as using TableData to load large tables of data dynamically. Generally, it is inadvisable to cache dialog boxes, with some caveats in that a dialog box that is expensive to create (heavy parsing or complex graphical operations required to display it) may be better off weakly cached. This avoids heavy memory consumption if multiple instances are serially created.

Once you have a highly-tuned module packed with features, how can you get it to your users? You will need to take steps to package it into a convenient form and learn how to maintain it for the long haul. The next chapter explains how to do so.

CHAPTER 27

Producing Modules (Packaging & Distribution)

Just writing a module JAR that works in your NetBeans test environment does not make it ready for end users. One critical consideration is the lifecycle of the module—how multiple versions of it may be maintained and user settings from them upgraded. Internationalization and accessibility can help your module be usable by people speaking various languages and people with disabilities or special needs for interacting with software. Online documentation can be provided via JavaHelp for novice users. If your module provides access to a Java API, you can make it more convenient for the user to work with this API. Production includes physical creation of the module and associated files using a robust build system and publishing it to be available for users without complicated installation procedures. Finally, it is desirable to make the module easily testable for bugs and regressions, as well as providing for diagnosis of problems in the field. All of these topics can perhaps be ignored during initial prototyping, but need to be addressed before a public release can be considered.

Versioning

Giving versions of your module and controlling how it may be used by other modules or what other modules it uses is an important production consideration—unless you can guarantee what environment a user is running NetBeans in and are willing to manually manage upgrades to all modules, the NetBeans module dependency and versioning system can help keep track of (and enforce) your assumptions.

This section will discuss how versioning and dependencies work. To make them effective, you also need a consistent policy of when to make releases, what dependencies are acceptable, and so on. The NetBeans Versioning Policy (*http://openide. netbeans.org/versioning-policy.html*) tries to provide this in the case of the NetBeans Open APIs, core, and common modules hosted on *netbeans.org* (and Forte for Java tries to follow this policy, too). You may want to use this document as a model or source of hints. It will also be helpful for understanding when certain NetBeans APIs became officially available, as well as when declaring dependencies on common Net-Beans modules.

Version Numbers and What They Mean

Modules can and should specify versioning information that controls how they may be installed and upgraded. Three different kinds of versions can be associated with a single module (all are optional), and it is important to understand the difference and what each is useful for. Consider the following manifest as a reference point:

```
Manifest-Version: 1.0
OpenIDE-Module: org.netbeans.modules.wombat/1
OpenIDE-Module-Specification-Version: 1.0
OpenIDE-Module-Implementation-Version: built A.D. 2001, Sunday, around tea-time
```

 Manifest-Version: 1.0 is fixed by the Java manifest specification and has nothing to do with NetBeans. Also take care that manifests end with a double newline.

- The module code name is given by the magic OpenIDE-Module attribute in the manifest, which every module must have. It consists at least of a code name base that uniquely identifies the module, then optionally a slash followed by a major release version. The major release version is usually present on modules that can serve as APIs to other modules. It changes only when incompatible changes are made to the module. This version must be a whole number.

  In the preceding example, the code name base org.netbeans.modules.wombat is a unique identifier for this module among all possible NetBeans modules; the release version 1 indicates that clients of the Wombat support module can cleanly upgrade to any later version with the *same* release version. If the module provided no API to other modules, org.netbeans.modules.wombat would suffice as the full code name (in which case the release version is understood to be less than 0).

- The specification version given by the OpenIDE-Module-Specification-Version attribute is the most useful version number, and almost all modules should have one. It must be in Dewey-decimal format, which means a sequence of one or more whole numbers (0, 1, ...) separated by decimal points (.), where earlier numbers are more significant and 1.2.0.0 is a synonym for 1.2. It *cannot* use non-numeric components as in 1.2.0-beta3. The specification version defines the normal forward progression of module versions. It can be used to control availability of compatible API features, but it is also used in simple modules to control automated upgrades.

- The implementation version may be given by the OpenIDE-Module-Implementation-Version attribute. It is not used for much by the IDE; it is mainly informational, and can be used to identify a particular build of the module, who built it on what machine, and so on. The text is free-form, and if it contains a number, NetBeans does not notice. It is intended mostly for tracking down the exact copy of a JAR that a user of that module has installed onsite—the implementation version of each installed module is printed in the log file when NetBeans starts.

The normal situation when upgrading a module is to simply increase its specification version by some amount and release the new version of the module. For example, if you started at 1.0, you might increment it to 1.1 (or 1.0.1 if you are just releasing a minor patch). The IDE will treat this as a regular upgrade; if you are using a module installer (org.openide.modules.ModuleInstall) its updated() method will be called with the old version instead of the usual restored(), which you might find useful when dealing with older settings, though normally this method would not be overridden.

Specifying Dependencies

By default a module is assumed to have no particular dependencies. That is, any version of NetBeans will assume that the module can be loaded and used, and the UI of the IDE will treat your module this way.

In practice most modules *do* have some dependencies. The most common dependencies include use of a particular version of the Open APIs (or later), and use of some other module (typically at least some version of it). The NetBeans Module API specifies four kinds of dependencies your module may declare. Let us use the manifest in Example 27-1 to demonstrate these.

Example 27-1. Dependency specifications in modules

```
Manifest-Version: 1.0
OpenIDE-Module: org.netbeans.modules.wombat/1
OpenIDE-Module-IDE-Dependencies: IDE/1 > 1.33
OpenIDE-Module-Java-Dependencies: Java > 1.4
OpenIDE-Module-Package-Dependencies: javax.help[HelpSet] > 1.0
OpenIDE-Module-Module-Dependencies: org.openidex.util/2 > 2.2
```

- **A dependency on the NetBeans Open APIs.** Here we request that at least version 1.33 be available.

   Do not be misled: > here really means "greater than or equal to."

If any version of NetBeans using APIs prior to 1.33 attempts to load this module, the loading will be refused, and the message will explain to the user that the IDE is too old.

If you use APIs that have not been in the Open APIs since the very beginning, you should always state such a dependency and give the version corresponding to the latest API you are using. It is not hard to find this out; a list of all API changes (going back several releases) is available on the NetBeans web site in the API Change List (*http://openide.netbeans.org/apichanges.html*). If you forget to do this and a user of an older version of NetBeans tries to load your module, it will seem to work at first but then `NoClassDefFoundErrors` might be thrown while the module is running, along with other nasty things.

- **A dependency on Java.** If your module uses specific features of later versions of Java—for example, it requires JDK 1.4 and will not run on 1.3—then you can specify such a dependency (as our example manifest does). This dependency applies to the specification version of the Java Platform APIs. It is also possible to indicate a dependency on the Java Virtual Machine specification using the keyword `VM` instead of `Java`.

- **A dependency on a Java package.** These dependencies are a little trickier syntactically, and you are advised to refer to the Modules API documentation for the full details. Our example requests that the package named `javax.help` be available (this is the JavaHelp extension), at least (specification) version 1.0. If JavaHelp is not present in the installation, or is present but not accessible to this module, or is older than 1.0, the dependency will fail and NetBeans will refuse to install the module (a message explaining the problem will be displayed to the user).

  The class name in brackets also gives NetBeans a hint that the package should be forcibly initialized if necessary by loading the class `javax.help.HelpSet`; for technical reasons, the Java VM will not automatically load definitions of available packages until some classes from them are requested, and there is no other way to reliably find them all. So you need to help a little by supplying an example of a class you expect to find.

- **A dependency on other modules.** The last and probably most important kind of dependency is on other modules. This example declares that the module whose manifest is displayed needs the `org.openidex.util` (API Extensions) module in order to function. Furthermore, it wants the exact major release version 2, and a specification version no earlier than 2.2.

  NetBeans is strict about module dependencies! If you do not declare a dependency on another module, you *cannot* use classes from it directly (`NoClassDefFoundErrors` will be thrown). Class loaders in NetBeans and how they relate are covered in detail in Chapter 15.

  After declaring a dependency on a module you can technically use any class it contains. However modules typically provide an API to other modules (if at all) only within a limited range of packages (again the NetBeans Versioning Policy describes conventions to use); check a module's API documentation to be sure.[*]

There are other details to how dependencies may be specified, as well as other infrequently used styles of dependency (for example, exact implementation version matches); for these, please refer to the Modules API documentation.

Managing Inter-Module Dependencies

It is common for a module to require one or more other modules as dependencies. These may provide some basic services or APIs used by the client module. As mentioned in the previous section, you must declare dependencies on the other modules in your module's JAR manifest. However, NetBeans permits users to dynamically upgrade or add modules, perhaps in ways you did not foresee. How are such changes handled?

Let us consider two modules, one provides some basic services including a Java-level API (see Example 27-2), and another uses these services (see Example 27-3).

Example 27-2. Providing services to a client

```
Manifest-Version: 1.0
OpenIDE-Module: wombat.service/1
OpenIDE-Module-Specification-Version: 1.0
```

Example 27-3. Specifying a required service in a client

```
Manifest-Version: 1.0
OpenIDE-Module: wombat.client
OpenIDE-Module-Specification-Version: 1.0
OpenIDE-Module-Module-Dependencies: wombat.service/1 > 1.0
```

Here the module `wombat.client` uses the module `wombat.service` for its interfaces and cannot run without `wombat.service`. For example, the service module might define classes `wombat.service.api.Wombat` (a general interface or abstract class) and `wombat.service.spi.DefaultWombatImpl` (an SPI, or service-provider interface). The client module might have a class `wombat.client.ComplexWombat` extending `DefaultWombatImpl` and a GUI class `wombat.client.WombatViewer` that displays a list of objects assignable to `Wombat`.

This example uses a Java-level API to illustrate the issues arising from module "version skew," but in fact everything here can be understood to apply equally to other types of APIs (for example, XML-based data interchange) that have notions of compatible and incompatible evolution of interfaces. The only real difference is that NetBeans helps you enforce Java-level APIs by employing `ClassLoader` hierarchies to

---

[*] NetBeans 3.4 will let API-providing modules enforce access to only those packages they really support as public APIs.

prevent them from being used without an explicit module dependency (discounting sneaky use of Java reflection of course).

Routine and compatible upgrades

There are four sorts of upgrade scenarios you might imagine starting from this point. In the first scenario, the module `wombat.client` is improved and a 1.1 version is released. `wombat.service` need not be changed. A user can retrieve the 1.1 version of *wombat-client.jar* and be ready to go.

The second scenario involves an upgrade to the service module `wombat.service`. Maybe some new convenience constructors were added to `DefaultWombatImpl` (that `ComplexWombat` does not need or use), or maybe there were simply some bug fixes in `DefaultWombatImpl`. The service manifest may now read:

```
Manifest-Version: 1.0
OpenIDE-Module: wombat.service/1
OpenIDE-Module-Specification-Version: 1.1
```

The client module does not need to change. The user upgrades to the 1.1 version of *wombat-service.jar* and is done.

In the third scenario, the service module adds APIs (for example, extra constructors for `DefaultWombatImpl`), and this time it is decided that `ComplexWombat` should use them. The service manifest is changed to give 1.1 as its specification version as before, and some note is made of this version in its APIs, for example:

```
package wombat.service.spi;
import wombat.service.api.Wombat;
public class DefaultWombatImpl implements Wombat {
  /** Simple constructor. */
  public DefaultWombatImpl() {}
  /** More powerful constructor.
   * @param x a parameter to configure me with
   * @since 1.1
   */
  public DefaultWombatImpl(int x) {...}
  // ...
}

package wombat.client;
import wombat.service.spi.DefaultWombatImpl;
class ComplexWombat extends DefaultWombatImpl {
  ComplexWombat() {
    super(3);
  }
  // ...
}
```

A 1.1 version of *wombat-service.jar* is released including the new `DefaultWombatImpl`. About the same time, the specification version of the client module is also increased to 1.1. Before releasing the new *wombat-client.jar* with the modified ComplexWombat, it is necessary to declare the updated dependency in its manifest:

```
Manifest-Version: 1.0
OpenIDE-Module: wombat.client
OpenIDE-Module-Specification-Version: 1.1
OpenIDE-Module-Module-Dependencies: wombat.service/1 > 1.1
```

Otherwise, a user might accidentally update the 1.1 client module while still keeping the 1.0 service module, and errors would be thrown when an attempt is made to instantiate ComplexWombat. The Update Center, discussed in more depth in Example 27-23, would ask a user selecting the 1.1 client to also select the 1.1 service (assuming it were available at the same update URL; otherwise, it might just prevent the download of the 1.1 client).

Incompatible upgrades

The fourth (and hopefully rarest) scenario is the trickiest. Here the author of wombat. service decides that the approach taken in its API is fundamentally flawed and can no longer be supported while continuing to develop the service (even @deprecations are not enough). So the decision is made to introduce an incompatible change. The Wombat APIs are rewritten in a cleaner way. The manifest is changed to match; the major release version must be incremented:

```
Manifest-Version: 1.0
OpenIDE-Module: wombat.service/2
OpenIDE-Module-Specification-Version: 2.0
```

> Actually increasing the specification version is not at all required here—the major release version always takes precedence. But it can help avoid confusion to increase it this way, as users are likely to be used to looking at this version when thinking about upgrades.

About the same time, the client module is altered to work with the new Wombat API. Or if a different person or organization works on the client module, this could be months later. In any event, a new client module is produced with a new manifest:

```
Manifest-Version: 1.0
OpenIDE-Module: wombat.client
OpenIDE-Module-Specification-Version: 1.2
OpenIDE-Module-Module-Dependencies: wombat.service/2 > 2.0
```

A user who updates both new modules (*wombat-service.jar* 2.0 and *wombat-client.jar* 1.2) at the same time should have no problems because they will work together. If the user tries to update just the client module, as with the compatible upgrade Net-Beans will refuse. The client module needs the second major release of the Wombat APIs and only the first is available. The difference is that if the user tries to update just the service module, NetBeans will also refuse; rather, the user will be able to install the service module, but must disable the client module. The old client will not work with the newer service. The client cannot be turned back on until the 1.2 release is obtained.

Note that a client module *cannot* declare that it can use any arbitrary major release of the service module. This would be a dangerous declaration, for it would mean that it knows about all future incompatibilities and will work with any of them.

Module dependencies and relative order

In addition to ensuring compatibility by means of version numbers, module dependencies can also be used for some less obvious purposes. One is installation order. In the example in the last section, it could happen that both the wombat.service and wombat.client modules had module installers (subclasses of ModuleInstall) that perform some special actions when the IDE starts up and shuts down (such as the methods restored() and closing() or close()). Normally the order in which such installers are run at startup time is arbitrary. However, since the client declares a dependency on the service, NetBeans will be sure to run the service's restored() method before it runs the client's. Conversely, when shutting down, closing() will be called on the *client* first, then the service (then close() in the same order). The same happens during installation (forward order) and uninstallation (reverse order). This means that if the service starts some general registry in its restored() method (and stops it in close() and uninstalled()), the client can safely add an entry to it in its own restored() (and if necessary remove it in uninstalled()).

A related point to note is that if one module overrides or removes some entries in another's XML layer, the modification should be accompanied by an explicit module dependency. This technique is not common but can be appropriate in a few cases. For example, the service module might declare a layer with a few files in it:

```
<filesystem>
  <folder name="WombatFiles">
    <file name="unobjectionable.txt">Untouched</file>
    <file name="replaceable.txt">Basic contents</file>
    <file name="deletable.txt">Get rid of me!</file>
  </folder>
</filesystem>
```

Suppose for some reason the client module wishes to replace the second file and suppress the third entirely. It could use the following in its layer:

```
<filesystem>
  <folder name="WombatFiles">
    <file name="replaceable.txt">Advanced contents</file>
    <file name="deletable.txt_hidden"/>
    <file name="added.txt">New contents</file>
  </folder>
</filesystem>
```

The resulting *WombatFiles* folder in the system filesystem will have three files: *unobjectionable.txt* with the contents Untouched, *replaceable.txt* with the contents Advanced contents, and *added.txt* with the contents New contents. The modifications cannot work reliably unless the client module declares a dependency on the service module because the dependency affects layer merge order.

This technique is rarely used because it requires fairly detailed and thus fragile assumptions on the part of the client module of what it should be modifying. Typically such modifications would be done on GUI objects such as menu items or windows when the basic variant is superseded by an "advanced" supplement module. In most cases it is appropriate for modules to only *add* files in their layers (never replacing or deleting files from other modules), and layer-based Open APIs are designed to make it convenient to follow this restriction. When only adding files, merge order is irrelevant, and module dependencies do not come into play.

Upgrading User Settings

Besides compatibility for module clients, an equally important consideration when upgrading modules is to ensure that user settings are preserved intact (or as much so as feasible). Since NetBeans modules are responsible for storing their own settings (with some infrastructural assistance from the Open APIs), they are also responsible for maintaining compatibility of existing settings between releases.

Settings History and Physical Format

Before going into detail on how to do this, it is worth reviewing what kinds of settings are possible and where they are stored, as well as the history of these choices. All 3.x versions of NetBeans have stored some kinds of user customizations in an area of disk known as the *user directory*. For example, in NetBeans 3.3 the default user directory name on Unix is *~/nbuser33/*, though a user can always pass -userdir to override this.

In NetBeans 3.0 only a few types of customizations were stored here in a human-readable form. The IDE would, on seeing a new user directory, prepopulate it with defaults for these configurations, and user customizations could then modify the files. The default filesystem in the Open APIs (Repository.getDefaultFileSystem()) was an alias for the *system/* subdirectory of this user directory where settings are stored.

NetBeans 3.1 introduced XML layers, which made provision of the defaults easier for a module writer and better for a user; the layer contains the default; only changes are written to disk, not unmodified settings. As of 3.1 the default system system is actually a MultiFileSystem that merges together all XML layers with the *system/* subdirectories of the user and installation directories. MultiFileSystem handles the "patching" logic and decides where to write out modifications.

NetBeans 3.2 expanded on the list of settings that can be stored via the layer-plus-system-directory combination, but did not fundamentally change settings storage.

 Actually one change was significant: prior to 3.2, the user directory was not by default distinct from the installation directory. Since it is much safer during upgrades to keep user settings apart from the distribution, beginning with 3.2 the user directory is separate.

NetBeans 3.3 converted almost all remaining kinds of settings to be registerable in layers, including all system options, filesystem mounts, the window system configuration, service types, and more.* Since each settings object is kept in an individual file with a predictable name, error recovery and expert manipulation become possible, as well as potential version control of settings. The list of installed modules and other module metadata is also kept in XML files in 3.3, with a separate file for each module.

NetBeans 3.3 also took the concept of project-specific settings storage (implemented already in 3.0) and updated it to be consistent with other settings: project-specific settings are stored exactly as other settings are, but the root of settings for a project is *userdir/system/Projects/projectname/system/* rather than *userdir/system/*. The default filesystem again handles the necessary merging and makes decisions about where to store modifications. Thus, a complete default system consists of some XML-provided defaults, some "global" settings, and some "project" settings.

The nature as well as location of setting storage has of course changed as well. Menu and toolbar items have always been stored as *action instances* in *Menu/* (a resource path in the system filesystem) and *Toolbars/*, typically using *.instance* files that provide an `InstanceCookie` with an instance of the action. Templates have always been stored simply as the template file in *Templates/*.

In NetBeans 3.3 the XML *.settings* format (documented in the Services API) was introduced, specifically to persist arbitrary objects in files. Most such settings are kept in a subfolder of *Services/*, though filesystem mounts are kept in *Mount/*. As of 3.3 user customizations are still written to disk using the Java serialization format (hexadecimal encoded in XML), though customized formats are possible in 3.4.

NetBeans 3.3 also introduced a new XML format for storing the window system configuration under *Windows/*, as documented in the Window System API. Likewise a new XML format for representing module metadata was added, with storage in *Modules/*, according to the Modules API. And some modules added their own storage formats in 3.3—most notably the `editor` module that defined an XML settings

---

* Only the data loader pool shown as **Object Types** and some possible customizations involving context menus are still stored in special ways in 3.3. A post-3.4 release is expected to convert all of these to layer-friendly storage.

format specific to editor settings—in response to user demands for fine-grained and robust storage of editor settings that tend to be complex.

It is important to remember that many of the same techniques used to provide user-customizable settings are also used to register static resources from modules. For example, the *Services/* folder can be used for both settings presented to a user and designed for customization, as well as for registration of services from one module to another, with no expectation of user visibility or modifiability. The "invisible" settings, however, pose no problem for upgrades (no modifications will ever be written to the user directory), so we will not consider them further in this section.

Upgrade Scenarios for Settings

Every sort of setting customizable by a user in an older version of a module should be imported into newer versions compatibly. Or when this makes no sense, at least a sensible default for the new setting should be chosen, and the upgrade proceed without apparent errors.

Exactly how to upgrade user settings properly depends on the nature of the settings storage. We will go through the common settings that modules can provide. Where there is a difference, it will be assumed that only settings from NetBeans 3.3 or later are involved, that is, upgrading from a pre-3.3 settings format is not covered. However, in practice the techniques are the same.

Above all, test! Keep old NetBeans releases and the versions of your module that run on them handy. For each such module version, start the IDE with a fresh user directory. Customize everything you can think of pertaining to your module in order to force many changes to be written to disk. Before releasing a new version, start the IDE with the new module and a copy of this old user directory and make sure the old settings are either retained as they were or quietly skipped.

Serialized settings

By far the most common issue when upgrading is serialized settings. These include system options, service types such as compilers and executors, certain other services in NetBeans 3.3 such as web browser types that work similarly to `ServiceType` without actually extending it, mounted filesystems, custom top components in the window system, node handles (`Node.Handle` instances can be saved when persisting Explorer selections), open or editor support "environments" (for example `DataEditorSupport.Env`), data loader configuration (such as list of extensions), and also any changes made programmatically to a `ModuleInstall` and externalized (though doing so is deprecated as of NetBeans 3.3).

In all of these cases, if you create a subclass of one of these serializable or externalizable objects, you are probably responsible for ensuring safe deserialization in future versions. To indicate your willingness to maintain compatibility for it, the first step is to add a `serialVersionUID` field to any serializable class you create. (The initial value is quite arbitrary, unless you "slipped" once and have already released a version with no declared UID.)

For `SystemOptions` deserialization is made safer for you by the Options API. Only one property at a time will be deserialized, and an exception thrown from this attempt will not affect other properties. (You should, nevertheless, give a `serialVersionUID`.) In all other cases, you are essentially left to the guidance of the JDK documentation, which discusses the mechanics of serialization and compatibility in full detail.

Some tips are still warranted:

- Externalization is often more flexible than plain serialization when there are significant changes in implementation between releases, so module authors are encouraged to declare their classes `Externalizable` even when the interface type only requires `Serializable`.

- When using `Serializable`, `readObject()` may be implemented to *not* call `ObjectInputStream.defaultReadObject()`, and instead explicitly find the `GetField` and examine the contained instance variables one by one.

- When using externalization, decide on a numbering scheme for versions of your format; start with 1, move to 2 when a major change is made, and so on. When reading, the protocol number is read from the stream first, and the rest of the decoding is switched according to this protocol version.

- Or learn how to use write replacers and read resolvers, which can help isolate per-version serialization information in clearly separated classes.

- Generally, deleting a class that might have been serialized is forbidden, as a `ClassNotFoundException` might result. If the class is really obsolete, try replacing its implementation with a dummy one. In some cases it is permitted to return `null` from `readResolve()`, causing the container that was reading the serialized object to skip it. In other cases it is possible to have `readObject()` do nothing special immediately, yet schedule a task to delete the bogus object from the system. (This is more work, so it should be reserved for important scenarios.)

Don't worry about refactoring and moving all your classes and packages around. In plain Java serialization, this would break all old storage, but since refactoring is common enough, NetBeans specially supports it. If the code that initiates the deserialization calls `org.openide.util.Utilities.translateName()` (as standard code in the NetBeans implementation should), refactoring is supported. The resource *org/openide/util/packages.txt* in *openide.jar* supplies a list of refactored classes and packages, permitting them to be deserialized from either the old or new name. NetBeans 3.4 decentralizes this system with *META-INF/netbeans/translate.names*, a per-module list.

As previously mentioned, NetBeans 3.4 includes a settings support module that provides a richer API for storing and upgrading settings in more robust and readable custom formats, though most settings are still stored in serial form in this release.

Templates and saved files

Templates customized by a user generally need no special treatment, assuming they will continue to be usable in future releases of the module. In the unlikely event that the kind of template supportable by the module changes, either warn the user or initiate some sort of automated conversion. These things could be done from the `ModuleInstall.updated()` method.

If you used any `TemplateWizard.Iterator` implementations to associate a wizard with a template, bear in mind that these are serializable and may be stored with a template if any modification is made to that template. So when changing a template wizard iterator, give thought to ensuring that old serialized versions of it can be safely restored. The same consideration applies to any serializable object that you might store as a file attribute using `FileObject.setAttribute()`. These are generally stored in serialized form in *.nbattrs* files and are expected to be safely deserializable later.

Actions

Menu and toolbar items (also related customizations such as keyboard shortcuts) stored as *.instance* files might be broken if the action thus represented is deleted from one module release to the next. Attempts to load the obsolete *.instance* file might then fail with a `ClassNotFoundException`. For this reason it is probably wise not to really delete actions if they have been placed in a menu or toolbar or added to the Actions pool (*Actions/* subfolders); rather, deprecate the action class, cease to reference it from anywhere, and make it into a no-op:

```
public class ObsoleteAction extends CallableSystemAction {
  protected void initialize() {
    super.initialize();
    setEnabled(false);
  }
  public void performAction() {}
  public String getName() {return "";}
  public HelpCtx getHelpCtx() {return null;}
}
```

If the action was only listed in the context menu of data nodes, by being included in `DataLoader.defaultActions()`, it should be safe to delete it, as long as you quietly handle the fact that it is missing in your `DataLoader.readExternal()`:

```
public void readExternal(ObjectInput oi)
    throws IOException, ClassNotFoundException {
  try {
    super.readExternal(oi);
  } catch (SafeException se) {
    if (se.getException() instanceof ClassNotFoundException) {
      ErrorManager err = TopManager.getDefault().getErrorManager();
      String msg = "Not to worry; SomeAction was deleted and will throw CNFE";
      err.annotate(se, ErrorManager.UNKNOWN, msg, null, null, null);
      // Print only to log file:
      err.notify(ErrorManager.INFORMATIONAL, se);
```

```
        } else {
          throw se;
        }
      }
    }
  }
```

Window system elements and custom formats

These two are easy to summarize. Window system XML files (such as workspace or mode definitions and references to top components) are in fixed XML formats not extensible by modules. So only upgrades of the Window System API, not your module, are relevant—meaning that as a module author, you need not be concerned. Such fixed-format files are not to be confused with the storage of the TopComponent state, which is done in the *Windows/Components/* folder and normally uses serialized *.settings* files like other settings—for these, all the considerations of serialized settings apply.

If you store settings in a format of your own devising—for example, in XML files according to a DTD you supply—then of course the burden of design and implementation of this format is up to you because it pertains to upgrade compatibility. In the specific case of DTDs (or similar techniques such as XML Schema), it is advisable to choose a new public ID with a new version number for each change in the format. For example, -//Your Org//DTD Something 1.0//EN could be revised as -//Your Org// DTD Something 1.1//EN. Then ensure that module code checks the public ID and can read any old version as well as the current one.

What Happens When a Module Is Disabled?

In addition to ensuring that your saved customizations are correctly restored into a new version of your module, you should check that these customizations *do no harm* if the module is disabled (or even deleted). As with upgrades, you should test your module out, to make sure its settings behave well in this regard.

Serialized settings can be a significant problem because, when a module is disabled or missing, its classes are not available for possible deserialization; if the system attempts to load customizations made by the user of objects your module defined, ClassNotFoundExceptions might result and alarm the user unnecessarily. So, the *.settings* format includes a standard way of guarding against this.

When declaring *.settings* files in an XML layer, always be sure to include the optional but recommended <<module/>> element. This element is also automatically included in settings saved to disk after customization of an object, if its implementing class is found to have been loaded from a module JAR. If the system is started *without* the mentioned module (or with an older version of it, which could be just as dangerous), the settings file is simply ignored. It will produce no instance and will thus be excluded from any container that looks for objects to deserialize. If the module is subsequently reenabled, the setting will become available once more.

The same <<module/>> element is also available in the XML formats used to persist window system objects (workspaces, modes, and top component references). While these would not actually throw ClassNotFoundExceptions were the originating module to be disabled, it is very common for changes to such objects to be written to disk (for example, after simply adjusting a window position), and it is quite apparent and ugly to have (for example) an empty workspace left in the IDE when the module for which it was intended is no longer enabled. It is advisable to declare the originating module when adding workspaces, modes, and top component references; if your module is disabled, the window system object will be removed from view. Again, actual top component state involves module-defined classes and is normally kept in *.settings files, so also use this element in such files to protect against ClassNotFoundExceptions.

As of NetBeans 3.3 *.instance files have no built-in way of being deactivated when they correspond to disabled modules. Such a mechanism may be added in the future. Or you can simply use *.settings files instead because these subsume all of the capabilities of *.instance files (albeit a bit more verbosely due to the XML declaration and so on). There are other less critical places where an explicit means of marking the associated module might be useful but not yet supported in 3.3—for example, serialized file object attributes.

User Development Data

It is worth drawing a distinction between *settings*, which refer to user-saved information about the desired configuration of the IDE and its embedded tools and *development data*, which is the actual data that the tool is producing. For example, in the NetBeans Form Editor, the settings would be the SystemOption specifying default access permissions on generated bean variables, the contents of the Component Palette (serialized beans in subfolders of *Palette*), the configuration of the *.form + *.java data loader, and perhaps other similar things. The development data is the actual *.form files produced by the Form Editor when building a form, as well as the matching *.java files with guarded code blocks and freely edited areas.

While it is excusable to ignore some details of old settings when they cease to become relevant to the operation of the new module or in extreme cases even to discard old settings (when things have changed so radically the user ought to re-create his configuration in the new system), it is never excusable to render old development data unloadable or unusable. Compatibility must be retained forever, as this is the fruit of the user's work. Either open old files as they are and save them the same way, or upgrade them to the new format before opening—only with the user's express permission, however.

Also it is general policy that settings need not be forward-compatible; that is, it is acceptable for a module to save settings that an *older* version cannot read. In the case of development data, this restriction may or may not be acceptable. Ideally converters would be available (in the module GUI or as standalone tools) permitting interchange between different versions of the format defined by the tool.

Bundling Extension Libraries

While many modules contain all the code they need to operate, in other cases an additional library is needed to complete the module. For example, a module might require special XML parsers, XSL processors, or similar standard libraries. Or it may be the case that part of a module is designed to function more generally outside of NetBeans and should be kept as a separate JAR file. In all these cases, a means is needed to separate the library functionality and make it available to the module.

Referencing Libraries with Class-Path

Let us assume that the Wombat module `wombat.service` needs a non-NetBeans-specific library, *wombat-lib-3.0.jar*. The first consideration is where to put this library JAR. While technically NetBeans permits it anywhere beneath (not in!) the *modules/* directory in an installation or user directory, conventionally the *ext/* subdirectory is used for such libraries. Thus a NetBeans installation will contain:

> *modules/wombat-service.jar*
> *modules/ext/wombat-lib-3.0.jar*

Placing a JAR in the extensions area does *not* automatically cause NetBeans to do anything—remember that this area is purely conventional. It is also necessary to add the `Class-Path` attribute to the module manifest, pointing to the extension's relative location. (You can have more than one extension as its value, separated by spaces.) This attribute is meaningful generally for Java JARs, not just NetBeans modules.

It is also a good idea (though not required) to make the library into a proper Java package and declare a dependency on it using `OpenIDE-Module-Package-Dependencies`, as discussed in the earlier section "Specifying Dependencies." Here is an example of both the module (see Example 27-4) and package (see Example 27-5) manifests showing their relationship.

Example 27-4. The module manifest

```
Manifest-Version: 1.0
OpenIDE-Module: wombat.service/1
OpenIDE-Module-Package-Dependencies: wombat.lib[WombatException] > 3.0
Class-Path: ext/wombat-lib-3.0.jar
```

Example 27-5. The package manifest

```
Manifest-Version: 1.0
Specification-Title: wombat.lib
Specification-Version: 3.0
Specification-Vendor: Wombat Enterprises
Implementation-Title: Wombat Library
Implementation-Version: built 2001.06.13
Implementation-Vendor: Wombat Enterprises
```

Here it is assumed that *wombat/lib/WombatException.class* is a loadable class in *wombat-lib-3.0.jar* that can be loaded quickly to force initialization of the package.

Consult the Java Versioning Specification (included in the JDK documentation) for details on declaring packages. You can also define different package information for each Java package (folder) in the JAR.

 Extensions added using Class-Path go directly into the module's class loader, which permits classes in the module to reference extension classes directly. (The reverse is also true, but very poor style.) For this reason, modules that *depend on* the wombat.service module will also be able to refer to wombat.lib.* classes directly.

You may have noticed that we included the version number of the library in its file-name, *wombat-lib-3.0.jar*. We did so because it is possible for more than version of the library to be loaded at once in the same NetBeans VM! Naturally this would make no sense for a single module. However, imagine that a different company also creates a Wombat support module, com.megacorp.wombatblaster, that uses the Wombat library—but currently only supports the older 2.0 library. Megacorp could keep the older library in the file *modules/ext/wombat-lib-2.0.jar*, and in their module manifest ask for it normally:

```
Manifest-Version: 1.0
OpenIDE-Module: com.megacorp.wombatblaster
OpenIDE-Module-Package-Dependencies: wombat.lib[WombatException] > 2.0
Class-Path: ext/wombat-lib-2.0.jar
```

The Wombat Service and Wombat Blaster modules can coexist in the same VM without conflicts.

 No other module should depend on *both of these modules* together, however; see Chapter 15.

Putting the version number in the JAR filename ensures that both can be present at once. So it is always a good practice to do this; you never know who else might be using the same library but a different version.

The flip side is that if two unrelated modules happen to have the Class-Path attribute set to ext/wombat-lib-3.0.jar, the 3.0 JAR will be loaded *twice*. This means they cannot share startup time loading the library, communicate with classes from the library (ClassCastExceptions would ensue), or see static variables set by the other. If you find yourself in this situation, there is no cause for immediate alarm; but consider converting the extension to an autoload module, as discussed in the next section.

An extension library should be distributed to the user along with the module it is used by. The best way to do this is via an NBM file, which will be covered in Example 27-21 later in this chapter.

Using Autoload Library Modules

For reasons just mentioned, class-path extensions are fine for simple libraries closely associated with a module that just need to be in separate JAR files—but they are not ideal for more complex situations where some functionality is generally useful and is intended to be shared among several modules. For these situations, you can make the common functionality into a NetBeans module.

The objections to doing so are mostly practical ones. In particular the user experience of adding an extra module that supplies no easily identifiable functionality is not good. That is why NetBeans 3.3 introduced autoload modules. In all respects they are much like regular modules; the only real difference is how they are turned on.

A regular module is displayed to a user in a list of all available modules and the user is presented with the option to turn it on or off, but this is not so for autoloads. They are displayed in a separate Libraries area to indicate that they are not of direct interest. The user cannot turn them on or off directly. Instead, if *any* regular module declaring a dependency on a given autoload module is enabled, the autoload is too. Conversely, if and when the *last* regular module with a dependency on that autoload is disabled, the autoload is disabled with it.

To make a module be treated as an autoload, just place it in the *modules/autoload/* directory of an installation or user directory, rather than *modules/*.

Figure 27-1 shows one configuration of modules in NetBeans 3.3. You can see various autoloads (as well as the pseudo-module IDE Core) in the Libraries subnode. Some, like Debugger Core, are turned on—just because JPDA Debugger is on too. Others like VCS Core are off; none of the modules depending on this autoload (Built-in CVS Client or VCS Generic Command-Line Support) are turned on at the moment.

In this way autoloads serve as libraries to the "real" modules that require them. However, they are normal modules in most respects: they can be updated from the Update Center independent of their client modules, they may have their own class-path extensions (conventionally under *modules/autoload/ext/*), and so on. They may even have XML layers, installers, or other installed objects; for example the Debugger

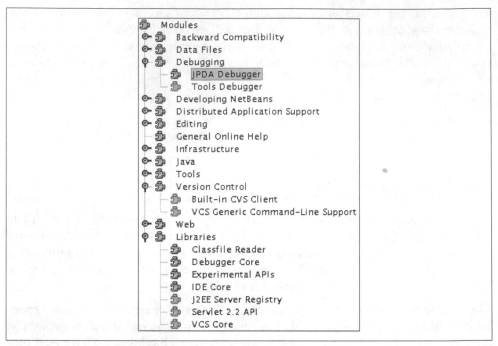

Figure 27-1. Autoload modules

Core adds the Debug menu and its menu items so that the user interface associated with debugging is enabled only when some debugger is enabled, too.

If you have a third-party library that you wish to make an autoload—for example an XSL processor—it is only necessary to add the `OpenIDE-Module` attribute to its manifest (as well as `OpenIDE-Module-Name` for the display name, probably) and place it in the *modules/autoload/* directory. If even such a small modification is impossible for legal reasons, a "dummy" autoload module with just a manifest can be placed in *modules/autoload/* and the real library in *modules/autoload/ext/*, permitting the third-party module to be used exactly as distributed. Remember that the `Class-Path` manifest attribute always points to the location of the extension relative to the module JAR's directory:

```
Manifest-Version: 1.0
OpenIDE-Module: org.myxsl.nbmodule
OpenIDE-Module-Specification-Version: 1.0
Class-Path: ext/myxsl-1.0.jar
```

Autoloads may also signal compatible and incompatible changes in the usual way, using their major release and specification versions. Note that NetBeans does not permit more than one version of a given module to be loaded at once; if an autoload module has undergone incompatible changes, rather than incrementing its major release version (forcing all clients to change to match this or be disabled), it might actually change its code name base, as exemplified here:

```
Manifest-Version: 1.0
OpenIDE-Module: wombat.lib.v2
OpenIDE-Module-Specification-Version: 2.0


Manifest-Version: 1.0
OpenIDE-Module: wombat.client
OpenIDE-Module-Module-Dependencies: wombat.lib.v2 > 2.0
```

Such a trick permits more than one "version" of the module to coexist in the system, since as far as NetBeans is concerned they are really unrelated modules. However the autoload in this case should be careful about what it installs from an XML layer. If more than one version of the module is enabled simultaneously, any overlaps in the filenames supplied by the different layers might produce conflicts. Only one version of any given file can be chosen for the system filesystem, and the choice is arbitrary.

Ad-Hoc Resources and Module Installer Validation

Sometimes the dependencies that can be specified declaratively on packages and modules are not enough to represent everything that a module needs to run. A typical situation is one in which a commercially sold module requires a license key to be activated. With an invalid or missing license key, the module should not be turned on. It is probably possible to explicitly disable every feature the module supplies to the user in case the license key is missing, but this is clumsy—the desired result is not to have the module turned on.

To accomplish this, you can override ModuleInstall.validate() to throw an IllegalStateException should it turn out that some critical resource is missing from the module's runtime. Throwing this exception will cause the module installer to abort any attempt to enable the module and prevent it from being turned on (in the current IDE session). You should provide a localized message for the exception using ErrorManager to be displayed to the user.

What if the external resource is a library? It sometimes happens that a large and self-contained Java application is installed on a computer and also adds a NetBeans integration module. Typically such a module needs to be linked against library JAR files present in another software installation. You cannot use Class-Path for this because the exact location of the external software is not known in advance. There is not a single good solution to this question, but the FAQs included in the Open APIs documentation include a few approaches that may be helpful.

A special note needs to be made for those modules that need to include particular versions of XML parsers as extensions. Various XML APIs (DOM, SAX, JAXP) are used by the NetBeans Open APIs and basic parts of the IDE infrastructure; for this reason, they are on the classpath of the VM and cannot be overridden.

As far as parsers (implementations of the APIs) are concerned, as of NetBeans 3.3 the Xerces and Crimson parsers are also on the classpath, making it difficult to use different parser versions in modules. While NetBeans 3.4 removes parser implementations from the module-visible classpath, making it easier to use a custom implementation, 3.3 users can get the same effect with a little more work. The NetBeans APIs FAQs (*http://www.netbeans.org/download/apis/org/openide/doc-files/faq.html#foreign-module-extensions*) shows you how.

Internationalization and Accessibility

While most Java programmers can probably read English well enough, not all can. Not all *want to* if it can be avoided, and NetBeans can serve as a framework for general applications where no such assumption can be made at all. For these reasons it is simply professional to support internationalization in every NetBeans module intended for general release, meaning that human-displayable resources such as text and images in the module can be cleanly substituted with variants according to locale (language or country). At least a default locale must be supported, which for practical reasons is usually English (the language—in some broadly used dialect). *Localization* means actually providing new locales to be supported by the module: Japanese, Chinese, and major European languages are common choices.

Another important consideration as a module approaches the release stage is accessibility. If a potential user has poor or no eyesight, cannot press modifier keys like Control, or has any of numerous other needs, will your module be a joy to use—or worthless?

I18N and L10N

The NetBeans web site includes current information on I18N and L10N at the I18N Page (*http://www.netbeans.org/i18n/*). You can refer to that page for the full details on what is supported, but an overview of important concepts will be given here.

The basic step when internationalizing a NetBeans module is to use `org.openide.util.NbBundle` to retrieve locale-sensitive resources. It is similar to the standard Java `ResourceBundle` but better tuned to NetBeans's needs. Example 27-6 is an example of basic usage.

Example 27-6. I18N: Basic src/org/module/SomeClass.java

```java
package org.module;
public class SomeClass ... {
  // ...
  public String getDisplayName() {
    return NbBundle.getMessage(SomeClass.class, "LBL_some_class");
  }
}
```

Example 27-7 is the accompanying *Bundle.properties*.

Example 27-7. I18N: Basic src/org/module/Bundle.properties

```
# A label for some object.
LBL_some_class=My first object
```

Example 27-8 an internationalized Java properties file in which the base-locale name *Bundle.properties* is searched for in the same package as the class.

Example 27-8. I18N: Basic src/org/module/Bundle_cs.properties

```
# A label for some object.
LBL_some_class=M\u016Fj prvn\u00ED objekt
```

The presence of such a localized bundle in the same package means that a user running in Czech locale (for example) will see the proper label instead of English. Note the use of Unicode escapes in the bundle, producing **MØj první objekt**.

A common mistake among programmers who are native English speakers is to underestimate the significance of word order and grammar in other languages. The code in Example 27-9 and Example 27-10 is not generally internationalizable.

Example 27-9. I18N: Incorrect src/org/module/SomeClass.java

```java
package org.module;
public class SomeClass ... {
  // ...
  private String warningMessage(int count, String missing) {
    return NbBundle.getMessage(SomeClass.class, "LBL_warning_1") +
           missing +
           NbBundle.getMessage(SomeClass.class, "LBL_warning_2") +
           count +
           NbBundle.getMessage(SomeClass.class, "LBL_warning_3");
  }
}
```

Example 27-10. I18N: Incorrect src/org/module/Bundle.properties

```
# Parts of warning.
LBL_warning_1=The name
LBL_warning_2=could not be found in
LBL_warning_3=file(s).
```

Such sentence fragments cannot be coherently translated into all languages. It would be better to use a *message format*, shown also with a translation, as in Example 27-11, Example 27-12, and Example 27-13.

Example 27-11. I18N: Revised src/org/module/SomeClass.java

```
package org.module;
public class SomeClass ... {
  // ...
  private String warningMessage(int count, String missing) {
    return NbBundle.getMessage(SomeClass.class, "LBL_warning",
                               new Integer(count), missing);
  }
}
```

Example 27-12. I18N: Revised src/org/module/Bundle.properties

```
# A warning.
# {0} - number of files
# {1} - the name
LBL_warning=The name {1} could not be found in \
            {0,choice,1#one file|1<{0} files}.
```

Example 27-13. I18N: Revised src/org/module/Bundle_cs.properties

```
# A warning.
# {0} - number of files
# {1} - the name
LBL_warning=V {0,choice,1#jednom souboru|1<{0} souborech} \
            chyb\u011Blo jm\u00E9no {1}.
```

The Javadoc for `java.text.MessageFormat` fully describes what message formats can do.

Besides text strings accessed from Java code, `NbBundle` supports loading other resources such as images in a locale-sensitive manner. Other parts of the Open APIs that permit a module to specify localizable text declaratively also use bundles. For example, the attribute `OpenIDE-Module-Localizing-Bundle` permits module metadata to be localized using bundles, and XML formats such as those used in the window system also permit bundle + key references to be used instead of literal strings. `NbBundle` also transparently permits any localizable resource to be *branded* with no change in code. This is discussed in depth in Chapter 28.

Where do localized resources go? In the simplest case, locale variants of resources such as bundles may be simply placed in the main module JAR file alongside the base-locale resources. More commonly, it is desirable to keep localization physically separate—besides making it easier for translation teams to work without interfering with other forms of development, separate files can be easily added to or removed from a NetBeans installation when new localizations become available or when existing ones are deemed by a user to be a waste of disk space. For this reason, NetBeans module JARs can be *split* into a basic JAR and some number of locale-variant JARs.

For example, Czech translations of a module *modules/wombat.jar* could be placed in the file *modules/locale/wombat_cs.jar*. There is no need to use Class-Path to refer to locale variant JARs; NetBeans will automatically load them when the corresponding locale is actually used. (Resource paths inside locale variants JARs still need to reflect the locale, for example, *org/module/Bundle_cs.properties*.) Even module extensions can have their own variant JARs, for example *modules/ext/locale/wombat-lib-3.0_cs.jar*.

A11Y

Accessibility refers to the ability of a module to support users who need various assistive technologies to interact with software. In the simplest case, the large proportion of people who cannot distinguish colors cannot easily distinguish certain objects (for example, node icons) solely on the basis of hue. More critically, people who are blind cannot rely on visual cues at all and in order to use screen readers, require every GUI component to be paired with a useful textual description. A11Y is now required by US law. Good A11Y also helps even users with no disabilities because it can improve the ease of keyboard navigation and many other aspects of the user interface.

In fact many modules need not do much to support A11Y. If most of your module's UI is mediated through the Explorer, Property Sheet, and other standardized GUI mechanisms, and you provide good localized display names and tool tips for everything, the Java and NetBeans infrastructure will take care of a number of concerns for you. Most of the work will be in testing, not changing, your code. Pay attention to APIs such as the window system XML formats that provide A11Y-specific options, and take advantage of them.

Modules that use any GUI components, however, need to be more carefully thought out. Prepare GUI forms with a clear tab traversal order; programmatically associate text labels with the components they describe; provide textual descriptions for certain components to assist screen readers; and be especially cautious when creating new Swing components, since it is then necessary to use the Swing Accessibility API to associate descriptions with components, as well as handle focus traversal issues. If you are designing your components inside NetBeans, you can find some helpful ideas in Chapter 8.

The NetBeans web site has plenty of information on the A11Y pages (*http://a11y. netbeans.org/*). Not only are tips given for common A11Y mistakes and how to correct them, but also the project includes testing tools (proven in the field by NetBeans UI developers) that can find A11Y-related problems in your module and suggest solutions.

JavaHelp—Writing and Distributing

Almost any module that provides functionality the user can see and interact with ought to be accompanied by helpful documentation. In NetBeans, this is done using the standard JavaHelp framework. Help sets created according to the JavaHelp specification can be added to NetBeans easily, and virtually all parts of the UI support association of help IDs pointing into the help set. The API class `org.openide.util.HelpCtx` is often used to wrap a help ID. JavaHelp integration is discussed in the Modules API.

As an illustration we will add help to the Mini-Composer module. The first step is to create a JavaHelp-compatible help set. Our help set will be simple and have just one navigator, a table of contents. A nontrivial help set ought to also have an index and a full-text search database.

Creating a Help Set

You should begin with an XML document describing your help set, as in Example 27-14.

Example 27-14. JavaHelp: src/org/netbeans/examples/modules/minicomposer/help-set.xml

```
<!DOCTYPE helpset PUBLIC
          "-//Sun Microsystems Inc.//DTD JavaHelp HelpSet Version 1.0//EN"
          "http://java.sun.com/products/javahelp/helpset_1_0.dtd">
<helpset version="1.0">

<title>Mini-Composer Help</title>
  <maps>
    <homeID>org.netbeans.examples.modules.minicomposer.HOMEID</homeID>
    <mapref location="help-map.xml"/>
  </maps>
  <view>
    <name>TOC</name>
    <label>Contents</label>
    <type>javax.help.TOCView</type>
    <data>help-contents.xml</data>
  </view>
</helpset>
```

You also need to map the help topics to HTML help files; Example 27-15 provides an example.

Example 27-15. JavaHelp: src/org/netbeans/examples/modules/minicomposer/help-map.xml

```
<?xml version="1.0" encoding="UTF-8"?>
<!DOCTYPE map PUBLIC
            "-//Sun Microsystems Inc.//DTD JavaHelp Map Version 1.0//EN"
            "http://java.sun.com/products/javahelp/map_1_0.dtd">
<map version="1.0">
```

```
    <mapID target="org.netbeans.examples.modules.minicomposer.HOMEID"
          url="help-main.html"/>
    <mapID target="org.netbeans.examples.modules.minicomposer.playing"
          url="help-playing.html"/>
    <mapID target="org.netbeans.examples.modules.minicomposer.explorer"
          url="help-explorer.html"/>
    <mapID target="org.netbeans.examples.modules.minicomposer.settings"
          url="help-settings.html"/>
    <mapID target="org.netbeans.examples.modules.minicomposer.visual"
          url="help-visual.html"/>
    <mapID target="org.netbeans.examples.modules.minicomposer.textual"
          url="help-textual.html"/>
</map>
```

Next add the table of contents for your help set, as shown in Example 27-16.

Example 27-16. JavaHelp: src/org/netbeans/examples/modules/minicomposer/help-contents.xml

```
<?xml version="1.0" encoding="UTF-8"?>
<!DOCTYPE toc PUBLIC
          "-//Sun Microsystems Inc.//DTD JavaHelp TOC Version 1.0//EN"
          "http://java.sun.com/products/javahelp/toc_1_0.dtd">
<toc version="1.0">
  <tocitem target="org.netbeans.examples.modules.minicomposer.HOMEID">
    Using the Mini-Composer
    <tocitem target="org.netbeans.examples.modules.minicomposer.visual">
      Visual Composition
    </tocitem>
    <tocitem target="org.netbeans.examples.modules.minicomposer.textual">
      Textual Composition
    </tocitem>
    <tocitem target="org.netbeans.examples.modules.minicomposer.playing">
      Playing Music
    </tocitem>
    <tocitem target="org.netbeans.examples.modules.minicomposer.explorer">
      Notes in the Explorer
    </tocitem>
    <tocitem target="org.netbeans.examples.modules.minicomposer.settings">
      Customizations
    </tocitem>
  </tocitem>
</toc>
```

And of course the six HTML files named by the help map are also placed in the *src/
org/netbeans/examples/modules/minicomposer/* directory. It is common to use a CSS
stylesheet as well.

With the Open APIs Support module installed, you can preview a JavaHelp help set
easily: select the help set file (in this example, *help-set.xml*) in the Explorer and press
Execute. A simple JavaHelp help viewer will open enabling you to confirm that the
mappings all work, the HTML looks fine, and so on.

Adding a Help Set to NetBeans

A help set can be added to a module simply by mentioning it in the manifest. As of NetBeans 3.3 this still works; however, it is preferred to install it from the XML layer, which also offers more possibilities for control of the UI.

The most important step is the registration of the help set as being available to the system. This can be accomplished with an XML file in a format specified by the Modules API (see Example 27-17). It must be placed in the service lookup area of the system filesystem, conventionally in *Services/JavaHelp/*.

Example 27-17. JavaHelp: src/org/netbeans/examples/modules/minicomposer/help-set-ref.xml

```
<?xml version="1.0" encoding="UTF-8"?>
<!DOCTYPE helpsetref PUBLIC
          "-//NetBeans//DTD JavaHelp Help Set Reference 1.0//EN"
          "http://www.netbeans.org/dtds/helpsetref-1_0.dtd">
<helpsetref
  url="nbresloc:/org/netbeans/examples/modules/minicomposer/help-set.xml"/>
```

The help set is pointed to using the nbresloc protocol that refers to a resource in a module JAR. nbresloc automatically handles localization (and branding) so that translations of the documentation can be added just by supplying extra help sets, for example *src/org/netbeans/examples/modules/minicomposer/help-set_cs.xml*. All other XML and HTML files used by the help set are found by relative URLs according to the JavaHelp syntax, so NetBeans is not concerned with them.

You also need to register your help set via your *layer.xml* document:

```
<filesystem>
  <folder name="Services">
    <folder name="JavaHelp">
      <attr name="org-netbeans-modules-usersguide-above-regular.txt/,↵
org-netbeans-examples-modules-minicomposer-help-set-ref.xml" boolvalue="true"/>
      <file name="org-netbeans-examples-modules-minicomposer-help-set-ref.xml"
            url="help-set-ref.xml"/>
      <attr name="org-netbeans-examples-modules-minicomposer-help-set-ref.xml/,↵
org-netbeans-modules-usersguide-below-regular.txt" boolvalue="true"/>
    </folder>
  </folder>
</filesystem>
```

Note the two ordering constraints asking that the reference to the help set be placed between two "marker" files in the *JavaHelp* folder. If the usersguide (General Online Help) module is installed, these markers are present. JavaHelp can merge help sets together (for example, each table of contents is concatenated), and it is often desirable for normal help sets to merge into a central area, while the core NetBeans help comes first, and manuals for third-party software last. Figure 27-2 shows the NetBeans merged help as opened with Help Contents and the Mini-Composer help selected.

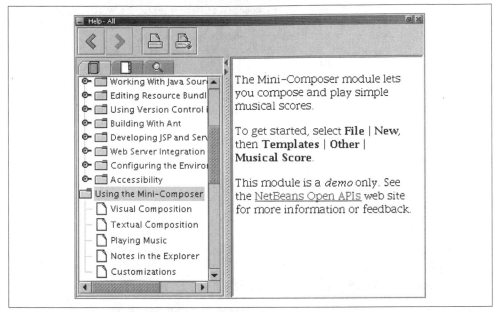

Figure 27-2. Minicomposer: JavaHelp start page

It is also desirable to add a shortcut to the help set so the user knows it is there. These are conventionally placed in a submenu of the **Help** menu. Again, a special XML format provides a menu presenter for a JavaHelp shortcut, shown in Example 27-18.

Example 27-18. JavaHelp: src/org/netbeans/examples/modules/minicomposer/help-main-page.xml

```
<?xml version="1.0" encoding="UTF-8"?>
<!DOCTYPE helpctx PUBLIC
          "-//NetBeans//DTD Help Context 1.0//EN"
          "http://www.netbeans.org/dtds/helpcontext-1_0.dtd">
<helpctx id="org.netbeans.examples.modules.minicomposer.HOMEID"/>
```

We just need to indicate the help ID. The map file translates this into an actual URL to an HTML file. Here is the change needed in your *layer.xml*:

```
<filesystem>
  <folder name="Menu">
    <folder name="Help">
      <folder name="HelpShortcuts">
        <attr name="org-netbeans-modules-usersguide-sep.instance/,↵
org-netbeans-examples-modules-minicomposer-help-main-page.xml"
              boolvalue="true"/>
        <file
            name="org-netbeans-examples-modules-minicomposer-help-main-page.xml"
            url="help-main-page.xml">
          <attr name="SystemFileSystem.localizingBundle"
                stringvalue="org.netbeans.examples.modules.minicomposer.Bundle"/>
          <attr name="SystemFileSystem.icon" urlvalue=
```

```
          "nbresloc:/org/netbeans/examples/modules/minicomposer/ScoreDataIcon.gif"/>
            </file>
            <attr name="org-netbeans-examples-modules-minicomposer-,↵
help-main-page.xml/org-netbeans-modules-usersguide-lower-sep.instance"
                boolvalue="true"/>
          </folder>
        </folder>
      </folder>
      <folder name="Actions">
        <folder name="Help">
          <file name="org-netbeans-examples-modules-minicomposer-help-main-page.xml"
                url="help-main-page.xml">
            <attr name="SystemFileSystem.localizingBundle"
                  stringvalue="org.netbeans.examples.modules.minicomposer.Bundle"/>
            <attr name="SystemFileSystem.icon" urlvalue=
            "nbresloc:/org/netbeans/examples/modules/minicomposer/ScoreDataIcon.gif"/>
          </file>
        </folder>
      </folder>
    </folder>
  </filesystem>
```

You also need to make additions to your *Bundle.properties* file:

```
Menu/Help/HelpShortcuts/org-netbeans-examples-modules-minicomposer-\
    help-main-page.xml=Mini-Composer Help
Actions/Help/org-netbeans-examples-modules-minicomposer-\
    help-main-page.xml=Mini-Composer Help
```

Again, the new shortcut is placed relative to usersguide-supplied markers. (If usersguide is not installed, this has no effect.) Note the use of a localized name (as given by the bundle) and an icon. Placing a second copy in *Actions/Help/* ensures that it will be visible in the Actions pool in the Options dialog box, enabling the user to copy and paste to other menus, toolbars, and so on.

The help menu then looks like Figure 27-3.

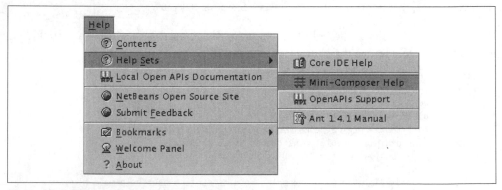

Figure 27-3. Minicomposer: Help Sets submenu

Selecting Mini-Composer Help opens the same help viewer as before, but showing only the Mini-Composer help set.

Adding Context Help

The last stage is to add context help to various objects in the module that are visible in the GUI. This means associating help IDs with them in various ways.

The easiest way to add context help is to look for places in the Open APIs where a `HelpCtx` object is requested. For example, we can add a help ID to the internal player referring the user to the page that discussed playing audio files (in *InternalPlayer.java*):

```
public HelpCtx getHelpCtx() {
    return new HelpCtx("org.netbeans.examples.modules.minicomposer.playing");
}
```

Pressing F1 (for help) on Internal AU Player in the Options dialog box will show this help, for example. Besides adding real help IDs in all of the places previously seen, we will add a `getHelpCtx()` to `ScorePanel.java` to supply help for the visual panel. Also the data loader as seen in Object Types in the Options dialog box can have help; this is done by adding the attribute to its bean descriptor (specified by the `ScoreDataLoaderBeanInfo` class):

```
public BeanDescriptor getBeanDescriptor() {
    BeanDescriptor desc = new BeanDescriptor(ScoreDataLoader.class);
    desc.setValue("helpID",
                  "org.netbeans.examples.modules.minicomposer.HOMEID");
    return desc;
}
```

Finally the *folder* for the audio players in the Options dialog box can get help, too. This is distinct from the help for particular players shown beneath it, and should also be added to the *layer.xml* document:

```
<filesystem>
  <folder name="Services">
    <folder name="Executor">
      <folder name="org-netbeans-examples-modules-minicomposer">
        <attr name="helpID"
              stringvalue="org.netbeans.examples.modules.minicomposer.playing"/>
        <!-- other attrs and contained files as before... -->
      </folder>
    </folder>
  </folder>
</filesystem>
```

Separating Help from Code

In our example we simply included the help set XML and HTML in the module JAR like any other resource. Sometimes it is desirable to separate the help into a different file; after all it can be used independently of NetBeans in any JavaHelp viewer.

If this is wanted, it is enough to create a separate ZIP or JAR file with the help set files and refer to it from the main module JAR. Conventionally such separated archives are placed in the *modules/docs/* directory of an installation or user directory. For example, we could have the following:

> *modules/minicomposer.jar*
> *modules/docs/minicomposer-help.zip*

For autoload or eager modules, the documentation could live in *modules/autoload/ docs/* or *modules/eager/docs/*, respectively, though it is less common for autoload and eager modules to include documentation.

The only other change needed, besides moving the JavaHelp-related files (the help set, navigators, and HTML) into the ZIP file, is the usual addition to the main attributes area of the module manifest described in Example 27-3:

```
Class-Path: docs/minicomposer-help.zip
```

Another convention you may wish to follow is to keep the JavaHelp files (both XML and HTML) physically separate from other module source code. In the NetBeans source base, help files are normally kept in a *javahelp/* subdirectory in the module's source tree, rather than in *src/*.

Supporting User-Level Java APIs

Many modules have as the primary, or a significant, purpose the support of a Java API—helping the user to write Java code using a published package. A NetBeans module can help several ways, involving little or no extra coding in the module.

Supplying a Parser Database

Code completion (automatic completion of partially typed class, method, or field names in the Source Editor) is a favorite and heavily used feature of NetBeans, and presence of code completion makes use of an unfamiliar API much more pleasant. It is easy to plug in new parser databases that support code completion. The same databases are also used for many other features, such as Fast Open.

Let us say your module is designed to work with the Wombat extension version 2.0, with public API classes in javax.wombat.*. You can interactively build a parser database by right-clicking the *wombat* source package in the Explorer and choosing **Tools → Update Parser Database....** When prompted for the file prefix, choose something meaningful, such as wombat20. Normally the access settings can be left at default values; only public and protected classes and members should be included.

When the dialog box closes and the database creation is done, you will have active completion in your own IDE for this API (so test it). The parser database files can be found in your user directory in *system/ParserDB/* and will be named *wombat20.jcb* and *wombat20.jcs*. To make them available to other users, just copy them to the *system/ParserDB/* directory of the destination IDE. Practically speaking, this means they should be put in that directory in the NBM file you make, as shown later in Example 27-21.

As of this writing, there is not a supported way to build parser databases off-line (outside the IDE, especially from automated environments such as a build script). It can be done starting from *.class files, but important information such as parameter names to methods is lost this way. However, such a system is planned for the future—check the Editor Module (*http://editor.netbeans.org/*) web pages and issue #8059 (*http://www.netbeans.org/issues/show_bug.cgi?id=8059*) for up-to-date information on whether this is supported.

Bundling Javadoc

Normally adding a new API also means providing easily-browsable documentation for it in Javadoc format. The NetBeans javadoc module supports browsing and search of Javadoc documentation sets. Other modules can easily add *Javadoc mounts* to the default list, saving the user the trouble of finding and mounting the documentation.

First, place the documentation somewhere in an installation (meaning that it should be present in the NBM file). A typical choice is the *docs/* directory, though it does not really matter. (This is *docs/* directly beneath the root of the installation or user directory, *not modules/docs/*.) To avoid clutter it is usually best to distribute it in a ZIP file, for example *docs/wombat-api-2.0.zip*. (Make sure the filenames inside the ZIP match Java package structure, for example, *javax/wombat/WombatException.html*. The Javadoc module needs to be able to find HTML pages corresponding to given class names.)

To add an automatic mount of the Javadoc ZIP, all you need to do is add an entry somewhere in the *Mount/* folder of the system filesystem (conventionally in *Mount/Javadoc/*), where the entry is a filesystem instance provided using an XML format defined by the javadoc module:

 If the javadoc module is disabled, the mount will not work.

```
<filesystem>
  <folder name="Mount">
    <folder name="Javadoc">
      <file name="com-wombatblaster-javadoc.xml" url="javadoc-mount.xml">
        <attr name="SystemFileSystem.localizingBundle"
              stringvalue="com.wombatblaster.Bundle"/>
        <attr name="SystemFileSystem.icon"
              urlvalue="nbresloc:/com/wombatblaster/docs.gif"/>
      </file>
    </folder>
  </folder>
</filesystem>
```

The referenced XML document, *javadoc-mount.xml*, is shown in Example 27-19.

Example 27-19. Bundling Javadoc: javadoc-mount.xml

```
<?xml version="1.0" encoding="UTF-8"?>
<!DOCTYPE Javadoc PUBLIC
        "-//NetBeans IDE//DTD JavadocLibrary//EN"
        "http://www.netbeans.org/dtds/JavadocLibrary-1_0.dtd">
<Javadoc>
  <Archive name="docs/wombat-api-2.0.zip"/>
</Javadoc>
```

Finally, make this addition to your *Bundle.properties*:

```
Mount/Javadoc/com-wombatblaster-javadoc.xml=Wombat 2.0 API Documentation
```

The `name` attribute of `<<Archive/>>` refers to a location within a user or installation directory. The localized display name of the file is polite, since it will be shown in the IDE's Filesystems Settings (see Figure 27-4).

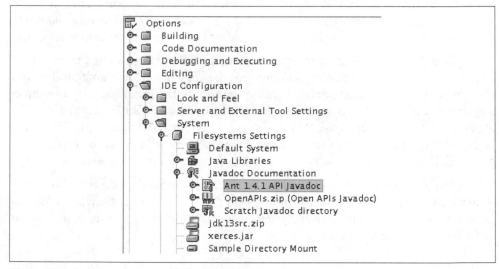

Figure 27-4. Javadoc automatic (declarative) mounts

Adding to the Default Classpath

A technique very similar to that used for Javadoc lets you add a library to the default user classpath—the list of directories and JARs used for compilation, execution, and debugging in a user's project (unless somehow overridden). If an API is intended to be compiled against, it is normally desirable to put it in the user's classpath so there is no need to mount it manually.

The style is almost exactly the same as for Javadoc automatic mounts. The JAR to be added to the classpath might be in `modules/ext/` (often such JARs are linked into the module too), or it might be anywhere else convenient in an IDE installation. There is a different XML DTD, and it is conventional to place such mounts in *Mount/java/*:

```
<filesystem>
  <folder name="Mount">
    <folder name="java">
      <file name="com-wombatblaster-lib.xml" url="lib-mount.xml">
        <attr name="SystemFileSystem.localizingBundle"
              stringvalue="com.wombatblaster.Bundle"/>
        <attr name="SystemFileSystem.icon"
              urlvalue="nbresloc:/com/wombatblaster/lib.gif"/>
      </file>
    </folder>
  </folder>
</filesystem>
```

Example 27-20 shows the *lib-mount.xml* document that defines the archive location.

Example 27-20. Adding to the User Classpath: lib-mount.xml

```
<?xml version="1.0" encoding="UTF-8"?>
<!DOCTYPE Library PUBLIC
          "-//NetBeans IDE//DTD JavaLibrary//EN"
          "http://www.netbeans.org/dtds/JavaLibrary-1_0.dtd">
<Library>
  <Archive name="modules/ext/wombat-lib-2.0.jar"/>
</Library>
```

You will also need another addition to *Bundle.properties*:

```
Mount/java/com-wombatblaster-lib.xml=Wombat 2.0 Library
```

Templates

When adding a new API, it is probably desirable to ship templates of classes using that API in a typical or illustrative way. This can be as simple as including them in the *Templates/* folder and marking them as templates:

```
<filesystem>
  <folder name="Templates">
    <folder name="WombatRenderers">
      <attr name="SystemFileSystem.localizingBundle"
            stringvalue="com.wombatblaster.Bundle"/>
      <attr name="templateWizardURL"
            urlvalue="nbresloc:/com/wombatblaster/renderers-desc.html"/>
      <file name="SimpleRenderer.java" url="SimpleRenderer.java.template">
        <attr name="template" boolvalue="true"/>
        <attr name="SystemFileSystem.localizingBundle"
              stringvalue="com.wombatblaster.Bundle"/>
        <attr name="templateWizardURL"
              urlvalue="nbresloc:/com/wombatblaster/simple-renderer-desc.html"/>
      </file>
    </folder>
  </folder>
</filesystem>
```

Example 27-21 is a sample template.

Example 27-21. Java Templates: SimpleRenderer.java.template

```
package Templates.WombatRenderers;
import javax.wombat.*;
public class SimpleRenderer implements WombatRenderer, WombatConsumer {
  public SimpleRenderer() {...}
  // ...
  public void render() {
    WombatUtils.runWithLock(new Runnable() {
      public void run() {
        WombatConsumer c = __NAME__.this;
        // ...
      }
    });
  }
}
```

You will need to make a corresponding addition to your *Bundle.properties*:

```
Templates/WombatRenderers=Wombat Renderers
Templates/WombatRenderers/SimpleRenderer.java=Simple Renderer
```

Note that you can provide not only a localized name (and if you like, icon) for the New template wizard, but also an HTML file to show in the description pane.

The template source file is named **.template* in the module sources (and in the module JAR) just to ensure that no attempt is made to compile it as part of the module's source code. Remember that in the system filesystem, it will be in some subpackage of Templates.*, so the template version should be written to match that. When actually instantiated, the Java package declaration and constructor names will be changed according to the package and class name the user has chosen for the new class. If you need to refer to the chosen class name elsewhere in the file, use macros such as __NAME__ (the NetBeans online help lists and describes these).

The Open APIs Support module provides a tutorial on adding a Java template that additionally shows how to associate a custom sequence of wizard panels with it, permitting some of the initial code to be customized by asking the user questions. Some modules also want to provide groups of files together to form a complex template. This can be accomplished by a using a **.group* file (a text file listing full resource paths to member files) and marking it as a template. Again the NetBeans online help discusses how to make such groups as a power user; module authors can do the same.

Bean Installation

If you are providing a JAR with one or more JavaBeans, you can also easily make them accessible to the NetBeans Form Editor without requiring the user to install them manually. Just place your bean JAR file in the *beans/* directory of the IDE installation, and the Form Editor should notice it and create a Component Palette category (based on the JAR file name). Alternatively, for more control you can make a Java mount of the bean JAR file and add this to the palette directory:

```
<filesystem>
  <folder name="Palette">
    <folder name="MyCategory">
      <attr name="SystemFileSystem.localizingBundle"
            stringvalue="com.wombatblaster.Bundle"/>
      <file name="javax-wombat-WombatPane.instance">
        <attr name="SystemFileSystem.localizingBundle"
              stringvalue="com.wombatblaster.Bundle"/>
        <attr name="SystemFileSystem.icon"
              urlvalue="nbreloc:/javax/wombat/WombatPaneIcon.gif"/>
        <attr name="beaninfo" boolvalue="false"/>
      </file>
    </folder>
  </folder>
</filesystem>
```

Here is the matching addition to *Bundle.properties*:

```
Palette/MyCategory=Wombat Beans
Palette/MyCategory/javax-wombat-WombatPane.instance=WombatPane
```

Creating the Module JAR File Within the IDE

If you have a simple module, you can create (and test) it right inside the IDE without any special tools. From the New wizard, select **Templates** → **NetBeans Extensions** → **Modules** → **API Module JAR**. Decide on a name and location for the completed JAR file. Add your source package or subpackages to the JAR in the next wizard pane. Also add the module manifest under the JAR resource name *META-INF/MANIFEST.MF*. You can make such a manifest using the Module Manifest template, if you have not done so already, and add NetBeans-specific attributes and sections visually from the Explorer (the Open APIs Support module documentation describes all this).

Once the JAR is created, just click Compile to build the JAR—this will also compile any classes in the module first if necessary (see the NetBeans online help for how to use the JAR Packager in more detail). You can run the module in test mode just by clicking Execute; if the module is already installed in test mode, this will reload it with any changes you made.

Creating a Build Script Using Ant

More complex modules are trickier to build with the JAR Packager because you do not have so much control over them. For such cases, it may be desirable to use the Ant build tool (which is integrated into NetBeans) to build the module. You probably want to use Ant to build your module if any of the following apply:

- You need reproducible builds that could be run easily from the command line (or via automated schedulers, and so forth).

- Creation of resources for the module requires special steps such as substituting text files. Or some Java source files require pre- or post-processing.

- There is more to the module than the JAR file. As described in other sections in this chapter, you may want to include additional files in an NBM package, such as Javadoc API documentation, extension libraries, and so on. These are most easily handled from an explicit build script.

- You wish to take advantage of several Ant tasks written especially for NetBeans module creation. NetBeans is built using Ant, so there are tasks that may be helpful for you, too.

There are many examples of how to write module build scripts in the NetBeans sources. Look for *build.xml* files in top-level module directories in the source tree. Some of the things you will find in such build scripts are specialized for integration into the NetBeans master build system, permitting a complete IDE to be built with a module configuration specified as a parameter. Most of the script content, however, just creates directories called *netbeans/* under the module source tree that hold that module's contributions to the NetBeans installation—the module JAR in *netbeans/ modules/* and any other files it may add (documentation, extensions, parser databases, and so on). This *netbeans/* directory can be *merged* into the master build directory (in *nbbuild/netbeans/*) or used as is to create an NBM (discussed below).

The NetBeans web pages devoted to building from source include some guides that you can use to find out what to include in a build script, especially the Extending Ant page (*http://nbbuild.netbeans.org/ant-extending.html*).

In *nbbuild/antsrc/org/netbeans/nbbuild/* are a number of Ant tasks that are of use to people creating modules. They are built by the NetBeans build process into *nbbuild/ nbantext.jar*, from which you can taskdef the tasks you want. For example, jhindexer runs the JavaHelp full-text search database indexer on a set of HTML files, making it easy to add full-text search to your module's help set without having to remember to manually keep it up to date. makelayer is helpful for creating an XML filesystem layer with a number of repetitive entries, for example if you have dozens of files to install in a similar way. And there are others; refer to the *nbbuild.netbeans.org* pages for Javadoc and other instructions.

When using Ant to build your module, you can still test it interactively in the IDE. With the Open APIs Support installed, use the nbinstaller task to install or reload a module JAR—naturally this task only works if you run the Ant script from inside NetBeans. If you normally have JavaHelp or library extensions referenced via Class-Path as external JAR files, nbinstaller only tries to reload the main JAR; however, you can test changes in these by packing them all into the same JAR file with the module sources; just add extra filesets to the jar task. Again see the Open APIs Support's online help.

Producing the .nbm File

An NBM file (NetBeans Module, *.nbm*) is a special higher-level archive that can package a module JAR file together with any other resources it might need—classpath extensions, external documentation files, and so on. The exact contents are essentially up to you, but it is assumed they will all be unpacked in the positions you specify within a NetBeans installation or user directory.

The NBM format is not very complex. It is just a ZIP file with some metadata in *Info/info.xml* describing the NetBeans module and with all the resources to be unpacked into the NetBeans installation placed under the *netbeans/* prefix. Let us take a look at the file list from one version of *ant.nbm*, the Ant integration module. You can use Unix ZIP tools, Windows WinZip, or even the JDK's own jar tool to create and examine NBMs (see Example 27-22).

Example 27-22. NBMs: Sample NBM File Contents

```
META-INF/MANIFEST.MF
META-INF/NB_IDE.SF
META-INF/NB_IDE.DSA
Info/info.xml
netbeans/modules/ant.jar
netbeans/modules/ext/ant-optional-1.4.1.jar
netbeans/modules/ext/ant-1.4.1.jar
netbeans/modules/docs/ant-manual.zip
netbeans/modules/patches/org-apache-tools-ant-module/README.txt
netbeans/system/ParserDB/ant141.jcb
netbeans/system/ParserDB/ant141.jcs
netbeans/docs/ant-api.zip
```

The manifest and signature files in *META-INF/* simply sign the NBM, as with the JDK's jarsigner tool, and do not contain anything specific to the NBM format. *Info/info.xml* is an XML file giving basic information about the module and how it may be downloaded and used. Example 27-23 is an example.

Example 27-23. NBMs: Sample Info/info.xml

```
<?xml version="1.0" encoding="UTF-8"?>
<module codenamebase="org.apache.tools.ant.module"
        homepage="http://ant.netbeans.org/"
        license="ant-license.txt"
        distribution="http://ant.netbeans.org/get/me/here/ant.nbm"
        downloadsize="0"
>
  <manifest OpenIDE-Module="org.apache.tools.ant.module/2"
            OpenIDE-Module-Specification-Version="2.7.1"
            OpenIDE-Module-Implementation-Version="200112012238"
            OpenIDE-Module-IDE-Dependencies="IDE/1 &gt; 1.35"
            OpenIDE-Module-Java-Dependencies="Java &gt; 1.3"
            OpenIDE-Module-Name="Ant"
            OpenIDE-Module-Short-Description="Supports Ant scripts..."
```

Example 27-23. NBMs: Sample Info/info.xml (continued)

```
            OpenIDE-Module-Long-Description="The Ant module..."
            OpenIDE-Module-Display-Category="Tools"
  />
  <license name="ant-license.txt">
    <!-- Omitted for brevity: -->
    <!-- first, license for Ant module (NetBeans code)... -->
    <!-- then license for Ant itself (Jakarta code)... -->
  </license>
</module>
```

The `module` element must be the root, and in its attributes gives basic information about the module. `distribution` and `downloadsize` are not important here; if the NBM is already available, clearly they are not needed. (See the next section for an explanation of these attributes.) The nested `manifest` element gives copies of important attributes from the main section of the module manifest; only attributes beginning with `OpenIDE-Module` and dealing with versioning, dependencies, or the module display name and description are relevant here. General JAR manifest attributes and NetBeans attributes giving instructions on installation (`OpenIDE-Module-Install`, `OpenIDE-Module-Layer`) may be omitted.

Every NBM may come with a license or other notice that the user will see (and must accept) before installing. The license name given in the `license` attribute of `module` should match the name given on the `license` element. In the next section we will see how licenses from several NBMs can be shared.

The rest of the NBM under *netbeans/* is unpacked into the user's NetBeans installation as is. One JAR file should be in *netbeans/modules/* (or *netbeans/modules/ autoload/*), the actual module represented by the NBM, but there may be any number of other files, such as libraries or documentation.

As of NetBeans 3.3, the Auto Update tool will keep track of each file installed from an NBM, so it is safe to change the set of files in an NBM between releases. As a rule, NBMs should not include files that might normally be modified by a user, as this will confuse the upgrade process. The standard NetBeans settings infrastructure lets settings be defined in layers and stores customizations in the *system/* folder, so for most modules the question would not come up.

There is a distinction made between *global* and regular NBMs. If the NBM includes any file to be installed in the *bin/* or *lib/* directories—most commonly an extension library in *lib/ext/* that for unavoidable technical reasons must be in the JVM's application classpath, and cannot be referred to via `Class-Path` from the module JAR— then the NBM is referred to as "global." In this case it cannot generally be installed (or upgraded) without a restart of the IDE, so the Auto Update tool will prompt the user to do so. Normal module NBMs will not need to place anything in these directories, so they can be installed "on the fly."

NBMs can be signed using the standard jarsigner tool or its equivalent. Signatures are acknowledged automatically if they are contained in the public keystore *lib/ide.ks* in the user's NetBeans installation. Other distributions may include alternate keystores. A user may also (with appropriate warnings) accept unsigned NBMs, accept NBMs with unknown signatures, and add novel signatures to his own keystore.

If you wish to create an NBM as part of an Ant-based build system, you can use the makenbm task, included in the NetBeans build infrastructure, which makes doing so easy. See the reference pages mentioned in "Creating a Build Script Using Ant" for information on this. All NetBeans standard modules use this task in their build scripts, so examples are plentiful.

More information about NBMs can be found on the Auto Update web pages (*http:// autoupdate.netbeans.org/nbm/nbm_package.html*).

How can an NBM actually be installed? The following section describes how to publish NBMs properly for wide distribution, but you can easily test them in a local NetBeans installation. Start **Tools** → **Update Center** and select Install Manually Downloaded Modules. You can select *.nbm* files to install, or you can double-click an NBM visible in the IDE's Explorer to initiate installation.

Publishing Using the Update Center

Once you have an NBM file, or several NBMs if you are making several modules, you can simply offer them for download or by other forms of distribution and let users install them directly. However, it can be annoying to a user to have to check for new versions on a web site, download them manually, and so on. Additionally, modules may have complex dependencies and a user might download a number of NBMs before realizing that they could not really be installed into the current IDE.

For these reasons the Auto Update module supports connecting to an update center that can both distribute NBMs and serve metadata about the available NBMs. The update client can thus make informed decisions about which NBMs to retrieve. The user can manage all this without touching a web browser; only sensible options are offered (for example, a user is not prompted to download a module he already has unless a newer version has been published). The Auto Update module can also perform automated update checks whenever the IDE is started (or at other intervals), for users with permanently on-line computers; the wizard will be opened if and only if updates have become available.

The metadata takes the form of an XML file served from a specific URL on the update server (presumably a web server). The XML file might be static or generated by a servlet or other dynamic means.

Let us take a look at a hypothetical update XML file that can serve two different modules (see Example 27-24). Both will be shown in the Wombat Software category in the Auto Update wizard and will use the same license.

Example 27-24. Update Center: Sample Update XML

```
<?xml version="1.0" encoding="UTF-8"?>
<module_updates timestamp="00/00/00/30/6/2001">
  <module_group name="Wombat Software">
    <module codenamebase="com.wombats.tools"
            homepage="http://www.wombats.com/products/tools/"
            license="wombats-inc-license.txt"
            distribution="http://www.wombats.com/download/tools-1.0.nbm"
            downloadsize="513110"
    >
      <manifest OpenIDE-Module="com.wombats.tools/1"
                OpenIDE-Module-Specification-Version="1.0"
                OpenIDE-Module-Implementation-Version="1.0 release #2"
                OpenIDE-Module-IDE-Dependencies="IDE/1 &gt; 1.33"
                OpenIDE-Module-Name="Wombat Tools"
                OpenIDE-Module-Long-Description="Infrastructure for wombats..."
      />
    </module>
    <module codenamebase="com.wombats.visualizer"
            homepage="http://www.wombats.com/products/visualizer/"
            license="wombats-inc-license.txt"
            distribution="http://www.wombats.com/download/visualizer-3.0.nbm"
            downloadsize="938112"
    >
      <manifest OpenIDE-Module="com.wombats.visualizer"
                OpenIDE-Module-Specification-Version="3.0"
                OpenIDE-Module-Implementation-Version="3.0 release #3"
                OpenIDE-Module-IDE-Dependencies="IDE/1 &gt; 1.33"
                OpenIDE-Module-Module-Dependencies="com.wombat.tools/1 > 1.0"
                OpenIDE-Module-Name="Wombat Visualizer"
                OpenIDE-Module-Long-Description="Wombat viewing tool..."
      />
    </module>
  </module_group>
  <license name="wombats-inc-license.txt"><![CDATA[Wombats Inc. License (WIL)

You may use wombats wherever the urge may lead you.
We are not responsible for wombat-related nuclear meltdowns.
Other terms and local restrictions may apply.

Copyright (C) 2001, The Wombat Trust
]]></license>
</module_updates>
```

As you can see, the format is very similar to that used in the *Info/info.xml* files in the NBMs. The document element module_updates gives a timestamp indicating when this set of NBMs was last updated (permitting an update client to quickly skip unchanged updates). Each `module_group` visually groups together related modules for the user's benefit; these may be nested. The `module` element is much like that used inside an NBM, but the `distribution` is now important—it points to the actual download URL for the NBM—and `downloadsize` should give the size in bytes of the NBM, permitting a progress bar to be displayed while downloading. All `license` elements come at the end of the XML file and may be shared according to name among several NBMs; in this example, a user selecting both NBMs would see the license only once.

If there are only a few modules involved and infrequent releases, it is not difficult to make such update description files manually. Or they may be generated dynamically, for example, by a servlet. NetBeans can include a registration number in the update URL; for example, this URL is used (as of this writing) by NetBeans development builds:

```
http://www.netbeans.org/updates/dev_{$netbeans.autoupdate.version}_,↵
{$netbeans.autoupdate.regnum}.xml
```

`{$netbeans.autoupdate.version}` is replaced with the protocol version of the update client, currently 1.5. `{$netbeans.autoupdate.regnum}` is by default the empty string, but a user may enter a registration number (the meaning is up to you) to get a special update page. The NetBeans web site currently serves a static page at *http://www.netbeans.org/updates/dev_1.5_.xml*.

Another way to make such XML files is using Ant (see "Creating a Build Script Using Ant"). The task `makeupdatedesc` can be configured with a list of NBM files (generated previously by `makenbm`) and some display group names, and can generate the complete update description XML file for you. This can be used to make it easy to publish a whole block of NBMs in one step.

Once you have a web server with a properly configured update description and NBMs available for download, how does a user see them? First of all, you can interactively add a new update URL. Just open the Options dialog, select **IDE Configuration** → **System** → **Autoupdate Types**, and click New to create a new update center reference. The URL can be configured. A user can use the NetBeans update center as well, or just the newly configured one. You can just use a `file:` URL for local testing.

If you are making a module, you can supply additional update URLs pointing to your web site so that the user does not have to configure this manually. Consult the autoupdate module's layer for the best way to do this, but here is a quick example (your module should depend on autoupdate to make this safer):

```
<filesystem>
  <folder name="Services">
    <folder name="AutoupdateType">
      <file name="com-wombats-updates.settings" url="updates.settings">
        <attr name="SystemFileSystem.localizingBundle"
              stringvalue="com.wombats.Bundle"/>
        <attr name="SystemFileSystem.icon" urlvalue=
```

```
        "nbresloc:/org/netbeans/modules/autoupdate/resources/updateAction.gif"/>
      <attr name="url"
            stringvalue="http://www.wombats.com/download/updates.xml"/>
      <attr name="enabled" boolvalue="true"/>
    </file>
  </folder>
 </folder>
</filesystem>
```

Here is the entry required in *Bundle.properties*:

```
Services/AutoupdateType/com-wombats-updates.settings=\
  Wombats Inc. Software Updates
```

Example 27-25 shows the XML document describing the update settings.

Example 27-25. Update Center: updates.settings

```
<?xml version="1.0" encoding="UTF-8"?>
<!DOCTYPE settings PUBLIC
        "-//NetBeans//DTD Session settings 1.0//EN"
        "http://www.netbeans.org/dtds/sessionsettings-1_0.dtd">
<settings version="1.0">
    <module name="org.netbeans.modules.autoupdate/1"/>
    <instanceof class="org.openide.ServiceType"/>
    <instanceof class="org.netbeans.modules.autoupdate.AutoupdateType"/>
    <instanceof class="org.netbeans.modules.autoupdate.XMLAutoupdateType"/>
    <instance class="org.netbeans.modules.autoupdate.XMLAutoupdateType" method=
  "org.netbeans.modules.autoupdate.XMLAutoupdateType.createXMLAutoupdateType"/>
</settings>
```

Here a new XML update configuration is created, parametrized by the file attributes
url and enabled. The same kind of configuration could be done using branding (see
Chapter 28 for more).

Again the Auto Update web pages discuss configuration of update servers.

Using ErrorManager to Log Problems

The 1.4 version of the Java 2 platform includes great improvements in logging, error
detection, and exception reporting, including the following new features:

- Assertions using the assert keyword
- Nested exception tracking using Throwable.getCause()
- Configurable logging facilities in java.util.logging.*

Unfortunately as of NetBeans 3.3, the 1.3 JDK must be supported, which lacks these
features.

JDK 1.3 support will probably be dropped when 1.5 is available, at which point 1.4's features can be used consistently in NetBeans.

As a temporary substitute for these facilities, the Open APIs include a simple utility class org.openide.ErrorManager with basic support for nested exceptions, exceptions annotated with additional information such as localized messages, and logging. (When 1.4 support can be assumed, ErrorManager will simply delegate to these standardized features.)

The three major features of the NetBeans ErrorManager are as follows:

Tracking the original cause of a rethrown or compound exception.
Any NetBeans code that throws a different exception than it catches or collapses a number of exceptions together should use this facility to avoid loss of critical debugging information. annotate(Throwable, Throwable) is the simplest way to use this facility. Examples in earlier chapters used this idiom where appropriate.

Localized exception messages.
This was discussed in earlier chapters in various contexts: annotate(Throwable, String) can be used to add a user-friendly message to an exception. You can also mark exceptions as being user errors and not real code bugs.

Logging.
log(String) and other overloads can log information about what a module is doing.

We will discuss the last facility in this section. Logging is very helpful during development of a module, as it helps a developer see exactly what steps the module is performing. It is just as useful in production. A user who has deployed a module in the field and is experiencing problems can turn on a flag and send trace information back to a support engineer to get the problems resolved quickly.

As an example, let us add logging support to the ScoreSupport class in the Mini-Composer example (discussed in detail in Chapter 22). The class is somewhat complex, and its state transitions can be subtle, so it is a good idea to permit logging of what it is doing.

To get started, let us make an ErrorManager instance specific to this class. There is one "master" ErrorManager in the system, and you can log to it; however, to be able to separately configure logging of particular sections of code, it is advisable to create a custom instance. You give an instance name, which conventionally looks like a Java package name; instances may be configured based on package prefixes. Here we will actually add the name of the score file to the instance name, permitting logging to be turned on for just one file if desired. The following changes belong in the ScoreSupport class constructor:

```
    private final ErrorManager err;
    public ScoreSupport(DataObject obj, EditorCookie edit) {
      this.obj = obj;
      err = TopManager.getDefault().getErrorManager().
        getInstance("org.netbeans.examples.modules.minicomposer.ScoreSupport." +
                      obj.getPrimaryFile().getPackageName('.'));
      this.edit = edit;
    }
```

Now it is easy to log messages from various methods doing interesting things:

```
    public void stateChanged(ChangeEvent ev) {
      err.log("Editor state changed");
      invalidate();
    }
```

By default this call to log() does nothing because logging is not enabled by default on this customized instance. However, if the user starts NetBeans with the option -J-Dorg.netbeans.examples.modules.minicomposer=0, logging is enabled for any code in the Mini-Composer. Then the *system/ide.log* file will receive this entry if *somescore.score* were closed in the Source Editor:

```
    [org.netbeans.examples.modules.minicomposer.ScoreSupport.somescore] Editor ,↵
    state changed
```

In this case the message is simple. Commonly a message should be logged that is expensive to compute (for example, listing all objects in a set), and it is of course undesirable to calculate a log message that will never be printed. For this reason, isLoggable() is useful:

```
    private synchronized void setScoreAndParseException(Score s, IOException e) {
      if (err.isLoggable(ErrorManager.INFORMATIONAL)) {
        err.log("parsed; exception=" + e + "; score size=" + s.getSize());
      }
      score = s;
      parseException = e;
      fireChange();
    }
```

The message is not computed if it would not have been used anyway.

Testing

Before putting a module into production, test it as thoroughly as possible. There are several basic kinds of testing:

- **Ad-hoc.** Start NetBeans with the module installed and go through a sequence of typical user actions, exercising all aspects of the module.

- **Automated GUI testing.** Tools are available that record sequences of interactions with the GUI and make sure they continue to work. Though very useful, these can be limited by the variability of the GUI during development.

- **Additional testing.** Similar to the above, some tools are available to test specific aspects of the module's GUI—for example, completeness of internationalization or accessibility.

- **Script-based unit tests.** These isolate particular pieces of the module's functionality (typically running non-visually) and ensure that they conform to internal or published API specifications.

- **Script-based regression tests.** These attempt to reproduce a sequence a steps that was known to at some point trigger a bug in the module—for example an exception. If the bug is fixed, writing a regression test helps to ensure that it will not reoccur (at least not in its original form) during future rewrites of the code.

The first style needs little more explanation. The second is possible with testing tools generally available for Java. Some tools are especially designed for use on NetBeans that may help you. Jemmy (*http://jemmy.netbeans.org/*) is a general GUI testing framework that permits automated exercise of a GUI application. Jelly (*http://jellytools.netbeans.org/*) builds on Jemmy and knows how to interact with common GUI components found in NetBeans, such as the explorer, source editor, and so on. Using these two together, you can verify that user-visible actions and workflows in your module continue to operate even after big changes "under the hood."

The third style is possible both with generic and NetBeans-specific tools. For example, the NetBeans Accessibility page (*http://a11y.netbeans.org/*) gives instructions for using an accessibility tool on NetBeans modules. Similarly, the I18N page (*http://www.netbeans.org/i18n/*) mentions a simple command-line switch that can quickly alert you to unlocalized resources displayed by a module.

The final two styles of testing require a proper test framework. For NetBeans modules, the XTest framework is ideal; it is based on JUnit and has extensions to make testing NetBeans code easier. For more information, see the XTest web site (*http://xtest.netbeans.org/*).

You can find out more about the different tools available to help with testing NetBeans on the Test Tools web site (*http://testtools.netbeans.org/*).

We have now covered all the essentials of creating and distributing a NetBeans module. Many developers, however, are really interested in creating a complete application, not just a plug-in to someone else's IDE. In the following chapter, we will show how to take this final step.

Building Your Distribution of NetBeans

Since the NetBeans project is open source and makes an effort to be friendly to people building all kinds of applications, you have the opportunity to create a custom distribution of NetBeans, or even a rather different application reusing some NetBeans code.

Do You Need Your Own Distribution?

The first serious question is whether creating your own distribution is necessary or even advisable. There are some good reasons to do it:

- NetBeans includes a number of modules your users do not want or need.

- NetBeans does not include a number of modules you produce that your users need, and it would be silly to force them to get vanilla NetBeans and then download these modules.

- You want the application to *look* like yours. This is known as a desire for *branding*.

- You wish to suppress some pieces of the NetBeans UI that are not appropriate for your purposes. For example, nothing you are interested in involves compilation; why should users see a Build menu they will never use?

- Your desired application does not really resemble an IDE at all. You just want to reuse some pieces of the NetBeans platform, for example the Filesystems library, the module activation system, or the Explorer GUI.

Memory Requirements

Note that while the NetBeans IDE requires 128 MB of physical RAM to run tolerably, if you are building an application around the NetBeans core, your application probably will not have such large memory requirements. The NetBeans IDE is a very large application, with a vast complement of modules. Most applications will not be so complex.

In light of these considerations, remember that the decision to create a distribution, rather than just supplying modules that can be added to a normal NetBeans installation, should not be taken lightly. There are disadvantages, too, depending on your target audience:

- New NetBeans releases do not automatically translate into new foundations for your product. You might be able to upgrade the underlying NetBeans version easily, but it will not be as smooth as if you distribute a module (for which the NetBeans team tries to guarantee compatibility).

- If you have removed some NetBeans modules, users who really do want them might have a harder time getting them (*netbeans.org* does not routinely host NBMs of standard modules, since it is assumed users already have them).

- If you have suppressed basic parts of the NetBeans UI (such as the **Build** menu), users will be unable to work with other standard modules or modules from other organizations, even if they want to.

- You will probably need to supply documentation for basic functions of the application that would otherwise be covered in the NetBeans online help.

- More development and testing time will be consumed, compared to shipping individual modules.

With these cautions, let us look at what is involved in creating a NetBeans distribution. Naturally the amount of complexity will depend mostly on how far you are planning to deviate from the structure of the NetBeans IDE.

Licensing

NetBeans is licensed under the *http://www.netbeans.org/about/os/license.html* Sun Public License (SPL). This is a variant of the Mozilla Public License. In fact, the primary differences are that where the Mozilla license says Netscape, the SPL says Sun Microsystems and that the SPL provides for the documentation being part of the open source project as well. Note that this is *not* the more restrictive Netscape Public License (NPL) that grants special rights to the Netscape company with regard to Mozilla (and which is being phased out) or the dual-licensing scheme, which is being phased in as of this writing.

The license allows you to freely redistribute NetBeans, including or not including whatever modules or pieces of code you wish, either commercially (as a for-pay product, probably including some modules or code of your own) or for free. The only significant restriction it imposes is that source code you modify that was *already* under the SPL has to *stay* under the SPL, and if it is distributed in binary form, it has to be made available somehow in source form, too. There is no limitation when removing SPL files or when adding your own non-SPL files; only modifying existing SPL files triggers this clause.

You should have no legal licensing problems if everything you distribute is licensed under the SPL, a commercial license, or licenses such as the BSD or Apache licenses. There may be issues with distributing code under the GNU Public License (GPL) along with the IDE. A full discussion of the knotty issues associated with licensing is beyond the scope (and liability) of this book, so we will leave it to you and your lawyer to deal with that discussion.

If you have comments or questions of a private nature regarding licensing, such as sometimes come up when preparing a commercial distribution, feel free to send them to *feedback@netbeans.org* for a personal response. However, most questions of this type, assuming there is no particular reason for them to be kept private, should be sent to the *nbdiscuss@netbeans.org* general-purpose mailing list.

Selecting a Baseline

Which version of NetBeans should your distribution be based on? There is no single answer, though some guidelines can be given.

Most redistributors should use a NetBeans stable release, such as 3.2.1 or 3.3.2. This choice provides the greatest reliability in a platform. It is best to choose the most recent available release: you get the latest and hopefully most feature-rich code, bugs left unresolved in earlier releases may well be fixed in the latest one, you will get much better support on the NetBeans mailing lists if you are using code close to what is currently being worked on by the developers, and the configurability of the NetBeans sources and their friendliness toward redistributors increases with each release, sometimes substantially (as with 3.3).

It may happen that an earlier release suits your purposes better because of bugs introduced in a later release; if so, please tell the NetBeans development team about it (on *nbdev@netbeans.org*)! Bug-fix-only releases such as 3.3.2 are often made, and your pet peeve might get solved in the next one. Minor, isolated problems that have already been fixed by developers in working sources may be best handled by applying a patch to the latest release—these are often available right in the bug report in Issuezilla, or if not please ask for one to be added to it. Core and Open API patches in the form of JAR files may be placed in *lib/patches/* in a NetBeans distribution; module patches may be placed in *modules/patches/modulename* where *modulename* is the code name base of the module, for example `org.netbeans.modules.java`. See Chapter 15 for an explanation of module patches.

If you are feeling more adventurous, you might want to build on top of newer development sources. The most current is the CVS trunk, to which new revisions are freely committed every day. It will surely have some bugs, but not critical ones—it should be buildable and runnable at all times. A compromise between new features and stability is the *http://qa.netbeans.org/processes/q-builds-program.html Q-Build*, a build made weekly that is based on the development trunk but in which the most egregious bugs introduced (or found) during that week have been fixed.

It may happen that you need to make extensive modifications or apply selected bug fixes in your version of the NetBeans sources. It could be cumbersome to try to keep a local copy of the sources and make patches to these, as you are not directly tied to the NetBeans CVS repository (so, for example, merging to a newer stable version would be more complex). If you wish to have a private branch made for your own purposes in the NetBeans CVS repository, just ask on *nbdev@netbeans.org*. Only SPL-licensed sources can be kept in such a branch, but what to do in this branch is at your discretion. Just avoid committing large numbers of new files or adding large numbers of CVS tags because such operations can slow down or clutter the repository for other users.

Finally, you might decide to base a distribution on *another* NetBeans distribution. For example, you may want to use some of the features of an edition of Sun's Forte for Java IDE. Such a choice could give you access to additional modules not available in NetBeans, though it might also complicate the process of creating a distribution. Such a choice is outside the scope of this book, but if you take this course, just contact the vendor you wish to build on (for example, Sun welcomes such partnerships and has a program to support them).

Getting the Sources

If you are basing your distribution on an official NetBeans release, source snapshots of these can be downloaded in **.tar.gz* or **.zip* formats from the NetBeans web site. Do not forget to download the "extra binaries" (non-SPL files such as third-party libraries) that correspond to them.

You can also get sources using CVS. All NetBeans development work is done on the *cvs.netbeans.org* server. For example, if you want to retrieve a copy of the sources used to build Release 3.3.x, use the following sequence of commands:

```
$mkdir -p ~/nb-src-33/nb_all
$cd ~/nb-src-33/nb_all
$cvs -d :pserver:anoncvs@cvs.netbeans.org:/cvs login
Press Enter
$cvs -d :pserver:anoncvs@cvs.netbeans.org:/cvs co -rrelease33 standard
should check out sources
$mkdir ~/nb-src-33/nbextra
$cd ~/nb-src-33/nbextra
$unzip /tmp/NetBeansIDE-release331-extbin.zip
```

More details on building NetBeans are available in Chapter 1.

Customizing the Build Process

If you are making a custom distribution including some standard NetBeans modules and some of your own, it may be easiest to run the normal NetBeans build process with appropriate substitutions. In effect, work with your modules from the perspective of the build process as if they were hosted on *netbeans.org* (of course if you are contributing a module to NetBeans, you will do this anyway).

Making such changes should not be difficult. Start with a complete and buildable NetBeans source distribution. Now choose a new subdirectory where your module or modules will be held—for example, *mystuff/*. If you have more than one module you want to build, you may want to create a subdirectory in *that* for each such module; it is up to you.

Each module subdirectory must then have a *build.xml* build script that does everything necessary to build that module when its `netbeans` target is called, placing all desired build products in a subdirectory named *netbeans/*. Conversely, a `clean` target ought to remove any files created by the build. The NetBeans *http://nbbuild.netbeans. org/ant-extending.html* Extending Ant Builds page discusses the exact contract with each subdirectory in more detail and gives pointers to a number of tasks and idioms you may want to use.

You need to do one more thing: in the master build script *nbbuild/build.xml*, add a target `all-modulename` for each module you have that might be included in a build. If you put it in the subdirectory *mystuff/*, use `all-mystuff`. If it was nested in *mystuff/ module1/*, use `all-mystuff/module1`. This target should call a subbuild in your module directory. It may depend on other `all-*` targets if your module needs other modules to be built before it can be built; at least `all-openide` should be included for any NetBeans module—for example:

```
<target name="all-mystuff" depends="all-openide,all-othermodule">
  <echo message="Building module mystuff..."/>
  <ant dir="../mystuff" target="netbeans"/>
</target>
```

Here then is a summary of the file structure you will end up with:

nbbuild/
nbbuild/build.xml—patched by you
nbbuild/
openide/
core/
ant/
applet/

mystuff/module1/build.xml—1st build script
mystuff/module1/manifest.mf—JAR manifest, conventionally

mystuff/module1/src/—sources, conventionally
mystuff/module1/netbeans/modules/my-first-module.jar—build product
mystuff/module1/netbeans/—anything else such as parser database files, etc.
mystuff/module2/—another module

The NetBeans *http://www.netbeans.org/devhome/sources/structure.html* Source Structure guidelines give conventions for how source files in modules ought to be arranged for consistency.

Now you just need to include your modules in a build:

```
$ cd nbbuild
$ant -Dmodules=... real-clean
removes all build products
$ant -Dmodules=ant,...,mystuff/module1,mystuff/module2
build should complete in a few minutes
$cp -v NetBeans-*.zip /dist
```

It can be cumbersome to type the complete list of modules to include in the build every time you run it. So you can also add a config to the configmods task in the init target of the master build script, say including some standard NetBeans modules and some of your own. In NetBeans 3.3:

```
<configmods property="modules" selectedconfig="${moduleconfig}">
    <!-- existing configurations, then add yours: -->
    <config name="myapp"
            modules="mystuff/module1,mystuff/module2,editor,classfile,clazz,java"/>
</configmods>
```

(In NetBeans 3.4 *nbbuild/build.properties* is used for this purpose instead.) Then you need only type:

```
$ant -Dmoduleconfig=mystuff
same result as above
```

To make a minimal configuration of NetBeans (just the basic platform), just use -Dmodules= for 3.3.x sources or -Dmoduleconfig=platform starting with 3.4.

If you want to begin building against a different version of NetBeans, it should suffice just to cvs update the NetBeans source directories and resolve any textual conflicts that might have occurred in *nbbuild/build.xml*. This style may also be appropriate if for some reason you need to patch existing NetBeans Java sources to get the results you want—but branding (described in "Branding") was designed to support many common types of customization more easily and maintainably than patching.

Here is a quick summary of the steps needed to add your modules to the NetBeans build process:

1. Get NetBeans sources and make sure you can build them as is.
2. Create some subdirectories for your modules. Make a build script for each module.
3. Add the names of your modules to the master list.

4. Optionally create a module configuration for your application.

5. Run the NetBeans build with your modules (or module configuration) selected.

6. Update CVS sources whenever desired and build again.

Adding Modules to a "Stock" Distribution

A different approach to take is to begin with a pre-built IDE and add your built module or modules to it. This is easiest if you are not trying to *remove* any modules from the baseline distribution, for then you would need to know exactly which files are associated with each module in the distribution—though you can find this out starting in NetBeans 3.3 by looking at the file *update_tracking.xml* in the root of a build. Starting with a pre-built IDE may be necessary if you are basing your distribution on something other than vanilla NetBeans, for example an edition of Sun's Forte for Java IDE. As of NetBeans 3.4, you can also download a small *platform* build designed for this purpose.

Such an approach may also be useful if you do not want to become too involved in the NetBeans build process and have your own means of creating your module. In this case all you should need to do is copy your module JAR and any other supporting files into the proper places in the IDE build, and it should be ready to run.

To be best-behaved, however, two other things should be done to the resulting build to indicate the presence of your module. Both of these things are done automatically by special tasks in the NetBeans build process, but if you are adding modules manually, you will need to do these things manually as well.

First, create an XML file in the *system/Modules/* directory named according to your module's code name base, and looking something like Example 28-1:

Example 28-1. Adding a Module: sample system/Modules/com-yourcorp-modulename.xml

```
<!DOCTYPE module PUBLIC "-//NetBeans//DTD Module Status 1.0//EN"
                        "http://www.netbeans.org/dtds/module-status-1_0.dtd">
<module name="com.yourcorp.modulename">
  <param name="autoload">false</param>
  <param name="enabled">true</param>
  <param name="jar">your-module.jar</param>
  <param name="origin">installation</param>
  <param name="release">1</param>
  <param name="reloadable">false</param>
  <param name="specversion">1.0</param>
</module>
```

Be sure to get the version information right: specversion must match your JAR's OpenIDE-Module-Specification-Version, and release should be included if and only if your JAR has a major release number after a slash in OpenIDE-Module. Autoload modules (Chapter 27) have autoload set to true and must have no enabled parameter, and must have an origin of installation/autoload.

If this file is not present in the installation, the module will still be turned on when a user runs the IDE—but the file will be created in the user directory, adding a little clutter. For the first start of the IDE the module will also be listed as a "new" module. So it is a little cleaner to create this file in advance.

The other desirable thing to do is to add information about the files associated with your module (or modules) to the *update_tracking.xml* file mentioned previously. Each module element should correspond to one potential NBM bundle of the module and should include basic metadata about the module as well as a list of all the files associated with it (including checksums). Ensuring that the update tracking XML file matches the actual state of the installation is useful because it helps Auto Update manage files better when new NBMs are installed, and in the future may permit incremental patching rather than downloading full NBMs. Here is an example addition:

```
<module codename="com.yourcorp.modulename/1">
  <!-- For install_time attribute, see java.util.Date: -->
  <module_version specification_version="1.0" origin="installer"
                  last="true" install_time="1020709484048">
    <!-- For crc attribute, see java.util.zip.CRC32: -->
    <file name="modules/your-module.jar" crc="1234567890"/>
    <file name="modules/ext/some-lib.jar" crc="2345678901"/>
  </module_version>
</module>
```

Since generating *update_tracking.xml* fragments by hand might be cumbersome, you could also use the Ant task genlist loaded from *nbbuild/nbantext.jar* and used in all module build scripts.

Naturally, if you are removing any modules from the distribution, you should also remove the matching module XML files and update tracking entries.

Here is a quick summary of the steps involved in adding modules to a stock distribution:

1. Start with a stock binary distribution of NetBeans or a related product.
2. Add your module JARs and any supporting files such as libraries to the proper places. Remove module JARs and supporting files for any modules you do not want.
3. Add an XML file to *system/Modules/* for each module you add. Remove a file for each module you remove.
4. Add a module entry to *update_tracking.xml* for each module you add. Remove an entry for each module you remove.

Remember, generally you will choose to *either* add modules by customizing the build process *or* by manually adjusting a pre-built distribution.

Creating Preconfigured Settings

In some situations you may wish to customize the *default settings* provided by Net-Beans for some kind of behavior—without changing the range of behaviors. This is easy to handle. You can select certain settings to override and include them in your distribution. Since NetBeans merges settings from an installation directory as well as a user directory (and sometimes a project directory, too), anything you place in the installation directory will serve as a default for the user.

First, you need to understand what is stored where—an overview of the NetBeans settings layout is given in Chapter 27. The easiest way to prepare customized settings is to actually run NetBeans (with a fresh user directory using the -userdir option) and adjust whatever you like using the GUI. Shut it down, then select the desired files from the user directory under *system/* and copy them to the corresponding parts of *system/* in your installation directory (the build). For example, *Services/org-netbeans-modules-java-settings-JavaSettings.settings* currently holds general settings for the Java sources module. (Such paths can be expected to be fairly stable, since they need to be in order to support upgrades of user directories between releases.)

In more advanced cases, if you know the technical details of how a customization is stored and what formats it can take, you can prepare more sophisticated changes. For example, using the Window System documentation relating to its XML persistence format, you can set up additional workspaces just by adding some files to your distribution. Or you can create special Java executors or compilers with particular program paths and arguments, and so on.

However, in general, you will just want to add new modules to support such things and place the added or modified settings in the layer; this will be easier and more powerful. As an example, without any added module, you could add a configuration for a new Java external compiler type that runs your optimized compiler (shipped in the distribution for out-of-the-box use). But you would be limited to the format substitution keys that the standard Java external compiler type defines: debugging and optimizing switches, classpath setting, and so on. Perhaps you want to refine the options available in the Property Sheet for the compiler relating to optimization: not just on or off, but intermediate settings. Or perhaps a different executable needs to be selected according to the user's platform. In such cases it is best to create a new subclassed compiler type based on the one used in the Java module (the basic pattern to follow was given in Chapter 24). This could provide more or fewer options, preconfigure some defaults programmatically, and more.

Branding

Branding is a general system used in NetBeans to permit alternate distributions of the application to selectively customize many aspects of its appearance and behavior. It is based closely on the internationalization infrastructure described in Chapter 27, and details of its workings are given on the NetBeans web site (*http://www.netbeans. org/devhome/docs/i18n/index.html#5*).

The first step in branding your distribution is to choose a *branding token*. This is a short suffix akin to a locale abbreviation. For example, if your distribution is the MacroModeler, you could choose the token macmod whatever you like. Branded resources will be identified with this suffix much like localized resources are. For example, if the plain NetBeans resource is a properties file *Bundle.properties*, your *variant* of it would be named *Bundle_macmod.properties*. This could override certain text keys in the bundle.

If you have finer-grained subdivisions within a product suite, you may wish to brand some resources generally for your organization and others more specifically for one product. This is done by using a compound branding token separated by underscores. For example, if you have a MacroModeler Basic Edition and a MacroModeler Advanced Edition, you could create a *Bundle_macmod.properties* giving some overrides applicable to all MacroModeler editions; *Bundle_macmod_basic.properties* for things applicable only to the basic edition, and similarly *Bundle_macmod_ adv.properties* for the advanced edition. There could be further subdivisions as well.

Branding is orthogonal to locale. While *Bundle_macmod.properties* applies to the MacroModeler in the default locale (normally English), there may be a Japanese translation as well. NetBeans already includes Japanese translations (maintained by Sun's Forte for Java team), for example *Bundle_ja.properties*, and as you read this book, there may be others contributed by users around the world. *Bundle_macmod. properties* will take precedence over this when running MacroModeler in Japanese locale; to provide the MacroModeler for Japanese users, you create a *Bundle_ macmod_ja.properties* file listing Japanese translations of the overrides given in *Bundle_macmod.properties*. Note that the branding suffix must precede the locale suffix when both are used.

Any resource that is requested using NbBundle can be branded automatically, as well as localized. In NetBeans, property files with localizable text are retrieved using NbBundle. Similarly, images such as icons can be loaded with it. The URL protocol nbresloc: does this automatically, so nbresloc:/org/netbeans/modules/foo/icon.gif will find an icon *org/netbeans/modules/foo/icon_macmod.gif* if you have provided one. XML layers from modules are also localized and branded automatically. So in most cases, if there is a resource used in the NetBeans core or a standard NetBeans module that you want to override, you can do it with branding—if not, file a bug about it! (And then work around it by adding a direct patch for the resource in your distribution.)

Implementing Branding on a Distribution

One key advantage of branding is that branded resources are kept physically separate from the "pristine" originals. For example, if *modules/foo.jar* contains the resource *org/netbeans/modules/foo/Bundle.properties*, you can brand it by creating a JAR file *modules/locale/foo_macmod.jar* containing *org/netbeans/modules/foo/Bundle_macmod.properties*. Always remember that the JAR resource path has to contain the branding suffix, and the name of the JAR file must match that of the original except for being located one directory down in a subdirectory named *locale/* and including the branding suffix in its name before the `.jar` extension. This naming convention is the same as the convention used to separate locale-specific JAR files during internationalization. You can physically separate subdivided branding JARs in the natural way: *modules/locale/foo_macmod.jar* with some customizations as well as *modules/locale/foo_macmod_basic.jar* and *modules/locale/foo_macmod_adv.jar* with further refinements.

How is branding turned on? By default, NetBeans runs unbranded, meaning branded resources are ignored (and branded JARs not opened). If you want to run with a certain branding for testing, pass it on the command line using `-branding yourtoken`. Your users will not know to do this, of course, so you can set it as the default branding by creating a file *lib/branding* in your distribution, which should have one line listing the branding token (for example `macmod_basic`). NetBeans will find it and use it as a default unless `-branding` overrides it.

The effect is that you can apply many kinds of customizations to NetBeans, making it look and act like a different product, without touching the NetBeans source code or even modifying files in the NetBeans installation—take a complete NetBeans release, add your branded JAR files and the *lib/branding* file, and you are done. You can just keep a ZIP of your branding additions and unpack it on top of a NetBeans build or release. This is a great way to insulate yourself from minor changes in NetBeans source code—no need to keep running patches. If the location or meaning of a JAR or resource within a JAR changes from one NetBeans release to the next, you will have to update your branding patches to match it. Such changes tend to be infrequent, however—branding tuned for one release will probably work tolerably well on the next one, or need only modest revision.

When replacing complete resources such as images, it is easy to create a branding variant with the correct name and add it to your JAR. Overriding parts of a resource such as a bundle file is more subtle; as these techniques are discussed in the next section, tools will be mentioned to make it easier.

Simple Branding: Text Strings and Images

The most elementary form of branding applies to atomic resources such as images. For example, in NetBeans the splash screen is loaded from *lib/core.jar* in the file *org/netbeans/core/resources/splash.gif*. To brand it, just create a new splash screen and put it in a file named (for example) *lib/locale/core_macmod.jar* under *org/netbeans/core/resources/splash_macmod.gif*.

 Actually in the specific case of the splash screen, you will usually want to take another step. NetBeans writes status information on the splash screen during startup. It also shows the splash screen in the About dialog box. If your splash is a different size or if it needs to place this text in a different place or in a different color for best visibility, these things can be overridden, too. Brand *org/netbeans/core/ Bundle.properties* (also from *lib/core.jar*) and replace keys such as SPLASH_WIDTH, SplashRunningTextBounds, AboutTextColor, and so on (see comments in that file).

Changing text strings loaded from bundles is not much harder. Remember all Java code should be retrieving displayable messages using some variation of this syntax:

```
String msg = NbBundle.getMessage(ThisClass.class, "LBL_something");
```

Other things that load messages from a bundle (localized module manifest strings, XML workspace names, and so on) also go through NbBundle. To brand such a message, assuming it came from *Bundle.properties*, just create a *Bundle_macmod. properties* containing *just this key* and its branded value. Here is a sample base *Bundle.properties*:

```
LBL_something=Show in NetBeans source editor
LBL_something_else=Make read-only
```

And here is a label for your branded distribution; this would go in *Bundle_macmod. properties*:

```
LBL_something=Show in MacroModeler source editor
```

When NetBeans is looking for a resource key, it always searches in more specific branded (or localized) bundles first, finally defaulting to the unmarked bundle. Remember that compound branding tokens are searched in a logical order, so you could also provide some more specialized keys, such as in *Bundle_macmod_adv. properties*:

```
LBL_something=Show in MacroModeler Advanced source editor
```

If you are branding a lot of keys from one bundle, you may find it convenient to use the NetBeans resource bundle support. Locate the original bundle from NetBeans sources in the Explorer. Create a new "locale" (really your branding token) by selecting Add Locale... from the context menu, and then you can make selected changes in the table view.

 NetBeans will try to copy all the keys from the base bundle for you. Just delete the ones you do not plan to change.

When you are done, move your branded *.properties* file to its real destination.

Figure 28-1 shows the core bundle of NetBeans being branded. The Explorer shows the newly added *Bundle_macmod.properties* as a node **macmod - macmod** beneath **Bundle.properties**. The upper part of the split pane on the right shows a table view where you can see all branded values alongside the originals; the lower part of the split pane shows the branded bundle being edited as text at the same time.

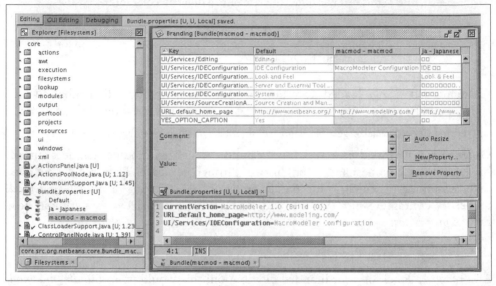

Figure 28-1. Branding: patching the core bundle

Configuration Branding: Menu Bar, Workspaces, and More

Most of NetBeans' configuration is managed by files in the system filesystem. For example, the menu bar in the main window is controlled by subfolders and action instance files beneath *Menu/*. Similarly, the complete setup of workspaces and the positions and contents of the windows within them is controlled by a hierarchy of XML files in the *Windows/* folder. Branding lets you patch these things and much more. The key is that when an XML layer from a module (including also the core layer) is loaded, any branding variants are also loaded at the same time.[*] All variants are merged together, with the more specific brandings taking precedence. The merging is done by `org.openide.filesystems.MultiFileSystem` and thus follows the same behavior used to merge project and user directory customizations with module-supplied defaults.

---

[*] It is also possible to give locale variants of layers, but this is rarely used since localizable text strings are normally stored in bundles anyway, rather than directly in the layer.

Let us start with a simple example. The utilities module defines the URL data type, recognizing *.url files (simple files containing just a URL). One of its features is that a URL file can be shown directly in a menu or toolbar. The data object has an InstanceCookie providing an instance of a menu presenter that, when clicked, displays the contained URL. This makes it easy to add web links to a menu.

The same module also provides a number of default URLs in the Help menu (at least in NetBeans 3.2 and 3.3). For example, here is one such link (shown as an abbreviated layer file with other parts omitted):

```
<filesystem>
  <folder name="Menu">
    <folder name="Help">
      <file name="netbeans-web-link.url">
        <![CDATA[http://www.netbeans.org/]]>
        <attr name="SystemFileSystem.localizingBundle"
              stringvalue="org.netbeans.modules.url.Bundle"/>
        <attr name="SystemFileSystem.icon"
              urlvalue="nbresloc:/org/netbeans/modules/url/webLink.gif"/>
      </file>
    </folder>
  </folder>
</filesystem>
```

Note that the display name and icon of the data object also serve as the name and icon of the menu item.

To modify virtual files using branding, you need to know which module (including the core) they came from. Unfortunately in NetBeans 3.3, there is not a simple way to do this. However, in most cases, it is easy to guess which module would provide a file, based on the kind of functionality it represents; just look at the XML layers of likely suppliers until you find it. A way to find this information directly will be added to the Open APIs Support module for NetBeans 3.4.

Replacing a file

It is probable that a branded distribution would want to change this web link. This is easy enough: just provide a branded layer (like *Layer_macmod.xml*) that overrides the contents of this file. The layer does not need to contain anything else, as all other files (including some invisible services, and so on) will be picked up from the plain utilities module:

```
<filesystem>
  <folder name="Menu">
    <folder name="Help">
      <file name="netbeans-web-link.url">
        <![CDATA[http://modeling.com/]]>
      </file>
    </folder>
  </folder>
</filesystem>
```

To change the link destination, just package this layer variant in *modules/locale/ utilities_macmod.jar*. In this case the display name and icon stay the same by default; you might also brand the bundle file (*org/netbeans/modules/url/Bundle_macmod. properties*) and/or brand the icon (*org/netbeans/modules/url/webLink_macmod.gif*).

Adding a file

Adding new virtual files to the system filesystem using branding is as easy as replacing the contents or attributes of existing files (present in the unbranded base layer); just write the new files you want. Example 28-2 illustrates this.

Example 28-2. Branding: .../Layer_macmod.xml with a new file

```
<filesystem>
  <folder name="Menu">
    <folder name="Help">
      <attr name="netbeans-web-link.url/some-other-link.url" boolvalue="true"/>
      <file name="some-other-link.url">
        <![CDATA[http://modeling.com/feedback.html]]>
        <attr name="SystemFileSystem.localizingBundle"
              stringvalue="org.netbeans.modules.url.Bundle"/>
        <attr name="SystemFileSystem.icon"
              urlvalue="nbresloc:/org/netbeans/modules/url/webLink.gif"/>
      </file>
    </folder>
  </folder>
</filesystem>
```

Here we add a new link to the Help menu pointing to a feedback page. The link is configured as a virtual file (file object) with the *.url* extension used by URL bookmarks.

Example 28-2 also shows that branded layers can add folder ordering constraints involving any files in the folder. Here we request that the newly added feedback link come *below* the main web site link. In a real situation we would also want to add a second constraint asking that it come *above* some other known menu item; otherwise, the feedback link might appear anywhere in the menu below the main link, not necessarily immediately after it.

The new file can be given a localized name and icon, too; we will need to add the name to the branded bundle, as shown in Example 28-3. As usual, the ampersands indicate menu mnemonics.

Example 28-3. Branding: .../Bundle_macmod.properties with a new file

```
# Change the name of the original link.
Menu/Help/netbeans-web-link.url=&More about Modeling
Menu/Help/some-other-link.url=MacroModeler &Feedback
```

Removing (masking) a file

Removing files using branding is not as easy, but doing so is not difficult once you know how. It is just necessary to create a mask file that is named by adding the suffix _hidden to the name of the real file. The mask can just be an empty file and serves to tell NetBeans (actually MultiFileSystem) to ignore the masked file—for example:

```
<filesystem>
  <folder name="Menu">
    <folder name="Help">
      <file name="netbeans-web-link.url_hidden"/>
    </folder>
  </folder>
</filesystem>
```

This example causes the URL to disappear from the folder and thus the Help menu. The semantics are logical but a little subtle, so it is worth looking at what is happening. Whenever a MultiFileSystem encounters a file in a container layer whose name shows that it is a mask (*_hidden), it excludes that mask file from the list of "real" files in the folder and also excludes the masked file (if there was one—no harm is done if the real file did not exist to begin with).* Whole folders can also be masked with one mask file, for example:

```
<filesystem>
  <folder name="Menu">
    <!-- Suppress the whole Versioning menu: -->
    <file name="Versioning_hidden"/>
  </folder>
</filesystem>
```

Figure 28-2 shows how layers are combined and files are masked.

Using the Open APIs Support to brand layers

While you can of course brand layers manually by typing in the proper XML for your branding layer, it can be cumbersome. You need to keep a copy of the original "base" layer open for comparison, as well as understand how to create mask files, and so on. Testing whether your branding worked correctly might involve creating a new branding JAR and restarting a test copy of the IDE to examine its appearance and behavior.

The Open APIs Support module provides a tool to make the process easier and more visual. Any layer can be opened as text (XML) in the editor; just look for the ✳ icon indicating that an XML file is a layer. You can also manipulate it visually. Expand its node in the Explorer and under the **<root folder>** that appears, make changes to files just like

---

* If the filesystem parameter propagateMasks is on, it leaves the mask there. This is normally done for technical reasons when the MultiFileSystem is contained as a layer in a higher MultiFileSystem and it is desirable to permit a layer to mask a file in a "cousin" rather than "sibling" layer. The topmost MultiFileSystem has the parameter off so that masks do not appear in the ultimately visible file list.

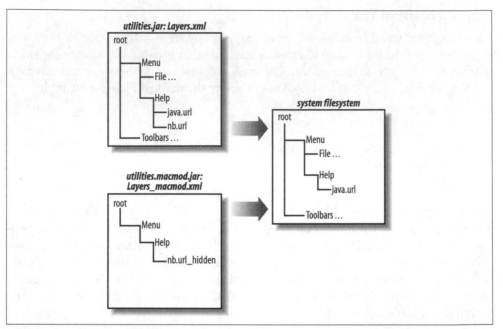

Figure 28-2. Branding: masking a file

What Happens to Changes Made on a MultiFileSystem?

The same principle used when branding layers works *in reverse* during modifications of a composite filesystem. Typically a MultiFileSystem has one or more writable layers and several read-only layers. In Chapter 14 you saw that the system filesystem has a writable session layer, a read-only global layer consisting mostly of module XML filesystems, and usually a writable project layer.

If a request is made to delete a file that originated in a read-only layer, it actually just creates a mask file on some writable layer, which effectively "deletes" the file. Modifications and additions simply write out the modified or new file to a writable layer.

The choice of writable layer is at the discretion of the MultiFileSystem. In "Registering the Players as Services" in Chapter 24, you saw the file attribute SystemFileSystem. layer set to project on the Minicomposer players—this serves as a hint to the system filesystem to try to write changes to the project layer, whereas by default it will write changes to the session layer.

User customizations in NetBeans are done using filesystem calls on the system filesystem (a MultiFileSystem) where the writable layers are the *system/* subdirectories of the user directory and project directory. If a user deletes a menu item, service, or anything else originally defined in a read-only module layer, this really means a mask file is written to disk.

you would on any mounted filesystem: copy, open in the Editor, delete, change file attributes such as **Template**, and more. Such changes are applied to the XML, and conversely changes in the XML will appear in the Explorer too.

 Some versions of the XML module can interfere with this structural layer editing feature. Look for any release notes on the Open APIs Support home page at *http://apisupport.netbeans.org/*.

For branding layers, you can also edit the **<root folder>** in the Explorer. More commonly, though, what you are really interested in is the *result* of the branding. To work this way, make sure an additional subnode appears beneath the layer node in the Explorer; this will happen automatically if the Open APIs Support detects that a layer is branding another layer based on its package and name, but consult this module's online documentation for details (you may be able to add branding views manually as well).

In Figure 28-3 you can see an example of branding in action. The file *Layer.xml* from the standard NetBeans utilities module is shown in the Explorer on the left, with its file contents expanded in a separate window (upper-center on the desktop). A branded *Layer_macmod.xml* has been created in the same Java package; you can see its text in the lower center of the desktop and its file contents in the window in the upper-right, along with the virtual result of merging it with the base layer.

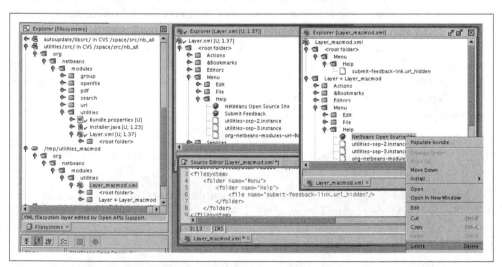

Figure 28-3. Branding a layer with the Open APIs Support module

The utilities module adds several items to the Help menu, including a couple of URLs specific to the NetBeans web site. In order to ensure that the MacroModeler application does not show these inappropriate links, you mask the **.url* files. Here a branding layer *Layer_macmod.xml* is open. One link named Submit Feedback has already been masked; there is a mask file in the XML (visible in the branding layer's **<root folder>**), and the corresponding link does not appear in the merged view beneath **Layer + Layer_macmod**, which tries to simulate the final configuration that will be present in the branded application. Deleting **NetBeans Open Source Site** from the merged view will automatically create a second mask file.

In a similar fashion, you can add or modify files in the merged view, and the proper entries will be made in your branding XML file. You can even change the order of items in folders—try the context menu on the item in the Explorer. To back out a change, simply delete associated elements from the XML and watch the merged view revert to the "pristine" version.

Advanced Branding: Patching Behavior

As time goes on, more and more aspects of the configuration of NetBeans are specified in XML layers, rather than ad-hoc configuration schemes or programmatically using Java installation hooks. Besides making it easier to find everything a module does and making module writing more declarative, this trend directly benefits those who create branded applications. *Any part* of an XML layer may be patched using the branding system, meaning that many aspects of how a given module (or the Net-Beans core) works can be customized declaratively without patching Java source code.

You should consult the documentation for the version of NetBeans you are working with to find out exactly what can be configured in a layer and how to do so. As of this writing, certain important aspects of the application are not controlled by branding, and the NetBeans web site lacks a complete registry of items known to be installable via layers. However, the NetBeans core developers and community are working on completing the transition to layers and creating documentation to improve the use of NetBeans as an application platform. Check the *http://www.netbeans.org/platform/* platform web site for the latest details.

To interactively browse through everything installed in layers in your copy of the IDE, just make the system filesystem visible in the Filesystems tab of the Explorer and look through it (see Figure 28-4).

To illustrate some techniques, let us take an example that could be used in NetBeans 3.3. The MacroModeler application should be updatable over the web, and so it is decided to use the standard NetBeans autoupdate module to support this. However, the full GUI behavior of this module is deemed too "heavyweight" for an average modeling user, who does not want to retrieve or manage arbitrary module downloads, but just an occasional update of the model editor and associated utilities from *modeling.com*. To control the behavior of the update feature, a branding JAR *modules/locale/autoupdate_macmod.jar* should be created containing just the file *org/netbeans/modules/autoupdate/resources/mf-layer_macmod.xml*. Such a file can be conveniently edited using the Open APIs Support module, as described in the previous section.

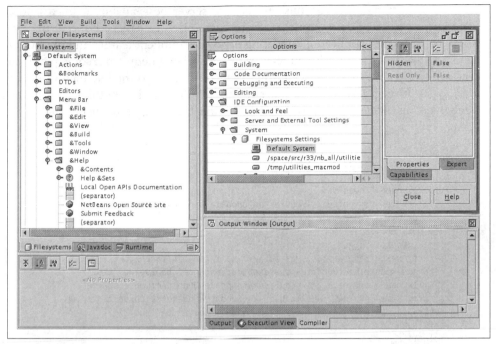

Figure 28-4. Showing the system filesystem in the Explorer

The first concern is to control the set of update servers available. In fact only one is really needed, *modeling.com*, but the NetBeans module ships with several server settings pointing to *netbeans.org*. We can simply mask out the unwanted URLs and add a new one:

```
<filesystem>
  <folder name="Services">
    <folder name="AutoupdateType">
      <!-- Hide the main NetBeans server. -->
      <file name="autoupdate_xml_type.settings_hidden"/>
      <!-- Alpha & beta servers too. -->
      <file name="autoupdate_xml_type_1.settings_hidden"/>
      <file name="autoupdate_xml_type_2.settings_hidden"/>
      <!-- Now add our own. -->
      <file name="com-modeling-updates.settings" url="updates.settings">
        <attr name="SystemFileSystem.localizingBundle"
              stringvalue="com.modeling.Bundle"/>
        <attr name="SystemFileSystem.icon" urlvalue=
        "nbresloc:/org/netbeans/modules/autoupdate/resources/updateAction.gif"/>
        <attr name="url"
              stringvalue="http://www.modeling.com/updates.xml"/>
        <attr name="enabled" boolvalue="true"/>
      </file>
      <!-- (Bundle.properties and updates.settings need to be created too) -->
    </folder>
  </folder>
</filesystem>
```

Since it is intentional that just this one update server be available, it makes little sense to provide a GUI option for the user to customize the servers. For that matter, in the MacroModeler application, updating is not a prominent feature and ought not be given so much visibility. We can remove update-related items from some places in the UI and also move the menu item from the Tools menu to the File menu (maybe Tools does not seem like the right place for something that has nothing to do with models). Let us add more customizations to the branding layer, using *mf-layer_ macmod.xml*:

```
<filesystem>
  <!-- Move the menu item: -->
  <folder name="Menu">
    <folder name="Tools">
     <file name="org-netbeans-modules-autoupdate-UpdateAction.instance_hidden"/>
    </folder>
    <folder name="File">
      <!-- Do not forget positioning: -->
      <attr name="Separator4[javax-swing-JSeparator].instance/,↵
org-netbeans-modules-autoupdate-UpdateAction.instance" boolvalue="true"/>
      <file name="org-netbeans-modules-autoupdate-UpdateAction.instance"/>
      <attr name="org-netbeans-modules-autoupdate-UpdateAction.instance/,↵
org-netbeans-core-actions-SystemExit.instance" boolvalue="true"/>
    </folder>
  </folder>
  <!-- Do not show a setup wizard panel asking about updates: -->
  <folder name="Wizards">
    <folder name="Setup">
      <file name="org-netbeans-modules-autoupdate-SetupPanel.instance_hidden"/>
    </folder>
  </folder>
  <!-- Nor update settings nor list of servers in the Options dialog: -->
  <folder name="UI">
    <folder name="Services">
      <folder name="IDEConfiguration">
        <folder name="System">
          <file name=
              "org-netbeans-modules-autoupdate-AutoupdateTypes.shadow_hidden"/>
          <file name="org-netbeans-modules-autoupdate-Settings.shadow_hidden"/>
        </folder>
      </folder>
    </folder>
  </folder>
  <!-- Nor permit new servers to be added. -->
  <folder name="Templates">
    <folder name="Services">
      <file name="AutoupdateType_hidden"/>
    </folder>
  </folder>
</filesystem>
```

We can keep one UI item that is added by the NetBeans module by its layer (*mf-layer.xml*):

```
<filesystem>
  <folder name="Welcome">
    <file name="org-netbeans-modules-autoupdate-UpdateAction.instance">
      <attr name="welcomeDescription" urlvalue=
"nbresloc:/org/netbeans/modules/autoupdate/resources/info-UpdateAction.html"/>
    </file>
  </folder>
</filesystem>
```

This entry causes a button to appear in the Welcome panel that, when pressed, launches the update wizard.* However, we may want to customize the HTML description that will appear to the right of the button. This can be done by including a branded HTML file in our JAR (see Example 28-4); it works because of the nbresloc URL protocol that automatically searches for localized and branded variants.

Example 28-4. Branding: org/netbeans/modules/autoupdate/resources/ info-UpdateAction_macmod.html

```
<html>
  <body>
    Get MacroModeler updates and beta plug-ins online.
  </body>
</html>
```

With such a branded *autoupdate_macmod.jar*, it is possible to suppress many aspects of the Auto Update user interface that might be distracting in a one-purpose application, yet retain much of the same functionality and make it look and feel integral.

Pat yourself on the back if you have read this far. If anyone offered certification for Qualified NetBeans Engineers, you would be a strong candidate! The appendixes at the end of this book will help you continue on the road to being a NetBeans guru. The first appendix shows you where to look in NetBeans sources for helpful design patterns. Go to the source! No programmer can afford to ignore the examples of others. You will also learn how to extend your module with functionality not covered in the basic Open APIs. After that, you can learn about some handy utility APIs, find out what is on the horizon for future NetBeans releases, learn to thrive in the open source community as a regular contributor to the NetBeans project, and finally take a look at what other individuals and companies are doing with NetBeans now. Best of luck and see you on *nbdev@netbeans.org*!

---

* The Welcome panel in NetBeans 3.4 is a complete rewrite and cannot be configured by modules. So this particular example will *not* work in 3.4. However, the same principle is used for other parts of the UI.

A Tour of Existing Modules

Many of the modules in NetBeans supply Service Provider Interfaces (SPIs) you can use to implement your functionality much more quickly. A good example of this is the XML set of modules that provides a variety of different types of support for XML.

Also, you may often find yourself implementing functionality that resembles something another module does, and having a template for how to do that is a very good way to avoid making mistakes or reinventing the wheel.

Modules That Expose Functionality You Might Need

While we've endeavored to provide a good start for building your own modules for NetBeans, there's nothing like learning from the experience of someone who has solved the problem you're facing. And since all of the modules mentioned in this appendix are open source and available in source code form on *netbeans.org*, there is nothing preventing wholesale borrowing of useful code and techniques from modules that do something you need to do. The following sections provide some useful sources of examples.

The XML Modules

As XML is used more and more in business and computing, it will be more and more common for modules integrating with NetBeans to either use XML internally in one form or another or handle specialized editing or construction of specific types of XML documents. The XML (*http://xml.netbeans.org/*) project is where to find detailed documentation on these modules. Support for XML in NetBeans is factored into a set of modules that address different needs for working with XML:

TAX Library

Not to fear, no fees will be assessed. TAX stands for "Tree API for XML." This library is what other XML support modules use for getting a structural representation of XML and DTD documents. It can handle dynamically updating them programmatically, firing events on changes, and more. The model is similar to DOM, but more specialized for a development environment.

XML Core

This module provides the basic support for parsing XML documents into the TAX library's representation of them, and is responsible for creating the basic XML data object type in NetBeans. The XML Core module contains provisional implementations of what will eventually become NetBeans' standard APIs, but currently are still under revision.

Tools

These are XML productivity tools, including such things as tools for generating a DTD from an XML document.

Catalog

This module allows NetBeans to use entity catalogs.

XML Text Editor

Provides an editor implementation with syntax highlighting, abbreviation support, and code-completion support for XML documents.

XML Tree Editor

Provides a structural visual editor for XML and DTD documents and filtering to customize how the document tree is presented (for example, showing or not showing whitespace elements).

CSS

Provides basic support for editing CSS (Cascading Style Sheet) documents in NetBeans.

The interesting thing about these modules is that you will be able to register a specific DTD or XML namespace that will represent your module's kind of XML content and register a data loader for that type of data. So a module can implement domain-specific behavior for XML documents, using the Looks infrastructure. For example, viewed as a text file, a Tomcat deployment descriptor looks much more intimidating than it needs to in order to expose its user-relevant characteristics. With a look registered for deployment descriptors, users will be exposed only to the relevant information, but if they just want access to the raw structure of the XML file, they just change the look being used on its property sheet. As of this writing, the API to the XML modules permitting this kind of customization is still under development.

The Editor

The editor is implemented in two parts:

- A drop-in replacement for Swing's editor kits.

  This is a set of Swing `EditorKit` implementations and base classes designed to make it easier to build your own editors. Programmatically, they behave similarly to Swing's built-in editors (and so can be used in stand-alone applications), but they have far more features and a mature SPI for building support for new content types. The JSP module can add JSP syntax-coloring support, and so on. This SPI, in turn, consists of a few different parts:

  — Editor kits for different content types.

  — Infrastructure for specifying a lexical analysis engine for a content type (with some support for using ANTLR, a popular open source parser generator). The new `lexer` module is intended to make this infrastructure more general.

  — Syntax coloring based on the tokenization provided by the lexer.

  — Formatting and indenting text based on the tokenization.

  — Code completion—you can plug in an engine that can supply completions based on cursor position and context. Compound documents in multiple languages, such as HTML with embedded JavaScript, can be supported as well.

  — Editor-specific base classes for actions that allow easy access to the editor's content. For example, adding a keyboard shortcut to line wrap a paragraph could be accomplished using one action subclass.

- A NetBeans-specific SPI allowing modules to integrate their own content types that uses the first half as a library. It supports the following things:

  — Registration of editor kits by MIME type.

  — Provision of system options for a new kit. These system options enable the user to customize the editor's visual appearance. For example, fonts and colors used in syntax coloring can be changed, printing behavior can be refined, abbreviations can be added, and keyboard shortcuts can be rebound.

  — Creation of new NetBeans "indentation engines," selectable by MIME type. This is based on the text formatting ability in the generic library.

  — The ability to add a toolbar appropriate for a content type. For example, Java sources can display a small toolbar with a method/field picker.

Version Control—the VCS Core Module

The VCS Core module handles most of the dirty work of integrating version control systems with the NetBeans Filesystems API. It handles caching, user interface, and versioning-specific submenus. Combining the SPI exposed by this module with the

---

annotation capabilities in the Filesystems API for modifying a file's display name and icon to indicate its status gives you everything you need to (fairly) painlessly integrate a version control system. For examples of its usage, investigate the sources of the JavaCVS or Generic VCS modules.

The Generic VCS module allows you to integrate with any command-line version control system without writing Java code, but by creating a profile for that version control system that includes commands and the syntax for issuing them to the system, along with regular expressions for parsing the output of those commands into results meaningful to NetBeans. This can also be an effective way to integrate a version control system, but often a tighter integration can perform better and be more effective at exposing the particular features of your version control system. You can incrementally tighten an integration using Generic VCS by writing small Java classes to handle particular commands. The resulting profiles can be packaged and distributed as first-class modules, for example, using the Update Center.

RemoteFS

Similarly to VCS Core, this module defines an SPI that makes it more convenient to build filesystem support for types of filesystems that store data remotely. It is currently primarily documented in Czech, however. For an example of its usage, see the FTPFileSystem implementation in the same module, which uses this support to provide filesystem support for FTP servers.

The Ant Module

The Ant module provides an SPI that allows other modules to register tasks that should be run from inside the NetBeans environment. For example, the Open APIs Support module uses this hook to implement uninstalling and reloading a module as an Ant task. Tasks thus registered are then available to any Ant script run from inside NetBeans.

The Java Module

Integrating with the Java module is somewhat problematic—in practice, it is widely and frequently done, but what is exposed by the module as official API/SPI is fairly minimal. The Java module exposes an interface that other modules can use to hook into the creation process of source element Nodes, allowing control over both the presentation and the properties of those Nodes. For examples of this usage, see the JavaBeans Support module (*http://beans.netbeans.org/*). The Form Editor, CORBA, and RMI modules go further to extend JavaDataLoader and JavaDataObject in various ways.

With the introduction of the Metadata Repository, the Java module is slated to be rewritten to use this technology and the Looks infrastructure. This rewrite will not necessarily mean any significant differences in appearance or behavior, but a much more standardized and extensible infrastructure for adding features such as Java-Beans, GUI form editing, and so on. This work is in progress at the time of this writing, and we refer you to the documentation at *http://java.netbeans.org/*, the Javadoc of the sources, and the public mailing lists for up-to-date details. The authors of this module are on the *nbdev@netbeans.org* mailing list; if there is something you need to do involving integration with the Java module, that is the place to go.

While all this may sound scary, bear in mind that at the time of this writing, more than 30 companies are shipping modules, four distributions of NetBeans as a Java IDE, and numerous applications using the NetBeans Platform. Every step possible will be made to ensure backward compatibility or document changes module authors will need to make. For cases such as extending the Java loader, which is not an official API, module authors may need to make some changes.

Debugger Core

This module provides a substantive SPI by which you can integrate different debuggers. There is additionally the JPDA Debugger module, which a few modules rely on, but the primary point of integration is the Debugger Core module.

J2EE Server

This is a pure SPI module—it does not, by itself, expose any user-level functionality or actions. It allows you to plug in integrations with new J2EE servers and register information about the deployment descriptors required to deploy objects to such servers. You can also add properties to an EJB specific to a given application server, or create execution services specific to that server, which will integrate smoothly with existing support for EJBs and web applications. To integrate support for an application server, write code to the SPI of this module and create a module that provides deployment ability for that server.

Form Editor

The Form Editor module is as problematic as the Java module to integrate with. There is extensive and powerful support for integrating new layout managers—this can be an entry point for integrations in that it allows you to define the semantics of drag-and-drop into forms, constrain what types of components can be added, and define customizers for a form layout. Adding new beans to the Component Palette is also straightforward.

For deeper integration, such as defining an entirely new kind of form, there is no specific API. Such support will need to be written from scratch, but the Form Editor sources can act as a guide for doing this effectively.

HTTP Server Module

Among its other functions, this internal server allows other modules to add their own Java servlets. Such servlets will be run inside the NetBeans VM, which can be useful for presenting some aspect of a module's functionality over HTTP.

Classfile Reader Module

This module is used by other Java-related support modules. Originally, to handle Java classes without associated sources, NetBeans relied on loading the classes into the NetBeans JVM and introspecting them. This technique is usually effective, but undesirable: poorly-behaved classes might have static blocks that run unknown initialization code.[*] The Classfile module provides a lightweight structural parser for Java bytecode, which is now used in preference to introspection and can provide information on deprecated methods and more.

The Metadata Repository—a Whole Host of APIs

As we write this appendix, the Metadata Repository is still being finished, so it is difficult to give specifics on it. The fundamentals are that, given a model for a programming language and a parser for that language, the Repository is capable of processing sources and generating metadata for those sources. See Appendix D for more information.

Socket-Based Editor Support—the External Editor Module

The External Editor module is used to replace NetBeans' internal editor with the popular Unix-based editors VIM or XEmacs. This is accomplished by creating a Swing EditorKit implementation that is a wrapper for a TCP/IP socket and that defines a protocol by which an external editor can interact with NetBeans. For those interested in integrating editors not written in Java or editors that will run on a machine remote to the one on which NetBeans is running, this not-for-the-faint-of-heart module provides an example of how to do it.

Those wishing to tightly integrate a new external editor into NetBeans will be able to implement the remote side of a text-based socket protocol defined in this module.

---

[*] Any code run in-VM from user classes is subject to a security manager. But this just changes the problem from a security hole to an annoyance, when SecurityExceptions are thrown just because you *looked at* a class file with a static block.

Incidental APIs, Utilities, and Extensions

The following modules are useful for common problems and tasks in programming NetBeans. Each helps you avoid repetitive coding, especially when someone has solved the same problem before.

The Utilities Module

The Utilities module is a grab bag of useful classes, APIs, and convenience implementations of miscellaneous interfaces. Components worth mentioning here are as follows:

Data loader for .url files

If you need to provide URL links from a menu or toolbar, you just create a file with the extension *.url* containing the desired URL. A suitable menu item (or toolbar button) will be created that displays the URL in the IDE's web browser (internal or external). You can control the menu item or button's appearance by giving a localized display name and icon for the *.url* file.

.group files

Allow a single file to act as a pointer to a collection of files. In particular this is used to implement group templates. If you have used some of the Open APIs Support templates mentioned in this book, you may have noticed that a template might cause more than one file to be created. For example, when you use the `CallableSystemAction` template (from the Actions API), an icon and a resource bundle are created along with the action class. *.group* files make this behavior easy to implement without the need to write a custom template wizard iterator.

API Extensions (openidex)

This library contains unofficial or proposed extensions to the Open APIs—rather like the utilities module except that its contents are not necessarily convenience classes for module authors, but things that have the potential to eventually become better supported APIs. A number of things currently present in openidex will eventually be split out into additional modules, and the current components deprecated but present for a few generations of NetBeans and eventually removed. What is useful there currently is:

Search API

Permits objects to be searched. The API in `org.openidex.search.*` consists of `SearchType` and `SearchGroup`. `SearchType` is a service and defines one way of searching, such as by object type or VCS status; the user can customize search types, save them, and reuse them. `SearchGroup` permits different kinds of objects to be searched—for example, data objects or uninterpreted file objects.

A separate SPI to help you create new search types more easily does not exist; however, some examples of concrete search types can be found in the Utilities module, which also provides a general UI for searching.

Old Looks API

An older version of the Looks API, used in NetBeans 3.3, is kept in `org.openidex.nodes.looks.*`. Newer code should, however, use the revised Looks API and SPI, available as a separate module for NetBeans 3.4.

Modules That Make Good Examples for Things You May Need to Implement

While we've written this book as a task-based guide to working with the Open APIs, one of the best ways to become quickly and deeply familiar with an API set is to modify existing code. And for most problems you'll need to solve in building modules for NetBeans, you will usually find modules that have had to solve problems similar to yours. Let this section be a guide to finding some examples for things you may need to code.

Annotations and Dynamic Editor Tool Tips— the Ant Module and the Debugger Core Module

Both of these modules do non-trivial work with annotations: marking up lines in the editor with alternative font styles or icons to indicate something to the user. These modules are worth a look if your implementation needs to add this type of functionality.

Adding Information to the View of Java Sources—the Beans Module

The Beans module (the one that creates the **Bean Patterns** node underneath the node for a Java source file) provides a good example for module authors writing code that needs to add functionality available on Java sources. Its implementation is likely to change with the pending revisions to the Java module, to use the Looks infrastructure rather than its current approach, but it provides an effective example of interacting closely with the Java module and integrating new functionality.

Adding a Debugger Type—the Applet Module

The Applet module adds support for applet debugging in NetBeans. For a simple example of integrating a new debugger type, it is quite effective.

Multiplexing DataObjects and Complex Cut/Copy/Paste Support—the Properties Module

The Properties module (which handles Java resource bundles) does some of the most complex things with DataObjects of the available examples. A set of *.properties* files related by locale form a single DataObject with a subnode for each locale. The various locale files for a given properties object need to sometimes be treated as a single entity, and sometimes as separate entities. For example, a graphical table view displays all locales side-by-side, while individual locale files can also be opened as text. You can cut and paste the entire object as a whole or manipulate just one locale file within it.

Working with Network Protocols to Access Files—JavaCVS and RemoteFS

For anyone integrating a new kind of filesystem storage, the JavaCVS and RemoteFS modules demonstrate the range of available possibilities.

Domain-Specific XML Support—the Tomcat and Ant Modules

If your module deals with XML files, but is only interested in those that conform to a specific DTD or schema or other constraint, these modules provide excellent examples. The Ant module provides support for managing Ant build files. It hides unnecessary details of the XML and makes it easy to create new tasks and launch them from within NetBeans. The Tomcat module provides support for Tomcat deployment descriptors (among other things).

In NetBeans 3.3, these modules internally rely on ad-hoc manipulation of the XML document structure, so they should be treated as examples of possible UI rather than implementation. For 3.4 or 4.0 the XML modules' infrastructure should be used to simplify the implementation and improve features and robustness.

Stretching the Limits—the Web Modules

In the immortal words of Mr. Glick, "The most ill-advised uses of the Datasystems API are in the Web modules. All the things that make API developers hold their heads and groan are done routinely by them." These modules are definitely a source of non-trivial examples of just how far the limits of NetBeans can be pushed, considering DataObjects that map their own filesystems, replace root directories, and so forth.

Many of these unusual use cases are actually symptomatic of some limitation in the APIs. For example, the current APIs identify the user-level classpath with the roots of mounted filesystems, which forces supports for web applications to mount many libraries just to ensure their existence in the classpath. This kind of problem should be solved in the future with a more sophisticated API for projects, currently in planning. See Appendix D for more details on how these issues will be addressed.

Complex Syntax Coloring—the JSP Module

The JSP module provides a great example of multi-language mixed-mode syntax highlighting and code completion, where a user edits a document that is in multiple languages and the editor needs to highlight and provide appropriate formatting, abbreviations, and syntax highlighting for multiple language contexts within a single document.

Multi-Stage Compilation—the JSP, RMI, and CORBA Modules

The JSP module lets you plug in an arbitrary Java compiler, but must first run a JSP preprocessor to generate the servlet code that will be fed to it as Java source. RMI takes a similar approach in almost the reverse order—an RMI source is a remote interface, which needs to be compiled and then have a postprocessor run against the result to generate client and server dynamic stubs. Both of these modules provide good examples of pipelining an existing compiler in a more complex build process. The CORBA module is also a good example of this.

Bridging to an Entirely Different Build System— the Ant and Makefile Modules

These modules provide excellent examples for cases where you need to perform a build process that walks and talks like NetBeans' notions of compilation but that relies on none of the existing infrastructure. The user invokes the UI for compilation in NetBeans, but on the back end an entirely different infrastructure is used.

Also do not overlook the cpp and cpplite modules that help the user create and run the C/C++ makefiles traditional on Unix systems.

Use of the Compiler Infrastructure for Non-Compilation Tasks—the JAR Packager Module

You can compile a recipe for a JAR file into an actual *.jar* archive using the JAR Packager module. This is a process that bears enough resemblance to a compilation process that it makes sense for the user (and for the developer of the module) to fit it into the same paradigm—you have a set of sources and a result that represents those sources transformed into a different type of file.

Successfully creating an archive requires that the contents of that archive first have associated processing applied to them, such as compiling Java sources to *.class* files. Failure at any stage is indicated to the user so that the problem can be corrected. If these stages complete, the archive will then be generated.

Here the final JAR generation stage is unaware of what type of compilation or processing is done to the content files—Java files use their associated compilers, as do RMI interfaces, and so on. The Compiler API is used to communicate between the JAR Packager module and the compilers associated with the content files.

Execution—the Applet and JSP/Servlet Modules

Each of these modules provides an example of performing user-invokable execution of a certain type of object that involves special initialization of an environment into which those objects need to be deployed, before the deployment itself. In the case of JSPs, a Tomcat server must be launched and a JSP load request sent to it. For applets, the applet viewer or a remote browser must be launched, which may also involve preparing a custom security policy file.

The I18N module also allows you to launch applications using the locale of your choice. This is a nice example of a very simple but useful executor.

Custom Hyperlinking in the Output Window— the Ant Module

The Ant module provides a good demonstration of the use of annotations for hyperlinking in the Output Window—for an example of this, create an Ant build file, intentionally introduce syntax or semantic errors into it, and then run it. The Output Window will indicate the location of the error with a hyperlinked message. You can double-click the message to navigate to the error in the editor, where you will see an error icon in the editor's gutter with a tool tip giving the error message.

Specifying Windows, Workspaces, and Components Using XML—the Core Window System and the Form Editor Module

The Window System API specifies how to define workspaces, what windows should appear on them, and what components should live in those windows, all using module layers. Since NetBeans has default components such as the Explorer, the best example of how to specify these things is to look at the core window system, which uses XML to define the default contents of NetBeans' workspaces and their windows. The Form Editor module is also a good example, since it does an interesting job of docking components together.

Complex Work with MIMEResolvers and Multi-File DataObjects—the CPP Module

The CPP module provides support for editing, compiling, and executing C++ (as well as C and FORTRAN). On Unix systems at least, there is not a simple naming convention for files used by these languages that can permit easy file classification. For example, standard C++ headers now have no extension (*stdio* rather than *stdio.h*). ELF object files are often named *.o* but not always, and linked executables traditionally have no extension.

To enable NetBeans to intelligently handle all such object types, a complex MIMEResolver is used to classify files by name and content and assign MIME types accordingly.

Completing the process of mapping raw file data on disk to structured DataObjects, complex data loaders know how to associate source files with the object files they compile to.

Cut/Copy/Paste—Data Transfer Support for Complex Elements—the Ant and Java Modules

The Java module allows you to use cut/copy/paste for manual refactoring of Java sources and provides hooks for such things as redefining package declarations when a source file is pasted into a different package. If your module supports a structural data type that may need some modification if its context is changed, look at this aspect of the Java module for an example.

The Ant module contains a straightforward implementation of the common data transfer operations within the context of structurally constrained XML files.

Interconversion between Different Types of Clipboard Contents—JNDI, CORBA, and RMI

Each of these modules provides a runtime interface to interact with remote objects on a live server, and each of them also provides a means for you to copy an entity in the Explorer window that exists on a remote server to the clipboard. The goal of such functionality is that what the user pastes into the editor from this operation is Java source code that will produce a reference to that remote entity. So this provides a good example of copying something to the clipboard, while performing a complex conversion to data meaningful for the paste context.

Integrating Other Programming Languages— the C++/Fortran, Scripting, and WebL Modules

While NetBeans may have started its existence as a Java-based IDE for Java, it is no longer exclusively for Java. The ongoing introduction of the Metadata Repository will result in a standardized technique for generating Java classes to support a language within NetBeans from an abstract metamodel of that language and a parser for the language.

Nevertheless, for building support for a new language against the current infrastructure, these modules can serve as an excellent guide, and many of the things they do to integrate tools for working with those languages will remain viable even when MDR is used for handling the language metadata. You can find examples of language-specific compilation and execution tools, syntax coloring, and more.

Fancy Footwork with Nodes—the Java Module

The Java module does some of the most complex operations with Nodes to be found in the NetBeans source base. This includes providing custom properties and context-sensitive property editors, copy and paste between different types of containers, customizable sorting and display formats, and accepting factories for other modules to create additional child Nodes of a module-provided Node.

Adding Nodes to the Runtime Tab in the Explorer— the RMI, CORBA, JNDI, and Database Explorer Modules

The Runtime tab of the Explorer window is generally used for representing transient internal data and live remote servers and objects residing on them. Generally, server-oriented modules add Nodes here for the type of server they support, which have context actions allowing the user to create and manipulate subnodes representing live servers.

The Bare Essentials of Non-Data-Driven Nodes— the System Properties Module

This module also adds a node to the **Runtime** tab in the **Explorer** window, displaying the Java system properties set in the VM that NetBeans runs in. It does a number of common tasks with Nodes: creating a hierarchy of subnodes lazily; refreshing Nodes based on internal changes; displaying properties in the property sheet, permitting the user to add, delete, and rename nodes; and so on. Its attraction as an example is that the data it represents is rather simple: the standard Java calls System.getProperties() and System.setProperty() suffice to manipulate it. For this reason, almost all of the code can serve as an example of using Nodes, without much distraction.

Wizards—the CORBA, Java, and New Module Wizard Modules

The CORBA Wizard provides a general, straightforward example of how to build a wizard using NetBeans' infrastructure. On the other hand, the Java module provides an example of a custom wizard iterator that extends the New Wizard. Creating a wizard well may require non-trivial logic for when the user can continue and for determining the subsequent sequence of steps based on the user's prior choices. This module provides a good example of such logic.

The New Module Wizard (apisupport/lite in sources) is also a good example for performing complex logic to determine whether the user may proceed and of using a wizard to create not one but a suite of resulting objects all of which are determined by the user's choices in the wizard.

Embedding Property Panels into Wizards— the Java Module

When you create a new Java object from a template, you will find a number of additional panels in the New wizard that are not present if you are creating, say, a plain text file. These panels are added by the Java module and allow you to specify such things as the superclass for your class and what initial fields or methods you want to create or inherit.

Complex Explorer Views—the Debugger Core Module

Probably the most complex window composed of explorer views in the NetBeans IDE is the Debugger window, which offers a set of panes for such things as sessions, breakpoints, and watches. If you need to expose complex but interconnected trees or lists of data to the user, this implementation can provide a good example of how to do that. It also demonstrates complete configuration of a window system workspace geared to a certain task (as does the Form module).

Enabling/Disabling Sets of Actions Based on Context—the VCS Core Module

The VCS Core module provides a toolbar for versioning-related operations that need to be active only when the user is interacting with version-controlled sources.

Useful Utility Classes

In any piece of software, developers will find there are some common tasks that need to be done in widely differing areas of the code, but none of which are of such significance that they merit their own API definition or package. This is as true of Net-Beans as any other large software project. Here we'll try to cover some of the convenient bits of utility code that are available to you as a module author.

XML Utilities

Increasing numbers of modules deal with XML, either for their own internal use or to support an XML-based user data format. There are a number of useful utilities you can use if your module deals in any way with XML data.

org.openide.xml.XMLUtil

The XMLUtil class consists entirely of static utility methods. Some are purely convenience methods that provide easier ways to access JAXP functionality to parse documents, create DOM documents, and so on. You can also serialize a DOM document to XML text—this functionality is provided in some parser implementations, but with XMLUtil you do not need to know which you are using. Finally, various methods help escape XML metacharacters, useful when manually generating XML markup from a data model.

org.openide.xml.EntityCatalog

EntityCatalog provides an entity resolver that is able to look in a local catalog for DTDs and other entities without having to connect to a network to download them. Modules can register DTDs in the system filesystem via their XML layers, and these local copies will be used in preference to downloading. The catalog implements the standard org.xml.sax.EntityResolver interface.

Visual Components and Extensions to Standard Swing Components

Visual components in NetBeans, outside the Window System API, fall generally into two categories: extensions to Swing components designed to hook into NetBeans' infrastructure and hacks or workarounds to either bugs or limitations in Swing. The former category can be useful; the latter category will ideally eventually be eliminated as Swing matures.

In the package `org.openide.awt`, you can find such classes as `MenuBar`, `Toolbar`, and so forth. Generally these are components that know how to create themselves from a NetBeans filesystem folder. For example, the main menu is essentially a component that, given a filesystem folder, will create menu item subcomponents for the contents and subfolders of that folder.

Lookup Implementations

`FolderLookup`, technically in the `loaders` package, is a specialized `FolderInstance` that makes it possible to look up object instances declared in *.instance* (or *.settings*) files. If one or more *.instance* files in the folder are an implementations of `Lookup`, the `FolderLookup` will delegate to them, splicing in their lookup results. Including subinstances of `Lookup` inside a folder that is searchable using the Lookup API is generally useful if your module creates many objects on the fly that you need to add to lookup.

This elegant approach bridges the declarative power of the XML filesystems specification to NetBeans at runtime; not everything you get back in a `Lookup.Result` has to be directly declared in a module's XML layer.

The `org.openide.util.lookup` package also contains a variety of base classes useful for creating certain kinds of in-memory lookups. You can easily make a `Lookup` implementation providing just a fixed set of instances.

Threading

`org.openide.util.Mutex` provides the classic mutex design pattern: a read-many, write-one lock.

`Task` is a frequently used and subclassed class representing a task that can be executed and monitored for its status. In particular, it goes hand-in-hand with the `RequestProcessor`.

`RequestProcessor` can execute `Tasks` or other `Runnables` in its own thread. It offers scheduling and priority options for posted tasks.

Miscellaneous Utility Classes in org.openide.util

The utilities package and its subclasses are a general grab-bag of classes and methods that have proven useful in one place or another as NetBeans has evolved. NetBeans APIs written before the availability of Java 2 Collections make use of java.util.Enumeration, and the org.openide.util.enum package contains some convenience classes for aggregating enumerations, enumerating arrays, and such. If you find yourself needing to do something complex with enumerations, check the Javadoc for this package—the class names are fairly self-explanatory, and you may save yourself some coding.

WeakListener

> Allows attaching listeners without creating strong references between objects. For details on its use, see Chapter 26.

Utilities

> This class is a smorgasbord of unrelated static methods for performing various random tasks, including for example:
>
> - Determining the OS on which NetBeans is running
> - Loading images with a cache
> - Merging images for icon badging
> - Comparing arrays
> - Converting arrays of objects such as Integer to equivalent arrays of primitive types and vice versa
> - Determining the screen size and centering windows, taking into account the Windows task bar and multi-screen displays
> - Breaking a string with newlines into an array of strings

For a complete overview of this package, refer to the Javadoc.

Serialization Helpers

The package org.openide.util.io contains various classes helpful when working with serialization. NbMarshalledObject serves as a unitary wrapper for a serialized data stream that can be unpacked on demand. It is often used when there is a "dangerous" object that might include arbitrary classes from foreign module code and that could easily throw exceptions when serialized or deserialized due to programming errors. Rather than embedding the dangerous object directly into a larger serialized data stream, you can wrap it in an NbMarshalledObject, which will isolate any problems without affecting the rest of the stream.

`NbObjectOutputStream` and the matching `NbObjectInputStream` are commonly used for serialization in NetBeans. Besides automatically using a classloader that can load classes from any NetBeans module, they make it easy to isolate dangerous serialized objects (using `NbMarshalledObject`). `SafeException` is thrown from these classes when serializing or deserializing one object to or from the stream fails but the rest of the stream stays intact.

 From time to time, you might need to look at the structure of a serialized object that NetBeans has saved in the user directory (for example). Perhaps a `SystemOption` does not seem to be storing what you expect, and you are not sure *what* is really on disk.

Let the IDE help you! If you have a *.ser* file in the Explorer in NetBeans 3.4, you can expand it to see the detailed structure of its serial data stream. If you have a *.settings* file with `serialdata` inside it, right-click it and choose Customize Bean, then Serialize As.... Pick any location and name, then browse to the new *.ser* file and look at what was really saved.

Resources

NetBeans' built-in CVS may be fully sufficient for your needs. But if you ever wish to fetch the standalone CVS program source and/or executables for your development platform as an adjunct to or replacement for NetBeans built-in CVS, here are some references.

CVSHome

CVSHome (*http://www.cvshome.org/*) is the upstream site for the Concurrent Versions System, the site where the maintainers post the main line of the open source code that makes up CVS. There is also excellent online documentation at this site.

GNU/BSD/Other Operating Systems

Pretty much all GNU and BSD operating systems include CVS in their base distribution.

- If you do not find CVS installed on a GNU Linux system after system installation, check your distribution CDs for the RPM package containing CVS. It's there for sure.

- If you do not find CVS installed on a BSD system after system installation, check the ports tree for a makefile that will download, build, and install CVS.

- On other Unix-like operating systems and on VMS, proceed to CVSHome (*http://www.cvshome.org/*) where you will find a source archive allowing you to build CVS on your platform.

- Microsoft Windows has Unix-like CVS under Cygwin (see *http://sources.redhat.com/cygwin*).

CVS GUI Clients

If you want a standalone CVS GUI for any platform, take a look at the open source software project at CvsGui.Org (*http://www.cvsgui.org/*).

Java Environments

The following are complete environments for compiling and running your Java code and programs:

- Javasoft (*http://www.javasoft.com*) is Sun's site for Java. The site offers many features, the majority of them freely downloadable, including:
  - — Java Development Kits
  - — Advanced APIs
  - — Books
  - — Tutorials
  - — White papers
  - — Discussion forums
- Software behemoth IBM's Developer Works Java (*http://www.ibm.com/developerworks/java/*) rivals Sun in wealth of environments and tools. IBM has ported high-performance JVMs to Linux, Windows, OS/2, AIX, OS/400 (i/OS), OS/390 (z/OS), VM/ESA (z/VM), and other environments. In addition, the IBM Developer Works has provided scores of libraries and API's, on their own and in conjunction with the Apache Software Foundation (*http://www.apache.org*), and other organizations, a good amount of which is open source.
- IBM's open source Jikes (*http://oss.software.ibm.com/developerworks/opensource/jikes/*) is a fast and rigorous Java compiler. You'll still need a Java Development Kit, but users who point the NetBeans external compilation feature at Jikes report rapid compile cycles, with occasional surprises as the pedantically strict Jikes rejects idioms swallowed by compilers that adhere less rigorously to the language specification. Jikes has (surprise!) its own bugs, reportedly in the arena of conformance and bytecode generation. As the late and lamented Douglas Adams, author of *Hitchhiker's Guide to the Galaxy*, recommended, "Don't Panic."
- Kaffe (*http://www.transvirtual.com/kaffe.htm*) is a complete open source Java virtual machine aimed at running anywhere on any type of device, including handheld devices.
- GNU gcj (*http://www.gnu.org/directory/gcc.html*) is a free software Java compiler integrated with the Free Software Foundation's ubiquitous GCC offering.

Java Tools

The following are tools specifically for aiding you in Java development:

Apache Software Foundation

The Apache Software Foundation (*http://apache.org/*) not only produces the world's favorite web server, it also produces an impressive array of Java tools and libraries.

Apache is an open source project staffed largely by volunteers. Their outflowing of productivity is grouped into categories of projects, including:

http://xml.apache.org/, XML-Apache
> Seven projects touching on all aspects of XML processing in C++ and Java

http://jakarta.apache.org/, Jakarta
> Aimed at providing commercial-quality server solutions

http://java.apache.org/, Java-Apache
> At this writing is just emerging as the overarching Apache Java project and promises to swallow up Jakarta

Of special note among the Jakarta projects is, of course, Jakarta Ant (*http://jakarta. apache.org/ant/index.html*). Ant is a build tool that in the Java world is coming to occupy the niche occupied in the C/C++ world by the *make* utility. As you have seen in this book, Ant is supported in NetBeans. You owe it to your skillset to get to know Ant better. Start at the source!

Secure Shell (SSH) Resources

The Secure Shell (SSH) allows encrypted logins and full session encryption. Today, remote CVS repositories often require SSH capability in order to log in and check files in and out. You can learn more about SSH at the following sites:

- OpenSSH (*http://www.openssh.com*) is a free software implementation of the SSH protocol.
- SSH Secure Communications (*http://www.ssh.com/*) is a commercial vendor and supporter of SSH.

Cygwin for Windows

If you are a Windows user working in Java and using NetBeans, you may find it useful to have an entire GNU-Linux-like environment under Windows in which to operate. The Cygwin Project (*http://www.cygwin.com/*) brings such an environment to Windows, and it's all open source. This amazingly rich project from Cygnus Support (now part of RedHat (*http://www.redhat.com*)) includes not only the typical text utilities (*grep*, *sed*, *awk*, and the like) but also:

- The full *GCC C/C++* compiler and toolchain, allowing you to recompile the whole Cygwin distribution, including GCC.
- CVS, the concurrent version system
- The *BASH shell* providing you a command-line enviroment more amenable than the DOS prompt for using the commands provided with Cygwin
- A port of the entire *XFree86 X Server*, allowing XWindows applications running on remote servers to appear in a Windows window

In sum, the Cygwin tools are an almost indispensible adjunct to Java development under Windows.

Newsgroups and Mailing Lists

All the official NetBeans public mailing lists are listed on the mailing lists page (*http://www.netbeans.org/about/community/lists.html*). Most lists also have a corresponding "digest" version to which you can subscribe to receive only one mailing a day. Furthermore, newsgroups on the server news.netbeans.org (*news://news.netbeans.org*) mirror the mailing lists in their entirety for those who would rather participate in the discussion via their newsreader. You will find that these discussions range from beginner questions to design debates between major participants in the NetBeans open source project itself. Enjoy!

Web Sites

The following sites all contain supplemental NetBeans information and resources:

Organization of Main NetBeans Web Site

The NetBeans website (*http://www.netbeans.org/*) was established to facilitate the open source NetBeans project. To this end it provides:

- A centralized source for information about NetBeans
- Downloads of NetBeans and related tools and projects
- Support for participating developers including version control
- A bug tracking system

Although you can browse the site, download NetBeans, and sign up for mailing lists without registering for the site, we suggest that you start off by registering. There's no charge, and once you are registered you can use the Issuezilla bug tracking system to search for bugs you suspect have already been found in NetBeans, or you can report new bugs.

Sun Sites

As noted in various places in this book, Sun Microsystems packages select releases of NetBeans as Sun ONE Studio 4 (formerly Sun Forte for Java). The main Sun ONE Studio 4 web site is *http://wwws.sun.com/software/sundev/jde/index.html*. Additionally, you might find other Sun sites relating to open source software and to Java programming interesting and helpful (aside from the obvious Javasoft web site (*http://www.javasoft.com*)), for example:

- SunSource.Net (*http://www.sunsource.net/*) is about Sun's involvement in open source software development.
- Sun Developer Connection Discussion Forums (*http://forum.sun.com/*) have topics on Java development and Sun ONE Studio 4 (formerly Sun Forte for Java).

NetBeans Open Source Projects with Design Forms in the Distribution

(*http://www.softwoehr.com/oss*) contains a few projects whose GUI portion was designed under NetBeans. These include the *FIJI ForthIsh Java Interpreter* and the *MEU Remote Source Physical File Member Editor for the IBM AS/400*. The JavaBeans and NetBeans design forms produced in the course of these projects are included.

Java-Oriented IDEs Other Than NetBeans

Freedom of choice is one of the finer aspects of the spirit of the Java programming community. In that spirit, we herewith offer a list of other popular IDE's aimed at Java development.

 The inclusion of any IDEs mentioned here should not be construed as disparagement of any IDE we fail to list. It's a pretty arbitrary selection.

Do a net search for Java + IDE, and you'll find many more listings than shown here.

- AnyJ (*http://www.netcomputing.de/*) is a Java IDE for Windows and Mac OS X.
- Borland JBuilder (*http://www.borland.com/jbuilder/*) is a popular commercial offering with extended enterprise support. Freely downloadable limited demo.
- IBM VisualAge for Java (*http://www.software.ibm.com/ad/vajava*) is a popular commercial offering with extended enterprise support. Freely downloadable limited demo.
- Eclipse (*http://eclipse.org/*) is an IBM-sponsored open-source universal tools platform. Its authors appear to have been somewhat influenced by NetBeans.
- IntelliJ IDEA (*http://www.intellij.com/idea/*) is a full-featured Java IDE with a high level of usability and outstanding advanced code editing and refactoring support.
- JCreator (*http://www.jcreator.com/*) has a free and trial version, in addition to a commercial version.
- JavaWorld Developer's Tools IDE Page (*http://www.javaworld.com/javaworld/tools/jw-tools-ide.html*) has a long list of various Java IDEs.

Future Plans

No software project is ever "finished"—and this is as true of NetBeans as any. While backward compatibility with older ways of doing things is almost always maintained, new ways evolve that are more efficient or easier. Old ways of doing things turn out to have limitations, new solutions are created, and the old ones deprecated and eventually removed. This is part of the lifecycle of any software project.

NetBeans has had a long time to evolve. Since its first incarnation in 1996 as a monolithic IDE, to its somewhat modular sibling NetBeans 2.0, to today's modern, modular architecture, a lot of thought has gone into what worked and what didn't. And in some cases, requirements simply changed. When NetBeans was originally designed, no one was expecting the huge proliferation of modules now available.

As with currents in history or culture, it is often possible to predict future directions, and that is what we will try to do in this appendix.

This appendix attempts to give an overview of expected major changes, not every detailed change between releases. The Upgrade Guide available as part of the Open APIs reference documentation is the best place to find specifics on changes made since the last release.

Declarative Instantiation

Probably the thing that is most predictable as NetBeans evolves is that more and more functionality is moving toward being declared using XML. That is to say, rather than incur the overhead of loading large numbers of classes on startup, you will define how NetBeans should instantiate classes that supply your functionality in an XML document that contains the class names and other information necessary to instantiate your objects on demand. In the long run, this translates to improved performance by reducing NetBeans' memory footprint, and makes NetBeans a more scalable environment.

As of 3.3, system settings and visual workspaces can be declared in XML; with 3.4 or 4.0, it will be possible to declare user invokable actions and when they should be enabled entirely in XML. The goal is that eventually, no classes from a module need to be loaded in order to present that module's functionality to a user—classes will be instantiated when the user actually begins to use the functionality.

Uniform Lookup

An effort is underway to make the mechanisms of finding objects inside NetBeans as consistent as possible. Generally this means using `org.openide.util.Lookup` wherever possible to register objects. Formerly programmatic registries are being made declarative, as mentioned in the previous section. Other forms of object registration will eventually also be moved to use lookup: `org.openide.TopManager` gets more methods deprecated with every NetBeans release, and `getCookie(Class)` methods on `Node` and `DataObject` will one day be replaced with `getLookup()`.

As of this writing, there is also an experimental effort to use JNDI to register objects by name. This style complements `Lookup`, which is effective for a pool of anonymous objects.

Datasystems II

The current Datasystems API suffers from many problems. As a central API in the NetBeans architecture, it has often borne the weight of new features and suffered in complexity. It also has insoluble performance limitations that hurt scalability, and it has a complicated threading model that has produced many race conditions and deadlocks. Finally, this API is cluttered with compile-time references to most other major APIs in NetBeans, making it very hard to use as a standalone library or in a reduced application.

Since all of these problems cannot be solved by compatible extensions to the existing API, work is underway to develop a complete replacement. The new Datasystems will be conceptually similar to the current API, but have a much smaller core and use cleaner design patterns for thread safety, extensibility, and performance. A runtime compatibility bridge is part of the new implementation, permitting clients of the new API to "see" old-style `DataObjects` and vice-versa.

The Looks API

The Looks API is an API that will probably be used heavily in NetBeans in the future. The Looks API is currently available in an experimental form. Many API and user interface issues surrounding Looks have yet to be resolved as of this writing, however.

One of the key aspects of Nodes is that they don't hold any data, they just present it—show a set of actions, properties, children, and Cookies for some other object that exists in the JVM. So more than one kind of node can represent the same data—in fact, this is exactly the kind of flexibility Nodes exist to provide.

Unfortunately, there is no standard way to switch the node used to display an object to mix and match pieces of existing nodes to create a customized appearance for the object. There is also no way for code holding a reference to an object from an unfamiliar data model to find a node that could display it appropriately.

Looks is a direct application of the MVC paradigm. Given an object from a certain data model, you can apply a Look to a LookNode displaying it, which will determine how the children, properties, and actions for that Node will appear. By changing the look on a node and combining and filtering looks, you can flexibly control the appearance of an object in the UI while keeping a clean MVC separation. You can search a registry of looks suited to a given object.

A clear example of the need for Looks is the presentation of XML data. In the DOM model, even whitespace adds elements to the document tree. For correctness, this kind of precise mapping between the data model and the document contents is absolutely necessary—a data model exists to represent its data, all of it, period. But to present a tree crammed with distracting whitespace Nodes to a user who needs to get something done is terrible UI. An intervening layer that can filter a data model and whittle it down to the content that is actually useful to the user is natural. Permitting modules that work with special XML subtypes like Ant scripts to supply optional customized appearances for these XML files is also natural. These are exactly the problems the Looks API intends to solve.

The Looks API is one of the newest APIs in NetBeans and is evolving even as this book is being written. It is important for XML support and key to the UI for the Metadata Repository. Revised Datasystems will probably use Looks natively as well. As with the Lookup API, its power is in its genericness, and as time goes on more and more modules will come to use this infrastructure to control how a data model is presented to the user.

Declarative Actions

One area that has not benefited as greatly as it could from the introduction of XML layers is actions. While they are installed in the module's XML layer, they are instantiated when the main menu for the IDE is built—context-sensitive action classes need to be called to determine if and when they should be enabled or disabled.

One of the things being worked on for NetBeans 4.0 is a specification for declaring the constraints on an action in XML layers. Since the primary mechanism for determining the enablement of actions is the Cookies available on the activated nodes, this specification will include ways to declare the required cookies as part of the definition of the action, along with specifying that action's display name and icon. The method to call to perform the action can be specified in much the same manner as factory methods are specified on *.instance* files. This should cover most cases, and in fact obviate the need for action classes at all; the method to call to perform the action can be in any implementation class within the module declaring it.

The current Actions API also does not provide an extensible way to manage context menus. The revised API should provide richer layer-based installation of all kinds of actions.

The new API and implementation are being developed as a separate module. The current actions support in the Open APIs will be left alone but deprecated in favor of the replacements.

Check the overview page for the Actions API in your version of NetBeans to determine the right way to install your actions.

Deprecation of IDE-Specific Functionality in the Open APIs

Because NetBeans has become a generic platform for applications, beyond simply being a platform for development tools, any functionality in the basic APIs that is specific to their application to development tools is considered a bug. Some items in the core APIs are inapplicable except for using the NetBeans platform to build development tools, and these are gradually being deprecated and retired.

Specific items planned for deprecation are as follows:

`org.openide.cookies.SourceCookie` *and* `org.openide.src.*`
These control parsing and regeneration of Java sources. In the future, such support should be removed from the Open APIs; the Metadata Repository in conjunction with a Java source language model will replace it.

The Compiler and Execution APIs
These APIs contain many constructions specific to development tools and even some specific to Java. Separate API modules will probably be created to house their replacements in the future. The Debugger API is already very minimal indeed; practically speaking, all debugger implementations already use much richer APIs under development in debugger modules.

The Metadata Repository

The metadata repository (MDR) is a very impressive piece of technology that promises to revolutionize the way new language support is built for NetBeans. While it was created in order to enable refactoring support in the NetBeans IDE and to more easily implement support for additional languages, it can be a very useful tool to other applications built on NetBeans that deal with complex sets of data. For example, Project XEMO (*http://www.xemo.org/*), a music composition environment based on NetBeans, is using the MDR to allow users of their tool to do things such as rapidly access bar 33 of the first cello part for a symphony being edited.

Reflecting its name, the MDR is a repository of information that can be queried. It makes possible things such as computing structural diffs between versions of classes, finding all of the references to an element such as a class, and even translation between languages.

The two core concepts behind the MDR are the following:

Metadata
> Metadata is information about data, describing that data. Examples of metadata are things like the relationship between Java source files in the IDE and places where they are referenced in the code.

Metamodels
> In the NetBeans IDE, a metamodel is like meta-metadata. A metamodel describes the structure data can have and the interrelationships possible between different entities. In the case of Java language support for the IDE, a metamodel of the Java language specifies things like the fact that classes can contain methods, inner classes, fields and constructors; that methods can be passed variables; and that code in one class can refer to these elements within the constraints of the Java language.

Some aspects of what the metadata repository offers to NetBeans appear almost like black magic. With this tool, building basic support for a language involves supplying NetBeans with a metamodel of the language in question, a parser for that language (such as one generated using ANTLR—*http://www.antlr.org/*), and a tool to generate code, written to an API supplied by the MDR. When the metamodel is installed, a set of JMI (Java Metadata Interface) compliant interfaces are generated. But not only that—NetBeans will also generate the bytecode necessary to structurally browse source code in that language!

As this chapter is being written, the Java module is in the process of being rewritten to use the MDR. Following this will come tools for refactoring and other technologies based on it.

An acute reader of Chapters 22–26 will have noticed many places where that module needed to implement fairly complex parse-regenerate-listen logic, all of which is conceptually similar to the logic already used in the Java module, XML module, and so on. MDR promises to unify this programming style. Score files will be defined by an ANTLR grammar and a metamodel developed in UML. Parse-regenerate code can then be generated automatically, rather than defining ScoreCookie and ScoreSupport manually. Furthermore, the metamodel will support fine-grained change notification—that is, just one note in the model changes when just one line of text is changed. This kind of generic structure diff is known to NetBeans developers as *nará æi çka*, or "the little smashing-together," of old and new structural trees to find where they differ.

The metadata repository is implemented as a separable library that can be used by standalone applications outside of NetBeans. For performance, the metadata it stores is kept in B-tree files on disk, but the storage mechanism is pluggable and can be replaced with, for example, a database if desired. For detailed information about the MDR, see the MDR web site (*http://mdr.netbeans.org/*).

Standards Employed by the MDR

One of the most important aspects of the MDR is that it is entirely based on open standards, many of them from the Object Management Group (*http://www.omg.org/*) (OMG). This means that any other tools that use these standards will interoperate easily with the metadata repository. The standards in question are as follows:

CWM
> The OMG's Common Warehouse Model (*http://www.cwmforum.org/*) is a standard for representing database schema. It provides standards for transformations and data mining on these schema.

MOF
> OMG's Meta-object Facility (*http://www.omg.org/technology/documents/formal/mof.htm*) is a standard for the storage of metadata. It defines what a repository is and how to access it.

XMI
> OMG's XML Metadata Interface (*http://www.omg.org/technology/xml/index.htm*) is a standard interchange format for models, which may be created using UML tools or other modeling tools that can export a model in XMI format.

JMI
> The Java Metadata Interface (*http://java.sun.com/products/jmi/*) (JSR-40) is a Java standard for metadata interchange. It implements the interfaces specified in Interface Definition Language (IDL) in the MOF standard.

Model driven architecture
> MDA is not so much a standard as it is what you get when you use the preceding standards. MDA is OMG's vision for the future of applications, in which platform-independent models define the application in an implementation-independent way.

Project Support

Coming in NetBeans 4.0 is a completely revamped project management system. This system has been under development for some time, and a prototype is available at the time of this writing. Historically, support for projects in the NetBeans IDE has been relatively weak, and has been reimplemented several times. The new projects module attempts to provide the Grand Unified Theory of projects, yet do so in a generic and lightweight way that will be applicable across languages and possibly in non-IDE applications.

Here are some of the primary requirements for the coming projects support in NetBeans:

Sharability
> Projects must be able to be shared by groups of users, using version control.

Intuitiveness
> In usability tests, users often expect the project to be the fundamental unit they will work with to get started in NetBeans. Currently this is not the case.

Language neutrality
> Project support should make no assumptions about the language being used for development and must not force alien concepts on a language.

Filesystems != Classpath
> This is probably the most profound change, since it has implications for the APIs and backward compatibility. The IDE will, on initial startup, mount all local disks; the classpath is then constructed from ad hoc subdirectories.

Different handling of libraries
> Many other IDEs have a concept of libraries that a user instructs the IDE to compile against. A generic concept of libraries that can be part of a project should exist.

Multiple simultaneous projects
> It should be possible to have more than one project open at the same time. For example, if you are working on a library and software that uses that library, both projects can be open at the same time if that suits your work style.

Object groups
> Projects can have groupings of objects, such as all GIF images.

Deliverables
> The purpose of a project is to produce a deliverable, so there is a *recipe* (for example, build script) for creating the deliverable.

Modules will supply specific project implementations
> A generic projects framework will provide basic infrastructure for project support. Specific kinds of projects, such as a Java project, will be provided by modules.

An extensive set of documentation and proposals, along with the prototype, is available on the projects module pages (*http://projects.netbeans.org/*), which go over the details of the new projects system. In particular the *http://projects.netbeans.org/openissues/DiscussionSummary.html* discussion summary of the planning for the new projects infrastructure is illuminating.

Working with Open Source and NetBeans

Many interesting texts are available on the value, philosophy, and practices of open source software development, so we'll stick to some practical advice and tips for working effectively in the NetBeans project.

Practices

Any community functions according to stated or unstated contracts between its participants. In the case of NetBeans, these "contracts" are relatively lightweight. To participate effectively in a community, it is helpful to know what the typical behavior patterns are. Read on to learn how NetBeans works as an open source project.

Governance

The NetBeans project has a "governance board" that can vote and make decisions if there is some irreconcilable problem. It is composed of two members chosen by the user and developer community on the mailing lists and one member appointed by Sun Microsystems, which donated the initial source code and sponsors the project. The governance board is the choice of last resort. As of this writing, it has never had to decide an issue. It exists to ensure that no party can hijack the project or cause NetBeans to evolve specifically in its private interest at the expense of others or the health of the project and code.

Heavyweight governance, with committees, hierarchies, and chairpeople is notably absent from the NetBeans project. The authors of this book were two of the individuals who set up the initial site and governance process, and we strongly believe that it is far better to evolve the structures you need as you need them than to create formal processes that may or may not prove useful. Think of the filibuster—Robert's Rules of Order were never created with that in mind. The point is that creating any structured social system inevitably creates perverse incentives you never realized were there until they are exploited, and to anticipate all possible loopholes and close them is both a never-ending process and an anticipation of antisocial behavior. What you anticipate, you communicate that you anticipate, and that just increases the likelihood that you'll get exactly what you don't want. So, when setting up the governance of *netbeans.org*, we concluded that less is more.

Consensus

Decision making happens by consensus, arrived at on the mailing lists. Generally, somebody proposes something, and others weigh in with concurring or differing opinions. The person making the proposal has the responsibility, after some time, to summarize and post what she finds to be the consensus. There is a convention that such emails will include [wrap up] or FINAL CALL in the subject line to indicate that this is happening.

The underlying notion is that consensus is an efficient means of getting things done. For many parts of NetBeans, only a handful of people will care passionately about a given change. But it is impossible, in an open community, to know who those people will be. Therefore, it's important to make sure those who are interested in a change have a voice and the ability to discuss the change. To create formal membership procedures would waste people's time and mean that the project could not benefit from the contribution of those who do not have formal membership.

Forking

In open source, there is always the option of last result—to "fork" the code: to create a possibly incompatible version of the program that implements some change a part of the community was opposed to. Probably the most famous example of this is the Emacs and XEmacs editors for Unix. The most interesting aspect of this example is that both survived, and that the maintainers of both would like to find a way of re-merging the codebases. But this is also an example of the tragedy of forking: It divides the community's efforts and doubles the maintenance load if the maintainers of one branch wish to incorporate changes from the other. It can also kill off both projects, and is thus the last resort. Generally, it is effective to be persuasive and to listen to the feedback you get on an idea—usually there is a way to implement a change so that it will not adversely affect others, and a consensus-based process optimizes for that outcome.

This is not to say that everyone is always happy with the results of a decision—there may be consensus with some amount of dissent. At that point, those who dissent are welcome to reopen the issue at a later time.

A truism of open source (and life) is that the only way to be sure you'll get something done in open source is to do it yourself. If the idea is compelling, it will probably attract other developers. At the same time, a significant percentage of the developers of NetBeans are being paid to work on it because they work for a company that has specific goals. Many of these people contribute some of their off-work time to working on projects within NetBeans that they're particularly passionate about. You will find plenty of help, answers, and encouragement on the NetBeans mailing lists. But a suggestion without the willingness to implement the suggestion is just that.

The mechanics of consensus

In talking about consensus, a concrete example is probably more illustrative than philosophy. The following conversation thread took place on the *nbui@netbeans.org* mailing list in the spring of 2001, starting with one of Sun's human interface engineers suggesting a change in the way basic and expert options were divided in NetBeans' wizards. For the sake of saving trees, it is not reproduced here in its entirety—you can browse the entire thread on the web at *http://www.netbeans.org/servlets/ReadMsg?msgId=83575&listName=nbui*.

```
Date: Wed, 21 Mar 2001 15:58:00 -0800
From: Dirk Ruiz
To: nbui@netbeans.org
Subject: [nbui] Erecting a novice/expert wall in wizards.

Folks,

Maya and I would like to propose a small wizard change.  The problem is that
some wizards need to present options for both the novice and expert user.  The
two best examples are the Setup Wizard and the New Wizard (aka the New From
Template wizard).  The Setup Wizard uses a checkbox at the bottom of the page to
give users access to expert options.  The New Wizard just enables the Finish
button after the user has set the object name and package.

Neither of these solutions is really adequate.  Jim Dibble pointed out, in a
private conversation, that making the user check a box for expert options is
a bit silly.  And, enabling the Finish button is too subtle.  It's easy to
blunder on, pressing Next, and find yourself in a bunch of screens you don't
want to be in.  (To my embarrassment, I find I do this frequently in the New
Wizard.)  What's worse is that these two solutions are inconsistent: we should
settle on one solution as soon as possible.

We need an obvious way to tell the user when she has specified enough, and when
she is about to stray into expert territory.  To this end, we would like to
propose the following.  Upon reaching a state where enough information has been
specified, the Next and Finish buttons are both enabled (as is done now).  If
the user clicks Finish, then the wizard is dismissed and the object created.
BUT, if the user clicks Next, a page like that shown in the two attached GIF
files (SetupWizardPage.gif and NewWizardPage.gif) is shown.  This page tells the
user she has entered enough information to get a sensible default, and to stop
here or to click Finish for expert options.

In addition, we would like to propose that the left panel explicitly show this
distinction between novice and expert steps with the "-- Expert --" separator.
```

What do you think? The left panel modification seems nice, but is not
absolutely essential; it could be saved for later. And, I suppose some could
debate the usefulness of this for the New Wizard, since it would force the user
to do an extra click in order to fill in fields and methods. But, at a very
minimum, I would like to use this kind of scheme for the Setup Wizard. Not only
would it be an unobtrusive way to put up a wall between novice and expert
options, but it would allow us to take out the "expert options" checkbox (and
replace it with something truly useful). Eventually, we would like to add this
back into the NetBeans Wizard Guidelines as the standard way to erect an
unobtrusive novice/expert wall for wizards.

Thanks!

Dirk

Terry Roberts replies to this by voting a "resounding YES," and Dirk mentions that
he meant click **Next** for expert options, not **Finish**. Jan Benway responds that the
expert/novice distinction may not be the right one and that users usually treat
"expert" as meaning "other." Dirk responds:

Good point. The problem is that, in the Setup pane, it very clearly is an
expert/novice type distinction. The first pane of the wizard should be
comprehensible by everyone; the later panes require knowledge of the IDE and how
it works. But I'm open to any label that clearly tells the user, "don't go here
unless you know what you're doing", particularly in the Setup wizard.

Maya Venkatraman responds to this, pointing out that perhaps a solution is some
kind of status area that indicates when there is or is not enough information to complete the wizard. She adds:

I think that the panel does introduce an irritating additional click -
but users will know to expect it - and click out of it right away
What we loose by introducing the panel is outweighed by what
we gain (my opinion).

At this point, Rochelle Raccah suggests:

2 possible ideas:

1) Have the "expertness" of the wizard be customizable in options. Users who
want the short/long version can set it there. I'm not sure what the default
would be.

2) Rename the Next button on the page which transitions between basic and expert
screens. "Further customization" or something like that?

After all of this, Dirk summarizes and comes up with a modified proposal based on
the feedback on the mailing list:

Date: Wed, 28 Mar 2001 16:04:49 -0800
From: Dirk Ruiz
Subject: Re: [nbui] Erecting a novice/expert wall in wizards. (FINAL CALL)

```
Folks,

The discussion on erecting a novice/expert wall in wizards seems to have yielded
some good conclusions.

1. "Novice/Expert" itself is the wrong distinction to be making.  A better
distinction would be "do now/do later" or maybe "basic/advanced".  In essence,
we should use categories that emphasize the characteristics of the wizard
contents, rather than the qualities of the user herself.

2. For the Setup Wizard, the wall page (the one that says, "You have specified
enough information to properly set up NetBeans") was seen as a reasonable way to
make the distinction.

3. For the New Wizard, the wall page page was seen as a possible irritant and
hindrance.  Several ways were considered to deal with this, including setting an
"Expertness" option for wizards, putting a "Don't show this again" checkbox on
the wall page, or putting a textual/graphical indication in the Steps pane.

4. The modifications to the Steps pane received little comment.  However, a
private conversation with one of the UI Team developers revealed that it would
not be possible to implement within the 3.2 timeframe, since the Steps pane is
not directly under the wizard developer's control.

With all this in mind, I would like to make the following amended proposal.  We
should have two types of walls between options: a high wall and a low wall.  The
high wall consists of a (mostly blank) wizard page that says, "You have
specified enough information...".  It is for things like the Setup Wizard, or
other wizards that have a strong distinction between easy options and difficult
options.  The low wall consists of adding a textual notification to a regular,
working wizard page; the text tells the user that she has specified enough
information to get something sensible.  It is for things like the New Wizard,
where there is not as strong a distinction between easy and hard options.  In
the New Wizard case, it would consist of a piece of text at the bottom of the
second page saying, "Ready to generate your &lt;object&gt;."  In neither of these
cases will the Steps panel change.

After 3.2, we should explore other options, e.g., adding graphics or text to the
Steps panel.

If this is OK with everyone, I will ask the UI Team developers to make the
changes to the Setup Wizard and New Wizard.

Many thanks!

Dirk
```

If you read the preceding thread, you can see a process happening here: Dirk introduces the idea. There are some objections and suggested modifications. At the end of the process, the idea has changed, but still retains its basic character. And what you see in NetBeans 3.2 and later is the functionality discussed here.

How to Get Involved

Too much is sometimes made of contributions of code to an open source project. There are many ways to participate—filing bugs and participation on mailing lists are just as valuable to the community as contributions of code! For details of the major mailing lists and resources on *netbeans.org*, see Chapter 13.

The mechanics of contribution

Contributing to NetBeans codebase is rewarding and a valuable contribution to the NetBeans community and the Java community at large. It even looks good on a resume! There are three basic ways to contribute code to NetBeans:

- Create a module project and contribute it to *netbeans.org*.

- Submit patches or bug fixes to the NetBeans core or modules—once you've submitted several that were accepted by the project maintainer, ask for CVS write access to the code you're interested in working with.

- Take over maintenance of an abandoned or unmaintained project—at present there are not many such projects on *netbeans.org* (nor should there be), but there are a few, such as the JUnit (*http://junit.netbeans.org/*) or ANTLR (*http://antlr. netbeans.org/*) modules, which are not receiving full-time attention from anyone.

The following is an example of that process in action, as it happens on the NetBeans mailing lists. This is also an abridged version of the original conversation—for the full version, see *http://www.netbeans.org/servlets/ReadMsg?msgId=188265&listName=nbui*.

```
From: "Michael Beauregard"
Date: Thu, 8 Nov 2001 21:52:49 -0700
To: nbui@netbeans.org
Subject: [nbui] code completion enhancements

I have started making my first contribution to Netbeans tonight. I want to
add the following two features to the code completion popup window:

1) When using code completion for methods with many parameters, it is
difficult to visually determine which parameter you must enter next. It
would be convenient to highlight/bold the current method parameter in the
completion view so that the user can quickly see what the next parameter is.

For example, "Hashtable h = new Hashtable( 10, " should have a corresponding
completion hint such as: "Hashtable( int initialCapacity, <B>float
loadFactor</B>)"

I have implemented this feature with minimal changes to the existing source
code and I have one issue remaining. Since I am using a 'bold' font to
highlight the current method parameter, it has different font metrics that
are not accounted for when the ScrollCompletionPane scroll ranges are set
(wherever that is??). The result is that if the method with bold chars is
the longest cell in the list, then the last few pixels of the method text
may be cut off in the scroll pane).
```

```
2) The next feature and issue are related to #1. Currently if you are coding
a method with many parameters, you have to manually scroll the code
completion scroll bar to view that last few parameters. I want the
completion scroll pane to scroll automatically as needed as method
parameters are being entered.

I am not sure how to manipulate the scroll pane in either case so any help
you can offer will probably assist both of these tasks.

Thanks in advance,

Michael.
```

Lea Anthony responds with an additional suggestion that the parameter type, rather than the name appear when you press the comma in code completion. Martin Roskanin jumps in to suggest that Michael look at `org.netbeans.editor.ext.java.` `JCCellRenderer` for font metrics information and suggest other places in the NetBeans source base to look to for examples. Michael then responds to Lea's suggestion:

```
Adding the first change is *very* easy, but I could see how some people
might not like having the type entered there. Maybe a better solution is to
have the code completion window stay open as you enter method parameters.
Personally, I find it a little annoying that it closes in between each
method parameter.

I would like some people to comment on this before I make any changes.

Meanwhile, I'll look into differentiating between local/inherited methods.
```

Riyad Kalla responds that Microsoft Visual Studio's code completion window stays open and that this is probably the better solution. Michael writes that he has implemented the initial feature (boldfacing the current parameter in code completion) and Lea's suggestion. John Richardson chimes in that he doesn't really like having the type show up, because often the suggested value is actually correct. Michael responds that he agrees, and Lea also mentions that keeping the window open is probably a better idea. Michael submits the patch as an attachment to the enhancement request he filed, and mentions this on the list. One bug is found and fixed, and the final messages in the thread are:

```
From: "Michael Beauregard"
Date: Tue, 20 Nov 2001 13:46:04 -0700

I have provided a fix for this problem.
http://openide.netbeans.org/issues/show_bug.cgi?id=17569

From: Martin Roskanin
Date: Thu, 22 Nov 2001 09:45:35 +0100

Thank you Michael,

I will commit your contribution during next week.
If there will be any problems, we can communicate via Issuezilla's
```

```
http://openide.netbeans.org/issues/show_bug.cgi?id=17569
Thank you,
Martin
```

Doing what Michael did is a good way to get a start in programming for NetBeans—there are always small improvements or enhancements that can be made, and one of the best ways to learn a language, a codebase, or a programming paradigm is to modify someone else's existing code.

The Lifecycle of Module Development

If you want to write a module and contribute it to NetBeans, here are the steps to take:

1. Post to *nbdev@netbeans.org* about it. If you're working on a module, probably you are already at least reading, if not participating in, this mailing list. You will probably want to include the following information:

   What you are creating or want to create
   So you can find out if anyone is already working in this area or if anyone else would be interested in contributing.

   Info on how far along the project is
   If you've already written some code.

2. Create a prototype or some working code. The *netbeans.org* approach to new projects is a little different than that of sites like SourceForge (*http://sourceforge. net/*). Generally, a module should exist in the form of at least a skeleton of code before a formal project is created—this is more interesting to the rest of the community and guarantees that *netbeans.org* does not become littered with projects that were good ideas with no implementation.

3. Make sure the source code's licensing is correct. All code hosted on *netbeans.org* must, for legal reasons, be licensed under the Sun Public License (SPL), the same open and unrestricted license NetBeans' source code is licensed under. All source and text files in your code should contain the SPL license notice, as can be found in any of NetBeans source files or the examples for this book.

4. Make sure your packaging and coding conventions are correct. The convention for organizing sources in NetBeans is that the base directory of a module should contain *src/* and *www/*. The *src/* directory should contain the first level package directory for your module. The source code should obey NetBeans' packaging convention—for example, `org.netbeans.modules.somemodule`. Since CVS does not handle renaming terribly well, it is best to have code packaged correctly before it is put in CVS. The *www/* directory is the root directory of your project's web site. There should also be an Ant build file for the module in the base directory of the project.

The coding standards are Sun Microsystems' recommended standards for Java, along with some NetBeans-specific items. These are detailed on the NetBeans web site (*http://www.netbeans.org/devhome/docs/code_conventions.html*). Coding conventions are a somewhat religious topic, but there is value in consistency—this being open source, other people will be reading and working with your code as well. Reading code that is formatted in ways you are not used to is more difficult than reading code that is formatted in a familiar way. Using consistent coding conventions ensures that everybody working on NetBeans will be accustomed to what they see on the screen and able to read it easily.

5. Contribute the source code. The *contrib.netbeans.org* project (at *http://contrib.netbeans.org/*), is designed to host your source code temporarily. Follow the instructions you see there. When your module becomes complete enough to need its own project, request creation of CVS space for it and a web site, including what you want it to be called.

6. Set up your module's web site. Modules have their own web sites, using virtual hostnames—if you are working on the humdinger project, your site would be *humdinger.netbeans.org*. Your module web site is managed through CVS. Once you've gotten notification that the code you've contributed is in CVS and the site is set up, perform a checkout of the sources from NetBeans' CVS server. You will find a *www/* folder is present in the top level folder of your checkout. In this folder you can create your module's web site, checking the images and HTML files into CVS just as you would source code. You can optionally set up mailing lists for users or developers of your module.

7. Release your alpha/beta module. When your module is mature enough to be feature-complete and functional but not necessarily bug-free, make a request on *nbdev@netbeans.org* to add the module to the alpha update center on *netbeans.org*. This will make your module available to all users of NetBeans. Announce the release on the *nbannounce@netbeans.org* mailing list and be available on the *nbusers@netbeans.org* mailing list to answer questions and encourage users of your module to test it and others to try it out. You can also submit a news item to appear on the main pages of the NetBeans web site.

8. Code, bug fix, test, and release. Use Issuezilla to track bug reports and requests for enhancement of your module. As you fix bugs and implement enhancements, update their entries in Issuezilla, so the people who reported them will know you're working on them. From time to time (every few weeks to month or two), update the version of your module that's in the update center so that users will be testing the latest bits. Announce the updates on *nbannounce@netbeans.org* so people will find out about them even if they don't habitually check for updates.

9. Request that your module be included in the standard NetBeans build or listed on the standard update center. When your module is stable and mature, you can request that it either be included in the standard NetBeans distribution (this is a

community decision that should take place on *nbdev@netbeans.org*). Including something in the standard distribution means that it is stable and generally useful enough to belong there. The decision is up to the entire community.

10. Write unit tests. Unit tests are a way of guaranteeing that functionality remains stable over time. The NetBeans source base is continually built and tested. Available from the NetBeans web site are tools for testing functionality, API/SPI backward compatibility, and performance. If you add your unit tests to the suite of standard tests, it will be easier to find out about problems as soon as they happen. See Chapter 27 for more information on unit tests.

Resources

CVS (Concurrent Versioning System)

The sources are stored in a CVS repository (*http://www.netbeans.org/devhome/sources/cvs.html*). CVS is an open source version control system. To use it you need a CVS client. The IDE includes a CVS client written in Java, in the JavaCVS module. CVS allows the tracking of version histories and functionality to allow users to check out, modify, and update files.

The sources to NetBeans can be downloaded via anonymous CVS; permission to write to the CVS repository is customarily granted on request, provided that the requester has submitted some patches or other code and that the other developers on the project agree to it.

The address of the CVS server is *cvs.netbeans.org*. The CVSROOT environment variable for a CVS client to check out the NetBeans sources should be :pserver:anoncvs@cvs. netbeans.org:/cvs with a blank password.

Projects

The site is divided into projects, each of which has a virtual hostname. So, for example, to find proposals regarding the Editor, go to *http://editor.netbeans.org/*. Some projects do have their own mailing lists, but most of the discussion happens on two main development mailing lists, *nbdev@netbeans.org* and *dev@openide.netbeans.org*.

Projects are mostly a web-site user interface abstraction; each module on *netbeans. org* has its own virtual hostname—but in some cases, there is not a justification for large amounts of web content about, say, support for sourceless Java *.class* files. Having a parent project allows for logical groupings of modules and the possibility of mailing lists based on topics common across a subset of projects.

The name of a project corresponds to its name as a CVS module—for example, cvs co editor checks out the source code to the Source Editor. cvs co all will download the entire NetBeans source base. For details on the NetBeans sources and CVS access to them, see the sources pages on *netbeans.org* (*http://www.netbeans.org/ devhome/sources/index.html*).

Mailing Lists

If you have a question, a problem, a solution, a module, or just want to get involved, these are the first places to go. Development decisions are made in public, on public mailing lists. Here is a breakdown of the major mailing lists:

nbusers@netbeans.org
> Discussion about using the IDE.

nbdev@netbeans.org
> General development discussion.

dev@openide.netbeans.org
> Discussion of the Open APIs and their usage, and requests for changes or enhancements.

nbui@netbeans.org
> User interface planning and discussion.

nbdiscuss@netbeans.org
> Discussion of issues relating to *netbeans.org* infrastructure, such as mailing lists and the web site and community issues.

nbnews_contrib@netbeans.org
> The weekly NetBeans newsletter contribution list. The NetBeans newsletter covers interesting threads from the mailing lists and is a "week in review" for the NetBeans project. If you'd like to see certain issues go out as part of the newsletter, send the information to this address so that the volunteer writing the newsletter that week knows about them.

Additionally, bear in mind that projects may have their own mailing lists—for example, dev@mdr.netbeans.org.

CVS mailing lists

If there are multiple participants in your module project, one of the most effective ways to keep up with what is going on in the project is to sign up for the project's CVS mailing list. Whenever someone commits code into the source base of your project, you will get an email with the log message detailing what they did. This is a tremendous resource for collaboration—please don't overlook it!

To subscribe to the CVS mailing list for a given module or project, send a blank email to *cvs-subscribe@someproject.netbeans.org*.

Issue mailing lists

Module owners are also expected to subscribe to the issues mailing list for their project. This mailing list receives emails whenever bug or enhancement reports for the project are created or updated.

To subscribe to the issues mailing list for a given module or project, send a blank email to *issues-subscribe@someproject*.netbeans.org.

Issuezilla

netbeans.org currently uses Issuezilla, scion of Bugzilla, the venerable bug-tracking tool from the Mozilla web browser project. Each virtually-hosted module also gets its own bug-tracking category in Issuezilla.

While the query interface to Issuezilla is somewhat terrifying at first glance, it becomes fairly easy to use with practice. A bug report specifies a number of things, such as these:

- The version of NetBeans in which the bug was observed
- The operating system on which it was observed
- The component (module) that has the problem
- The subcomponent, such as code, documentation, or user interface
- A summary of the bug
- A description of the bug
- Keywords to help classify the bug
- Who (if anyone) is responsible for fixing it

Part of contributing bug reports is making sure that they are clear and specific. Where possible, include the exact steps to produce the bug and attach your log file, which contains platform information and many diagnostics. Note that a BugSubmitter module is now in progress that will mine this information directly from a running copy of NetBeans and save time and effort. As of April 2002, it is not yet included in the standard builds, but probably soon will be. For more information on writing effective bug reports, see the HOWTO document on the NetBeans web site (*http://qa.netbeans.org/bugzilla/reportbug.html*). Two other good resources on writing effective bug reports are

- Simon Tatham's entertaining How to Report Bugs Effectively (*http://www. chiark.greenend.org.uk/~sgtatham/bugs.html*)
- The Mozilla project's How to write effective bug reports (*http://www.mozilla.org/ quality/bug-writing-guidelines.html*)
- Elisabeth Hendrickson's insightful treatise on the subject (*http://www. qualitytree.com/feature/webr.pdf*)

Interacting Effectively on Mailing Lists

The social context of open source projects is mailing lists, and yet there is remarkably little written about how to be an effective participant on them. While this is an area that is under-researched, we can share some of the things that have worked for us.

Lurk before posting
> If you have just signed up to a mailing list, read it for a while before posting to it, and get a sense of who the people there are and what the community is like.

Read the entire thread (or a lot of it) before responding
> A fast way to lose credibility in a public community is to sound like you don't know what you're talking about. Take some time to know the context in which you're responding.

Assumptions are as important as what you say explicitly
> Indirect communication is sometimes more important than direct communication. That which is directly communicated is more likely to arouse resistance than what is indirectly communicated. Another way of saying this is that tone means a lot.

You catch more flies with honey
> Even if someone replies to you with overt hostility, treat them with respect and make sure that the assumptions underlying your response are that they are trying to help. That makes it much more likely that the next response will have constructive content.

Greet people when replying
> Simply including "Hi, David," (or whomever you're addressing) dramatically changes the tone of a message, and it shows that you've taken the time to read and appreciate the message you are replying to.

Be concise
> A message that covers a huge range of information is less likely to draw responses—it's too much work to read it. Also, if there are several important points, it is likely that the resulting thread of responses will not address all of them. By having a topic for a post and sticking to it, it keeps the conversation focused and makes it easier for other people to respond. Also, since not everybody reads every post on the mailing lists, some people who may have something valuable to contribute to the conversation may never end up reading it, because the subject didn't indicate it was of interest to them.

The NetBeans mailing lists are remarkably free of the flame wars found elsewhere on the Internet, largely because of this type of interaction. It is a wonderful community of bright, interesting people, and we hope to meet you there!

Additional Modules and Where to Find Them

One of the key values of the NetBeans IDE is extensibility, and of course plenty of extensions are available, from debuggers and profilers, to UML tools, to at least one Minesweeper game. A number of online resources list and allow you to download modules for NetBeans. The primary ones are as follows:

The netbeans.org update server

There are a number of open source modules for NetBeans that are not currently in the standard distribution. Some are simply too esoteric to be of interest to most users; others are useful, but not currently maintained; others are alpha, beta or experimental modules that may at some point end up in the main IDE distribution.

Probably the easiest way to find new modules is by using the Update Center on the Tools menu. This is a tool for downloading extension modules directly into the IDE and installing them. It works by connecting to an update server (multiple servers can be specified), querying it for available modules, and comparing that with the list of installed modules. If there is anything you don't have, you can download and install it. Some modules do have cross-dependencies, so dependency checking is also done.

The NetBeans third-party page (http://www.netbeans.org/about/third-party.html)

this page lists companies building applications based on NetBeans and modules for NetBeans. Not all companies listed have shipping products yet. Many vendors have demo versions of their modules available from their web sites.

If you are building modules or an application based on NetBeans, send email to *feedback@netbeans.org* to be listed.

The Flashline (http://www.flashline.com/forte_modules/) modules marketplace

This page was created for Sun Microsystems' Forte for Java partners program. It is possible to purchase or download demo versions of modules here. The Update Center in the Forte for Java IDE is slightly different than the one in NetBeans—it includes authentication, thus it is e-commerce enabled. Users can purchase modules from Flashline and then download them using the update center, after entering their Java Developer Connection username and password. It is anticipated that the authentication code will be contributed to the NetBeans project by Sun in the near future.

If you are building commercial modules for NetBeans that you would like to sell through Flashline, contact Sun Microsystems' partner program (*http://forte.sun. com/ffj/partnerprograms/partnercontact.html*).

This chapter contains information about various modules available for the NetBeans IDE and various applications and projects based on NetBeans. The descriptions of these products are the vendors' as they appear on the web. This listing is included as a convenience to the reader, and should not be interpreted as an endorsement of these products. While we have made every effort to make the lists complete and ensure that the information here is accurate, it may not be.

Open Source Modules Available Via the Update Center

Open source modules available via the Update Center at the time of this writing include the following:

Database Explorer
A tool for browsing and editing databases via JDBC. If you are writing a module that interacts with databases, this module may be useful in your own code as well.

CORBA
Tools for working with CORBA technology, including browsing and code generation.

File Copy
An execution service which deploys a file to a remote server.

Object Browser
This is NetBeans' old and unmaintained Object Browser module. Its functionality is to be replaced by more language-neutral and robust tools based on the metadata repository.

Jini
Tools for working with Jini technology.

Makefiles
Provides support for working with the traditional build tool, make.

Serial Version UIDs
Tools for working with serializable classes.

CPP support
Basic support for editing and compiling C++ code.

Unit tests

Support for generating and running tests using the open source JUnit (*http://www.junit.org/*) unit testing framework.

FTP Filesystem

A handy tool for mounting a remote filesystem via FTP (File Transfer Protocol). Loading and saving happen via FTP, but you can interact with files just as if you had mounted a local directory.

The Modules Marketplace on Flashline

A large number of commercial modules are available on Flashline (*http://www.flashline.com/forte_modules/*), running the gamut from profiling tools to UML modeling tools and more. The Flashline marketplace is part of the Sun Microsystems' Forte for Java partner program. The following is a listing of what is available at the time of this writing. Many companies that are developing modules that are not yet commercially available, so it is a good idea to check the web site for up-to-date information.

Zenaptix BeanStork

BeanStork delivers compiled JavaBeans classes directly from XML Schema instances. XML Documents can be marshaled to and from JavaBeans objects, on the fly. BeanStork provides Javadoc™ documentation for generated classes, direct Bean Scripting Framework support, and, vetoable property change support.

Imperial Software Technology Visaj-Visual Application Builder for Java

Visaj is a rapid visual application builder for Java. It pioneers a new style of Java development tool centered on a visual representation of the application. Visaj enhances developers' productivity by providing a fast and intuitive point-and-click environment for rapidly building Pure Java applications.

Jcorporate Expresso Framework

An open source application development (AD) framework featuring a foundation set of reusable, standards-based software components designed to shorten time-to-delivery of Web-based, business transactional applications enabling the developer to concentrate on application logic.

Virtuas Solutions JtagCommunity

The Virtuas Jtag libraries are based on Sun Microsystems' JavaServer Page 1.1 specification. The libraries are broken into nine distinct packages: Community, Output, Object, Flow Control, Enterprise, Credit Card, LDAP, SQL, and Wireless. The Community library is available free via download and the other libraries are available through subscription, which gives the subscriber access to the over 60 custom JSP tags available, all relevant documentation, newsgroups and FAQs, plus all new libraries and tags released by Virtuas throughout the year.

Cava Soft CavaTools

CavaTools is a Java component framework designed specifically for building scalable, cross-platform web applications.

SoftwareAG Tamino

The Tamino Module for Forte is a Software AG provided Extension to the Forte for Java Integrated Development Environment (IDE) that enables the Java Developer to very easily access the Tamino XML Server and implement XML Enabled Enterprise Solutions.

Alberg Software, Inc. Applese

Using "Model-based Code-Generation Technology", Applese simplifies EJB based Application Development. Applese offers record-time development and deployment, a reduced learning curve, and lower maintenance by generating EJBs, Home Interfaces, Remote Interfaces, Client-Servlet Code, HTML based User-Interfaces, Swing Based User-Interfaces and more!

Information Architects™ SmartCode™ 4.2

SmartCode is a complete, three-dimensional product—a different way to view the Web. Information Architects designed and developed SmartCode, the first and only RDF server, to allow the Web to do what it was designed to do—move content, make content more accessible and meaningful, and to do those things better and more efficiently than any method before it.

Headway Software Headway reView

Headway reView is a Source Code Visualization and Comprehension Tool for Java and C++ developers. It parses class files and source code to reverse engineer a visual representation of the composition and dependencies of the application. The Headway reView diagrams called hiGraphs, are intuitive, interactive, visual environments in which a developer can gain a truer understanding of how their applications are structured.

Embarcadero Technologies Describe Developer Edition

Describe Developer is an application programmer's utility that adds live UML round trip engineering within the leading Java IDEs to create, manipulate, view and document source code more efficiently. It is designed for the individual professional or corporate developer implementing complex Java applications where better design visibility during the construction phase allows better coding decisions.

Yospace SmartPhone Emulator Forte Module Edition

SmartPhone Emulator Forte Module Edition is an adapted version of Yospace's core SmartPhone Emulator product, which emulates many of the world's leading WAP handsets.

No Magic Magic Draw UML 5.1

MagicDraw is a visual UML modeling and CASE tool designed for the Business Analyst, Software Analyst, Programmer, QA Engineer, Documentation Writer, or Corporate Executive. The tool allows the developer or business professional to draw, design, and view UML diagrams of Object Oriented systems. Besides UML diagramming it also provides industry's best code engineering mechanism—full round-trip support for the Java, C++ and CORBA IDL programming languages.

HYWY Software POPE.J Basic Plus–Integrated Support for FFJ

POPE.J™ Basic Plus is a full-featured Productivity Environment for Java that allows new and experienced Java developers alike to model, build, test and deploy production-ready Java applications.

Class IQ IQ Test for Java

IQTest for Java is a component testing tool that does not require scripting or coding and makes the unit testing of Java components straightforward.

IDEs That Are Distributions of the NetBeans IDE

Currently listed on the NetBeans third-party page are the following IDEs[*][†]:

Sun Microsystems Forte for Java

Sun's Forte for Java software is the only development tool needed for building Java applications on any platform. It is completely modular and easily extensible because it's completely open and based on the NetBeans Platform. The Forte for Java IDE enables you to easily and quickly create internet services and solutions with 100% Pure Java code on the Windows, Linux, or Solaris Operating Environments.

Compuware OptimalJ

OptimalJ is an advanced development environment enabling the rapid design, development and deployment of J2EE applications. OptimalJ simplifies the development of J2EE applications, enabling developers of varying experience levels to rapidly produce reliable applications. OptimalJ generates complete, working applications directly from a visual model, using sophisticated patterns to implement accepted best practices for coding to the J2EE specs. To allow developers to add custom code to the generated code in so-called free-blocks, OptimalJ includes the NetBeans IDE version 3.2.

INFORMATION ARCHITECTS IA SmartCode™ Interactive Development Environment

IA SmartCode™ IDE is designed as a plug in for the open source NetBeans platform, making it compatible with Sun's Forte for Java development environment. IA SmartCode's metadata framework provides interactive support for state-of-the-art application and data modeling capabilities based on the open Resource

---

[*] As with the preceding list of modules, the information here is vendor-supplied and the authors take no responsibility for the accuracy or completeness thereof.

[†] This list omits companies already listed in the previous Flashline section.

Description Framework (RDF) standard from the World Wide Web Consortium (W3C) as well as industry standards that include the Simple Object Access Protocol (SOAP). IA SmartCode includes a commitment to J2EE, including Enterprise JavaBeans (EJB), Java Database Connectivity (JDBC), Java Server Pages (JSP) and Java Naming and Directory Service (JNDI). IA SmartCode's™ support for Java Servlet API and EJB enables seamless interoperability with all leading Web servers and Java application server platforms.

Compaq NetBeans for OpenVMS

Compaq is announcing a slew of new products, technologies, initiatives, and programs—including NetBeans for OpenVMS—as part of its strategy of constantly updating and broadening the capabilities of OpenVMS. In NetBeans, Compaq sees not only the e-business, Java IDE of choice, but also the potential of becoming a multipurpose IDE for OpenVMS—one in which modules for a range of non-Java languages can be developed.

Incomit iWarf

The iWarf Service Creation Environment (SCE) is designed to create telecom applications in a easy and convenient manner without having to have thorough knowledge about the telecom network or JAIN SPA. It provides an easy-to-learn Integrated Development Environment (IDE) based on NetBeans. iWarf makes development of telecom applications a matter of drag-and-drop using the NetBeans IDE, together with some basic Java™ programming. Template wizards that automatically generates the fundamentals for an iSea application are provided, as wells as a wizard for easy deployment of applications. For high performance applications and/or applications that will provide full access to the telecom applications provided by the Parlay gateway, it is recommended to use the more powerful JAIN SPA APIs. Since the JAIN SPA provides more functionality, they are more complex and requires a bit more work than the E-SPA APIs. There is no support for directly using the JAIN SPA APIs in iWarf.

Open Source Application Projects Based on NetBeans

NetBeans has spawned a number of open source projects that use the NetBeans core for the application's infrastructure and that are building communities around developing modules in their domain:

Center for Computational Geography, Leeds University, UK

An open source GIS application with a particular emphasis on spatial analysis—By removing the Java specific modules from the NetBeans IDE and replacing them with mapping, visualization and analysis modules we are building a robust, modular, environment for spatial analysis and visualization. The framework provided by NetBeans provides support for an abstract file system, integrated help system, built in support for scripting languages—such as Python, excellent project and workspace management, a well designed and documented plug in system, an API which covers the ideas of services, editors, hierarchical organization and a whole host of other key features.

Department of Computing Science, University of Glasgow's BioBeans

BioBeans (*http://bioinf.gla.ac.uk/biobeans/*) is an open source project with the aim of providing biologists with a complete integrated data analysis environment. This goal will be achieved by removing the IDE specific modules from the NetBeans™ Tools Platform and replacing them with biological data visualization and analysis tools. By building on the NetBeans core the application will be completely modular and easily extensible allowing researchers to tailor the analysis environment to their needs. We want the development process to be as open as possible and we encourage bioinformatics software developers to become involved in the design and contribution of modules. Further details and an evolving vision statement can be found at the *biobeans.org* development website.

Project XEMO

An open source, modular software environment for the development and delivery of interactive music, audio and sound applications—The NetBeans Platform provides Project XEMO with a strong application architecture and infrastructure, including advanced windowing services, project management, remote update and other utilities. XEMO ICE—the Integrated Composition Environment—is the desktop delivery platform for the integration of application modules into an interactive musical application. It provides those services needed for all musical applications, such as common data representations, music file formats and common interface components, e.g. playback controls. These services are implemented as a set of shared APIs that are available to music application developers.

Commercial Applications Built on the NetBeans Platform

Below are non-IDE commercial applications built using NetBeans as an application platform.

BEA Campaign Manager for WebLogic™

BEA is a proud partner of NetBeans. The San Jose-based company, which provides e-business software infrastructure, recently launched Campaign Manager for WebLogic®, built leveraging public NetBeans tools. Designed by marketers for marketers and running on the BEA WebLogic E-Business Platform™, Campaign Manager is a complete, integrated e-business solution for targeting customers with personalized promotions and campaigns that stimulate awareness, interest and action.

ECSI MINEX V integrated mine planning application

Australian mining software company ECS International are the authors of MINEX, the world's leading totally integrated software solution for the evaluation and planning of open-cut and underground mines for both coal and minerals. ECSI, an employee owned company formed in 1996 (from ECS Pty Ltd an innovative and pioneering Australian mining software company founded in 1966) will release its next version, Minex V, with a re-designed Graphical User Interface (GUI) and infrastructure based on NetBeans. The new version makes the program strictly a server, with the NetBeans GUI acting as the client. NetBeans has been modified to suit an advanced OpenGL/PEX/Phigs graphics environment and socket communication to the server program. Thanks to the NetBeans community we hope to also release Japanese, Spanish, and French versions.

Whitehead Institute / MIT Center for Genome Research

A collection of gene expression related modules—GenePattern is a collection of gene expression related modules connected to the NetBeans application framework. The use of modules will have the advantage that users can add new features as modules to GenePattern without modifying GenePattern's code. Software developers can implement analysis algorithms as modules to plug in to the GenePattern-NetBeans framework.

e-Sim, Inc. RapidPLUS

e-SIM is using NetBeans as the basis for the user interface of the new generation of its simulation-based development toolset for embedded systems, code named "Interstate". Interstate will provide developers of electronic product software and embedded Java applets with the capability to simulate their products' user interfaces, generate code to run in the products directly from the simulation and publish the simulation on the Internet.

Equilibrium MediaRich

Server-based software that automates image production and enables dynamic delivery of images anywhere. Equilibrium MediaRich is server-based software that automates image production and enables dynamic delivery of images anywhere. MediaRich brings true state-of-the-art automation tools to the Enterprise, allowing companies to create more engaging customer experiences while reducing production time and costs.

Commercial Modules Available for NetBeans

The following is a list of companies producing commercial modules that integrate with the NetBeans IDE, along with those companies' descriptions of their products.

Hybris J2EE components for e-procurement and e-commerce applications

Hybris jakarta is the rapid deployable, component-based software platform for sophisticated e-commerce and e-procurement solutions. Hybris jakarta enables a short time-to-market thanks to pre-built components and the easy-to-use hybris jakarta logic API. The open J2EE and XML architecture offers almost unlimited flexibility for the optimization of existing and creation of new business processes.

Yospace SmartPhone Emulator Forte Edition

The Yospace SmartPhone Emulator Forte Edition allows the user to view and interact with WAP content and services in a manner that accurately reproduces a variety of WAP enabled devices. The module facilitates the development of WAP content, allowing the user to quickly and easily produce content tailored for many of the world's most popular handsets. The Yospace Application Platform for J2ME is available from the Yospace J2ME developer site,

DataMirror Corp. DataMirror

DataMirror's DB/XML Transform provides a powerful engine for bi-directional data transformation between XML, database and text formats. Through XML, transformation from or to other formats such as HTML, XHTML, WML, EDI can be easily achieved. And DataMirror's DB/XML Vision automatically creates XML documents containing hierarchical data from any database for B2B applications, EDI, database integration and conversion.

Drala Software NetBeans plug-ins

The company develops infrastructure components for enterprise Java applications including Drala Workflow Engine and Drala Event Broker which will be available as NetBeans plug-ins to maximize developer productivity.

Embarcadero Technologies Describe™ Integrated UML Modeling & Java Development

We have embedded award-winning UML functionality and Live Round Trip Engineering natively within the NetBeans interface to create a single seamless environment. Describe features also include: Markerless Reverse Engineering for Java, C++ and IDL, real-time collaboration, integrated UML/ER modeling, Inter-model synchronization; Web system reports; and automated development and deployment of Enterprise JavaBeans. Full featured evaluation copies are available on our Web site.

Gentleware AG Poseidon for UML

Gentleware AG offers a UML modeling tool called Poseidon for UML that fully integrates into NetBeans and Forte. Gentleware was founded by major contributors to the open source modeling tool ArgoUML (*http://www.argouml.org/, www.argouml.org*). A Community Edition is free of charge and can be downloaded from (*http://www.gentleware.com/, www.gentleware.com.*) The commercial editions include round-trip engineering, template-based code generation (Velocity), documentation generation, OCL support etc. and come at a very moderate price.

HiT Software Allora Wizards Build XML-RDB Access

HiT Allora is the XML platform for data exchange. Allora leverages the power of XML for data exchange by providing real-time, read-write XML access to relational databases. Allora includes XML schema/catalog mapping, data binding interfaces, support for Message Queues (JMS), SAX and DOM. Wizards make XML-RDB data exchange fast and easy.

HYWY Software Corp Java Productivity Environment (JPE)

HYWY Software Corp.'s Java Productivity Environment (JPE) offers an object-oriented development environment enabling technical solutions to be conceptualized and generates the required Java code to solve business problems more effectively. HYWY's comprehensive and integrated solution incorporates object-oriented application modeling, code generation, re-generation, testing and object persistence through a high performance object cache. HYWY's PopeTools™ JPE supports persistent business objects running in a high-performance object cache for use by application servers supporting the J2SE, or J2EE standards.

I-Ware NBAM (NetBeans Annotation Module)

NBAM allows users to add "sticky notes" to their projects. Annotations can be attached to: your system, project, files or data in files. NBAM will provide you with a way to include TODOs in your code and keep track of them. The functionality of NBAM is not limited to only TODOs but any annotation of something that you need in your development, be it annotating old code in your sources, links to documentation or distribution of responsibilities in your development team.

IONA Technologies Enterprise-class Java and CORBA deployment servers

IONA Technologies provides enterprise-class Java and CORBA deployment servers. IONA is working on modules that will facilitate rapid development of J2EE and CORBA componentry with high-speed deployment to their execution engines and application servers.

Modelistic CASE tool

Modelistic is a Java-only CASE tool. It lets programmers create models diagrammatically, saving them as Java source, or make models from Java source without the need for any other storage format. It is designed to be used in conjunction with the IDE, and act as an alternative mode for viewing and editing work.

mslinn.com, inc. JSP Explorer

Mslinn.com is customizing NetBeans to support their JSP Explorer product. JSP Explorer is a novel method of "bringing Javadocs to life", and is available at *http://www.mslinn.com/jspExplorer*. The NetBeans customization allows a programmer to highlight sample code and generate HTML buttons in the Javadocs that invoke the JSP Explorer.

PushToTest

Test automation software to assure Web Services for functionality, scalability and performance.—TestMaker enables a developer, QA analyst or IT manager to build intelligent test agents to assure Web Services (HTTP, HTTPS, SOAP, .NET, JDBC, etc.) for functionality, scalability and performance. The agents are written using a scripting language to drive a library of test objects which handle the protocols. The Web Service thinks real users are making requests which enables TestMaker to simulate real world environments to test. The same agents act as service level monitors for Web services in production.

SIP Technologies Limited

Integrates NetBeans with JBoss Application Server. One of SIPtech's major activities is to carry out system integration in the open source software area. Some of the recent initiatives of the company include integrating leading IDEs with popular application servers. A case in point is the integration of Forte for Java/NetBeans with the open source JBoss application server.

Systinet

Systinet WASP (Web Applications and Services Platform) enables companies to develop internal applications based on emerging Web Services standards (SOAP, UDDI, XML, etc.), integrate enterprise applications and databases using a service-oriented approach, and integrate business processes with customers, suppliers and partners.

WASP Developer supports the NetBeans IDE and makes creating Web services a natural and simple extension of the existing development process. WASP Server is a sophisticated runtime environment that supports remote references and advanced security. WASP UDDI is a v2 compliant UDDI registry.

Thought Inc. CocoBase Enterprise O/R mapping tool

CocoBase Enterprise O/R is an O/R mapping tool, optimized for NetBeans/Forte for Java. CocoBase maps database tables, generates scalable/high performance Java, CMP, BMP, JSPs and effortlessly deploys to all the most popular EJB J2EE application servers.

Virtuas Solutions Virtuas Jtag JSP tag library

Virtuas is creating a floating palette which will contain Virtuas' tag libraries, enabling Java developers to drag and drop the tags into their development environment to accelerate the creation of Web applications.

Should You Create Your Own Update Server?

The specification for the update server is public—the simplest implementation is an XML file on a web server, which contains information about the available modules, dependencies, and so on. So anyone wanting to operate their own update server is welcome to—if you are doing this, please make it known on the mailing lists at *www.netbeans.org*.

If you are a vendor building an application on top of NetBeans who wants to deliver modules to customers, then probably your modules would not make sense in the context of an IDE, in which case it makes sense for you to operate your own update server.

There are several advantages to using this technology. You can deliver incremental product updates faster, and your customers will appreciate not having to download and install the entire application again. Also you will be able to deliver new functionality asynchronously—it is not necessary to do an entire software release process in order to offer new functionality to your customers.

However, for IDE-related modules, your own update server probably isn't the ideal solution, since potential users will have to find it in order to install your modules. In this case, it may be a better choice simply to go to one of the existing update servers. *netbeans.org* is happy to host open source module projects as long as the module is open source, relevant to NetBeans, and licensed under the same license as the rest of NetBeans. Sun's partner program offers co-marketing and promotion resources to vendors wishing to distribute commercial modules for NetBeans.

Index

We'd like to hear your suggestions for improving our indexes. Send email to *index@oreilly.com*.

creating bindings, 59
global key bindings, 103

L

languages, support, 62–63
launching, 12
  NetBeans, 9–14
  NetBeans Source Editor, 53–54
layers, xiv
  filesystems, 224–225
  formatting URLs, 497–503
  installing, 238
  Minicomposer module, 384
  modules, 223–224
  RMI, xiv
  XML, 496–497, 497–503
layouts
  AbsoluteLayout, 143
  GridBagLayout Customizer, 143–146
  GUI containers, 139
  Null, 143
lazy initialization, 495
  avoiding ModuleInstall classes, 496–497
libraries, bundling extensions, 519–523
licenses, 551–552
  applications, 211–212
  source code, xx, 211–212
lifecycles
  modules, 504, 609
  score files, 406
linking
  events, 142
  Javadocs, 178
loading, partial, 497
localization of NetBeans, 306
locating modules, 615–626
  Flashline, 617–619
  Update Center, 616–617
Log CVS, 124
logging, ErrorManager, 546–548
Looks API, 596–597
lookups
  APIs, 255–257
  implementing, 587
  NetBeans, 296–297
  uniform, 596

M

Macintosh, 10
  binary distributions, 6
  NetBeans, 10

macros, recording, 105–108
mail clients
  creating workspaces, 377–382
  DataLoaders, 356–363
  interfaces, 356
  views, 363–377
mail-based filesystems, 329
  building mail readers, 329–339
  configuring accounts, 345–355
  creating folders for attachments, 340–341
  marking unread messages, 341–343
  viewing properties, 343–344
MailFileSystem.java, implementing, 331
mailing lists, 612, 614
Makefile modules, 581
management of projects, 47–50
manifests
  Minicomposer module, 384
  modules, 247
mapping files to Java objects, 222–223
marking unread messages, 341–343
matching words, 60
MDI (Multiple Document Interface), 14
memory
  formatting URLs, 497–503
  optimizing, 491, 492–494
  runtime/startup, 492
  techniques, 494–497
menus
  configuring, 99–100
  context, 54
  GUI, 138
  View, 46
merging source paths, 127
messages
  DataLoaders, 356–363
  editing, 357–361
  marking unread, 341–343
  multipart, 362–363
  viewing, 357–361
Metadata Repository, 577, 598–600
methods
  drop-downs, 319–324
  RMI, xiv
Methods subnode, 319
migration, 11
MIME (Multipurpose Internet Mail Extensions), 389
MIMEResolvers, 228
Minicomposer module
  Compiler cookie, 426–430
  compilers, 420–425

About the Authors

Jack J. Woehr is an independent consultant specializing in building and mentoring programming teams at high technology startup ventures. His practice over the past two decades has ranged from microcode to mainframes. Jack is also a Contributing Editor for *Dr. Dobb's Journal*, one of the world's most popular programming magazines. His web site is *http://www.softwoehr.com*.

Vaughn Spurlin began his programming career in 1967 on the physically largest computer ever built, the SAGE system's house-sized AN/FSQ-7. A freelance consultant since 1975, he worked with a wide range of computer hardware and languages, including several early personal computers before they were known as such. Vaughn currently writes technical articles about Sun ONE Studio and develops training materials for Sun.

Simeon Greene currently lives with his wife Nikki in Philadelphia, PA, but is originally from the sunny island republic of Trinidad and Tobago. In the pursuit of money, education, and all else that corrupts, he left his island paradise and currently works as a developer for Hewlett-Packard. Although he misses tropical breezes and an idyllic lifestyle, he enjoys being a software developer and the opportunity to work with interesting technical people like those on the NetBeans project. Besides technology, Simeon also enjoys poetry, classical literature, travel, and underground hip-hop—of course.

Jesse Glick has worked on NetBeans since January 1999 in several capacities, including developing NetBeans core software, editing API documentation, and providing assistance for integrators. He joined Sun with the acquisition of NetBeans in the Fall of 1999. He has spoken twice at JavaOne on NetBeans module development.

Tim Boudreau is a native of Massachusetts who has worked in the IT industry as a developer, writer, and graphic artist on and off since the age of twelve. Following a hiatus as a literary theory major and musician, he returned to the world of computers at the age of 23 in response to the marvelous career opportunities for a student of literature during a recession, and the clamour of the IT world for his return.

In the Spring of 1999, he moved to the Czech Republic to work for a small company called NetBeans, which was soon to be acquired by Sun Microsystems, where he still lives and works. Tim can be found at most times perched with an underpowered laptop, deep in ascetic concentration in his monastic quarters high in the towers of Sun Microsystems in Prague. He is occasionally led outside, blinking in the twilight, to belt out blues tunes in smoky bars, on the advice of his physicians and Sun Microsystems' "Great Place to Work" program.

Colophon

Our look is the result of reader comments, our own experimentation, and feedback from distribution channels. Distinctive covers complement our distinctive approach to technical topics, breathing personality and life into potentially dry subjects.

The animals on the cover of *NetBeans: The Definitive Guide* are European tree frogs (*Hyla arboria*). These tiny amphibians inhabit verdant European forests. Like most tree frogs, they have suction pads on the end of each toe that allow them to cling to plants, but European tree frogs can be distinguished from other species by a white-bordered black line that runs from their nostrils to their hind legs. They are generally green in color, though their shade often changes to match their surroundings and help them hide from predators. Less than two inches long, tree frogs are an attractive snack for snakes, lizards, birds, and large fish. Because they are cold-blooded, tree frogs often stay in the sun, snapping up flies and other tiny insects with their long sticky tongues.

The most distinctive feature in the males is a well-developed vocal sac; when calling this sac can expand to be larger than the frog's head. The male's sac is creased and usually darker than the rest of his body, while the female's is smoother, smaller, and lighter in color. European tree frogs usually spawn in ponds during spring or early summer. At dusk, males claim an area from which to call females, who arrive later in the evening and choose a mate if they are ready to spawn. The female lays up to 1,000 eggs, which sink to the bottom of the pond. Tadpoles hatch in 12–14 days, and develop their hind legs a month later. Once the tadpoles become frogs, they will leave the water until they are old enough to spawn. An individual female will spawn only once a season, but males do so throughout the summer. These frogs are notoriously difficult to breed in captivity, but are often kept as pets because of their expressive features, distinctive coloring, and ability to stick to the sides of glass terrariums.

Phil Dangler was the production editor for *NetBeans: The Definitive Guide*. Argosy provided production services and wrote the index. Emily Quill and Jane Ellin provided quality control.

Hanna Dyer designed the cover of this book, based on a series design by Edie Freedman. The cover image is a 19th-century engraving from *Animal Creation, Volume 5*. Emma Colby produced the cover layout with QuarkXPress 4.1 using Adobe's ITC Garamond font.

David Futato designed the interior layout. This book was converted from XML to FrameMaker 5.5.6 with a format conversion tool created by Erik Ray, Jason McIntosh, Neil Walls, and Mike Sierra that uses Perl and XML technologies. The text font is Linotype Birka; the heading font is Adobe Myriad Condensed; and the code font is LucasFont's TheSans Mono Condensed. The illustrations that appear in the book were produced by Robert Romano and Jessamyn Read using Macromedia FreeHand 9 and Adobe Photoshop 6. The tip and warning icons were drawn by Christopher Bing. This colophon was written by Philip Dangler.